Lecture Notes in Computer Science 550

Edited by G. Goos and J. Hartmanis

Advisory Board: W. Brauer D. Gries

T0230054

A. van Lamsweerde   A. Fugetta (Eds.)

ESEC '91

3rd European Software Engineering
Conference, ESEC '91
Milan, Italy, October 21-24, 1991
Proceedings

Springer-Verlag

Berlin Heidelberg New York
London Paris Tokyo
Hong Kong Barcelona
Budapest

Series Editors

Gerhard Goos
GMD Forschungsstelle
Universität Karlsruhe
Vincenz-Priessnitz-Straße 1
W-7500 Karlsruhe, FRG

Juris Hartmanis
Department of Computer Science
Cornell University
Upson Hall
Ithaca, NY 14853, USA

Volume Editors

Axel van Lamsweerde
Université Chatolique de Louvain, Unité d'Informatique
Place Sainte Barbe 2, B-1348 Louvain-La Neuve, Belgium

Alfonso Fugetta
CEFRIL
Via Emanueli 15, I-20126 Milano, Italy

CR Subject Classification (1991): D.2

ISBN 3-540-54742-8 Springer-Verlag Berlin Heidelberg New York
ISBN 0-387-54742-8 Springer-Verlag New York Berlin Heidelberg

© Springer-Verlag Berlin Heidelberg 1991
Printed in Germany

Typesetting: Camera ready by author
Printing and binding: Druckhaus Beltz, Hemsbach/Bergstr.
45/3140-543210 - Printed on acid-free paper

Foreword

The third European Software Engineering Conference follows ESEC '87 and ESEC '89 which were held in Strasbourg and Warwick, respectively. This series of conferences was set up by the European computer societies with the aim of providing an international forum for researchers, developers and users of software engineering technology. The need for a meeting point to discuss new results and useful experiences was felt quite naturally in view of the large amount of high-quality software engineering research which originated in Europe and which was stimulated over the last years through major European research programmes.

ESEC '91 has been organized jointly with two other international events: the Sixth International Workshop on Software Specification and Design (IWSSD-6), and an industrially oriented symposium and fair on Software Quality (CQS '91). The synchronization of these three events aimed to offer a unique opportunity to combine advanced research, ongoing developments and current practice in the field.

It appeared from the beginning of ESEC that these conferences also attracted distinguished work from elsewhere in the world. Internationalization has become even more pronounced with ESEC '91 where 133 papers were submitted from 26 different countries spanning four continents. The papers in these proceedings reflect this expansion.

The 22 papers published here represent those judged best by the Program Committee. They cover a fairly broad range of themes such as formal methods and practical experiences with them, special techniques for real-time systems, software evolution and re-engineering, software engineering environments and software metrics. The reader will perhaps identify some trends that are emerging from these papers, such as the search for systematic approaches to handle real-time systems, the need to fill the gap between unusable but sound formal methods and used but unsound "arrows and boxes" techniques, the need for developing environments equipped with reasoning capabilities, or the wish to learn or to rebuild from existing products and processes.

Invited talks were organized to address important areas that were felt to be insufficiently covered by the regular papers. Perspectives on configuration management, software factories, user interface design, computer security, and technology transfer were discussed by well-known experts. A number of invited papers covering these themes have accordingly been added to the regular papers. A few position papers by panel participants have also been included to provide some flavour on these panels.

We would like to express our warmest thanks to all members of the Program Committee who have been working hard reviewing papers and making numerous suggestions regarding the organization of the conference. The final shape of the program owes much to their help and advice. We are also indebted to the other referees who provided additional assistance in the difficult process of selecting good papers.

The software crisis has been recognized for 25 years now. Some people are currently talking about a software engineering crisis, that might be measured in terms of the number of problems raised versus the number of problems really solved. We hope that the contents of these proceedings will make a modest contribution to decreasing this measure.

August 1991

Axel van Lamsweerde
Alfonso Fuggetta

Program Committee

Program Chair

Axel van Lamsweerde, Université Catholique de Louvain (Belgium)

Executive Chair

Alfonso Fuggetta, CEFRIEL (Italy)

Tutorial Chair

Véronique Donzeau-Gouge, CNAM and INRIA (France)

Tools Fair Chair

Alberto Cazziol, ETNOTEAM (Italy)

Members

A. Endres (Germany)	J. McDermid (U.K.)
S. Fickas (USA)	E. Milgrom (Belgium)
J.P. Finance (France)	R. Mittermeir (Austria)
M.C. Gaudel (France)	J. Musa (USA)
C. Ghezzi (Italy)	F. Orejas (Spain)
E. Girard (France)	C. Potts (USA)
S. Greenspan (USA)	S. Prehn (Denmark)
H. Horgen (France)	H. Tardieu (France)
P. Hruschka (Germany)	R. Taylor (USA)
C. Jackson (U.K.)	W. Tichy (Germany)
R. Jacquart (France)	P. Torrigiani (Italy)
H. Jonkers (Netherlands)	B. Warboys (U.K.)
K. Lohr (Germany)	H. Weber (Germany)
T. Maibaum (U.K.)	J. Winkler (Germany)
M. Maiocchi (Italy)	P. Wodon (Belgium)
D. Mandrioli (Italy)	J. Wordsworth (U.K.)

Reviewers

Abowd J.
Anderson J.
Belanger D.G.
Bernot G.
Botella P.
Boullier P.
Bril R.
Brown A.W.
Burns A.
Canzi U.
Castro J.
Cazin J.
Celiman M.M.
Coen-Porisini A.
Colemar D.
Cunningham J.
Dardenne A.
Deransart P.
Dewayne P.
Di Giacomo P.
Dissmann S.
Dix A.
Donnelly M.
Donzeau-Gouge V.
Durney B.
Eisenbach S.
Emmerich W.
Endres A.
Enrlich W.K.
Feldman S.
Fickas S.
Finance J.P.
Finkelstein A.
Fladeiro J.
Franchi P.
Freestone D.
Fuggetta A.

Garzia M.
Gaudel M.C.
Ghezzi C.
Gimeres I.
Girard E.
Goldsack S.J.
Greenspan S.
Guarro B.
Hardin T.
Helm R.
Higgins C.
Hochmueller E.
Horgen H.
Hruschka P.
Hulin G.
Incerpi J.
Jackson L.A.
Jacquart R.
James D.
Jonkers H.
Junkermann G.
Khouri B.
Kramer J.
Lacroix M.
Lee S.K.
Lemoine M.
Levine D.
Liditinghagen K.
Lohr K.
Maibaum T.
Maiocchi M.
Mandrioli D.
Marre B.
Matthews T.S.
McDermid J.
Michel P.
Milgrom E.

Mittermeir R.
Moineau T.
Morasca S.
Musa J.
Norris M.T.
Orejas F.
Phillips I.
Potts C.
Pozzi S.
Prehn S.
Rafsanjani G.H.B.
Robinson B.
Robinson G.A.
Runciman C.
Ryan D.
Schmedding D.
Schulke F.
Schumann H.
Stokes D.A.
Tardieu H.
Taylor R.
Thevenod P.
Tichy W.
Tinker R.
Torrigiani P.
Vanhoedenaghe M.
van Lamsweerde A.
Vercoustre A.M.
Warboys B.
Weber H.
Winkler J.
Wodon P.
Wordsworth J.
Wu X.
Young P.
Zage D.

Table of Contents

Invited Papers

Software Configuration Management: Past Uses and Future Challenges..............1
Stuart I. Feldman

Architectural Design for User Interfaces 7
Joëlle Coutaz

The Eureka Software Factory: Concepts and Accomplishments......................23
Christer Fernström

Formal Approaches

Integrating Structured and Formal Methods: A Visual Approach to VDM..........37
J. Dick and J. Loubersac

Rational Design of Distributed Applications...60
T. Cattel

Experience With Formal Methods

Test Data Selection From Algebraic Specifications:
Application to an Automatic Subway Module.......................................80
P. Dauchy and B. Marre

Specification in COLD-1 of a CAD-Package for Drawing Shadow Masks........101
F. J. van der Linden

Real-Time Systems I

ASTRAL: An Assertion Language for Specifying Real-Time Systems............122
C. Ghezzi and R. A. Kemmerer

Execution Environment for ELECTRE Applications.................................147
D. Creusot, P. Lemoine, O. Roux, Y. Trinquet, A. Kung, O. Marbach and C. Serrano-Morales

Real-Time Systems II

An Engineering Approach Towards Hard Real-Time System Design..............166
H. Kopetz, R. Zainlinger, G. Fohler, H. Kantz, P. Puschner and W. Schütz

An Application of Artificial Intelligence to Ptototyping Process in
Performance Design for Real-Time Systems..189
S. Honiden, N. Uchihira and K. Itoh

Coping With Changes

Dynamically Replaceable Software: A Design Method...............................210
J. Amador, B. de Vicente and A. Alonso

Software Merge: Models and Methods for Combining Changes to Programs 229
V. Berzins

Software Re-Engineering

A Theory for Software Design Extraction 251
B. A. Sijtsma and J. W. Mager

SESADA: An Environment Supporting Software Specialization 266
A. Coen-Porisini and F. De Paoli

Metrics

Metric-Driven Classification Analysis...290
R. W. Selby and R. K. Madsen

A Dynamic Failure Model For Predicting the Impact that a
Program Location Has on the Program 308
J. Voas

Relation Between Source Code Metrics and Structure Analysis Metrics...........332
I. Rozman, J. Györkös and T. Dogsa

Formal Bases

Algebraic Validation of Software Metrics...343
M. Shepperd and D. Ince

An Algebraic View of Inheritance and Subtyping in Object Oriented
Programming..364
F. Parisi Presicce and A. Pierantonio

Environments I

Scaling Up Rule-Based Software Development Environments 380
N. S. Barghouti and G. E. Kaiser

Inference-Based Support for Programming in the Large 396
G. Snelting, F. J. Grosch and U. Schroeder

Environments II

TICKLE: Object-Oriented Description and Composition Services
for Software Engineering Environments.................................409

T. Collins, K. Ewert, C. Gerety, J. Gustafson and I. Thomas
Integrated Project Support Environments,
Text Generation and Technical Writing.................................424
C. Tattersall

The Arcs Experience 443
D. Schefström

Position Papers

*Panel 1: Impact of Software Engineering Researches
on Industrial Practice*

Panel Presentation 465
A. Fuggetta

The Production of Software in the FINSIEL Group 468
V. Frasca

The Impact of Software Engineering Researches on Industrial Practice -
A Personal View..472
C. Jackson

Impact of Methods on Productivity and Quality 480
R. Troy

*Panel 2: Requirements Engineering: The Neats Versus
the Scruffies*

Requirements Engineering: Getting Right from Wrong................485
M.S.Feather

A (Neat) Alphabet of Requirements Engineering Issues.............489
A. Finkelstein

The Scruffy Side of Requirements Engineering 492
Sol Greenspan

Expediency and Appropriate Technology:
An Agenda for Requirements Engineering Research in the 1990s.............495
C. Potts

Panel 3: CASE Support for the Software Process

CASE Support for the Software Process 497
P. Hruschka

CASE Support for the Software Process: a Research Viewpoint...................499
J. Kramer

CASE Support for Large Systems...504
D. Robinson

CASE Seen From Both Sides of the Fence...509
W.E. Fischer

CASE Support for the Software Process:
Advances and Problems 512
B. Lang

Software Configuration Management: Past Uses and Future Challenges

Stuart I. Feldman

Bellcore, Morristown, New Jersey, USA

1. Meaning and Goals of Software Configuration Management

Software Configuration Management is one of the established sub-fields of Software Engineering, and one that provides recognized benefits to practitioners and managers, SCM tools have been in widespread use for decades, there is a historical hardware model on which to build, and a variety of commercial tools are on the market. Our work is not yet done, and most of the needs remain unmet. This essay presents some views on where we are and the areas of future growth.

2. Past of SCM

Configuration management began as a tool for keeping track of complex physical devices. There are some very important differences between these worlds (the software is directly accessible to the computer, whereas only an identifier for the hardware is in the computer.) Some problems (e.g., identifying the objects) are traditionally addressed very differently in hardware and software. However, with the appearance of self-identifying sub-systems, some of these differences (e.g., labeling the objects) may be eradicated. The frequent changes and customization of software seems to lead to much more complex configuration problems than are faced in hardware. (As hardware gets more logically complicated, SCM concepts will be needed to do HCM.)

As software grew in complexity and the needs for delivering different forms became more common, specific tools were created to avoid errors and to speed the activities of software construction. Problems of versions and building were usually intertwined and handled manually or by the language translation systems. General purpose systems (e.g., Make) appeared in the 1970's, as did languages (e.g., Ada) that added CM aspects to their official definitions.

3. Some Present Practice of Software Configuration Management

It is probably fair to say that such elementary tools predominate real practice. Integrated environments (e.g., PC compilation systems, Ada environments) include a specific notion of SCM in their worlds. More open environments provide means of describing configurations and utilizing them to control activities (e.g., the Make family).

More aggressive SCM systems are in use in some large software companies; combinations of process management, standards enforcement, and data sharing are provided in very complex support systems. Use of these is not yet widespread, and most users get by with the more basic mechanisms. In part, the simplicity of use, low software cost, and ease of entry entice users, who then find they can get by without moving to more elaborate structures. Nonetheless, we expect further use of more general SCM systems as software practice matures.

4. Future Pressures and Opportunities

Research proceeds in a number of directions, and one should expect important progress. This is not just pious hope, as experience with complex systems is growing and related areas of computing are providing new tools and insights. The following are some needs that are not being met generally, and reasons why improvements are plausible.

4.1. Scale

As in virtually all areas of software engineering, the challenge of scale is paramount. It is easy to make most approaches work on toys, but generalizing to industrial scale work is perilous, either because algorithms have super-linear complexity or because limits of human comprehension are surpassed.

As an example, Bellcore's development area has around 2500 software people. The supported inventory (not counting versions) is around 50 million lines of code. A dozen variants of a single system may be in the field simultaneously. Other large software organizations have similar problems. When the software becomes huge, understanding and reasoning about dependencies becomes a large part of the work, and the SCM system must provide most of the information and structure. The SCM systems must provide very serious assistance in archiving, retrieving, building, tracking, and managing the software.

Luckily, storage and processing resources are also increasing, and one naturally takes advantage of them to support the work. In the future, distributed databases and object stores can be expected to provide many of the services that are now specially crafted inside SCM.

4.2. Full Life Cycle Support

SCM was first introduced to assist the build operations typical of the implementation and delivery phases. It is recognized that management of documents from other phases (requirements, designs, test sets, field installation manuals) is an essential and onerous tasks. Providing baseline control and association among versions and variants of these related documents is an increasingly important part of practical SCM. Many conceptual problems are exacerbated by broadening the scope, since relationships among different historical versions and semantically related variants become harder to describe and support. Describing connections while creating a new version is particularly tricky, since the structure will be inconsistent until all elements are in place and linked together.

The use of rule-based and database techniques appear to be essential to solving these problems. The size of the archives and the number of links will clearly grow rapidly as upstream and downstream information is managed along with the more traditional, code-related data.

4.3. Tailorability

Different developers and software groups work in different ways and have different requirements for SCM. A solo practitioner may not need as much help, be able to afford all of the hardware and software, or be willing to accept all the discipline needed for large and changing organizations. The software process supported by the SCM system must be tailorable to these various demands. The problem is further complicated because the user's needs may change radically and the process and SCM data may need to be upgraded without losing historic information.

4.4. Interoperability of SCM Systems

SCM is becoming a competitive business, and users make choices about what (portions of which) systems to buy and use. There will therefore be a growing need to be able to share information among independently developed SCM systems. At present, the problem is usually handled by building specialized translators between data and model description formats. In future, it will be necessary to have some standards, both for data interchange and for primitive operations, to simplify these tasks. These are the unavoidable costs of a maturing field.

4.5. Formal Models

There is a growing perception of a need for better agreement about underlying concepts and perhaps for more general (mathematical) frameworks for describing what SCM systems do. For example, it turns out to be extraordinarily difficult to find a consistent yet useful definition for "revision" and "variant". There have been several dissertations that provide more formal bases for parts of SCM. There is clearly room for deeper modeling of SCM. The boundaries of SCM are not obvious; it is easy to view SCM as a general purpose programming language, process model, database, and distributed systems paradigm. Informally, it is clear that there are problems specific to the SCM domain, and a need for crisper descriptions of SCM problems that are susceptible of analysis. New insights in certain areas of logic databases and of object-oriented programming suggest approaches for scientific progress.

5. User View of SCM

The user (programmer, manager, tester) can view SCM in a number of ways, and the systems need to cater to these requirements. Even if the underlying system can accommodate all approaches, individual will want systems that operate in particular modes.

5.1. Tools vs Integration

In a truly integrated environment, configuration management could be almost invisible as one of the behind-the-scenes services. Many SCM activities are predictable parts of the software process, and certain activities can be viewed as concomitants of approvals or commits. Even in such a future complete software development environments there would be occasions when explicit SCM activities are required.

5.2. Programming vs Graphical Interfaces

The face the SCM system presents to the user depends on usage patterns and complexity. For many purposes, an interface based on menus, buttons, graphical displays is excellent, and decreases training time and error rates. When the problem becomes very complex, textual or command interfaces become profitable, and are easier to implement. It is also possible to build specialized tools if there is a well-defined programmable interface.

Therefore, good quality interfaces of both sorts must be supported.

5.3. Automatic vs Manual Invocation

In some systems, all significant actions are started manually. In others, useful work is done in the background, or triggered automatically by events. If extra computing capacity is available, it may be useful to perform compilations, builds, or even regression tests optimistically. On the other hand, choosing the right operations to perform can be very difficult. Some operations should be delayed until certain inconsistencies have been relieved. Deciding which variants to process requires expert knowledge. (If a system can be configured for 10 operating platforms and 10 instruction sets and 10 windowing systems, it is unlikely that each test for each of the 1000 cases should be run each time a file is changed.) Expert systems technology can provide assistance in these cases.

6. Data View of SCM

SCM provides ways to save and manipulate information relating to changing software. It is therefore crucially important to consider the data and ways to manipulate and store it.

6.1. Data Models

It is necessary to describe the data associated with different configurations and versions. In the simplest case (the baseline), a literal list of entities that go together is maintained. This representation is essential for auditing purposes and shipping lists. It is not adequate for supporting variegated products, since it is necessary to parametrize the descriptions, or preferably, to provide more general rules or connections among the parts. When creating a test version or experimenting with a new variant, one does not wish to specify thousands of obvious cases, so general rules and defaults are needed.

There are further advantages to a more general representation, which permits concise descriptions that can be understood and analyzed. It also permits examination of various slices through the sets of possible configurations, and analyses of properties of sets of controlled objects. On the other hand, a fully general representation is just an arbitrary database or programming language, and not very convenient for the specific purposes of SCM. A major challenge is to find solutions that are sufficiently general while being usefully expressive.

6.2. Rules and Constraints

A natural way to represent the relationships among data is constraints they should satisfy and rules to be performed. Even the simplest SCM systems implement a restricted form of rules. The problems of scale intrude rapidly: large numbers of rules are very hard to understand, and can be expensive to support. The rules themselves need to be configurable, so the representation problems can proliferate. There are many interesting ideas and prototypes that apply rule-based techniques; scaling them to factory-sized systems remains a challenge.

6.3. Granularity

The granularity of the data is crucial. Common systems operate at an excessively coarse level: the source file or deliverable program. An ideal system would permit manipulation of a wide range of sizes. The most popular grain size appears to be the function, procedure, or class definition. There are times when programs need to manipulate even finer grains, but handling this directly in the SCM system this can lead excess overhead and poor performance. Having a huge number of tiny objects can also clutter the human interface and interfere with the user's work. A major challenge is to provide mechanisms for all sizes, while providing special mechanisms for purposes of efficiency.

6.4. Data Storage

SCM systems specialize in the representation of huge numbers of related entities, many of which are never actually created or used. This has led to creation of a variety of compression and differencing techniques for storing related sequences (versions, etc.), and complex naming techniques for describing what is needed. These ideas need to be extended sensibly to a world of overlapping complex entities made up of objects (in the object-oriented sense).

7. Builder's View of SCM Systems

The architecture of SCM systems requires a balancing of many techniques. A modern large-scale SCM system makes serious demands on human interface, database, and distributed systems technologies. To make a system that operates well, one must choose to use some standard components and to build others from scratch. For example, SCM systems do not demand a solution of the fully general distributed database problem, and special techniques can be used to reconcile inconsistent data stores. A system that wishes to handle fairly general objects does not require full-scale object-oriented database facilities, but special care for representing links and for storing many slightly different data may be essential for success.

8. Gaining User Acceptance

After the technical points above are addressed, there are still major barriers to getting acceptance and use of the advanced technology. There is a fine balance between delivered functionality and difficulty of learning and utilization. Some hurdles to be jumped before achieving success are:

-   Evolution: It is crucial that good tools be provided to ease the transition from crude SCM to new systems, both to preserve data and semantics without requiring continual human intervention.

-   Performance: Performance must be perceived to be excellent.

-   Reliability: The system must be of unquestioned reliability, since all of the crucial project data will be managed by the SCM system and the final products will be created by it.

- Functionality: It must provide actual assistance to the user, not just make the managers happy.
- Productivity: It should enable the individuals and the organization to perform qualitatively better, not just provide a small incremental improvement.

ARCHITECTURAL DESIGN FOR USER INTERFACES

Joëlle COUTAZ

Laboratoire de Génie Informatique (IMAG)
BP 53 X, 38041 Grenoble Cedex, France
fax: (33) 76 44 66 75, tel. (33) 76 51 48 54
email: joelle@imag.fr

Summary

This article discusses software architecture modelling for the design and development of interactive systems. Software architecture models should support properties and constraints prescribed by the software and cognitive psychology communities. From these observations, we derive a multi-agent framework applicable to the software design of interactive systems. An example shows how this general model can be engineered to fit practical problems. We then discuss the ability of the model to support a number of properties and constraints relevant to software engineering.

Keywords

multi-agent architecture, user interface, software architecture.

1. Introduction

Rapid improvements in computer technology have increased the opportunities for developing highly interactive user interfaces. At the same time, progress in psychological studies and human factors have increased the potential for designing high quality user interfaces. These advances, however, have not alleviated the task of the user interface software designer. Requirements continue to overpass current practices. In order to fully exploit innovation in a systematic way, new and clear software architectures are needed.

This article discusses software architecture modelling for the design and development of interactive systems. Software architecture models should support properties and constraints prescribed by the software and cognitive psychology communities. A number of software properties and constraints are presented in section 2. From these observations, we then propose a framework useful for organizing interactive software (Section 3). In Section 4, a complete example is used to explain how the notions conveyed by the model can be engineered to fit a practical problem. In the last section, we analyse the ability of the model along the dimensions defined in section 2.

2. Properties and Constraints

Properties are the idealized characteristics which define the dimensions of a design space. They can be judiciously exploited to define design trade offs. Constraints are imposed attributes which reduce the design space. In general, they cannot be modified. The intent of this section is to enumerate a number of salient properties and constraints related to human computer interaction (HCI) and software engineering. Although the list is not exhaustive, it serves as a basis for evaluating our architecture model and for presenting our terminology.

HCI properties that we will consider here include: the control of the interaction, the notions of feedback and thread of dialogue; As for software engineering properties, we will pay attention to performance, concurrency, reusability, modifiability and portability. The platform used for software development and the existence of the functional core are two interesting constraints.

2.1. HCI properties

Control of the interaction. In HCI, one makes the distinction between system-driven interaction and user-driven interaction. In system-driven interaction, the user must respond to questions from the system. In user-driven interaction, the user is free to choose among a number of currently valid options.

Feedback covers expressions produced by the system in response to user's actions. It may be semantic (i.e. domain dependent) or syntactic and lexical (i.e. presentation dependent).

A *thread of dialogue* denotes some user's task. A dialogue is multi-thread when the user is able to undertake multiple tasks in parallel. Threads are interleaved when multiple tasks can be initiated but only one of them is processed at a time.

2.2. Software engineering properties and constraints

Performance. Response time of the system must match the expectation of the user. For example, datagloves require that the visual representation of the hand on the screen matches the physical hand gesture "instantaneously". Even if the user is capable of adjusting hand and finger movements to the slowness of the system, interaction becomes impossible [Sturman 89]. Clearly, performance is crucial to the usability of the system.

Concurrency is required to support parallism at the user's level: multiple physical actions may be performed simultaneously on a variety of devices and multi-thread dialogue are made possible.

Reusability is a key element in the evaluation of the development cost: Experience shows that the user interface portion of an interactive system represents up to 80% of the whole code. The ability to reuse and to port existing user interface components is thus an important feature.

Modifiability is a necessary property of an interactive system since good user interface design relies necessarily on iterative refinement [Norman 86].

The *development platform* includes the reusable software imposed to the implementer, such as the underlying operating system and tools fro building user interfaces. It is often the case that design decisions must be revisited to take into account the limiting factors of the platform.

Existence of the functional core. An interactive system is composed of two components: the functional core (FC) and the user interface system (UIS). The FC implements domain dependent concepts such as the notions of document, chapter, section, etc., in a document editor. The UIS implements the interaction between the user and the FC. For example, the UIS of the document editor presents the editing commands as well as the document in a WYSISYG manner. (We call UIMS, the user interface tool that helps in building a UIS). The existence of the FC may constrain the properties of the UIS.

The properties and constraints considered so far result from the analysis of the interaction between a human and a computer system. When considering architectural issues, this analysis leads to the following remarks: there are concepts (those modelled by the functional core) and presentation objects (those perceivable to the user and implemented in the UIS). Concepts and presentation objects must be linked by some mechanism. Since they serve different purposes, they may not use the same formalism. In addition to mapping functions, there must be some transformation mechanisms which smoothly bridge the gap between concepts and presentation objetcs. These preliminary observations are refined in the following section.

3. Overall Organization of an Interactive System

Figure 1 shows a general model of an interactive system based on the Seeheim model [Pfaff 85]. One salient property of this model is the symmetry organized around a key component: the dialogue controller. At the two extremes, the functional core and the user play a symmetric role at a high level of abstraction: both of them manipulate task domain concepts. Next, come two interface components: the functional core adaptor (the FCA) and the presentation component (the PC). A second salient property of the model is the multi-agent architecture of the dialogue controller.

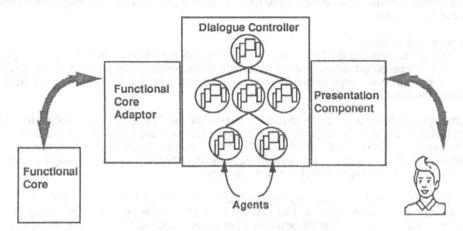

Figure 1: The basic components of an interactive system.

In the following paragraphs, we first consider the two extreme components of the model (the user and the functional core), then we discuss the two interfaces (the functional core adaptor and the presentation component) and close with the key element (the dialogue controller).

3.1. The user and the functional core

The user and the functional core both produce and consume information through the dialogue controller via the interface components. This symmetric view of the general functioning of an interactive system where the key component, the dialogue controller, is equally driven by the functional core and the user does not impose any model on the control of the interaction. The question of external VS internal VS mixed control [Tanner 83] is irrelevant at this level of description. Clearly, the choice between the alternatives is guided by the case at hand.

3.2. The functional core adaptor

The functional core adaptor (FCA) serves as a buffer between the dialogue component and the domain specific concepts implemented in the functional core. It is designed to absorb the effects of change in its direct neighbors. As any boundary, it implements a protocol. A protocol is characterized by temporal strategies, by the nature of data exchanged and by some linking mechanisms [Coutaz 91a].

Temporal issues
The transfer of information between two communicating entities such as the functional core and the UIS, must be coordinated over time. The coordination may be fully synchronous or fully asynchronous or may alternate between the two techniques.

Synchronous coordination implies that the sender waits for the receiver before its own processing can resume. In the context considered here, synchronous coordination models the mutual control of the functional core and the UIS: either one has the initiative but the initiator is directly controlled by its partner. Asynchronous coordination allows communicating entities to exchange information without waiting for each other. With such a communication scheme, the functional core and the UIS are two equal partners sharing a common enterprise: that of accomplishing a task with the user.

When considering interaction styles, synchronous coordination results in single threads of dialogue or, at best, in interleaved threads. Asynchronous coordination supports multiple concurrent threads of dialogue: the user may issue multiple commands simultaneously (using for example, a combination of voice and hands) while the functional core may have its own processing going on.

Nature of data exchanged
Data exchanged between the functional core and the UIS is performed in terms of conceptual objects. The term object should be considered here in the general sense as an entity. It does not suppose any particular implementation technique such as a class, a function, or a shared data structure but covers all of them.

A conceptual object is an entity that the designer of the functional core wishes to make perceivable to the user. Consequently, it is an object that both the functional core and the UIS understand. It belongs to the FCA. Ideally, a conceptual object is the electronic media independent representation of a domain dependent concept. Conceptual objects can be characterized by their type and their semantic purpose.

The type of a conceptual object may be elementary or constructed depending on the nature of the concept to be conveyed to the user through the UIS. The purpose of a conceptual object may be specific to the task domain or it may be of general interest. For example, the notions of paragraph, section, chapter, and document are specific to structured text editing. General purpose conceptual objects refer to notions that cognitive psychologists and human factors people have identified as useful for any interactive system. They include the concepts of error, cut-copy-paste, undo-redo, procedural and contextual help.

So far, we have identified two dimensions for the FCA: concurrency and the nature of data exchanged in terms of conceptual objects. We need now to analyze how conceptual objects relate to entities in the UIS components.

View Mapping
A presentation object is a UIS component whose purpose is to make a conceptual object perceivable to the user by using a combination of the human perceptual systems: auditory, visual, tactile systems, and eventually smell when the technology will be available. View mapping defines the correspondence between conceptual objects and presentation objects. This correspondence can be characterized along five axes: direction, connectivity, instantiability, accessibility, and responsiveness [Coutaz 91a].

Direction refers to the direction of the transfer of information between a conceptual object and a presentation object. It may be a one-way correspondence either from the functional core to the UIS or the other way round; It may be a two-way correspondence. A correspondence between a conceptual object and a presentation object implies that the UIS is able to automatically maintain the servoeing between those objects.

Connectivity refers to the cardinality of associations between conceptual objects and presentation objects. Experience reveals two useful configurations: connectivity 1-to-n and connectivity n-to-1. Connectivity 1-to-n may express the decomposition of a compound conceptual object into simpler units of presentation; it may also model the multiple representation of the same concept. For example, the concept of temperature may be presented to the user with two complementary views: a thermometer and a plot which respectively show the current value and the evolution of the temperature over time. Connectivity n-to-1 expresses the composition of multiple conceptual concepts into a unique presentation object.

Instantiability covers the dynamic creation and destruction of conceptual objects. Typically, computer aided design involves the dynamic creation and destruction of instances of concepts. The consequence for the UIS is to dynamically maintain the correspondence between conceptual objects and presentation objects through the FCA.

Accessibility expresses the semantic validity of the connection between conceptual objects and presentation objects. For example, the connection between the function "delete" implemented in the functional core and the menu item "delete" is semantically valid if at least one destroyable conceptual object exists in the system.

Responsiveness specifies the condition under which communication between conceptual objects and presentation objects can occur. Active data react immediately on changes. In some circumstances, immediate reaction need to be delayed.

So far, we have defined the dimension space at the boundary between the functional core and the UIS. This dimension space identifies the properties of the FCA. We need now to investigate the second interface of the model: the presentation component.

3.3. The presentation component

The presentation component implements the physical interaction with the user via hardware and software. It includes a set of presentation objects that defines the "image" of the system [Norman 86], i.e. the perceivable behaviour of the interactive system.

The presentation component is the location for handling low level multi-media events (for input as well as for output). For example, low level input events produced by voice and gesture input devices may be time-stamped and queued in the same way mouse events and keyboard events are currently processed by windowing systems. Multi-media events are combined into higher level events in the same way keyboard and mouse events are currently combined into higher abstractions by presentation objects.

3.4. The dialogue controller

The dialogue controller is the keystone of the model. Contrary to a number of user interface models, the dialogue controller is not a monolithic "obscure potato"! Instead, it is organized as a set of cooperating agents which smoothly bridges the gap between the functional core adaptor and the presentation component. An agent is a complete information processing system [Bass 91, Coutaz 90]. The nature of the agents involved in a particular interactive system and their relationships will be further described in paragraph 3.4.2. For now, we need to justify the overall functionality of the dialogue controller.

The overall functionality
The dialogue controller has the responsibility for task-level sequencing. Each task or goal of the user corresponds to a thread of dialogue. This observation suggests the choice of a multi-agent architecture. An agent or a collection of cooperating agents can be associated to each thread of the user's activity. Since each agent is able to maintain its own state, it is possible for the user (or the functional core) to suspend and resume any thread at will.

The dialogue controller receives events both from the functional core via the functional core adaptor (FCA), and from the user via the presentation component (PC). Bridging the gap between an FCA and a PC has a number of consequences. In addition to task sequencing, the dialogue controller must perform data transformation and data mapping:

1) A FCA and a PC use different formalisms. One is driven by the computational considerations of the functional core, the other is toolkit/media dependent. In order to match the two formalisms, data must be transformed inside the dialogue controller.

2) State changes in the FCA must be reflected in the PC (and vice versa). Therefore links must be maintained between FCA conceptual objects and PC presentation objects. A conceptual object may be rendered with multiple presentation techniques. Therefore, consistency must be maintained between the multiple views of the conceptual object. Such management is yet another task of the dialogue controller.

The dialogue controller at multiple resolution
Bridging the gap between the FCA and the PC covers task sequencing, formalism transformation, and data mapping. Experience shows that these operations must be performed at multiple levels of abstraction and distributed among multiple agents.

Levels of abstraction reflect the successive operations of abstracting and concretizing. Abstracting combines and transforms events coming from the presentation objects into higher level events until the FCA is reached. Conversely, concretizing decomposes and transforms high level data from the FCA into low level information. The lowest level of the dialogue controller is in contact with presentation objects. Since agents should carry task sequencing, formalism transformation, and data mapping at multiple levels of abstraction, it is tempting to describe the dialogue controller at multiple grains of resolution combined with multiple facets.

At one level of resolution, the dialogue controller appears as a "fuzzy potato". At the next level of description, the main agents of the interaction can be identified (see the example described in Section 4). In turn, these agents are recursively refined into simpler agents. This description applies the usual abstraction/refinement paradigm used in software engineering. Figure 1 shows the recursive description of the dialogue controller at multiple grains of resolution.

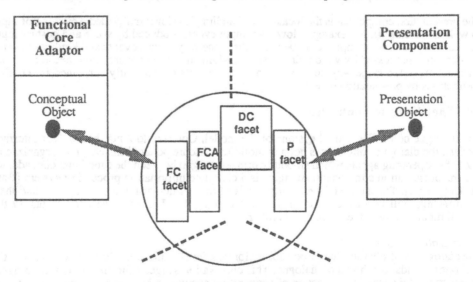

Figure 2: An agent of the dialogue controller. Dashed lines represent possible relationships with other agents. Dimmed arrows show the possible links with the surrounding components of the agent.

In addition to the refinement/abstraction axis, we introduce the "facet" axis. Facets are used to express the different but complementary and strongly coupled computational perspectives of an agent. These perspectives are similar to those identified for the whole interactive system:

• the functional core facet (FC facet) defines the competence of the agent in the chain of abstracting and concretizing. It may be related to some conceptual objects in the functional core adaptor;

- the functional core adaptor facet (FCA facet) performs formalism translation between the FC facet and the dialogue controller facet of the agent;

- the dialogue controller facet (DC facet) controls event sequencing inside the agent, maintains a mapping between the FCA facet and the presentation facet of the agent;

- the presentation facet (P facet) is involved in the implementation of the perceivable behaviour of the agent. It is related to some presentation object in the presentation component.

Figure 2 shows an agent of the dialogue controller and its relationships with the surrounding components. The model presented so far is kept general intentionally. The example described in the following section shows how it can be applied to a practical problem.

4. An example

Let us consider a tourist information system. As illustrated in Figure 3, this system splits the screen into two parts. A schematic view is used to display the map of the whole tourist area at low resolution (details such as town names and churches, are not visible). The detailed view contains a close-up view of a subset of the schematic view determined by a movable rectangle. As the user moves the rectangle with the tracker-ball, the detailed view is updated accordingly.

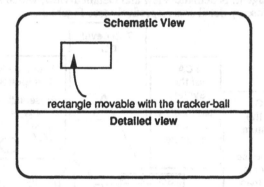

Figure 3: The split screen of the tourist information system.

In the following paragraphs, we describe the steps involved in the software design process of the tourist information system. We show how software design considerations can be combined to the principles advocated by our architecture model. More details on the software design rules can be found in [Coutaz 91b].

4.1. Step 1: Identifying conceptual objects and view agents

The tourist information system must model the notions of road, site of interest, name, etc. as well as their relationships. As shown in figure 4, the relationships between these elements can be modelled as a semantic network. This network, which is an abstract media-independent representation of the map, is maintained by the functional core portion of the interactive system. This functional core is considered here to be a data base server.

The purpose of a data base system is to express logical relationships between units of information such as "road R connects towns A and B". On the other hand, the notions of "close-up" and "schematic" views, which are user interface issues, may not be modelled in the data base. If so, an intermediary data structure, adequate for the automatic generation of the two complementary views, must be defined. This structure acts as a perspective on the tourist map maintained in the functional core. It adapts the content of the functional core to the need of the UIS. Therefore, it belongs to the functional core adaptor (see Figure 4).

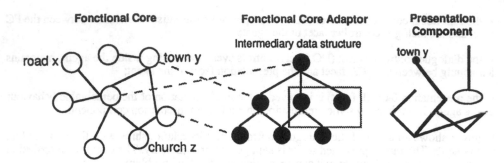

Figure 4: An intermediary data structure maintained in the FCA as the interface between the data-base world and the graphics tools. The rectangle shows the subset of the intermediary data structure that is currently displayed in the detailed view. Dashed lines between the FC and the intermediary elements represent the mapping maintained through the FCA.

So far, we have considered the abstract conceptual side of the interactive system. At the other end of the spectrum, we observe that the tourist information system provides the user with two different views of the map. Since a view acts as an interlocutor of the user, each view should be implemented as an agent: Schematic-View and Detailed-view, which model the schematic diagram area and the close-up detail area respectively (see Figure 5).

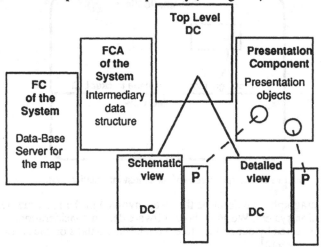

Figure 5: Step 1: Defining one agent per view. Dashed lines indicate the links with the presentation objects. Plain lines denote the expansion of the DC of the system.

According to the model, an agent is modelled along multiple perspectives. In particular:

• The P facet of Schematic-view is linked to a presentation object implemented in the presentation component of the system. This presentation object interprets graphics primitives to generate the visual representation of the map as well as the rectangle attached to the displacement of the tracker-ball. It also interprets input events when the tracker-ball is moved (see 4.5 for more details).

• Conceptually, the FC facet of Schematic-view is the intermediary representation of the map: Schematic-view is supposed to produce an image from the intermediate data structure designed as one step towards rendition. Since this representation holds for Detailed-view as well, it must be factored out (*software design criteria: memory resource sharing*). As advocated above, the FCA of the interactive system is the good candidate for maintaining such sharing.

• The DC facet of Schematic-view translates primitives received about the intermediary representation into graphics primitives interpreted by the associated presentation object.

• Since the FC facet of Schematic-view is empty, its FCA is empty.

An identical design process holds for the definition of Schematic-view. At this stage of the design, we can observe the abstraction/concretization/transformation phenomenon between the abstract representation of a map in the functional core, the intermediate media-independent data structure of the FCA suited for rendering, and the graphical representation of the view agents whose interpretation produces perceivable information.

4.2. Step 2: Introducing control agents

The functions of Detailed-view and Schematic-view are tightly coupled: the first one shows a close-up subset of the second one. Therefore a Multiple-view agent must be introduced to control their relationships. By doing so:
• automatic visual consistency is maintained between the two views, and
• Schematic and Detailed views ignore their mutual existence (*software design criteria: reusability*). (If the views referenced each other directly, they would not be reusable independently.)

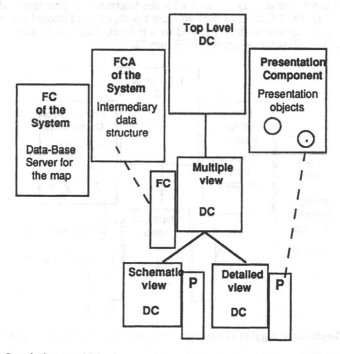

Figure 6: Step2: Introducing a multiple view agent to maintain visual consistency. Dashed lines denote links.

Since Multiple-view controls the multiple rendering of a map, its FC facet becomes a good candidate for maintaining the intermediary representation. There is a conflicting design decision, here: conceptually, the intermediary representation belongs to both the FCA of the interactive system and the FC facet of Multiple-view. Having an explicit interface with the functional core is a strong principle. Thus, the intermediate representation should explicitly sit

in the FCA of the interactive system. As for the FC facet of Multiple-view, the alternative is the following:
1) replicate the intermediary representation,
2) download portions of the intermediary representation and use it as a cache in the UIS,
3) access the intermediary representation when needed.

Clearly, solutions 1 and 2 minimize information transfer and ameliorate response time but require more resource memory. Although this is not the case in our example, they also imply the maintenance of semantic consistency. Solution 3 should be preferred if all the agents share the same address space. In our design, we will suppose that solution 3 is adequate: for example, the FC facet of Multiple-view contains pointers to the intermediate data structure of the FCA of the interactive system.

The DC facet of Multiple-view maintains the consistency between the two views it controls. Given the definition of the FC facet, there is no need for an FCA facet. The P facet is empty since Multiple-view is a controller with no direct representation on the screen. Figure 6 shows the current output of the software design process.

4.3. Step 3: Factoring out functionality

We observe that the FC and FCA facets of Schematic-view and Detailed-view are empty (functions already factored out in the higher levels of abstraction of the system). We also observe that the DC facet of Schematic-view is functionally identical to that of Detailed-View. Both contain the same operator (i.e. layout) with the intermediary structure and the level of detail as inputs. Thus, the DC facet of the two view agents can be factored out into Multiple-view. Since, the view agents are now reduced to a P facet, they can be converted into two presentations for the Multiple-view agent (See Figure 7).

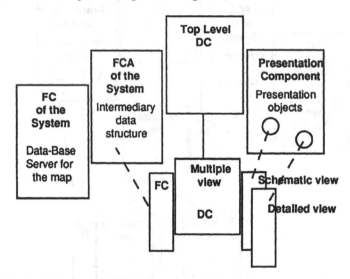

Figure 7: Step3: Converting the two view agents into two P facet for the Multiple-view agent.

4.4. Step 4: Bundling Agents

An agent of the dialogue controller may control multiple agents or perform data transformation (abstraction/concretization). When an agent controls a single subagent, then the functionalities of these agents may be combined. Since the DC of the system is controlling one single agent (i.e. Multiple-view), the functionalities of DC and of Multiple-view can be bundled up into one unit. Figure 8 shows the final architecture.

4.5. The final architecture

As shown in Figure 8, the tourist information system consists of the following components:

• a functional core, FC, for modelling the notion of map at a high level of abstraction,

• a FCA for adapting the abstract FC map to the UIS requirements,

• a DC which 1) includes a translation mechanism for switching between the formalism used in the FCA and the formalism used in the presentation component; 2) maintains visual consistency in the presentation component.

• a presentation component made of two presentation objects: Schematic and Detailed, corresponding to the schematic diagram area and the close-up detail area respectively.

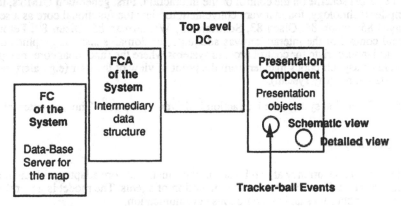

Figure 8: One possible architecture for the tourist information system.

We are now able to describe the information flow as the user acts on the tracker-ball to select a new area of interest:

• When receiving a tracker-ball event, Schematic view computes the relative displacement of the focus of interest (dx, dy). The software designer must then make a choice between two possibilities:
  a) either Schematic notifies DC of the traker-ball event, and DC asks Schematic to move the rectangle,
  b) or Schematic processes the event (it moves the rectangle), then notifies DC of the state modification.

Solution b) is preferable in terms of message passing but solution a) is more appropriate in terms of semantic feedback. In b), Schematic immediately reacts at the lexical level without waiting for potentially useful computationnal feedback: Schematic's behaviour is wired. Since Schematic's behaviour is semantic independent, we will opt for solution b).

• Schematic informs DC of a "new focus". DC maps the parameters of the focus into the new portion of the intermediate data to be shown;

• DC gets the new portion from the FCA, transforms the FCA description into graphics primitives;

• Graphics primitives are sent to the Detailed presentation object which then is able to redraw the new close-up view.

As discussed in the following section, this design solution may be modified by the properties and constraints of the development platform.

5. Architecture modelling with constraints and properties

This section is concerned with the impact of properties and constraints on the design process. When relevant, the discussion will be illustrated with the design example of section 4.

5.1. The control of the interaction

The balance between the functional core and the user does not imply any scheme for controlling the interaction. This is in constrast with earlier interpretations of the Seeheim model which imposed an *a priori* scheme on the control of the interaction. First generation UIMS's, inspired by the compiler technology, found it very convenient to view the functional core as a semantic server [Hayes 85, Jacob 84, Olsen 83, Schulert 85, Wasserman 85, Olsen 89, Petoud 89]. This external control of the interaction was adequate for domains such as graphics and text editing; it was inappropriate for control process systems where the functional core may produce information in an asynchronous manner from the point of view of the user (e.g., alert messages in a nuclear station security system).

In the tourist information system, the interaction is driven by the user. Thus, an external control is desirable.

5.2. Concurrency

The model refers to concurrency at two levels: in the functional core adaptor with the notion of protocol, and in the dialogue controller with the notion of agents. The model is general enough to support both synchronous and asynchronous communication.

Concurrency at the dialogue controller level makes it possible to implement concurrency at the user's level. For example, in the case of the tourist information system, concurrency at the user's level would allow simultaneous verbal requests (such as "show me this") and physical actions (such as the selection of the location of interest on the screen). Concurrency at the FCA level, allows for parallel processing between the functional core and the UIS.

The development platform may not provide facilities for the expression of parallelism (e.g. the Macintosh system). Then, in order to handle concurrency between the functional core and the UIS, the UIS is constrained to periodically poll the functional core. This functionality may be handled by the DC facet of the system (i.e. the top level DC).

In the domain of user interface, concurrency control has a strong impact on the usability of the system. As discussed in [Robertson 89], agents in animation systems have different time constants and vary in their computational requirements. If the underlying platform is not able to support these variations, then some animated objects may jump instead of showing a smooth evolution over time, or they may appear too fast or too slow. Again, a top level DC facet can be implemented to control computational resources between the agents of the UIS.

5.3. Reusability

The model stresses reusability in a number of ways. First, with the notion of adaptors, then through a judicious organization of agents. The advantages of the adaptors will be developed in the next paragraph. Cement and multiple view agents are good examples of reusability.

The cement agent controls a number of sibblings (say a palette and a scratch area). It behaves like a syntax analyzer which controls the local automata maintained in its subagents. By doing so, input for syntax analysis may come in any order from multiple sources. If, in addition, the cement agent is able to handle the construction of several commands simultaneously, it provides an easy way to implement multi-thread dialogues.

By doing so, none of the sibblings has a privileged role over the others and they need not be aware of each other. Being unaware means that they do not send any message to each other. Being aware would make them dependent; They would not be reusable individually but as a cluster only. The multi-agent framework provides a natural way for satisfying agent reusabilty through the use of intermediary control agents.

Similarly, the multiple view agent is driven by reusability considerations. Agents which implement the views of a concept do not need to know each other. Considering that the views are created dynamically by the user, it may be difficult for the view agents to track their alter ego. Consistency maintained by a special control agent solves the problem in a simple way.

5.4. Modifiability

The model suports modifiability in multiple ways: the existence of adaptors and the possibility for semantic enhancement.

Adaptors
The two adaptor components, the functional core adaptor and the interaction toolkit adaptor, enhance modifiability and portability. They alleviate the constraints imposed by the functional core and the interaction toolkit available from the development platform.

The functional core adaptor defines a clear interface with the functional core. As long as the modification of the functional core does not affect this interface, the rest of the system is left unchanged. If the interface is to be modified, then the modification is necessarily concentrated in one location. This centralization facilitates the maintenance of the interactive system and limits development cost.

As shown in Figure 9, the interaction toolkit adaptor defines a virtual toolkit used for the expression of presentation objects. This expression is then mapped into the formalism of the actual toolkit used for a particular implementation. Switching to a different toolkit requires rewriting the mapping rules but the expression of the presentation objects remains unchanged.

Presentation Component

Extension Layer
Interaction Toolkit Adaptor
Toolkit

Figure 9: Details of the Presentation Component.

Presentation objects are generally constructed from entities made available in interaction toolkits. In general, interaction toolkits such as the X Intrinsics [OSF 89], provide an abstraction mechanism for defining new presentation objects. However, it is not always possible to build new presentation objects from the predefined building blocks of the toolkit. For example, in an earlier version of the X intrinsics, widgets (i.e. presentation objects) would occupy rectangular areas only. In such conditions, the notion of a wall in a floor plan drawing editor, could not be implemented as a diagonal line widget. Instead, a presentation object "wall" would be defined as a new abstraction outside the toolkit.

This example shows that the presentation component should be structured into three layers. Specific presentation objects which can be built from the building blocks of the toolkit belong to the toolkit. Those which cannot be built with the toolkit are part of a third layer, the extension layer. The interaction toolkit adaptor (ITA) such as XVT [Valdez 89] defines the boundary between these two layers.

An ITA defines a policy for the acquisition of user events. An event may or may not be automatically dispatched to the presentation object where the event occurred. If the tourist information system is to be implemented on top of an ITA with automatic dispatching, then Schematic receives tracker-ball events (as in section 4). At the opposite, if events are not dispatched, a special DC facet should be implemented for this purpose. In general, the top level DC of the system is a good candidate for event acquisition whether such events come from the FCA or from the ITA. In the example of the tourist information system, events would be acquired by the top level DC. This DC would then determine the new focus in the FCA, notify Detail to update its content as well as Schematic to move the rectangle at the appropriate location.

Semantic Enhancement
The notion of conceptual object in the functional core adaptor may be exploited to perform semantic enhancement. A conceptual object is supposed to match the mental representation that the user elaborates about a particular domain concept. It may be the case that the functional core, driven by software or hardware constraints, implements a domain concept in a way that is not adequate for the user. In the case of the tourist information system, the notion of "detail/schematic" was not modelled.

Semantic enhancement may be performed in the FCA by defining conceptual objects which reorganize the information of the functional core. Reorganizing may take the form of aggregating data structures of the functional core into a single conceptual object or, conversely, segmenting a concept into multiple conceptual objects. It may also take the form of an extension by adding attributes (such as "detail/schematic") which can then be exploited by the UIS.

5.5. Performance

Performance may be enhanced through semantic delegation. The semantic quality of feedback may require frequent round trips with the functional core. This long chain of data transfer may be costly with respect to time. Therefore, it may be inconsistent with the expectation of the user. Semantic delegation, which consists of down-loading functional core knowledge into the user interface is a way to reduce transmission load. In particular, if the functional core is implemented as a distinct process running on a distinct processor, it may be judicious to use the FCA as a local cache of the functional core.

Semantic delegation may be performed in the dialogue controller as well. Functional core facets of agents provide a natural means for maintaining domain dependent information at multiple levels of abstraction. In the example of the tourist information system, semantic delegation could have been exploited with the FC facet of the Multiple-view agent.

5.6. Feedback

The possibility of representing any concept, from simple up to compound information, may have a strong impact on the quality of the semantic feedback. In particular, if the UIS supports simple data types only, then concepts which "naturally" match compound structures must be artificially decomposed by the functional core into elementary entities.

In order to reconstruct a representation adequate for the user, the UIS must provide the user interface designer with an abstraction mechanism in the presentation layer. In the absence of such a mechanism, the "glue" must be explicitly programmed. Then, the next problem for the implementor is to identify the appropriate location for such coding. A number of UIMSs, such as FormsVBT [Brown 89], do not support compound conceptual objects. In addition, most of them do not provide any abstraction mechanism in the presentation layer nor do they convey a clear architectural model to guide the decision process and identify which portion of the interactive system should be in charge of the conceptual glue.

An explicit expression of accessibility in the FCA allows the UIS to automatically produce an appropriate feedback and prevent the user from performing illicit actions. For example, the menu item associated with the delete operator would be dimmed until accessibility becomes legal.

An explicit expression of responsiveness in the FCA can be used to control the granularity of semantic feedback. For example, consider the task of a customer filling up an order. The form contains fields specific to the task including the customer's name. Concerning the validity of the customer's name, the designers of the system have two options: either check the validity as soon as the name is specified or perform the verification when the user validates the order form. In the first case, the user is provided with immediate semantic feedback, whereas with the second option, the order is processed in one burst.

6. Conclusion

Despite the development of a large number of UIMSs and interaction toolkits, there is currently no satisfactory product. In particular, automatic generation of user interfaces may be applied in only a limited number of cases. As a result, software designers still have to face the difficult problem of implementing the missing pieces or overloading the inadequate portions produced with user interface tools. The architecture model and the engineering issues presented in this article address the shortcomings.

Acknowledgements

This paper was influenced by stimulating discussions with our colleagues and observers of the IFIP WG 2.7, and with members of the AMODEUS project: G. Abowd, Bala, L. Bass, M. Beaudouin-Lafon, M. Harrison, I. Newman, P. Dewan, J. Larson, C. Unger, H. Stiegler. A. Chabert and L. Nigay of the IHM group of LGI and V. Normand of Bull-Imag also deserve special thanks for their contribution to our model.

References

[Bass 91] L. Bass, J. Coutaz: Developing Software for the User Interface; Addison Wesley Publ., 1991.

[Brown 89] M.H. Brown, G. Avrahami, and K.P. Brooks: A Two-View Approach to Constructing User Interfaces. In Proceedings of SIGGRAPH'89 (Boston, 31 July-4 august). Computer Graphics, 23, 3 (July), ACM, 1989.

[Coutaz 90] J. Coutaz : Interface Homme-Ordinateur : Conception et Réalisation; Dunod Publ., 1990.

[Coutaz 91a] J. Coutaz, S. Balbo: Applications: A Dimension Space for UIMS's; Proceedings of the Computer Human Interaction Conference, ACM ed., May 1991, pp. 27-32.

[Coutaz 91b] J. Coutaz, L. Nigay: Software design rules for multi-agent architectures. Amodeus BRA 3066 Deliverable.To appear, August 1991.

[Hayes 85] P.J. Hayes, P. Szekely, R. Lerner : Design Alternatives for User Interface Management Systems Based on Experience with Cousin; Proceedings of the CHI'85 Conference, The Association for Computing Machinery Publ., April, 1985, 169-175.

[Jacob 84]   R.J.K. Jacob : An Executable Specification Technique for Describing Human-Computer Interaction; Advances in Human Computer Interaction, H.R. Hartson, ed. Alex Publishing Co., 1984.

[Norman 86] D. A. Norman, S. W. Draper : User Centered System Design; Lawrence Erlbaum Associates Publ., 1986.

[Olsen 83] D.R. Olsen, E.P Dempsey : Syngraph : A Graphical User Interface Generator; Computer Graphics, July 1983, 43-50.

[Olsen 89] D.R. Olsen : A Programming Language Basis for User Interface Management; CHI'89 Conference proceedings, K. Bice, C. Lewis editors, ACM Press publish., April, 1989, 171-176.

[OSF 89] OSF : OSF/Motif, Programmer's Reference Manual, Revision 1.0; Open Software Foundation, Eleven Cambridge Center, Cambridge, MA 02142, 1989.

[Petoud 89] I. Petoud, Y. Pigneur : An Automatic and Visual Approach for User Interface Design; IFIP WG2.7 Working Conference Proceedings, Engineering for Human-Computer Interaction, Napa Valley, August, 1989.

[Pfaff 85] User Interface Management Systems; G.E. Pfaff ed., Eurographics Seminars, Springer Verlag, 1985.

[Robertson 89] G. Robertson, S. Card, J. Mackinlay: The Cognitive Coprocessor Architecture for Interactive User Interfaces; 2nd symposium on UIST, November, 1989, pp. 10-18.

[Schulert 85] A.J. Schulert, G.T. Rogers, J.A. Hamilton : ADM - A Dialog Manager; Proceedings of the CHI'85 Conference, The Association for Computing Machinery Publ., April 1985, 177-183.

[Sturman 89] D.J. Sturman, D. Zeltzer, S. Pieper: Hands-on Interaction with Virtual Environments; 2nd symposium on UIST, Nov., 1989, pp. 19-24.

[Tanner 83] P. Tanner, W. Buxton: Some Issues in Future User Interface Management Systems (UIMS) Development. IFIP Working Group 5.2 Workshop on User Interface Management, Seeheim, November, 1983.

[Valdez 89] Valdez : XVT, a Virtual Toolkit; Byte 14(3), 1989.

[Wasserman 85] A. Wasserman : Extending State Transition Diagrams for the Specification of Human-Computer Interaction; IEEE Transactions on Software Engineering, 11(8), August, 1985.

The Eureka Software Factory: Concepts and Accomplishments

Christer Fernström
Cap Gemini Innovation, Grenoble Research Centre
7, Chemin du Vieux Chêne, ZIRST, 38240 Meylan, France
e-mail: christer@capsogeti.fr

ABSTRACT

The Eureka Software Factory project has been active since late 1986. This paper describes the overall aims and technical approach of the project and provides a status report as of mid 1991.

The need to adapt the computerized part of a software factory to the total needs of the factory is important, while at the same time the needs change over the life-time of the factory. Flexible adaptation is therefore important and is in ESF achieved through process modelling and process enactment, which is applied within the framework of a factory evolution model.

The factory evolution model of ESF is supported by a set of functionalities given the name *ESF Support*. The first full implementation of ESF Support, which will be available mid 1992, is described, together with the experimental prototypes which are currently under evaluation.

1. BACKGROUND

The software factory concept, which was introduced a number of years ago, symbolizes a desired paradigm shift from labour intensive software production to a more capital intensive style, where investments can be applied at a well understood level of risk. The focus of a software factory is not a project, but an organization, and return on investment is consequently measured in global terms with respect to the software producing organization. The scope of a software factory is therefore also much larger than the scope of more traditional software engineering environments or "integrated project support environments", IPSEs. Given the larger context, the lifetime is also considerably longer than for an IPSE and a software factory must be able to survive changes in the organization it supports and be adaptable to new tools and technologies. Providing an adequate basis for building and introducing software factories in practice is a major effort, which goes beyond what any individual CASE vendor or system house is currently prepared to manage.

With the intention to address the full scale of this problem, the Eureka Software Factory (ESF) project was established in 1986 by a consortium of IT companies, universities and research institutes under the auspices of the Eureka programme. The aim of the ESF

This work was supported by the Eureka Software Factory project.

project is to provide the necessary infrastructure (including technology, standards and organizational support) in order that software factories may be constructed and tailored from components marketed by independent developers. The ESF consortium, which comprises fourteen partners from five European countries, represents different software "interest groups": computer manufacturers, research institutes, CASE tool providers and system developers. The consortium has the following members:

- Cap Gemini Innovation (F)
- Dresdner Bank (D)
- EB (N)
- ICL (UK)
- Imperial College (UK)
- INRIA (F)
- Matra Espace (F)
- Sema Group (F)
- Sema Group (UK)
- SI (N)
- Softlab (D)
- Systemhaus GEI (D)
- TeleSOFT (S)
- University of Dortmund (D)

The project has a central management team located in Berlin and development is carried out in subprojects, which are organized as smaller projects at different locations in Europe. Subprojects involve one or several ESF partners and are set up in answer to internal calls for proposals. Since 1989 the total effort has been over 200 man years per year. The workplan divides the planned project time into four phases with different focuses: a definition phase (86-87) focussing on requirements and choice of technologies; a kernel phase (88-92) focussing on reference architecture, environment standards, development of integration technology, re-engineering and experimental integration of existing tools and factory demonstrators; a factory instance phase (92-94) focussing on introducing factories into organizations and on the continuous adaptation of factories to the (changing) requirements of specific organizations; a market phase (92-96) focussing on the organizational support for a market of ESF conformant components, factories and services. This paper provides an overview of the project and presents the major results achieved to date.

2. ESF SOFTWARE FACTORIES

ESF stresses the existence of both computerized and non-computerized parts in a software factory. The scope of a factory accordingly embraces both the organization and its work force on the one hand, and the tool support given to individuals and teams on the other. The term *factory support environment*, FSE, is introduced to denote the computerized support part of a software factory.

The need to adapt the FSE to the organizations rather than the other way around cannot be over-emphasized. A fundamental concept in ESF is therefore what has been called *model driven support* of the software process, and the technology commonly referred to as "process modelling" plays an important role. The bridge between the organizational aspects and the FSE is technically achieved by placing the individuals in *work contexts*, derived from explicit models of the software production process. Not only does this contribute to providing better support for the work of the individuals but, equally important, it helps achieving better predictability of the process. This is accomplished by using the process model as a focal point for accumulating experience from earlier or ongoing projects. Process models thus become tangible containers of methodological know-how in a format which makes them readily accessible for future use. The remainder of the present section of the paper will elaborate on the role of process models in the organization of software factories.

2.1 Software Factory Evolution Model

A general model for the areas of concern of software factories is outlined in figure 1. The model shows the four areas of: general framework, tools and components, models or descriptions of specific factories, and implementations of specific factories. The name given to the areas are respectively: *Generic ESF, Component Base, Factory Model* and *Software Factory (Instance)*.

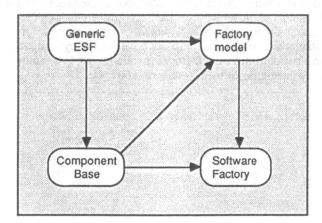

Figure 1. General model for the areas of concern of software factories. Arrows indicate flow of information.

The Generic ESF level defines a reference architecture for software factories, conformance criteria for ESF compliant factory components, a factory meta-model (i.e. a formal model of the factory life-cycle) called the *ESF Software Factory*

Evolution Model, and notations (languages) for describing components and factory processes.

The component base level denotes the base of available components for population of factory support environments. This base, which is the result of implementation or re-engineering of existing CASE tools in conformance with the generic ESF definitions is continuously extended. In addition to tools and tool fragments (tool fragments are software components that serve as reusable building blocks for tools), the component base level includes specific knowledge of the software engineering domain in the form of reusable specifications of software processes (e.g. descriptions of standard methods) and support environments (e.g. conceptual information models for software engineering or tool models).

The factory model level describes *specific* software factories in terms of models of the processes to be supported and the characteristics of the (desired) support environments. These models are provided in accordance with the generic ESF. The reuse of models of processes and support environments, present in the component base level, plays an important role in building a specific factory model.

The software factory (instance) **level** denotes the customized software factories which are put into place within the software development organizations.

Figure 2 provides a semi-formal description of the factory evolution process which is defined as part of the Generic ESF. The notation used in the figure is SA/DT actigram and the model is simplified to include only the major activities and information flows.

The six activities, or sub-processes, defined in the model are: component implementation & re-engineering, component certification, formal customization, factory instantiation, the target software process, and model and software reuse deduction. These processes are partly carried out within the context of the target organization's software factory (as indicated by the shadowed part in the figure), partly within other organizations. For example: the tool implementation & re-engineering process is carried out by component providers, whereas the formal customization and factory instantiation processes may either be carried out by factory integrators or by the target organization.

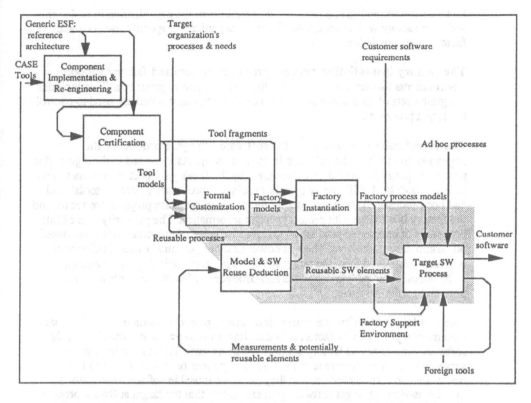

Figure 2. ESF software factory evolution model expressed in SA/DT notation.
The scope of the target organization's software factory is shadowed.

The six sub-processes, and the information flow between them, can be summarized as
follows:

The **component implementation and re-engineering process** produces
various building blocks for factories, of which the most important are tools and
tool fragments. The process is controlled (as indicated by an incoming arrow at the
top of the process box in the figure) by the reference architecture and component
conformance criteria of the Generic ESF. Tools on the CASE market serve as
input for re-engineering. The output of the process also includes tool models that
describe the behaviour of the tools. Tool models are expressed in the ESF
Component Description Language (CDL).

The **certification process** verifies that independently produced components
fulfill the ESF conformance criteria.

The **formal customization process** produces customized factory models, i.e.
models of specific software factories. Inputs to the process includes: tool models
produced by the implementation & re-engineering process, reusable process and

factory support models and informal descriptions of the organization in which the software factory will be set up. At this level organization specific methods and factory roles are defined.

The factory instantiation process produces customized factory support environments that are used to support the target software processes. This includes integrated sets of tools and executable model specifications that are used to control the target processes.

The target software process is the software life-cycle process of the organization in which the software factory is set up. As indicated in the figure, this process is partly supported and controlled by the factory support environment and process models of ESF, partly by other tools and processes ("foreign tools" and "ad hoc processes"). As a first step in the process, software projects are set up and the factory is initiated with project specific information. The primarily role of this process is of course the production and maintenance of customer software, based on customer requirements. There is however other potentially useful information that may be derived from the target software process, including measurements, information about ad hoc processes and produced software elements that has a potential for future reuse.

The model and software reuse deduction process manages the feedback information produced by factories in use. Its aim is to produce reusable models of software processes and factory support environments. These reusable models serve two purposes: they extend the ESF component base which is used in the formal customization process, and they generate reusable software elements that may be used in the target software process. (Note that the target software process may also include a local reuse process within a single factory instance).

2.2 ESF Support

Although not shown in figure 2 for simplicity reasons, all processes above are supported by what is called *ESF Support*. ESF Support is thus the common name denoting the set of functionalities that support the total factory life-cycle process. It comprises two distinct parts:

* **Evolution Support**, with the role to assist in factory evolution.

* **Operation Support**, with the role to assist factory operation within the target software process.

ESF Evolution Support may in fact be considered as an ESF software factory in its own right, where the software process supported is the ESF factory evolution process. It should however be noticed that different types of organizations may be in charge of different parts of the factory process. Thus if a tool vendor, active in the the implementation & re-engineering process, has one factory instance, a system house, specializing in factory building, will have a slightly different factory instance that mainly aids the formal customization and instantiation processes.

An instance model for the ESF Evolution Support factory is defined by the ESF Project that also provides one implementation of such a factory. The current status of availability is described in Section 4 below. The principal elements of ESF Evolution Support are the following:

- The component implementation & re-engineering process is supported by syntax-directed editors, stub-generators and reuse libraries for the ESF CDL (Component Description Language). Furthermore, it is supported by tools for user interface generation and object oriented database management systems that relieve component builders of the tedious tasks of dealing with user interaction or management of persistent objects.

- Component conformance, which is verified by the certification process is controlled by component conformance criteria and supported by an ESF certified test harness for components.

- The formal customization process is supported by graphical editors for process and information modelling, and by tools for reuse of the component base.

- The factory instantiation process is assisted by process model compilers and by the plug-in mechanism of the ESF Software Bus[1] (see below) that supports component interoperation and integration.

- The model and software reuse process is supported by tools for process metrics, model acquisition and reuse classification.

The target software process is supported by the ESF Operation Support, which comprises the communication mechanism of the ESF Software Bus, process program interpreters and mechanisms for process supported user interaction.

3. OPERATIONAL VIEWS OF AN ESF SOFTWARE FACTORY

The support environment of an ESF software factory can, as any information system, be considered from various viewpoints. Each sub-process of the factory life-cycle process described above has its view (or even sets of views) of the support environment. In this section, three important views will be described, namely that of the individual taking part in the target software process; that of the process manager who defines and customizes the factory process definitions in the factory customization process, and that of the component integrator in the factory instantiation process. These views are respectively referred to as the *user interaction view*, the *interworking view* and the *interoperation view*[2].

---

[1]"Plug-in mechanism" and "ESF Software Bus" are registred trademarks of the ESF Project.

[2]The interworking and interoperation views were referred to as the "process view" and the "structural view" respectively in earlier technical descriptions of ESF (e.g. [ESF 89])

3.1 The User Interaction View

The user interaction view focuses on the universe of discourse in the interaction between individuals and their support environment. How the interaction takes place or how various concepts are represented to the users may vary between different factories or between different users in the same factory (e.g. depending on the type of interaction media they use) and will most certainly vary over time, since user interface technology and style is continuously evolving. The ESF user view is therefore focussed on a conceptual model of the factory concepts that influence the interaction.

The user interaction view is based on the concepts of *user work context* and *user interaction environment*. A user work context is a user-role-task specific collection of interaction objects. Interaction objects encapsulate information and tool functionality and may appear as distinct elements in an object oriented user interaction model, or as independent data and tools. A user work context may be used and customized (e.g. in terms of look and feel) by the person who owns it. Every task in which the person is involved is represented to him in terms of a work context, and the set of all work contexts that are available to him at one point in time constitutes his user interaction environment. This is schematically represented in figure 3.

A useful paradigm for user interaction based on these concepts is that of office environments, where information flows between "desks" in the form of office envelopes containing more or less self-contained information to be processed by the recipient. Such office oriented environments have been built in ESF, where user work contexts represent office envelopes with their contents, a specific "agenda" tool represents the in-trays and out-trays, and the desktop, on which the contents of opened envelopes are disposed, the user interaction environment [Fernström and Ohlsson 91].

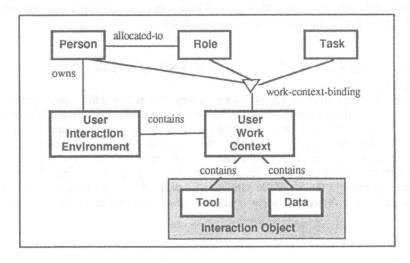

Figure 3. User work contexts provide individuals with access to task and role specific tools and data.

3.2 The Interworking View

The interworking view is the place for describing the software process of a factory. It describes the working procedures supported in the factory and shows the factory support environment as a programmable system: how it is customized to fit the methods of organizations and projects and how the users are to be actively supported. In this view are represented: methods, working procedures and rules, the organization in which the software process takes place, products, and the support functionality available in the factory. An essential characteristic of ESF is that process descriptions are enacted, meaning that the people-oriented software process and an executable model of this process are executed simultaneously and in a synchronized manner, with the aim to enhance the computer-based support given to the human-oriented process, e.g. through automatic provision of user work contexts.

Process models describe the relationships between entities such as *role, task, activity* and *tool*. Task descriptions (or, more precisely, task type descriptions) serve as templates for specific tasks, which are instantiated from the process models during process enactment. Instantiation of tasks may be triggered by various events in the process, the most obvious one being a project manager's decisions about planning and resource allocation. Instantiation involves parametrization and binding to real persons, tools, etc. Obviously, not all bindings may take place at the same time; the binding of persons to tasks typically takes place during project planning, while the binding to tools may be deferred until the task is actually started. An important quality of process programming languages is therefore the ability to allow incremental instantiation of generic elements, meaning that certain elements may be bound while others remain generic.

Process support for managers, teams and individuals can take different forms, and the ESF model does not enforce any particular view on the nature of process support in software factories. Depending on the needs of the organization, the process support may be authoritarian with the aim to enforce procedures and rules, or relaxed and supportive with the aim to help focus the user's attention or to automate trivial but time-consuming tasks.

Different styles of process support put different requirements on the languages used to express the processes, and ESF therefore proposes several languages for process modelling, but with a common frame of reference for basic concepts [Schäfer 90]. To date, three languages and their corresponding process support environments are available for use in ESF factories (see [Schäfer 90] for an overview) :

- OPIUM combines structured analysis charts with Petri-nets into a graphical language suitable for describing and automating information flow between individuals. The OPIUM environment currently supports process enactment in a distributed environment.

- FUNSOFT combines a type-definition language with Petri-nets into a graphical language suitable for automating or simulating complex activities. The FUNSOFT environment currently supports simulation and dynamic modification of processes, but not full scale enactment.

- MERLIN combines an extensible knowledge base with a rule-based language with forward and backward chaining semantics into an expert system shell suitable for describing role interactions and providing automatic tool invocation. MERLIN currently supports enactment in a distributed environment.

3.3 The Interoperation View

The interoperation view of a factory describes how the various building blocks of a factory support environment interoperate within the framework of an open systems interaction model. The ESF reference architecture is communication oriented, based on client-server and peer-to-peer interoperation. Functionality is provided by *Service Components* which are entities with private address space and which may be allocated over a computer network. Interaction between users and the functionality provided by the Service Components is handled by *User Interaction Components*, which are programs running locally at the users' workstations. *Tools* in the traditional meaning do not exist as distinct entities, but should be seen as compositions (or bindings) between User Interaction Components and Service Components, as described by process models.

The *ESF Software Bus* [ESF 91] manages various aspects of integration between components, including:

- the matching of services that are required by one component to those offered by others

- the provision of new services through combination of services already available

- the communication between components with little structural and semantic loss of information, across heterogeneous language and system platforms

The Software Bus is a language-based set of mechanisms that use component models expressed in the ESF *Component Description Language* to enable the integration of components. It covers data integration, control integration and platform integration:

Data integration is supported by the Software Bus through "specification level interoperability" [Wileden et al. 90], meaning that the semantics of data is treated separately from its syntax and representation. Integration takes place over semantic data descriptions, while data representation problems are handled by syntax transformation. For the purpose of data integration, the CDL includes a type manipulation sub-language, called SADL ("service abstraction description language"), and a data representation sub-language, called SRDL ("service representation description language"). Separation of the two concepts also allows alternative implementations of the same semantic concepts, but with different representations, in a manner similar to programming with abstract data types.

Control integration is supported by the provision of a set of interoperation primitives with different semantics. There are two built-in primitives, namely RPC (remote procedure call) which provides synchronous communication with procedure call semantics, and buffered asynchronous communication which allows communication with components that are temporarily off-line. Event queue management, selective broadcast and notification services can all be built on top of the software bus communication primitives in order to extend the control integration facilities.

Platform integration is supported by letting the communication mechanisms run on a platform independent communication layer - TCP/IP in the present implementation - and by providing dynamic system reconfiguration and late binding between components. This allows for example a service component running on one computer in the system to be dynamically replaced by a new component running on another computer, possibly of a different type, without client components being aware of the change.

4. ACHIEVEMENTS

After four and a half years of existence, the project has built up a considerable amount of technology and know-how which will be summarized in this section. For more details, see [ESF 90, Rockwell 91].

The first group of results is concerned with the Generic ESF, i.e. *specifications, definitions and standards*. Internal results are available in terms of a reference architecture for ESF software factories, a component description language (which implicitly specifies the ESF software bus), a frame of reference for process modelling, language proposals for reusable software elements and for user dialogues, and an outline reference model for engineering environments. Due to the importance of formal languages and notations in the project, a language definition standard has been established. Within a wider scope, the ESF project is participating in European standardization efforts, including the ECMA standardization works on PCTE and software engineering environment architectures.

The second group of results consists in *implementations of ESF Support*. A first full release of ESF Support will be available in May 1992. However, prototype versions of the various elements are available and under evaluation within the project. These include:

- Two successive implementations of a software bus (HAPPI and SHIVA).

- Four implementations of process support (OPIUM, FUNSOFT, MERLIN and PEBA Process Support).

- Build and run-time support for User Interaction Components, including an editor generator for visual languages (SEMDRAW), a multi-view application interface (XTV), a dialogue generator (XCB) and a view server for managing consistency between views of shared information (NEXUS).

- An integration framework for constructing federated databases (OSS).

The third group of results involves the *ESF component base*, which includes software components for populating ESF factory support environments, ready-to-use process models of standard methods, and reusable software elements in general. This includes:

- User Interaction Components and Service Components supporting the following type of activities: project management, configuration management, quality control of software modules, metrication, document creation and manipulation, documentation management (hypertext with versions), design (graphical and textual support for several design methods), test generation, reuse, programming (syntax-directed or textual editors, in some cases with semantic verification and completion), debugging, testing, specific support for Ada programming and testing, prototyping. Many of these components are the result of re-engineering of commercial CASE products.

- Process models for standard methods: DoD 2167A, GAMT17, HOOD, as well as a number of proprietary standards, e.g. PERFORM of Cap Gemini Sogeti. Model fragments are also developed for specific aspects, including change management and reuse.

- Reuse libraries of common packages/class structures for Ada and C++.

The fourth group is concerned with *factory models*. Currently there are three models available, two for software factories for real-time applications (ESF-MINI, FERESA) and one for commercial applications (PEBA).

The fifth group involves *prototypical instances of partial factory support environments*. The most ambitious effort along these lines was based on factory requirements for the production of real-time software [Bégou and de Torcy 90, Fernström 91]. This sample FSE, called the "ESF-Mini", incorporates more than twenty components provided by eight organizations in ESF and gives a realistic view of a software factory according to the principles of ESF. It was publicly demonstrated at an ESF seminar in November 1990. Other trial FSEs with specific focus on process support and work context management include: SITE [SI 89] (user-definable work contexts, delegation of work), HAPPI [Hubert and Perdreau 90] (process enactment, a posteriori integration of commercial tools), PEBA [Franckson 91] (relationships between process and product models, process guided interaction with product models) and ARCHIPEL [Fernström and Ohlsson 91] (process enactment and integration with project management, delegation, work contexts, tool activation)

Finally, research efforts within the context of the ESF Advanced Technology Programme (see below) have produced results in the areas of extensible type systems and formal languages.

5. PROJECT ORGANIZATION

The ESF project is organized into work programmes coordinated by a management framework which includes centralized and decentralized management teams. Individual subprojects are set up by sub-consortia in order to carry out work within the context of the work plans of the programmes. At present there are three active work programmes:

- **A technology development programme**, with the purpose to develop specifications, prototypes and products. In the present phase of the project, called the "kernel phase" (1988-92), the role of the technology development programme is to provide implementations of ESF Support, component conformance criteria/standards, elements of the ESF component base and factory demonstrators.

- **A factory introduction programme**, with the aim of helping to establish ESF software factories within software development organizations inside and outside the ESF consortium. This work programme is currently being established and will gain importance during the next project phase: the "factory instance phase" (1992-94).

- **An advanced technology programme,** with the purpose to prepare the future work programme for the technology development programme. The majority of the work carried out by the research institutes and academic partners of ESF fits into this work programme.

Figure 4 depicts the organizational structure of the project. The *Control Board*, which includes representatives of all partners and with equal voting rights, continually evaluates and defines the strategic targets of the project. The Control Board is supported by two advisory boards: the *ESF Research Focus* which gives scientific advice and helps position the project in the context or world-wide research efforts, and the *ESF Council* which gives advice with respect to the market position of the project. Both advisory boards include distinguished individuals from outside the consortium.

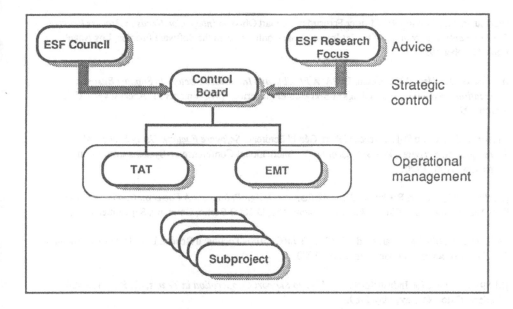

Figure 4. The ESF project organization

Operational management and project support is carried out by a project management team which consists of two bodies: the *Technical and Administrative Team (TAT)* which is centrally located in the project headquarters in Berlin, and the *ESF Management Team (EMT)* which consists of the operational managers of all partners and which is a decentralized team meeting on a regularly basis. Working teams are grouped into *Subprojects*, each with a project manager and a technical manager/chief architect.

ACKNOWLEDGEMENTS
The author is grateful to Kjell-Håkan Närfelt and Lennart Ohlsson for providing ideas and input to the paper, and to Robert Rockwell and Maurice Schlumberger for many helpful comments to an early version of this paper.

REFERENCES

[Bégou and de Torcy 90] Philippe Bégou, Eric de Torcy: *ESF Real-time Factory*, in [ESF 90].

[ESF 89] ESF Technical Design Group: *ESF Technical Reference Guide, ver 2.0,*ESF, Hohenzollerndamm 152, D-1000 Berlin, Germany. July 1989.

[ESF 90] The ESF Project: *ESF Project Overview and Technical Reports*, ESF Seminar, ESF, Hohenzollerndamm 152, D-1000 Berlin, Germany. November 1990.

[ESF 91] The ESF Software Bus subproject: *The ESF Software Bus - An Overview*, ESF Technical Report. ESF, Hohenzollerndamm 152, D-1000 Berlin, Germany. May 1991.

[Fernström 91] Christer Fernström: *An ESF Pilot Factory for Real-time Software*, Proceedings of Software Engineering Environments 91, Aberystwyth, UK, March 1991.

[Fernström and Ohlsson 91] Christer Fernström, Lennart Ohlsson:*Integration Needs in Process Enacted Environments*. Proceedings of the 1st International Conference on the Software Process, Los Angeles, USA, October 1991.

[Franckson 91] Marcel Franckson: *PEBA: A Flexible and Integrated Factory to Support Business Application Production*, Proceedings of Software Engineering Environments 91, Aberystwyth, UK, March 1991.

[Hubert and Perdreau 90] Laurence Hubert, Gérald Perdreau: *Software Factory: Using Process Modeling for Integration Purposes*, Proceedings of the 1st International Conference on Systems Integration, Morristow, April 1990.

[Rockwell 91] Robert Rockwell: *Software Factory Design Priorities: A Focus on Communication*, ESF Technical Report, ESF, Hohenzollerndamm 152, D-1000 Berlin, Germany, September 1991.

[Schäfer 90] Wilhelm Schäfer (ed.): *ESF SPECIMEN*, ESF Technical Report. ESF, Hohenzollerndamm 152, D-1000 Berlin, Germany. November 1990.

[SI 89] SI: Senter for Industriforskning: *How to Support Cooperation in Teams*, SI, P.O. Box 124, Blindern, Oslo, Norway, May 1989.

[Wileden et al. 90] Jack C. Wileden, Alexander L. Wolf, William R. Rosenblatt, Peri L. Tarr: *Specification Level Interoperability*, Proceedings of the 12th International Conference on Software Engineering, Nice, France, May 1990.

Integrating Structured and Formal Methods: A Visual Approach to VDM

Jeremy Dick, Jérôme Loubersac
Bull Corporate Research Centre,
Rue Jean-Jaurès, 78340 LES CLAYES-SOUS-BOIS, France

Abstract

Two barriers to the widespread industrialisation of formal methods are a lack of methodology, and the use of mathematical notations that are not easily understood by the non-specialist.

The work presented in this paper addresses these problems by defining diagrams which may be used to visualise aspects of formal specifications. The diagrams used are adaptations of classical approaches such as entity-relationship and state-transition diagrams.

The approach described imposes a methodology on the early stages of system specification, and provides the analyst with a choice of notations, visual and non-visual, while maintaining an underlying formality. During the process of analysis, the notation most appropriate for the expression and communication of the concepts required can be selected.

Two sorts of diagram are discussed: Entity-Structure Diagrams, and Operation-State Diagrams, the former in detail, the latter in sketch form.

A tool is envisaged that assists the analyst in moving between diagrams and VDM. Each diagram can be mapped onto parts of a common VDM specification, which forms the central underlying system description. Consistency can then be checked by a VDM type-checker.

Keywords

integration, structured methods, formal methods, visual notations, VDM

Acknowledgement

This work is partially supported by the ESPRIT project Atmosphere, Ref. #2565. The main partners are CAP Gemini Innovation (coordinator), Bull, Philips, Siemens, SNI and SFGL (contractor).

1 Introduction

Formal notations have a reputation in industry for being hermetic. Their terse textual nature, with frequent use of mathematical symbols, does not provide a good medium for communication with the non-mathematician. This creates a barrier to the uptake of formal methods in an industry where 'methodology' is frequently equated with the use of graphical techniques, especially in the early stages of system conception.

Some formalists have expressed the opinion that pictures are not an appropriate medium for formality, because they are too open to misinterpretation and ambiguity. Along with other authors (see for instance [PKP91], [CunGold88], [MTW90], [Harel87] and [Naftalin91]), we feel that this dismissal of visual notations is unfair. We see no reason why diagrams cannot be used as a concrete image of an abstract syntax with a formal semantics as in, for instance, [BFO89].

Such notations could combine formality with visual intuition, alleviate the communication problem with non-specialists, and accelerate the uptake and integration of formal methods into industry.

1.1 Formal Notations

Formal notations are those whose semantics have been formally specified using mathematics. A typical approach to the definition of such languages is to define the syntax (often abstractly), to define a domain of mathematics in which the semantics will be modeled, and to define a mapping from syntactic constructs to sets of models.

The Vienna Development Method [Jones90] makes use of a formal notation (referred to hereafter as VDM) for the specification of functional properties of systems. It is not a programming language, since it contains non-executable constructs. It is intended for the definition of the functional requirements in a very abstract but formal manner, before designing a system in detail.

The use of formality at the specification stage of system development can increase confidence in the correctness of software by permitting

- proof of properties of the system before it is implemented. Design errors can be avoided before they become very costly to correct.

- proof of properties of the system during implementation: Implementation is carried out by successive refinements, each of which can be proven correct with respect to the previous stage.

Some of the tools required to assist in formal development are an editor, a static analyser (parser and type checker) and others to assist in the refinement process.

As part of the ESPRIT project Atmosphere, the formal specification group at the Bull Research Centre are integrating a range of such tools for VDM into a PCTE [BGMT88] programming environment for the development of distributed systems.

One of these tools will be a Specification Assistant, designed to support the creation of VDM specifications through the use of visual notations.

1.2 A Specification Assistant

As we have mentioned above, the ability to present in diagrammatic form the essential structures defined by a formal specification could improve communication. Thus a tool for generating, for instance, Entity-Relationship Diagrams [Chen76] from VDM specifications is an attractive idea.

The ability to do the converse - to extract VDM specifications from diagrams - would address another current difficulty: the lack of methodology for the early stages of formal system development. If requirements analysis could be carried out in graphic form, and formal specifications derived, at least in part, from the diagrams, then the route to the adoption of formal methods would be still easier.

It is with these goals in mind that we have set about creating a prototype analysis assistant which can manage the consistency of a VDM specification and a set of annotated diagrams. The analyst may either

- create a VDM specification from a collection of diagrams

- create a set of diagrams from a specification showing different aspects of the VDM specification

- make changes to the VDM, and have the tool make the appropriate changes to the diagrams, or

- make changes to the diagrams, and have the tool make the appropriate changes to the VDM.

The work involves, in part:

selecting appropriate diagrams: Our goal is to find three or four types of diagram, each giving a significantly different dimension of the problem, and yet which, when taken together, give an as complete as possible formal specification. Where information cannot conveniently be represented diagrammatically, annotations will be used to make the meaning of symbols precise.

defining the well-formedness of diagrams: A certain level of consistency and completeness will be required in diagrams before successful translation into VDM can be achieved. We plan to define the kinds of intelligent assistance that could be given by a tool in this domain.

developing appropriate styles of VDM specification: It is evident that some styles of specification will be a great deal easier to represent diagrammatically than others, especially by automatic translation. Without unduly constraining the analyst, we need to define the styles preferred. These styles will contribute to the methodology imposed by the use of diagrams.

giving a formal semantics to selected diagrams: By defining transformations from annotated diagrams to VDM, we are in effect giving the diagrams a formal semantics in VDM[1]. To formally define these transformations, we must provide an abstract syntax for each type of diagram, and functions mapping objects of this syntax to and from the abstract syntax of VDM.

making a prototype implementation: Our role in the Atmosphere project is to demonstrate feasibility rather than provide a production quality toolset. Our approach is therefore to formally specify (in VDM) the transformations required, and make a fully working prototype in Prolog or Lisp. We have adopted the diagraming tools of IDE's "Software thru Pictures" for the creation and editing of diagrams, and the Atmosphere editor and type-checker for VDM specifications. Using an early prototype, we have already succeeded in generating VDM domain expressions from extended Entity-Relationship diagrams.

An obvious relationship exists between Entity-Relationship Diagrams and VDM domains. Less obvious is how to represent VDM operations diagrammatically. State-transition diagrams are an immediate choice for examination, and it is here that the style of specification becomes critical. The VDM notation does not have the same notion of state as that usually intended in a state-transition diagram. However, an appropriate methodology surrounding VDM could encourage a style in which it is easy to identify states and transitions. Whether such a style is compatible with ease of proof in the later stages of refinement is a question we do not expect to be able to address in this work.

1.3 Related Work

The work of the FOREST project [CunGold88], where diagrams are used to capture requirements, and formal texts derived from them, is close in spirit to the work presented here, although the underlying formalism is a modal logic designed to express rather different aspects of functionality than those addressed in VDM.

Work is being carried out on the relationship between the Z notation and structured analysis. In one approach [SA91] aimed at integrating the Yourdon methodology with Z, Entity-Relationship Diagrams (ERDs) are used to model system state, and Data-Flow Diagrams (DFDs) are used to create operation schemas. Another project called SAZ [Polack91] aims at integrating SSADM with Z in a similar way. Whereas we have felt able to depart from the classical entity-relationship diagram to create a formal visual notation closer to VDM, the emphasis in the Yourdon and SAZ work is in the integration of Structured Analysis with formal notations. For this reason, they have chosen not to depart from the classical diagrams, and they study how to move from SA diagrams to specification using Z.

Recent work at the Delft University of Technology [PKP91] has studied different approaches to modelling the transformation of DFDs into VDM. The semantics of DFDs is sufficiently complex, however, that it is doubtful whether the corresponding VDM specifications help in understanding the system.

---

[1]This supposes, of course, the existence of a formal semantics for VDM. We are in touch with the British Standards Institute committee on the standardisation of VDM who are currently defining such a semantics [BSI90b].

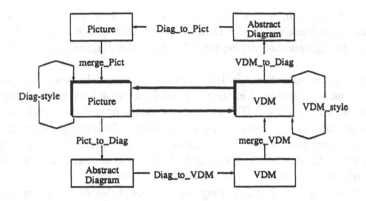

Figure 1: Tool functionality for each diagram

1.4   Contents of the Paper

In Section 2, we describe our view of the process of analysis, and how the analyst interacts with the tool. In Section 3, we describe in detail the use of a form of entity-relationship diagram called Entity-Structure Diagrams. In Section 4 we describe the transformations between Entity-Structure Diagrams and VDM. Section 5 contains a sketch of a plan for Operation-State Diagrams. Section 6 discusses the use of "Software thru Pictures" for creating and editing such diagrams, and finally Section 7 draws conclusions and describes the direction of future work.

2   The Process Of Analysis

The process of requirements analysis involves communication and interaction with the commissioners of the system, taking, analysing and presenting information in many different forms, until (in this context) a complete formal specification has been drawn up and agreed.

It is our view that there are advantages in being able concurrently to build diagrams and formal texts during the analysis process. The diagrams assist in communicating the structure of the system in a clear visual manner, and the formal texts encourage the analyst to ask the right questions to remove inconsistencies and ambiguities from the system description.

We envisage, therefore, analysts working alternately on diagrammatic and textual descriptions of the system. They may choose from one of a number of different kinds of diagram, or the formal text, as the most appropriate medium for developing a particular concept. Tool support, then, should enable analysts to move freely from diagram to text and back again, automatically translating changes as required.

Within this scheme also, several analysts may be able simultaneously to work on different diagrams, developing different aspects of a system, and use tools to bring all aspects together in a unified, structured formal text.

Figure 1 represents the functionality required of a tool for each kind of diagram supported. The boxes and arcs in bold represent the overall functionality required, i.e.

the ability to translate from pictures to VDM and back again. The other boxes and arcs represent the smaller steps from which the main transformations are composed. Both transformations pass through an abstract representation of the diagram, and finish with a merge.

Merging is necessary, because there is information contained in both the picture form and the VDM form, not contained in the abstract form, which we wish to preserve across updates. On the one hand, a VDM text may contain operation definitions, for instance, which are not affected by the content of an entity-relationship diagram. The operation definitions should not be lost. On the other hand, pictures carry implicit information about, for instance, the positioning and size of nodes and arcs which we may wish to retain whilst other details of the diagram are altered.

For translation to be successful, there may be various styles of visual or textual notation which must be used. The style arcs marked on the emboldened boxes of Figure 1 represent functions intended to give intelligent assistance in completing the information content of a diagram or text. Such tools will ask appropriate questions whose answers will supply missing information, lead to the removal of ambiguity or inconsistency, or promote a particular style of specification.

A set of these transformations is required for each kind of picture used. In the following sections of this paper, we shall describe two kinds of picture. One kind, based on entity-relationship diagrams, we shall describe in detail. The other, based on states and transitions, we shall only sketch.

3 Entity-Structure Diagrams

The purpose of this section is to describe Entity-Structure Diagrams (ESDs), an extended form of entity-relationship diagram that we have chosen to depict VDM type definitions, and the relationship between the ESD and VDM notations.

In Section 3.1 we discuss VDM composite types, motivating the ideas in an intuitive step-wise fashion. Section 3.2 similarly discusses VDM modules. Section 3.3 then defines the full ESD notation.

3.1 Composite Types in VDM

In VDM, complex types can be created from certain basic types (Booleans, Naturals, Characters, Reals, ...) using type constructors such as sets, sequences, products, maps and functions. A frequently used construction is the so-called *composite* type, a form of product type with named fields. An example of this is

> *Cabin* ::
>   *position* : **N**
>   *speed* : **R**
>   *buttons* : **B**-set

which defines a new type called *Cabin* composed of three fields of types natural, real and set of Boolean, respectively. Fields may be referenced using a Pascal-like dot notation; e.g. if *c* is of type *Cabin*, one can write *c.speed* to reference the real-valued field of *c*.

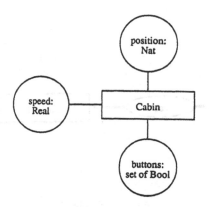

Figure 2: A simple entity-attribute diagram

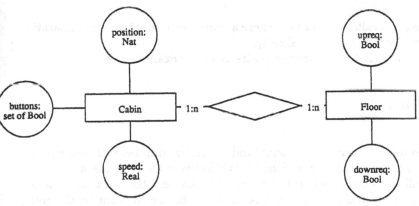

Figure 3: A simple unnamed relationship

If one views composite type as entities, and fields as attributes, there exists an obvious transformation between composite type definitions and entity-attribute diagrams. Figure 2, for example, could be used to represent *Cabin*, where rectangles signify entities (composite types) and circles represent attributes (fields).

Relationships can be added to entities and attributes to represent products or maps between composite types. If, for example, there exists a second composite type:

Floor ::
    upreq : **B**
    downreq : **B**

the product type *Cabin* × *Floor* could be represented by a many-to-many relationship, as in Figure 3, for example. A map type *Cabin* $\xrightarrow{m}$ *Floor* and one-to-one map type *Cabin* $\xleftrightarrow{m}$ *Floor* could be represented by one-to-many and one-to-one relationships respectively.

Note that it is not clear at this stage what the name of the relationship should be. Attributes have names drawn from the names of the fields in the composite type.

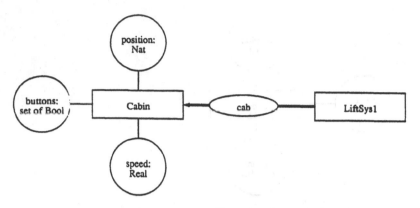

Figure 4: A simple has-a relationship

What the relationship is called depends on where abouts the product or map declaration occurs. We shall address this problem shortly.

The type of a field may be another composite type, for example

> *LiftSys1* ::
>   *cab* : *Cabin*

It is convenient to interpret this as a special kind of relationship between two entities, namely a has-a relationship called *cab*. Since it is effectively an attribute with a composite type, we will use a shape rather like a circle to represent the has-a relationship. The relationship is directional, so an arrow is used on the arc to point to the entity owned. It is depicted in Figure 4.

This notation can be extended to cater for more complex relationships between entities. For instance, a cardinality can be placed on a has-a relationship to indicate sets of attributes. Consider, for example, the composite type *LiftSys2*

> *LiftSys2* ::
>   *cab* : *Cabin*
>   *floors* : *Floor*-set

which has a field whose type is a possibly empty set of *Floor*. This is depicted in Figure 5 in which the has-a relation is marked with a cardinality of 0:n to indicate zero or more occurrences in the set.

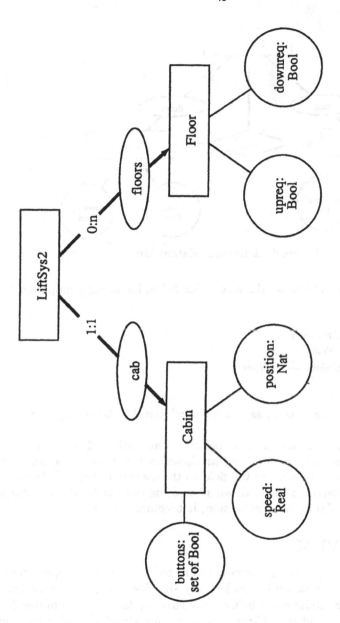

Figure 5: A has-a relationship with cardinality

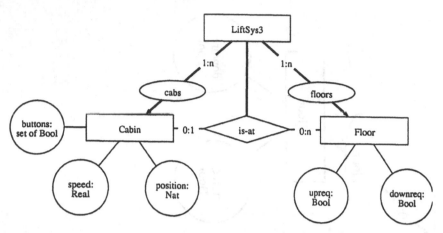

Figure 6: A named relationship

Now consider *LiftSys3* which has three complex fields, including a mapping:

> *LiftSys3* ::
>   *cabs* : *Cabin*-set
>   *floors* : *Floor**
>   *is-at* : *Cabin* $\xrightarrow{m}$ *Floor*

We can depict the third field, *is-at*, as a named relationship belonging to the entity *LiftSys3*, as shown in Figure 6.

We insist that every relationship must belong to an entity. The owner entity is attached to the relationship by a thick arc, as shown in the figure. The name of the relationship is now always the name of the field in the composite type. This insistence is not an unreasonable constraint; indeed, when we come to consider the structuring of a specification into modules in the next section, it becomes natural.

3.2 Modules in VDM

The ability to structure a specification is vital in any software engineering environment. Until recently, The VDM notation has lacked any significant structuring facilities. A number of proposals for modules are being considered by the BSI committee for the standardisation of VDM, and it is likely that a module structure will appear as an appendix to the first draft standard. We use here the syntax as currently suggested by that committee [BSI90a].

We shall reflect the structure of a specification by drawing a separate ESD for each module. We encourage a style in which each module defines a type which carries the same name as the module. This main type becomes the central entity in the ESD. Other local types (local entities) may be defined within the module. All relationships are defined within a module, and thus belong to the central entity of that module. Has-a relationships attached to the central entity point to references to the central entities of other ESDs, and depict the importation of other modules within a module. In this way,

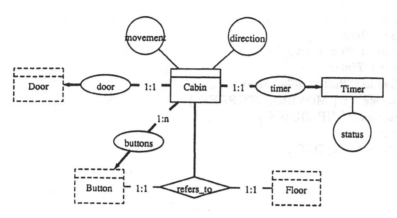

Figure 7: An Entity-Structure Diagram

we impose a hierarchical structure on ESDs, and no single ESD becomes over complex. Circular importations are not permitted.

We now need to extend an ESD to cater for three different kinds of entity: central, local and imported. Figure 7 shows an example of an ESD with these extensions. The solid barred rectangle is the central entity; dashed barred rectangles are imported entities, and the ordinary rectangle is a local entity.

The informal meaning of this diagram is as follows: a cabin consists of a single door, a set of buttons and a single timer. It has attributes indicating movement and direction, and it has associated with it a one-to-one mapping from buttons to floors. The timer, a local entity, has an attribute indicating status.

The VDM corresponding to this diagram could be as follows:

```
module Cabin
   interface
      export
         types Cabin
         ....
      imports
         from Door
            types
               Door
         ....
         from Button
            types
               Button
         ....
         from Floor
            types
               Floor
         ....
   definitions
      types
```

Cabin ::
   door : *Door*
   buttons : *Button*-set
   timer : *Timer*
   refers-to : *Button* $\xleftarrow{m}$ *Floor*
   movement : { MOVING, STOPPED }
   direction : { UP, DOWN }
 Timer ::
   status : { ON, OFF }
 ....
end *Cabin*

The parts marked .... could be definitions relating to operations which are not relevant to an ESD, and would have to be depicted by some other kind of diagram. The types of the attributes are not shown to avoid to much clutter. Invisible annotations which can be inspected and edited are used to hold such information.

The order in which the arcs appear on the diagram is, of course, completely arbitrary; an entity, for instance, will be modeled as having a set of attributes, ordering being unimportant. However, the order in which fields occur in a VDM composite type definition is not arbitrary; in the abstract syntax of VDM, a composite type is defined as having a *sequence* of fields. This difference has to be resolved in the transformation between ESDs and VDM modules, and will be handled by the merging process described in Section 4.3.

3.3   Abstract Syntax of ESDs

The previous subsections have strongly suggested a concrete visual syntax for ESDs, which we used to motivate the concepts involved. We will now abstract away from any particular representation by giving an abstract syntax for an ESD which contains all the information necessary to define the transformations in Figure 1. The syntax will be presented in the form of VDM type definitions.

First an ESD consists of a name, some imported entities, some local entities, some has-a arcs and some other relationships.

Esd ::
 name : *Id*
 imported : *Id*-set
 local : *Id* $\xrightarrow{m}$ *Entity*
 has-arcs : *HasRel*-set
 rel-arcs : *Relation*-set

 inv *esd* $\triangle$ *well-formed-esd(esd)*

By using a map of names to entities, we ensure that no two local entities have the same name. An invariant is placed on ESDs, which ensures, for instance, that the *name* field names a local entity, and that arcs are properly connected. Full details can be found in [DickLoub91].

An Entity consists of a number of optional components: a type, a VDM invariant (pattern and boolean expression), and a possibly empty set of attributes.

> *Entity* ::
>   *type* : [*TypeDef*]
>   *invar* : [*Invariant*]
>   *attribs* : *Attribute*-set

The type component is optional because it is often possible to deduce a composite type just from the set of attributes and relationships attached to the entity.

An Attribute consists of two obligatory components: a name and a VDM type definition for the attribute.

Attribute ::
    name : *Id*
    type : *TypeDef*

Each attribute corresponds to a field in a VDM composite type.

A has-a relationship comprises a name, an optional type, references to the owner and owned entities, a cardinality (defaults to ONE if omitted) and a Boolean value indicating whether or not the ownership is optional.

HasRel ::
    name : *Id*
    type : [*HasType*]
    owner : *Id*
    owned : *Id*
    cardin : [*HasCard*]
    opt: B

HasType = { SET, SEQ }
HasCard = { ZERO_MANY, ONE, MANY }

The type of a has-a relation indicates whether a multiple cardinality is to be modeled as a set or as a sequence. Note that the optionality of an attribute can be expressed as part of its VDM type definition by using square brackets round the type expression. This is not possible for a has-a relation, hence the explicit optionality field.

Other relationships consist of a name, a VDM type definition, the name of the owner entity, and a number of connections to other named entities, each connection having an associated cardinality.

$Relation$ ::
   $name : Id$
   $type : TypeDef$
   $owner : Id$
   $connects : Id \xrightarrow{m} RelCard$

$RelCard = \{$ ZERO_ ONE, ONE_ ONE, ZERO_ MANY, ONE_ MANY $\}$

The type definition is obligatory, because there is often insufficient information embodied in the cardinalities of the connections alone to construct the VDM type. The given type must, however, be consistent with the connections, but we have not attempted to define an appropriate invariant at this stage.

4 Translation Between ESDs and VDM

In this section we discuss the relationship between ESDs and VDM modules. Complete VDM specifications of the two transformations, *ESD-to-VDM* and *VDM-to-ESD* can be found in [DickLoub91]. The specifications make use of the abstract syntax for ESDs described in Section 3, and an abstract syntax for VDM taken from the BSI VDM draft standard [BSI90a]. Here the discussion of the transformations takes an informal approach, concentrating on the relationship between constructs in ESDs and VDM.

4.1 Transformation of an ESD into a VDM Module

ESDs only describe the data aspects of a system, corresponding to the type definitions in a VDM specification. The correspondence between the notations is as follows.

A central entity becomes a VDM module of the same name, exporting a local type definition of the same name.

Local entities become a local type definition of the same name in the module. If the entity's type field contains a VDM type, the type definition in the module takes this value; otherwise the type definition is composite, containing fields as described below, or **is not yet defined** if the entity has no attributes or relations.

Imported entities become a module instantiation of the same name in the module interface. The name of the entity also appears as an imported type in the instantiation, so that it may then be referenced in the module.

Has-a relations become a field of the same name in the composite type corresponding to its owner entity. The type of the field is essentially the name of the owned entity (which will become a composite type in the module) modified by "-set", "*" (sequence) or "+" (non-empty sequence), depending on the values of the cardinality of the relation. In addition, the type may be optional if the entity's optionality field is set.

Relations become a field of the same name in the composite type corresponding to its owner entity. The type of the field is taken directly from the relation's type field. The cardinality of the relation must agree with the type.

Attributes become a field of the same name in the composite type corresponding to its owner entity. The type of the field is taken directly from the type field of the attribute.

The order in which fields are placed in composite types is discussed in Section 4.3.

4.2   Transformation of a VDM Module into an ESD

Here the reverse transformation is described, an ESD into a VDM module.

A module becomes a main entity of the same name.

Instantiations become imported entities of the same name.

Type definitions become local entities of the same name (except if the type definition has the same name as the main entity). Composite types are defined by their fields which become attributes and relations as described below. All other types are defined by a the VDM type attribute on the entity.

Simple fields become has-a relations of the same name, owned by the entity corresponding to the enclosing composite type, and owning the entity of the same name as the field type name. (A simple field is either a VDM TypeName, or TypeName-set, or a sequence of TypeName, or an optional one of these. The cardinality and optionality of the has-a relation are set accordingly.)

Products or maps become relations of the same name between the entities whose field names appear in the type definition. Simple products and maps only can be treated in this way. The cardinality of the relationship is constructed as follows:

$$T1 \xrightarrow{m} T2 \qquad \text{one-to-many}$$
$$T1 \xleftrightarrow{m} T2 \qquad \text{one-to-one}$$
$$T1 \times T2 \qquad \text{many-to-many}$$

Other fields become attributes of the same name owned by the entity corresponding to the enclosing composite type, with its VDM type used to define the attribute type.

4.3   The Merging Operations

A typical mode of working with the Specification Assistant is to create an ESD, extract a VDM module from it, make modifications to the VDM, and recreate the corresponding diagram using the VDM to ESD transformation function. Typical changes to the VDM might be to change the order of fields in a composite type, or add fields to a composite type, or to add operation definitions to the module.

When the diagram is recreated, much of the information has remained unchanged. It is the role of the merge function to take the new version of diagram, and merge it into the old version in such a way as to retain diagram-specific details such as symbol sizes and positions.

A similar merge function must exist in the opposite transformation also, where the transformation of a diagram creates a new version of a VDM module. Here the kind of VDM specific information that should be retained is the order of fields in a composite type, for instance.

The transformation functions will assign default values to variables specific to the target notation. For instance, symbols will be of a default size, and assigned a position according to some predetermined algorithm. Similarly, field orders will depend, perhaps, on the order of creation of the arcs in the diagram. The merge function will then compare the new version with the old, and where common elements can be identified through non-notation specific attributes, the notation-specific values will be copied from the old version. Of course, if the user is not happy with the default values assigned by the tool, the editors can be used to change them.

5   Operation-State Diagrams

We discussed VDM type definitions in Section 3, and how ESDs could be used to visualise them. Here we discuss how Operation-State Diagrams (OSDs) can be used to visualise operations in VDM.

Operations in VDM are defined by the effect they have on the state of a system. There are two ways of defining them: *explicitly*, by giving a direct definition in a functional style; and *implicitly*, by stating a post-condition constraining the possible results of the operation. Both styles may optionally use a pre-condition to express partiality.

Pre-conditions are predicates on the arguments of the operation and on system state before the operation. Post-conditions are predicates on the operation's arguments and result, and the state of the system before and after the operation.

An example of an operation *start* on a *Cabin* is given below. The composite type for *Cabin* is also given for clarity.

Cabin ::
      position : $\mathbb{N}$
      speed : $\mathbb{R}$
      dir : *Direction*
      buttons : $\mathbb{B}^{*}$
      door : *Door*

$Direction = \{\ UP,\ DOWN\ \}$

$start(\ floor{:}\mathbb{N}\ )\ dir{:}Direction$
wr $c{:}Cabin$

      pre $c.speed = 0.0\ \wedge$
              $c.door.closed\ \wedge$
              $floor \neq c.position$

      post $c.speed > 0.0\ \wedge$
              $c.door.closed\ \wedge$
              $c.dir = $ if $\ floor > c.position$
                   then UP
                   else $DOWN\ \wedge$
              $dir = c.dir\ \wedge$
              $c\prime.position = c.position$

Since *start* has a certain effect on the state of the cabin *c*, it is tempting to view the operation as a state transition, with the pre- and post-conditions defining the source and target states respectively. The difficulty with this, however, is that pre- and post-conditions allow one to express properties far more general than can be conveniently represented in a classical state-transition diagram. For instance, states are disjoint in state-transition diagrams; that is, only one state can be occupied at a time. But here we wish to handle more complex states, where, for example, the cabin can be moving or not moving, and quite independently its direction indicator may be set to up or down.

Another idea is to use Petri nets, by associating a place to each predicate, and a transition to each operation. Pre- and post-conditions can be decomposed into smaller logical pieces to reflect more closely the complexity of the VDM. Even this, however, does not allow enough flexibility, since we wish to have some operations which have no pre-condition, and, in the case of explicitly defined operations, no post-condition. This would lead to ill-formed Petri-nets. In any case, we feel that to mix the formalism of Petri-nets with that of VDM in this context would lead to confusion.

Instead we have chosen to encourage a particular style of VDM in which states of interest are explicitly identified by auxiliary predicate definitions. These states do not have to be disjoint. We adapt the classical notion of a state-transition diagram by allowing non-disjoint states and operations which are loosely connected to states. The resulting diagrams we call Operation-State Diagrams (OSDs).

First we define some explicit states of a cabin, *idle* and *moving*:

$idle : Cabin \rightarrow \mathbf{B}$
$idle(c) \quad \underline{\Delta} \quad c.speed = 0.0 \ \wedge$
$\qquad\qquad c.door.closed$

$moving : Cabin \rightarrow \mathbf{B}$
$moving(c) \quad \underline{\Delta} \quad c.speed > 0.0 \ \wedge$
$\qquad\qquad c.door.closed$

Now we are able to recast the operation *start* making use of these definitions:

$start(\ floor{:}\mathbf{N}\ )\ dir{:}Direction$
wr $c{:}Cabin$

> pre $\quad idle(c)\ \wedge$
> $\qquad floor \neq c.position$
>
> post $\quad moving(c)\ \wedge$
> $\qquad dir = $ if $\ floor > c.position$
> $\qquad\qquad$ then UP
> $\qquad\qquad$ else $DOWN$

Figure 8 shows what an OSD for the cabin module with a number of operations might look like. States are pictured as circles, and operations as rectangles. Double circles represent initial states. Short, thick lines join sets of disjoint states. Arrows represent dependencies between operations and states as pre- and post-conditions. For instance, the two states *idle* and *moving* are attached to the operation *start* as pre- and post-conditions respectively, as shown by the direction of the arrows, representing the requirement that the operation is only valid on an idle cabin, and the effect of the operation is to leave the cabin in the moving state.

The diagram does not represent all the requirements. Other parts of pre-conditions (for example, that the destination be not equal to the cabin's current position) have to be expressed as non-visual attributes of the operation. Similarly with the details of the arguments of operations, and the other parts of post-conditions.

It is reasonable to interpret the operation *start* in Figure 8 as a state transition, since the states *idle* and *moving* are disjoint. Other operations, however, cannot be so viewed. Take for example the operations *set_dir_up* and *set_dir_down*: these partial operations are only applicable when the cabin is NOT in the *moving* state (as represented by the "not" annotation on the corresponding arrow.) It is clear that the operations in this case cannot be interpreted as state transitions, their only effect being to set the direction, and the states *down* and *up* are independent from the other states.

There is a certain amount of information implicit in an OSD which has to become explicit in a VDM module. For instance, nothing is explicitly stated about how the

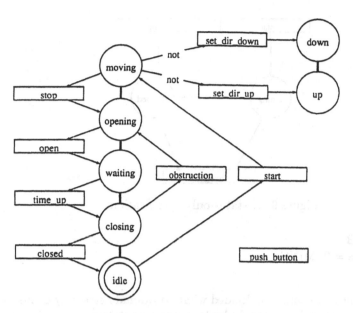

Figure 8: A Operation-State diagram

the moving-opening-waiting-closing-idle state component changes under the operations *set_dir_up* and *set_dir_down*; it is assumed implicitly to remain unchanged. A feature of VDM is that, if components of the state remain unchanged, the fact must always be explicitly stated. Therefore, in translating operations such as these into VDM, information about the unchanging state components must be stated.

The disjointness of those states connected by disjointness arcs could be represented in the VDM by an invariant in the composite type (in this case *Cabin.*) It is not clear at this stage how such invariants will be handled in the semantics of VDM. If this would prevent operations from being implemented in a way that allowed the entity temporarily to pass through other states during a transition, then an invariant is not the best way of handling the problem. Another, perhaps better, way would be to generate a proof obligation to show that the various states are disjoint.

Note that the operation *push_button* is not connected to any state. This means, in effect, that the operation is applicable in any state of the cabin, without affecting any of the named states. Its definition must be contained entirely within non-visual annotations.

In some cases all that one may want to say abstractly about an entity is that it can be in one of several states; other than these details, there are no identifiable attributes, etc. Consider for instance the two diagrams in Figure 9, an ESD on the left and an OSD on the right. In order to define these disjoint states in a VDM module, the type *Timer* will have to be composed of at least one field, so that the different states can be represented. In this case it is clear that a single field, called perhaps *state* taking the values *TIMING* and *STOPPED* would be sufficient, and this could be automatically generated in the transformation process, along with the appropriate predicate definitions for the states, e.g.

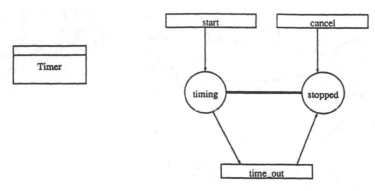

Figure 9: A states-only specification

$timing : Timer \rightarrow B$
$timing(t) \triangleq t.state = \text{TIMING}$

In general, however, it cannot be decided what additional fields may be necessary to determine the state. One solution would be to generate a state attribute in every case, and where no predicate describing the state is provided, generate one by default. We are currently working on better approaches to this problem.

6 Software Thru Pictures

The design of the two kinds of diagram described in previous sections has been influenced by the choice of diagram editor used as a medium for implementation and integration. Local constraints lead us to choose the Picture Editor from "SoftWare thru Pictures"[2] (StP).

StP is a tool designed to support structured methods using classical diagrams such as entity-relationship, state-transition, data-flow and structure charts. The different kinds of diagram each interact with a common data-base of definitions, which provides a central mechanism for controlling consistency between diagrams.

The tools offer a wide variety of symbols, and allow easy creation and editing of diagrams. An ascii representation of each diagram is available in a published format, which can be manipulated directly.

StP offers a number of pre-defined diagram editors which are specialisations of a basic diagram editor. The entity-relationship editor, for instance, includes three symbols and a single type of arc, sufficient for classical entity-relationship diagrams. To create the proposed diagrams, we have used the so-called Picture Editor, which offers the symbol shapes and arc types we require. Indeed, the figures in the paper where drawn in this manner.

The symbols and the arcs which join them carry two kinds of attribute: *visible* attributes, shown by shape and arc type or by textual labels; and *hidden* attributes,

---

[2] A product from Interactive Development Environments, Inc.

made up of structured text which may be inspected and edited separately from the diagram.

The hidden attributes of symbols allow diagrams to be linked to an underlying database of definitions. Each type of diagram is in essence a different view of the contents of the data-base.

It is possible in StP to personalise symbols by redefining the structure of the hidden attributes. Each attribute has an identifier, a cardinality and a value. The cardinality specifies the number of attributes of that kind that may be assigned to a single symbol.

StP also provides a mechanism for traversing a hierarchy of diagrams by use of a PUSH-POP function. This allows us, for instance, to move from one ESD to another by following the hierarchy of imported entities.

In the work reported here, the role of the underlying data-base is replaced by a collection of interrelated VDM modules. This permits control on consistency, by passing the VDM specification through a type checker. In this way, entities referred to in an OSD but not defined in an ESD, for instance, can be identified. Thus we make no use of the StP data-base.

Our approach to the definition of a concrete syntax for each type of diagram is to first define an abstract syntax for an StP picture. Then we define transformations to and from the abstract syntax of StP pictures and the abstract syntax of each type of diagram. We also define a picture merge function which updates an existing picture from a new version, but retains information such as symbol coordinates and size.

7 Conclusions and Future Work

We have described two visual notations for the expression of aspects of VDM specifications: Entity-Structure Diagrams, covered in detail, and Operation-State Diagrams in sketch form. The transformation of ESDs to and from VDM were relatively simple to specify, and have been presented here. The transformations for OSDs are more complicated due to the desire to give the diagrams a rest-unchanged semantics. They also required the VDM to be in a particular style.

We have chosen to depart from the classical entity-relationship and state-transition diagram because neither expressed exactly the kinds of aspects we required for a VDM specification. ESDs allows us to express a containment hierarchy, and OSDs allow us to express non-disjoint states.

For the present, we are continuing with the work of specifying the transformations for OSDs. We shall then make prototype implementations of the ESD and OSD transformations, and try them out on some case studies.

In due course, other diagrams should be considered as alternatives or as complementary to those described here. For instance, it would be interesting to examine a possible role for data-flow diagrams and structure charts.

We are keen also to look at diagrams for other specification languages, such as the RAISE specification language, which has aspects of process, channel, communication and concurrency not present in VDM. Finding a diagram for representing such aspects is an interesting challenge. Also of interest to us are notations for object-oriented concepts, adding aspects of class and inheritance.

Another very interesting line of work would be to study the refinement of diagrams. Initially, one could study the differences in diagrams of VDM specifications and their refinements, and from there try to devise direct diagrammatic refinement techniques. Interesting approaches to diagrammatic refinement can be found in [Naftalin91], and more formally in [Back91] where programs are derived using HOL and diagrams.

References

[Back91]   R. J. R. Back, *Refinement Diagrams*, In Proc. Fourth Refinement Work-shop, Wolfson College, Cambridge, Jan 1991

[BFO89]   R. D. van der Bos, L. M. G. Feijs, R. C. van Ommering, *POLAR, A Picture-Oriented Language for Abstract Representations*, Philips Research Laboratories, Research report No. RWR-113-RB-89021-RB, October 1989

[BGMT88]   G. Boudier, F. Gallo, R. Minot, I. Thomas, *An Overview of PCTE and PCTE+*, ACM Symposium on Software Development Environments 1988, pp. 248-257

[BSI90a]   British Standards Institute, *The BSI/VDM Proto-Standard*, Draft of 7 Sept 1990, Brian Richee (Ed.)

[BSI90b]   British Standards Institute, *The Dynamic Semantics of the BSI/VDM Specification Language*, Draft of August 1990, Peter Gorm Larsen (Ed.)

[Chen76]   P. P. Chen, *The Entity-Relationship Model: towards a unified view of data*, ACM Transactions on Database Systems, Vol 1, No 1, March 1976

[CunGold88] R. J. Cunningham, S. J. Goldsack, *Why FOREST?*, In Proc. of UK IT88, IEE, 1988, pp. 91-94

[DickLoub91] J. Dick, J. Loubersac, *A Visual Approach to VDM: Entity-Structure Diagrams*, Bull Research Center Report, DE/DRPA/DMA/91001, Jan 1991.

[Harel87]   D. Harel, *Statecharts: A visual formalism for complex systems*, Sci. Comput. Programm. Vol. 8, pp. 231-274, 1987

[Jones90]   Cliff B. Jones, *Systematic Software Development using VDM*, Second Edition, Prentice Hall Int., 1990

[MTW90]   M. W. Maimone, J. D. Tygar, J. M. Wing, *Formal Semantics for Visual Specification of Security*, in *Visual Languages and Visual Programming*, Shi-Kuo Chang (Ed.), Plenum Publishing Corp., 1990

[Naftalin91] Maurice Naftalin, *A Formal Framework for Opportunistic Design*, Univ. of Stirling Tech. Report TR72, April 24 1991

[PKP91]   Nico Plat, Jan van Katwijk, Kees Pronk, *A Case for Structured Analysis/Formal Design*, Submitted for publication.

[Polack91]   Fiona Polack, *Integrating Formal Notations and Systems Analysis: Using Entity Relationship Diagrams*, University of York Research Report, SAZ 91/004, Feb. 27, 1991

[SA91]   Lesley Semmens, Pat Allen, *Using Yourdon and Z: an Approach to Formal Specification*, In Proc. 5th Z Users Group Meeting, December 1990, (to be published by Springer Verlag in Workshops in Computing Science.)

RATIONAL DESIGN OF DISTRIBUTED APPLICATIONS

Thierry Cattel
Digital Equipement, Centre Technique Europe Sarl
Chemin du Levant, 01210 Ferney-Voltaire
Laboratoire d'Informatique, URA CNRS 822
Université de Franche-Comté
25030 Besançon cedex
France
Phone : +33 81.66.64.58   Fax : +33 81.66.61.77
E-mail : cattel@emc2.enet.dec.com

Abstract

Although numerous distributed programming facilities have been developed, the lack of methodologics to support the design of distributed applications makes the task of designers very difficult. The aim of our work is to contribute to the design of complete distributed applications, stressing first and foremost the quality of the final systems. To reach this goal we propose a software development environment based on a three-phased approach : analysis, design and construction. We will focus on the design and construction phases so as to define the architecture of the application, and to propose an implementation on a technical environment based on a distributed application model including the virtual node concept. Our approach uses the VDM formal method to support the design phase and the Conic distributed language and environment as the target for the implementation.

Keywords

Distributed application, programming in the large, reliability, formal specification, refinement, virtual node, module, port, communication.

1. Introduction

Today the software engineering community is convinced that there is a need to master the design of software. Developed software is becoming bigger and bigger and it is obvious that its complexity increases with its size. The maintenance costs is evaluated at 70% of the overall development cost. The aim of software engineering is clearly to find means to build quality software[21], and it is commonly accepted that the best ways to achieve this is particularly by abstraction, modularity, reusability[9].

However the recent development of workstations and communication networks proves that distributed programming is now a reality and the task of software designers is all the more difficult. The support available is mainly distributed operating systems, for instance : Amoeba [27], Chorus[24], Mach[1], parallel languages such as Ada, Occam, realtime languages like

Esterel[3] or distributed environments : Conic[17], Diadem, Dragoon[2]. Regarding methods, work is just started and is mostly algorithm based ; we quote for instance techniques of systolic array design as described in[23], or methods consisting in expressing a calculus problem thanks to a set of recurrence equations, which will be derivated and interpreted as a concurrent processes network[10]. Numerous approaches of rigorous program development exist, in particular program transformations[11], possibly assisted by program derivation support tools like SACSO[12] for instance. To our knowledge, few attempts have been made to distributed applications[22].

The aim of our work is to contribute to the design of distributed applications, proposing a rational approach applicable to complete applications, stressing the reliability of the final systems. This approach will be integrated into an open multiwindowing sofware engineering environment. It will be possible to refine a distributed application from its formal specification, stepwise transforming it by applying elementary tactics one after the other, or a succession of elementary tactics gathered into a strategy. This environment will allow to represent and manipulate the used objects in a graphic way. It will be totally open so as to accept and integrate the definition of new tactics or new strategies suggested by the designer.

Our contribution is part of a general stepwise design approach of distributed application. This approach is composed of three steps : analysis, design and construction. The goal of the analysis is to produce a first specification of the application from the requirements of the problem. From this model the design step leads to the architecture of the application. Eventually the construction step will effectively produce the code of the executable application.

The temptation is to jump directly from the application specification to an implementation on the technical target architecture, but we would be forgetting away a very determinant phase for quality of the application : the design step. Therefore we will concentrate on the design step (Fig.1) rather than the analysis and the low-level parts of construction. From an initial VDM formal model[13], the design step leads to the architectural structure of the application which complies to the underlying model of Conic distributed environment[17].

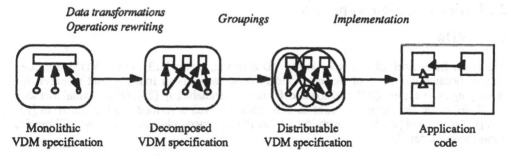

Data transformations Operations rewriting	Groupings	Implementation

Monolithic VDM specification	Decomposed VDM specification	Distributable VDM specification	Application code

Fig.1 - Rational design steps

From the architecture of the distributed application produced by the design phase, the construction phase will generate the code of the application itself, and determine its physical configuration. The choice of the technical target architecture is defined by its underlying concepts of modularity, abstraction and communication and its configuration facilities. It is not our goal to define a total implementation on the technical architecture, the configuration on the physical architecture or the execution control of the resulting applications are not our purpose, and we will propose straightforward solutions so as to illustrate the treated examples.

The design phase is based on data transformations. The techniques applied are the essential features of VDM, namely the specification refinement technique and the refinement correctness proofs. We apply syntactical transformations to the data of the model so as to make it more suitable for distribution, and we consider that they are analoguous to data refinements. Hence we may prove that each transformation is correct (adequacy of the representation). This proof is carried out only once. The application of a correct transformation necessarily leads to a correct result. Syntactical transformations are easy to formalize, and then to automatize. When the data has been transformed, it is necessary to echo the impact of the transformation onto the operations of the model and to prove their correctness (domain rule, result rule).

We refine the initial model in several equal distributable models. The greater the number of obtained distributable models is, the greater the probability of reaching a satisfying solution. Our work provides general rules of transformation application strategy.

The originality of this work is on one hand the application of formal techniques on *programming in the large* problems ; our aim is to provide software tools based on a rigourous approach suitable for developing rationally complete distributed applications. Besides, we want to explicitly express the designers *savoir-faire*, including it in the tools, while allowing the approach to be extensible at the tactic level as well as at the strategic level.

The rest of the paper describes each step of the approach while illustrating each with an example. We first give an overview of the VDM method, describe its formal language and give an initial VDM model of the example. We then study the general problem of distribution and how it may appear inside a VDM model and how it may be modified by means of transformations. We explain the general principle for applying the transformations. We present their formalism, which property to be proved to ensure their validity ; we give a non comprehensive list of the main rules, showing their objectives, possibly formally justify their validity, and study strategy application issues. We apply the transformations on our example, obtaining a new model. We show how to sum up the model structure with a graph, describe the grouping phase which consists of a logical configuration and finally give hints for implementing the architecture of the resulting model into a Conic environment.

2. Rational design approach

2.1. VDM

The main framework of our work is the VDM formal method[13], [14]. VDM has been chosen because it is one of the most widely used methods in industry and research for specifying large systems[20], and some tools are now available[6], [25]. Other formal methods like Z[26] could also have been chosen. This method is well described and illustrated in [13] and [14] so we will provide an overview, explaining its general philosophy and we will precise some syntactic details.

2.1.1. General philosophy

VDM is based on a formal language and a stepwise method. The formal language allows the definition of model-oriented specifications in terms of states and operations acting on these states. The state is an instance of an abstract data type which is described by high level constructors such as sets, maps, etc., by classical constructors such as composite structures, and basic types : integers, boolean, quote literal, etc. ; the state may be constrained by an invariant property which must be verified before and after the application of any operation. The operations are approximatively analoguous to Pascal procedures ; their signature may encompass input and output parameters, and the model state too if the operation uses it ; however their body is described in a non procedural way with a precondition and a postcondition written as expressions of a formal language based on the set theory and first order logic ; the precondition expresses the condition that the parameters used by the operations must satisfy for the postcondition to be applicable ; the postcondition expresses the condition verified by the results after the application of the operation.

The classical VDM stepwise method consists in writing an initial specification, then successively refining it until the distance to a possible implementation is negligible. The validity of the initial model must be proved with regard to a set of certain properties : *operation implementability, state invariant preservation by each operation*, etc. ; then refinements are made. The validity of the new model must be proved with regard to another set of properties : *adequacy of the representation, domain rule, result rule*, etc. [13].

2.1.2. Language syntax

VDM is provided with a formal language whose syntax is subject to various dialects, but since tools exist and since standards organisations such as the British Standard Institute have begun to work on it, a general standard has been defined. This definition is included in [13], which has been taken as our reference. However, we have decided to slightly modify the language, keeping only things necessary for our purpose, changing the symbols into names, etc. We present the syntax we use, in BNF format ; the keywords are in bold. A specification is a module with a name, containing some definitions :

    *<module> ::= **module** <identifier> <definitions> **end***
    <definitions> ::=   ***state** <state definition>*
                     ***types** <type definitions>*
                     ***operations** <operation definitions>*

A type definition may concern a type not totally defined or may associate a type to a type name :

    *<type definition> ::= <identifier> **is not yet defined***
    <type definition> ::= <identifier> = <type >

A type is a type construction, possibly constrained by an invariant :

    <type> ::= <type construction> [<invariant>]

A type construction is either a basic type, a quote literal, a type name, the union of two or several types, a set, a map, or a composite type of one or several fields characterised by a name and a type :

    <type construction> ::=   ***integer** / **boolean** / **@**<identifier> / <identifier> /*
                          <type>{ / <type> }+ /
                          *<type> **-set** /*
                          <type> -> <type> /
                          record** { <identifier> : <type> }+ **end

An invariant is a boolean function that limits the possible type construction and is expressed as a lambda function[7] :

    *<invariant> ::= **inv** <lambda function>*

The state definition describes the state of the model ; it is an instance of an abstract data type. The adopted syntax quotes three things : the abstract data type, the state of the model itself which is an instance of this type and the initial value of the state :

    <state definition> ::=   ***state** <type> **init** <expression>*

An operation definition is composed of a heading and a body ; the heading describes the possible input parameters and result, and quotes the possible parts of state used ; the body expresses the precondition and the postcondition of the operation :

    <operation definition> ::= <operation heading> <operation body>
    <operation heading> ::= <identifier> ({<identifier> : <type>}) [<identifier> : <type>]
                           *[**ext** [**rd** {<identifier>}+] [**wr** {<identifier>}+]]*
    <operation body> ::=   *[**pre** <expression>]*
                     ***post** <expression>*

An expression may be a literal value, an arithmetic expression, a logical expression, a set expression, a map expression, or a composite data expression. We slightly changed the syntax of some expressions, but their reading remains natural. We will need the corresponding abstract syntax of this language for formalizing the transformations, but we do not present it here.

2.1.3. Specification example : Bank management

We now present parts of an example of a specification in order to illustrate the above considerations and to serve as input for our rational design approach.

2.1.3.1. Requirements

This example is partly inspired by [13] ; it consists in managing a set of accounts and a set of clients as explained below. Each client is characterised by a unique number and may own at least one or several accounts. A client is allowed to have a maximum overdraft for each of his account. This maximum overdraft is the same for all his accounts. The balance of an account must always be greater than the allowed overdraft. An account belongs to a single client. It must be possible to add a new client into the system, to remove a client if the balance of all his accounts is null, to create a new account for an existing client, to delete an account if its balance is null, to modify the overdraft of an existing client, to credit an account, to debit an account, to see the allowed overdraft of a client, to see the account list of a client and to see the balance of an account.

2.1.3.2. Specification

```
module bank1
    state
        record
            bank : Bank
        end
    init  (bank->{})


    types
        Bank = Cnumber -> Ainfo
                inv λx. all(cnb1,cnb2) in dom(x) .
                    cnb1<>cnb2 => dom(accounts(x(cnb1))) inter dom(accounts(x(cnb2))) = {}
        Ainfo =    record
                        overdraft : Overdraft
                        accounts : Accounts
                    end
                    inv λx. all anb in dom(accounts(x)) . accounts(x)(anb) >= overdraft(x)
        Accounts =    Anumber -> Balance
                        inv λx. x<>{}
        Cnumber is not yet defined
        ...

    operations
        CLIENT_CREAT()cnb:Cnumber
            ext    wr bank
            post   cnb notin dom(bank) and
                   anb notin union{dom(accounts(ai)) | ai in rng(bank)} and
                   bank = bank' union {cnb->(overdraft->0, accounts->{anb->0})}
```

CLIENT_DEL(cnb:Cnumber)
    ext   wr bank
    ...

ACCOUNT_CREAT(cnb:Cnumber)anb:Anumber
    ext   wr bank
    pre   cnb in dom(bank)
    post   anb notin union{dom(accounts(ai)) | ai in rng(bank)} and
           bank = bank' overwrite {cnb->(overdraft->overdraft(bank'(cnb)),
                            accounts->(accounts(bank'(cnb)) union
                                        {anb->0}))}

ACCOUNT_DEL(anb:Anumber)
    ext   wr bank
    ...

OVERDRAFT_MOD(cnb:Cnumber, over:Overdraft)
    ext   wr bank
    pre   cnb in dom(bank) and all b in rng(accounts(bank(cnb))) . b >= over
    post   bank = bank' overwrite
                 {cnb->(overdraft->over, accounts->accounts(bank'(cnb)))}

ACCOUNT_CRED(anb:Anumber, val:integer)
    ...

ACCOUNT_DEB(anb:Anumber, val:integer)
    ext   wr bank
    ...

OVERDRAFT_SEE(cnb:Cnumber)val:integer
    ext   rd bank
    pre   cnb in dom(bank)
    post   val = overdraft(bank(cnb))

ACCOUNTS_SEE(cnb:Cnumber)al:Anumber-set
    ext   rd bank
    ...

ACCOUNT_SEE(anb:Anumber)val:integer
    ext   rd bank
    ...

end

2.2. Distribution

Distribution consists in dividing and then dealing. Dividing consists in splitting into several parts, dealing consists in allocating according to a certain order or to bring in miscellaneous places. If we take an example of distribution in everyday life, it is possible to easily understand the conditions and steps. Let us consider a set of 4×k loafs to be fairly shared between 5×k persons, k ∈ ℕ. A possible solution consists in dividing each loaf into five equal parts, putting together the fifths by groups of four and allocating a group to each person. It clearly appears that the distribution is applicable to an objet, here a loaf set, and consists of three steps : a division phase, a grouping phase and an allocation phase. These steps are of course influenced by the object divisibility and by the grouping and allocation criterias ; they are still valid for our work and we call them division, grouping and configuration.

In our topic, the object to be distributed is a software application. When done, this application will execute according to an expected behaviour. The incentives of the distribution may be to harness the parallelism of the machines so as to reduce the calculation time, or to balance the calculation load on the machine network ; they are in fact more general and consist of best utilization of the available machines for the particular application to be built. The division and grouping steps will be defined. Regarding the configuration step, it consists in putting the obtained fragments of the application onto the machine network, and ensuring good performance of the whole system ; we will not study it, but hints may be found in the literature[5].

Unless the object to be distributed is totally indivisible, it always exists several distribution choices. The distribution choices are directly dependent of the object divisibility ; a finer division allows to reach all the distribution choices resulting of a coarser division ; it is necessary to divide the object as much as possible to get a better chance to reach a good distribution solution.

We will now study how to distribute a VDM specification composed of a state and a set of operations. It could be possible to jump to the following steps of grouping and configuration, but the divisibility limits of the specification would not be reached. Indeed, we may wonder whether the operations or the state are divisible and what would be the consequences of it.

The division of an operation would lead to decompose it into subprograms or coroutines and would satisfy the incentive of using the potential parallelism of the machines. An operation has two parts : a precondition and a postcondition which are first order predicates that may be expressed as the conjunction of terms possibly bound by calculus dependencies. The set of terms and dependencies is a graph that could be implemented as a system of synchronised parallel tasks. It is not our main goal, but it could easily be done.

The division of the state will lead to more interesting cases of distribution. The state is a data structure built by means of VDM basic data types and constructors and its divisibility depends on them. We consider that data not totally defined or defined as integer, boolean, quote literal or union are not divisible. On the opposite a data defined as a record or a set could be considered as divisible : a record owns a fixed number of fields for its whole life, a set may have a varying number of values depending on the moment of its life. Last, map may be expressed in terms of sets and records, then its divisibility is the concern of what is said upper. In fact, the application distribution normally takes place before its execution. However it might evolve during the execution ; this situation is called dynamic configuration and is supported by environment such as Conic[13]. We deliberately decide to totaly define the distribution of an application before its execution for sake of simplicity. For this reason we only consider data expressed with the record contructor as divisible.

The state structuration choice of the initial model is partly arbitrary for there are always multiple intuitively equivalent possibilities. Among these possibilities, some are more suitable for distribution since they are more divisible. In compliance with what has been said before, a state defined with a n fields record is more divisible than an equivalent state defined with a m fields record, if n>m. Here is a first state definition, it has a single field which is a map whose elements of the codomain are separate maps :

state

    record m:M end

    inv λx.true

    init (m->{})

types

    M=T1->(T2->T3)

    inv λx.all (x1,x2) in dom(x) .

        x1<>x2 => dom(x(x1)) inter dom(x(x2)) = {}

It is intuitively equivalent to the following one. The initial map has been split into two maps and the state has now two fields and so is more divisible :

```
state
    record
        m1 :M
        m2 :T2->T3
    end
    inv λx.union rng(m1(x))=dom(m2(x))
    init (m1->{}, m2->{})
types
    M=T1->(T2-set)
    inv λx.all (x1,x2) in dom(x) .
        x1<>x2 => x(x1) inter x(x2) = {}
```

More formally the intuitive idea of data type equivalence must be related to the VDM concept of data refinement. VDM is based on specification transformations that are of two kinds : data refinements and operation decomposition. First are applied data refinements that consists in changing abstract data into concrete ones ; each time a data refinement takes place, the operations must be rewritten to take it into account. When the data are considered enough concrete, operation decomposition may occur and it consists in rewriting the preconditions and postconditions of each operation in a procedural way close to the implementation language.

A data refinement is characterized by two things : the transformation of a data type into another one and the inverse transformation called *retreive function* ; of course any inept data refinement might be expressed and a mean is needed to identify only valid ones. This mean consists in proving the so called *representation adequacy* property. A valid data refinement in fact formally expresses the intuitive idea of data type equivalence.

These observations suggest us to take an inventory of all the possible data refinements and to identify those that will allow the increasing of data divisibility. We will dispose on a set of tactic tools, the basic bricks of our design system, and it will be possible to find application strategies in compliance with the ideas exposed above. These data refinements will be defined as data transformations rules whose denotational semantics will be presented in the natural semantics style[15].

2.3. State refinements

2.3.1. Notation conventions

Data types

The data refinements will act on types presented as abstract syntax trees. All manipulated types, except if they are not totally defined, will be unfold, i.e. all reference to intermediate type definition will be replaced with the definition itself. We recall that each type is a type construction and an invariant. If the invariant is omitted in the specification that means it is implicitly λx.true. As abstract syntax is not very readable we will use concrete syntax for denoting lambda functions, but it is only a convenience, abstract syntax alone should be used. For instance the type of the following state:

```
state
    record
        f1 :Number_set
        f2 :Name
    end
    inv λx.true
    init ...
```

types
    Number_set=Number-set inv λx.card(x)<20
    Number=integer invλx.x>10
    Name is not yet defined
will be written :
    t(rect[fd(id f1, t(sett(t(intt(),
                                λx.x>10)),
                     λx.card(x)<20))
        fd(id f2, t(id Name,
                    λx.true))],
    λx.true)

Lambda functions

Let $E, L1, L2, LE1, LE2$ be some expressions such as $L1=λx.LE1$ and $L2=λx.LE2$. $L1(E)$ denotes the application of $L1$ on E. $L1$ *and* $L2$ is equivalent to $λx.LE1$ *and* $LE2$. $L1 • L2$ denotes the composition of $L1$ and $L2$ and is defined by $L1•L2=λx.L1(L2(x))$.

2.3.2. Data refinement formalization

A data refinement is characterised by a data type transformation (Fig.2) and the associated *retreive function*. The data refinements are presented in the natural semantics style as a formal system (called T) of inference rules of the form :

$$⊢P–\ PRED\ ...\ ⊢T–...$$
$$\overline{⊢T–TYPE1→TYPE2,\ RETF}$$

where *TYPE1* is of the form $t(D1,I1)$ and *TYPE2* is of the form $t(D2, I2)$. The rule means that any instance $d1$ of $D1$ verifying the invariant $I1$ may be transformed, under some conditions, into an instance $d2$ of type $D2$ that verifies $I2$; the retreive function *RETF* is such that $d1=RETF(d2)$. Applicability conditions may reference other transformation rules or first order predicates ; in this latter case we express them as a theorem prover with another formal system (called P) whose judgments are of the form : $⊢P–PRED$

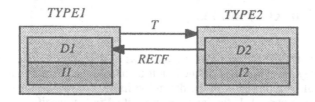

Fig.2 - Data refinement

2.3.3. Data refinement validity

The *representation adequacy* property ensures the validity of a data refinement and its proof consists in the formal verification of the meaning of the associated inference rule, namely :
    all x in { d1 in D1 | I1(x) } . (exists y in { d2 in D2 | I2(d2) } . x=RETF(y))
or in an equivalent way using the logic rules *all-in-eq* et *exists-in-eq* (See appendix) :
    all x in D1 . (I1(x) => (exists y in D2 . I2(y) and y=RETF(x))

2.3.4. Rule examples

2.3.4.1. Set simplification

This is a simple example of a transformation rule. The set constructor enables the expression of objects composed of a varying number of elements ; if it is proved to always be composed of a single element, the set constructor is useless and we may remove it.

$\vdash T-$ $t(sett(D), \lambda x.card(x)=1) \rightarrow D, \lambda x.\{x\}$ *set-simpl*

For instance the type : *integer-set inv $\lambda x.card(x)=1$* will be changed into : *integer* and an example of instance of the first type : *{10}* will become *10*.

Validity proof
As said before, this refinement is correct if the following property may be proved :
   all d in D-set . ($\lambda x.card(x)=1$)(d) => (exists d' in D . ($\lambda x.true$)(d') and d=($\lambda x.\{x\}$)(d'))
or in an equivalent way :
   all d in D-set . card(d)=1 => (exists d' in D . d=\{d'\})

   The proof is presented as in [13], by use of boxes. The keyword *from* introduces a hypothesis, the keyword *infer* introduces the corresponding conclusion. The inside boxes *from/infer* are some intermediary proofs. A line is true inside the box it is contained in. The right part is the justification of the line. The prefix quotes the name of the invoked logic rule (See appendix), and inside the parenthesis are the numbers of the lines used or the name of a well-know theory. A line number prefixed with *h* is related to the hypothesis of the quoted subproof, a line number not prefixed with *h* is related to the whole subproof.

	from	
1	*from d in D-set*	
1.2	*from card(d)=1*	
1.2.1	*d=\{d'\} and d' in D*	*set(h1,h1.2)*
1.2.2	*d=\{d\}*	*and-E(1.2.1)*
1.2.3	*d' in D*	*and-E(1.2.1)*
	infer exists d' in D . d=\{d'\}	*exists-I(1.2.2,1.2.3)*
1.3	*card(d)=1 in boolean*	*invariant*
	infer card(d)=1 => (exists d' in D . d=\{d'\})	*=>-I(1.2,1.3)*
	infer all d in D-set . card(d)=1 => (exists d' in D . d=\{d'\})	*all-I(1)*

2.3.4.2. Record codomain map split

This rule expresses that a map whose codomain is a record with two fields may be split into two maps which are the respective projections of the map on both fields of the elements of the codomain.

$\vdash T-$ $t(mapt(D, rect[fd(F1,CD1), fd(F2, CD2)], RI),$ *rec-codom-map-split*
         $\lambda x.true)$
   $\rightarrow$
   $t(\ rect[\quad fd(F1, t(mapt(D,CD1), \lambda x.true)),$
               $fd(F2, t(mapt(D,CD2), \lambda x.true))], RI1)\ , RETF$
where RETF = $\lambda x.\{ d\text{->}(F1\text{->}F1(x)(d),F2\text{->}F2(x)(d)) \mid d\ in\ dom(F1(x)) \}$
   RI1 = $\lambda x.dom(F1(x))=dom(F2(x))\ and\ all\ x1\ in\ rng(RETF(x)) . RI(x1)$

Example

Let us take an example close to our main example so as to illustrate this tranformation :

    Cnumber -> record
                    overdraft:Overdraft
                    accounts:Accounts
                end

will become :

    record
        overdraft:Cnumber->Overdraft
        accounts:Cnumber->Accounts
    end,
    inv λx.dom(overdraft(x))=dom(accounts(x)))

The instance :

    {   101->(overdraft->1000,accounts->{10140->100, 10160->-50}},
        105->(overdraft->500,accounts->{10560->10} }

is now :

    (overdraft->{101->1000, 105->500},
        accounts->{101->{10140->100, 10160->-50}}, 105->{10560->10}})

2.3.4.3. Map decomposition

This rule expresses that a map whose elements of the codomain are maps may be split into two maps provided all the map of the codomain have separate domains.

⊢T—   t(mapt(D1, t(mapt(D2, D3), MI2)), MI1)   **map-decomp**
      →
      t(rect[fd(F1, t(mapt(D1, t(sett(D2), λx.true)), MI3)),
                 fd(F2, t(mapt(D2, D3), λx.true))], RI))
      , RETF

where

    MI1 = λx. all (x1, x2) in dom(x) . x1<>x2 => dom(x(x1)) inter dom(x(x2)) = {}
    RETF = λx.{ d->m | d->s in F1(x) and cd in s and cd->cdd in F2(x) and cd->cdd in m}
    RI = λx. union(rng(F1(x)))=dom(F2(x)) and all x1 in rng(RETF(x)) . MI2(x1)
    MI3 = λx. all (x1, x2) in dom(x) . x1<>x2 => x(x1) inter x(x2) = {}

2.3.4.4. Record flattening

It is possible to flatten a record inside another record.

⊢T—   t(rect[fd(F1, D1),   **rec-flat**
                 ...,
                 fd(Fi, t(rect[fd(Fi1, Di1), ..., fd(Fim, Dim)], RI)),
                 ...,
                 fd(Fn, Dn)], λx.true)
      →
      t(rect[fd(F1, D1),
                 ...,
                 fd(Fi1, Di1), ..., fd(Fim, Dim),
                 ...,
                 fd(Fn, Dn)], RI) ,
      λx.(F1->F1(x), ..., Fi->(Fi1->Fi1(x), ..., Fim->Fim(x)), ..., Fn->Fn(x))

2.3.4.5. Substitution in a record

A transformation may be applied on a single field of a record without affecting the others.

$\vdash T-$ $Di \rightarrow Di'$, RETFi   *rec-subst*

$\vdash T-$ $t($ rect[fd(F1, D1), ..., fd(Fi, Di), ..., fd(Fn, Dn)], $\lambda x.true$)

$\rightarrow$

$t($ rect[fd(F1, D1), ..., fd(Fi, Di'), ..., fd(Fn, Dn)], $\lambda x.true$)

,

$\lambda x.(F1 \rightarrow F1(x), ..., Fi \rightarrow RETFi(Fi(x)), ..., Fn \rightarrow Fn(x))$

2.3.4.6. Invariant weakening

It is always possible to replace the invariant of a type by a weaker one. This rule is quite natural but is useless alone, it will allow the introduction of the *invariant weakening consequence* rule.

$\vdash P-$ $I(x) => I1(x)$ *inv-weak*

$\vdash T-$ $t(D, I) \rightarrow t(D, I1), \lambda x.x$

2.3.4.7. Invariant weakening consequence

This rule will allow us the extension of the application span of the refinements. Indeed the refinements express the minimal invariant that the data type must verify for the refinement to be applicable. Of course if the invariant is stronger the refinement is still applicable. Let us take a simple example. It is clear that the type :
  integer-set inv $\lambda x.card(x)=1$
may be refined, applying the *set-simpl* rule, into :
  integer
but it should be possible for :
  integer-set inv $\lambda x.x <> \{\}$ *and card(x)<2 and 10 notin x*
to be transformed into :
  integer inv $\lambda x.x <> 10$
Thus it is necessary to take into account the case where the invariant verifies some extra conditions, not to loose these extra conditions during the transformation and to echo them on the result.

$\vdash P-$ $I(x) => I1(x)$ *inv-weak-csq*
$\vdash T-$ $t(D, I1) \rightarrow t(D1, I2), RETF$

$\vdash T-$ $t(D, I) \rightarrow t(D1, I2$ and $I \bullet RETF), RETF$

A particular case is when $I1 = \lambda x.true$. It expresses the fact that the initial refinement requires no particular condition on the invariant since for all invariant I, $I(x) => true$.

2.3.4.8. Refinements composition

This rule allows the successive application of several refinements. The retreive function obtained is the composition of the retrieve functions.

⊢T—   t(D0, I0)→t(D1, I1), RETF1   ***ref-comp***
⊢T—   t(D1, I1)→t(D2, I2), RETF2
──
⊢T—   t(D0, I0)→t(D2, I2), RETF1 •RETF2

2.3.5. Bank example

We now consider our main example and see how it could be refined using these rules. We give an idea of how to apply the refinements and what are the obtained results ; doing it formally would be a bit cumbersome and long. We are currently implementing a tool to automatize this tedious task. Let us remind the unfold state of the initial specification :

> *state*
> > *bank : Cnumber ->   record*
> > > > *overdraft :   Overdraft*
> > > > *accounts :   Anumber -> Balance*
> > > > *inv λx. x<>{}*
> > >
> > > *end*
> > > *inv λx. all anb in dom(accounts(x)) .*
> > > > *accounts(x)(anb) >= overdraft(x)*
> >
> > *inv   λx. all((cnb1,cnb2) in dom(x) . cnb1<>cnb2 =>*
> > > *dom(accounts(x(cnb1))) inter dom(accounts(x(cnb2))) = {}*
>
> *inv   λx. true*
> *init   (bank->{})*
> ...

Applying in an ad hoc way the rules ***ref-comp, rec-subst, rec-codom-map-split, map-decomp,*** and ***rec-flat*** will lead to obtain the following new state :

> *state*
> > *om : Cnumber -> Overdraft*
> > *am : Cnumber -> Anumber-set*
> > *bm : Anumber -> Balance*
>
> *end*
> *inv   λx.dom(om(x))=dom(am(x)) and union rng(am(x))=dom(bm(x)) and*
> > *all (cn1,cn2) in dom(am(x)) . cn1<>cn2 => am(x)(cn1) inter am(x)(cn2) ={} and*
> > *all anb in dom(bm(x)) . anb in rng(am(x)(cnb)) and bm(x)(anb) >=*
> > > > > > *overdraft(x)(cnb)*
>
> *init   (om->{}, am->{}, bm->{})*
> ...

The difference now is that the state is composed of three fields instead of only one as before. The data of the specification is now much more divisible and will allow the application to be more easily distributed as we will see in the following paragraphs.

2.3.6. Refinement application stategies

We have presented some tactical tools for refining the data of a VDM specification. They in fact provide the basic bricks of our design system. We have formalized them as inference rules and a prototype tool for automatizing their application is being developed. This tool will allow us to experiment with the application of successive refinements in order to bring out elements of strategy. We plan to integrate ways of defining application stategies within the tool.

2.4. Operations rewriting

When the data of a specification is refined, the operations acting on them must be changed to take the refinement into account. Here is for instance the new definition of the operation *ACCOUNT_CREAT* after the refinement of our example proposed §2.3.5 :

    ACCOUNT_CREAT(cnb:Cnumber)anb:Anumber
      ext   *rd om*
            wr am, bm
      pre   *cnb in dom(om)*
      post *anb notin dom(bm) and*
            am = am' overwrite {cnb->(am'(cnb) union {anb})} and
            bm=bm' union {anb->0}

We do not intend to explain this point any further. Note that a system of transformation rules should be defined and its implementation and integration into the support tools should be possible.

2.5. Structure graph

Our aim is to divide a VDM specification in order to distribute its parts but its underlying structure is not explicit when looking at the VDM text. It is possible, however to graphically represent a specification so as to clearly show its different parts and their interconnections. Since a specification is composed of data and operations using these data, it is natural to represent it as a bipartite graph with two types of vertices : one type corresponding to data and one type to operations ; the edges linking the vertices correspond to the way the operations use the data and may be of two types : read and/or write. Here is for instance the graphical representation related to the first specification of the bank example :

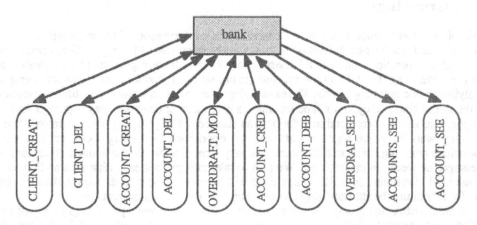

Fig.3 - Example initial structure graph

and the one related to the refined specification :

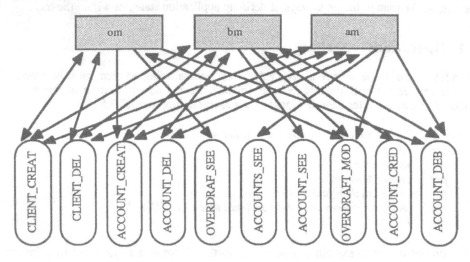

Fig.4 - Example final structure graph

Some remarks may be made. No edge a priori link two operations together ; this is because there is no relation between operations ; it sometimes happens that an operation is defined by reusing another one but such relations would be of design concern only and do not interest us for distribution. When there is a write edge from an operation towards a data, then there is always a read edge from the data to the operation ; this comes from the fact that VDM does not allow to make the distinction between data used in write and read mode and these used in write mode only ; of course this thiner distinction could be done at the VDM level for special aims. There is as much data as there are fields in the state definition and the division of the specification now clearly appears. Besides some operations are now decoupled from some data they do not use and it will be interesting in distribution.

2.6. Groupings

This phase is very important since it concerns the configuration of the application onto a virtual logical architecture. It consists in grouping the fragments of the application, namely the data and the operations, into several classes ; each class will correspond to a Conic module at the implementation level. From the structure graph, we must produce a set of extracted graphs applying ad hoc grouping criteria. The extracted graphs do not necessarily constitute a partition of the initial graph : they may not be separate ; a given data or operation may appear in several graphs, that would correspond to a duplication situation. The grouping criteria are multiple ; we may want to group together data and the operations modifying them, or data with operations requiring quick access to them ; we may want to minimize the number of exchanged messages between the modules, etc. We plan to take into account execution information such as the kind of machine on which an operation will execute, the kind of database a data will be, etc. by decorating the structure graph so as to allow realistic grouping strategies.

Without justifying the way it has been obtained, Figure 5 shows a possible grouping of our refined bank example. It corresponds to three classes without duplicated object. Each class will later become a Conic module, and the edges going from one class to another clearly show the future message exchanges.

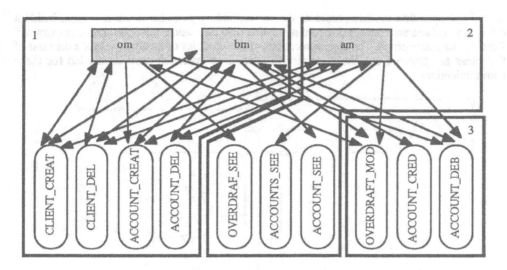

Fig.5 - Example groupings

3. Implementation

This phase consists of producing the Conic architecture and code of the distributed application from the last VDM specification and the groupings choices. This transition is systematic and brings the executable semantics of Conic to the application.

3.1. Conic environment

Conic[17], [18] is a technical environment based on a distributed application model including the virtual node concept. Its essential features are modularity, abstraction and communication. A distributed application is represented by a network of interconnected modules ; a module may itself be a network of modules. Each module has a well-defined interface composed of input output ports and communicates with the modules it is linked to by messages passing. There are two different communication semantics and then two kinds of communication ports : an asynchronous one and a synchronous one. In the asynchronous mode, the sender sends a message and waits until it has been taken into account by the system, but does not care if the message arrives at the receiver or not. In the synchronous mode, the sender waits for an answer from the receiver. All the connection topologies are possible including bipoint, broadcasting and merge connections, except for synchronous ports which do not support broadcasting. In the case of a port receiving messages from several senders (merge), messages are buffered and treated in FIFO order. Conic also provides support for physical configuration, through its dynamic modification and sophisticated graphical execution monitoring[16].

3.2. Implementation principles

The technique we adopt to generate the Conic architecture of a distributed application is very straightforward. It consists in creating a module of every data, operation, and grouping class. Each data module will be a server for the data it encapsulates ; it will be interfaced with two ports : a synchronous one for reading the value of the data, a asynchronous one for writing the data. Each operation module possesses the corresponding ports for the data it uses. Inside a class, the modules are connected according to their data utilization, this information is extracted from the structure graph. The communications of the modules of a class towards a data out of this class are grouped and the class module then owns as much ports as needed for these communications.

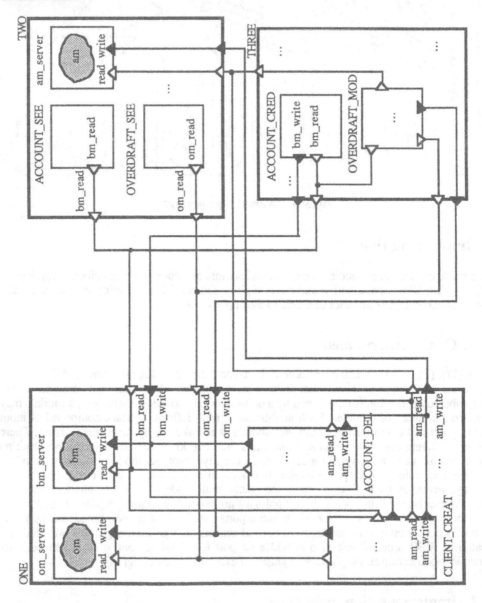

Fig.6 - Example implementation

This solution is an example to illustrate the upstream approach but it is not very efficient nor reliable. Indeed the data are always manipulated globally, and it is certainly unrealistic to copy a whole database from a machine to another just for a query ; the read and write accesses are too coarse for manipulating the data and some thiner ones must be identified. Besides, this solution chooses to have unitelligent data servers but intelligent operation modules. The problem is that the parallelism grain of the application is thiner than an operation and mutual exclusion or deadlock issues may arise. This may certainly be tackled by introducing synchronisation accesses to the data (semaphor-like), in addition to the read/write access. Another extreme solution may consists in defining intelligent data servers and unitelligent operation modules, but in the previous solution the system was very easily modifiable in case of functionnalities addition, now it is no longer true. A good compromize might be to define a set of synchronisation accesses, a set of possible data accesses depending on the manipulated data but not on the problem so that an efficient and reliable implementation may be systematically derived from the result of the design. The modules' code is not our first concern but their derivation from the operation postconditions may be performed manually.

3.3. Bank example

For our purpose we use the Conic graphical representation of the application architecture since it clearly shows the modules, ports and connections and drop the module code (Fig.6). Each module and port is named. The synchronous ports are represented with empty triangles, asynchronous ones with filled triangles. The direction of the communication is in the direction of the arrows.

Conclusion

In this paper, we have sketched out a possible approach for designing distributed applications. We have given a precise framework with concrete steps and intermediary formalisms. We have proposed a first solution for solving the issues occuring at each step, and also gave hints for more sophisticated solutions.

From now onwards the span of our work is well defined and the design of most of its parts is about to be achieved. We are currently implementing prototype tools under CENTAUR[4] which is an environment for developing and manipulating languages. CENTAUR allows the expression of very clean concrete and abstract syntaxes but also semantics in a formalism very close to the natural semantics.

We plan to integrate tools in our development environment, such as VDM toolsets[6], [25] or theorem provers[19], [8] because the proposed approach will always need an interactive operation for the designer, it will never be totally automatic and such tools will ease designer intervention.

But for the moment it is more important is to provide an initial version of a tool for each phase of the approach in order to test its suitability on larger examples, to discover relevant application strategies and then to enrich the approach itself.

Appendix : logic rules

$E1$ and $E2$ and ... and En **and-E**

———————————— $1 \leq i \leq n$

Ei

$E1 \vdash E2$; $E1$ in **boolean**   **=>-I**

————————————

$E1 => E2$

$$exists\ e\ in\ \{\ x\ in\ X\ /\ p(x)\ \}.q(x) <=> exists\ x\ in\ X\ .\ p(x)\ and\ q(x)$$

exists in-eq

$$\frac{s\ in\ X\ ;\ E(s/x)}{exists\ x\ in\ X.E(x)}$$

exists-I

$$all\ e\ in\ \{\ x\ in\ X\ /\ p(x)\ \}.q(x) <=> all\ x\ in\ X\ .\ p(x)=>q(x)$$

all in-eq

$$\frac{x\ in\ X\ \vdash E(x)}{all\ x\ in\ X\ .\ E(x)}$$

all-I

References

[1]   M. Accetta, R. Baun, W. Bolosky et al. : *Mach : a new kernel foundation for Unix development* ; Proceedings of the Summer Usenix Conf., Atlanta, July, 1986.

[2]   C. Atkinson, A. Di Maio : *From DIADEM to DRAGOON ;* Distributed Ada Symposium, Southampton, December 1989.

[3]   G. Berry, L. Cosserat : *The synchronous programming language ESTEREL and its mathematical semantics ;* INRIA research report N°327, 1987.

[4]   P.Borras, D.Clément, T.Despeyroux et al. : *CENTAUR : The system* ; Proc. of SIGSOFT'88 third annual symposium on sotfware development environments, Boston, 1988

[5]   A. Billionnet, M.C. Costa, A. Sutter : *Les problèmes de placement dans les systèmes distribués* ; Techniques et sciences informatiques Vol. 8, N°4, p. 307-337, 1989.

[6]   R. Bloomfield, P. Froome, B. Monahan : *Specbox : a toolkit for BSI-VDM* ; Adelard, internal report, February 1989.

[7]   J. Barwisi, D. Kaplan , H.J. Reisler et al. : *The lambda calculus, its syntax and semantics ;* North Holland, 1984.

[8]   J. Despeyroux : *Theo : an interactive proof development system* ; INRIA research report N°116, 1990.

[9]   D. Colnet, D. Léonard, G. Masini et al. : *Les langages à objets* ; Interéditions, Paris, 1989.

[10] M.C. Eglin, J. Julliand, G.-R. Perrin : *Compiling Equations in Asynchronous Communicating Processes ;* Fourth ISMM/IASTED International Conference on PARALLEL & DISTRIBUTED COMPUTING & SYSTEMS , Washington, U.S.A., 8-11 October 1991.

[11] M.S. Feather : *A survey of classification of some program transformation approaches and techniques* ; Program specification and transformation, p.165-195, Elsevier science publishers, Holland, 1987.

[12] J.P. Finance, N. Lévy, J. Souquières et al. : *SACSO : un environnement d'aide à la spécification* ; Techniques et Science Informatiques, Vol.9, N°3, p. 245-261, 1990.

[13] C.B. Jones : *Systematic Software Development Using VDM* ; Prentice Hall International, 1990 (second edition).

[14] C.B. Jones, R.C. Shaw : *Case Studies in Systematic Software Development Using VDM* ; Prentice Hall International, 1990.

[15] G.Kahn : *Natural Semantics* ; Proc. of STACS'87, LNCS 247, 1987.

[16] J. Krammer, J. Magee, K. Ng : *Graphical configuration programming* ; IEEE Computer, 1989.

[17] J. Kramer, J. Magee, M. Sloman : *Constructing distributed systems in CONIC* ; IEEE transactions on software engineering, Vol. 15, N° 6, June 1989, p. 663-675.

[18] J. Kramer, J. Magee, M. Sloman : *Managing evolutions in distributed systems* ; Software Engineering Journal, November 1989, p. 321-329.

[19] C. Lafontaine, Y. Ledru, P.Y. Schobbens : *An experiment in formal software development : using the B theorem prover on a VDM case study* ; Proc. 12th Int. Conf. on Software Engineering, IEEE Computer society press, 1990.

[20] Y. Ledru, P.Y. Schobbens : *Applying VDM to large developments* ; Proc. ACM SIGSOFT Int. Workshop on Formal methods in software development, p. 55-58, Napa, May 1990.

[21] B. Meyer : *Object-oriented Software Construction* ; Prentice Hall, 1988.

[22] M.Mühlhäuser : *Software engineering in distributed systems - Approaches and issues* ; Proc. of Phoenix conf. on computers and communications, Scottsdale, March 1990.

[23] P.Clauss, G.R.Perrin : *Synthesis of process arrays ;* CONPAR'88, Manchester , Cambridge University Press 88, September 1988.

[24] M. Rozier, V. Abrossimov, F. Armand et al. : *Chorus Distributed Operating Systems* ; Chorus systèmes, technical report 88-7.5, 1988.

[25] *RAISE overview* ; RAISE/CRI/DOC/9/V2, Computer ressources international, denmark, June 1990.

[26] J.M. Spivey : *The Z notation* ; Prentice Hall, 1989.

[27] A.S. Tanenbaum, R.V. Renesse, H. VanStaveren et al. : *Experiences with the AMOEBA distributed operating system*; Communications of the ACM Vol. 33, N°12, December 1990.

Test data selection from algebraic specifications: application to an automatic subway module

Pierre Dauchy, Bruno Marre
dauchy@frlri61.bitnet, marre@frlri61.bitnet

Laboratoire de Recherche en Informatique, U.A. CNRS 410
Université PARIS-SUD F-91405 Orsay Cedex

Abstract:

A method and a tool for black-box program testing are applied to a realistic example, a part of an automatic subway driving system. Test data sets are automatically selected from an algebraic specification of the system via selection strategies derived from well-chosen hypotheses. This selection is done in a modular way and can be tuned by the user of the system.

Key Words: software testing, algebraic specifications, program correctness, transportation systems, software reliability.

Introduction

[Ber 90] and [BGM 91] present a method and a tool for black-box testing of programs: given an algebraic specification of the program to be tested, test data sets are selected via a tool based on equational logic programming.

This paper presents a first experiment on a non academic example, namely a module of an automatic subway driving system. This experiment is based on a case study on structured algebraic specifications: starting from a version of the informal specification of the system ([Gui 89]), the embedded part of the system has been specified ([Dau 89]). The case study was performed in parallel with and independently of the actual development and validation process. This paper reports more precisely the application of the method and the tool for the selection of test data sets from the specification of the door monitoring module.

The paper is organized as follows: part 1 introduces the specification case study; then, part 2 describes the method and the system; and part 3 reports the actual experiment done.

1 Specification of the door monitoring module

1.1 The context and the informal specification

MAGGALY (Métro Automatique à Grand Gabarit de la Région Lyonnaise) is an unmanned subway driving system, where most of the safety functions such as alarms control are taken care of by software. The embedded driving system gets necessary data from ground based units. Our concern is the door monitoring module, whose function is to raise an alarm when a door opening might be dangerous.

Doors may not be open on the way side, except when the train is stopped on a side-track. Platform doors should not normally be open while the train is moving. However, to increase the passenger flow, the doors may be opened in station when the speed is less than some value spd_open_doors, thus anticipating the halting. But care must be taken to ensure safety:

- the train must not accelerate again beyond the speed limit above;

- it must stop before it has covered some distance limit dx_max;

- it must not pass the end of the station with its doors open.

When a forbidden situation happens, the alarm al_doors is set and emergency braking occurs.

In addition to the informal specification, an automaton describing possible "states" of the train w.r.t. the doors was given:

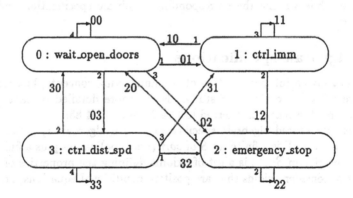

Figure 1: The doors automaton

The transitions are numbered according to their initial and final states. The small numbers on each transition define priorities. Thus, the transition 22 may be fired only if the transition 20 cannot. We give hereafter the respective firing conditions for each transition:

01 $\neg$(closed_pf $\wedge$ closed_way) $\wedge$ on_sidetrack $\wedge$ (speed = 0)

where closed_pf means that the platform-side doors are closed and closed_way that the way-side doors are closed

03 `located` ∧ `in_station` ∧ (`speed` < `spd_open_doors`) ∧ `closed_way` ∧ ¬`closed_pf`

where `located` means that the locating system works properly and `in_station` that all platform-side doors face the platform

02 ¬(`closed_pf` ∧ `closed_way`)
∧ ¬(`located` ∧ `in_station` ∧ (`speed` < `spd_open_doors`) ∧ `closed_way`)

10 `closed_pf` ∧ `closed_way`

12 `speed` ≠ 0 ∨ ¬`located` ∨ ¬(`on_sidetrack` ∨ `closed_way`)

20 `closed_pf` ∧ `closed_way`

32 ¬(`located` ∧ (`delta_x` < `dx_max`)
∧ (`speed` < `spd_open_doors`) ∧ `in_station` ∧ `closed_way`)

where `delta_x` is the distance covered by the train since the doors opened

30 `closed_pf` ∧ `closed_way`

31 `speed` = 0

Four more transitions (00 . . . 33), may be fired when no state change can take place. Their firing conditions were not made explicit in the automaton description we had; they were elaborated while writing the corresponding algebraic specification and we will present them later.

1.2 Algebraic specifications

We will not give a full presentation of the underlying concepts, but focus on the points which are relevant to this case study. For a more detailed presentation of Algebraic Specifications, the reader is referred to [ADJ 76] or [EM 85].

We use structured algebraic specifications. An algebraic specification is a pair (Σ, Ax); the signature Σ is a finite set S of *sort* (i.e. type) names plus a finite set of *operation* names with arity in S; Ax is a set of axioms defining the properties of the operations of Σ. We only consider axioms that are positive conditional equations, i.e. of the form:

$$(v_1 = w_1 \&...\& v_k = w_k) \implies v = w$$

where v_i, w_i, v and w are Σ-terms which may contain variables, i.e. terms built over the signature Σ and a set of typed variables $\mathcal{X}$.

Among the operations of the signature, we single out a subset of *generators* such that any term can be proved equal to a term built from the generators only. The other operations will be called *defined operations*. We only consider specifications with no equation between generators.

Moreover, specifications are structured. This structure is expressed by the "USE" construction which allows a specification module to use other ones. All the operations declared in a used specification module are known in the specification modules which use it. The "USE" construction is transitive, i.e. if a module SP uses SP_1 which uses SP_2, then SP uses SP_2.

1.3 The door monitoring algebraic specification

This specification is structured as shown on Figure 2.

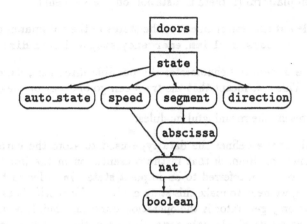

Figure 2: The specification modules and their dependencies

On this graph, the nodes are specification modules and the links represent the "USE" relation. Since every module (except **doors**) defines only one sort, we name each module according to the defined sort. The modules in oval boxes are the auxiliary ones and will be presented shortly.

- The modules **boolean** and **nat** are classical specifications of booleans and natural numbers, the latter being generated by 0 and a successor operation $s \_ : \textbf{nat} \rightarrow \textbf{nat}$.

- The module **speed** defines the sort **speed** by coercion of the naturals. A speed is thus given by its measure (in km/h). The operation **null_spd** tests whether a speed is 0 (this eases the expression of some axioms). The constant **spd_open_doors** is defined as the value 3.

- The module **abscissa** similarly defines the sort **abscissa** by coercion. An abscissa is given by its measure (in meters). The following constants are also defined:

  - **dx_max**, the maximum distance the train is allow to cover in station with doors open, has value 2;

  - **delta_door_1** and **delta_door_6**, distances between the front of the train and the first (resp. last) door, have values 33 and 3 respectively.

- The way is divided into pieces called *segments*; the train's position is given by a segment and an abscissa on this segment. The module **segment** defines the segments by coercion of naturals (a segment is designated by its number). It also defines four operations:

- the boolean operations sidetrack_segment and station_segment test the nature of a segment;
- abs_min_pf and abs_max_pf are the abscissas of the entry and exit point of the station platform (if there is a station on the segment).

• The module auto_state enumerates the states in the automaton of Figure 1. They are wait_open_doors, ctrl_imm, emergency_stop and ctrl_dist_spd.

• The module direction enumerates the possible directions, direction1 and direction2. This just means that the train can go one way or the other...

Now let us present the meaningful modules:

• The module state defines the data type used to store the current values of the train parameters. Remark that in the presentation of the informal specification, each firing condition referred to an implicit state. In order to build an algebraic specification, we need to make this state explicit. We specify it as a "record" of ten values. The only generator is the operation cons that builds a value of sort state from ten arguments of adequate sorts. Ten operations allow access to these fields, each taking a state as argument:

- the current value of the door alarm is given by the boolean operation al_doors;
- the boolean located is true if the locating system works correctly;
- the booleans closed_pf and closed_way are true respectively if the doors are closed on the platform side and on the way side;
- auto_state is the state in the automaton;
- segment is the segment on which the train currently is;
- abscissa is its abscissa on this segment;
- abs_ctrl stores the abscissa the train had on the last normal door opening in station; it is used to compute the distance the train covered since then;
- direction and speed are self-explanatory.

Additional operations are defined in the module state. From now on, S will denote a variable of sort state.

- in_station _ : state → boolean determines whether the train is in station with all doors facing the platform, as shown on Figure 3 .
  The axioms defining in_station are given below:

```
i1 : station_segment(segment(S)) = true
& on_sidetrack(S) = false
& lt(abs_min_pf(segment(S)),
      sub(abscissa(S), delta_door_1)) = true
& lt(sub(abscissa(S), delta_door_6),
      abs_max_pf(segment(S))) = true
    => in_station(S) = true
```

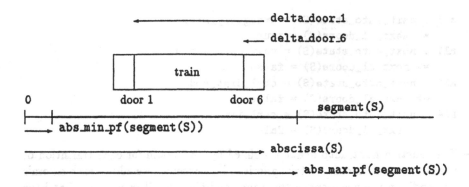

Figure 3: A train in station

```
i2 : station_segment(segment(S)) = false
     => in_station(S) = false
i3 : station_segment(segment(S)) = true
 & on_sidetrack(S) = false
 & lt(abs_min_pf(segment(S)),
       sub(abscissa(S), delta_door_1)) = false
     => in_station(S) = false
i4 : station_segment(segment(S)) = true
 & on_sidetrack(S) = false
 & lt(sub(abscissa(S), delta_door_6),
       abs_max_pf(segment(S))) = false
     => in_station(S) = false
```

- **on_sidetrack** is true whenever the current segment is a sidetrack segment;

- **delta_x** is the distance covered in station since the doors opened, as defined by the following axioms:

```
d1 : direction(S) = direction1
     => delta_x(S) = sub(abscissa(S), abs_ctrl(S))
d2 : direction(S) = direction2
     => delta_x(S) = sub(abs_ctrl(S), abscissa(S))
```

- The module **doors** defines the transitions in the automaton. A new value for the state, **next_auto_state**, is computed from the current state and the other train parameters. Moreover, new values **next_al_doors**, and **next_abs_ctrl** for the fields **al_doors** and **abs_ctrl** are computed.

  - The function **next_al_doors** has value true if and only if the next automaton state is **emergency_stop**. This is expressed in four simple axioms:

```
al1 : next_auto_state(S) = emergency_stop
   => next_al_doors(S) = true
al2 : next_auto_state(S) = wait_open_doors
   => next_al_doors(S) = false
al3 : next_auto_state(S) = ctrl_dist_spd
   => next_al_doors(S) = false
al4 : next_auto_state(S) = ctrl_imm
   => next_al_doors(S) = false
```

- The function next_auto_state is defined by one axiom for each transition of the automaton. In order to take priorities into account, we add to each axiom's precondition the negations of the firing conditions of all transitions that have priority. Furthermore, each transition from a state to itself has as precondition all negations of the firing conditions of all transitions leaving this state. The following axioms are named as the transitions they correspond to. For instance, the axiom

```
01 : auto_state(S) = wait_open_doors
 & and(closed_pf(S), closed_way(S)) = false
 & on_sidetrack(S) = true & speed(S) = (0)
   => next_auto_state(S) = ctrl_imm
```

specifies that the transition from state wait_open_doors to state ctrl_imm occurs when some door is open and the train is stopped on a sidetrack. Notice the parentheses around the speed value (0); this is the expression of the coercion of a natural into a speed. The coercions into abscissas or segments are expressed in the same way. The complete specification of next_auto_state can be found in appendix.

- The function next_abs_ctrl gives a new value for the reference abscissa used when computing the distance the train covered since the doors opened in station. This abscissa is updated to the current train's abscissa when the transition 03 leading from wait_open_doors to ctrl_dist_spd is fired. In all other cases, it is not modified. This is expressed in the following axioms:

```
act1 : auto_state(S) = wait_open_doors
 & next_auto_state(S) = ctrl_dist_spd
      => next_abs_ctrl(S) = abscissa(S)
act2 : auto_state(S) = ctrl_imm
      => next_abs_ctrl(S) = abs_ctrl(S)
act3 : auto_state(S) = emergency_stop
      => next_abs_ctrl(S) = abs_ctrl(S)
act4 : auto_state(S) = ctrl_dist_spd
      => next_abs_ctrl(S) = abs_ctrl(S)
act5 : next_auto_state(S) = ctrl_imm
      => next_abs_ctrl(S) = abs_ctrl(S)
act6 : next_auto_state(S) = wait_open_doors
      => next_abs_ctrl(S) = abs_ctrl(S)
```

```
act7 : next_auto_state(S) = emergency_stop
       => next_abs_ctrl(S) = abs_ctrl(S)
```

2   The test data set selection method and the system

2.1   Overview of the testing method

Most current methods and tools for software testing are based on the program to be tested: they use some coverage criteria of the structure of the program. With the emergence of formal specification languages, it becomes possible to use the specification to define some testing strategies in a formal framework. These strategies provide a formalization of the black-box testing approaches. Such strategies allow to test whether all the cases mentioned in the specification are actually dealt with in the program. It is now generally agreed that black-box and white-box testing are complementary.

Let P be the program which implements a specification (Σ, Ax). Let us consider the set *Exhaust* of all ground instances of the axioms obtained by replacing each variable by all ground terms of the same sort built from the generators in the signature. If the program validates each formula of *Exhaust*, it is correct w.r.t. the specification. Remark that to be able to compute the values of terms, P must implement all operations in Σ. Moreover, when we assume that the success of *Exhaust* implies the correctness of P, we assume in particular that every computed value is denoted by a term. As a matter of fact, if "junk" values existed, no test in *Exhaust* could detect an error involving such a value. If P satisfies both stated conditions, we say that it defines a *finitely generated* Σ-algebra.

Each formula in *Exhaust* being a ground instance of an axiom, it is a *test* of this axiom. To decide the success of a test $t_1 = t'_1 \& \ldots \& t_n = t'_n \Rightarrow t = t'$ in P, we need to:

1. compute in P the values $t_i^P, t'_i{}^P, t^P, t'^P$ denoted by the terms t_i, t'_i, t, t';

2. verify that whenever t_1^P *equals$_P$* $t'_1{}^P$ and ... and t_n^P *equals$_P$* $t'_n{}^P$, we have t^P *equals$_P$* t'^P,

where *equals$_P$* is a decision procedure of the equality in P. The existence of such a decision procedure is an important problem; it has been studied in [Ber 90] and is based on the notion of observability.

Among the tests of *Exhaust*, some are conditional and their precondition can be false. It seems useless to verify such formulae since they do not mean anything about the program correctness. Thus we can define an exhaustive equational test data set *EqExhaust* as the set of all ground instances of the *conclusions of the axioms* such that the instantiations validate the preconditions *in the specification*. The success of this exhaustive test data set is also equivalent to the correctness of the program w.r.t. its specification if the preconditions are observable ([Ber 90]).

But most of the time *EqExhaust* is not finite; we need to consider only a finite subset of it. Since we want to cover all the properties defined by the axioms, our method suggests to select a finite subset of *EqExhaust* for each axiom.

Let ax be an axiom of the specification, *EqExhaust$_{ax}$* the subset of *EqExhaust* containing all ground instances of the conclusion of ax that validate the preconditions and T_{ax} a finite subset of *EqExhaust$_{ax}$*. When we *select* T_{ax}, we make the following *selection* *hypothesis H* on the program *P* (recall that elementary tests are formulas; moreover, we identify a test set with the conjunction of its elements):

$$T_{ax} \Rightarrow EqExhaust_{ax}$$

Such hypotheses are usually left implicit. We claim that they are a good conceptual tool for the selection of test data sets: it seems sound first to state some general hypotheses and then to select a test set corresponding to them. Actually, the method suggests to build these hypotheses by combination and specialization of some general hypothesis schemas.

We require both following properties of the pair (H, T_{ax}):

- Under the hypothesis *H*, the test data set rejects all programs not validating *ax* (T_{ax} is *valid*, it detects every incorrect program that validates the hypothesis):

$$(H \wedge (P \models T_{ax})) \Rightarrow (P \models ax)$$

- Under the hypothesis *H*, the test data set does not reject programs validating *ax* (T_{ax} is *unbiased*, it accepts every correct program that validates the hypothesis):

$$(H \wedge (P \models ax)) \Rightarrow (P \models T_{ax})$$

If (H, T_{ax}) has both these properties and T_{ax} is finite, the success of T_{ax} is equivalent to the correctness of the program w.r.t. *ax*: (H, T_{ax}) is *practicable*.

It is shown in [BGM 91] that the pair (*P* defines a finitely generated Σ-algebra, *EqExhaust*) is practicable, and, moreover, that the strategies and selection hypotheses we will use hereafter only lead to practicable such pairs.

Another important point of the method is that the test selection can be done in a modular way, following the specification organization in modules. We can assume that when all the test data sets for the axioms of a given specification module SP_i have been selected, we have a sufficient test data set of the properties of the operations defined in this module. Furthermore, when one considers a module *SP* that uses a module SP_i, it seems useless to test again the properties of the operations of SP_i. Thus we can assume strong selection hypotheses for the variables occurring in the arguments of these operations in *SP*. Similarly, for other occurrences of variables of imported sorts, it is sometimes useful to assume strong hypotheses in order to select small test data sets.

2.2 Selection hypotheses and strategies

We describe here some general schemas of selection hypotheses and their corresponding selection strategies. We do not describe all the schemas mentioned in [BGM 91] but only those that will be used for our study.

Let us consider the axiom *al1* of the specification module doors:

```
next_auto_state(S) = emergency_stop  ⇒  next_al_doors(S) = true
```

We assume that we have already selected a test data set for each axiom of each used specification module. The sort of the variable *S* is state, defined in the used specification module state.

2.2.1 Uniformity hypothesis for a variable

Since the properties of all the operations of sort state have already been tested, it seems useless to test again these properties in the axiom *al1*. We first assume that the operations having S as an argument are correct (in the program) for every value of S. This hypothesis is a *uniformity hypothesis for the variable* S *of sort* state. It can be expressed as follows:

$$(\forall x_0 \in \text{state}) \, (al1(x_0) \; \Rightarrow \; (\forall S \in \text{state}) \, al1(S))$$

where *al1(x)* is the instance of the axiom *al1* obtained by replacing S with x.

Assuming that this formula is true in the program under test, we can select only one instance *al1(x_0)* of the axiom for any term x_0 of sort state built from generators only. Since we know the signature and the generators, the corresponding selection strategy is very easy to implement. Then, we can select the following term for x_0:

```
cons(false,true,false,true,ctrl_imm,(1),(0),(1),direction1,(0))
```

Unfortunately, this term does not satisfy the precondition of the axiom *al1*. From the specification, we can prove that next_auto_state(x_0) is ctrl_imm, not emergency_stop. Thus, we cannot select the test made of the instance of the conclusion of *al1(x_0)*.

The previous hypothesis was not appropriate. In fact, the hypothesis we make is that it is sufficient to test *al1* for any instance such that its precondition is satisfied. This hypothesis is a *uniformity hypothesis on the domain* of the precondition of *al1*.

2.2.2 Uniformity hypothesis on a domain

For the axiom *al1*, this *uniformity hypothesis* can be expressed as follows:

$$(\forall x_0 \in \mathcal{D}om(\text{next\_auto\_state}(S) = \text{emergency\_stop}))$$

$$(al1(x_0) \; \Rightarrow \; (\forall S \in \text{state}) \, al1(S))$$

Assuming that this formula is true in the program under test, we can select only one instance *al1(x_0)* of the axiom, for one arbitrary term x_0 which denotes some value of the validity domain of the precondition.

From the form of our specifications, the kind of domains on which uniformity hypotheses can be made are defined by conjunctions of equations:

$$u_1 = v_1 \, \& \dots \& \, u_n = v_n$$

where u_i, v_i are terms built from the signature.

In order to implement the selection strategy associated with a uniformity hypothesis on the domain of this conjunction, we need an equational resolution procedure enabling to compute *any* of its solutions. Such a resolution procedure exists for our form of axioms: the conditional narrowing proposed in [Hus 85], [Fri 85]. Given such a procedure, we can compute any solution of the conjunction of equations defining a uniformity domain.

In the case of the axiom *al1*, we can select as element of the domain of the equation next_auto_state(x_0) = emergency_stop the non-ground solution:

```
x₀ = cons(A1, Loc, true, false, emergency_stop, Seg,
    Train_Abs, Ctrl_Abs, Dir, Spd)
```

where A1, Loc, Seg, Train_Abs, Ctrl_Abs, Dir, Spd are variables of the appropriate sorts. This solution corresponds to one of the cases described by the axiom *22* which says that when the train is in the emergency_stop state and platform doors or way doors are opened, its next state is emergency_stop. Such a solution can be computed by narrowing the goal

$$\text{next\_auto\_state}(x_0) = \text{emergency\_stop}$$

Since we do not want to select always the same solution of a given goal, we made it possible in our system to use a "random" strategy for the choice of the axiom to be applied during this narrowing. This enables us to compute the solutions in a non-deterministic order. Thus, the first solution of a goal is not always the same.

In order to select a ground instance of the conclusion of the axiom *al1*, we can make uniformity hypotheses on the variables occurring in x_0. The corresponding selection strategy can be implemented by narrowing a typing goal of the form is_a_state(x_0) = true with the random choice strategy previously described.

The axioms defining such boolean typing operations are automatically generated by our system (using the generators of the signature).

For the axiom *al1*, one possible test selected by our system is:

```
next_al_doors(cons(true,true,true,false,emergency_stop,(0),(0),
    (3), direction1,(0))) = true
```

Note that under the hypotheses previously made, this test is itself a *valid* and *unbiased* test data set for the axiom *al1*.

2.2.3 Coverage of a validity subdomain

We can remark that the coverage of the cases where the precondition is true is very poor. The above test covers only one of the cases described in the axiom *22*. Since this coverage is unsatisfying, we need weaker hypotheses in order to cover other interesting cases.

Four axioms describe the transitions leading to the state emergency_stop: *02, 12, 22, 32*. In order to cover the validity domain of the precondition of the axiom *al1*, we want to cover each firing condition described in these axioms. We can reach this coverage by applying uniformity hypotheses on the domains of the preconditions of the axioms *02, 12, 22, 32*. Such a decomposition into uniformity subdomains can be done by *unfolding* the defined operations occurring in the domain definition. This unfolding mechanism is well-known in the area of program transformation ([BD 77], [Kot 80]). In our case, the unfolding mechanism consists in using the axioms to replace equals by equals in order to uncover interesting subdomains.

Let us illustrate this unfolding on the decomposition of the validity domain of *al1*. By unfolding the definition of the operation next_auto_state in the precondition, we get the following definitions of four subdomains:

```
02 : auto_state(S) = wait_open_doors
 & and(on_sidetrack(S), null_spd(speed(S))) = false
 & and(closed_way(S),
       or(closed_pf(S),
          and(located(S),
              and(in_station(S), lt(speed(S), spd_open_doors))))) = false
12 : auto_state(S) = ctrl_imm
 & and(closed_pf(S), closed_way(S)) = false
 & and(null_spd(speed(S)),
       and(located(S), or(on_sidetrack(S),closed_way(S)))) = false
22 : auto_state(S) = emergency_stop
 & and(closed_pf(S), closed_way(S)) = false
32 : auto_state(S) = ctrl_dist_spd
 & and(lt(delta_x(S), dx_max),
       and(lt(speed(S), spd_open_doors),
           and(in_station(S), and(closed_way(S), located(S))))) = false
```

If these subdomains seem "too big" to apply uniformity hypotheses, we can go further in the decomposition and unfold e.g. the boolean operations and, or which are defined by their truth tables. This leads to much more uniformity subdomains on which we can assume weaker uniformity hypotheses.

Another way to define the previous decomposition strategy is to say that we do no want to unfold the occurrences of the operations different from next_auto_state, and and or in the subdomains obtained by the unfolding of their occurrences.

Since it tries to apply each relevant axiom at each occurrence of a defined operation, the narrowing of the definition of a domain is itself an implementation of decomposition by unfolding. All we need is to enrich narrowing with a way of expressing the conditions under which it should be stopped.

Our system provides some control specifications allowing the user to define the conditions under which the unfolding of an operation is forbidden. This control allows to specify some elementary uniformity subdomains: such subdomains are defined by forbidding the unfolding of some equations. This is expressed with "wait" declarations of the form

$$\texttt{wait}(f(t_1 \ldots t_n) = t) : - < \text{condition} > .$$

where f is a defined operation and the t_i and t are terms built from variables and generators. These "waits" affect the resolution procedure during the narrowing of a subgoal containing the definition of the domain to be decomposed. When the procedure chooses an occurrence to be narrowed, it consults the "wait" declarations corresponding to the operation at this occurrence. If some "wait" can be applied at this occurrence, i.e. if the equation argument of the wait matches the occurrence and condition is satisfied, the resolution procedure chooses another occurrence in the subgoal. If all occurrences of defined operations are blocked by "waits", the current subgoal is returned together with the current computed substitution of the variables of the initial goal. This pair *(substitution, waiting subgoal)* defines a uniformity subdomain of the domain of the initial goal according to the elementary uniformity subdomains defined by the wait declarations.

This surprising use of a control mechanism to implement decomposition was first suggested in [Cho 86] using the control facilities of NU-Prolog [Nai 82].

We will later see some examples of "wait" declarations that will be used to implement some decomposition strategies.

So our system is essentially a parameterized narrowing procedure for our form of structured algebraic specifications. Its main parameters can be set using the following commands:

- `constraints(true/false)` allows the narrowing to stop when a subgoal only contains blocked equations;

- `random_choice(true/false)` activates a random choice strategy for the choice of the axiom to be applied;

- `factorize(true/false)` allows different occurrences of the same subterm to be shared between equations in a goal;

- `rewrite(true/false)` turns on or off an additional simplification mechanism: the rewriting of subgoals between two steps of narrowing.

Furthermore, a narrowing request may be composed of the following elements:

- *<conjunction of equations>*: parameterized resolution of these equations;

- `?()`: first solution of the constraints resulting from the parameterized resolution of the previous part of the request, with a random choice strategy for the axiom to be applied and no stop on constraints;

- `?(<conjunction of equations>)`: same as above, except that the equations are added to the constraint list;

- `nodisplay`: just give the number of solutions and the CPU time used by the narrowing.

3 Application of the method to the example studied

We have already sketched the selection of a test data set for the axiom *al1*. We give here all the hypotheses and strategies used to select a test data set for each axiom defining the operation `next_al_doors`: *al1*, *al2*, *al3*, *al4*.

We want to decompose the domain of these axioms in such a way that every possible kind of train behaviour is covered by a test. In particular, we want to cover every transition, leading to an alarm or not. Remark that the axioms defining `next_al_doors` already exhibit the four possible next automaton states. Thus, we want to test all possible transitions leading to these states. Furthermore, since the firing conditions of these transitions cover many interesting cases, we also want to decompose them into smaller subdomains. The corresponding unfolding is described in the following "rules":

- First, unfold all occurrences of `next_auto_state`.

- Then, the introduced occurrences of and and or, which leads to the coverage of their truth tables; thus, each accessor of a boolean field in a state appearing in a boolean expression is decomposed in its two possible values.

- in_station is unfolded in the four domains described by its axioms (see part 1).

- The operation lt in lt(speed(S), spd_open_doors) is unfolded in three domains (lower, equal, greater) corresponding to the axioms defining lt on natural numbers. The special case where the speed is equal to the limit seems as interesting as the other ones.

We do not want to unfold the other operations which may occur. In particular, an inequality on segments or abscissas is not decomposed. This forbids to further decompose the subdomains reached by the unfolding of in_station and, in general, helps avoid enumerating abscissas or segments. This is done by use of the "wait" clause

$$\texttt{wait(lt(A, B) = C)}.$$

where A and B denote any term of sort abscissa and C any boolean term.

The operation delta_x is not unfolded either, for its definition makes use of the train direction and we assume that the train behaviour does not depend on its direction. So we define a similar "wait"

$$\texttt{wait(delta\_x(S) = A)}.$$

Similarly, since sidetrack_segment and station_segment only enumerate the adequate segment numbers, we do not want to unfold them. This is specified by the following meta-clauses:

$$\texttt{wait(sidetrack\_segment(Sg) = B)}.$$
$$\texttt{wait(station\_segment(Sg) = B)}.$$

We now have everything we need to implement the selection strategies. Note that all we said above just gives a means to decompose the validity domain of the axioms *al1 ... al4* into uniformity subdomains. We still do not know what these subdomains are. They will be defined by the pairs (substitution, constraints) returned by the narrowing of the preconditions of these axioms.

Now let us show some actual examples of decompositions using the system. For the axiom *al4*, the described decomposition strategy is implemented by the narrowing of the following goal:

```
??- next_auto_state(S:state) = ctrl_imm.
```

where "??-" is the system prompt. We comment hereafter the result given by the system.

From the axiom *01*, we obtain the following uniformity subdomains:

```
S = cons(_v0:boolean,_v1:boolean,true,false,wait_open_doors,_v2:segment,
         _v3:abscissa,_v4:abscissa,_v5:direction,(0))
constraints = { sidetrack_segment(_v2:segment) = true }
```

```
S = cons(_v0:boolean,_v1:boolean,false,true,wait_open_doors,_v2:segment,
         _v3:abscissa,_v4:abscissa,_v5:direction,(0))
constraints = { sidetrack_segment(_v2:segment) = true }

S = cons(_v0:boolean,_v1:boolean,false,false,wait_open_doors,_v2:segment,
         _v3:abscissa,_v4:abscissa,_v5:direction,(0))
constraints = { sidetrack_segment(_v2:segment) = true }
```

These correspond to the three false cases in the truth table of and.

From the axiom *11*:

```
S = cons(_v0:boolean,true,true,false,ctrl_imm,_v1:segment,_v2:abscissa,
         _v3:abscissa,_v4:direction,(0))
constraints = { sidetrack_segment(_v1:segment) = true }

S = cons(_v0:boolean,true,false,true,ctrl_imm,_v1:segment,_v2:abscissa,
         _v3:abscissa,_v4:direction,(0))
constraints = { sidetrack_segment(_v1:segment) = false }

S = cons(_v0:boolean,true,false,true,ctrl_imm,_v1:segment,_v2:abscissa,
         _v3:abscissa,_v4:direction,(0))
constraints = { sidetrack_segment(_v1:segment) = true }

S = cons(_v0:boolean,true,false,false,ctrl_imm,_v1:segment,_v2:abscissa,
         _v3:abscissa,_v4:direction,(0))
constraints = { sidetrack_segment(_v1:segment) = true }
```

Of the preconditions of the axiom *11*, two offer possible decompositions:

$$\text{and}(\text{closed\_pf}(S), \text{closed\_way}(S)) = \text{false}$$

$$\text{or}(\text{closed\_way}(S), \text{on\_sidetrack}(S)) = \text{true}$$

If closed_way(S) = true, the first one has the only solution closed_pf(S) = false and the other one offers both values for on_sidetrack(S). If closed_way(S) = false, we symmetrically get both values for closed_pf(S) and only one for on_sidetrack(S). These are the four cases above.

Remark that since the narrowings involving on_sidetrack(S) are blocked by a "wait", each equation involving this operation is returned as a constraint.

The remaining case comes from the axiom *31*. There is no decomposition: the equation in_station(S) = true has only one uniformity subdomain and the other defined operations are either deterministic or blocked by "wait" meta-clauses.

```
S = cons(_v0:boolean,true,false,true,ctrl_dist_spd,_v1:segment,(_v2:nat),
         _v3:abscissa,_v4:direction,(0))
constraints = {
  delta_x(S) = _v5:abscissa, lt(_v5:abscissa,(2)) = true,
  station_segment(_v1:segment) = true,
  sidetrack_segment(_v1:segment) = false,
  sub(_v2:nat,33) = _v6:nat, lt((24),(_v6:nat)) = true,
  sub(_v2:nat,3) = _v7:nat, lt((_v7:nat),(96)) = true }
```

We must now select instances of S belonging to the uniformity subdomains defined by the answers above. The corresponding selection strategy is achieved by adding at the end of the previous goal the construction ?(). This enables to compute the first solution of each set of constraints with random_choice(true).

These instances may contain variables. We make uniformity hypotheses on them. We can thus select any ground instances of them. This is achieved by appending a typing equation ?(is_a_state(S) = true) to the previous goal. This typing equation will be solved with random_choice(true). All the selection strategies associated to the hypotheses made are implemented through the narrowing of the following goal:

$$next\_auto\_state(S : state) = ctrl\_imm, ?(), ?(is\_a\_state(S) = true).$$

This returns eight ground instances of S, belonging to the previous uniformity subdomains. From these instances, we build the following test data set for $al4$.

```
next_al_doors(cons(false,false,true,false,wait_open_doors,(0),(1),(2),
                 direction2,(0))) = false

next_al_doors(cons(false,false,false,true,wait_open_doors,(0),(0),(1),
                 direction1,(0))) = false

next_al_doors(cons(false,false,false,false,wait_open_doors,(1),(3),(0),
                 direction2,(0))) = false

next_al_doors(cons(false,true,true,false,ctrl_imm,(0),(0),(0),
                 direction1,(0))) = false

next_al_doors(cons(false,true,false,true,ctrl_imm,(9),(1),(1),
                 direction2,(0))) = false

next_al_doors(cons(false,true,false,true,ctrl_imm,(2),(0),(3),
                 direction1,(0))) = false

next_al_doors(cons(true,true,false,false,ctrl_imm,(0),(4),(0),
                 direction2,(0))) = false

next_al_doors(cons(false,true,false,true,ctrl_dist_spd,(7),(60),(0),
                 direction2,(0))) = false
```

Using the same unfolding strategy for the axioms *al1*, *al2* and *al3*, we get other uniformity subdomains. These are expressed by conjunctions of elementary uniformity subdomains defined by the "wait" meta-clauses. For the sake of brevity, we will not give them here, nor the test data sets they enable to build. The narrowing of the following requests implements the selection strategies used for their selection. The use of the `nodisplay` command allows to show only the number of selected ground instances.

For the axiom *al1*:

```
??- next_auto_state(S:state) = emergency_stop, ?(),
    ?(is_a_state(S) = true), nodisplay.
```

Number of solutions = 230

For the axiom *al2*:

```
??- next_auto_state(S:state) = wait_open_doors,?(),nodisplay.
```

Number of solutions = 4

For the axiom *al3*:

```
??- next_auto_state(S:state) =ctrl_dist_spd,?(),nodisplay.
```

Number of solutions = 2

The large number of cases selected for the axiom *al1* is mainly due to the unfolding of `next_auto_state` through the axioms *02* and *32*. The boolean operations occurring in their preconditions lead to an important combinatory. To be more pragmatic, what is tested in these cases is all possible conjunctions of a number of dangerous circumstances. These circumstances being *a priori* rather infrequent, it may seem unnecessary to test so much conjunctions, which are still less likely to happen. Less extensive decompositions can be obtained in two ways:

- we can add "waits" on boolean operations in order to stop the decomposition sooner; but then the reached uniformity subdomains will not tell apart different dangerous circumstances;

- or we can rewrite the specification a little. For instance, on the axiom *32*, if we wish to single out the situation where the locating system fails, we can write two axioms

```
32a : auto_state(S) = ctrl_dist_spd & located(S) = false
      => next_auto_state(S) = emergency_stop

32b : auto_state(S) = ctrl_dist_spd
      & located(S) = true
      & and(lt(delta_x(S), dx_max),
            and(lt(speed(S), spd_open_doors),
                and(in_station(S), closed_way(S)))) = false
      => next_auto_state(S) = emergency_stop
```

Thus, we will cover the dangerous situation located(S) = false and all conjunctions involving the other conditions. This new expression of the transition $S2$ leads to half the number of test cases we got before. We can even push this further and write as many axioms as we wish in order to express the basic unfolding we wish to obtain.

As a final remark, this short presentation cannot show the repeated backtracking needed to elaborate the control meta-clauses shown here. Since they dynamically affect the narrowing, each one indeed had to be "tested"! This is an important difficulty often encountered when using the system. The nodisplay command is of particular interest since it allows to know how many test cases will be selected and thus to tune the strength of the hypotheses accordingly.

Conclusions

We have presented an application of a method and a tool for black-box testing of a program against its algebraic specification. Test data sets have been selected from a specification module describing the door functionality of an automatic subway driving system.

In the specification module we used, the chosen "record" data structure for the representation of an internal state may seem rather awkward. Another specification of states, based on the use of an history, has been experimented for the same test data sets selection and has led to similar results. Moreover, the used specification language is currently being extended to support a more natural representation of a state.

Our results seem promising: despite the use of standard test selection strategies, the automatically selected test cases mostly concern the firing of the alarm, which is the main topic of this specification module.

The underlying method suggests that each selection strategy can be seen as the proof of some existential theorems (computing some solutions of an equational problem). The tool used for this selection is based on equational logic programming techniques, mainly narrowing. Furthermore, from a more theoretical point of view ([BGM 91]), a test can be defined as a theorem of the specification and the decision of its success (resp. failure) as its proof (resp. refutation) in the program under test. The relationship between proof techniques and test data selection mechanisms deserves to be further investigated and extended to deal with other testing methods.

Acknowledgments

The approach described here comes within the Software testing project directed by Marie-Claude Gaudel. It is a pleasure to acknowledge her numerous judicious suggestions about our work. We are also grateful to Patrick Ozello from INRETS (Institut National de Recherche et d'Etudes sur les Transports et leur Sécurité) for his constant help during the elaboration of the algebraic specification used here.

This work has been partially supported by the PRC "Programmation et Outils pour l'Intelligence Artificielle" and by a contract with INRETS.

References

- [ADJ 76] J. Goguen, J. Thatcher, E. Wagner
  "An initial algebra approach to the specification, correctness, and implementation of abstract data types"
  Current Trends in Programming Methodology, Vol.4, Yeh Ed., Prentice Hall (1978)

- [BD 77] R. Burstall, J. Darlington
  "A transformation system for developing recursive programs"
  J. Assoc. Comput. Mach., 1 (1977)

- [Ber 90] G. Bernot
  "Testing against formal specifications: a theoretical view"
  TAPSOFT 91, Brighton (April 91)

- [BGM 91] G. Bernot, M.-C. Gaudel, B. Marre
  "Software testing based on formal specifications: a theory and a tool"
  Software Engineering Journal, to appear in November 1991
  Also: LRI internal report n° 581 (June 1990)

- [Cho 86] N. Choquet
  "Test data generation using a PROLOG with constraints"
  Workshop on Software Testing, Banff, Canada, IEEE Catalog Number 86TH0144-6, pp. 132-141 (July 1986)

- [Dau 89] P. Dauchy
  "Application de la méthode PLUSS de spécification formelle à une fonction du métro de Lyon"
  Journée AFCET-INRETS "Conception et Validation des Logiciels de Sécurité dans les Transports Terrestres", Lille (June 1989)

- [EM 85] H. Ehrig, B. Mahr
  "Fundamentals of Algebraic Specification"
  EATCS Monographs on Theoretical Computer Science 6, Springer-Verlag (1985)

- [Fri 85] L. Fribourg
  "SLOG, a logic programming language interpreter based on clausal superposition and rewriting"
  International Symposium on Logic Programming, Boston (July 1985)

- [Gui 89] M.-C. Guillaumin
  "Spécification de l'UGE sécuritaire (édition 8)"
  Internal MAGGALY document, September 1988

- [Hus 85] H. Hussmann
  "Unification in Conditional-Equational Theories"
  Technical Report MIP-8502, U. Passau (January 1985)
  Résum. Proc. EUROCAL 85 Conf., Linz.

- [Kot 80] L. Kott
  "Des substitutions dans les systèmes d'équations algébriques sur le magma, application aux transformations de programmes et à leur correction"
  Thèse d'Etat, Université Paris 7 (June 1980)

- [Nai 82] L. Naish
  "An introduction to MU-PROLOG"
  Technical report, 82/2, Dept. of Computer Science, U. of Melbourne (1982)

Appendix: the automaton specification

```
00 : auto_state(S) = wait_open_doors
 & closed_pf(S) = true & closed_way(S) = true
   => next_auto_state(S) = wait_open_doors
01 : auto_state(S) = wait_open_doors
 & and(closed_pf(S), closed_way(S)) = false
 & on_sidetrack(S) = true & speed(S) = (0)
   => next_auto_state(S) = ctrl_imm
02 : auto_state(S) = wait_open_doors
 & and(on_sidetrack(S), null_spd(speed(S))) = false
 & and(closed_way(S),
       or(closed_pf(S),
          and(located(S),
              and(in_station(S), lt(speed(S), spd_open_doors))))) = false
   => next_auto_state(S) = emergency_stop
03 : auto_state(S) = wait_open_doors
 & located(S) = true & in_station(S) = true
 & lt(speed(S), spd_open_doors) = true
 & closed_pf(S) = false & closed_way(S) = true
   => next_auto_state(S) = ctrl_dist_spd

10 : auto_state(S) = ctrl_imm
 & closed_pf(S) = true & closed_way(S) = true
   => next_auto_state(S) = wait_open_doors
11 : auto_state(S) = ctrl_imm
 & and(closed_pf(S), closed_way(S)) = false & speed(S) = (0)
 & located(S) = true & or(closed_way(S), on_sidetrack(S)) = true
   => next_auto_state(S) = ctrl_imm
12 : auto_state(S) = ctrl_imm
 & and(closed_pf(S), closed_way(S)) = false
 & and(null_spd(speed(S)),
       and(located(S), or(on_sidetrack(S),closed_way(S)))) = false
   => next_auto_state(S) = emergency_stop

20 : auto_state(S) = emergency_stop
 & closed_pf(S) = true & closed_way(S) = true
   => next_auto_state(S) = wait_open_doors
22 : auto_state(S) = emergency_stop
 & and(closed_pf(S), closed_way(S)) = false
   => next_auto_state(S) = emergency_stop
```

```
30 : auto_state(S) = ctrl_dist_spd
 & closed_pf(S) = true & closed_way(S) = true
 & located(S) = true & lt(delta_x(S),dx_max) = true
 & lt(speed(S), spd_open_doors) = true & in_station(S) = true
   => next_auto_state(S) = wait_open_doors
31 : auto_state(S) = ctrl_dist_spd
 & closed_pf(S) = false & closed_way(S) = true & located(S) = true
 & lt(delta_x(S), dx_max) = true & in_station(S) = true & speed(S) = (0)
   => next_auto_state(S) = ctrl_imm
32 : auto_state(S) = ctrl_dist_spd
 & and(lt(delta_x(S), dx_max),
       and(lt(speed(S), spd_open_doors),
           and(in_station(S), and(closed_way(S), located(S))))) = false
   => next_auto_state(S) = emergency_stop
33 : auto_state(S) = ctrl_dist_spd
 & lt(delta_x(S),dx_max) = true & null_spd(speed(S)) = false
 & lt(speed(S), spd_open_doors) = true & in_station(S) = true
 & closed_way(S) = true & closed_pf(S) = false & located(S) = true
   => next_auto_state(S) = ctrl_dist_spd
```

RWR-513-fl-91011-fl

Specification in COLD-1 of a CAD package for drawing shadow masks

F.J. van der Linden

Philips Research Laboratories

P.O. Box 80000

5600 JA Eindhoven

The Netherlands

July 1, 1991

Abstract

The specification language COLD-1 is used in the formal specification of the FSM package, a specialized CAD package, that is used for shadow mask design within Philips. The case study shows that formal techniques can be used in an industrial context; in particular the language COLD-1 is a good vehicle for writing the specifications. In addition it is shown that an object-oriented style can be used within this wide spectrum language, without changing it.

keywords COLD, formal specification, industrial application, CAD package, image tubes.

Introduction

In the summer and fall of 1990 a case study has been carried out in the Technology Centre Display Components (TCDC) of Philips Components. Display Components manufactures *image tubes*, both for the consumer market (TV sets) and for the professional market (e.g. computer displays). The TCDC designs new tubes using a CAD system. The present package is not satisfactory and TCDC is in the course of reimplementation of the CAD system. Therefore a specification is needed. The reimplementation and specification should use an object-oriented technique in order to reuse software components and to facilitate maintenance. The FSM package (Forming Step Mask) is only a part of the complete CAD system. It is used in the *shadow mask* design. A shadow mask is a part of a colour tube. The actual software component that is specified deals with the drawing process, i.e. mechanical deformation, of those masks. The purpose of the case study was the formal specification in COLD-1 of the FSM package.

The FSM package is only one of the many steps in the tube design process. However, many aspects of the complete design process are covered in the FSM specification, such as dealing with complex geometrical structures and dealing with complex data structures. The COLD-1 specification gives a rigorous definition of the geometrical structures and algorithms, which makes it easy to reuse them for other parts of the CAD system.

In this paper we report on the use of COLD-1 in an industrial environment. The success of our approach was enabled because a researcher on formal methods was actively participating in the design process. The formal specifications were supplemented by the usual informal specifications, such as entity relation diagrams and plain English texts. The users of the FSM package were confronted with the informal specification and they were asked to give more precise requests in cases where the COLD-1 specification was faced with ambiguities.

The application domain already has a mathematical formalization. This formalization could be reused in the COLD-1 specification of the FSM package. This is an advantage of a wide spectrum language like COLD-1.

It was requested that the specification was designed to be object-oriented. This was realized by the mapping of types of objects in the application domain onto sorts in the COLD-1 specification. The introduction of sorts and the specification of the operations on them are grouped together. Each component describes only one class of objects. Data hiding was enabled by export lists. Inheritance in object-oriented languages has two aspects: subtyping and code sharing. The first aspect cannot be expressed in COLD-1. Instead explicit inclusion functions are used. The second aspect may be different in a specification and corresponding implementation. However, in COLD-1 code sharing may be performed with explicit imports. The wide spectrum aspects of COLD-1 made it possible to work in an object-oriented way without changing the language.

In section 1 we describe the functionality of the image tubes, the shadow masks and the drawing process. Some parts of the shadow masks are given special attention: distributions and slots. Section 2 gives a survey of the language COLD-1. We show some aspects of modeling the basic operations of the FSM package in section 3. The standard components that are used, real-analysis and geometry matters are discussed in this section. The FSM specific geometrical structures and functions are treated in section 4. Finally the combination of all operations, in order to operate the FSM package is dealt with in section 5. Notice that the mathematical structure of the application domain is reflected in the structure of the COLD-1 specification. The COLD-1 parts that occur in sections 3, 4 and 5 combine into a correct, type-checked COLD-1 specification, which is a simplified specification that covers many aspects of the real specification. The final section gives some conclusions.

The TCDC designs image tubes both for the consumer market (TV sets) and for the professional market (e.g. computer displays). There are two kinds of image tubes: monochrome tubes and colour tubes. Monochrome tubes only display images in one colour (e.g. black-grey-white). Colour tubes display images in all colours. In this paper we only discuss colour tubes for the consumer market. In a colour tube there are three *electron guns* (called red, green and blue). On the *display panel* of the tube there are lines of phosphorous material that illuminate in one of the three colours red, green or blue. All colours can be made by a weighted combination of red, green and blue light. The *shadow mask* is a part of a colour tube, that blocks the way of the electrons which otherwise would land on lines of the wrong colour. It is a metal screen with holes, placed near the glass panel of the tube at the inner side of the tube.

The shadow mask has a curved surface that is almost parallel to the glass panel. This surface contains rectangular holes (slots) to let through the electrons from the guns. The mask is made from a flat piece of metal, the flat mask, that is drawn over a drawing die in order to get its final shape. The slots are already in the flat mask. The slots are all at the inner side of a contour, the *picture size*. During the drawing process the positions of the slots and their sizes change. Also the picture size is given a different shape and dimension. The FSM package computes the places and the sizes of the slots and the picture size, as they appear on the flat mask, from the geometry of the shadow mask and from several drawing process parameters.

Because we cannot cover all aspects of the FSM package, we select a small part to show how COLD-1 is used to specify the behaviour. In particular we focus on the slot sizes as they are handled by the package.

1 Informal description of the problem domain

A shadow mask is a component of a colour display tube. We sketch the construction of such a tube in section 1.1. In section 1.2 we go into more detail about the function and geometry of the shadow mask. In section 1.3 we deal with the rectangular holes that appear in the masks. In section 1.4 so-called distributions are presented, which are mathematical structures to represent the places of the holes in a shadow mask. In section 1.5 we describe the drawing process, which is used to manufacture shadow masks.

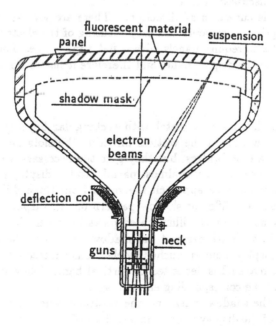

Figure 1: Sketch of a colour display tube

1.1 Tubes

Figure 1 shows a colour display tube. It has a glass housing with deflection coils around it. At one end (at the bottom of the picture), there are three electron guns, one for each of the colours red, green and blue. At the other end is the display panel, on which there are lines of fluorescent material. When electrons hit this material, it emits light in its characteristic colour, red, green or blue. The intensity of this light is dependent on the number of electrons that hit the material in a given time. The light from the fluorescent line is emitted through the glass panel and can be observed at the outside of the tube. The place where the electrons hit the panel is dictated by deflection coils that are placed around the neck of the tube. The electrons from the electron guns are repeatedly directed to move over the panel in a zig-zag pattern, in such a way that the complete panel is touched in $\frac{1}{25}$th of a second. By varying the current of the electron guns according to a video signal, a picture is displayed in this time. Each $\frac{1}{25}$th of a second a new picture is displayed.

In order to obtain colours on the panel the electrons from the 'blue' gun should only touch fluorescent material that emits blue light. Similarly this holds for green and red. Because the electrons from the three guns come from different directions, it is possible to build a shadow mask that blocks the electrons from the 'blue' gun to land on the spots of green or red fluorescent material. The same shadow mask blocks electrons from the 'green' gun from landing on spots of red or blue fluorescent material and the electrons from the 'red' gun from landing on spots of blue or green fluorescent material. The geometrical shape of this mask is discussed in section 1.2.

The display panel is curved in all directions. There are several reasons for this curvature, such as strength requirements and easy focusing of the electron beams. However, the consumers of TV sets require panels with a flat appearance. The shadow mask has to be almost parallel to the display panel and therefore it has to be curved itself.

1.2 Masks

A shadow mask is a thin piece of metal with rectangular holes (slots) arranged in a regular pattern, see figure 2. In the vertical direction the slots are separated by small bridges. Ideally there are no bridges, but they give the necessary strength to the mask. The shadow mask is placed close and almost parallel to the display panel. The electrons from the different electron guns approach the mask from three different angles. Thus each electron gun creates a different shadow pattern on the display panel. The shadow mask has a correct shape when the illuminated parts in the shadow pattern of one gun completely falls within the dark parts of the shadow pattern of the other guns. In this way each part of the display panel is touched by electrons emitted by at most one electron gun. The fluorescent material is deposited in vertical bands following the light spots of the shadow pattern of the corresponding electron gun.

The geometry of the shadow mask and the positions where the slots should be are dictated by the form of the display panel, the positions of the electron guns and deflection coils and by requirements of image resolution. All slots are placed within a contour that defines the size of the picture as it appears on the display panel.

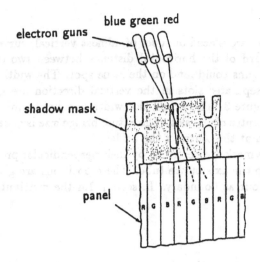

Figure 2: Functionality of a shadow mask

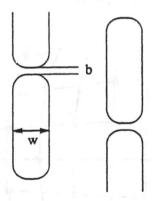

Figure 3: Slots, w = width, b = bridge size

1.3 Slots

The slots are rectangular holes that are placed on a set of, almost vertical, curved lines. The width of a slot is less than $\frac{1}{3}$rd of the horizontal distance between two of them. Otherwise electrons from different guns could land on the same spot. The width of slots and the size of the bridges that separates slots in the vertical direction are given by functions of two parameters, see figure 3. The actual slot width is equal to the value of the corresponding function at the centre of the slot. The actual bridge size is equal to the value of the corresponding function at the centre of the bridge.

The positions of the slots on the mask are described by their perpendicular projections on a plane that is perpendicular to the axis of the tube. These positions are given by a distribution of points, with a contour as boundary. In section 1.4 the distributions are discussed.

1.4 Distributions

A distribution is a collection of points in the plane, see figure 4. Each point of the distribution is (the projection of) a midpoint of a slot in the mask. The distribution is described by two collections of lines: the *horizontal line set* $\mathcal{H}$ and the *vertical line set* $\mathcal{V}$. Each curve in $\mathcal{H}$ is almost horizontal, each curve in $\mathcal{V}$ is almost vertical. For each real number $x \in \mathbb{R}$ there is a curve $\mathcal{H}_x \in \mathcal{H}$ that intersects the y-axis and there is a curve $\mathcal{V}_x \in \mathcal{V}$ that intersects the x-axis. The places of intersection are monotonously increasing, continuous functions of x, called the *pitch formulas*. To each pair of integers $m, n \in \mathbb{Z}$ there correspond two points in the distribution, viz. the point of intersection in $\mathcal{H}_m \cap \mathcal{V}_n$ and the point of intersection in $\mathcal{H}_{m+1/2} \cap \mathcal{V}_{n+1/2}$.

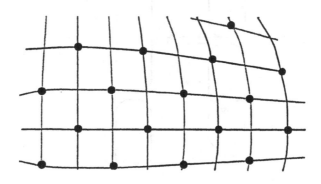

Figure 4: A distribution

The form of the lines in $\mathcal{V}$ is chosen in such a way that their image on the panel forms vertical lines. The form of the lines in $\mathcal{H}$ is dependent on several conditions in order to obtain the best images. The pitch of $\mathcal{H}$ and $\mathcal{V}$ is dependent on the required resolution and the strength requirements of the material that is used for the mask.

1.5 The drawing process

A shadow mask is manufactured from a flat piece of metal with holes in it. This piece of metal is called the *flat mask*. The flat mask is drawn over a drawing die to give the mask its final shape, called the *formed mask*, see figure 5. During the drawing process the positions and the form of the slots are changed. The form of the boundary contour is also changed. These changes are dependent on the shape of the formed mask, the drawing process and the material used.

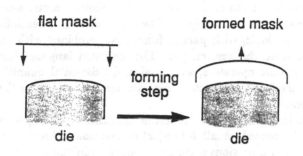

Figure 5: Forming step mask

The flat mask is designed in such a way that the positions and sizes on the formed mask are as required by the designer of the formed mask. Therefore, the distribution and boundary contour (and other parameters) of the flat mask are derived from those of the formed mask together with some process parameters.

2 Survey of COLD-1

The language COLD-1 is a wide spectrum language for design, which was developed at the Philips Research Laboratories (Nat. Lab.), in the context of the ESPRIT project 432: METEOR. The name COLD is an acronym for Common Object-oriented Language for Design. It is a formal language. Descriptions in the language are unambiguous and there is a high level tool support available. The use of formal techniques guarantees a high quality of the development process. The language COLD-1 offers enough expressive power to cover all intermediate stages of the design of a software system. It can be viewed as a combination of a specification and a programming language.

The language COLD-1 is based on COLD-K. In fact, COLD-1 is a syntactically sugared extension of the language COLD-K and there is an exact mapping from texts in COLD-1 to texts in COLD-K. There is a mathematically defined syntax and semantics for COLD-K, cf. [3, 6]. For a complete introduction to COLD-K we refer to [2, 5].

Axiomatic specifications, pre- and postcondition style specifications and algorithmic definitions are supported in COLD-1. States and invariants are concepts that can be used in COLD-1. This enables users to express their specifications in the way they prefer. COLD-1 specifications are intended to be used for programs in existing imperative language, mostly C in recent applications.

There are two major advantages of COLD-1 as compared with more widely known approaches such as VDM [1] and Z [7, 8]. First the expressions in COLD-1 are strongly typed, with the consequence that mechanical type checking is possible. Second, COLD-1 has more powerful constructs for modularization, parameterization and designs. These are essential for describing systems of realistic size and complexity.

The key notion of COLD-1 is that of a class. Within a class a complete system can be modeled. Each class has a collection of states and an initial state. The state of a class can be changed by means of procedures. Classes can be used to build other classes.

The constructs of COLD-1 can be divided into the following sorts: *assertions, expressions, definitions, components* and *designs*. The assertions are essentially assertions in a many-sorted first-order logic, with partial functions, combined with some dynamical aspects to model the state changes, cf. [4]. The assertion language includes propositional connectives, dynamic operators, universal and existential quantifications over a sort, equality and definedness of objects, predicate application and a 'let-construct' to make local declarations.

Among the expressions are the usual function applications and operator expressions. There are expressions for procedure call, for object declaration and reference, modification, the value of expressions in a previous state and nondeterministic selection.

Names for sorts, predicates, functions and procedures can be defined. The meaning is given by axioms (e.g. invariants), pre- and postconditions for functions and procedures, (inductive) definitions for predicates, functions and procedures and criteria that procedures should satisfy (e.g. the creation of a new object of some sort). Sorts can only be defined by the functions, procedures and axioms about objects of the sort. It is possible to define pre-, in- and postfix operators of a given priority and associativity behaviour.

The 'components' of COLD-1 are a means for modularization and parameterization. A component has a name and possibly some parameters, which are sorts. A component may import other components, whereby the arguments for the parameters of these other components should be provided. Renaming is possible for elements exported by the imported components. Selective import of sorts, functions, predicates and procedures is possible as well. In addition, a collection of definitions may be given and some axioms may be stated. An export list may reduce the visibility of the definitions in the class. A component may have a specification part and an implementation part, where the implementation part provides more details.

A system is the final collection of components that the design is meant for. It explicitly names a collection of components and all components that are used by these components are part of the system.

3   Mathematical basis of the drawing process

The COLD-1 specification of the FSM package consists of a specification of three major structures, together with their parts. These three structures are the descriptions of the formed mask, the flat mask and the drawing input data. In addition, some geometrical operations are specified to compute the flat mask out of the formed mask and the drawing input data.

The input of the FSM package is the formed mask description, which is computed by another package. The user of the FSM package introduces the drawing process parameters for the mask, which are dependent on the way of drawing and the material used. The computed flat mask will be used for further processing and finally be manufactured.

In this section we concentrate on the mathematical basis of the drawing process. In the section 4 we define some mathematical structures that are specific for the FSM package and in section 5 we deal with the main structures of the FSM package.

3.1 Basic components

The specification uses a collection of standard components out of a component library designed by others.

The standard components that are included are a (partial) specification of the real numbers, records and tuples (unchangeable records). Because COLD-1 does not allow higher-order logic in its specifications, the real numbers cannot be specified completely. The specifications of records contain functions val1, val2, ... to select the components of records and procedures upd1, upd2, ... to change fields of records. New, empty, records are created by the procedure create. Fields of tuples are selected by the functions proj1, proj2, ... A tuple with given components is returned by the procedure tup. In the actual specification many more standard components are included.

The inclusion of operators enhances the readability of the specification, e.g. addition and multiplication can be used as infix operators with the normal priorities. The declaration of the used operators is as follows:

```
OPERATORS
  PREFIX        -
  INFIX LEFT    *,  /
  INFIX LEFT    +,  -
  INFIX         contains, encloses, over
  INFIX         <,   >,   <=,  >=
```

This declaration means that the prefix operator - has the highest priority and the infix operators <, ... have the lowest priority.

3.2 Real analysis

In the FSM package many functions of one, two or three variables are needed. Because COLD does not support higher order logic, we cannot use function spaces directly. However, we can define sorts to model these function spaces. For our small example we need a part of the function space of two variables. This is specified in the component FUNC2:

```
COMPONENT FUNC2 SPECIFICATION
EXPORT
  SORT Func_R2toR
  FUNC app: Func_R2toR # Real # Real -> Real,
       -  : Func_R2toR # Func_R2toR  -> Func_R2toR
IMPORT REAL
CLASS
```

```
DECL f, g: Func_R2toR, x, y: Real

SORT Func_R2toR
FUNC app: Func_R2toR # Real # Real -> Real

AXIOM ( f = g <=> FORALL x, y ( app(f, x, y) = app(g, x, y) ))

FUNC - : Func_R2toR # Func_R2toR -> Func_R2toR
IN   f, g
OUT  h
POST FORALL x, y ( app(h, x, y) = app(f, x, y) - app(g, x, y) )
END
```

The component starts by giving it a name, viz. FUNC2. It ends with the keyword END. The export list describes the external interface of the component. The exported sort and the two functions are defined in the corresponding class. In the import list the component REAL is imported which describes the real numbers. This is a component described in the standard library. The sort Real and many functions and predicates on Real are imported into the component FUNC2. The part of the component after the keyword CLASS gives additional specifications. In this case the sort Func_R2toR, the functions app and - and an axiom. The part after the keyword DECL defines types of logical variables that are used in the component. In this case f and g have type Func_R2toR and x and y have type Real.

The sort Func_R2toR is the type of functions of two real variables. The function app is the application of such a function on two arguments. Functions are determined by their behaviour under app. This is stated by the axiom. The operator - defines the pointwise subtraction of two functions. Notice that - is an infix operator because it appears in the operator list.

3.3 Geometry

The FSM package needs many geometrical objects. These include vectors and points in two and three dimensional space. Moreover surfaces in space and curves in the plane and in space are introduced. There are several ways to describe curves, such as the graph of a function of one variable or the zero set of a function of two variables or in a special way, such as lines, circles, ellipses and parabolas. The computation of the intersections of curves and projections from space to the plane are dealt with. In our example, we only specify a few of these objects and functions and do not give a complete definition of all axioms that are satisfied by them.

```
COMPONENT POINT2 SPECIFICATION
EXPORT
  SORT Point2
  FUNC point: Real # Real -> Point2,
       0    : -> Point2,
       x    : Point2 -> Real,
       y    : Point2 -> Real,
       dis  : Point2 # Point2 -> Real
```

```
IMPORT
  REAL,
  TUP2'[Real, Real] RENAMING
     SORT Tup2  TO Point2
     FUNC tup   TO point,
          proj1 TO x,
          proj2 TO y
  END
CLASS

  FUNC 0: -> Point2
  DEF  point(0, 0)

  FUNC dis: Point2 # Point2 -> Real
  IN   P, Q
  DEF  sqrt(sqr(x(P) - x(Q)) + sqr(y(P) - y(Q)))
END
```

The component POINT2 describes points in the plane. It imports the standard component REAL. The sort Point2 of points in the plane is defined to be tuples of two real numbers. This sort is defined by importing the standard component TUP2 and do some renamings. The two components of a point can be selected by the functions x and y. The origin of the plane is denoted by the point 0. The distance of two points in the plane is given by the function dis. The definition of this function uses the functions sqr and sqrt for squaring and taking the square root, which are defined in the component REAL.

```
COMPONENT CONTOUR2 SPECIFICATION
EXPORT
  SORT Contour2
  PRED contains: Contour2 # Point2,
       encloses: Contour2 # Point2
IMPORT
  REAL,
  FUNC2,
  POINT2
CLASS
  DECL ct, dt: Contour2, P: Point2
  SORT Contour2
  PRED contains : Contour2 # Point2

  AXIOM ( ct = dt <=> FORALL P ( ct contains P <=> dt contains P ))

  PRED encloses: Contour2 # Point2
END
```

Contours are closed curves in the plane without self intersection. They are of the sort Contour2, which is described in the component CONTOUR2. For this example we only need an operator predicate contains to denote whether a point is on a contour and a predicate operator encloses to denote whether a point is at the inner side of the contour. Both operators are declared as infix in the operator list. Two contours are equal if they contain the same points. Notice that ∈ is not an ASCII-symbol, therefore `contains` is used in its place.

In the actual specification there are different representations for elements of the sort `Contour2`. In the implementation this will be modeled by inheritance (in fact subtyping).

```
COMPONENT SURFACE SPECIFICATION
EXPORT
  SORT Surface
  FUNC arc_dis: Surface # Point2 # Point2 -> Real,
       arc_dis: Surface # Func_R2toR -> Func_R2toR
  PRED over: Surface # Point2
IMPORT
  REAL,
  FUNC2,
  POINT2
CLASS
  DECL P, Q: Point2

  SORT Surface
  FUNC arc_dis: Surface # Point2 # Point2 -> Real
  PRED over: Surface # Point2

  FUNC arc_dis: Surface # Func_R2toR -> Func_R2toR
  IN   S, f
  OUT  g
  POST FORALL P
       ( S over P =>
         EXISTS Q
         ( arc_dis(S, P, O) = dis(Q, O) AND
           x(P) * y(Q) = y(P) * x(Q) AND x(P) * x(Q) + y(P) * y(Q) >= O AND
           app(f, x(P), y(P)) = app(g, x(Q), y(Q))
       ) )
END
```

A surface in space is of the sort `Surface`. They are described in the component `SURFACE`. The surfaces that are used have an injective orthogonal projection on the xy-plane, i.e. they are the graph of a function of two variables. Functions on the surface are defined to be functions on the x- and y-coordinates. For our purposes we need to compute the arc-distance of two points on the surface. The function `arc_dis: Surface # Point2 # Point2 -> Real` gives this distance depending on the projections of the points on the plane. This function gives rise to another function `arc_dis: Surface # Func_R2toR -> Func_R2toR`. This function transforms function on the projection of the surface to functions on the coordinate system that uses the arc distance to the origin. The infix predicate `S over P` is true whenever P is an orthogonal projection of some point on the surface S. In our example we do not give the specification of the function and predicate because it would consume too much space.

4 FSM specific structures

4.1 Slots and distributions

The sizes of the slots on the surface are dependent on the position where they occur. The sort Slot_format is a tuple of two functions in the plane: the width and the size of the bridges in vertical direction. For the formed mask these functions are given on its projection on the xy-plane. The component SLOT_FORMAT defines them:

```
COMPONENT SLOT_FORMAT SPECIFICATION
IMPORT
  FUNC2,
  TUP2'[Func_R2toR, Func_R2toR] RENAMING
    SORT Tup2  TO Slot_format
    FUNC proj1 TO width,
         proj2 TO bridge_size,
         tup   TO slot_format
    END
END
```

A distribution is a collection of points in the plane. Again we only show a part of the signature information, omitting axioms and defining clauses. In the actual FSM specification, DISTRIBUTION is a non-trivial specification, based on the ideas of section 1.4.

```
COMPONENT DISTRIBUTION SPECIFICATION
IMPORT
  INT,
  POINT2
CLASS
  SORT Distribution

  FUNC point1: Distribution # Int # Int -> Point2
  FUNC point2: Distribution # Int # Int -> Point2
END
```

For our example we only need the definition of the sort and two functions point1 and point2 that select points of the distribution.

4.2 Apertures set

The sort Set_apertures models all aspects of the set of slots in a mask. Its elements are tuples consisting of a distribution, a contour and a slot format.

```
COMPONENT SET_APERTURES SPECIFICATION
EXPORT
  SORT Set_apertures
  FUNC distribution: Set_apertures -> Distribution,
       picture_size: Set_apertures -> Contour2,
       slot_format : Set_apertures -> Slot_format,
```

```
              apertures: Distribution # Contour2 # Slot_format -> Set_apertures
IMPORT
  DISTRIBUTION,
  CONTOUR2,
  SLOT_FORMAT,
  TUP3'[Distribution, Contour2, Slot_format] RENAMING
      SORT Tup3  TO Set_apertures
      FUNC proj1 TO distribution,
           proj2 TO picture_size,
           proj3 TO slot_format,
           tup   TO apertures
  END
END
```

4.3   Inverse drawing process

The inverse drawing process models the computation of the attributes of the flat mask
out of the attributes of the formed mask and the drawing input parameters. The main
attributes that are needed for such a transformation are the distribution, the contours
and the slot sizes. In this section we specify the inverse drawing process for these objects.
Only for slots we give several details.

```
COMPONENT DRAW_SLOT SPECIFICATION
EXPORT
  SORT Delta_Slot
  FUNC delta_width: Delta_Slot -> Func_R2toR,
       bridge_size: Delta_Slot -> Func_R2toR,
       draw: Delta_Slot # Slot_format # Surface -> Slot_format

IMPORT
  REAL,
  FUNC2,
  SURFACE,
  POINT2,
  SLOT_FORMAT
CLASS
  SORT Delta_Slot
  FUNC delta_width: Delta_Slot -> Func_R2toR
  FUNC bridge_size: Delta_Slot -> Func_R2toR

  FUNC draw: Delta_Slot # Slot_format # Surface -> Slot_format
  IN   ds, sl, sh
  OUT  sl1
  POST width(sl1) = width(sl) - delta_width(ds);
       bridge_size(sl1) = bridge_size(ds)
END
```

The sort Delta_Slot contains the information that is needed to compute the slots in
the flat mask out of the slots of the formed mask. It consists of tuples of two functions

of two variables. The first function denotes the change in slot width due to the drawing process. The second function denotes the bridge size formula for the flat mask. The bridges on the formed mask ideally have size equal to 0. However for strength requirements the bridges have to have a minimal size. This size is given as the second component of the tuple.

The function draw computes the slot formats on the flat mask out of an element of type Delta_Slot, a surface and the formula on the formed mask. The computed slot width formula is combined from a projection of the surface onto the plane that keeps the arc distance to 0 constant, after which the correction is subtracted. The bridge size formula is directly copied from the Delta_Slot information. Of course the specification of the function draw looks simple. This is because in the actual specification the function arc_dis is involved and the way the values of the function delta_width is determined is not shown here.

For the distributions and the contours we have similar draw functions.

```
COMPONENT DRAW_CONTOUR SPECIFICATION
IMPORT
  CONTOUR2,
  SURFACE
CLASS
  SORT Delta_Contour
  FUNC draw: Delta_Contour # Contour2 # Surface -> Contour2
END

COMPONENT DRAW_DISTR SPECIFICATION
IMPORT
  SURFACE,
  DISTRIBUTION
CLASS
  SORT Delta_Distr
  FUNC draw: Delta_Distr # Distribution # Surface -> Distribution
END
```

5 Main FSM structures

In the sections 3 and 4 the application domain is specified. In those sections the formalization is the formalization of mathematics. In the present section the FSM packet is specified. In this section the formalization is directed to the CAD package and computer science. It involves the manipulation of structured objects in a clear way.

The main FSM structures are the formed and flat masks and the drawing input. This section gives a simplified version of the COLD1 specifications for these structures.

5.1 Formed masks

A formed mask consists of a surface, a mask size, which is a contour, and a set of apertures. The mask size completely surrounds the picture size of the set of apertures. There is an area without holes in between the picture size and the mask size at the border of the mask.

```
COMPONENT FORMED_MASK SPECIFICATION
EXPORT
  SORT Formed_mask
  FUNC shape    : Formed_mask -> Surface,
       mask_size: Formed_mask -> Contour2,
       apertures: Formed_mask -> Set_apertures
  PROC create: Surface # Contour2 # Set_apertures -> Formed_mask
IMPORT
  CONTOUR2,
  SURFACE,
  SET_APERTURES,
  REC3'[Surface, Contour2, Set_apertures] RENAMING
       SORT Rec3 TO Formed_mask
     FUNC val1 TO shape,
          val2 TO mask_size,
          val3 TO apertures
  END
CLASS

  PROC create: Surface # Contour2 # Set_apertures -> Formed_mask
  IN   s, c, sa
  OUT  fo
  SAT  NEW Formed_mask
  POST shape(fo)    = s;
       mask_size(fo) = c;
       apertures(fo) = sa
END
```

The procedure create returns a new formed mask with the given attributes. The satisfaction clause SAT NEW Formed_mask means that the side effects consists of adding a new object of type Formed_mask and the function values on all other objects remain the same. The new object is the result (fo) of the procedure. The postcondition of the procedure create states what are the values of the relevant functions for the newly created object.

5.2 Drawing input

```
COMPONENT DRAWING_INPUT SPECIFICATION
EXPORT
  SORT Drawing_input
  FUNC delta_distr    : Drawing_input -> Delta_Distr,
       delta_pict_size: Drawing_input -> Delta_Contour,
       delta_slot    : Drawing_input -> Delta_Slot,
       delta_mask_size: Drawing_input -> Delta_Contour,
       draw_apertures : Drawing_input # Set_apertures # Surface
                        -> Set_apertures,
       draw_mask_size : Drawing_input # Contour2 # Surface
                        -> Contour2
  PROC add_delta_distr   : Drawing_input # Delta_Distr ->,
```

```
        add_delta_pict_size: Drawing_input # Delta_Contour ->,
        add_delta_slot     : Drawing_input # Delta_Slot ->,
        add_delta_mask_size: Drawing_input # Delta_Contour ->,

        drawing_input: -> Drawing_input,
        drawing_input: Delta_Distr # Delta_Contour
                       # Delta_Slot # Delta_Contour -> Drawing_input
   PRED complete: Drawing_input
IMPORT
  DRAW_DISTR,
  DRAW_CONTOUR,
  DRAW_SLOT,
  SET_APERTURES,
  SURFACE,
  CONTOUR2,
  REC4'[Delta_Distr, Delta_Contour, Delta_Slot, Delta_Contour] RENAMING
      SORT Rec4 TO Drawing_input
      FUNC val1 TO delta_distr,
           val2 TO delta_pict_size,
           val3 TO delta_slot,
           val4 TO delta_mask_size
      PROC upd1 TO add_delta_distr,
           upd2 TO add_delta_pict_size,
           upd3 TO add_delta_slot,
           upd4 TO add_delta_mask_size,
           create TO drawing_input
   END
CLASS

  PROC drawing_input: Delta_Distr # Delta_Contour
                      # Delta_Slot # Delta_Contour -> Drawing_input
   IN   dd, dps, ds, dms
   OUT  di
   SAT  NEW Drawing_input
   POST delta_distr(di)     = dd;
        delta_pict_size(di) = dps;
        delta_slot(di)      = ds;
        delta_mask_size(di) = dms

   PRED complete: Drawing_input
   IN   di
   DEF  delta_distr(di)! AND delta_pict_size(di)! AND
        delta_slot(di)! AND delta_mask_size(di)!


   FUNC draw_apertures: Drawing_input # Set_apertures # Surface
                    -> Set_apertures
   IN   di, sa, sh
   OUT  sa1
```

```
PRE   complete(di)
POST  distribution(sa1) = draw(delta_distr(di), distribution(sa), sh);
      picture_size(sa1) = draw(delta_pict_size(di), picture_size(sa), sh);
      slot_format(sa1)  = draw(delta_slot(di), slot_format(sa), sh)

FUNC draw_mask_size: Drawing_input # Contour2 # Surface
                     -> Contour2
IN    di, c, sh
PRE   complete(di)
DEF   draw(delta_mask_size(di), c, sh)
END
```

The sort Drawing_input is specified as a record of 4 fields: the corrections in the distribution, in the picture size, in the slot formula and in the mask size. There are two ways to create a formed mask, either by calling the procedure drawing_input without arguments, or by calling it with all component fields as arguments. The first procedure is defined in the component REC4 and renamed here. The second one is defined in the component DRAWING_INPUT. It results in a drawing input where all fields are already defined. A drawing input exists only after creation.

The values of the functions (attributes) delta_distr, delta_pict_size, delta_slot and delta_mask_size may change during the lifetime of the system. Because the collection of drawing inputs will change during the lifetime of the system, these functions also apply to different sets of arguments. Initially they may be undefined for a given drawing input, dependent on the way it is created. The procedure add_delta_distr applied on the Drawing_input di and the Delta_Distr dd has as a side effect that the value of delta_distr(di) is changed into dd. This is the only side effect that this procedure has, as is specified in the component REC4. Similarly the procedures add_delta_pict_size, add_delta_slot and add_delta_mask_size change the values of the functions delta_pict_size, delta_slot and delta_mask_size.

The predicate complete is true when all four functions delta_distr, delta_pict_size, delta_slot and delta_mask_size are defined for a given drawing input. This definedness is denoted by the exclamation mark. Thus delta_distr(di)! means that the function delta_distr is defined for the argument di.

The function draw_apertures computes a set of apertures for the flat mask out of drawing input, the set of apertures of the formed mask and the surface of the formed mask. This function is only defined when the drawing input has enough defined fields. It results in the set of apertures that has as components the application of the drawing functions to the components of the given set of apertures. Similarly the flat mask size may be computed, when the mask size correction of the drawing input is defined.

5.3   Flat masks

A flat mask is a tuple consisting of a mask size and a set of apertures:

```
COMPONENT FLAT_MASK SPECIFICATION
EXPORT
  SORT Flat_mask
```

```
FUNC mask_size: Flat_mask -> Contour2,
     apertures: Flat_mask -> Set_apertures
PROC draw: Drawing_input # Formed_mask -> Flat_mask
IMPORT
FORMED_MASK,
DRAW_CONTOUR,
DRAWING_INPUT,
SET_APERTURES,
REC2'[Contour2, Set_apertures] RENAMING
     SORT Rec2 TO Flat_mask
     FUNC val1 TO mask_size,
          val2 TO apertures
END
CLASS

PROC draw: Drawing_input # Formed_mask -> Flat_mask
IN   di, fo
OUT  fl
SAT  NEW Flat_mask
POST mask_size(fl) = draw_mask_size(di, mask_size(fo), shape(fo));
     apertures(fl) = draw_apertures(di, apertures(fo), shape(fo))
END
```

A flat mask may be computed out of a drawing input and a formed mask when both have all their fields defined.

Now the specification is almost complete. We only have to specify that the component FLAT_MASK is the one for which the specification was meant. This is done specifying the system to be the following.

```
SYSTEM
IMPORT FLAT_MASK
END
```

6 Conclusions

The purpose of using COLD-1 for the specific FSM application is the use of formal methods in an industrial context. As a research group in formal methods we received a request for help in specifying a part of the new CAD system. We worked together with people from TCDC to obtain the information needed for the specification. At their site a more informal specification is written, containing signatures and comments in the English language, interwoven with pictures and mathematical formulas. The users of the FSM package were confronted with the informal specification. They were requested to give comments on this specification and these comments were included in both specifications. Problems caused by undefinedness of functions or conflicting requirements were mainly signaled by writing down the formal COLD-1 specification. They were returned to the users to obtain adequate answers.

During the construction of the specification we used a state-based description of the larger data structures, because in the real system only a few elements of these structures are used at the same time. Moreover, changes should be possible during the lifetime of the system. This means that the identity of formed masks and drawing inputs must remain the same even if there is an update of one of their attributes.

For specifying the basic objects we used a top-down approach. First the main objects were treated and later their components. In the mean time we investigated which pre-defined basic objects and structures could be used. These were mainly sets, tuples and records, but also the specifications of the integers and real numbers. The mathematical formalization of the application domain is reflected in a similar formalization in the COLD-1 specification.

It was required that the specification was focused on an object-oriented implementation. The example included in this paper already shows how this is done. Each component has an export list that determines which sorts, procedures and functions are exported. Most components in the example also have such an export list. All operations on data structures are specified near the definition of the data structures itself, in one component. In each component only one sort is defined and exported. All functions and procedures in the module have this sort as first argument, or is a procedure creating members of the sort. In order to make the example specification small, most export lists are removed (thus everything is exported) and some components are combined.

Other parts of the CAD system may also be specified and newly implemented by using COLD-1. A main advantage is that many geometrical objects and functions are firmly specified and can be reused in the other parts of the CAD system.

Many aspects dealing with the administration of the masks and the coupling of the right masks to the right drawing input are not included in this paper, but are a large part of the specification. These aspects are needed to obtain good functioning of the FSM package.

7 Acknowledgements

The author would like to thank TCDC for many discussions about the specification and the way the flat masks are computed. He would also like to thank T. Winter for his contributions that lead to the specification and this paper.

References

[1] D. BJÖRNER, C.B. JONES (eds.), *The Vienna development method: the meta-language*, Springer Verlag, LNCS 61 (1978).

[2] L.M.G. FEIJS, H.B.M. JONKERS, J.H. OBBINK, C.P.J. KOYMANS, G.R. RE-NARDEL DE LAVALETTE, P.H. RODENBURG, *A survey of the design language COLD*, in: ESPRIT '86: Results and Achievements, Elseviers Science Publishers B.V. (North Holland), pp. 631–644 (1986).

[3] L.M.G. FEIJS, H.B.M. JONKERS, C.P.J. KOYMANS, G.R. RENARDEL DE LAVALETTE, *Formal definition of the design language COLD-K*, ESPRIT document METEOR/t7/PRLE/7 (1987).

[4] D. HAREL, *Dynamic logic*, in.: D. Gabbay, F. Guenther (eds.), Handbook of Philosophical Logic, vol. II, D. Reidel Publishing Company, pp. 497–604 (1984).

[5] H.B.M. JONKERS, *Introduction to COLD-K*, in: M. Wirsing, J.A. Bergstra (eds.), Algebraic Methods: Theory, Tools and Applications, Springer Verlag LNCS 394 pp. 139–206 (1989).

[6] H.B.M. JONKERS, *A concrete syntax for COLD-K*, ESPRIT document METEOR/t8/PRLE/2 (1988).

[7] J.M. SPIVEY, *Understanding Z, a specification language and its formal semantics*, Cambridge Tracts in Theoretical Computer Science 3 (1988).

[8] J.M. SPIVEY, *The Z Notation: A reference manual*, Prentice Hall (1989).

ASTRAL: an Assertion Language for Specifying Realtime Systems

Carlo Ghezzi ‡ §
Dipartimento di Elettronica, Politecnico di Milano
Milano, Italia

Richard A. Kemmerer §
Reliable Software Group, Department of Computer Science
University of California, Santa Barbara, CA 93106

Abstract: ASTRAL is a formal specification language for realtime systems. This paper discusses the rationale of ASTRAL's design and shows how the language builds on previous language experiments. ASTRAL is intended to support formal software development; therefore, the language itself has been formally defined. ASTRAL's specification style is illustrated by discussing a case study taken from telephony.

1. Introduction

Realtime computer systems are increasingly being used in critical applications such as aircraft avionics, nuclear power plant control and patient monitoring. These systems are generally characterized by complex interactions with the environments in which they operate, and strict time constraints whose violation may have catastrophic consequences. The need for these software systems to be highly reliable is evident.

The best way to improve software quality is to develop it formally. Existing informal software development methods and tools [HP 88, Qui 85, Gom 86] are simply unable to provide acceptable levels of assurance for many realtime applications, because of the combination of complexity and critical requirements. On the other hand, existing formal methods, while capable in principle of providing higher levels of assurance, generally lack tool support, do not address the special requirements of realtime systems, and for the most part are based on languages that non-mathematicians find difficult to read and write [Sof 90,TSE 90,Win 90]. Therefore, formal methods are not being used in developing realtime systems.

The solution to this problem is to develop a formal specification language for writing requirements and design specifications of realtime systems, a formal proof system for

‡ This research was conducted while Carlo Ghezzi was visiting the Reliable Software Group at UCSB. Carlo Ghezzi has been partially supported by CNR-Progetto Finalizzato Sistemi Informatici e Calcolo Parallelo.
§ This research was partially supported by the National Computer Security Center under grant MDA904-88-C-6006

proving properties about these specifications, and tools to support the construction and use of specifications. The ASTRAL formal specification language for realtime systems and its associated tools are intended to provide that solution.

The Reliable Software Group at UCSB has designed and implemented a language for formally specifying and verifying sequential software systems, called ASLAN [AK 85]. In addition, they have designed an extension of the ASLAN specification language called RT-ASLAN, for specifying realtime systems [AK 86]. The ASLAN specification language served as a basis for the ASTRAL language and some of the RT-ASLAN approaches for specifying timing constraints were also adapted to ASTRAL. The ASTRAL language, however, was developed as a new language. Although the ASLAN state machine approach with layering is retained, ASTRAL uses a novel approach to modeling interprocess communication, and many new specification ideas for expressing timing relationships are introduced.

TRIO is a logic language designed at the Politecnico di Milano as a formal notation for specifying and verifying timing requirements [GMM 90, MGG 90]. In particular, the research and experimentation on TRIO addressed the issue of executing TRIO specifications. TRIO is a formally defined language, which means that its proof theory and its executability can be mathematically defined. It lacks, however, many of the qualities that would make it a practically usable language for specifying real life systems. It is hard to read and understand; there are no mechanisms for modularizing a complex specification nor for arranging it as a hierarchy of abstraction levels. Due to these weaknesses, TRIO appears more like a realtime machine level formal language than a language to be used by a system specifier. On the other hand, its strengths make it a perfect candidate as the internal (machine level) representation to be used in a specification support environment for a higher level language.

Using this ASLAN and TRIO experience, a new formal specification language for realtime systems has been developed (ASTRAL), and several case studies have been developed using this language. The semantics of the language have also been formally defined as a translation scheme from ASTRAL into TRIO. This provides a firm theoretical basis for the development of an ASTRAL support environment, which constitutes one of the future research directions. Due to the space limitations for this paper, it is not possible to give the details of the translation nor of the approaches one can follow to verify ASTRAL specifications through such a translation. These details can be found in [GK 90].

The experience of basing the ASTRAL language on ASLAN and translating ASTRAL specifications into the TRIO logic language prompted the selection of the name for the language: an ASlan based TRio Assertion Language.

This paper concentrates on ASTRAL, by discussing its motivations (section 2) and providing a detailed description of the language through a realistic case study (sections 3 and 4). Finally, in the last section conclusions drawn from this work and future areas of research are discussed.

2. Goals and Assumptions

Because there is no point in developing another language that no developer would choose to use, usability was emphasized as a main goal in the design of ASTRAL. Whenever more than one language design choice existed, the option that made the language more usable was picked. Similarly, developing a language without state-of-the-art tools to support its use inevitably results in an unused language. Therefore, the development of ASTRAL proceeded in parallel with the initial design of tools for supporting the language. The plausibility of modifying and/or extending existing tools, such as the ASLAN specification processor or the TRIO Executor, for use with ASTRAL specifications was also constantly factored into the language design process, although this was not a primary factor in the decision making process.

In addition to having a language that is usable with tool support, the other primary goals for the ASTRAL specification language were that it support specifications that are layered, compositional, and executable. Layering and composition are two complementary approaches to hierarchical system development. A layered specification method allows one to refine the specification of a process to show more detail, without changing the interface of the specified system. This is important because it allows designers to prove, test, or otherwise examine properties of a process whose behavior is specified abstractly, then iteratively refine the behavioral specification to be as close to an implementation as appropriate for a given assurance level. In this way errors can be found early in the design process, before spending time and money adding details.

A compositional specification method allows one to reason about the behavior of a system in terms of the specifications of its components [Zwi 89]. That is, the behavior of a system comprising several component processes is completely determined by the component specifications. This is important because it modularizes a system's proof and allows for bottom-up development.

An executable specification language allows developers to treat specifications as prototypes. This is important because testing in the design stage, even before attempting proofs, can be a cost-effective means of finding design flaws [Kem 85].

The ASTRAL computational model is a state machine model and assumes maximal parallelism, noninterruptable and nonoverlapping transitions in a single process instance, and one-to-many message passing communication. Some motivation for and the details of these assumptions are presented in section 3.

Formal specification of realtime system has recently become an active research area. The main approaches can be classified in two categories: operational approaches based on different kinds of automata and descriptive approaches based on logic. The first category includes extensions to finite state machines, such as Statecharts [Har 87, HLN 88], and various kinds of high level Petri nets, such as [MF 76] and [GMM 89]. The latter category includes [JM 86, KR 85, KKZ 87, Koy 89, Mor 89, JL 89], previous work on temporal logic (such as [Pnu 81]), and the authors' previous work mentioned above. There is also on-going work on temporal extensions to algebraic languages like CCS [Mil 83] and Constrained Expressions [DAW 88]. Related approaches also include synchronous realtime languages, such as ESTEREL [BCG 87] and LUSTRE [CHP 87]. Both describe programs which react instantaneously to external events. The former is an imperative language, providing assignments, conditionals, loops, etc. The latter is a dataflow language.

3. The ASTRAL Language

The ASTRAL formal specification language is based on ASLAN and its realtime extension RT-ASLAN. ASTRAL uses a *state machine* process model and has types, variables, constants, transitions, invariants, and constraints as in ASLAN. The process being specified is thought of as being in various *states* with one state differentiated from another by the values of the *state variables*. The values of these variables can be changed only via well defined *state transitions*. Like RT-ASLAN, an ASTRAL system specification is comprised of a collection of ASLAN-like state machine specifications. Each of these specifications may be layered and the interlayer proofs are an extension of the RT-ASLAN approach.* However, unlike RT-ASLAN, ASTRAL does not use interface specifications for interprocess communication. The multicast communication model that is used in ASTRAL is discussed in the next section.

In ASTRAL a realtime system is modeled by a collection of state machine specifications and a single global specification. Each state machine specification represents a process type of which there may be multiple instances in the realtime system. State variables and transitions may be explicitly exported by a process. This makes the variable values readable by other processes and the transitions executable by the external environment. Interprocess communication is via these exported variables, and is accomplished by inquiring about the value of an exported variable for a particular instance of the process. A process can inquire about the value of any exported variable of a process type or about the start or end time for an exported transition of the type. *Start(op)* is used to give the start time of the last occurrence of transition op, and *Start-k(op)* is the start time of the kth previous occurrence of op. Inquiries on a specific transition can also specify a specific value for one or more of the parameters of the operation. For example, Start(op(-,y,-)) is the start time of the last execution of transition op for which the value of the second parameter was y. Inquiries about the end time of a transition are specified similarly using *End(op)* and *End-k(op)*. The ASTRAL language also includes a *past(var,t)* specification function, which is used to specify the value the exported variable var had at time t. These inquiries are the only means of interprocess communication.

For inquiries where there is more than one instance of that type, the inquiry is preceded by the unique id of the desired instance, followed by a period. For example, i.Start(op) gives the last start time that transition op was executed by the process instance whose unique id is i. The exception to this occurs when the process instance performing the inquiry is the same as the instance being queried. In this case the preceding id and period may be dropped.

The type ID is one of the primitive types of ASTRAL. Every instance of a process type has a unique id. An instance can refer to its own id by using "Self". There is also an ASTRAL specification function IDTYPE, which returns the type of the process that is

---

* Due to space limitations, the layering is not discussed in this paper.

associated with the id.

The ASTRAL global specification contains declarations for any nonprimitive types that are shared by more than one process type as well as global invariants and scheduling constraints. A globally declared type must be explicitly imported by a process type specification that requires that type. The global invariants represent properties that need to be proved about the realtime system as a whole. The global scheduling constraints specify ordering of transitions from different process instances and the time between executions of different transitions. Some of these constraints may be proved and others are used by the TRIO translation of the specification to determine whether the specification is satisfiable. That is, the scheduling constraints are used by the TRIO executor to determine whether there is *some* schedule that satisfies the scheduling constraints. Only exported variables and the start and end times of exported transitions can be used in the global scheduling and invariant specifications.

ASTRAL Computation Model

The computational model for ASTRAL is based on nondeterministic state machines and assumes maximal parallelism, noninterruptable and nonoverlapping transitions in a single process instance, and implicit one-to-many (multicast) message passing communication.

Maximal parallelism assumes that each logical task is associated with its own physical processor, and that other physical resources used by logical tasks (e.g., memory and bus bandwidth) are unlimited. In addition, a processor is never idle when some transition is able to execute. That is, a transition is executed as soon as its precondition is satisfied (assuming no other transition is executing). The maximal parallelism approach was chosen on the basis of separating independent concerns; that is, first demonstrate that a design is satisfactory, then, and only then, consider the scheduling problem imposed by a particular implementation's limited resources. This approach, advocated in [FP 88] for realtime systems and in [CM 88] for parallel systems, allows for much cleaner designs than an approach that starts with scheduling concerns. A design based on the structure of the system rather than on its scheduling problems will usually be easier to maintain and/or modify. In addition, architectures that meet the maximal parallelism assumptions are becoming more prevalent.

Process cooperation, which involves both communication and synchronization, may be achieved in essentially two ways: either by data sharing or by message passing [BST 89]. The interface specification of RT-ASLAN is an example of modeling communication with shared data in a realtime specification language. Although *physical* data sharing has obvious performance advantages, and is, therefore, often used in current realtime systems, there is no apparent advantage in using *logical* data sharing in describing process interactions at an abstract level. There are, however, obvious disadvantages. For example, contention for shared data must be addressed in the design, which implies that mutual exclusion also must be addressed. Furthermore, future realtime systems are likely to be less tightly-coupled than existing systems. For these reasons, in ASTRAL cooperation is modeled with implicit message passing rather than with data sharing. Implicit rather than explicit message passing was chosen to further simplify the design and to concentrate on the structure of the realtime system.

The specifics of the implicit multicast message communication model are that whenever a process instance starts executing an exported transition it broadcasts the start time and the values of the actual parameters to all interested processes (i.e., any process that may refer to the start time). Furthermore, when the transition is completed the end time as well as the new value of any exported variables that were modified by the transition are broadcast. Of course, any exported variables that are modified by a nonexported transition are also broadcast by the process when the transition completes execution. Thus, if a process is inquiring about the value of an exported variable while a transition is being executed by the process being queried, the value obtained is the value the variable had when the transition commenced. That is, the ASTRAL computation model views the values of all variables being modified by a transition as being changed by the transition in a single atomic action that occurs when the transition completes execution. These broadcasts are also assumed to be instantaneous.

The assumption that transitions in a logical process are nonoverlapping, allows the use of the existing ASLAN proof methods to prove properties about the behavior of the individual tasks.

4. Example System

The example system used in this paper is a simple phone system in which there is a central control through which all connections are made. The motivation for this example came from the telephony example in a paper by Dasarathy [Das 85]. Using Dasarathy's example as a starting point and the local phone system in Santa Barbara for further clarification, the example specification was developed. The system is clearly a simplification of a real phone system; for example, all phone numbers are exactly seven digits long, a customer can be connected to at most one other phone, and ongoing calls can not be interrupted. Although the example is simplified, it does point out many of the problems that arise in realtime specifications and serves as a good vehicle for presenting the ASTRAL specification language.

The phone system consists of two process type specifications: Phone and Central_Control, and the global specification Phone_System. Most of the examples of the specification that appear in this section are from the Central_Control specification. All three specifications can be found in the appendix.

Types

ASTRAL is a strongly typed language. Integer, Boolean, ID, and Time are the only primitive types in ASTRAL. All other simple and constructed types used in a process specification must be either declared in the type section of the specification or must be declared in the global specification and explicitly imported by the process type specification.

No local types are declared in the Central_Control specification, however, the imports clause

```
IMPORT Digit, Digit_List, Phone_ID, Enabled_State
```

indicates that all of the types that are declared in the Phone_System global specification are imported. Each of these global type declarations are discussed in the following paragraphs.

The declaration

```
Digit: TYPEDEF d:Integer (d≥0 & d≤9)
```

indicates a subtype declaration, and the declaration

```
Digit_List IS LIST OF Digit
```

declares Digit_List as a list of Digits.

The declaration

```
Phone_ID: TYPEDEF pid:ID (IDTYPE(pid)=Phone)
```

is another subtype declaration. It declares Phone_IDs to be exactly those ids that are of type Phone. This declaration demonstrates the use of the ASTRAL specification function IDTYPE.

The final global type declaration

```
Enabled_State = (Idle,Ready_To_Dial,Dialing,Ringing,
                 Waiting,Talk,Disconnect,Busy,Alarm)
```

is for the enumerated type Enabled_State and indicates the various modes that a customer's phone can be in. These different modes are used to determine what transitions the phone can execute and how the central control should respond to certain actions of a customer's phone.

Returning to the central control specification,

```
EXPORT Phone_State, Enabled_Ring_Pulse,
                     Enabled_Ringback_Pulse
```

indicates that three of the five state variables of the central control process are exported, and none of its transitions are made available to the external environment. In contrast, the exports clause for the phone process type

```
EXPORT Offhook, Next_Digit, Pickup, Enter_Digit, Hangup
```

specifies that three of its transitions are exported: Pickup, Enter_Digit, and Hangup.

Variables, Constants, and Definitions

As was mentioned above, in ASTRAL one state is differentiated from another by the values of the state variables, and it is the state variables that are referenced and/or modified by the state transitions. All of the state variables must be declared in the variable section of the formal specification.

In the central control specification there are five state variables. They are all parameterized variables, parameterized by Phone_ID. The first

```
Phone_State(Phone_ID): Enabled_State
```

indicates the central control's view of the mode of each of its customer's phones.

The reader should note that the central control's view may differ from the actual mode of a phone. For instance, when a customer P first picks up his/her handset the central control may view that particular phone as being idle (i.e., Phone_State(P)=Idle), but it is actually active. The central control, however, will not treat P as active until P's offhook response (i.e., P.Offhook) is processed by executing the Give_Dial_Tone transition for P. Clearly, this is an action that should occur in a timely fashion. In fact, the global scheduling constraint that is used for the phone system example addresses this issue.

The next two variables

```
Enabled_Ring_Pulse(Phone_ID),
Enabled_Ringback_Pulse(Phone_ID): Boolean
```

are necessary because the central control actually pulses the ring of the callee's phone and the ringback tone of the caller's phone, and they are pulsed independent of each other. When Enabled_Ring_Pulse(P) is true and the mode of phone P is "ringing", this indicates that phone P should be ringing its bell (i.e., Ring = true for phone P). Note that the central control does not ring the bell, but rather indicates by means of an exported variable that the bell should be ringing. The transition that actually rings the bell is the Start_Ring transition of process Phone. Enabled_Ringback_Pulse is used in an analogous fashion to pulse the ringback tone in the caller's phone.

The remaining two variables

```
Connected(Phone_ID): Phone_ID,
Number(Phone_ID): Digit_List
```

indicate to what other phone each phone is connected and the number (or partial number) that is being dialed. Connected(P) is meaningful only if P is in waiting, ringing, or talk mode. Likewise, Number(P) is only meaningful when P is in ready to dial or dialing mode.

In ASTRAL definitions are used to make the specification more readable. Only one definition is used in the central control specification. It is

```
DEFINITION Count(P:Phone_ID):Integer==LIST_LEN(Number(P))
```

ASTRAL definitions may contain zero or more parameters. When generating proof obligations the expression that follows the "==" replaces any occurrence of the definition in the specification with the appropriate substitution of the actual parameters for the formal parameters. The Count definition is used to track how many digits have been processed for each customer. LIST_LEN is an ASTRAL specification function that indicates the number of items in the list.

Constants in ASTRAL are values that cannot change over the lifetime of the system. The first four constants in the central control specification

```
Uptime_Ring,Downtime_Ring,
Uptime_Ringback,Downtime_Ringback: Time
```

are of type Time and are used to indicate the pulse rate for ringing a customer's phone and for giving the ringback tone. The next constant

```
Get_ID(Digit_List): Phone_ID
```

is an example of a parameterized constant. It indicates the id of the particular phone that is associated with each phone number.

In this simple phone system phone numbers are assumed to never change. If it were desirable to change phone numbers, then it would be necessary for Get_ID to be a state variable rather than a constant.

The constants Time1, ..., Time10 are used in the central control specification to indicate the amount of time that each of the transitions requires for execution.

Invariants and Constraints

For a realtime system there are two types of critical requirements: behavioral and temporal. In ASTRAL, the behavioral critical requirements for a process are expressed as invariants and constraints, and the temporal critical requirements are expressed as schedules. The invariants express the critical requirements that are to hold in every reachable state, and the constraints express the critical requirements that must hold between any two consecutive states. The scheduling requirements are requirements that determine how transitions must be scheduled. They deal explicitly with the timing requirements for the process type.

The ASTRAL specification processor will generate the necessary proof obligations to assure that the invariants hold in every reachable state and that any two consecutive states satisfy the constraints. This proof methodology is identical to that used in ASLAN and the interested reader is referred to [AK 85] for further details.

For the central control process type the invariant clause specifies two restrictions on Count and several on phone modes. The first part of the invariant

```
FORALL P:Phone_ID ( Count(P) ≥ 0  &  Count(P) ≤ 7 )
```

indicates that the number being dialed by a user can never be more than seven digits long and that it is always greater than or equal to zero. This invariant demonstrates the use of the definition Count.

The second part of the invariant in the central control specification expresses the requirement that when one customer is waiting for another to answer, the other customer's phone is ringing. Similarly if one's phone is ringing then the phone of the caller should be waiting for an answer. Finally, if a phone is in talk mode the phone it is connected to should also be in talk mode. The invariant is expressed as follows

```
FORALL P:Phone_ID (
        Phone_State(P)=Waiting
                    → Phone_State(Connected(P))=Ringing
      & Phone_State(P)=Ringing
                    → Phone_State(Connected(P))=Waiting
      & Phone_State(P)=Talk
                    → Phone_State(Connected(P))=Talk ).
```

The only constraint in the central control specification is

```
FORALL P:Phone_ID (
    (  Phone_State'(P)=Busy
    |  Phone_State'(P)=Alarm
    |  Phone_State'(P)=Disconnect)
    & Phone_State(P) ≠ Phone_State'(P)
→
    Phone_State(P)=Idle ).
```

This constraint specifies that if a user reaches a busy number, doesn't dial quickly enough and gets into alarm mode, or is disconnected because the other party hangs up the phone, then the only choice for the customer is to hangup (i.e., enter idle mode). Note that in an ASTRAL expression a primed variable (eg., x´) indicates the value that variable had in the previous state.

There are six scheduling constraints for the central control process type, and they are specified by the six conjuncts composing the schedule clause of the specification. Because the scheduling constraints involve some of the transitions for the central control specification, they are presented in a separate section after the initial conditions and the state transitions are discussed.

Initial Clause

The initial clause of a process specification expresses the restrictions on the initial state of the process type. That is, for each state variable it is necessary to express the restrictions that are to be placed on its initial value. Since the initial state is a reachable state it is necessary for the initial state to satisfy the invariant (In fact, this is one of the proof obligations that will automatically be generated by the ASTRAL specification processor.). Therefore, one might choose to use the invariant itself as the initial expression. A more realistic approach is to choose a degenerate case that reflects the initial introduction of an instance of the process type being specified into the operational environment while still satisfying the invariant. This is the approach used in the central control process specification.

The initial condition specifies that in the view of the central control initially all phones are idle, no digits have been processed, and no phones are ringing nor are any receiving a ringback tone. It is not necessary to specify an initial value for the Connected variable because it is only meaningful when a phone is in either waiting, ringing, or talk mode. By reviewing the transitions for the central control process one can see that before a phone can be placed in one of these modes its connected value will be updated appropriately (See the Process_Call transition.).

State Transitions

ASTRAL transitions are used to specify the ways in which an instance of a process type can change from one state to another. A transition is composed of a header, an entry assertion, and an exit assertion. The header gives type information for the transition's parameters and specifies the amount of time required for the transition to execute. The *entry* assertion expresses the enabling conditions that must hold for the transition to occur, and the *exit* assertion specifies the resultant state after the transition occurs. That is, it specifies the values of the state variables in the new state relative to the values they had in the previous state.

In an ASTRAL specification exceptions are dealt with explicitly. That is a transition can have except/exit pairs in addition to the standard entry/exit pair. An *except* assertion expresses an exception that may occur when a transition is invoked. The corresponding exit assertion specifies the resultant state after the transition occurs.

In the control center process type specification there are ten transitions. They are

Give_Dial_Tone – response to the customer taking the handset offhook when in idle mode. It changes the phone from an idle mode to a ready to dial mode.

Process_Digit – processes each digit entered by a customer.

Process_Call – processes the number after the customer has entered seven digits. It can result in either a busy state or a waiting/ringing state.

Enable_Ring – enables the ring pulse for the callee's phone.

Disable_Ring – disables the ring pulse for the callee's phone.

Enable_Ringback – enables the ringback pulse for the caller's phone.

Disable_Ringback – disables the ringback pulse for the caller's phone.

Start_Talk – response to the callee taking the handset offhook. It changes the caller and the callee's mode to talk.

Terminate_Call – response to customer hanging up the phone.

Generate_Alarm – puts the phone in an alarm mode if dialing exceeds allotted times.

Several of these transitions are discussed in detail in the following paragraphs.

The Process_Call transition represents the central control attempting to establish a connection for a caller who has entered seven digits. It has both a normal entry/exit pair and an except/exit pair. The entry/exit pair corresponds to the case where the called party is in idle mode and the except/exit case corresponds to the case where the callee is busy. The value Time3 is the execution time for this transition. *

The entry assertion for the successful case specifies that the caller's phone must be offhook, a seven digit number must have been processed, the phone is in dialing mode, and the phone to be connected to must not be offhook and it must be idle. The exit assertion specifies that the caller's phone is now in waiting mode, the callee's phone is in ringing mode, and the mode for all other phones is unchanged. Furthermore, the caller is indicated as being connected to the callee and vice versa, and the value of connected for all other phones is unchanged. The last conjunct

```
FORALL i:ID ((i≠P & i≠Get_ID(Number'(P))
          → (  NOCHANGE(Phone_State(i))
             & NOCHANGE(Connected(i) ) )
```

is necessary, because without it the value of the parameterized variables Connected and Phone_State would be undefined for all phones other than the caller and the callee.

The entry assertion for the busy case is identical to the success case except that the phone being called is either not in idle mode or is offhook. The exit assertion for this

---

* For simplicity, in this paper it is assumed that the same amount of time is required for executing both the success case of a transition and any exception case. In the actual language design different times are provided for each entry/exit or except/exit pair.

case indicates that the mode of the caller's phone is now busy and the mode for all other phones is unchanged. The "BECOMES" operator that is used in this expression is a shorthand provided by ASTRAL for asserting that the value of a parameterized variable changes for some particular arguments, but remains unchanged for all of the other arguments. Thus

```
Phone_State(P) BECOMES Busy
```

is equivalent to

```
FORALL P1:Phone(
        Phone_State(P1) =
                IF P1=P
                        THEN Busy
                        ELSE Phone_State'(P1)
        FI )
```

This approach was adapted from ASLAN. The ASTRAL specification processor transforms BECOMES statements to this form when constructing the proof obligations.

The Enable_Ring and Disable_Ring transitions are used for modulating the Enabled_Ring_Pulse exported state variable to control the ringing of a customer's phone. The Enable_Ring transition sets this variable to true and the Disable_Ring sets it to false. The Phone process type then inquires about the value of the Enabled_Ring_Pulse variable to determine when to ring its bell. The length of time for the ring pulse to be enabled is determined by the constant Uptime_Ring and the time for it to be disabled is determined by the constant Downtime_Ring.

The entry assertion for the Enable_Ring transition requires the mode of the phone to be ringing, the phone not to be offhook, and the ring pulse to currently be disabled (~Enabled_Ring_Pulse). The last conjunct of the entry assertion controls the space between ring pulses. This expression provides an example of the use of the ASTRAL keyword *Now*, which represents the current value of time, and of the End inquiry applied to the Disable_Ring transition with parameter value P. The conjunct

```
Now - End(Disable_Ring(P)) ≥ Downtime_Ring
```

specifies that it has been at least Downtime_Ring time units since the last occurrence of the Disable_Ring transition with parameter P completed execution. The reader should note that because Disable_Ring is a transition of the process that is performing the End inquiry, it is not necessary to precede the inquiry with a unique id. The exit assertion for the Enable_Ring transition specifies that the ring pulse for phone P is now enabled (Enabled_Ring_Pulse(P)).

The Disable_Ring transition works in an analogous manner accept that its entry assertion allows for the ring pulse for phone P to be disabled early if phone P is taken offhook.

The Enable_Ringback and Disable_Ringback transitions are specified similarly except that they use the Downtime_Ringback and Uptime_Ringback constants to control their pulse rates.

The last transition to be discussed is the Generate_Alarm transition. This transition represents three of the dialing timing constraints that Dasarathy presented in his paper

[Das 85]. The restrictions are that

"After receiving a dial tone, the caller shall dial the first digit within 30 s."

"After the first digit has been dialed, the second digit shall be dialed no more than 20 s later." and

"A dialer should dial seven digits in 30 s or less ..." *

The first two conjuncts of the entry assertion for the Generate_Alarm transition

```
P.Offhook
& (  Phone_State(P)=Dialing
   | Phone_State(P)=Ready_To_Dial)
```

specify that the caller is about to begin dialing or in the process of dialing. The last conjunct captures the three constraints from Dasarathy's paper. The first disjunct

```
Count(P)=0
& (Now - End(Give_Dial_Tone(P))) > 30
```

specifies that no digits have been processed since the dial tone was enabled (Count(P)=0) and that more than 30 time units have elapsed since phone P was put in ready to dial mode (Now - End(Give_Dial_Tone(P)) > 30). The second disjunct

```
Count(P)>0 & Count(P)<7
& (Now - End(Process_Digit(P))) > 20
```

specifies that one or more, but less than seven, digits have been processed for phone P, and that it has been more than 20 time units since the last digit was processed. Finally, the third disjunct

```
Count(P)<7
& (Now - End(Give_Dial_Tone(P))) > 100
```

specifies that less than seven digits have been processed for phone P and more than 100 time units have elapsed since phone P was put in Ready_To_Dial mode.

The exit assertion specifies that phone P is put in the alarm mode.

Scheduling Requirements

As discussed above, proof obligations generated by the ASTRAL specification processor assure that the invariants hold in every reachable state and that any two consecutive states satisfy the constraints. These restrictions will be satisfied no matter what the transition execution order is and independent of the time between executing different transitions. Of course, a transition needs to have one of its entry or except assertions true before it can be executed. Scheduling restrictions, on the other hand, deal explicitly with the ordering of transitions and with the length of time between occurrences of transition executions.

Scheduling constraints are part of both process type specifications and global specifications. Process type scheduling clauses deal with timing constraints for that process only. They can not contain variables or inquiries from another process. The global

---

* For the example specification the second constraint was extended to cover the time between *any* two digits, and the total dial time was changed to 100 s, which seemed more reasonable.

scheduling clause, in contrast, specifies timing constraints which involve multiple processes.

Unlike invariants and constraints, which must all be proved, some scheduling requirements may be proved, but others may not. When a scheduling expression can not be proved it is necessary to test whether such a schedule is feasible. That is, is it possible to get a schedule that will satisfy these constraints. Scheduling requirements that can not be proved will be tested for feasibility by transforming them to TRIO and using the TRIO Executor to find a schedule that satisfies the requirements. If such a schedule can be found, then the satisfiability of the specification will have been demonstrated, but not the validity.

The six scheduling constraints that compose the schedule clause of the central control specification deal with the pulsing of the Enabled_Ring_Pulse and the Enabled_Ringback_Pulse. In the case of the Enabled_Ring_Pulse it is desirable that the pulse be enabled (Enabled_Ring_Pulse) for exactly Ring_Uptime time units and that it be disabled (¬Enabled_Ring_Pulse) for exactly Downtime_Ring time units. However, the entry assertion for the Enable_Ring transition requires that it be "at least" Downtime_Ring units since the ring pulse was enabled, and similarly for the Disable_Ring transition. Thus, it is not possible to prove that the timing will be exact for a realtime system that satisfies these specifications.

The second conjunct of the scheduling constraint for the control center captures the idea of the ring pulse being enabled exactly Uptime_Ring time units. The conjunct

```
FORALL P:Phone_ID (
        Phone_State(P)=Ringing
    & End(Enable_Ring(P))
                    > End(Process_Call(Connected(P)))
    & Now ≥ End(Enable_Ring(P)) + Uptime_Ring
→
    End(Disable_Ring(P)) =
                    End(Enable_Ring(P)) + Uptime_Ring )
```

specifies that if phone P is currently in the ringing mode, the most recent Enabled_Ring_Pulse transition has completed execution for phone P since P entered this mode, and it has been more than Uptime_Ring time units since the most recent enabling of the ring pulse for phone P, then the ring pulse was disabled exactly Uptime_Ring time units after it was enabled. Note that because phone P is the callee, the query for the most recent process call uses parameter "Connected(P)", which is the unique id of the caller.

The third conjunct works similarly to specify that the length of time that the ring pulse is disabled is exactly Downtime_Ring time units, and the last two conjuncts of the scheduling expression are written in an analogous manner for the pulsing of the ringback tone.

What these four conjuncts do not express is a constraint on how quickly the first ring pulse and/or the first ringback pulse should be enabled. This is expressed in the first and the fourth conjuncts. These expressions make use of the End-n notation, where End-n(op) is the end time of the nth previous occurrence of transition op. The first conjunct

```
FORALL P:Phone_ID (
      Phone_State(P)=Ringing
   & Now - End(Process_Call(Connected(P)))
                   ≥ Downtime_Ring
→
   EXISTS n:Integer (
      End-n(Enable_Ring(P))
                   > End(Process_Call(Connected(P)))
   & End-n(Enable_Ring(P))
                   ≤ End(Process_Call(Connected(P)))
                        + Downtime_Ring ) )
```

specifies that if phone P is currently in the ringing mode and it has been at least Downtime_Ring time units since P entered this mode, then the ring pulse for phone P was enabled in at most Downtime_Ring time units after P entered the ringing mode.

The fourth conjunct is specified similarly for the ringback pulse. The only difference that may need clarification is the expression

```
End-m(Enable_Ringback(Connected(P)))
                   ≤ End-n(Enable_Ring(P)) + .5
```

which is the result of trying to capture another of the timing constraints from [Das 85]. The constraint expressed in that paper is "After a connection has been made, the caller will receive a ringback tone no more than 0.5 s after the callee has received a ring tone." This English expression is somewhat ambiguous: should every ringback tone occur .5 s after a ring tone or should only the first ringback tone occur .5 s after the first ring tone? Or should the first ringback tone occur within the period that starts with the connection and ends .5 s after the ring tone? After talking with some of the telephony people on campus, it was decided that the ringback tone and the ring should be independent. That is, they can have different pulsing cycles (Thus, the need for the additional constants Uptime_Ringback and Downtime_Ringback.). Following this approach it was determined that the first ringback pulse should be enabled no more than .5 time units after the first ring pulse is enabled, but possibly before the first ring pulse is enabled.

The global scheduling requirements specify restrictions on the ordering of transitions from different process instances and on the time between different transition occurrences. Some of these restrictions will be provable from the process type specifications and others will need to be tested to determine whether the specification is satisfiable. That is, the scheduling constraints that can not be proved or that have not yet been proved can be analyzed to determine whether there is a schedule that satisfies the scheduling constraints. Only exported process type variables and the start and end times of exported transitions can be used in the global scheduling clause.

The global schedule clause for the example system specifies another of Dasarathy's timing constraints: "The caller shall receive a dialtone no later than 2 s after lifting the phone receiver." The corresponding specification clause is

```
FORALL P:Phone_ID (
        P.Offhook
      & Now - P.Start(Pickup) ≥ 2
      & past(Phone_State(P),P.Start(Pickup))=Idle
   →
        EXISTS t:Time (
               t > P.Start(Pickup)
             & t ≤ P.Start(Pickup) + 2
             & past(Phone_State(P),t)=Ready_To_Dial ) ).
```

The first conjunct of the antecedent specifies that phone P is currently offhook. The second conjunct is an example of the use of the Start inquiry for a particular instance of the process type phone. It specifies that it has been 2 or more time units since the start of execution of the transition Pickup by phone P. The third conjunct specifies that phone P was in idle mode when it last began execution of the Pickup transition. This conjunct is necessary because if P was in ringing mode when the receiver was picked up, then the customer should not get a dialtone. The consequent specifies that at some time during the two time unit period that started with the execution of the Pickup transition (expressed by the first two conjuncts of the consequent) the mode of phone P as viewed by the central control was ready to dial, which enables the phone P to execute its Start_Tone transition.

Note that this expression does not specify that phone P actually gets a dialtone, but that it *can* get a dialtone. In order for the global schedule clause to express that phone P gets the dialtone the variable Dialtone would have to be exported by the phone process type.

5. Conclusions and Future Work

This paper is about ASTRAL, a new formal specification language for realtime systems. The language is an outgrowth of the authors' previous work on realtime formal specification languages. ASTRAL builds on ASLAN by introducing time and by providing a formal semantics to the language. It builds on TRIO by adding structuring mechanisms. Although ASTRAL retains some of the best features of (RT-) ASLAN and TRIO, the resulting language provides a novel approach to the problem.

ASTRAL retains the nondeterministic state machine modeling style of ASLAN, where states are specified via predicates, and state changes occur as a consequence of the application of atomic operations. Modularity and hierarchy of specifications are also inherited from ASLAN, along with the proof obligations of invariants and constraints. Finally, ASTRAL retains the syntactic flavor of ASLAN. The most important influence of TRIO is the fact that it allows ASTRAL to be given a formal semantics, so that the concepts related to ASTRAL's proof theory and executability can be mathematically defined.

ASTRAL also inherits some features from synchronous languages, such as ESTEREL and LUSTRE. For example, ESTEREL's intermodule communication via signals transferred in an instantaneous broadcast network is mirrored by ASTRAL's interobject communication. ASTRAL differs from these languages, however, in that the actions performed by the system in response to external stimuli take a nonnull time (i.e., there is a delay between external events and responses). Thus, ASTRAL's model is asynchronous, whereas ESTEREL and LUSTRE are synchronous. As is the case with LUSTRE, validation of ASTRAL specifications can be supported by model checking. ASTRAL differs from LUSTRE, however, in that model checking for ASTRAL performs specification testing by restricting the analysis to finite subdomains.

Future work will proceed in several directions. One direction is to experiment with the approach in real life cases. The authors did some ASTRAL experimentation on several case studies; one such case study has been included in this paper. The case studies have shown that the language is highly expressive and powerful. More experimentation, however, will be needed in order to further assess the approach.

Another research direction will deal with the implementation of an ASTRAL support environment. This will require at least the implementation of an ASTRAL editor and syntax checker, the implementation of a translator from ASTRAL to TRIO, the acquisition of the TRIO execution tools that are currently implemented and those under development, and the generation of proof obligations for hierarchically defined ASTRAL specifications.

Yet another research direction consists of enhancing and extending the theory behind the approach. On the one hand, the relationship between the target physical architecture and the ASTRAL computation model needs to be examined more closely. Which assumptions need to be relaxed or modified in order to fit target architectures more closely? A typical example is the assumption that as soon as a task terminates a transition, the changed values of the exported variables are immediately visible to all other tasks. Assumptions about communication delays and a global clock must also be investigated. Other theoretical issues concern the development of a proof theory for the language, including a careful analysis of their composability, so that the proofs of individual tasks can be combined to produce a proof for the entire system.

References

[AK 85]   Auernheimer, B. and R. A. Kemmerer, ASLAN User's Manual, Report No. TRCS84-10, Department of Computer Science, University of California, Santa Barbara, March 1985.

[AK 86]   Auernheimer, B. and R.A. Kemmerer, "RT-ASLAN: A Specification Language for Real-Time Systems," *IEEE Transactions on Software Engineering*, Vol. SE-12, No. 9, September 1986.

[BST 89]   Bal, H.E., J.G. Steiner, and A.S. Tanenbaum, "Programming Languages for Distributed Computing Systems," *ACM Computing Surveys*, Vol. 21, No. 3, September 1989.

[BCG 87]   Berry, G., P. Couronne', and G. Gonthier, Synchronous Programming of Reactive Systems, an Introduction to ESTEREL, INRIA Report No. 647, 1987.

[CHP 87]   Caspi, P., et al. "LUSTRE: a Declarative Language for Programming Synchronous Systems", *Proceedings of the 14th Annual ACM Symposium on Principles of Programming Languages*, Munich, 1987.

[CM 88]   Chandi, K.M. and J. Misra, *Parallel Program Design: A Foundation*, Addison-Wesley, 1988.

[Das 85]   Dasarathy, B., "Timing Constraints of Real-Time Systems: Constructs for Expressing Them, Methods for Validating Them," *IEEE Transactions on Software Engineering*, Vol. SE-11, No. 1, January 1985.

[DAW 88]   Dillon, L.K., G.S. Avrunin, and J.C. Wileden, "Constrained Expressions: Toward Broad Applicability of Analysis Methods for Distributed Software Systems," *ACM Transactions on Programming Languages and Systems*, Vol. 10, No. 3, pp. 374-402, July 1988.

[FP 88]   Faulk, S.R. and D.L. Parnas, "On Synchronization in Hard Real-Time Systems," *Communications of the ACM*, Vol. 31, No. 3, March 1988.

[GK 90]   Ghezzi, C. and R.A. Kemmerer, ASTRAL: an Assertion Language for Specifying Realtime Systems, Report No. TRCS90-25, Department of Computer Science, University of California, Santa Barbara, California, November 1990.

[GMM 89]   Ghezzi, C. et al., "A General Way to Put Time in Petri Nets," *Proceedings 4th International Workshop on Software Design and Specification*, Monterey, California, April 3-4, 1987.

[GMM 90]   Ghezzi, C., D. Mandrioli, and A. Morzenti, "TRIO: A Logic Language for Executable Specifications of Real-Time Systems," *Journal of Systems and Software*, June 1990.

[Gom 86]   Gomaa, H., "Software Development of Real-Time Systems," *Communications of the ACM*, Vol. 29, No. 7, July 1986.

[Har 87]   Harel, D., "Statecharts: A Visual Formalism for Complex Systems," *Science of Computer Programming*, Vol. 8, No. 3, pp. 231-274, June 1987.

[HLN 88]   Harel, D. et al., "STATEMATE: A Working Environment for the Development of Complex Reactive Systems," *Proceedings 10th International Conference on Software Engineering*, pp. 396-406, Singapore, April 11-15, 1988

[HP 88]   Hatley, D.J. and I.A. Pirbai, *Strategies for Real-Time System Specification*, Dorset House, 1988.

[JL 89]   Jaffe, M.S. and N.G. Leveson, "Completeness, Robustness, and Safety in Real-Time Software Requirements Specification," *Proceedings 11th International Conference on Software Engineering*, Pittsburgh, Pennsylvania, May 15-18, 1989.

[JM 86]   Jahanian, F. and A.K. Mok, "Safety Analysis of Timing Properties of Real-Time Systems," *IEEE Transactions on Software Engineering*, Vol. SE-12, No. 9, September 1986.

[Kem 85]   Kemmerer, R.A., "Testing Software Specifications to Detect Design Errors," *IEEE Transactions on Software Engineering*, Vol. SE-11, No. 1, January 1985.

[KKZ 87]   Koymans, R., R. Kuiper, and E. Zijlstra, "Specifying Message Passing and Real-Time Systems with Real-Time Temporal Logic," *ESPRIT '87 Achievement and Impact*, North Holland, 1987.

[Koy 89]   Koymans, R., *Specifying Message Passing and Time-Critical Systems with Temporal Logic*, PhD Thesis, Eindhoven University of Technology, 1989.

[KR 85]   Koymans, R. and W.P. de Roever, *Examples of a Realtime Temporal Logic Specification*, LNCS 207, Springer Verlag, Berlin, 1985.

[MF 76]   Merlin, P.M. and D.J. Farber, "Recoverability of Communication Protocols, Implications of a Theoretical Study," *IEEE Transactions on Communications,* Vol. COM-24, September 1976.

[Mil 83]   Milner, R., "Calculi for Synchroni and Asynchroni," *Theoretical Computer Science,* Vol. 25, 1983.

[MGG 90]   Morzenti, A., D. Mandrioli, and C. Ghezzi, A Model Parametric Real-Time Logic, Politecnico di Milano, Dipartimento di Elettronica, Report 90.010, 1990.

[Mor 89]   Morzenti, A., *The Specification of Real-Time Systems: Proposal of a Logic Formalism,* PhD Thesis, Dipartimento di Elettronica, Politecnico di Milano, 1989.

[Pnu 81]   Pnueli, A., "The Temporal Semantics of Computer Programs," *Theoretical Computer Science,* Vol. 13, 1981.

[Qui 85]   Quirk, W.J., *Verification and Validation of Real-Time Software,* Springer Verlag, Berlin, 1985.

[Sof 90]   *IEEE Software,* Special Issue on Formal Methods, Vol. 7, No. 5, September 1990.

[TSE 90]   *IEEE Transactions on Software Engineering,* Special Issue on Formal Methods in Software Engineering, Vol. SE-16, No. 9, September 1990.

[Win 90]   Wing, J.M., "A Specifier's Introduction to Formal Methods," *IEEE Computer,* Vol. 23, No. 9, pp. 8-24, September 1990.

[Zwi 89]   Zwiers, J., *Compositionality, Concurrency, and Partial Correctness,* LNCS 321, Springer Verlag, Berlin, 1989.

Appendix   ASTRAL Formal Specification for the Example Phone System

```
GLOBAL SPECIFICATION Phone_System

USES        Phone, Central_Control

TYPE
        Digit: TYPEDEF d:Integer (d≥0 & d≤9),
        Digit_List IS LIST OF Digit,
        Phone_ID: TYPEDEF pid:ID (IDTYPE(pid)=Phone),
        Enabled_State = (Idle,Ready_To_Dial,Dialing,Ringing,Waiting,
                                Talk,Disconnect,Busy,Alarm)


SCHEDULE
        FORALL P:Phone_ID (
                P.Offhook
            & Now - P.Start(Pickup) ≥ 2
            & past(Phone_State(P),P.Start(Pickup))=Idle
        →
            EXISTS t:Time (
                    t > P.Start(Pickup)
                & t ≤ P.Start(Pickup) + 2
                & past(Phone_State(P),t)=Ready_To_Dial  )  )

END Phone_System
```

```
SPECIFICATION Central_Control
LEVEL Top_Level

IMPORT  Digit, Digit_List, Phone_ID, Enabled_State
EXPORT  Phone_State, Enabled_Ring_Pulse, Enabled_Ringback_Pulse

VARIABLE
        Phone_State(Phone_ID): Enabled_State,
        Enabled_Ring_Pulse(Phone_ID): Boolean,
        Enabled_Ringback_Pulse(Phone_ID): Boolean,
        Connected(Phone_ID): Phone_ID,
        Number(Phone_ID): Digit_List

DEFINITION
        Count(P:Phone_ID): Integer == LIST_LEN(Number(P))

CONSTANT
        Uptime_Ring,Downtime_Ring: Time
        Uptime_Ringback,Downtime_Ringback: Time,
        Get_ID(Digit_List): Phone_ID,
        Time1,Time2,Time3,Time4,Time5: Time,
        Time6,Time7,Time8,Time9,Time10: Time

INITIAL
        FORALL P:Phone_ID ( Phone_State(P) = Idle
                          & Number(P) = EMPTY
                          & ~Enabled_Ring_Pulse(P)
                          & ~Enabled_Ringback_Pulse(P) )

INVARIANT
        FORALL P:Phone_ID (
                Count(P) ≥ 0 &  Count(P) ≤ 7
            & Phone_State(P)=Waiting
               → Phone_State(Connected(P))=Ringing
            & Phone_State(P)=Ringing
               → Phone_State(Connected(P))=Waiting
            & Phone_State(P)=Talk
               → Phone_State(Connected(P))=Talk )

CONSTRAINT
        FORALL P:Phone_ID (
                ( Phone_State'(P)=Busy
                | Phone_State'(P)=Alarm
                | Phone_State'(P)=Disconnect)
                & Phone_State(P) ≠ Phone_State'(P)
          →
                Phone_State(P)=Idle )

SCHEDULE
          FORALL P:Phone_ID (
                Phone_State(P)=Ringing
              & Now - End(Process_Call(Connected(P)))
                  ≥ Downtime_Ring
            →
                EXISTS n:Integer (
                    End-n(Enable_Ring(P))
                    > End(Process_Call(Connected(P)))
                  & End-n(Enable_Ring(P))
                    ≤ End(Process_Call(Connected(P)))
                            + Downtime_Ring ) )
```

```
        & FORALL P:Phone_ID (
                Phone_State(P)=Ringing
              & End(Enable_Ring(P))
                              > End(Process_Call(Connected(P)))
              & Now ≥ End(Enable_Ring(P)) + Uptime_Ring
          →
                End(Disable_Ring(P)) =
                            End(Enable_Ring(P)) + Uptime_Ring )

        & FORALL P:Phone_ID (
                Phone_State(P)=Ringing
              & End(Disable_Ring(P))
                              > End(Process_Call(Connected(P)))
              & Now ≥ End(Disable_Ring(P)) + Downtime_Ring
          →
                End(Enable_Ring(P)) =
                            End(Disable_Ring(P)) + Downtime_Ring )

        & FORALL P:Phone_ID (
                Phone_State(P)=Waiting
              & Now - End(Process_Call(P)) ≥ Downtime_Ring
          →
                EXISTS n,m:Integer (
                    End-n(Enable_Ring(Connected(P)))
                        > End(Process_Call(P))
                  & End-n(Enable_Ring(Connected(P)))
                        ≤ End(Process_Call(P)) + Downtime_Ring )
                  & End-m(Enable_Ringback(Connected(P)))
                        > End(Process_Call(P))
                  & End-m(Enable_Ringback(Connected(P)))
                        ≤ End-n(Enable_Ring(P)) + .5     )

        & FORALL P:Phone_ID (
                Phone_State(P)=Waiting
              & End(Enable_Ringback(P)) > End(Process_Call(P))
              & Now ≥ End(Enable_Ringback(P)) + Uptime_Ringback
          →
                End(Disable_Ringback(P)) =
                        End(Enable_Ringback(P)) + Uptime_Ringback )

        & FORALL P:Phone_ID (
                Phone_State(P)=Waiting
              & End(Disable_Ringback(P)) > End(Process_Call(P))
              & Now ≥ End(Disable_Ringback(P)) + Downtime_Ringback
          →
                End(Enable_Ringback(P)) =
                        End(Disable_Ringback(P)) + Downtime_Ringback )


TRANSITION Give_Dial_Tone(P:Phone_ID)      Time1
  ENTRY
        P.Offhook
      & Phone_State(P) = Idle
  EXIT
        Phone_State(P) BECOMES Ready_To_Dial
      & Number(P) BECOMES EMPTY
```

```
TRANSITION Process_Digit(P:Phone_ID)     Time2
   ENTRY
           (Phone_State(P)=Ready_To_Dial | Phone_State(P)=Dialing)
         & P.End(Enter_Digit) > End(Process_Digit(P))
         & P.End(Enter_Digit) > End(Give_Dial_Tone(P))
         & Count(P) < 7
         & P.Offhook
   EXIT
           Number(P) BECOMES Number'(P) CONCAT LISTDEF(P.Next_Digit)
         & Phone_State(P) BECOMES Dialing

TRANSITION Process_Call(P:Phone_ID)     Time3
   ENTRY
           P.Offhook
         & Count(P)=7
         & Phone_State(P)=Dialing
         & (  ~Get_ID(Number(P)).Offhook
           & Phone_State(Get_ID(Number(P)))=Idle )
   EXIT
           Phone_State(Get_ID(Number'(P))) = Ringing
         & Phone_State(P) = Waiting
         & Connected(P) = Get_ID(Number'(P))
         & Connected(Get_ID(Number'(P))) = P
         & FORALL i:ID  ((i≠P & i≠Get_ID(Number'(P))
                 →    NOCHANGE(Phone_State(i))
                    & NOCHANGE(Connected(i) )
   EXCEPT
           P.Offhook
         & Count(P)=7
         & Phone_State(P)=Dialing
         & (  Get_ID(Number(P)).Offhook
           | Phone_State(Get_ID(Number(P)))≠Idle)
   EXIT
         Phone_State(P) BECOMES Busy

TRANSITION Enable_Ring(P:Phone_ID)     Time4
   ENTRY
           Phone_State(P)=Ringing
         & ~P.Offhook
         & ~Enabled_Ring_Pulse(P)
         & Now - End(Disable_Ring(P)) ≥ Downtime_Ring
   EXIT
         Enabled_Ring_Pulse(P) BECOMES True

TRANSITION Disable_Ring(P:Phone_ID)     Time5
   ENTRY
           Enabled_Ring_Pulse(P)
         & (  Now - End(Enable_Ring(P)) ≥ Uptime_Ring
           | P.Offhook)
   EXIT
         Enabled_Ring_Pulse(P) BECOMES False

TRANSITION Enable_Ringback(P:Phone_ID)     Time6
   ENTRY
           Phone_State(P)=Waiting
         & P.Offhook
         & ~Enabled_Ringback_Pulse(P)
         & Now - End(Disable_Ringback(P)) ≥ Downtime_Ringback
   EXIT
         Enabled_Ringback_Pulse(P) BECOMES True
```

```
TRANSITION Disable_Ringback(P:Phone_ID)      Time7
   ENTRY
            Enabled_Ringback_Pulse(P)
         & (  Now - End(Enable_Ringback(P)) ≥ Uptime_Ringback
            | ~P.Offhook)
   EXIT
            Enabled_Ringback_Pulse(P) BECOMES False


TRANSITION Start_Talk(P:Phone_ID)      Time8
   ENTRY
            Phone_State(P)=Ringing
         & P.Offhook
   EXIT
            Phone_State(P)=Talk
         & Phone_State(Connected'(P))=Talk
         & FORALL i:ID((i≠P & i≠Connected'(P))
                          → NOCHANGE(Phone_State(i)) )


TRANSITION Terminate_Call(P:Phone_ID)      Time9
   ENTRY
            Phone_State(P)≠Idle & Phone_State(P)≠Ringing
         & ~P.Offhook
   EXIT
            Phone_State(P)=Idle
         & IF (Phone_State'(P)=Talk | Phone_State'(P)=Waiting
              THEN
                   IF Phone_State'(P)=Talk
                      THEN Phone_State(Connected'(P))=Disconnect
                      ELSE Phone_State(Connected'(P))=Idle
                   FI
                 & FORALL P1:Phone_ID (P1≠P & P1≠Connected'(P)
                                  → NOCHANGE(Phone_State(P1)) )
              ELSE
                   FORALL P1:Phone_ID (P1≠P → NOCHANGE(Phone_State(P1)))
           FI


TRANSITION Generate_Alarm(P:Phone_ID)      Time10
   ENTRY
            P.Offhook
         & (Phone_State(P)=Dialing | Phone_State(P)=Ready_To_Dial)
         & (  Count(P)=0 & (Now - End(Give_Dial_Tone(P))) > 30
            | Count(P)>0 & Count(P)<7
                           & (Now - End(Process_Digit(P))) > 20
            | Count(P)<7 & (Now - End(Give_Dial_Tone(P))) > 100 )
   EXIT
            Phone_State(P) BECOMES Alarm


END Top_Level
END Central_Control
```

```
SPECIFICATION Phone
LEVEL Top_Level

IMPORT    Digit, Phone_ID, Enabled_State
EXPORT    Offhook, Next_Digit, Pickup, Enter_Digit, Hangup

VARIABLE
          Offhook,Dialtone,Ring,Ringback,Busytone: Boolean,
          Next_Digit: Digit

CONSTANT T1,T2,T3,T4,T5,T6,T7,T8,T9,T10,T11: Time

INITIAL
          ~Offhook
        & ~Dialtone
        & ~Ring
        & ~Ringback
        & ~Busytone

INVARIANT
          Dialtone → ~Ring & ~Ringback & ~Busytone
        & Ring → ~Dialtone & ~Ringback & ~Busytone
        & Ringback → ~Dialtone & ~Ring & ~Busytone
        & Busytone → ~Dialtone & ~Ring & ~Ringback


TRANSITION Pickup    T1
  ENTRY
          ~Offhook
  EXIT
          Offhook


TRANSITION Start_Tone    T2
  ENTRY
          Offhook
        & Phone_State(Self)=Ready_To_Dial
        & ~Dialtone
  EXIT
          Dialtone


TRANSITION Stop_Tone    T3
  ENTRY
          Offhook
        & Phone_State(Self)=Dialing
        & Dialtone
  EXIT
          ~Dialtone


TRANSITION Enter_Digit(D:Digit)    T4
  ENTRY
          Offhook
        & (  Phone_State(Self)=Ready_To_Dial & Dialtone
          | Phone_State(Self)=Dialing)
  EXIT
          Next_Digit=D
```

```
TRANSITION Start_Ring      T5
   ENTRY
           ~Offhook
        & Phone_State(Self)=Ringing
        & Enabled_Ring_Pulse(Self)
        & ~Ring
   EXIT
        Ring


TRANSITION Stop_Ring      T6
   ENTRY
        Ring & ~Enabled_Ring_Pulse(Self)
   EXIT
        ~Ring


TRANSITION Start_Ringback      T7
   ENTRY
           Offhook
        & Phone_State(Self)=Waiting
        & Enabled_Ringback_Pulse(Self)
        & ~Ringback
   EXIT
        Ringback


TRANSITION Stop_Ringback      T8
   ENTRY
           Ringback
        & ~Enabled_Ringback_Pulse(Self)
   EXIT
        ~Ringback


TRANSITION Start_Busytone      T9
   ENTRY
           Offhook
        & Phone_State(Self)=Busy
        & ~Busytone
   EXIT
        Busytone


TRANSITION Stop_Busytone      T10
   ENTRY
           Busytone
        & Phone_State(Self)≠Busy
   EXIT
        ~Busytone


TRANSITION Hangup      T11
   ENTRY
        Offhook
   EXIT
        ~Offhook


END Top_Level
END Phone
```

Execution environment for ELECTRE applications

Denis Creusot, Philippe Lemoine, Olivier Roux, Yvon Trinquet

LAN-ENSM, Ecole Nationale Supérieure de Mécanique, Equipe Temps Réel

1, rue de la Noë, F-44072 Nantes Cedex 03, France

Antonio Kung, Olivier Marbach, Carlos Serrano-Morales

TRIALOG Informatique

9, rue du Château d'Eau, F-75010 Paris, France

Abstract

This paper describes an execution environment for reactive systems specified in ELECTRE. ELECTRE allows the specification of a real-time application's temporal behaviour in terms of sequential entities called modules, of events, of relations between modules like parallelism, and of relations between modules and events like preemption. ELECTRE is based on a design and implementation approach enforcing the separation of the sequential part of the application (i.e. module specification), the event part of the application (i.e. event specification), and the control part of the application (i.e. reaction to events). This separation is also reflected at the execution level which includes a control unit, a module unit and an event unit. The execution environment is supplemented by a display system, which can be used for simulation, debugging or monitoring purposes. The display system is a multiwindow facility based on two main types of representations : a structural representation and a temporal representation.

Keywords: Reactive systems, real-time parallel systems, visualisation and monitoring, execution system.

1 Introduction

This paper describes a specification, programming and execution environment based on ELECTRE [Elloy 85], acronym for Exécutif et LangagE de Contrôle Temps-réel REparti (Language and Executive for Distributed Real-Time Control), a language allowing the description of the temporal behaviour of real-time control processes.

ELECTRE is one among several approaches intended to model a real-time system during its specification stage in order to be able to perform tasks such as analysis and formal checking of timing and event properties. Other approaches are specific "Real-Time Logics" [Jahanian 86, Ostroff 90], the use of event histories [Dixon 86, Faulk 88], the use of data-flow diagrams [Ward 86] or petri net analysis [Valette 88], and specific languages [Harel 90, Aeuernheimer 86]. The approaches of CCS [Milner 80] and Lotos [Brinksma 85] have influenced our work. ELECTRE is a specific language allowing the specification of behaviours concerning such notions as process preemption and process blocking. It does not support the description of the sequential process itself. ELECTRE can be classified as an asynchronous language, adapted for the programming of reactive systems, real-time systems in particular.

Among other functions, ELECTRE can be used in the following three ways :

- Validation of temporal behaviour specification. A simulator [Creusot 88] is currently available. It accepts external stimuli representing events, and shows to the user the modification of the state of the ELECTRE specification.

- Monitoring the dynamic behaviour of an application. ELECTRE expressions are used as redundant specifications, either to support debugging as in [Bruegge 83], or in order to provide a fault-tolerant mechanism for limiting detection latency of faults due to synchronization errors.

- Programming specification of the application's concurrency aspects. ELECTRE is used as a programming language. This is the approach which we have chosen and that we describe in this paper.

The rest of the paper is structured as follows. We first briefly describe ELECTRE. The kind of specification and programming environment in which ELECTRE can be included is then sketched, and the resulting execution environment, with a particular emphasis on display facilities, is presented in detail. Finally a conclusion with a description of current research is provided.

This project is partially funded by the French Ministry of Industry under the STRIN programme. The initial development of a simulator [Creusot 88] within the Electre project has been funded by Renault-Automobiles. It was used as a specification tool in the field of embedded systems.

2 Brief description of the ELECTRE language

Like some other languages [Benveniste 91], the ELECTRE language emerged from research concerning effective ways to express process behaviour and synchronization in reactive systems. [Pnueli 86, Harel 85, Benveniste 91] characterize those systems (e.g. real-time systems) by their reactions to external stimuli (e.g. sensors signals) in order to produce outputs (e.g. actuator commands). Moreover, those systems have to react to and act on an environment that constraints the reaction rate.

ELECTRE is based on path expression theory [Campbell 74]. Path expressions were mainly developed for the synchronization of concurrent processes sharing a resource. They allow the description of how concurrent processes are coordinated in the sharing of a resource. They are a convenient way of expressing constraints that processes must meet in order to guarantee that actions concerning a given shared object are executed in an orderly manner.

Path expressions have also been used as a debugging mechanism to monitor the dynamic behaviour of a computation [Bruegge 83]. In this case, path expressions are used as redundant specifications of the expected behaviour of the program being debugged in order to detect potential deviations. ELECTRE uses path expressions to specify the temporal behaviour of reactive systems.

The basic idea in the design of the ELECTRE language is to separate process synchronization constraints from algorithmic descriptions which are encapsulated in entities called *modules*. Four different behaviours concerning how modules may run with regard to other modules are available : modules may execute sequentially, in parallel, or exclusively, or a module may be repeated. These are denoted in the language by syntactic symbols **space** , ∥ , | , and ∗ respectively.

ELECTRE can express whether the execution of a module has to start upon a certain event occurrence, and whether it can be interrupted by another event occurrence. ELECTRE actually deals with two entities, modules and events. These entities are designated by identifiers appearing in ELECTRE programs together with operators. The operators ↑ and / correspond to two different types of preemption operators, and : corresponds to a module activation operator :

- The ↑ operator associates a module with an event (e.g. $M \uparrow e$). It indicates that the occurrence of e while M is active has the effect of preempting M.

- The / operator associates a module with an event (e.g. M/e). It also indicates that the occurrence of e while M is active has the effect of preempting M, but preemption is mandatory. If e has not occurred while M is active, M must wait for the occurrence of e upon completion.

- The : operator associates an event with a module (e.g. $e : M$). It indicates that upon occurrence of event e, the module M must be activated.

Thus modules can be considered as task sections which include no synchronization or blocking point. Their execution code may be expressed in any sequential language (e.g. C). A module may be in one of the following states :

- not existing. It has not been activated, or it has completed,

- active. It has been activated,

- interrupted. An event occurrence preempted its execution, and the module may be either resumed or restarted.

Since an event is linked to the ordered history of the occurrences of a specific signal, an event may be in one of the following states :

- not existing. No occurrence was memorized,

- memorized. There were one or several occurrences which have been noted but not yet acted upon,

- active. An occurrence was taken into account and it gave way to the activation of a module which has not yet completed.

In order accurately to express the temporal control in a synchronous or asynchronous application, some further properties may be associated with events and with modules.

Properties concerning events express how an event occurrence is memorized. After an event is used, it is erased from memory, i.e. *consumed* in ELECTRE terms.

There are four properties qualifying the memory of events : the default property, the @ property, the # property and the $ property. Events are qualified by preceding their identifiers by one of the three symbols (e.g. $e) or no symbol in the case of the default property. In the default property, an event occurrence is consumed upon the completion of the module it activated. The @ symbol qualifies "fleeting" events. Their occurrence cannot be memorized. Therefore, such events are either taken into account and consumed when they occur, or their occurrence is lost. The # symbol qualifies an event for which all occurrences are memorized. Finally, the $ symbol qualifies events which activate a module and whose occurrence is deleted from the memory upon the activation.

Properties concerning modules express preemption properties. There are three properties qualifying modules : the default property, the > property and the ! property. Modules are qualified by preceding their identifiers by one of the two symbols (e.g. > M) or no symbol in the case of the default property. In the default property, a module may be preempted at any time, and if it has to be activated again, it is resumed at the point where it was preempted. The > symbol qualifies modules which are restarted rather than resumed when they are reactivated. The ! symbol qualifies modules which cannot be preempted when they are active.

The above description describes the basic semantics of the language. The reader may refer to [Perraud 92] for an exhaustive and formal description of the operational semantics of the language. Figures 1 and 2 provide two temporal diagrams illustrating the execution of an ELECTRE program :

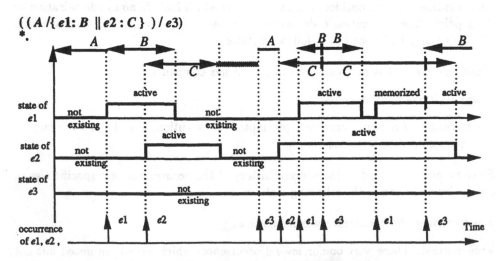

Figure 1. Execution of an ELECTRE program.

This first example shows the preemption of module A by the occurrences of events $e1$ and $e2$, which have the effect of activating modules B and C respectively. This sequence is itself preempted by the occurrence of event $e3$, which provokes the repetitive execution of the sequence (and leads either to the resumption or to the reactivation of A). Note that the second occurrence of $e3$ preempts modules B and C transiently. Since $e2$ and $e1$ are not consumed yet, they must be taken into account again, leading to the immediate resumption of modules B and C. The thick grey lines correspond to waiting states. For instance, C is waiting the occurrence of event $c3$.

$$(A / \{\, e1 : B \mid \{ e2 : C \parallel e3 : D \} \,\} : E\,)*.$$

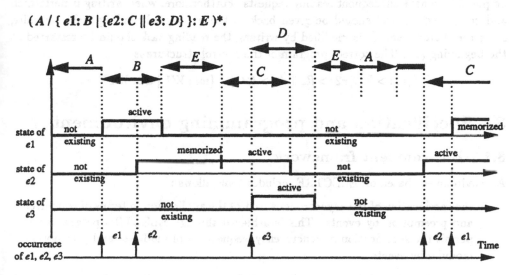

Figure 2. Execution of an ELECTRE program.

In this example, A starts to run and may be preempted by either $e1$ to activate B exclusively, or $e2$ or $e3$ to activate respectively modules C or D in parallel. Moreover, the completion of B, or of C or D, activates module E, and this whole sequence is then repeated.

An example of an ELECTRE program specifying the behaviour of processes is the well-known Readers-Writers problem [Elloy 85]. Assume that a given resource can be read simultaneously by three reader processes $R1$, $R2$, $R3$ or written by one of the two writer processes $W1$ and $W2$, but $W1$ and $W2$ cannot write at the same time. Events $r1$, $r2$, $r3$ and $w1$, $w2$ refer to read and write requests made from the modules $R1$, $R2$, $R3$, $W1$, $W2$ respectively.

If no priority is given, the control structure is given by :

$$(1/\{\{r1 : R1 \parallel r2 : R2 \parallel r3 : R3\} \mid w1 : W1 \mid w2 : W2\}) *.$$

The interrupt structure enclosed in the brackets following the ' / ' symbol indicates that all the events are at the same level and may preempt the background task, designated by 1. Writing by $W1$ and writing by $W2$ must take place exclusively, and reading must take place exclusively from writing. The inner brackets indicate that when reading occurs, concurrent reading is allowed. With such a control structure, it is possible that writers never take control. Any time there is a reader, starvation of writers can occur. In order to avoid this, the control structure below gives priority to writers. Each writer can preempt any running task in the following control structure :

$$((1/\{r1\colon R1\,\|\,r2\colon R2\,\|\,r3\colon R3\})/\{w1\colon W1\,|\,w2\colon W2\})*.$$

As a result, any writing request will preempt on-going readings. However, this structure is not totally correct, since events initiating the writers are mandatory : that is when reading is completed it is mandatory to await a write request, although it should be possible to have subsequent reading requests. Furthermore, when writing is performed and completed, control should be given back to the preempted reading tasks. Finally, since the shared resource is modified by writers, the reading task should be restarted at the beginning ($>$). The correct program of the control structure is :

$$((1/\{r1\colon > R1\,\|\,r2\colon > R2\,\|\,r3\colon > R3\})\uparrow\{w1\colon W1\,|\,w2\colon W2\})*.$$

3 Specification and programming environment

3.1 Environment framework

An environment based on ELECTRE includes tools allows :

- the specification of the asynchronous part of the application in terms of concurrency and preemption by events. This is achieved through ELECTRE programs which permit the specification of concurrency, sequencing of modules, and preemption of modules by events.

- the specification of the sequential part of the applications, i.e. modules created with standard tools and languages such as editors and compilers.

- the specification of events. Many entities can be represented as events (e.g. interrupts related to physical external events, software or hardware internal events). Those events can be combined into higher-level events (e.g. every four clock ticks). Ideally tools for expressing relations between events and tools allowing the specification of ELECTRE events are necessary. This area is beyond the scope of the project and will be part of future research.

3.2 Design and generation

The methodology follows the following steps :

- Isolate events which affect execution.

- Refine parallel entities into smaller entities, i.e. modules which contain no synchronisation point. They may contain request for signalling events.

- Derive an ELECTRE specification to describe the behaviour of the application.

Once the specification is available, tools for application compilation and generation can be used.

4 Execution environment

4.1 Execution subsystem

This section presents the ELECTRE execution system. It first explains its basic architecture and the dependencies between its main units. It then describes the control unit and the module unit.

4.1.1 Architecture

The execution system is based on the architecture shown in the figure below.

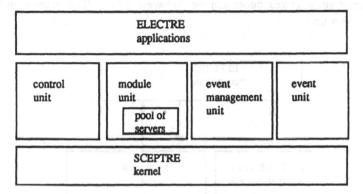

Figure 3. Execution architecture.

This architecture is based on the SCEPTRE standard [SCEPTRE 84], a real-time kernel on top of which higher level services can be provided. Most services are provided by the VDX executive services [Kung 89] to which specific services have been added to support ELECTRE.

The specific ELECTRE services are the following :

- **ELECTRE control unit** : this unit "interprets" ELECTRE control expressions and controls activation of modules. In order to do so, the event unit notifies each ELECTRE event occurrence to the control unit. The control unit then decides upon actions to be performed concerning modules. This entails requests to the module unit. The module unit notifies the control unit of module terminations. Basically, the control unit checks the occurrence of the notified event against a specification represented as a tree.

- **module unit** : this unit handles services allowing the control unit to request activation, termination, preemption, and resumption of a module. For efficiency reasons, modules are not implemented as processes of the underlying real-time executive. Execution of ELECTRE modules is ensured by a pool of server processes. Activation requests are enqueued on a first come / first serve basis.

- **event unit** : this unit receives notification of lower level events, and then decides whether an ELECTRE event has occurred. For instance the ELECTRE event *time out of 50 ms* might be handled by the 50th occurrence of the lower level event *tick 1ms* . Upon detection of occurrence, the event unit calls the event manager unit.

- **event manager unit** : this unit allows the specification of dependencies between ELECTRE events. Those dependencies concern logical and temporal combination of events which cannot be expressed in an ELECTRE specification (e.g. *e1* and *e2* occurred, *e1* or *e2* occurred, *e1* and then *e2* occurred).

4.1.2   Dependencies between subsystems

The picture below summarizes dependencies between units. The arrows indicate the interactions between units.

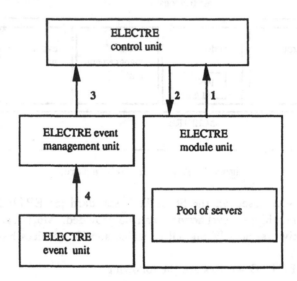

Figure 4. ELECTRE subsystem interfaces.

4 interfaces are identified :

- interface 1 : the module unit notifies the control unit of module termination.

- interface 2 : the control unit "interprets" the ELECTRE specification upon receiving event stimuli and requests the module unit for activation, preemption, resumption, or termination of modules.

- interface 3 : the event manager unit handles dependencies between ELECTRE events and interacts with the control unit.

- interface 4 : the event unit notifies the event manager unit of an ELECTRE event occurrence.

4.1.3 Control unit

The control unit uses ELECTRE expressions to determine which actions to perform in response to the notification of event occurrences. According to the kind of event and the current state of the expression, the control unit can activate or preempt modules or simply memorize the occurrence.

The control unit does not directly interpret the ELECTRE expressions but instead interprets data structures which contain :

- static parameters associated with modules (e.g. identifiers, initialization parameters),

- characterization of the events (e.g. identifiers, type),

- specification of the application represented by an "interpretation tree" which is computed from the ELECTRE sentence before the execution. This tree contains the semantics of the ELECTRE sentence, i.e. all the causal relations between modules or between modules and events.

Two interpretation trees are created. One is directly based on the syntactic and semantic structure of the control expression (structural interpretation tree), and the second one is an optimized version of the first. Figure 5 shows two examples of non-optimized structural interpretation trees.

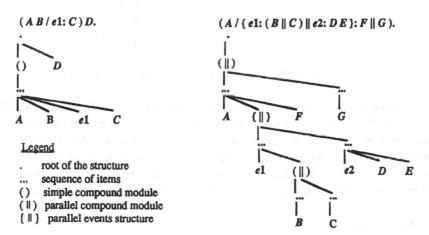

$(AB/e1:C)D.$

$(A/\{e1:(B\|C)\|e2:DE\}:F\|G).$

Legend

.	root of the structure
...	sequence of items
( )	simple compound module
(‖)	parallel compound module
{ ‖ }	parallel events structure

Figure 5. ELECTRE non-optimized structural interpretation trees.

While the building of structural interpretation trees at compile time is fairly simple, interpretation algorithms are often complicated because it is necessary to perform a systematically recursive analysis of the tree. Algorithms for on-line interpretation and off-line compilation can be found in [Creusot 88].

The control unit accesses the tree data structure after receipt of :

- the notification of an ELECTRE event issued from the event manager unit, or

• the notification of the completion of a module issued from the module unit.

As a consequence of the notification, the control unit uses the current state of the tree to activate or preempt modules with the services of the module unit, or it simply memorizes the occurrence according to the type of the event. In the latter case, active modules are not preempted and the occurrence will be taken into account later.

In a real-time context, interpretation algorithms must be efficient which is not the case when using the non-optimized tree. Since the interpretation tree is a structural copy of the initial ELECTRE expression, it "sinks" the entities which direct evolution of the application, i.e. the events. Consequently, a search must be performed for each event occurrence.

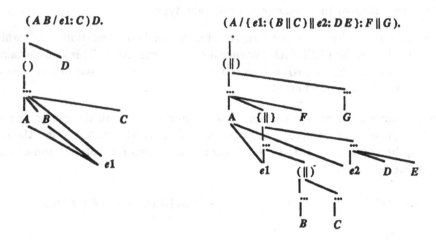

$(AB/e1:C)D.$ $(A/\{e1:(B\|C)\|e2:DE\}:F\|G).$

Figure 6. ELECTRE optimized structural interpretation trees.

Another approach based on an optimized interpretation tree has been proposed [Lemoine 90]. All events (those in the sentence and module completion events) are direct entry points of a new structure. The major interest of this approach is to "wire" the causal relations between events, modules and underlying structures (e.g. parallel, compound) in the tree. On-line analysis of such a structure is more efficient even though there are still cases when a recursive search is necessary. Figure 6 shows the result of optimization.

4.1.4 Module unit

The module unit interacts with the control unit. It provides services for activation, preemption, abortion, and resumption. It also calls a termination service of the control unit.

Activation is a service of the module unit requested by the control unit upon event occurrence (e.g. $e : M$), or in a sequence of modules (e.g. $M1M2$) or in a repetition (e.g. $(M1/e2 : M3)*$).

Preemption is requested upon event occurrence (e.g. M/e) . It is assumed that the ! preemption property qualifying modules is directly handled by the control unit which therefore does not request the preemption service. To implement preemption, the module unit uses the preemption services made available by the underlying SCEPTRE kernel.

Abortion is requested for event occurrences implying termination (e.g. $> M/e$). In this case subsequent references to the module correspond to activation (e.g. $(> M/e)*$).

Service resumption is requested in order to resume a module after preemption. For instance, if (M/e) is executed in a loop, the second reference to M corresponds to its resuming.

Termination is reported to the control unit by the module unit in order to allow it to proceed in the interpretation of the ELECTRE control expression.

The implementation of modules is based on a client-server model. A pool of task servers is preallocated when the system starts. This implementation is more efficient because tasks need not be created upon module activation. The number of tasks in the pool is decided by the application. While a known upper bound is the number of modules in an ELECTRE expression, it is not known how to compute statically the exact degree of concurrency of a given ELECTRE expression. If the actual degree of concurrency is greater that the number of tasks in the pool, requests for module activation are enqueued on a FIFO request queue.

4.2 Display subsystem

This section presents the ELECTRE display subsystem. Its purpose is to display in real-time or in pseudo real-time (i.e. possibly with some latency) information on ELECTRE execution states. Two types of representation display are used. One focuses on structural aspects, and the other on temporal aspects.

The display subsystem is a key element of an ELECTRE execution system. It is mainly intended for debugging and monitoring needs and to some extent for simulation and validation purposes. Most aspects of the display system are generic and could be generalized to other language approaches.

Figure 7 shows the display environment. The display system is entirely dependent on the ELECTRE control unit, in the sense that it interacts with it. In order to limit display overhead at the main processor level and to allow future extensions for a distributed version of the ELECTRE control unit, the display system runs on another processor connected to the main processor though a local area network. Communication is based on facilities provided by VDX. The display system is based on the Microsoft Windows environment.

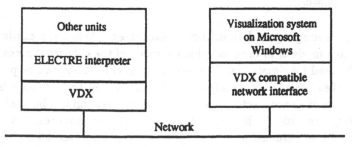

Figure 7. Display system environment.

4.2.1 Display system organisation

Static and dynamic data structures. The display system manipulates data structures describing static and dynamic aspects of an ELECTRE control expression. Static aspects relate to information which is independent of execution. This concerns the text of the ELECTRE expression, the interpretation tree structure, and preemption relations between events and modules. Static information is provided at compile time and loaded on the display system before execution starts. Dynamic aspects relate to information concerning a given execution. It mainly concerns modifications of the state of the interpretation tree, i.e. the beginning or the end of an ELECTRE sentence, an event, or the end of a module. These modifications are called *occurrences* in the rest of the document.

Static data are used to implement the various types of display representations explained below. Dynamic data can be saved in an execution history file in order to be reused later. The user of the display system can switch the input of data at any time from the stream provided by the ELECTRE control unit to a history file. To achieve this, the display system is divided in two units : the interface unit and the visualization unit. The interface unit either receives information from the control unit and dispatches it to a history file and to the visualization unit, or it reads information from a history file and dispatches it to the visualization unit. The visualization unit reads dynamic data from the interface unit and displays them.

Display modes. When the overall system is started, static information must be made available to the display system through loading directives. At this point, the default display mode is the *disconnected*, or off-line, mode, that is, the display system is not connected to the ELECTRE control unit, i.e. to the application itself. In this mode, the visualization unit obtains information directly from history files. In the *connected*, or on-line, mode, the display system is connected to the application. Data come directly from the control unit and can subsequently be saved in a history file.

Two further submodes are defined in the connected mode, the *decoupled* and the *coupled* submode. The coupled submode is the default submode. In this submode, data transmitted from the control unit is directly displayed. A user wishing to replay a sequence during the execution can set the decoupled submode. In this submode, data coming from the interpreter are redirected to a temporary file while a history file (typically the current one) can be replayed as in the unconnected mode. Upon returning to the coupled mode, the temporary file is first used to update the display with all changes that occurred during the decoupled phase.

Simulation, debugging and monitoring facilities. When the display system is in the disconnected mode or in the decoupled submode of the connected mode, the resulting system can be used for simulation. The display of modifications can be performed either on a step by step basis or by an adjustable timer. When the display system is in the coupled submode of the connected mode, the resulting system can be used for debugging and monitoring. In order to help in detecting specific occurrences, the display system can be stopped and resumed at specific points. The user can define breakpoints and decoupling points on a given occurrence. Breakpoints have the effect of stopping the application itself. Decoupling points have the effect of forcing the display system to be in the decoupled submode.

4.2.2 Display representations.

Two main types of representation are discussed here : structural representation and temporal representation. The examples below use the following ELECTRE sentence.

$$((A \| B) * / \{e1\} : (C/e2 \| D/\{e3 : E \mid e4 : FG \mid \{e5 : H \| e6\}\} : I \| J)) \uparrow e7.$$

Structural representation. This kind of representation is mainly based on a tree structure derived from the syntactic and semantic structure of an ELECTRE expression. Figure 8 shows the representation icons used to display basic entities (modules, events), basic relations (sequentiality of modules, necessary preemption, optional preemption), and syntactic non-terminal entities (simple compound module, parallel compound module, repetitive module, simple compound event, exclusive compound event and parallel compound event). Non-terminal entities have two representations : a simplified representation and an extended representation.

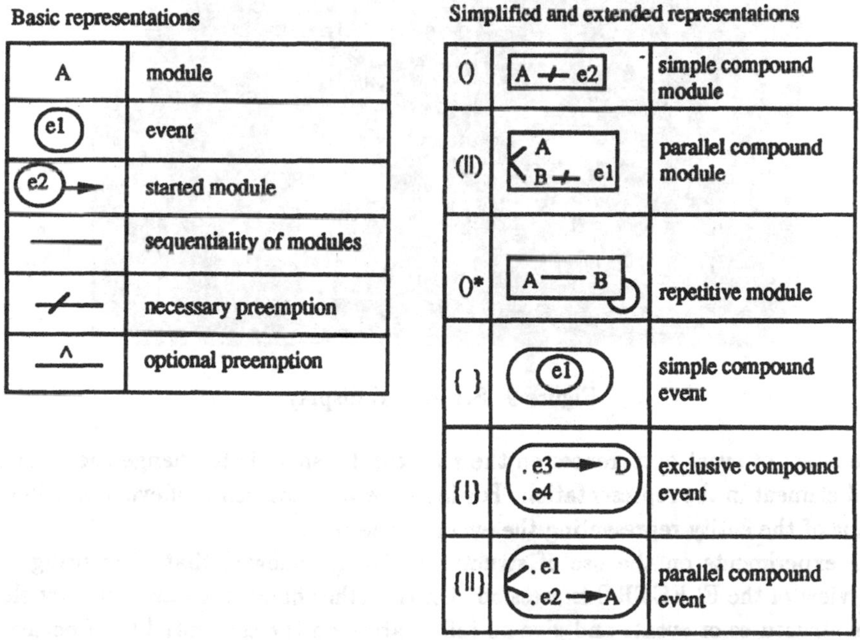

Figure 8. Structural display icons.

The user can select between the simplified and the extended representation by clicking on the representation. Figure 9 shows an example of a display with all extended representations. When the simplified representation is used, all details concerning the corresponding non-terminal entities are hidden.

The purpose of the simplified representation is twofold. It helps in encapsulating some parts of the ELECTRE sentence and it also reduces the size of the overall display. Vertical and horizontal scrolling are also supported, but it was felt that they did not preclude for the need of a simplified representation.

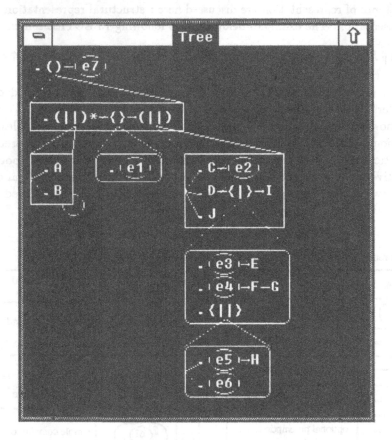

Figure 9. Structural display.

The effect of event occurrences on the structural display is to change the color of the affected element in the representation. For instance the occurrence of event e5 will change the color of the entity representing the event in the tree.

Our experiments on the use of structural displays showed that they bring a good overall view of the ELECTRE expression. On the other hand, they are not very clear for parallel structures or events and give no information on the sequentiality of occurrences.

Temporal representation. Temporal display representations are based on chrono-grams. They focus on the state of events (memorized, not existing, active), on the sequencing and states of modules, and on the concurrency of modules. Figure 10 shows the representation icons used to display basic entities.

◄—A——	module start	—— A)	module preempted
— A ►►	module end	—— A |	module stopped
— A——	no change	(A ——	module restarted
— — —	parallel sequence ended	[ ]	parallel structure
0	event awaited		

Figure 10. Temporal display icons.

The display representation uses the horizontal axis to represent time. To avoid scaling problems, the temporal axis is not defined by dates, but by occurrences. Horizontal lines show the behaviour of a given module. Figure 11 shows a temporal representation display.

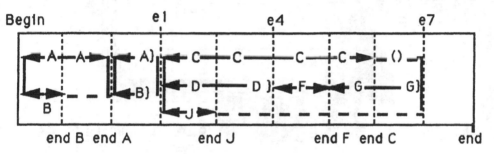

Figure 11. Temporal representation display.

The effect of occurrences on the temporal display is to scroll the window from right to left. Our experiments on the use of temporal displays showed that they bring a good overall sense of concurrency aspects of ELECTRE expressions.

Other representations. Other display facilities that have been made available are

- the textual display of the ELECTRE expression.

- the display of preemption relations between events and modules.

- a map corresponding to a simplified display of the structural representation. It is used to locate points and navigate in the structure. Clicking in a location of the map will cause the structural display window to show the corresponding part of the tree structure.

- the display of information concerning occurrences. This is obtained by clicking directly in the corresponding representation of the structural display. Temporary windows are used to provide information like the state of an occurrence, the date of an event, the location in the structure, and so forth.

Figure 12 is an example of an overall display.

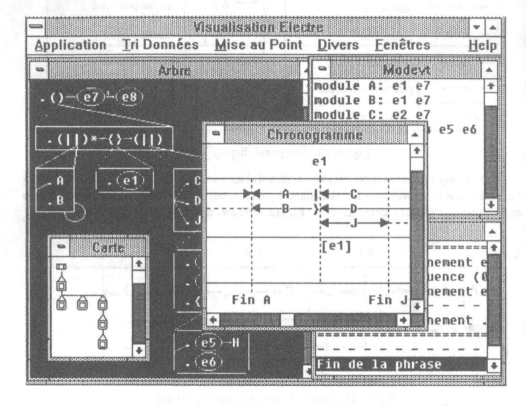

Figure 12. Overall display.

5 Conclusion

The project began in mid-1989 and was completed early in 1991, on a 250Kbit/s CSMA/CD network supplied by Compex at Annecy, France, using the VDX distributed executive provided by Renault. It runs on PCs. Experimentation on the resulting system is continuing. The project has shown the feasibility of directly using ELECTRE expressions for execution and constitutes only one step toward the identification and provision of a comprehensive range of tools for the specification and programming of safety-critical, distributed, real-time applications.

To this end, four main research directions are currently being investigated : the direct generation of an ELECTRE compiler from its formal semantic specification, fault-tolerance support, expression of timing constraints and distributed systems.

Compiler generation is based on the building of a rewriting system based on an attribute grammar describing ELECTRE. This system leads to the generation of a transition system which can be used as a compiler.

Concerning fault-tolerance, the ability to specify fault-tolerant behaviours of real-time applications in ELECTRE is being investigated. In particular, extensions have already been studied to allow the programmer to express either active or passive software redundancy techniques applied to modules.

Research is being carried out on the specification of critical timing constraints. Those specifications are associated with modules. The objective is to use the specifications in order to help select the appropriate scheduling policy.

The distribution of modules in a Local Area Network environment is also investigated. The goal is to have ELECTRE programs describe the behaviour of a global distributed system. Thus, the main issue is to make sure that each local action is compatible with the global ELECTRE program. The approach involves replicating the ELECTRE program at each site of the network and adding distributed synchronization techniques to ensure that the control sequence progress is the same everywhere.

6   Acknowledgements

We would like to thank Jean-Pierre Elloy, the head of the ENSM (Ecole Nationale Supérieure de Mécanique) real-time research team for the support he provided for our project. We are also grateful to Jérome Billion, Adam Mirowsky and Nabil Zakhama for their participation in the implementation of the ELECTRE execution environment.

Bibliography

[Aeuernheimer 86] B. Aeuernheimer, R.A. Kermmerer. *RT-ASLAN : A Specification Language for Real-Time Systems.* IEEE Transactions on Software Engineering, Vol. SE-12, n. 9, pp. 879-889, September 1986.

[Benveniste 91] A. Benveniste, G. Berry. *Real-Time Systems Design and Programming.* Special section of the Proceedings of the IEEE on real-time programming. To appear in autumn 1991.

[Bruegge 83] B. Bruegge, P. Hibbard. *Generalized Path Expressions : A High Level Debugging Mechanism.* ACM SIGSOFT/SIGPLAN Software Engineering Symposium on High-Level Debugging, pp. 34-44, March 1983.

[Brinksma 85] E. Brinksma. *A tutorial on Lotos.* IFIP Workshop on Protocol Specifications, Testing and Implementation, Moissac, 1985.

[Campbell 74] R.H. Campbell, A.N.Habermann. *The Specification of Process Synchronization by Path Expressions.* Lecture Notes in Computer Science, Vol. 16, Springer-Verlag, pp. 89-102, December 1974.

[Creusot 88] D. Creusot. *Guide d'utilisation du système ELECTRE Version PC.* Rapport de contrat Renault, VEH-ELE-D1, October 1988.

[Deplanche 88] A.-M. Deplanche, J.-P. Elloy, O. Roux. *Redundancy in Fault Tolerant Real-time Process Control Systems*. Congrès mondial IMACS, Paris, July 1988.

[Dixon 86] R.D. Dixon, D. Hemmendinger. *Analyzing Synchronization Problems by Using Event Histories as Languages*. pp. 183-188, 1986.

[Elloy 85] J.P. Elloy, O. Roux. *ELECTRE : A Language for Control Structuring in Real-Time*. The Computer Journal, Vol. 28, n. 5, 1985.

[Faulk 88] S.R. Faulk, D.L. Parnas. *On Synchronization in Hard-Real-Time Systems*. ACM, Vol. 31, n. 3, March 1988.

[Harel 85] D. Harel, A. Pnueli. *On the Development of Reactive System : Logic and Models of Concurrent Systems*. NATO ASI Series, Vol. 13 (K.R.Apt, ed.), Springer-Verlag, New-York, pp. 477-498, 1985.

[Harel 90] D. Harel, H. Lachover, A. Naamad, A. Pnueli, M. Politi, R. Sherman, A. Stull-Trauring, M. Trakhtenbrot. *STATEMATE : A Working Environment for the Development of Complex Reactive Systems*. IEEE Transactions on Software Engineering, Vol. 16, n. 4, (K.R.Apt, ed.), pp. 403-414, April 1990.

[Jahanian 86] F. Jahanian, A. Mok. *Safety Analysis of Timing Properties in Real-Time Systems*. IEEE Transactions on Software Engineering, Vol. SE-12, n. 9, pp. 890-904, September 1986.

[Kung 89] A. Kung, I. Lacrouts-Cazenave, C. Serrano-Morales. *Interconnection of Vehicle Software Components*. Working conference on decentralized systems. IFIP W.G.10.3, Lyon, December 1989.

[Lemoine 90] P. Lemoine, Y. Trinquet, J. Perraud. *Une proposition de modification de la structure d'arbre ELECTRE*. Internal report LAN, 1990.

[Milner 80] R. Milner. *A Calculus of Communicating Systems*. Lecture Notes in Computer Science, Springer-Verlag, n. 92, 1980.

[Ostroff 90] J.S. Ostroff. *A Logic for Real-Time Discrete Event Processes*. IEEE Control System Magazine, pp. 95-102, June 1990.

[Perraud 92] J. Perraud, O. Roux, M. Huou. *Operational Semantics of a Kernel of the Electre Language*. To appear in Theoretical Computer Science, n. 100, November 1992.

[Pnueli 86] A. Pnueli. *Applications of Temporal Logic to the Specification and Verification of Reactive Systems: a Survey of Current Trends*. Current Trends in Concurrency (Bakker & Al. eds.). Lecture Notes in Computer Science, Vol. 224, Springer-Verlag, Berlin, pp. 510-584, 1986.

[SCEPTRE 84] SCEPTRE. TSI, Vol. 3, n.1, January-February 1984.

[Valette 88] R. Valette, M. Paludetto, B. Porcher-Labreuille, P. Farail. *Approche Orientée Objet HOOD et Réseaux de Petri pour la Conception de Logiciel Temps-Réel.* Journées Internationales sur le Génie Logiciel et ses Applications, Toulouse (France), December, 1988.

[Ward 86] P.T. Ward. *The Transformation Schema: an Extension of the Data Flow Diagram to Represent Control and Timing.* IEEE Transaction on Software Engineering, Vol. SE-12, n. 2, pp. 198-210, February 1986.

An Engineering Approach to Hard Real-Time System Design *†

H. Kopetz, R. Zainlinger, G. Fohler
H. Kantz, P. Puschner, W. Schütz

Institut für Technische Informatik
Technische Universität Wien
Treitlstr. 3/182
A-1040 Vienna, Austria

Abstract

This paper presents a systematic methodology for the design of distributed fault tolerant real-time systems. The methodology covers the stepwise refinement of the given requirements, expressed in the form of real-time transactions, to task and protocol executions. It also includes a timing analysis and dependability evaluation of the still incomplete design. The testability of the evolving system is considered to be of essential concern. A set of coherent tools for the support of the methodology is described in some detail. The methodology assumes that the run-time architecture is based on static scheduling and a globally synchronised time-base is available to co-ordinate the system actions in the domain of real-time.

Keywords: System Design, System Evaluation, System Testing, Design Methodology, Design Environments, Real-Time Systems

1 Introduction

Real-time systems have to produce the correct results within the specified time intervals. If a result is incorrect or arrives too late, then the real-time system has failed. The potential consequences of such a failure depend on the characteristics of the particular application context. If these consequences are possibly catastrophic, then we call the system a *hard* real-time system. Examples of such systems are flight control systems or train signaling systems. In this paper we discuss an engineering approach to the design of hard real-time systems.

---

*This work was supported in part by the ESPRIT Basic Research Project 3092 "Predictably Dependable Computing Systems"

†A related version of this paper has been accepted for publication in the "IEE Software Engineering Journal"

At present the design of many real-time systems resembles more an occult art than a rational engineering approach. In many real-time system projects the design starts from the functional specification, supplemented by some timing information, without a clear understanding of the peak-load the system is required to handle (the load hypothesis) and of the faults the system must be able to tolerate (the fault hypothesis). Such a practice is unthinkable in a classical engineering discipline. Consider the example of a civil engineer who does not know the load a bridge is supposed to carry or the earthquake severity the bridge must withstand, before starting his design.

System design focuses on closing the "semantic gap" between the given application requirements and the chosen run-time hardware/software architecture. The design process is expedited if both endpoints of the design process are well specified and if the abstractions provided by the run-time hardware/software architecture support the needs of application requirements. Real-time applications require run-time mechanisms that guarantee upper bounds for the maximum execution time of tasks and for the maximum duration of the interprocess communication protocols. There are few general purpose operating systems providing these guarantees. In this paper we assume that the MARS architecture [Kop89] is chosen as the run-time architecture, since it provides these necessary guarantees.

The paper is structured as follows: Section 2 elaborates the most relevant characteristics of an engineering approach to hard real-time system design. In Section 3 we then develop a novel design methodology for hard real-time systems that fulfills all the characteristics considered important in Section 2. The methodology is assisted by a specifically tailored set of coherent tools integrated in a design environment which is presented in Section 4.

2 Motivation

2.1 Characteristics of an Engineering Approach to Hard Real-Time System Design

This section elaborates the principal characteristics of an engineering approach to hard real-time system design. All characteristics have one central issue in common, namely to increase a system's dependability and clarity. Our major goal is to build systems that are easy to comprehend, simple but not simplistic.

Predictability

Predictable performance in peak-load situations is of utmost interest in hard real-time systems. Due to the crucial importance of temporal correctness in addition to functional correctness, timing analysis cannot simply be restricted to performance evaluation after the system has been designed and implemented. Instead, the design methodology has to integrate and support consideration of the timing requirements so that the only systems allowed to emerge from the design methodology are those for which their adherence to the specified timing behaviour under all anticipated peak-load and fault situations can be *verifiably guaranteed*.

Testability

Close to half of the resources spent in the development of hard real-time systems is allocated to testing. Therefore, any rational design methodology for dependable and predictable real-time systems has to produce testable systems, i.e. systems which are as easy to test as possible. This can only be accomplished with a suitable test methodology integrated with the design methodology. The most important aspects of testability are the following:

- *Test Coverage:* The test coverage indicates what fraction of the anticipated real world scenarios can be covered by corresponding test scenarios. Ideally this coverage is one, in reality there are significant limitations due to the combinatorial explosion of possible event combinations.

- *Observability:* Observability is important for determining whether the system under test performs correctly or not. There are two aspects. First, one must be able to observe every significant event generated by the environment and – much more important – to determine the correct ordering and timing of events. Secondly, it is necessary to observe the actions and outputs of the system during testing, but without disturbing its timing behaviour.

- *Controllability:* During testing, one must be able to control the execution of the system so that it is possible to reproduce arbitrary test scenarios such that the system's reaction is deterministic.

Testability is to a great extent determined by the properties of the underlying system architecture. However, software design and test methodology must carefully preserve and take advantage of these properties. For a discussion of the properties of our underlying system model and how these promote the testability of distributed real-time systems see [Sch90b].

Fault Tolerance

Real-time systems are characterised by a close interaction between the system and the environment. Modern technology allows the development of complex computer-environment interactions which humans are no longer able to control. Delegating control from humans to computers increases the importance and criticality of computers and demands dependable computer systems. Fault-tolerance is a promising approach to fulfill the demanded dependability of service.

Basically, two different types of real-time system applications can be distinguished: Fail-stop and fail-operational. In the former approach, there exists a safe state (e.g. in a train control system: all trains are stopped and all signals are turned to red). Applications where such a safe state does not exist (e.g. an avionic system), are called fail-operational. In such systems continuous service, even in the presence of faults, is of utmost importance.

Since system failures' impact and their handling are application dependent, an estimation and analysis of failures and their impact on the system behaviour is demanded during early phases of system design. System development is therefore characterised by the fact that the designer has, apart from functional requirements, to face fault tolerance aspects as well.

System Design

In contrast to conventional software design the development of real-time software is fundamentally influenced by the characteristics of the underlying hardware (peripheral devices, communication medium, CPU) and the operating system. The construction of the application software without considering the characteristics of the target system is inadequate. In conjunction with real-time systems we therefore rather talk about *system* design than *software* design.

Any design methodology for hard real-time systems must thus provide mechanisms that allow the simultaneous consideration of hardware and software in a concise and consistent manner.

Systematic Decomposition

Systematic decomposition is one of the basic concepts of system design. Starting from the initial requirements the system under design has to be gradually *decomposed* into smaller units (or modules) that are easier to understand and can be treated fairly independently of one another. The necessary prerequisite for the concept of gradual decomposition is the concept of *abstraction* that is based upon the idea of separating the essential from the inessential in a particular situation. Only then can a complex system be understood.

The process of gradual decomposition should be a continuous one that spans the overall system development cycle. In conjunction with real-time system design the uniform and thorough treatment of the *time* dimension has to be particularly emphasised.

Evaluability

Before initiating the time consuming test phase it is desirable to evaluate the designed system. In order to avoid costly revisions of major parts of the system this evaluation should ideally start as soon as possible in the system life-cycle, i.e. it should form an integral part of the system design process. In the context of real-time systems *dependability* evaluation and *timing* analysis constitute the most relevant evaluation activities.

For the dependability evaluation it is of crucial importance to deal with simple structures and (partially predefined) models that require only a small number of parameters to be specified. Only then can be guaranteed that

- a system designer is capable of specifying dependability parameters, and

- the results gained are to a large extent trustworthy.

An early timing analysis based on estimated task execution times provides the certainty that all deadlines will be met by the designed system provided that the estimated execution times can be met by the implementation.

2.2 Related Work

Many different methodologies for the design of real-time systems have been proposed in the literature. Some approaches tried to enrich existing conventional design methodologies with mechanisms that allow the specification of time related properties, e.g. SDRTS (Structured Design for Real-Time Systems) [War86], and DARTS (Design Approach for Real-Time Systems) [Gom86], other design methodologies for real-time systems have been built from scratch, sometimes having a particular application domain in mind, e.g. SDL (Specification and Description Language) [Bel89] for Telecommunication Systems, SCR (Software Cost Reduction) [Par84], MASCOT (Modular Approach to Software Construction, Operation and Test) [Sim86], EPOS (Engineering and Projectmanagement Oriented Support) [Lau89], and SREM (Software Requirements Engineering Methodology) [Alf85] for unmanned weapons systems.

We found that none of the existing methodologies does qualify in all aspects as presented above. Particularly mechanisms that can help to achieve predictable system behaviour (even under peak-load conditions) are missing.

For a detailed description of any of the design methodologies mentioned the reader is referred to the literature.

The following section presents a novel design methodology that considers all aspects highlighted above.

3 A Design Methodology for Predictable Hard Real-Time Systems

3.1 Architectural Assumptions

Reasoning about a design methodology for hard real-time systems is not possible without having a particular system architecture in mind. Our methodology is based on a reference architecture that corresponds closely to the MARS architecture as described in [Kop89].

We assume that a distributed hard real-time system consists of a set of components each of which executes a fixed set of tasks. Components are interconnected by a real-time bus with deterministic communication characteristics.

The communication among components (and thus tasks) is realised exclusively through periodic state messages.

Components with a high inner logical connectivity (i.e. components responsible for the same or closely related system functions) form a so-called *cluster* (Figure 1).

3.2 The Methodology - An Overview

The design methodology as sketched in Figure 2 is composed of design creation and design verification steps. For reasons of simplicity conventional verification steps (e.g. checking for completeness) which take place after each design step are not mentioned.

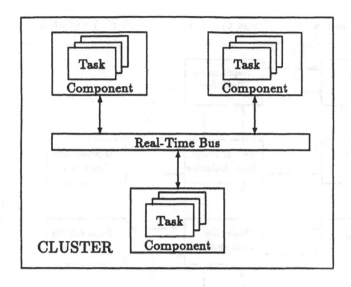

Figure 1: The Reference Architecture

In principle we distinguish between *static verification* (evaluation) which takes place simultaneously with the design creation activities and *dynamic verification* (testing) which requires that the system is (partially) completed and can be (partially) exercised.

The horizontal line separates the "Programming-in-the-Large" from the "Programming-in-the-Small" activities.

The following sections will briefly describe the basic principles of the various design activities and their co-ordination.

3.3 Design Creation

3.3.1 Basic Concepts

In our methodology, design objects, along with their interrelationships, constitute the basic mechanism to gather and maintain design information. Each design object is characterised by a set of attributes reflecting the object's properties. This approach is very similar to the one adopted in SDL [Bel89].

Our design methodology provides only a small number of different design objects. Most of them repeatedly occur in the various design steps. To keep this report compact we confine ourselves merely to the important ones. A detailed description of all design objects is contained in [Zai89].

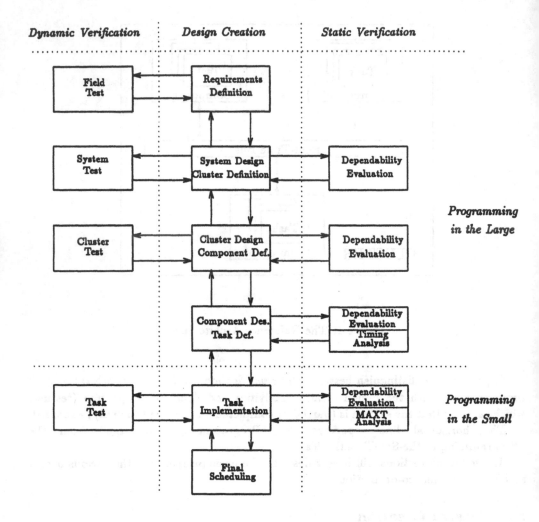

Figure 2: Design Steps

Transactions

The MARS design methodology is mainly influenced by a real-time transaction model as introduced in [Kop91]. For the rest of this paper we use the terms transaction and real-time transaction interchangeably.

Transactions are applied to express both the functional and the timing behaviour of a system or parts of it. We found that the concept of a transaction is particularly well suited to bridging the often perceived gap between the specification of a system and its actual design. Transactions serve two purposes, the initial specification of a system as well as its gradual refinement (= design).

A transaction is triggered by a *stimulus* and results in a corresponding *response*. The stimulus determines a condition under which the transaction is triggered, e.g. "temperature > 80 and pressure > 2", where *temperature* and *pressure* represent so-called *data items*. The response is represented as a set of data items along with their newly computed values, e.g. "valve-position = closed".

During design a transaction is repeatedly refined into a sequence of subtransactions finally becoming a set of tasks and protocol executions. Depending on the level of abstraction (sub-)transactions are attached either to the overall system, to a *cluster* or *cluster-path* (i.e. the interface between two clusters), or to a *component*.

Crucial parameters of a transaction are MART, the Maximum Response Time, and MINT, the Minimal Interval between two invocations of the same transaction (see Table 1). Furthermore, each transaction is characterised by a criticality classification indicating the consequences of a transaction failure.

Transaction	
Attribute	**Semantics**
name	the transaction's name
description	informal description
stimulus	name of the triggering stimulus
response	name of the resulting response
MART	"maximum response time". The time within which the transaction has to complete successfully (dictated by the environment)
MINT	"minimal interval" between two invocations of the same transaction
criticality	classification of the consequences of a transaction failure (low, medium, high, fatal)
failure costs	a list of costs and associated probabilities

Table 1: Attributes of a Transaction

Data Items

Data items are used to describe data oriented requirements. Data items represent both the external state of the environment as well as the internal state of the controlling system. Since the state of the environment in a real-time system permanently changes with the progress of time, a validity time is associated with each data item, that helps to maintain consistency between the actual state of the environment and its representation within the computing system.

3.3.2 Design Creation Steps

The design process is neither fully formal nor fully informal. We do not provide a formal design language spanning the complete development cycle. We also do not believe that the design process can be handled in a totally informal and unstructured way. Our philosophy tries to combine the advantages of informal and formal approaches by establishing "fill-in forms" for each design object; each form reflects the attributes of the particular design object. In each design step the corresponding form for each relevant design object is completed, thus representing the design information for the succeeding design step(s).

Concurrently, these more or less "isolated" objects are embedded into a semantic context by establishing relationships between the different design objects.

Requirements Definition

During the initial *requirements definition* phase the basic system requirements are detailed. Global system transactions are described as well as the peripheral devices (physical elements) and the data consumed and/or produced by these devices (using data items).

System Design and Cluster Definition

The second phase comprises the decomposition of the system into clusters, the refinement of the system transactions into sub-transactions and the allocation of the resulting cluster transactions to the clusters. Each system usually consists of at least two clusters, one representing the controlled, the other representing the controlling object. Very often a third cluster, the operator cluster, is introduced.

Although clusters are connected loosely, they are coupled. Thus, the inter-cluster dependencies have to be established as well, and the corresponding design objects are called *cluster paths*.

Cluster Design and Component Definition

In this phase each cluster of the controlling system is designed independently of the rest of the system. A cluster is refined into a number of components. Concurrently, the cluster transactions are refined into sub-transactions and allocated to the components, thus becoming component transactions.

Furthermore, external messages, i.e. messages exchanged between different components, are defined. These messages directly correspond to the data items exchanged by the allocated component transactions.

Component Design and Task Definition

In the component design and task definition phase the inner software structure of a component is detailed.

Each component transaction is refined into a set of tasks exclusively communicating via internal messages (which are specified as well). The resulting communication structure implicitly determines precedence constraints between the co-operating tasks. At the end of this phase, all information required for the timing analysis (see Section 3.4.2) is available. If the timing analysis fails to determine a valid schedule the software has to be redesigned. It is worthwhile mentioning that this redesign takes place at a stage where no coding activity has been initiated.

Task Implementation

The final step in the method chain deals with the implementation of the single tasks as derived from the component design and task definition level. The implementation has to consider the $MAXT_E$ constraints and to create tasks that adhere to their deadlines.

Final Scheduling

Once all tasks have been implemented, the task set is scheduled according to the constraints derived from the design. This scheduling is done similarly to the preceding timing analysis carried out after the Component Design and Task Definition phase (see Section 3.4.2). The only difference is that the $MAXT_E$ values are replaced by the actual $MAXT_C$ (*calculated maximum execution time*) values as established by the MAXT analysis (Section 3.4.3).

3.4 Design Evaluation

3.4.1 Dependability Evaluation

Dependability evaluation accompanies all design creation phases, thus providing an immediate feed-back to the designer with respect to the expected or actually achieved dependability [Kan91]. The results of the dependability evaluation thus trigger, if necessary, design changes and a return to a previous design creation phase. It is likely that several such iterations are necessary to assure the required dependability. During the design process, some parts of the system may already be designed in more detail than others; therefore, dependability evaluation must be capable of dealing with such incomplete designs. This is achieved by a particular structural input language [Mul88] that is used in all design phases.

At the *System Design and Cluster Definition* stage the designer can attach estimated dependability attributes to each cluster and each cluster transaction, checking if specified system dependability requirements are still fulfilled under the assumption that each cluster meets its specified dependability requirements. The designer can use this information as a confirmation or as a starting point for a (partial) redesign of the application. Dependability data for clusters and transactions can be estimated from related projects, or derived from standards.

After a further refinement in the *Cluster Design and Component Definition* phase the arrangement and the number of components are determined. At this level, the physical realisation (i.e. hardware used, degree of redundancy) is not considered. Each component and each component transaction is augmented with dependability attributes refined from the System Design and Cluster Definition step. Since the system structure on the component level is now established, a more detailed dependability evaluation can be initiated. Different architectural variants, parameter variations, and sensitivity analysis reveal the critical parts and bottlenecks of the system and suggest ways for their improvement.

In the *Component Design and Task Definition* phase the used hardware, the degree of redundancy of the logical units, and the set of tasks are specified. Precise dependability attributes of the hardware as well as estimated dependability attributes of the defined tasks can be taken into account. It can now be checked if the hardware fulfills the dependability requirements as derived from the previous design phase. If this is not the case, additional redundancy can be introduced, or more reliable components can be used.

After the *Task Implementation* phase is completed for all tasks of a particular cluster the software failure rate of the tasks can be estimated more precisely. The data are obtained from the failure history of test runs performed during the Cluster Test phase (see Section 3.5).

3.4.2 Timing Analysis

Timing analysis is concerned with the analysis of the temporal requirements of the system and its transactions in order to construct a schedule for the tasks' CPU usage and for message transmission over the real-time bus. In our approach, scheduling is done *statically*, before the run-time of the application. Scheduling has been shown to be NP-hard in the general case (see e.g. [Mok83]). In any dynamic scheduling scheme, guarantees that all required deadlines will be met can only be given under rather restrictive assumptions [Liu73]. Static scheduling is the only approach we know that guarantees predictable system behaviour even under peak-load conditions. In addition, static scheduling offers a low run-time overhead because only table look-up is needed.

In the following we briefly describe the information that is needed to construct a static schedule. Remember that a schedule for the specified peak-load situation must be found, so the worst-case values of all the necessary parameters have to be used always.

- **Application-dependent Inputs**

  Most of the needed information is application-dependent and must thus be obtained from design creation (see Section 3.3). First, the *transactions* which are to be scheduled must be known, along with their execution rate and an upper bound for their completion time (MART). MART has been specified during the design and is a hard deadline, dictated by the environment.

  Second, the *tasks* into which these transactions have been decomposed are needed. Each task is already allocated to one particular component. At present, task allocation is done by the designer; work is underway to delegate this job to Timing Analysis and to have the scheduling tool perform it automatically. All tasks are invoked with the invocation rate of the transaction to which they belong. Further, knowledge about the execution time of each task is necessary (see Section 3.4.3).

  Finally, we need information about the *precedence constraints* which describe the synchronisation requirements between tasks. In MARS, we may further assume that an application task reads all its input messages right after its invocation and sends its output messages at the end. Therefore, the schedule is constructed such that a task does not begin execution before all its predecessors have completed and before it has received all messages it needs. Precedence constraints may be determined by the communication structure of co-operating tasks of a transaction. Other sources of precedence constraints are, for example, tasks accessing a common output device, or the application demanding a particular starting-point of a task within a transaction.

- **System Parameters**

  The knowledge of the following system parameters is necessary for the construction of schedules that meet timing, communication, and synchronisation constraints: (a) The maximum execution time of the communication protocol between tasks and (b) CPU time usable for application-tasks (CPU availability): This requires that the time overhead caused by the operating system is bounded and known. This overhead includes times for task switching, periodic clock interrupt, and CPU cycles used by DMA, e.g. for network access.

All this information can now be analyzed and a schedule is constructed such that all transactions are executed with their specified period, and all task precedence constraints are fulfilled. Most importantly, the schedule must satisfy all MARTs of its transactions. MART includes the latency of the stimuli due to the sampling rate of the reading tasks, the execution time of tasks, communication times, and idle times of CPUs. Some of these components of MART are given to the scheduler as parameters which it cannot influence or change. The scheduler can experiment with different orders of task execution and of message transmission (within the bounds of the precedence constraints) and thus vary the idle times of CPUs and the communication times. If a schedule that satisfies all MARTs cannot be found, the designer will be notified. A (partial) redesign (e.g. a different allocation of tasks to components) is then necessary.

Therefore, Timing Analysis is used at two points in the design process (see Section 3.3). After task definition Timing Analysis is supplied with $MAXT_E$, the *estimated maximum execution time* at this point in design for all tasks. This is the first schedulability check for the designer. It takes place before any coding activity has been initiated, thus following the principle that errors should be detected as early as possible.

After task implementation, Timing Analysis is repeated to find the final schedule (see Section 3.3), based on $MAXT_C$, the *calculated maximum execution times* for all tasks (see Section 3.4.3). Final Scheduling is not necessary, if no $MAXT_C$ is larger than the corresponding $MAXT_E$.

3.4.3 MAXT Analysis

The MAXT analysis evaluates the worst case timing behaviour of the implemented tasks and checks it against the $MAXT_E$. An upper bound for the maximum execution time of all tasks is calculated ($MAXT_C$), from which we demand that it is tight and safe. In this context, safe means that the result must guarantee to be an upper bound for the actual MAXT which can under no circumstances be exceeded at run time. The tightness requirement is necessary to prohibit too pessimistic results. The probability that a task's maximum execution time is inappropriately qualified as too high by comparing $MAXT_C$ and $MAXT_E$ has to be reasonably low.

The code based MAXT calculation requires detailed knowledge about the timing properties of the hardware used, the principal system concepts (maximum interrupt frequency, possibility of task preemption), and the semantics of the language constructs used. These data, which are represented in the hardware and system description table, are combined with the information about the control structure of the task in the so-called timing tree, to calculate the task's $MAXT_C$.

In order to calculate the MAXT of a task, the MAXT for all parts of that task – sequences, loops, alternatives, etc. – must be computable. Full information about the timing semantics must be available for each construct used. Therefore programs, whose MAXT has to be determined, must not contain any recursive procedure calls or gotos. Furthermore, all loops have to be bounded [Sha89,Pus89].

3.5 Testing the Application Software

In this section we give an overview of the different phases into which the test methodology has been structured. We emphasise the objectives of each phase and pinpoint the contributions of each phase to a complete system evaluation. More information can be found in [Sch90b].

Each test phase is associated with a particular design phase (see Figure 2) such that the test phase evaluates the result(s) produced by the corresponding design phase, e.g. the System Test tests a complete system. The test phases have been derived as a compromise between the hardware and the software structure of MARS. A Component Test is not included since a component executes a collection of tasks which may or may not exchange information and which may or may not belong to the same transaction. It was judged to be much more useful to test a complete transaction rather than an "arbitrary" set of tasks. Testing can therefore immediately proceed from the task to the cluster level.

It should be noted that Figure 2 shows only a static relation between design phases and test phases. This does not imply that testing can begin only after the object to test has been completely implemented. It is increasingly recognised [Adr82,Gel88,Las89] that testing involves more than just executing test cases; it also comprises organisational, planning, analysis, design, implementation, and maintenance activities. A lot of these activities can be carried out in parallel with design creation.

Task Test

The *Task Test* is conducted entirely on the host system, with the advantage that rapid switching from executing test runs to program editing (error correction) and vice versa is possible. Emphasis is placed on functional testing (see for instance [How87]) of each individual task.

There is no difference to non-real-time testing because the only way a task can "know about time" is via time-stamps. These are provided automatically by the operating system, or are requested by the task through a special system call. All the time information that a task can see is already mapped into the value domain. Therefore we can view all the time-stamps a task encounters as additional inputs in the value domain, and the problem of testing a real-time task is the same as testing any non-real-time piece of code.

The only property of a task which cannot be assessed is its execution time; this is, however, handled by the MAXT Analysis (see Section 3.4.3).

Cluster Test

From the *Cluster Test* onwards, all tests are conducted on the target system. There are two variants of the Cluster Test, the *open-loop Cluster Test* and the *closed-loop Cluster Test*.

In the *open-loop mode*, test data are generated off-line, the resulting sequence of input messages is sent to the cluster under test at predetermined points in time, and the responses of the cluster are observed and stored for later evaluation. The tested entities are a MARS cluster from the physical point of view and any subset (except the empty one) of the set of its cluster transactions from the software standpoint. It is required that a *cluster schedule* has been computed and that all transactions and tasks have been allocated to the components of the cluster. Then, after all the tasks of a given transaction have been programmed and task-tested, this transaction can be down-loaded into the MARS cluster and Cluster Test can begin with respect to this transaction.

The objectives are to check both the functional correctness (semantic integration test) and the timeliness of task and component interaction (e.g. task execution time, transaction response time), and to verify cluster behaviour in the presence of anticipated faults (message loss, component loss).

In order to actually execute test runs, one has to set up a test bed. This is identical to the target system, except that the interfaces to the environment are replaced by "test driver components". Their task is to send test data to the cluster at the correct times; in addition they can be used to simulate faults in the cluster (message loss, component loss). Further, one or more monitor components are used to receive and store the results of the test run. Since these do not send any messages, they can be added to the cluster without disturbing its internal behaviour. More information on the test bed architecture for the open-loop Cluster Test can be found in [Sch90b].

In the *closed-loop mode*, the outputs (responses) of the tested cluster are fed to a model of its environment which dynamically computes the reaction of the environment on the cluster's output which in turn is used as the new input to the cluster under test, thus closing the loop. It is required that all transactions of this cluster have been completely implemented.

The objectives of the closed-loop Cluster Test are basically the same as those of the open-loop Cluster Test. In addition, however, "higher-level" test objectives can be gradually emphasised. These include extended test runs with highly realistic inputs, evaluating the quality of the (control) algorithms the cluster implements, demonstrating peak-load performance and the handling of other critical and stressful situations, and observing and evaluating the reaction of the cluster on both hypothesised and unforeseen errors in its environment (robustness test).

Execution of closed-loop tests requires the development of an environment simulation. This is an application-dependent test tool, which also must be a real-time system since both the functional and the time behaviour of the environment must be simulated. Therefore we propose to use the MARS Design Methodology again to design and implement the environment simulator. The test bed for closed-loop tests consists then of the application cluster which is interconnected with a simulation cluster executing the environment simulation software. The architecture of this test bed is also shown in more detail in [Sch90b]. Real-time simulation is discussed extensively in [Sch90a].

System Test

The *System Test* can begin after the Cluster Test has been completed for all clusters. The objectives are in principle the same as for the closed-loop Cluster Test, only that they are applied to the system as a whole. Thus, the System Test is (usually) performed in closed-loop mode, and the test bed architecture is similar to that of the closed-loop Cluster Test. The System Test is equivalent to the closed-loop Cluster Test if the system consists of just one cluster.

Field Test

Finally, during *Field Test*, the system is tested within its real environment and with its real peripheral devices. The purpose is to test the system in its production environment and to conduct the customer acceptance test.

4 MARDS - The MARS Design System

4.1 An Overview

The design methodology as described in the former section is supported by a fully integrated design environment populated with numerous tools reflecting the various design creation and verification steps. The principal structure of the design environment is sketched in Figure 3.

Central to the environment is the Tool and Project Management System that is centered around a contract handling system (CHS) whose development has been inspired by the ISTAR [Dow87] project. The CHS manages the storage and exchange of documents (e.g. *orders, deliveries, reclamations, etc.*) among different members of a project. A document serves two purposes. First, it is used as a management aid (orders may be split into suborders thus giving a project hierarchy), secondly, documents transport design information generated or consumed by tools of the environment.

The upper left hand box contains the particular design creation tools that cover the "Programming-in-the-Large" activities. As it is very likely that the work in this phase of a project is carried out by a group of persons the communication among these tools is realised via the CHS as indicated by the double arrow between the Tool and Project Management System and the "Programming-in-the-Large" box.

On the other hand the implementation of a single task is usually performed by a single person, i.e. the "Programming-in-the-Small" tools (located in the lower left hand box) have direct communication links, in order to keep the turn around cycles as short as possible.

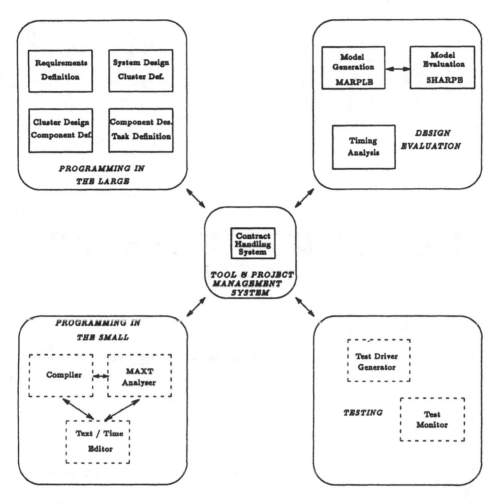

Figure 3: The Design Environment

The upper right hand box represents the design evaluation tools for the dependability and timing analysis while the lower right hand box displays the test tools.

All tools except those represented as dashed lined boxes exist in a prototype version. For the rest of this section we will confine ourselves to the particular tools of the environment. More detailed information on the overall structure of the design environment as well as on the various integration mechanisms can be found in [Sen88,Sen89,Zai90a,Zai90b].

4.2 Programming-in-the-Large

Programming-in-the-Large activities are covered by a set of four tools each of which corresponds to exactly one of the design methodology's creation steps. Figure 4 illus-

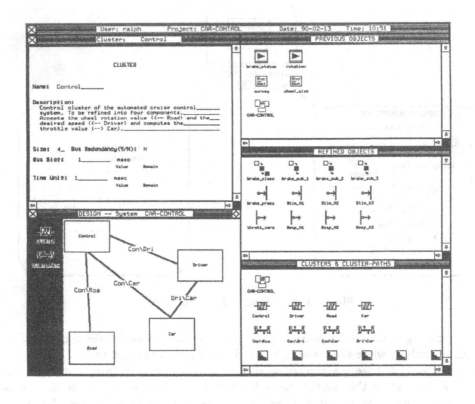

about the timing behaviour of a task is desirable during the overall implementation phase. Our programming environment [Pus90] is conceived such that it not only gives the programmer very detailed documentation, but also allows him to immediately observe the effects of code modifications on the execution time.

The programming environment is composed of three tightly co-operating components, an *editor* (incorporating a text and a so-called time editor), a *compiler*, and the *MAXT analysis* tool. These components exchange timing information via a so-called timing tree that represents both the structure and the execution time information of the task currently developed.

The text editor differs from other editors in that it co-operates with the time editor which represents worst case execution times of programs and their constructs by means of Nassi-Shneiderman diagrams.

The text editor is based on a "segment oriented approach", i.e. each program is developed and interpreted as a sequence of possibly nested segments. These segments directly correspond to structural units of the associated Nassi-Shneiderman diagram in the time editor. Text segments easily allow to implement and experiment with different code variants whereas Nassi-Shneiderman diagrams additionally support the process of experimenting with different hypothetical time values of program parts. This technique which we call *time editing* visualises how changes in the timing behaviour of certain program parts would effect the timing behaviour and the MAXT of the whole task.

The compiler not only translates programs but also generates output for the MAXT analysis containing information about the program structure as well as basic timing information.

The MAXT analysis tool then calculates the $MAXT_C$ for all constructs and the whole task. This calculation can be based on timing information derived by the compiler from the source code, on hypothetical values entered through the time editor, or on a combination thereof.

4.4 Evaluation

4.4.1 Dependability Evaluation

A textual formal design description augmented with dependability attributes serves as input for the dependability evaluation. However, generating a dependability model from this design information is still a challenging and error-prone task. Recently developed tools, as surveyed in [Mul86,Joh88,Gei90], revealed the need and aim for assisting the modeler in the model generation process.

In our implementation we have split up the process of dependability modelling into model generation and model evaluation phases.

In the first pass the design description augmented with dependability attributes is transformed into a PMS model [Kan89] (i.e. a combinatorial model describing the computer system and its communication network as an undirected graph) by a tool called MARPLE [Mul88]. The basic elements of the MARPLE input language are objects (clusters, components, sensors, tasks, ...), information items (notions for the abstract entities of information exchange), and transactions (describing the functionality of objects). This description is augmented with dependability attributes including: Degree and kind (active, passive) of redundancy, failure distribution of objects, and coverage values.

In the second step these PMS models are evaluated with the dependability evaluation tool SHARPE [Sah87].

The method of a fully automatic model generation is well suited for describing components where the dependability behaviour can be expressed in that simple way. Often there is a need to express a more complicated behaviour, like component dependencies, different failures, and repair modes. In such cases the user can define his own detailed submodels (e.g. as elaborated in [Kop90]). These models are then hierarchically included into the PMS model.

4.4.2 Timing Analysis

The scheduling algorithm has to find a feasible schedule for accessing CPUs and the communication medium for a set of transactions off-line, i.e. before run-time, that holds given MARTs. If a schedule is found, it will be stored, and is available to be interpreted by a task dispatcher at run-time with minimal CPU usage.

The scheduling problem is represented as search through a search tree. A heuristic function is used to guide the search, by omitting useless subtrees of the search tree or retracting the search at "promising" nodes.

We use IDA*, a heuristic search strategy for scheduling developed by Korf [Kor85]. The scheduler is not required to find an optimal schedule, any feasible one will do. IDA* has therefore been modified [Foh89]. Our heuristic function estimates the period of time needed to complete the execution of the transaction, called TUR (Time Until Response).

4.5 Testing

Tools to support testing are still very much under consideration. It is planned to integrate support for task testing with the programming-in-the-small environment so that the task programmer is supplied with a consistent and easy-to-use tool set. Possibilities include an animated debugger and a coverage analyzer.

For open-loop tests, a tool that generates a test driver from a description of the intended test run is currently under development. This description includes information about both the values and the timing of test inputs.

For closed-loop tests, in particular for implementing environment simulators, design creation, scheduling, and timing analysis tools are re-used.

Tools for evaluating test results are largely application-dependent, and have not yet been considered in detail.

Conclusions

An engineering approach to hard real-time system design must start from the relevant specifications concerning the functional and performance requirements of the intended system and must guide the designer through a sequence of design steps towards the final implementation. Furthermore, appropriate tests must be provided such that the system designer can establish the compliance of a particular design step with the given specifications. These tests must cover the functional and the performance properties of the evolving system.

Fundamental to our methodology is the notion of a real-time transaction, which is used to express the concerns about functionality and timeliness of a sequence of computational and communication steps in a single concept. A real-time transaction starts with the occurrence of a stimulus event within the environment and terminates with the functionally and temporally correct responses of the computer system to the environment. Real-time transactions are used to capture the requirements, to refine the design, and to describe the run-time behaviour of the computer system.

The predicted behaviour of any real-time computer system is based on a set of regularity assumptions concerning the future. If no such assumption can be made, it is not possible to predict anything. The other extreme, complete determinism, i.e., everything about the future is known apriori, is just as absurd. The load-hypothesis has to identify temporal constraints for the occurrence of stimulus events of real-time transactions (e.g., the specification of a minimum interval between two real-time transactions of the same type). Provided the events in the environment happen in conformance with these constraints, the system must deliver the functionally and temporally correct responses to the environment.

Although events will happen in the environment at arbitrary points in time (within the specified temporal constraints), it is possible to impose a regularity on those points in time when the occurrence of an event is recognised by the computer system. Without this imposed regularity, we find it difficult to design a real-time computer system with predictable behaviour. In our design methodology, this imposed regularity is used to reason about the temporal properties of the design, to find satisfactory execution schedules for real-time transactions and to reduce the plurality of test cases. It also forms the basis for the timing analysis and the test support tools we have described.

We feel that some of our regularity assumptions may be too stringent and can be relaxed without sacrificing the predictability of the design. Our future work will be directed towards finding minimum regularity assumptions that are required to build dependable distributed real-time computing systems.

Acknowledgments

We are grateful to Günter Grünsteidl, Johannes Reisinger, and Alexander Vrchoticky for their comments on an earlier version of this paper. We also want to thank our colleagues from the PDCS project, particularly John McDermid and Lorenzo Strigini, for their helpful remarks.

References

[Adr82]   W. R. Adrion, M. A. Branstad, and J. C. Cherniavsky. Validation, Verification, and Testing of Computer Software. *ACM Computing Surveys*, 14(2):159–192, June 1982.

[Alf85]   M. Alford. SREM at the Age of Eight; The Distributed Computing Design System. *IEEE Computer*, 18(4):36–46, Apr. 1985.

[Bel89]   F. Belina and D. Hogrefe. The CCITT-Specification and Description Language SDL. In *Computer Networks and ISDN Systems 16*, pages 311–341. Elsevier Science Publishers B.V. (North Holland), 1988/89.

[Dow87]   M. Dowson. ISTAR and the Contractual Approach. *Communications of the ACM*, 30(3):287–288, Mar. 1987.

[Foh89]   G. Fohler and C. Koza. Heuristic Scheduling for Distributed Real-Time Systems. Research Report 6/89, Institut für Technische Informatik, Technische Universität Wien, Vienna, Austria, April 1989.

[Gei90]   R. Geist and K. Trivedi. Reliability Estimation of Fault Tolerant Systems: Tools and Techniques. *IEEE Computer*, 23(7):52–61, July 1990.

[Gel88]   D. Gelperin and B. Hetzel. The Growth of Software Testing. *Communications of the ACM*, 31(6):687–695, June 1988.

[Gom86]   H. Gomaa. Software Development of Real-Time Systems. *Communications of the ACM*, 29(7):657–668, July 1986.

[How87]   W. E. Howden. *Functional Program Testing and Analysis*. Software Engineering and Technology. McGraw-Hill, New York, 1987.

[Joh88]   A. M. Johnson and M. Malek. Survey of Software Tools for Evaluating Reliability, Availability and Serviceability. *ACM Computing Surveys*, 20(4):227–269, Dec. 1988.

[Kan89]   H. Kantz and M. Mulazzani. Modeling of PMS - Structures in SHARPE. In *IFAC Proceedings SAFECOMP 89*, pages 97–102, Vienna, Austria, Dec. 1989.

[Kan91]   H. Kantz. Integrating Dependability Analysis into the Design of Distributed Computer Systems. In *IEEE CompEuro 91*, pages 762–766, Bologna, Italy, May 1991.

[Kop89]   H. Kopetz, A. Damm, Ch. Koza, M. Mulazzani, W. Schwabl, Ch. Senft, and R. Zainlinger. Distributed Fault-Tolerant Real-Time Systems: The MARS Approach. *IEEE Micro*, 9(1):25–40, Feb. 1989.

[Kop90]   H. Kopetz, H. Kantz, G. Grünsteidl, P. Puschner, and J. Reisinger. Tolerating Transient Faults in MARS. In *Proc. 20th Int. Symposium on Fault-Tolerant Computing*, pages 466–473, Newcastle upon Tyne, UK, June 1990.

[Kop91] H. Kopetz. Real-Time Systems. In J.A. McDermid, Editor, *Software Engineer's Reference Book*, pages 56/1–56/9. Butterworth-Heinemann Ltd., Oxford, U.K., 1991.

[Kor85] R. Korf. Depth-First Iterative-Deepening: An Optimal Admissable Tree Search. *Artificial Intelligence*, 27(3):97–109, 1985.

[Las89] J. Laski. Testing in the Program Development Cycle. *IEE Software Engineering Journal*, 4(2):95–106, Mar. 1989.

[Lau89] R. Lauber. Forecasting Real-Time Behavior During Software Design using a CASE environment. In *Proc. 22nd Annual Hawaii International Conference on System Sciences, Vol. II*, pages 645–653, Kailua-Kona, HI, USA, Jan. 1989.

[Liu73] C. L. Liu and J. W. Layland. Scheduling Algorithms for Multiprogramming in a Hard-Real-Time Environment. *Journal of the ACM*, 20(1):46–61, Jan. 1973.

[Mok83] A. K. Mok. *Fundamental Design Problems of Distributed Systems for the Hard Real-Time Environment*. PhD Thesis, Massachusetts Institute of Technology, 1983. Report MIT/LCS/TR-297.

[Mul86] M. Mulazzani and K. S. Trivedi. Dependability Prediction: Comparison of Tools and Techniques. In *IFAC Proceedings SAFECOMP 86*, pages 171–178, Sarlat, France, Oct. 1986.

[Mul88] M. Mulazzani. *Generation of Dependability Models from Design Specifications of Distributed Real-Time Systems*. PhD Thesis, Technisch Naturwissenschaftliche Fakultät, Technische Universität Wien, Vienna, Austria, Apr. 1988.

[Par84] D. Parnas, P. Clements, and D. Weiss. The Modular Structure of Complex Systems. In *Proc. 7th IEEE Intern. Conference on Software Engineering*, pages 408–417, Orlando, Florida, Mar. 1984.

[Pus89] P. Puschner and Ch. Koza. Calculating the Maximum Execution Time of Real-Time Programs. *Real-Time Systems*, 1(2):159–176, Sep. 1989.

[Pus90] P. Puschner and R. Zainlinger. Developing Software with Predictable Timing Behavior. In *Proc. 7th IEEE Workshop on Real-Time Operating Systems and Software*, pages 70–76, Charlottesville, VA, May 1990.

[Sah87] R. Sahner and K. S. Trivedi. Reliability Modeling using SHARPE. *IEEE Transactions on Reliability*, 36(2):186–193, June 1987.

[Sch90a] W. Schütz. Real-Time Simulation in the Distributed Real-Time System MARS. In *Proc. 1990 European Simulation Multiconference*, pages 51–57, Nürnberg, FRG, June 1990. The Society for Computer Simulation International.

[Sch90b] W. Schütz. A Test Strategy for the Distributed Real-Time System MARS. In *IEEE CompEuro 90, Computer Systems and Software Engineering*, pages 20–27, Tel Aviv, Israel, May 1990.

[Sen88] Ch. Senft. A Computer-Aided Design Environment for Distributed Realtime Systems. In *IEEE CompEuro 88, System Design: Concepts, Methods and Tools*, pages 288–297, Brussels, Belgium, Apr. 1988.

[Sen89] Ch. Senft and R. Zainlinger. A Graphical Design Environment for Distributed Real-Time Systems. In *Proc. 22nd Annual Hawaii International Conference on System Sciences, Vol. II*, pages 871–880, Kailua-Kona, HI, USA, Jan. 1989.

[Sha89] A. C. Shaw. Reasoning About Time in Higher-Level Language Software. *IEEE Transactions on Software Engineering*, SE-15(7):875–889, July 1989.

[Sim86] H. Simpson. The MASCOT Method. *IEE Software Engineering Journal*, 1(3):103–120, May 1986.

[War86] P. Ward. The Transformation Scheme: an Extension of the Data Flow Diagram to Represent Control and Timing. *IEEE Transactions on Software Engineering*, 12(2):198–210, Feb. 1986.

[Zai89] R. Zainlinger. Data Objects in the MARS Design System. Research Report 17/89, Institut für Technische Informatik, Technische Universität Wien, Vienna, Austria, Sep. 1989.

[Zai90a] R. Zainlinger. Building Interfaces for CASE Environments: An Object Oriented Interaction Model and its Application. In *Proc. of the IFIP International Conference on Human Factors in Information Systems Analysis and Design*, pages 65–80, Schärding, Austria, June 1990.

[Zai90b] R. Zainlinger and G. Pospischil. DIAMOND - An Object Oriented Graphics Library for Software Development Environments. In *Proc. of the Autumn 1990 EUUG Conference*, pages 157–166, Nice, France, Oct. 1990.

An Application of Artificial Intelligence to Prototyping Process in Performance Design for Real-Time Systems

Shinichi Honiden[1] Naoshi Uchihira[1] Kiyoshi Itoh[2]

1 Systems and Software Engineering Laboratory, Toshiba Corporation
70 Yanagi-cho, Saiwai-ku, Kawasaki 210, Japan
honiden@ssel.toshiba.co.jp

2 Faculty of Science and Technology, Sophia University
7-1 Kioi-cho, Chiyoda-ku, Tokyo 102, Japan
itohkiyo@hoffman.cc.sophia.ac.jp

ABSTRACT

This paper describes an application of artificial intelligence technology to the implementation of a rapid prototyping method in Object-Oriented Performance Design (OOPD) for real-time systems. A prototyping process is composed of three steps: Prototype construction, Prototype execution, and Prototype evaluation. The authors present the following artificial intelligence based methods and tools to be applied to each step. In the prototype construction step, a rapid construction mechanism, using reusable software components, is implemented based on the *planning* method. In the prototype execution step, a hybrid inference mechanism is used to execute the constructed prototype which is described in declarative knowledge representation. In the prototype evaluation step, an expert system, which is based on *qualitative reasoning*, is implemented to detect and diagnose bottlenecks and generate an improvement plan for them.

1. INTRODUCTION

Object-oriented technology can provide designers with practical, productive ways to develop software in most of application areas. As for real-time applications, object-oriented technology has been practically employed in a number of systems. Recently, various multiprocessors have become commercially available and have been used in many applications. Since stringent performance requirements are inevitable for real-time applications, it is very important to predict the target system performance precisely during the design phase, in order to determine the optimal software and hardware configurations which will satisfy users' requirements. However, in some real-time systems on multiprocessors, it is quite difficult to adjust some of the performance factors, such as load-balance on a given multiprocessor architecture, to satisfy the performance requirements. In practice, the performance design activities in the object-oriented design (called Object-Oriented Performance Design: OOPD) process tend to be empirical, because there are few algorithms which can derive the optimal software configurations that satisfy the performance requirements under a given hardware configuration. In other words, OOPD activities are usually carried out on a trial-and-error basis. These activities may compose a prototyping approach to improving ill-defined problems where only few algorithms are available. Artificial intelligence technology has been effectively used to tackle ill-defined problems. Various ill-defined problems are actually seen in the software engineering field including programming tasks. Several attempts have been made in applying the artificial intelligence techniques to these ill-defined problems in the software engineering field. Typical ones are GIST [Coh84, Swa83], Programmer's Apprentice [Ric78], $\phi 0$ [Bar82], Glitter [Fic85], Data-Representation Advisor [Kat81], SC [Dow90], and AFFIRM [Ger80]. These methods seem to be successfully applied to the particular phases or domains. Individual methods can be used to handle several steps in the software development process, but none of them can cover the overall development process nor can be used to fully implement the prototyping process.

A prototyping process is defined to be composed of three steps: prototype construction, prototype execution, and prototype evaluation [Ito89a]. The authors present the following artificial intelligence based methods and tools to be used in these three steps.
1) In the prototype construction step, a rapid construction mechanism, using reusable software components, is implemented, based on the *planning* method.
2) In the prototype execution step, a hybrid inference mechanism is used to execute the prototype which is described in declarative knowledge representation.
3) In the prototype evaluation step, an expert system, which is based on *qualitative reasoning*, is implemented to detect and diagnose bottlenecks and generate appropriate improvement plans.

In this paper, Section 2 describes the requirements of the prototyping process for real-time systems. Section 3 describes the presented method which satisfies the requirements. Section 4 describes OOPD which consists of three prototyping phases with application examples. Section 5 compares the presented method with related work and Section 6 evaluates it.

2. REQUIREMENTS OF PROTOTYPING PROCESS FOR REAL-TIME SYSTEMS

This section describes the requirements that should be satisfied for artificial intelligence to be applied or used to implement a prototyping process for real-time systems. In the previous section, the authors have mentioned that a prototyping process consists of the prototype construction, execution, and evaluation steps, as shown in Fig.1. This process may be repeated until the constructed prototype satisfies all the users' requirements. Note that, since rapidness is essential to prototyping, all the three steps need to be accomplished quickly and the number of iterations should be minimized. The characteristics and requirements of the three steps vary depending on the target applications. This section describes the fundamental requirements for implementing the three steps in the performance design for real-time systems.

Generally, a performance design task is composed of the following activities: performance model construction, performance measurement, performance diagnosis and generation of improvement plans. The prototype construction step, prototype execution step, and prototype evaluation step correspond to the performance model construction, the performance measurement, and the performance diagnosis and generation of improvement plans, respectively, as shown in Fig.1.

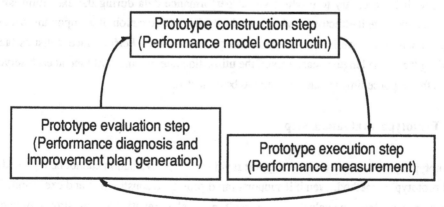

Fig.1 Prototyping process in performance design

2.1 Prototype construction step

Because most of the real-time systems contain many software modules, it is essential to any prototyping method to be able to treat large-scale programs, and increased software productivity during prototyping is required in order to construct prototypes rapidly. Software reuse methods have been considered as one of the most effective methods for increasing software productivity, and are employed in several domains [Hon86b, Jon84]. Various finding mechanisms, such as keyword, case grammar, and formula, have been proposed to retrieve reusable components. However, these methods can retrieve only one reusable component, using one specification statement at a time. The number of the specification statements is then proportional to the number of desired reusable components. To satisfy the rapidness requirements in the prototype construction step, the number of specifications necessary to retrieve the reusable components must be minimized.

2.2 Prototype execution step

One of the major properties essential to prototyping is executability, meaning that the following requirements should be satisfied.
(a) Rapid execution.
(b) Execution without complex preparation.
(c) Visual execution.
(d) Arbitrary interruption and re-starting during execution.
(e) Execution while displaying results which are easy to evaluate.
From the standpoint of performance design, since the execution of simulation usually takes a long time, it is necessary to produce visual performance data during the execution, and to collect and evaluate it effectively. For example, during the execution, it is important to display the queue lengths, as well as dead-lock detection in real-time. Performance statistics factors including the queue length at each server, the utilization rate and the wait time at each server as well as the response time are also required to be collected.

2.3 Prototype evaluation step

A prototyping method that does not support rapid prototype evaluation cannot be regarded as a rapid prototyping method, even if it supports rapid prototype construction and execution. This is because an inadequate evaluation may result in a useless repetition of the prototyping cycle and a time-consuming evaluation may slow down the whole prototyping process. These factors violate one of the main prototyping property of rapidity. To solve this problem in the prototype evaluation step, the following requirements should be satisfied.

> *Rapid detection of a bug which would produce undesired output and rapid generation of appropriate improvements.*

From the viewpoint of performance design, the functions that achieve the above requirements are indispensable for rapid detection of bottlenecks and rapid generation of performance improvement plans which include several appropriate performance parameters. At present, because there are few standard methods which can offer support to satisfy these requirements, it is time-consuming and difficult for a non-expert designer, who has limited experience and is not familiar with performance design, to satisfy these requirements. It is necessary to automate this step, for non-experts to accomplish the design tasks accurately, rapidly, and appropriately. As mentioned previously, using a simulator generally takes a much longer time to accomplish the prototype execution step. Therefore, the prototyping cost can be lowered by reducing the iterations in the prototype execution step. Reducing the prototyping cost also depends on the rapid generation of appropriate improvement plans. In real-time systems on multiprocessors, it is important to validate the performance of the constructed prototype, which is mapped to given multiprocessors. The constructed prototype must be evaluated on the given multiprocessors in the prototype evaluation step.

3. PROTOTYPING PROCESS

This section describes the prototyping process support tools used to satisfy the requirements described in Section 2.

3.1 Prototype construction and execution steps

In real-time systems, the combination of declarative knowledge description and actor-based object modeling is considered to be one of the effective methods to develop a prototype. The inter-relationships among objects are described with actor-based object modeling and the inner behaviors of each object are described using declarative knowledge. The authors adopted MENDEL as the executable specification language which provides the above functions. MENDEL is a Prolog based concurrent object-oriented language [Hon86a, Uch87, Hon89, Hon90], which can be used as a functional and performance prototype construction tool and a prototype execution tool.

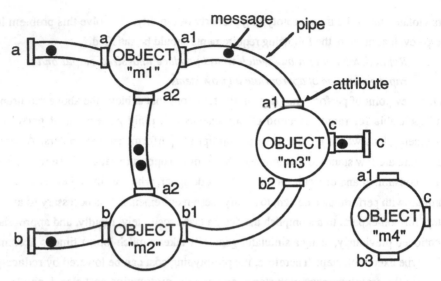

Fig. 2 Interconnection among MENDEL OBJECTs

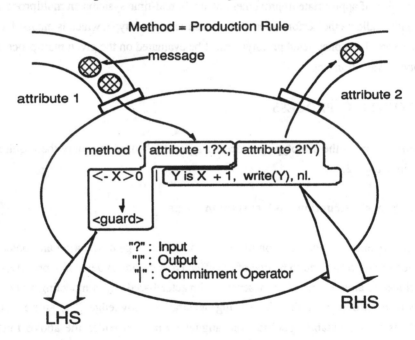

Fig.3 A MENDEL OBJECT

3.1.1 MENDEL object : A concurrent reusable component

Since an OBJECT in MENDEL is a concurrent processing unit, it can be regarded as a task or a process. Each OBJECT has pipe caps and can transmit messages only through the pipe caps, as shown in Fig.2. An attribute is assigned to each pipe cap and is used to identify input/output messages. Messages are transmitted between OBJECTs through the transmission pipe attached to the pipe caps. Each OBJECT consists of a block of working-memory and several METHODs, as shown in Fig.3. Each message consists of an attribute name, an input/output identifier- "?" or "!", and a variable name. If a message preceded by a "?" is received for a METHOD's variable, the METHOD's Prolog clauses are invoked. When the METHOD is executed, the variable preceded by an "!" will be unified and sent to the other OBJECTs as a message. Each METHOD is regarded as a production-rule and is used in the forward inference mechanism. A METHOD consists of a left-hand side (LHS) and a right-hand side (RHS). An LHS contains input messages and an RHS contains output messages. Both LHS and RHS contain internal state variables, which are stored in the working-memory. METHOD selection in a conflict set is non-deterministic. The body part of a METHOD consists of Prolog clauses. Since the Prolog system can be regarded as a backward inference engine, each METHOD includes a backward inference engine. The overall architecture is a distributed production system, in which each OBJECT has inherent working-memory and both forward and backward inference mechanisms. In MENDEL, a simple synchronization mechanism is achieved by using a METHOD selection mechanism, similar to Dijkstra's guarded command. The OBJECT is suspended, until it receives all required messages.

3.1.2 Planning

The authors extended MENDEL to contribute to rapid prototype construction, using reusable components, by introducing a *planning* method. One method to satisfy the requirements, mentioned in Section 2.1, is *planning* which can generate an action sequence or action program for an agent, such as a robot [Nil82]. Input to *planning* includes the initial world, a set of actions which change the world, and the final world. Output from *planning* is a sequence of actions which is represented by an acyclic-directed graph. As each action can be regarded as a reusable component and the world can be input and output specifications, the sequence of actions is a set of reusable components necessary to satisfy the input and output specifications. Each reusable component contains its own specification, called an *F-rule* [Nil82]. An *F-rule* consists of *preconditions*, *add formulas*, and *delete lists*. A *precondition* is corresponding to an input data item into the component, an *add formula* is corresponding to an output data item from the component, and a *delete list* includes the input data which has not appeared in the *add formula*. In an acyclic-directed graph, each node corresponds to a reusable component and each arc corresponds to the data flow between reusable components. Also, an acyclic-directed graph can be translated into a *task graph*, which has been used for resource allocation in multiprocessors [Gon77]. By using the *planning* method, the designer can retrieve and interconnect several reusable components at one time, only by giving input and output specifications.

MENDEL has employed the software reuse approach to increase software productivity. In MENDEL, the connection between pipe caps is accomplished automatically by the *planning* method. The *planning* method selects the required OBJECTs and connects the transmission pipes to create the message passing route from input specifications to output specifications. It carries out reusable component retrieval and interconnection by determining the reusable components which will satisfy the given input-output specifications. An automatic retrieval and interconnections are accomplished according to the following principles:

(a) A pair of pipe caps, having the same or similar attributes, can be interconnected using a semantic network, which consist of several attributes.

(b) All required output specifications must be reachable from given input specifications through connected objects and pipes.

The authors explain basic mechanism of the retrieval and interconnection using Fig.2. In Fig.2, input specification consists of "a" and "b" as external inputs, and output specification is "c" as an external output. At first, system retrieves OBJECT "m1", because OBJECT "m1" has attribute "a" which corresponds to the external input "a." Next, system retrieves OBJECT "m2", because OBJECT "m2" has attributes "a2" and "b" which correspond to "a2" of OBJECT "m1" and the external input "b." Finally, system retrieves OBJECT "m3," because OBJECT "m3" has attributes "a1", "b2", and "c" which correspond to "a1" of OBJECT "m1", "b1" of OBJECT "m2", and an external output "c", respectively. In this case, OBJECT "m4" can also be retrieved. It is assumed that "b2" of OBJECT "m3" is more similar to "b1" of OBJECT "m2" than "b3" of OBJECT "m4." The similarity is computed by the distance between nodes on the semantic network.

MENDEL has a hierarchical planning mechanism, similar to [And89]. In MENDEL, the strategy for assigning *criticality values* to the literals of an *F-rule's precondition* is based on the information from the reusable component generation process of *Object-Oriented analysis* (OOA) [Coa90]. That is, in OOA, attributes in an object are classified into two groups: attributes which are newly declared in the object and those which are inherited from its upper objects. In this case, MENDEL assigns a higher value to the former attribute and a lower value to the latter attribute.

As a prototype execution tool, MENDEL provides visual execution, where an activated object can be recognized as a blinking one displayed on the screen and message queues and message contents are displayed in real-time. Interconnected OBJECTs in MENDEL form a queueing network, in which each OBJECT in MENDEL represents a server and each message in MENDEL represents a transaction. The statistical data, collected during execution, are passed to the prototype evaluation step to be analyzed.

3.2 Prototype evaluation step

In the prototype evaluation step, any bottlenecks should be detected rapidly and appropriate performance improvement plans for the bottlenecks should be generated. In particular, the reduction of prototyping cost depends on the ability to produce improvement plans. In other words, the prototyping evaluation step should accomplish appropriate parameter tuning to reduce prototyping cost.

In MENDEL, the parameters to be tuned are as follows:
(1) The distribution of messages among OBJECTs.
Assume that identical OBJECTs are distributed among several processors for load-balancing, and that a particular OBJECT is busy and the others are not so busy. In this case, a message sent from an OBJECT to the busy OBJECT can be sent to an alternative OBJECT which is not so busy.
(2) A reusable component itself, which corresponds to an OBJECT on a particular processor.

Generally, there exist several reusable components in the library to satisfy the functional requirements. In this case, an alternative reusable component can be selected. Note that the reusable component having the shortest execution time, does not always satisfy the performance requirements of the given hardware configuration, and an important factor for performance is load-balancing. Viewpoint from the queueing network, as shown in Fig.4, the parameters to be tuned are, "μ"s for servers which indicate the OBJECT execution time and "r"s for entities on branching points which indicate the number of messages among OBJECTs. Note that "r"s having a functional meaning, such as the message attribute, should not be changed and that "r"s indicating a load-distributed factor can be changed.

In performance design, there are a large number of parameter candidates to be tuned. For non-experts, in order to select appropriate parameters, the authors adopt a knowledge engineering technique based on *qualitative* and qualitative reasonings. These reasoning methods can be designed by modeling the performance design experts' reasoning process. On the basis of heuristics and knowledge obtained from evaluation experts, the authors have developed two knowledge-based expert systems, BDES (Bottleneck Diagnosis Expert System) and BIES (Bottleneck Improvement Expert System). BDES qualitatively diagnoses or identifies bottlenecks and their sources, and generates qualitative improvement plan. BIES quantitatively estimates the effects of the improvement for bottleneck and their sources on the whole qucucing network [Ito89b, Ito90]. BDES and BIES are based on "*qualitative reasoning*" and "quantitative reasoning," respectively.

3.2.1 Bottleneck diagnosis expert system (BDES)

BDES diagnoses bottlenecks and their sources by reviewing for the queueing network and all its parameters. The bottleneck sources are the factors which govern bottlenecks, for example, low "μ"s or high "λ"s for servers, high "r"s on branching points, and their inter-relationships in the whole queueing network. The servers with the highest "ρ"s are bottlenecks, i.e., they are very busy. BDES judges that the servers whose "ρ"s >= 0.7 are or may be bottlenecks. 0.7 is called a bottleneck landmark (BL) in a *qualitative reasoning*. Moreover, BDES detects one or more alternative improvement plans for one bottleneck. On the basis of *qualitative reasoning*, the authors have designed qualitative behavior expressions for a single server, as shown in Fig.4.

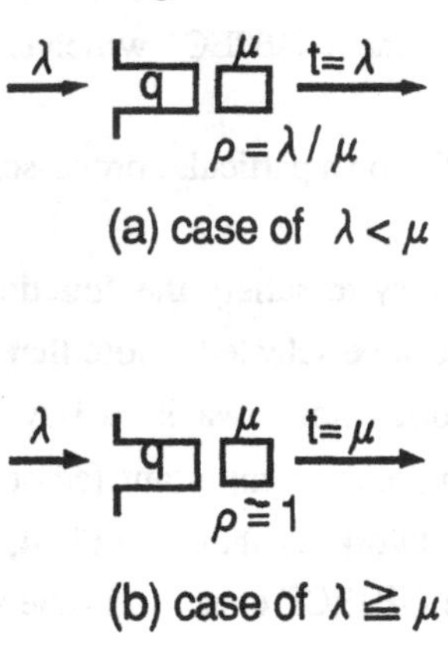

$$\rho = \lambda / \mu$$

(a) case of $\lambda < \mu$

(a) in the case of $\rho <$ BL,i.e., $\rho = -$
(a1) for λ
$d\rho = \pm <-- d\lambda = \pm$ (λ and ρ change in the same direction.)
$dt = \pm <-- d\lambda = \pm$ (λ and t change in the same direction.)
(a2) for μ
$d\rho = \mp <-- d\mu = \pm$ (μ and ρ change in the reverse direction.)
$dt = 0 <-- d\mu = \pm$ (although μ changes, t does not change.)

$$\rho \cong 1$$

(b) case of $\lambda \geq \mu$

(b) in the case of $\rho >$ BL,i.e., $\rho = +$ or $\rho = 0$
(b1) for λ
$d\rho = - <-- d\lambda = -$ (as λ decreases, ρ decreases.)
$dt = 0 <-- d\lambda = -$ (although λ decreases, t does not change.)
(b2) for μ
$d\rho = - <-- d\mu = +$ (as μ increases, ρ decreases.)
$dt = + <-- d\mu = +$ (as μ increases, t increases.)
(b3) for q
$dq = - <-- d\rho = -$ (as ρ decreases, q decreases.)
$d\rho = - <-- dq = -$ (as q decreases, ρ decreases.)

λ : average arrival rate of entities for a server
μ : average servicing rate of a server for entities
t : average throughput of entities by a server
ρ : average utilization rate for a server
q : average queue length of entities in front of a server

Fig. 4 Unit server model

In order to increase or decrease some parameters of a particular server, all the equations for servers included in the queueing network must be considered. For example, it is assumed that the bottleneck server "s4" in Fig.7 is to be improved. In order to decrease "λ" of server "s4," the designer may decrease "r" from "s2" to "s4" and increase "r" from "s2" to "s5." Increasing "r" from "s2" to "s5" may cause "λ"s of the servers such as "s5", "s9" and "s10" to be increased. That is, new other bottlenecks may occur downstream from the change point. All equations for the servers included in the queueing network are necessary to improve a particular bottleneck. Since the number of states and state transitions is big, qualitative simulation takes much time. Then, BDES introduces the heuristics on queueing network substructures, such as loop, joint, branch, and tandem, into *qualitative reasoning* for effective qualitative simulation.

Several kinds of the queueing network have been utilized in various applications. Two major categories are open and closed types. In each category, typical examples are the synchronized type of queueing network and the multi-entity type of queueing network. Then, the authors have also developed BDES-S (BDES for open Synchronized queueing network) [Ito91ab] and BDES-MF (BDES-S for Multi-Flow network).

3.2.2 Bottleneck improvement expert system (BIES)

Based on the qualitative improvement plan produced by BDES, BIES quantitatively improves the bottleneck and bottleneck sources, i.e., it increases low "μ"values, decreases high "λ"values and decreases high "ρ"values. Moreover, BIES estimates the effects of its operations on the whole queueing network. The effects are estimated by computing new "λ" and "t" values for servers in the whole queueing network to be affected by the improvement. Based on the flow balancing, BIES forces "ρ" to decrease to a constant value, called BIF (Bottleneck Improvement Factor):
Only if a bottleneck server can be improved,

$$\text{new "}\mu\text{" = original "}\lambda\text{" / BIF.}$$

Otherwise,

$$\text{new "}\lambda\text{" = original "}\mu\text{" / BIF.}$$

The BIF value is varied from 0.7 to 0.6, according to the "q" of the server. When "q" is pretty high, its BIF is automatically set to 0.6, on the basis of the experts' heuristics. After applying this equation, the "ρ" and "t" values of the server can be improved so that "ρ" = BIF and "t" = "λ." The new "t" can be transmitted as the "λ" of the just downstream servers.

The authors have also developed BIES-S (BIES for open Synchronized queueing network) and BIES-MF (BIES-S for Multi-Flow network).

4. OBJECT-ORIENTED PERFORMANCE DESIGN

4.1 Overview

This section describes OOPD which consists of three prototyping phases for real-time systems. In designing real-time systems, it is important to consider both functional and performance aspects. This implies that two prototypes exist in designing real-time systems: functional and performance prototypes. The functional design should be accomplished while satisfying performance requirements. That is, during the function implementation, the performance requirements must be satisfied under several constraints. Examples of constraints are the number of processors and a task configuration. These constraints may affect the real performance and are determined in accordance with the functional design actually developed. Therefore, prototyping should be accomplished under the defined constraints at various design phases.

The prototyping process of OOPD is shown in Fig.5. Each of the three phases has prototyping processes as follows;

<Phase1>
Prototype construction and execution steps
OOPD starts by logical architecture construction. OOPD assumes that all necessary objects for object design have already been stored in the object library at the object-oriented analysis stage. In the prototype construction step, the logical architecture, which consists of several objects that satisfy the functional requirement, is designed and mapped into the physical architecture of the given multiprocessors. The logical architecture is constructed rapidly using the planning method. Each object in the logical architecture is specified by MENDEL. In <phase1>, since object design is not yet done, only the functional outlines of objects are clarified and the contents of objects are not refined. Since objects are black boxes here, the processing time for each object is estimated by its functional outline taken into account. At the same time, the number of messages arriving at each object is estimated. This estimation data is used to perform simulation. The simulation result is used as the input data in the prototype evaluation step.
Prototype evaluation step

The prototype evaluation step enables the re-estimation of the logical architecture from the viewpoint of message quantity and processing time for objects. In OOPD, the initial logical architecture which consists of appropriate objects is very important to minimize corrections in the subsequent design steps. The estimation of the objects' structure in terms of their performance here has much significance.

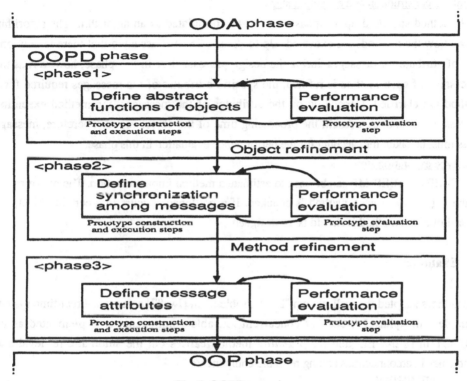

Fig.5 OOPD overview

<Phase2>

Prototype construction and execution steps

In <phase2>, an object obtained in <phase1> is refined by defining input and output of the methods that compose the object. With regard to the processing of the methods, the problem of synchronization of several messages arriving at the method must be managed. If a method needs several messages, it must wait until all messages arrive. Generally, the synchronization that affects the performance of concurrent programs must be examined.

Prototype evaluation step

BDES-S and BIES-S can be used to examine the performance degradation caused by synchronization. Also, message distribution among objects and method assignment in objects are checked.

<Phase3>

Prototype construction and execution steps

Each method specified up to <phase2> must be formulated as an algorithm. The algorithm shows how the methods are executed. Up to <phase 2>, it is assumed that there is only one type of attribute for messages during the design process. Here in this phase, however, as the processing of each method is refined, the specific attributes of the messages required for a method are clarified. Depending on the attributes of the messages, the method execution process varies and, as a result, the processing time of the object varies. Therefore, message types must be taken into account for the performance evaluation in this phase.

Prototype evaluation step

BDES-MF and BIES-MF can be used to estimate a method implementation. The performance of the algorithm of each method is checked. If a bottleneck occurs in a certain object, the algorithm of the method is should be re-designed.

4.2 Example

The authors adopted the well-known "LIFT Problem" in [Iws87] as a typical real-time system example. In <phase1>, each of concurrent reusable components is implemented as an OBJECT in MENDEL, and the *planning* method carries out the automatic retrieval and establishes interconnections among reusable components.

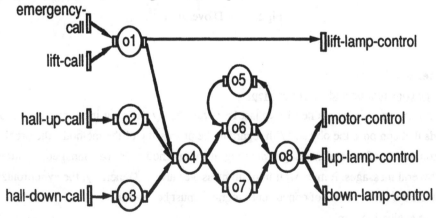

Fig. 6 Interconnected MENDEL OBJECTs which correspond to the functional model

For this example, by giving the input specification (hall-up-call, hall-down-call, emergency-call, lift-call) and the output specification (lift-lamp-control, up-lamp-control, down-lamp-control, motor-control), several OBJECTs are retrieved and interconnected, as shown in Fig.6.

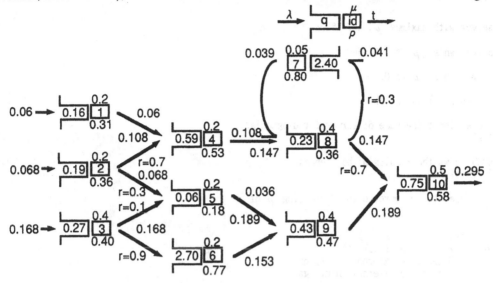

Fig. 7 Queueing network mapped from MENDEL OBJECTs in Fig.6

In Fig.6, OBJECTs "o1", "o2", "o3", "o4", "o5", "o6", "o7" and "o8" are retrieved and interconnected by the *planning* method. Interconnected objects in MENDEL form the queueing network, in which each object in MENDEL corresponds to a server and each message in MENDEL corresponds to a transaction. It is assumed that each OBJECT is assigned to each processor in a multiprocessor system which consists of 10 processors, as shown in Fig.7. OBJECTs "o1", "o2", and "o3" are assigned to "s1", "s2", and "s3", respectively. OBJECT "o4", including the main lift control, is distributed to three processors "s4", "s5", and "s6", because of load-balancing. And, OBJECTs "o5", "o6", "o7", and "o8" are assigned to "s7", "s8", "s9", and "s10", respectively. Lift-call, hall-up-call, and hall-down-call correspond to external inputs to "s1", "s2", and "s3" (called ga, gb, and gc), respectively. Figure 7 also shows the performance data from the simulation. For example, lift-call's arrival rate is 0.06 sec and "s7"'s utilization rate is 0.8 which shows a bottleneck. Emergency-call and lift-lamp-control are omitted from this queueing network, because they are out of statistical measurement. "r" from "s2" to "s4" and "r" from "s2" to "s5" indicate the load-distributed factor, because the message from "s2" may be sent to either "s4" or "s5." "r" from "s3" to "s5" and "r" from "s3" to "s6" indicate the load-distributed factors. In a queueing network in Fig.7, "μ"s for all servers, "λ"s for the entries into the network, "r"s, and the network structure are given, from the prototype construction step before the prototype execution. "ρ"s and "t"s for all servers and "λ"s for all servers can be obtained by the prototype execution.

server with maximum ρ : (s7 .800)

server whose $\rho \geq 0.9$ none.

server whose $\rho \geq 0.7$

(s6 .770) (s7 .800)

Please input the name of server for diagnosis.
: s7

BDES shows the results of bottleneck
diagnosis.

Parameter to be improved for decreasing ρ of
s7.

*plan-1 increase μ (s7)
*plan-2 decrease r (s2,s4)
*plan-3 decrease external input, gb
*plan-4 decrease external input, ga

Fig. 8 Improvement plans generated by BDES diagnosis

The designer can determine and locate bottlenecks by BDES. Figure 8 shows a list of servers and their "ρ"values by BDES. In Fig.8, for example, the designer can select bottleneck "s7." For improving the bottleneck on "s7", qualitative simulation can be applied. Block 2 in Fig.9 shows that only $\rho7$ and t4 are used in the loop consisting of "s7" and "s8." Figure 9 shows the bottleneck improvement process for "s7" with these heuristics, in which a dotted line box at the top represents the goal of *qualitative reasoning*, i.e., "decrease $\rho7$." The other 4 dotted line boxes represent the results from *qualitative reasoning*, i.e., the improvement plans for decreasing $\rho7$. BDES diagnoses the sources of the bottleneck "s7" and produces 4 improvement plans for bottleneck improvement, which are alternatives for the bottleneck "s7." For example, the designer can select Plan 2. BIES quantitatively improves the parameters, as shown bellow.

$$r(s2,s5) \quad 0.300 \quad ---> \quad 0.780$$
$$r(s2,s4) \quad 0.700 \quad ---> \quad 0.220$$

In order to improve the bottleneck of "s7", BIES can quantitatively modify "r" from "s2" to "s4." In this case, "r" from "s2" to "s4" can be modified, because this "r" indicates the load-distributed factor and the message from "s2" can be sent to either "s4" or "s5." In MENDEL, the message from OBJECT can be sent to the same OBJECTs on individual processors. The designer can accomplish the measurement using new parameters and obtain a new measured quantity. They can compare the second quantity with the first. Table 1 shows a comparison between two kinds of "ρ" values obtained by the first and second measurements, of the tuning process performed by BDES and BIES. Table 1 shows an appropriate improvement for bottleneck.

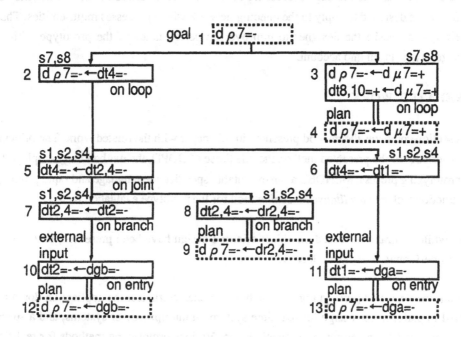

Fig. 9 Qualitative reasoning process for improving ρ's value on server "s7"

Table 1. Comparison of ρ's and queue length between two measurements

	measurement1		improved by BIES	measurement2	
	ρ	q		ρ	q
s7	0.80	2.40	0.65	0.58	0.52

In \<phase 2\>, how the synchronization affects the performance of concurrent programs must be examined. By refining each object, the designer can find that OBJECT "o8" starts only when it receives messages from both OBJECTs "o6" and "o7." OBJECT "o8" is assigned to "s10" in Fig.7. Then, "s10" can start only when "s10" receives both messages from "s8" and "s9", and it may be bottleneck server. BDES-S and BIES-S are able to model such "s10" as a synchronized server and can generate improvement plan for "s10." In this case, "r" from "s2" to "s4" should be modified.

In <phase3>, by refining each method in each object, the designer can find that the types of messages arriving at OBJECT "o4" from OBJECT "o1" are different from those from OBJECT "o2", and the message processing time is different between them. BDES-MF and BIES-MF are designed to apply to the queuing network which processes multi-entities. These expert systems assist the designer to improve the performance of the prototype with the messages' types taken into account.

5. RELATED WORK

This section compares the method presented in this paper with the related work. The principal characteristics of the presented method include those of OOPD, the methodology employed in the prototyping process, MENDEL as an executable specification language and rapid prototype construction tool, and *qualitative reasoning* used for the prototype evaluation method.

First, while several tools based on object-oriented design have been presented, few of them support performance design as does OOPD.

Second, the presented prototyping process has two characteristics; the application domain is limited to performance design for real-time system on multiprocessor systems, and a special emphasis is put on the prototype evaluation step. Various prototyping methods for real-time systems have been proposed [e.g. Luq88]. However, these methods do not support the overall performance design for statistical features. No prototyping method, which emphasizes the prototype evaluation step, has been presented. The authors' method is considered to be general-purpose and applicable to several other domains, in which the prototype evaluation step is needed for a more complex system.

Third, as for MENDEL, two points, one of which is for executable specification language and the other is for *planning* methods, should be discussed. Various executable specification languages have been presented and experimentally used. They are classified into two groups: the Operational approach, such as GIST [Coh84] and PAISLey [Zav84], and the Functional approach, such as MODEL [Pry84] and RPS [Dav82]. MENDEL employs the operational approach. Concerning the combination of actor-model and declarative knowledge representation, one of the languages most similar to MENDEL is Orient 84/K [Ish87], which is an object-oriented concurrent programming language. The main difference between MENDEL and Orient 84/K is that Orient 84/K has several message-scheduling mechanisms and a parallel control mechanism as a programming language and does not support a hybrid inference engine. As for planning, MENDEL's planning ability is very simple compared with [And89].

Fourth, as for *qualitative reasoning*, the relation to queueing theory and the main difference from other work should be discussed. General analytical method based on queueing theory generates "ρ"s , "t"s and "λ"s for all servers, using given "λ"s from external, all "μ"s and "r"s. On the other hand, BDES&BIES generates some "μ"s and some "r"s in order to improve the bottleneck, using given "ρ"s , "t"s and "λ"s for all servers. Several applications of *qualitative reasoning* to a design process have been proposed [e.g. Wil90]. The difference from other work in applying qualitative reasoning to software engineering [e.g. Dow90] resides in the prototype evaluation step, where *qualitative reasoning* is indispensable to effectively implement a human's heuristics in performance design. Furthermore, no related work on the queueing network model has been presented in the *qualitative reasoning* domain. BDES&BIES present a combination method for *qualitative reasoning* and quantitative reasoning on a queueing network model. BDES selects several parameters to be tuned using *qualitative reasoning*, and BIES determines the parameter value using quantitative reasoning.

6. CONCLUSION

This paper describes the role of artificial intelligence in implementing a prototyping process in performance design for real-time systems. The presented method has several limitations and assumptions as follows;
(1) Dynamic object creation is not permitted.
(2) Communication cost is not considered.
(3) Closed type queueing network is not supported.
(4) When required messages are received, the object execution is started without waiting for completion of another object execution.
Among above points, (4) may be the most critical limitation from the viewpoint of applicability. In MENDEL execution, it is assumed that individual objects are assigned to individual processors in a multiprocessor system. In practice, several objects may be mapped to the same processor. Then, the authors are now implementing a hierarchical queueing network version in order to solve this problem.

Acknowledgments

The research in Section 3.1 has been partially supported by the Japanese Fifth Generation Computer Project and its organizing institute ICOT. The authors would like to thank Ryuzou Hasegawa of ICOT for his encouragement and support. The research in Section 3.2 has been partially supported by the Japanese Ministry of Education, Science and Culture. The authors arc grateful to Seiichi Nishijima and Yutaka Ofude of Systems & Software Engineering Laboratory, Toshiba Corporation, for providing essential support. The authors also wish to thank Jun Sawamura and Keisuke Shida, Sophia University, for their helpful cooperation in developing BDES&BIES.

References

[And89] J.S.Anderson and S.Fickas : A Proposed Perspective Shift : Viewing Specification Design as a Planning Problem, *Proc. of 5th International Workshop on Software Specification and Design*, pp.177-184, 1989

[Bar82] D.Barstow et al. : An Automatic Programming System to Support an Experimental Science, *Proc. of 6th ICSE*, pp.360-366, 1982.

[Coa90] P.Coad and E.Yourdon : *Object-Oriented Analysis*, Prentice-Hall, 1990

[Coh84] D.Cohen : A Forward Inference Engine to Aid in Understanding Specifications, *Proc. of AAAI-84*, pp.56-60,1984.

[Dav82] A.M.Davis : Rapid Prototyping using Executable Requirements Specifications, *ACM SIGSOFT*, Vol.7,No.5, pp.39-44, 1982

[Dow90] K.Downing and S.Fickas : Specification Criticism via Policy-Directed Envisionment, CIS-TR-90-05, University of Oregon, 1990

[Fic85] S.Fickas : Automating the Transformational Development of Software, *IEEE Trans. Software Eng.*, Vol.11, No.11, pp.1268-1277, 1985

[Ger80] S.Gerhart et al. : An overview of AFFIRM: A Specification and Verification System, *Inform. Proc.*, Vol.80, pp-343-347, 1980.

[Gon77] M.J.Gonzalez : Deterministic Processor Scheduling, *Computing Surveys*, Vol.9, No.3, pp.173-204, 1977

[Hon86a] S.Honiden et al. : MENDEL: Prolog based Concurrent Object Oriented Language, *Proc. of Compcon '86*, pp.230-234, 1986.

[Hon86b] S.Honiden et al. : Software Prototyping with Reusable Components, *Journal of Information Processing*, Vol.9, No.3, pp.123-129, 1986, also in IEEE tutorial 'Software Reuse: The State of the Practice', 1988.

[Hon89] S.Honiden et al. : An Application of Structural Modeling and Automated Reasoning to Concurrent Program Design, *Proc. of HICSS-22*, 1989.

[Hon90] S.Honiden et al. : An application of Structural Modeling and Automated Reasoning to Real-Time Systems Design, *The Journal of Real-Time Systems*, Vol.1, No.3, Kluwer Academic Publishers,1990

[Ish87] Y.Ishikawa and M.Tokoro : Orient 84/K : An Object-Oriented Concurrent Programming Language for Knowledge System, *Object Oriented Concurrent Programming* (ed. by Yonezawa and Tokoro), MIT Press, 1987

[Ito89a] K.Itoh et al. : Tools for Prototyping for Developing Software, *JOHO SHORI*, Vol.30, No.4, pp.387-395, 1989

[Ito89b] K.Itoh et al. : Knowledge-based Parameter Tuning for Queueing Network Type System -A New Application of Qualitative Reasoning, *Proc. of IFIP CAPE' 89.*

[Ito90] K.Itoh et al. : A Method for Diagnosis and Improvement on Bottleneck of Queueing Network by Qualitative and Quantitative Reasoning, *Trans. on JSAI*, Vol.5, No.1, 1990.

[Ito91a] K.Itoh et al. : Qualitative Reasoning Based Parameter Tuning on Bottleneck of Synchronized Queueing Network, *Proc. of Compsac '91*, 1991

[Ito91b] K.Itoh et al. : Parameter Tuning on Bottleneck of Synchronized Queueing Network by Qualitative Reasoning, *Trans. on JSAI*, Vol.6, No.6, 1991

[Iws87] *Proc. of 4th International Workshop on Software Specification and Design*, CS Press, Los Alamitos, Calif, 1987.

[Jon84] T.C.Jones : Reusability in Programming: A survey of the State of the Art, *IEEE Trans. Software Eng.*, Vol.SE-9, pp.488-494, 1984.

[Kat81] S.Katz et al. : An Advisory System for Developing Data Representations, *Proc. of 7th. IJCAI*, pp.1030-1036, 1981.

[Luqi88] Luqi et al. : Rapidly Prototyping Real-Time Systems, *IEEE Software* September, pp.25-36, 1988. .

[Nil82] N.J.Nilson, *Principles of Artificial Intelligence*, Springer-Verlag, 1982

[Pry84] N.S.Prywers : Automatic Program Generation in Distributed Cooperative Computation, *IEEE Trans. Syst. Man. Cyber.*, Vol.14, No.2, pp.275-286, 1984

[Ric78] C.Rich et al. : Initial Report on a LISP Programmer's Apprentice, *IEEE Trans. Software Eng.* ,Vol.4, No.6, 456-467, 1978.

[Swa83] W.Swartout : The Gist behavior explainer, *Proc. of AAAI-83*, 1983

[Uch87] N.Uchihira et al. : Concurrent Program Synthesis with Reusable Component using Temporal Logic, *Proc. of Compsac '87*, pp.455-464, 1987.

[Wil90] B.Williams : Interaction-based Invention : Designing Novel Devices from First Principles, *Proc. of AAAI-90*, 1990

[Zav84] P.Zave : The Operational versus the Conventional Approach to Software Development, *Comm. ACM*, Vol.27, No.2, pp.104-118, 1984

Dynamically Replaceable Software: A Design Method

Jorge Amador
GMV S.A.
Isaac Newton, s/n, E-28760 Madrid (Spain)
jamador@gmv.es

Belén de Vicente
Teice Control
General Rodrigo, 6 5th., E-28003 Madrid (Spain)
belen@teice.es

Alejandro Alonso
E.T.S.I de Telecomunicación
Ciudad Universitaria, Universidad Politécnica de Madrid, E-28040 Madrid (Spain)
aalonso@gic.etsitm.upm.es

Abstract.- The usual maintenance techniques are not useful when dealing with non-stop software systems. It is not possible to stop the system execution to update some of its components. Dynamic software replacement is a mechanism that allows components updating without stopping the whole system. For this purpose, the Software Replaceable Unit (SWRU) concept has been introduced.

In this paper we present a design method for software systems including replaceable components. The executable unit (i.e. the process) is selected as the minimal software unit (SWRU) that can be dynamically replaced. This way, the strong relation between SWRU based software and distributed software is shown. This fact is used to extend the HOOD method in order to design SWRU based systems.

A replacement model is defined to implement the above concepts. The requirements that a SWRU has to fulfil, according to the above model, are identified. Finally, a method and a set of support modules to assist in the detailed design and coding phases are presented.

Key words.-   dynamic replacement, maintenance, non-stop systems, distributed systems, design methods.

1. Introduction.

It is not possible to develop software systems that do not need to be modified during their operational life. This process, which is known as maintenance, is the longest phase in the software life cycle, specially when dealing with long-lived systems. In addition, the cost of software maintenance is significantly higher than the development cost. Software maintenance falls into three categories [Sommerville 89]:

- *Perfective*: Changes which improve the system in some way, without improving its functionality.
- *Adaptive*: modifications due to changes in the environment of the program.
- *Corrective*: modifications due to the corrections of system errors.

The usual software maintenance techniques are performed by stopping the whole system, installing the new version, and finally resuming the whole system execution. Under this approach, during a certain period of time the system is not operational and this can cause various types of problems (economical, safety problems, ...).

There are systems that cannot be stopped without large risks. This is the case of the *Columbus* space platform, whose operational life is estimated at 30 years. Stopping an on-board software system may cause major problems. In this case the classical approach is not valid. The alternative is to develop a system that can replace parts of its code dynamically, while the rest of the system continues working. This approach is forced by the requirements of non-stop systems.

Some work on this area was promoted by the European Space Agency (ESA) for the *Columbus* project. In this project a new software concept was introduced: the Software Replaceable Unit (SWRU) [Antler 87]. Indeed, all the COLUMBUS on-board software shall be configured as a set of SWRUs [COLUMBUS 90]. An implementation of this concept was studied in the Ada Real Time Test (ARTT) project [Amador 88], and its results were the starting point of the further works reported in this article.

Our research work has followed two directions:

- Study of the influence of the SWRU concept on the architecture of a software system as well as the integration of this concept into an existing software design method.

- The definition of SWRU implementation method for its use in the detailed design and coding phases. It has been performed by defining a Replacement Model, and designing a standard procedure and a set of support modules to implement the model.

All these ideas have been implemented and validated for the special case of a software system designed with the HOOD [HUM 89] & [HRM 89] method and implemented with the Ada language [Ada 83].

Section 2 addresses those questions that are open about dynamic replacement. In section 3, the minimal programming unit that can be replaced is defined. Section 4 identifies the relationship between distributed software and SWRUs. In section 5 a proposal of some HOOD extensions to design systems with replaceable units is presented. In section 6, the Replacement Model chosen is presented while section 7 introduces a procedure and a set of support modules to assist in the detailed design and coding phases.

2. Problem statement.

A SWRU may be defined as [Amador 88]:

> *a piece of code, data or textual documentation that can be treated and considered as a unit that can be replaced within its operative environment under specific conditions.*

It is important to note that not only code may be replaced, but also data and text (e.g. a file to be used to provide some on-line help). In this paper we are going to consider only dynamic replacement of code, as it appears to be the most critical issue.

First of all, it is important to note that one of the hardest problems is to determine the granularity of replacement [Burns 89], defined as the smallest unit of software that can be replaced. The unit must be a meaningful object in the design method used, and in the replacement process, furthermore, its performance depends on its nature.

When dealing with SWRUs there are two main issues: how can SWRUs be designed and integrated in the overall software design process, and what is the replacement process going to be like.

The SWRU concept must be taken into account from the very first moment of the software design process. In order to do this, it is necessary to integrate this concept with a software design method.

Another critical feature is determining when and how the SWRU should be replaced. It is only possible to achieve this process at prefixed states that assure the right execution of the system after the replacement.

Finally, it is also necessary to give some support to the detailed design and coding phases. This should be done hiding from the implementer of a SWRU, as much as possible, the details of the replacement process.

3. The Replacement Unit.

Two different approaches have been studied for the selection of the replacement unit:

a) The single program approach, where a software system including SWRUs is designed as a unique program whose components (i.e. program units: procedures, functions, tasks) are dynamically replaceable.

b) The distributed program approach, where a software system including SWRUs is designed as a distributed program which is mapped to a set of processes communicating via message passing. Each process should correspond to a replaceable unit [Amador 88].

If we implement our software system as a single program, then the implementation language should provide dynamic linking between program units [Laws 87]. Thus, the actual address of each program unit is calculated each time its code is called.

Some work has been done in this way using Object Oriented Programming Techniques [Stadel 91]. This approach uses the features of inheritance and dynamic linking provided by object oriented languages (Smalltalk [Goldberg 83], Eiffel [Meyer 88], C++ [Stroustrup 86], etc) to provide dynamic replacement in a natural way.

These languages are not usually used in those typical software systems requiring dynamic replacement (e.g. the *Columbus* and *Freedom* space stations). Instead, the typical languages used are C and (in the examples above) particularly Ada. The latter languages do not provide dynamic linking features. So non-standard extensions to these languages are needed. Moreover, the use of dynamic linking wastes the advantages of strong typed languages like Ada, since static type checking is not performed.

In [Burns 89] a discussion on what should and should not constitute legal Ada replacements may be found. In [Tindell 90] a set of requirements and mechanisms for dynamic change of Ada code is presented, although the issue of concurrent and distributed Ada is not contemplated.

In the second approach, the software system is configured as a set of communicating processes, and therefore they seem to be the most appropriate candidate for being the replacement units. In this case, most languages used in the industry are not designed for the implementation of distributed software, but it is possible by designing in a certain way. Thus, no extensions to the language are needed, but it must be used with certain restrictions. Moreover, a communication layer enabling the inter-program communication (IPC) is needed.

The second approach was taken for our work, keeping in mind the important fact that most applications with replaceable components will have a distributed nature.

4. SWRUs as Distributed Software.

[Bal et al 89] states that a logically distributed software system consists of multiple software processes that communicate by explicit message passing. In this sense, the choice of the program (process) as the unit of replacement makes us consider a software system including SWRUs to be logically distributed. This contrasts with logically non distributed software systems, in which communication between processes is performed using shared data [Bal et al 89].

This could lead us to think that software systems including SWRUs must always run on a physically distributed system, but this is not really true. Logically distributed software may run on both physically distributed (computer networks) and non physically distributed (monoprocessor and multiprocessor) hardware.

4.1 Distributed Software Development.

Some languages have been specially designed for the development of applications for distributed systems. The best known one is CONIC [Kramer 88] & [Kramer 89]. In particular, this language addresses the issue of code replacement. But, as object oriented languages, they have the disadvantage that they are not the most typical ones used for the software systems in study.

On the other hand, the assumption of a single memory (i.e. a single process) is a feature that exists in most of standard, widely extended languages, such as Ada, C, etc. However, some strategies have been used for developing distributed software with standard languages. These strategies include [Atkinson et al 88]:

- Development of separate programs communicating via standard I/O.
- Making the distribution transparent to the developer (post-partitioning) [Jha et al 89] [Volz et al 89]
- The use of Virtual Nodes (pre-partitioning) [Burns 90] [Atkinson et al 88].

The first approach lacks flexibility, since the exact hardware configuration must be known from the beginning. The second strategy has as its main problem the high overheads due to remote communication.

In the last approach, a program must be designed and coded taking into account the distributed nature of the target (but not the exact configuration). So a program must be designed as a set of abstractions of independent network nodes which group together strongly cohesive components. Inside such abstractions the language may be used freely, but a set of restrictions are imposed for its use outside their boundaries. This abstractions are called Virtual Nodes [Atkinson et al 88] [Burns 90].

4.2.   Virtual Nodes

The Virtual Node concept as defined in the DIADEM project [Atkinson et al 88] has been the one taken for our study. Virtual Nodes are highly cohesive components, encapsulating functions that are strongly related, and loosely coupled to each other, so that the communication between virtual nodes may be handled in an efficient way. The following properties are defined as fundamental for Virtual Nodes [Atkinson et al 88]:

1) They must completely encapsulate their internal state, providing no access to internal state variables by other virtual nodes.

2) They must make no reference to any shared components having an internal state. If they

share components with other virtual nodes, these shared components must have no internal state.

3) They must communicate with other virtual nodes through well-defined interfaces, using a message passing protocol (not shared variables).

4) Each must have its own flow of control, being able to execute on a separate machine of a network.

A very important issue for virtual nodes is the communication. Since virtual nodes are considered distributed components of a single program, inter-node communication should be expressed in terms of normal intra-program mechanisms, such as the rendezvous or procedure call [Burns 90]. Sharing of data, as defined above, is unacceptable.

All the properties described above may be applied to SWRUs. Thus, we may derive that an SWRU may be implemented, from the distributed software point of view, as a Virtual Node. But since the fundamental feature of SWRUs is the replacement, we must add the following property:

5) Each SWRU shall provide specific support for dynamic replacement, including facilities to store and retrieve its internal state.

Therefore, a software system including SWRUs may be implemented as a distributed program partitioned into a set of communicating and *replaceable* Virtual Nodes.

5. SWRUs Design with HOOD.

The properties defined for both SWRUs and Virtual Nodes show that they are analogous to the object concept defined in Object Oriented Design [Booch 86] [Booch 90] [HRM 89]. A SWRU may be seen as an active object that provides not only operations to other SWRUs, but also operations for its replacement. This feature leads us to think in OOD techniques as a natural way to design software with replaceable components.

We have chosen the HOOD (Hierarchical Object Oriented Design) method [HRM 89] & [HUM 89] for our study. It is an architectural design method that can be extended to the detailed design phase and is specially oriented towards Ada program development. HOOD supports the identification of an object architecture and leads naturally into detailed design where operations are further refined.

5.1. HOOD Overview

A brief explanation of HOOD and its design process is included in this section. More information may be found in [HRM 89] and [HUM 89].

OOD is a technique that uses the object as the basic unit of modularity in system design [Booch 86]. Within OOD, a software system is a set of interconnected objects, and HOOD is a technique that enforces structuring of these objects according to [HRM 89]:

- Abstraction, information hiding and encapsulation principles: an object is defined by the services it provides to its users, whereas the internal structure is hidden to the user. The services are described in the OPCS (Operation Control Structure) and the behaviour of the object is described in the OBCS (Object Control Structure).

- Hierarchy principles:

    - Objects may be decomposed into other objects, so that a system can be represented as a parent object including child objects (*INCLUDE* relationship).

    - Objects may use operations of other objects, so that a system can be represented as senior objects using junior objects in hierarchy (*USE* relationship).

- Control structuring principles: operations of objects are activated through control flows. There may be several control flows operating simultaneously in an object. In HOOD two different kinds of objects are defined depending on whether the control flows are interacting within the object (*Active* objects) or not (*Passive* objects).

Finally, we must note that provided operations for Passive objects are *unconstrained* (i.e. the control flow is passed inmediately to that operations when requested). On the other hand, for Active objects, the OBCS *constrains* the way in which the operations are provided (the execution of an operation depends on the internal state of the object and/or the type of execution requested).

The HOOD design process is globally top-down, and consists of a set of basic design steps, in each of which a given object, called a parent object, is decomposed into a set of components called child objects which together provide the functionality of the parent object. This process of decomposition starts with the decomposition of the top level parent object called the root object which represents an abstract model of the system to design. Each component object in turn may be decomposed into other lower level objects in the following design steps until the bottom level or terminal object is reached. Terminal objects are designed without further decomposition, i.e. the design provides for direct implementation into code.

HOOD supports in some way the design of distributed software providing the Virtual Node object. This feature makes HOOD specially well suited for the design of SWRU based software. Anyway some extensions should be made, as the definition of a new kind of object, the SWRU object; and the extension of the HOOD design steps in order to identify and implement these objects.

5.2.   The SWRU Object

HOOD provides the Virtual Node object for the design of distributed software. Virtual node objects have the same properties as Active objects but they have some restrictions on the *USE* and *INCLUDE* relationship, due to their distributed nature (i.e. they are in different processes):

- *INCLUDE* relationship: The Virtual Node object may only be decomposed either into virtual node objects or into active and/or passive objects, but not a mixture [HRM 89].

- *USE* relationship: All operations provided by a virtual node object shall be constrained [HRM 89].

An SWRU object may also be considered as an active object with some special features. The main property of a SWRU object is the replacement, thus an SWRU object must provide:

- the specific operations provided to other objects of the system and,
- a set of operations to allow its replacement.

Replacement operations shall not be used by other objects. They shall be used by a human operator or by a special replacement process. They shall allow at least to start and stop the SWRU object execution, as well as to read and store its internal state, in order to start the new SWRU in an appropriate state.

The *INCLUDE* restriction may also apply to SWRUs:

An SWRU object shall be decomposed either entirely into SWRU objects or into active and/or passive objects, but not a mixture.

Each SWRU object is implemented as a separate program. On this basis, if we have a SWRU object (i.e. a replaceable object), that has any SWRU object as a child, this child object shall be implemented as a separate program. That implies that the rest of child objects interacting with it will be in at least one different program (i.e. a different SWRU).

On the other hand, replacing a parent SWRU object means replacing all its child objects, as far as a parent object is only a higher level abstraction of its child objects. Thus, we have two possible types of replacement (from the objects point of view):

- Replacement of a terminal SWRU object means replacing the corresponding process.
- Replacement of an SWRU object, including child SWRU objects, means replacing the processes corresponding to the child SWRUs.

The *USE* restriction does not apply to SWRUs:

An SWRU object shall provide both constrained and unconstrained operations.

Developing an appropriate communication layer, it is possible to support both constrained and unconstrained operations.

5.3.   HOOD design with SWRUs.

A HOOD design of a software system should be the same, independent of the existence of SWRUs. However, this is not possible since the use of SWRU object implies certain restrictions that must be taken into account in the design of objects and operations. Thus, we must extend the HOOD method twofold:

a) by adding some steps to identify SWRU objects and their replacement operations, and performing some changes to the existing ones.

b) by taking into account the restriction on the *USE* and *INCLUDE* relationship in the case of SWRU objects.

The basic design steps for each HOOD object are described in the HOOD Chapter Skeleton (HCS) [HUM 89]. The HCS steps, the changes to them, and the new steps added (marked with "R") are described below:

1   Problem Definition
   1.1   Statement of the problem
   1.2   Analysis and structuring of requirement data

2   Elaboration of an informal solution strategy

3   Formalisation of the strategy
   3.1   Identification of objects
   3.2   Identification of operations
   3.3   Grouping objects and operations
   3.4   Graphical description
   3.5   Justification of design decisions

2R   Elaboration of a replacement informal strategy

3R   Formalisation of the replacement strategy
   3.1R   Identification of SWRU objects
   3.2R   Identification of replacement operations
   3.3R   Grouping SWRU objects and replacement operations
   3.4R   Graphical Description of SWRU objects for replacement

4   Formalisation of the solution
   4.1   Object Description Skeleton (ODS)

In step 1.2, the replacement requirements are identified. The possible states of the system in which the replacement is possible are defined.

Steps 2 and 3 remain unchanged. Step 2R is introduced to elaborate a replacement strategy from the replacement requirements described in 1.2. In step 3.1R SWRU objects are identified, taking into account the *USE* and *INCLUDE* restrictions. In step 3.2R and 3.3R the replacement operations needed are identified and grouped with the corresponding objects. Step 3.4R shows graphically each SWRU object only with its replacement operations.

In step 4.1 the internal structure of all objects shall be formally described. Here we will define in each object two replacement features:

- in the Object Control Structure (OBCS), we will define the states in which it is possible to accept a replacement operation.

- in the Operation Control Structure (OPCS) of each replacement operation, we will define specific internal features such as internal data to be saved or restored, etc.

Figure 1 shows a simple example of a HOOD diagram including 2 SWRU objects using each other.

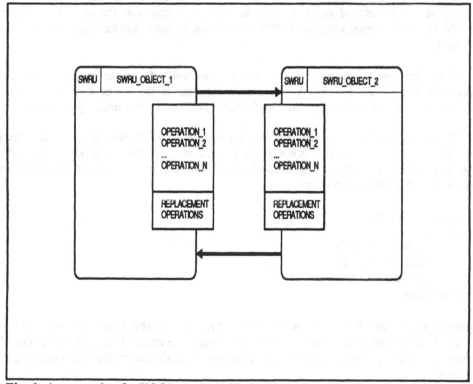

Fig. 1: An example of a HOOD design with SWRUs.

6. The Replacement Model.

In the previous sections we have described a design method for applications with replaceable software components. In this section we describe in more detail the replacement model that can be applied to these components.

6.1. The internal state of a SWRU.

The main consequence of the replacement process is that when an SWRU is replaced (we will call it the replaced SWRU), the SWRU replacing it (the replacing SWRU) system can continue the execution of the replaced SWRU from the point at which this one left it. So the rest of the units are not aware of what has happened in so far as they are not involved in the replacement process.

Obviously, the replacing SWRU must know which data of the replaced SWRU are meaningful (i.e. its internal state), in order to start its execution in the right state. We can identify two main internal states in an SWRU. These are its initial internal state and its current internal state.

Using the same terminology as [Amador 88], we will refer to the internal state as the checkpoint data of the SWRU. A unit checkpoint data is the set of data that gives us information about the value of the meaningful items (variables, structures, ...) at a given time.

When one SWRU replaces another, it must assume as its initial checkpoint data the current checkpoint data of the replaced SWRU. As an example, consider an SWRU designed to measure the pressure of valves in a chemical conversion machine. The checkpoint data of this unit includes the following values:

```
type VALVE is
record
     number : INTEGER;
     name : STRING;
     pressure : REAL;
end record;
```

During execution, this SWRU will be measuring, say, the pressure applied to the valve number 417 and it will obtain a value of 13.4. If at that moment we decide to replace this SWRU by another one that implements a more accurate measurement algorithm, this one should start at that state.

Actually, it is of major importance to the replacement process success, that the checkpoint data of every SWRU contains all the needed information related to its operational environment. This information should be carefully chosen in order to have a well defined starting point for the new SWRU.

6.2.   Replacement Supervision.

Once we have decided to replace one SWRU by another, there should be somebody in charge of the supervision and control of the replacement process. We have given the name of *Supervisor Unit* to the unit that will achieve this operation.

It must be noted that the HOOD design of the whole system is not affected by the nature of the *Supervisor Unit*, since this unit does not belong to the application, but to the replacement environment.

6.3.   SWRU Operation Mode

An SWRU may be executing in two modes:

- Normal Mode
- Replacement Mode

An SWRU is said to be operating in normal mode when it is achieving the functions that it was designed for. As the SWRU receives the first replacement request, its mode changes to replacement mode and stays in it while the SWRU is receiving this kind of requests. Requests to normal operations while the SWRU is in replacement mode are queued until the new SWRU is operational. Then the new SWRU will execute them.

6.4.   Replacement Phases.

The decision to replace a unit within a software system can be taken at any time. The Supervisor Unit will provide this service.

In [Amador 88] five operations (Run, Stop, Continue, Store Checkpoint Data and Retrieve checkpoint Data) were considered to achieve the replacement. Keeping the sequence of operations provided by them and applying the remote rendezvous concept, we have divided the replacement process into the following four phases:

Phase 1: Storing the checkpoint data.

As soon as the *Supervisor Unit* gets an indication to start the replacement of an SWRU, phase starts. The *Supervisor Unit* requests the unit that is going to be replaced to store its checkpoint data and waits for an answer from this unit. The mentioned unit carries out the service requested and confirms it to the *Supervisor Unit*. The replaced SWRU then enters the *Replacement Mode*. At the next step, the *Replaced SWRU* sends its checkpoint data to the *Replacing SWRU*.

Phase 2: Retrieving the checkpoint data.

When the *Supervisor Unit* gets the confirmation from the *Replaced SWRU*, it requests the *Replacing SWRU* to pick up the checkpoint data that the former has sent to it. The *Replacing SWRU* starts its execution in *Replacement Mode*. It performs this action and confirms the reception of this checkpoint data to the *Replaced SWRU*. At the following step, the *Replacing SWRU* is able to acknowledge the *Supervisor Unit* that the operation of obtaining the information has been completed (see figure 2).

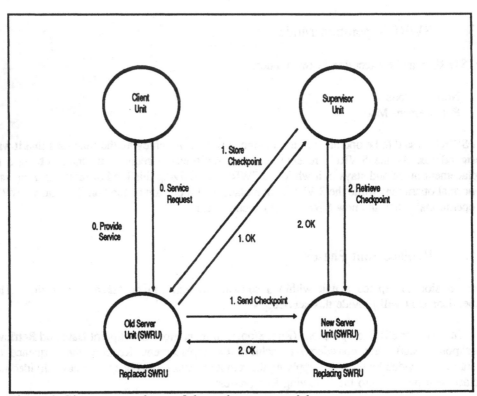

Figure 2: Phases one and two of the replacement model

Phase 3: Stopping the replaced SWRU.

When the replacement process reaches this phase, the Supervisor Unit already knows whether the exchange of information between the two SWRUs involved in the replacement has succeeded or not. If it has received the confirmation of this operation from the *Replacing SWRU*, the *Supervisor Unit* requests the *Replaced SWRU* to stop its execution, since the *Replacing SWRU* has the data to reproduce *Replaced SWRU* operation environment. When *Replaced SWRU* is asked to carry out this service, it sends confirmation back to the *Supervisor Unit* and exits.

On the other hand, if the exchange of data between both SWRUs has not succeeded, the *Supervisor Unit* requests the *Replaced SWRU* to enter the *Normal Mode* and resume its execution from the state in which it was before starting the replacement process. The process is considered to be failed, since the SWRU has not been replaced.

Phase 4: Starting the new SWRU.

As soon as *Replaced SWRU* has exited, phase 4 takes place. There is only one operation that should be done during this phase: the *Supervisor Unit* requests the *Replacing SWRU* to start its execution from the state defined in the checkpoint data. When the *Supervisor Unit* gets the answer back to this request, it considers that the replacement process has successfully finished since the new SWRU belongs to the executing system. Then the new SWRU starts its execution in *Normal Mode* (See figure 3 and figure 4).

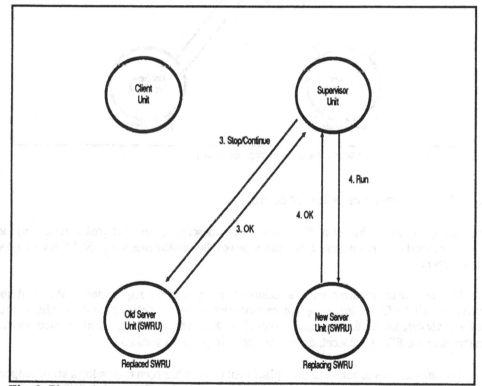

Fig. 3: Phases three and four of the replacement model

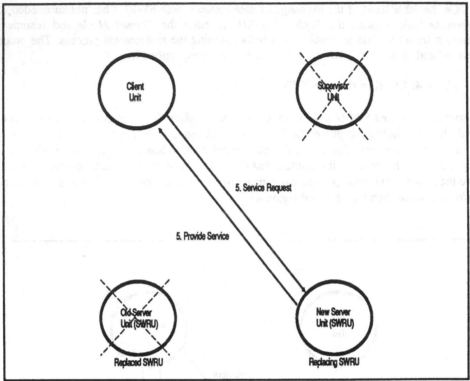

Fig. 4: Application view after a correct replacement.

7. SWRU Implementation Method.

Once the Replacement Model of SWRUs has been described, our next goal is related to the way the method can be automated, in order to make the implementation of SWRUs easier for the designers.

Maintaining the modularity and structure of the system is a requirement that should not be changed by the fact of including replacement concepts in the design of system units. In this way the appearance of the application should be kept and the design method used should contemplate the SWRU concept, as we have seen in previous sections.

The selected way to automate the replacement process has been to develop a set of support modules that transform a unit into a SWRU. From this point of view the SWRU continues looking like a module integrated in the system.

If the implementation language supports inheritance it could be used for this purpose [Stadel 91]. In our study a set of Ada generic units were developed.

7.1.   The Support Modules.

Two kinds of support modules should be provided. One of them should deal with the communication between SWRUs, in order to implement a remote communication interface for all the system units. It is necessary due to the distributed nature of the application. The external interface of this support module should be as general as possible, since it should fit all the variety of primitives provided by each communication mechanism selected to implement the remote communication.

The other module should provide the operations and the environment needed to add the replacement concepts within a selected unit. Some of these concepts are related to operations, such as attending replacement requests (store checkpoint data, retrieve checkpoint data, stop, run, continue) obtaining the checkpoint data from the unit, etc. Communication with the supervisor unit and the new SWRU is provided by the first module. The main functionality of the second support module should be to hide the mechanics of the replacement process to the designers. Otherwise the SWRU design would end in a work overload.

On the other hand, there is a wide variety of software applications. Each of these applications deals with specific data that the support modules do not know about. In this sense a cooperation with the designers is required. This cooperation is related to topics such as the selection of the data to be considered as checkpoint data.

As Fig. 5 shows, each SWRU is made up of an SWRU Object including the Replacement Support module and the Communication Support Module. These support modules have been implemented for the case of using Ada. They have been implemented as generic packages that are instantiated within the code of the SWRU object.

7.2. How to implement an SWRU.

Once the designers have decided to implement a selected unit as an SWRU, some actions should be performed.

1)   The designers have to define the contents of the unit checkpoint data.

2)   Integration of the support modules within the unit, in order to make available the checkpoint data and to add the replacement functionality to the unit. Some information should be provided to these support modules from the unit so they adjust well.

3)   Writing of SWRU code. At this point some areas should be covered:

- Identify the points in the code where the replacement could be done. These points should define safe moments for the replacement in order to maintain data consistency.
- Code the SWRU using structures that belong to the checkpoint data in a way to assure its correctness.

We have proposed a template to help this process, in order to ease the detailed design and coding phases.

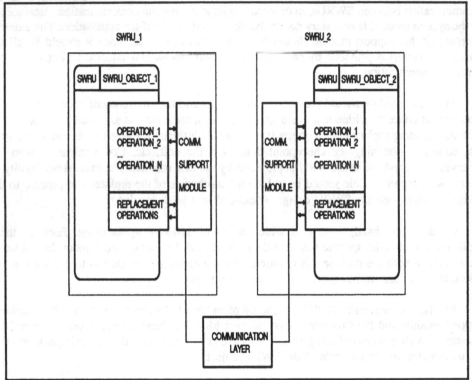

Figure 5: Implementation of a HOOD design including SWRUs

8. Conclusions.

We may summarize the main conclusions of this paper as follows:

- It is possible to replace software components dinamically in a running system.

- The process -fragment of a distributed program mapped to a process- seems to be an appropriate replacement unit.

- There is an analogy between distributed software and SWRU based software. In particular, the Virtual Node concept is strongly related to SWRUs.

- From the design method point of view (HOOD), an SWRU is seen as an active object with some special properties.

- A new kind of object must be defined in HOOD to support replacement features. We have called it the *SWRU object*.

- A replacement model is defined. In this model every SWRU can accept five replacement operations: *Run, Stop, Continue, Store Checkpoint Data and Retrieve Checkpoint Data.*

- The replacement model requires the existence of a replacement supervisor, managing the replacement process.

- The main steps of the replacement process are (1) storing the checkpoint data from the old SWRU, (2) obtaining the checkpoint data by the new SWRU, (3) stopping the old SWRU, (4) starting the new SWRU.

- The cooperation of the design team of the system is required in order to define the values that should be included in the checkpoint data of each SWRU.

- A set of guidelines and support modules have been developed which fulfils the above requirements hiding most replacement details to the implementer.

9. Acknowledgements.

We are grateful to Patricia Rodriguez, Juan Luis Redondo and Juan Antonio de la Puente. We also want to give special thanks to Javier Campos. Without his inestimable participation in the ARTT project, this paper would not have been possible. Work at UPM supported by the Spanish National Research program in Information and Communications Technologies, contract TCI-397/89.

10. References.

[Ada 83] DoD, *Ada Language Reference Manual*, ANSI/MIL-STD-1815A-1983.

[Amador 88] J. Amador, J. Campos, *SWRU Concept for ARTT*, GMV, Madrid, Spain, Doc. No. COL-GMV-ARTT2-TNSWRU, 1988.

[Antler 87] J. Antler, W. Häbel, *SWRU End-to-end Concept*, MBB/ERNO, Bremen, West Germany, 1987.

[Atkinson et al 88] C. Atkinson, T. Moreton, A. Natali, *Ada for distributed systems*, Cambridge University Press, 1988.

[Bal et al 89] H.E. Bal, J.G. Steiner, A.S. Tanenbaum, "Programming Languages for Distributed Systems", *ACM Computing Surveys*, vol. 21, no. 3, p. 261-322, 1989.

[Booch 86] G. Booch, *Software Engineering with Ada*, 2nd Edition, Benjamin Cummings, 1986.

[Booch 90] G. Booch, *Object Oriented Design with Applications*, 1st Edition, Benjamin Cummings, 1990.

[Burns 89] A. Burns and A.J. Wellings, "Dynamic Change Management and Ada", *Software Maintenance: Research and Practice*, vol.1, no.2, p121-131 (December 1989)

[Burns 90] A. Burns and A.J. Wellings, *Real Time Systems and their Programming Languages*, Addison-Wesley, 1990.

[COLUMBUS 90] European Space Agency (ESA), *COLUMBUS System Requirements Document*, Doc. No. COL-RQ-ESA-001, 1990.

[Goldberg 83] A. Goldberg, D. Robson, *Smalltalk-80: The language and its implementation*, Addison-Wesley, 1983.

[HRM 89] *HOOD Reference Manual*, Issue 3.0, HOOD Working Group, 1989.

[HUM 89] *HOOD User Manual*, Issue 3.0, HOOD Working Group, 1989.

[Jha et al 89] R. Jha, J.M. Kamrad, D.T. Cornhill, "Ada Program Partitioning Language: A Notation for Distributing Ada Programs", *IEEE Transactions on Software Engineering*, vol. 15, no.3, p. 271-280, 1989.

[Kramer 88] J. Kramer, J. Magee, "A Model for Change Management", *IEEE Conference on Distributed Computing Systems in the 90's*, Hong Kong, September 1988.

[Kramer 89] J. Kramer, J. Magee, "Constructing Distributed Systems in CONIC", *IEEE Transactions on Software Engineering*, p663-676, June 1989.

[Laws 87] R. Laws, M. Shopland, *Implications of SWRUs implemented in Ada for On-board Software*, Logica Space and Defence Systems, Cobham, England, 1987.

[Meyer 88] B. Meyer, *Object-Oriented Software Construction*, Prentice Hall, 1988.

[Sommerville 89] I. Sommerville; *Software Engineering*, 3rd edition; Addison-Wesley, 1989.

[Stadel 91] M. Stadel, "Object Oriented Programming Techniques to Replace Software Components on the Fly in a Running Program", *ACM SIGPLAN Notices*, vol. 26, no. 1, p. 99-108, January 1991.

[Stroustrup 86] B. Stroustrup, *The C++ programming language*, Addison-Wesley, 1986.

[Tindell 90] K. Tindell, "Dynamic Code Replacement and Ada", *Ada Letters*, vol. X, no. 7, p. 47-54, 1990.

[Volz et al] R.A. Volz, T.N. Mudge, G.D. Buzzard, P. Krishnan, "Translation and Execution of Distributed Ada Programs: Is it Still Ada?", *IEEE Transactions on Software Engineering*, vol.15, no.3, p. 281-292, 1989.

Software Merge: Models and Methods for Combining Changes to Programs[1]

Valdis Berzins

Computer Science Department, Naval Postgraduate School

Monterey, CA 93943

Abstract. We outline a model for programs and data, and present a formal definition of an ideal change merging operation. This model is used to develop a new semantically based method for combining changes to programs. We also evaluate the appropriateness of the change merging operation, and examine some circumstances where the specifications of a program as well as the implementations can be used to guide the change merging process in cases where the implementations conflict but the specifications do not.

Keywords: Software merging, configuration management, maintenance.

1. Introduction

Combining changes to a system is a critical issue in software development and maintenance. Software systems are created and evolve in a series of extensions and changes as requirements are extended, reformulated, or dropped, and as system faults are discovered and repaired. The versions of the system produced by this process can be arranged in a rooted acyclic graph representing the development history of the system [12]. A formalism is needed to develop accurate methods for automatically constructing new versions of the system by combining changes present in the development history. This paper presents such a formalism and a derived method for combining changes to a program. An operation for combining changes can be useful in the contexts of parallel enhancements, alternative designs, and alternative implementations.

Different branches of the version history can represent *enhancements developed in parallel* by different engineers or teams. Semantically based tools for combining changes are useful for combining the results of such parallel efforts. Different people working concurrently on a large software system usually have incomplete knowledge of what the others are doing. Semantically based tools for combining changes are essential for preserving the integrity of such systems, since people can detect inconsistencies only if they have knowledge of conflicting decisions.

---

[1]This research was supported in part by the Army Research Office under grant number ARO-145-91.

Different branches of the version history can represent *alternative designs* for the same enhancement. Automated tools for combining changes can be used to explore alternative choices for decisions in the context of software prototyping and exploratory design. The speed and accuracy provided by tool support can enable exploratory evaluations of design alternatives based on experimental measurements. These processes may be impractically slow and expensive if done manually, especially when exploring combinations of several interacting design decisions.

Different branches of the version history can also represent *alternative implementations* of a system for different operating environments that are derived from a common base version of the system. An enhancement to such a software family can be developed once based on the common root version, and propagated automatically to all of the environment-dependent variations by a tool for combining changes, as illustrated in Fig. 1 for the case of just two alternative variations. The grey boxes represent the software components that could be automatically generated based on models and methods such as those proposed in this paper. In the general case, there can be many branches of the development affected by a change, and there can be long chains of indirectly induced modifications, as discussed in [12]. Similar patterns of change propagation occur when a fault in a design decision is discovered only after several subsequent changes have been based on the faulty decision.

The problem of change propagation is also closely related to the treatment of inheritance in object-oriented programming languages. If a base version of an object-oriented program is represented by a set of class definitions, and an enhancement by a set of subclasses that inherit from the subclasses comprising the base version, then updates to the base version should ideally be automatically propagated to the enhanced version. However, in the context of current object-oriented programming languages, the effect of such a process depends very much on the internal details of the design and implementation of both the original method and the enhanced method, and there is no guarantee that the results of the process will be predictable or correct. If the enhanced method completely overrides the base version of the method, then updates to the base version will be ignored, and if it uses the base version as a subroutine, then arbitrary changes to the base version are likely to invalidate the principles on which the design of the enhancement depends, unless all of the subclasses are reviewed and redesigned in response to each update of the superclass. The

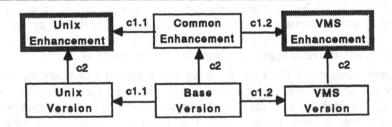

Fig. 1 Automatically Propagating Changes to Software Families

semantic model developed in this paper may lead to automated assistance for such a review process. Methods for merging programs based on this model may also enable future object-oriented programming languages with multiple inheritance to successfully coalesce several inherited methods for the same message if they do not conflict, rather than always reporting an error or forcing the choice of just one of the inherited methods.

Many software errors can be attributed to the difficulty of understanding interactions between scattered pieces of code [9]. Global inconsistencies in large software systems can be particularly difficult to detect using manual approaches because no single person may be aware of all the decisions in a mutually inconsistent set. The goal of our work is to develop accurate and reliable methods for automatically combining *changes* to a system that either guarantee correctness of the combination or pinpoint conflicts if the changes to be combined conflict with each other. Such facilities should make software development less error prone, and increase software productivity by reducing the need to repair inconsistencies introduced by system modifications, and by reducing the amount of manual effort required for combining a set of changes into a consistent version of a system. We have focused on the semantic models defining the requirements for such a system, and on formal systems for accurately deriving combinations of software changes. More work remains to develop efficient algorithms addressing complete programming languages in practical use.

Section 2 reviews some relevant previous work. Section 3 describes a semantic model for describing program behavior. This model extends approximation lattices to Boolean algebras. The purpose of these structures is to extend the ordinary data, program, and function domains to include improper values representing combinations of incompatible design decisions. This lets us formulate software merging as a total operation on this extended domain, which locates conflicts in cases where changes cannot be consistently combined. Section 4 uses the algebraic structures developed in Section 3 to provide a formal definition of an ideal operation for combining the semantics of software modifications, and determines some of the properties of this formal model. Section 5 uses the formal model developed in Section 4 to develop a new method for merging imperative programs and shows some examples of its application. Section 6 presents some conclusions and directions for future work.

2. Previous Work

There should be more work in this area, because of its potential impact on software maintenance. However, this is a new and difficult area. A general theory of combining changes is hard to formulate because such a theory should be independent of the source language to have a wide area of application. A sound theoretical framework is needed to enable the construction of software tools for combining changes, since such tools must be trustworthy and accurate to be useful in practical applications.

Automatable methods for combining two versions of a functional program are given in [2], which addresses a simplified version of the problem considered in this paper. The goal of the previous work was to construct the least common extension of two partial functions. This is a formalization of the problem of combining two upwards-compatible extensions to a common base program. An upwards-compatible extension preserves all of the behavior of the original version, but adds new functionality in some cases where the original version is not defined, i.e. produces an error message or fails to terminate. The restriction to upwards-compatible extensions enabled a formulation [2] in terms of versions rather than in terms of changes between versions, and allowed the common base program to remain implicit in the formulation. However, a solution to the restricted problem is not sufficient in many practical situations where software modifications are responses to changes in the requirements and produce incompatible changes. Such incompatible changes result in modified program behavior for some input values for which the previous version has a well-defined but inappropriate response. This paper extends the earlier work to treat such incompatible changes, and addresses imperative programs in addition to functional programs. We extend the semantic model from complete lattices to complete Boolean algebras to support incompatible changes in behavior and to increase the accuracy of conflict location. In the extended model, conflict elements identify which data elements are in conflict, in addition to indicating that a conflict has occurred. The semantic model is used to propose a method for formally deriving three-way merges that combine two potentially non-monotonic (incompatible) modifications to a base program.

The problem of merging monotonic (compatible) extensions is undecidable [2]. Since this problem is a special case of the problem addressed in the current work, the undecidability result and the conclusion that we must be content with reliable approximate solutions carry over to the current context. The intended semantics of merging compatible extensions was expressed using lattices and the approximation ordering $\sqsubseteq$ used in traditional approaches to denotational semantics of programming languages [15]. These lattice structures are also useful for formulating the intended semantics of combining incompatible changes, but they must be embedded in larger Boolean algebras to support a suitable difference operation, as explained in Section 3.

An approach to integrating both modifications and compatible extensions to while-programs is the HPR algorithm [7]. This algorithm uses program slices [16] and program dependency graphs. The method is based on principles similar to those used in compilers for data flow analysis. The HPR algorithm reports a conflict whenever the computation sequences of the two enhanced versions differ, even if they produce the same final states. The more recent YHR algorithm [17] is a more accurate version of the HPR algorithm that recognizes some equivalences between programs that compute the same results by different methods. The approximations used in both of these algorithms give partial but reliable results: in the cases for which the algorithms terminate without reporting a conflict, the results are correct with respect to reasonable criteria. Both the HPR algorithm and the YHR algorithm report conflicts when combining changes that can affect the same output variable.

This paper characterizes the intended semantics of combining changes independently of the algorithms used and the programming languages on which they operate, and proposes a method which can produce correct and conflict-free results in some cases where previous algorithms report conflicts [7, 17].

3. Semantic Domains for Software Merging

This section describes the semantic domains used to construct a formal model of the software merging operation in the next section. We embed the normal data values on which our programs operate in larger mathematical structures containing additional improper data elements to let us define the software merging operation as a total function. This has the advantage of providing diagnostic information for conflicts, since our representation allows us to show exactly which parts of the programs to be combined contain conflicts, thus locating problems, and also to show exactly which constraints conflict for each problematic point. A merge operation succeeds without producing any conflicts when all of the components of the merged program are proper data elements.

We introduce improper data elements to represent overconstrained values and undefined values to let' us represent programs that result from the combination of conflicting changes and programs that may diverge or terminate abnormally for some inputs. Specifically, our semantic domains are complete Boolean algebras which contain the complete lattices commonly used in the denotational semantics of programming languages as substructures.

A lattice is a partially ordered set that contains least upper bounds for all finite subsets. In denotational semantics the partial ordering relation of a complete lattice is written $\sqsubseteq$, and $f \sqsubseteq g$ is interpretated to mean that g is a compatible extension of f. The semantic domains for traditional programming languages and the data domains corresponding to composite data structures are mostly special kinds of function spaces. If f and g are interpreted as elements of functions spaces or as composite data structures such as arrays or trees, $f \sqsubseteq g$ means that g agrees with f at all points where f is defined, and that g may be defined at some points where f is not.

A complete lattice has a least upper bound operation $\sqcup$, a greatest lower bound operation $\sqcap$, a least element $\bot$, and a greatest element $\top$. The complete lattices used in denotational semantics contain least upper bounds for some infinite sets as well as for all the finite ones. This completeness property guarantees the existence of minimal fixed points, which are used to provide well-defined interpretations for recursive definitions of elements of the lattice. The significance of the components of a complete lattice in the context of the change merging problem can be outlined as follows.

(1) The elements of the lattice represent the software objects to be combined, where different lattices are used to represent different kinds of objects, or different aspects of the same object. For example, the elements of a syntactic domain represent program texts, and the elements of the corresponding semantic domain represent the functions computed by the programs. The data value domains represent the data values on which the semantic functions act.

(2) The bottom of the lattice $\bot$ represents a completely undefined (unconstrained) element, since every element of the lattice must be a compatible extension of $\bot$. The element $\bot$ can represent the result of a decision that has not yet been made, such as a fragment of a program text that is "to be determined", the result of a computation that diverges, or the result of a computation that terminates abnormally without delivering a result. The bottom element is an artificial value that represents the absence of useful information.

(3) The top element ⊤ of the lattice represents a completely overconstrained element, since it must be a compatible extension of all the elements in the lattice. The element ⊤ can represent the result of merging incompatible elements, and is useful in our context for representing and marking places where two or more software objects to be combined are in conflict with each other. The top element is an artificial value that represents an inconsistency.

(4) The least upper bound of two elements in a lattice is the least common extension of the two elements, which represents the intended semantics of an ideal merging operation for compatible extensions. Any upper bound is simultaneously a compatible extension of both versions to be combined. The least upper bound must be compatible with every upper bound, and hence must have minimal information content. The least upper bound of two software objects has all the features exhibited by at least one of the two objects, and no other features. For example, in a syntactic domain the least upper bound of two versions of a program contains the parts of the text that appear in both versions, and the parts of the text in each version that correspond to an undefined element ⊥ in the other version. The result contains the overconstrained element ⊤ in all the places where both versions are well defined and incompatible with each other, and the undefined element ⊥ in all of the places where both versions are undefined. In a semantic domain the least upper bound produces a function whose graph agrees with the union of the pairs in the graphs of the two partial functions, except that input values which are associated with multiple output values by the union are associated with the overconstrained value ⊤ by the least upper bound.

(5) The greatest lower bound ⊓ of two elements of the lattice represents their common part: both elements are compatible extensions of their greatest lower bound. The greatest lower bound operation is used in defining the meaning of incompatible changes. The greatest lower bound of two software objects has all of the features present in both objects, and no other features. For example, in a syntactic domain the greatest lower bound of two versions of a program represents the parts of the program text that appear in both versions, and contains undefined elements ⊥ in the places where the texts of the two versions are incompatible. The greatest lower bound in the corresponding semantic domain is a partial function which is compatible with the functions computed by both programs. This function has a defined value only for those input values for which both versions of the program compute compatible values, and has the undefined value ⊥ in all other cases.

Lattice structures are sufficient for describing operations that combine versions or that combine compatible extensions of partially defined software objects [2]. Compatible extensions are monotonic, in the sense that they add information without changing any previously defined features of the two versions. However, in practical situations, changes often remove or modify existing features of a software object in addition to adding new features. To model such nonmonotonic changes, we need a richer semantic structure.

Boolean algebras provide an appropriate structure for describing nonmonotonic modifications to software objects. Such modifications can change or remove previously defined functionality of a software object as well as adding new functionality. We use a class of countably based, complete Boolean algebras to model such modifications.

Every Boolean algebra is a lattice with respect to the partial ordering defined by the relations $x \sqsubseteq y \Longleftrightarrow xy = x \Longleftrightarrow x + y = y$. In addition to the lattice properties, a Boolean algebra also has a complement operation, which can be used to define a difference operator

$x - y = x\bar{y}$. This difference operator is the additional primitive we need to model incompatible changes and to show how they can be combined.

We use notations for operations on Boolean algebras common in circuit design. Unfortunately, these notations are not the same as those used for lattice operations in the context of denotational semantics. The correspondence is shown in Fig. 2. The notations for the Boolean constants and operators obey all the familiar algebraic properties of Boolean expressions. We have followed circuit designers in interpreting + as the inclusive-or operation, rather than as exclusive-or. (The exclusive-or interpretation for + is used in the study of Boolean rings, because this operation has all of the usual algebraic properties of addition.) The properties of the difference operator are the same as those of the set difference operator in ordinary set theory.

Although they obey the same algebraic laws, the Boolean algebras we are using have different interpretations than those used in digital circuit design, and typical models are larger. Circuit designers usually assume that the value sets of their Boolean algebras consist of the truth values T and F, or fixed-length vectors of truth values. For this class of models the cardinality of the value set is finite, and equal to a power of two. In contrast, the Boolean algebras we use are mostly function spaces, and the cardinality of the value set is typically infinite. The spaces we use are closely related to those used by circuit designers in the sense that they are generated by countable sets of atoms. An *atom* is an element that is distinct from the bottom element 0 and has no lower bounds other than itself and 0.

The Boolean algebra representing a scalar data domain is constructed as follows. The value set of the Boolean algebra is the power set of the domain of proper data elements. The proper data values are represented as singleton sets, and these values are the atoms of the Boolean algebra. The approximation relation $\sqsubseteq$ is interpreted as the subset relation, and the operations $x + y$, xy, and $x - y$ are interpreted as union, intersection, and set difference operations in the model structures. The completely undefined element 0 is represented as the empty set, and the completely overconstrained element 1 is represented as the set of all the proper data values. Each set of proper data elements represents the least upper bound of those elements.

Lattice	Boolean Algebra	Interpretation
$\top$	1	Conflict
$\bot$	0	Undefined
$x \sqsubseteq y$	$x \sqsubseteq y$	Compatible extension predicate
$x \sqcup y$	$x + y$	Compatible combination
$x \sqcap y$	xy	Common part
	$\bar{x}$	Complement
	$x - y$	Difference

Fig. 2 Correspondence between Lattice Notation and Boolean Notation

This construction is illustrated in Fig. 3 for a traffic light data type whose proper values are given by the enumeration (red, yellow, green). The normal data values are represented by the atomic elements {red}, {yellow}, and {green} of the Boolean algebra. The undefined element 0 is represented by the empty set { } in this model. The improper element {red, yellow} represents the least upper bound {red} + {yellow}, which is an over-constrained element that is obliged to be simultaneously compatible with both of the normal data values {red} and {yellow}, and hence represents the result of combining two conflicting design decisions.

Function spaces are defined by pointwise extension based on the set of all functions from atoms (normal data values) to atoms, using the rule that the functions of the Boolean function space must preserve least upper bounds of arbitrary sets. Each atom of the function space is a function whose value is the undefined element 0 everywhere except for a set of points consisting of all upper bounds for a single atom of the Boolean algebra representing the domain of the function.

4. Language-Independent Model of Software Merging

In this section we develop a formal definition of an operation for combining changes to software objects in terms of the operations of the Boolean algebras constructed in the previous section. We explore some of the properties of this definition to show that it correctly captures the informal intentions of software developers, and to clarify some aspects of software evolution.

4.1. Definition of the Model of Software Merging

We identify the meaning of a program with the function it computes. These functions are treated as elements of the Boolean function spaces defined in the previous section. The Boolean function spaces contain all ordinary partial functions as a subset. The Boolean

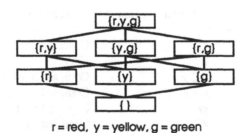

r = red, y = yellow, g = green

Fig. 3 Boolean Algebra Induced by an Atomic Data Type

spaces have been completed to include additional improper functions whose results are overspecified by conflicting constraints. These improper functions represent results of combining conflicting versions of a program, and contain information about the location and nature of the conflicting constraints. This provides a context in which the process of combining software objects can be treated as a total operation, and the results of that process can be analyzed to determine if they free of conflicts, or to identify the parts of the input space of the combined object that produce results subject to conflicting constraints.

Informally, an operation for combining changes to software objects should be able to apply the change defined by the difference between two versions v_1 and v_2 of a software object to some other version v_3 of the software object. We can characterize the change between two software objects f and g by decomposing each version into a common part and a changed part, as illustrated in Fig. 4. The diagram shows that the version g can be decomposed into two disjoint components, the greatest lower bound fg and the Boolean difference $g - f$. These two components contain all of the information in the version g because it can be recovered from them via the relation $g = (fg) + (g - f)$.

Derivation: $fg + (g - f) = fg + \bar{f}g = (f + \bar{f})g = 1g = g.$

The two components are disjoint because they satisfy the relation $(fg)(g - f) = 0.$

Derivation: $fg(g - f) = fg\,g\bar{f} = f\bar{f}g = 0g = 0.$

The software object fg represents the aspects of the object common to both versions f and g since $fg \sqsubseteq f$ and $fg \sqsubseteq g$. In terms of the functions computed by the software objects, fg is the partial function which gives the same result as both f and g for all inputs where the two versions agree, and gives the undefined value 0 for all other inputs. The software object $g - f$ represents the part of version g that differs from version f. In terms of the functions computed by the software objects, $g - f$ is the partial function which agrees with g for all inputs where f and g differ, and gives the undefined value 0 for all other inputs. The functions (fg) and $(g - f)$ are disjoint in the sense that there is no point in their domain for which both are defined (differ from the undefined element 0).

This decomposition views both versions f and g as compatible extensions of their greatest common subfunction fg. If we consider a change that transforms the initial version f into the new version g then the component $f - g$ represents a retraction: this is the behavior present in the original version f but not in the revised version g, which must be removed to transform f into g. This property is expressed by the relation $fg = f - (f - g)$.

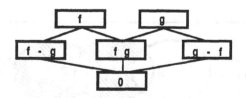

Fig. 4 Characterizing Software Changes

Derivation: $f - (f - g) = \overline{f(\overline{f\,g})} = f(\overline{f} + \overline{\overline{g}}) = 0 + fg = fg$.

Conversely, $g - f$ represents an extension: this is the new behavior added by a transformation from f to g. The roles of $f - g$ and $g - f$ are interchanged in the context of the reverse transformation from the new version g to the previous version f. The retraction and the extension characterizing a change are also disjoint from each other: $(f - g)(g - f) = 0$.

Derivation: $(f - g)(g - f) = f\overline{g}\,g\overline{f} = f\,0\,\overline{f} = 0$.

In the special case where the change from f to g is a compatible extension ($f \sqsubseteq g$), the retraction is empty ($f - g = 0$) and the common part is the entire original version ($fg = f$).

The previous discussion characterized a change in terms of its effect on one particular version of a software object. If we wish to apply that change to a different software object, then we must have some criterion for determining the intended effects of the change on all possible objects. This is an extreme form of the inductive inference problem: we are trying to infer an entire function (the intended change transformation) from its effect at only one point (the given initial version f). Clearly, this problem does not have a unique solution. One plausible approach to our extrapolation problem is the principle of minimal change, according to which no behavior other than that contained in the retraction $f - g$ may be removed by the general change transformation, and no behavior other than that contained in the extension $g - f$ may be added. This principle suggests the change transformation $\Delta[f, g]$ induced by an initial version f and a revised version g should be defined as follows:

$$\Delta[f,\ g](h) = (h - (f - g)) + (g - f).$$

This transformation removes exactly the behavior contained in the retraction ($f - g$) and adds exactly the behavior contained in the extension ($g - f$). This operation is illustrated in terms of set-theoretic operations in Fig. 5. The shaded portion shows the result of the change transformation. The diagram is simple because it shows an abstract view of the operation, in terms of the power set representation of the Boolean algebra. The elements of the sets in the diagram are the atoms of a Boolean function space, and each set represents the least upper bound of the atomic functions in the set. More concrete examples follow after we explore some of the properties of change transformations.

There is no guarantee that the principle of minimal change will always correctly capture a programmer's intentions. For example, it may be the case that the programmer intended to add some behavior h in a modification that produces version g, but that behavior was already present in the base version f ($h \sqsubseteq f$). In this case there is an

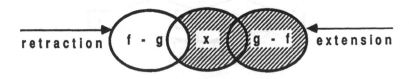

Fig. 5 The Change Transformation $\Delta[f,\ g]$

accidental overlap between the base version and the intended modification. Sine the behavior h is not contained in $(g-f)$, it will not be added when the transformation $\Delta[f, g]$ is applied to a different version that does not contain h. Only experience will tell how well our formal model captures the changes that programmers actually carry out.

4.2. Properties of the Model

We can also express the change transformation as $(g-f)+gh+(h-f)$, since

$$\Delta[f, g](h) = (h-(f-g))+(g-f)$$

$$= h\overline{(f\overline{g})}+g\overline{f}$$

$$= h(\overline{f}+\overline{\overline{g}})+g\overline{f}$$

$$= h\overline{f}+hg+g\overline{f}$$

$$= (h-f)+hg+(g-f)$$

$$= (g-f)+gh+(h-f)$$

Since $gh-gh(f+\overline{f})=gfh+g\overline{f}h$ and $g\overline{f}h\sqsubseteq\overline{f}h=(h-f)$, we note:

$$\Delta[f, g](h) = (g-f)+gh+(h-f)=(g-f)+gfh+(h-f)=g[f]h$$

where $g[f]h$ is the negmajority operation defined in [6] and corresponds to the integration operation defined in [14][2]. For economy and notational consistency, we will write $g[f]h$ for $\Delta[f, g](h)$ and $g[f]$ for $\Delta[f, g]$ in the rest of this paper. We can check that the change transformation $g[f]$ has the expected effect on the initial version f as follows.

$$g[f]f = (g-f)+fg+(f-f) = g\overline{f}+gf+0 = g$$

The intended use of a change transformation is to apply a change between two versions to a third version. However, there are two ways to do this, as illustrated in Fig. 6(a). We can view the pair of versions a and b as defining the change transformation $b[a]$, which is applied to the version c, or we can view the pair of versions a and c as defining the change transformation $c[a]$, which is applied to the version b. The following calculation shows these two processes are equivalent.

$$b[a]c = (b-a)+bc+(c-a) = (c-a)+cb+(b-a) = c[a]b$$

If we treat $[a]$ as a binary operation, this result says $[a]$ is commutative. A related question is whether the transformations $b[a]$ and $c[a]$ commute when applied to an arbitrary initial version, as illustrated in Fig. 6 (b). The following calculation shows this is indeed the case.

---

[2] The program integration operation is defined in terms of the pseudo-difference operation of a Browerian Algebra, instead of the difference operation of a Boolean algebra, because the graphs used in the algorithm do not satisfy all the properties of a Boolean algebra. Every Boolean algebra is a Browerian algebra, but Browerian algebras need not satisfy the law $1-(1-x)=x$.

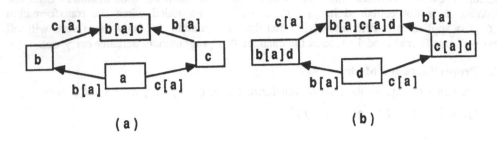

Fig. 6 Commutativity of Change Transformations

$b[a](c[a]d) = (b - a) + b(c[a]d) + ((c[a]d) - a)$

$\quad = (b\bar{a}) + (c[a]d)(b + \bar{a})$

$\quad = (b\bar{a}) + (c\bar{a} + cd + d\bar{a})(b + \bar{a})$

$\quad = (b\bar{a})(1 + c + d) + (c\bar{a})(1 + d) + d\bar{a} + cbd$

$\quad = (b + c + d)\bar{a} + bcd$

$\quad = ((b + c + d) - a) + bcd$

Interchanging b and c in this result we get

$c[a](b[a]d) = ((c + b + d) - a) + cbd = ((b + c + d) - a) + bcd = b[a](c[a]d)$

We conclude that both diagrams in Fig. 6 (b) commute: the results do not depend on which of the two possible paths we follow. Using this result and the commutativity of [a] we can show that the operation [a] is also associative.

$(c[a]d)[a]b = b[a](c[a]d) = ((b + c + d) - a) + bcd$

Substituting $(b \rightarrow d, c \rightarrow b, d \rightarrow c)$ gives us

$(b[a]c)[a]d = ((d + b + c) - a) + dbc = ((b + c + d) - a) + bcd = b[a](c[a]d)$

The significance of these results is that a set of modifications to the same base version can be combined in any order without affecting the result. This lets us view change combination with respect to a common base version as a set operation. We extend our notation to represent the result of a set of changes c_i ($1 \leq i \leq N$) to a base version b as follows:

$$[b]c_i = \bigsqcup_{i=1}^{N} \bar{b}c_i + \bigcap_{i=1}^{N} c_i.$$

5. A Method for Combining Programs

To develop a concrete method for combining changes to programs based on the theoretical framework developed in the previous section we need a representation for the function represented by a program. For programs over a language whose states consist only of the values bound to the program variables, one candidate for such a representation is the program function notation proposed in [10]. This notation identifies the meaning of a program statement with a function from states to states, where a state consists of a value for each variable in the program. Meaning functions are represented as sets of pairs, and states are represented as n-tuples of values. By convention, we arrange the variables of the program in alphabetical order to determine a unique position in the state tuple for each variable.

We illustrate our approach by using the proposed representation to construct the semantic merge for the example shown in Fig. 7 as follows. Our objective is to construct the merged version M = A[B]C, where B is the base version of the program, and A and C are two different modifications of B. The version M can be viewed as the result of applying the change A[B] to the version C, or equivalently of applying the change C[B] to the version A. We formally derive M via the meaning functions m(A), m(B), and m(C) corresponding to the versions A, B, and C. These meaning functions can be obtained from the program code as described in [10], with the following results.

$$m(B) = (x > 0 \rightarrow \{((x, y), (x, 1))\} \mid x \leq 0 \rightarrow \{((x, y), (x, -1))\})$$
$$m(A) = (x > 0 \rightarrow \{((x, y), (x, 1))\} \mid x \leq 0 \rightarrow \{((x, y), (x, 0))\})$$
$$m(C) = (x > 0 \rightarrow \{((x, y), (x, x))\} \mid x \leq 0 \rightarrow \{((x, y), (x, -1))\})$$

The state space of this program consists of pairs of values for the program variables (x, y). Thus the meaning of the base program B is a mapping that leaves the value of the state variable x invariant, and assigns either a 1 or a -1 to the state variable y, depending on the initial value of x. The notation is a shorthand for defining functions by cases, with a structure similar to guarded commands. For example, the expression $(p(a) \rightarrow \{(a, f(a))\} \mid q(a) \rightarrow \{(a, g(a))\})$ represents the set of pairs $\{(a, b) \mid (p(a) \& b = f(a)) \text{ or } (q(a) \& b = g(a))\}$, where a and b are program state tuples representing the initial state and the final state of the program, respectively.

We derive the meaning function for the merged program directly from our semantic definition of the change merging operation A[B]C, using the interpretations of the Boolean algebraic operations as unions, intersections, and set differences with respect to the

---

Base version B: if x > 0 then y := 1 else y := -1 fi

First changed version A: if x > 0 then y := 1 else y := 0 fi

Second changed version C: if x > 0 then y := x else y := -1 fi

Merged version M: if x > 0 then y := x else y := 0 fi

Fig. 7 Example of a Conditional Merge

powerset construction for our extended semantic domains.

$m(M) = m(A[B]C)$
$\quad = m(A)[m(B)]m(C)$
$\quad = (m(A) - m(B)) \cup (m(A) \cap m(C)) \cup (m(C) - m(B))$

$\quad = (x > 0 \rightarrow \{((x, y), (x, 1))\} - \{((x, y), (x, 1))\} \,|\, x \leq 0 \rightarrow \{((x, y), (x, 0))\} - \{((x, y), (x, -1))\}) \cup$
$\qquad (x > 0 \rightarrow \{((x, y), (x, 1))\} \cap \{((x, y), (x, x))\} \,|\, x \leq 0 \rightarrow \{((x, y), (x, 0))\} \cap \{((x, y), (x, -1))\}) \cup$
$\qquad (x > 0 \rightarrow \{((x, y), (x, x))\} - \{((x, y), (x, 1))\} \,|\, x \leq 0 \rightarrow \{((x, y), (x, -1))\} - \{((x, y), (x, -1))\})$

$\quad = (x > 0 \rightarrow \{\} \,|\, x \leq 0 \rightarrow \{((x, y), (x, 0))\}) \cup$
$\qquad (x > 0 \rightarrow \{((x, y), (1, 1))\} \,|\, x \leq 0 \rightarrow \{\}) \cup$
$\qquad (x > 0 \rightarrow \{((x, y), (x, x)) \,|\, x \neq 1\} \,|\, x \leq 0 \rightarrow \{\})$

$\quad = (x > 0 \rightarrow \{((x, y), (x, x))\} \,|\, x \leq 0 \rightarrow \{((x, y), (x, 0))\})$

$\quad = m(\text{if } x > 0 \text{ then } y := x \text{ else } y := 0)$

$\quad = m(M)$

The first element of each pair of state tuples contains variables that are free to range over the entire state space, while the second element of the pair contains expressions in which all occurrences of the state variables are implicitly bound by their occurrences in the first element of the pair. For example, the function $\{((x, y), (x, 1))\}$ is equivalent to the set of pairs $\{((x, y), (z, w)) \,|\, z = x \,\&\, w = 1\}$. We obtained the intersection by unifying the range descriptions (x, x) and $(x, 1)$ to obtain the intersection $(1, 1)$ via the substitution $(x = 1)$. This kind of unification yields an exact result whenever the unification succeeds. In the general case, it is possible for two syntactically distinct symbolic expressions to denote the same value, and in such cases the unification may fail even though the exact intersection may not be empty. Some stronger but possibly costly methods for recognizing the equivalence of two symbolic expressions are described in [2].

As noted in the introduction, we must be content with safe approximations or with exact methods that may in some cases fail to deliver a result because the exact change merging operation is not computable in general. It is safe but inexact to assume that inter-sections for which the unification fails are empty. Such inexact approximations can lead to merged programs that are partially correct, but may be undefined in some cases where the exact change merging operation produces a proper result. An exact representation of an intersection of the form $\{(a, f1(a))\} \cap \{(a, f2(a))\}$ is $\{(a, b) \,|\, b = f1(a) \,\&\, b = f2(a)\}$, but this representation is not easy to transform back into a program.

After deriving the meaning function of the merged program, we must reconstruct the program text from the meaning function. In this case the result is a program function representing a conditional statement, corresponding to the combined program shown in Fig. 7. This reconstruction can be determined by combining parts of the original programs: the if-then-else structure is common to all three, and the meaning functions for the subcomponents of the if-then-else match exactly the meaning functions of fragments of the original versions. The meaning functions of these fragments were determined as part of the derivation of $m(A)$, $m(B)$, and $m(C)$, so that corresponding parts of this derivation can be retraced in reverse to perform the synthesis.

Note that the result is a proper program even though both of the changes to be combined affect the same output variable y, so that both the HPR and the YHR algorithms report conflicts for this example. There is no semantic interference in this case because the two changes affect disjoint regions of the initial state space. Since the program function notation directly represents the functions computed by the programs, and the method for combining changes is directly based on the semantic definitions characterizing an ideal change combination process, correct results are assured whenever the symbolic expressions for the meaning function of the merged version can be transformed back into a program.

The transformation back into a program may be difficult or impossible to perform, and there may not be a unique solution. The conditions under which a meaning function can be realized by a program of a given form have been explored, and closed form characterizations of these conditions can be found in [10]. Automating this part of the process is subject to a tradeoff between the success rate and time spent on searching for possible solutions. The method described above is potentially capable of finding merged programs with algorithms and control structures that differ from both the base version and the two modified versions, but such solutions may be computationally expensive. To find a practical resolution of this tradeoff, we are exploring heuristics for guiding the search based on the structures of the three program versions to be combined, and on estimates of the relative efficiency of different program structures.

The process we have described is more difficult to carry out for programs containing loops. An example is shown in Fig. 8. The meaning functions for this example are shown below.

$$m(B) = m(C) = (x \geq 0 \rightarrow \{((x, y, z), (0, y, x * y))\} \mid x < 0 \rightarrow \{((x, y, z), (x, y, 0))\})$$

$$m(A) = \{((x, y, z), (0, y, x * y))\}$$

The programs in the example are simple loops for implementing multiplication. Version C has the same meaning function as the base version B, but it has been transformed to improve efficiency. Both B and C implement multiplication for only positive values of the input variable x. Version A has been modified to implement multiplation for both positive and negative values. The meaning function for the desired merge is derived as follows:

$$m(M) = m(A[B]C)$$
$$= m(A)[m(B)]m(C)$$
$$= (m(A) - m(B)) \cup (m(A) \cap m(C)) \cup (m(C) - m(B))$$

$$= \{\} \cup (x \geq 0 \rightarrow \{((x, y, z), (0, y, x * y))\}) \cup (x < 0 \rightarrow \{((x, y, z), (0, y, x * y))\})$$

$$= \{((x, y, z), (0, y, x * y))\}$$

$$= m(A)$$

We see that the meaning function for the merged version is the same as for the enhanced version A, so that A is a possible candidate for the merged version. We have instead constructed the merged version M by replacing B by C in A. This is sound because we know B and C have the same meaning function. It is desirable because C is more efficient than B, and the replacement is suggested by a heuristic that prefers implementation structures in the enhanced versions over the corresponding implementation structures in the base version. We seek to preserve the style of the original programs as far as possible by matching

Base version B:
  z := 0; while x > 0 do z:= z + y; x := x - 1 end

First changed version A:
  if x < 0 then x := -x; y := -y end;
  z := 0; while x > 0 do z:= z + y; x := x - 1 end

Second changed version C:
  z := 0;
  while x > 0 do
    if x mod 2 = 0 then x := x div 2; y := y + y
    else z:= z + y; x := x - 1 end
  end

A merged version M:
  if x < 0 then x := -x; y := -y end;
  z := 0;
  while x > 0 do
    if x mod 2 = 0 then x := x div 2; y := y + y
    else z:= z + y; x := x - 1 end
  end

Fig. 8 Example of Merging Loops

parts of the derived meaning function for the preserved program against the meaning functions for the fragments of the three given versions, and using corresponding parts of the original code in the synthesis of the merged program whenever suitable parts can be found.

We have made use of specification information in the above derivation, since we have identified the meaning of the loop with the multiplication function. The automatic procedures for deriving meaning functions give recursive equations for the meaning function of a program containing loops. We have taken the expected meaning function from the specification for the program, and checked that it satisfies the recursive equation derived directly from the program according to the methods described in [10]. If specifications are not available, then it is sometimes possible to derive a closed form for the meaning function using techniques for solving difference equations. If the recursive equations cannot be solved in closed form, it is sometimes possible to check that two recursively defined functions are equal by showing that each satisfies the equations defining the other. This allows loops to be merged whenever one of the two changes preserves the meaning function of the loop, as in the example above. This approach thus enables treatment of changes that improve the efficiency of a program.

Derivations involving loops can involve some difficult reasoning, and the method is not guaranteed to terminate in the general case. However, as we have illustrated above, this method can be used to successfully merge changes to a program even if some of the changes involve choice of different algorithms. In the HPR algorithm [7] the merged version is restricted to simulating the three original versions exactly (the same sequence of values must be read and written by corresponding program statements), where different statements in the merged version may come from different versions of the original program. The YHR algorithm allows merging of different algorithms for the same function, and can be used together with any congruence checking method, but the congruence checking method described in [17] is fairly limited in the equivalences it can recognize.

The transformation process we have described can also locate conflicts in changes that are not compatible with each other. In general, the result of the merging process is a set of pairs representing a relation on pairs of states (the initial and final states of the program). Although we would like this relation to be a function, this need no always be the case, because the union operations can associate more than one final state with an initial state. If the programs A, B, and C are free of conflicts themselves, then m(A), m(B), and m(C) are functions, and m(A)[m(B)]m(C) is a relation that associates at most two final states with each initial state. If the resulting relation is not a function, we say that it contains a conflict for each initial state that is associated with more than one final state. The programming language we consider is completely deterministic: the primitives are assignment statements, sequencing, if-then-else statements, and while-loops. Multiple-valued program relations resulting from the combination of several program modifications represent over-constrained rather than nondeterministic behavior: the program does not have a free choice of which final state to enter, but instead the unique final state of the program is required to be simultaneously compatible with all the final states associated with the initial state by the program relation. For this reason we adopt a rule that transforms multiple-valued program relations into improper functions as follows:

$$m(A[B]C)(\sigma) = \sqcup \{\tau \mid (\sigma, \tau) \in m(A)[m(B)]m(C)\},$$

where σ represents the initial program state and τ represents the final program state. Thus our structure has the inverse interpretation from the relational model for non-deterministic programs described in [13]: multiple-valued relations represent conflicts rather than non-deterministic choices.

The formulation in [13] has a discontinuous interpretation: smaller images under the relation represent more constrained behavior, except in the case of the empty image, which represents completely unconstrained behavior (for all inputs outside the domain of the relation representing the requirements). We can eliminate this discontinuity as follows. The image of a point outside the domain of the requirement is changed from the empty set to the set of all values, which is the natural representation for a "don't care" constraint. An empty image set is reinterpreted as a conflict: an unsatisfiable requirement. In this representation, the relation R' is *more defined than* R [13] (R $\sqsubseteq$ R') becomes the same as R $\supseteq$ R', but we lose the distinction between partial correctness and "don't care" conditions that require program termination but do not put any constraint on the final state. This ordering defines a Boolean algebra which supports a change merging operation for non-deterministic requirements according to the usual abstract formulation: a[b]c = $(a - b) \sqcup (a \sqcap c) \sqcup (c - b)$. In this representation, $x \sqcup y$ is $x \cap y$, $x \sqcap y$ is $x \cup y$, and $x - y$ is $x \cup \bar{y}$. For example, {a, b}[{b, c}]{b, c, d} = {a, b, d}: the merging operation removes the possible behavior {c} from the image set {b, c} (which represents a non-deterministic choice) because the left enhancement does not allow it, adds the possible behavior {a} because the left enhancement allows it, and adds the possible behavior {d} because the right enhancement allows it. This algebra also supports the familiar property {a}[{a}]{b} = {b} via a quite different calculation than in the deterministic algebra defined earlier in the paper. The details of merging code for nondeterministic programs, as opposed to merging relational specifications of nondeterministic programs, are left to a future paper.

Returning to the deterministic formulation that is our main theme here, we illustrate a combined program relation containing conflicts, the improper program function it represents, and the corresponding improper program via a simple example.

A: x := 1   m(A) = {((x), (1))}
B: x := 2   m(A) = {((x), (2))}
C: x := 3   m(A) = {((x), (3))}

m(A)[m(B)]m(C)
  = {((x), (1))} - {((x), (2))} ∪ {((x), (1))} ∩ {((x), (3))} ∪ {((x), (3))} - {((x), (2))}
  = {((x), (1))} ∪ {} ∪ {((x), (3))}
  = {((x), (y)) | y = 1 or y = 3}
  = {((x), (1 ⊔ 3))}
  = {((x), ({1} ∪ {3})))}
  = {((x), ({1,3})))}
  = m(x := {1,3})

We have converted the multiple-valued program relation into an improper function, assuming that the function space has been embedded in a Boolean algebra according to the construction explained in Section 3. The final form of the program function represents an assignment statement which binds an improper value to the -variable x. This improper value pinpoints the two inconsistent design decisions in the modified versions A and C: the value must be simultaneously compatible with both 1 and 3 to carry out both modifications. Note that the value 2 does not appear because it has been superceded by both modifications.

A software designer has several alternative approaches to resolve a conflict situation such as the one outlined above, depending on whether or not the requirements changes motivating the modifications A and C are incompatible.

The requirements changes corresponding to A and C might be compatible even though the particular program functions A and C are not compatible, because a requirement might only partially constrain program behavior, and might thus be consistent with several different program functions. This situation is illustrated in Fig. 9. We represent a requirement by the set of program functions that satisfy it (thus a requirement is formalized as a

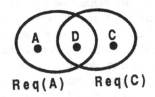

Fig. 9 Partially Overlapping Requirements

predicate on program functions, which distinguishes conforming behaviors from nonconforming behaviors). In terms of this representation, two requirements are compatible if their intersection is nonempty. In such a situation, the designer may choose to merge the two modifications A[B] and C[B] to produce a program D which computes a function D which is incompatible with both A and C, but which is compatible with both of the requirements that motivated the initial choices of the behaviors A and C. This kind of transformation requires knowledge of the requirements as well as the programs and involves the design and implementation of a completely new function D without much guidance from existing implementations of compatible subfunctions. We expect such situations to be handled by a skilled human designer. Tool support requirements are similar to those for the initial design and implementation. Providing such tool support is difficult and requires a formal approach at the conceptual modeling and functional specification stages [1, 4].

If the two requirements are incompatible, there are two ways to proceed: either evaluate the priorities of the goals supported by each and abandon the one with the lower priority, or examine the higher level goals that motivated the requirements, and seek to loosen the requirements in such a way that the higher level goals are still met but the loosened requirements have a nonempty intersection. Because the higher level goals are usually not completely formalized, we expect this part of the process to be carried out mainly by skilled people rather than by software.

6. Conclusions and Future Work

Large programming projects are characterized by concurrent efforts of a group of software engineers. The new problems that arise on such a scale involve coordinating, propagating, and reconciling the consequences of design decisions made by different people. A reliable method for combining changes to programs is an essential aspect of the computer-aided design capabilities that should be provided by software development environments for large programs. Such a capability would enable different people to concurrently develop updates to the same software object without the need for locking or mutual exclusion, and would allow the results to be combined after the independent updates have resulted in two alternative versions of the software object. Such situations may be common in large projects with aggressive schedules. A capability for combining changes is also useful in the situation where a design decision is found to be faulty after some subsequent decisions and software modifications have already been made. In such a case, the developer would back up to the version before the faulty decision, make an alternative enhancement corresponding to a different choice for the faulty decision, and then use the computer-aided change combination facilities to combine the alternative enhancement with the modifications that had been made based on the faulty decision. Such a tool would locate the places where these modifications conflict with the new design, and would guarantee the integrity of the results if no conflicts were detected.

We have provided a characterization of the semantic properties of an operation for combining changes to software objects. This characterization is independent of the programming language in which the software objects are described, and can be applied in many contexts. For example, the algorithm in [7] is correct with respect to our characterization for the cases in which it does not report any conflicts. The theory can also be applied to requirements and specifications, if we accept the view that a specification is a predicate that characterizes the set of all acceptable system behaviors, although the details of this are not explored in the current paper.

We have applied our ideal characterization of the change combination process to propose a new method for integrating changes to programs. The new method for combining changes is correct because it is based on direct representations of the functions computed by programs. Our approach has also been applied to other languages, notably PSDL. PSDL is a language for prototyping large, real-time systems, which is based on an enhanced data flow model of computation [11]. This language includes features for expressing concurrency and real-time constraints. A formal semantics of PSDL can be found in [8]. An initial version of a method for combining changes to PSDL programs has been developed [5]. We are also investigating the application of this framework to the development of program transformations that change the semantics of a program in a disciplined way [3]. Such transformations are important in software evolution, and form a complement to the meaning-preserving transformations that are used in implementing executable specification languages and in program optimization.

This paper outlines a method for merging changes to monolithic (small) imperative programs based on our semantic model. These results represent a single step towards reliable automated software merging and computer-aided configuration management. We have defined a sound calculus for deriving merged programs, and have not yet found an example of a correct conflict-free merge that cannot be derived in the calculus. However, some of these derivations can be very difficult to find. The process of deriving merged programs is nondeterministic and may fail to terminate. Heuristics for speeding up the process and limiting the search without losing the power of the method are needed, and better efficient algorithms for high resolution change merging would be useful. This paper has addressed only some of the issues that arise in small scale applications. Much more work remains to be done before this technology can be routinely applied in large-scale software development projects. The interactions between change merging and modular design should be clarified and design disciplines that limit the impact of change propagation need to be developed. Most of the work on change merging to date has focused on functions and procedures. Change merging for data types and state machines should also be explored. It is also important to recognize that the intentions of a programmer cannot always be accurately inferred from the code. Industrial strength change merging is likely to require explicit representation and processing of the requirements as well as the code.

The method reported here is a partial solution because it does not explicitly consider the requirements, and implicitly assumes that the requirements for different points in the input space are independent. This is true for any requirement of the form ALL(x: input SUCH THAT pre(x) :: SOME(y: output :: post(x, y)), which includes many but not all requirements. Some examples of diffuse requirements that do not fit this pattern are that the function to be computed must be strictly increasing and that all of the functions in an interface must provide consistent interpretations for the menu buttons.

Current practice in software development is to assign changes to different modules to different people, and to combine the results by assuming that changes to different modules do not interact. While this may be true for most of the input space in designs with loosely coupled modules, such an assumption is not safe if there is any direct or indirect data flow between the modules. Our preliminary investigations of change merging on a large scale indicate that interference can occur in sparse subsets of the input space (i.e. can be difficult to detect via testing), that a global analysis is necessary to ensure safety, and that the problems have no easy solutions.

Our vision of future facilities for software development and maintenance includes a configuration management system that provides more functions than most of the systems in current use. We expect such future systems to be sensitive to the semantics of the programming and specification languages used, to be capable of automatically merging changes and automatically analyzing the structure and content of a software design. In the long run such systems should have many capabilities related to the semantic compatibility relation ⊑ at the root of our model, such as factoring software objects into prime independent components and storing design histories in terms of prime decompositions of design decisions, with possible alternatives for each decision. A reliable change merging facility is needed to get the maximum benefit from such a vision, because engineers cannot rely on mechanically merged versions of software objects unless they have predictable properties. Such a facility would enable automatic synthesis of system variants driven by different combinations of stored choices for sets of independent design decisions. Many of the combinations that could be realized by such a system will not have been explicitly created by human designers.

A representation for software systems that decomposes software objects into independent design decisions promises to be a more useful record of a design history that the chronological sequence of steps that lead to the current configuration, because the logical dependencies are needed to understand and change a design. This logical structure may be only weakly related to the chronological order in which changes were made. It would be useful to formalize this logical structure to the point where computer-aided factoring and recombination of software objects becomes feasible. However, realizing this vision may require integrated change merging at the levels of software requirements and behavioral specifications as well as algorithms and data structures.

References

1. V. Berzins, M. Gray and D. Naumann, "Abstraction-Based Software Development", *Comm. of the ACM 29*, 5 (May 1986), 402-415.

2. V. Berzins, "On Merging Software Extensions", *Acta Informatica 23*, Fasc. 6 (Nov. 1986), 607-619.

3. V. Berzins, B. Kopas, Luqi and A. Yehudai, "Transformations in Specification-Based Software Evolution", Technical Report NPS 52-90-034, Computer Science Department, Naval Postgraduate School, 1990.

4. A. Berztiss, "The Set-Function Approach to Concptual Modeling", in *Information Systems Design Methodologies: Improving the Practice*, T. Olle, H. Sol and A. Verrijn-Stuart (editor), North-Holland, Amsterdam, 1986, 107-144.

5. D. Dampier, "A Model for Merging Different Versions of a PSDL Program", M. S. Thesis, Computer Science, Naval Postgraduate School, Monterey, CA, June 1990.

6. C. A. R. Hoare, "A Couple of Novelties in the Propositional Calculus", *Zeitschrift fur Mathematische Logik und Grundlagen der Mathematik 31*, 2 (1985), 173-178.

7.   S. Horowitz, J. Prins and T. Reps, "Integrating Non-Interfering Versions of Programs", *Trans. Prog. Lang and Systems 11*, 3 (July 1989), 345-387.

8.   B. Kraemer, Luqi and V. Berzins, "Denotational Semantics of a Real-Time Prototyping Language", Technical Report NPS 52-90-033,, Computer Science Department, Naval Postgraduate School, 1990.

9.   S. Letovsky and E. Soloway, "Delocalized Plans and Program Comprehension", *IEEE Software 3*, 3 (May 1986), 41-49.

10. R. C. Linger, H. D. Mills and B. I. Witt, *Structured Programming: Theory and Practice*, Addison Wesley, Reading, MA, 1979.

11. Luqi, V. Berzins and R. Yeh, "A Prototyping Language for Real-Time Software", *IEEE Trans. on Software Eng. 14*, 10 (October, 1988), 1409-1423.

12. Luqi, "A Graph Model for Software Evolution", *IEEE Trans. on Software Eng. 16*, 8 (Aug. 1990), 917-927.

13. A. Mili, W. Xiao-Yang and Y. Qing, "Specification Methodology: An Integrated Relational Approach", *Software Practice and Expereience 16*, 11 (Nov. 1986), 1003-1030.

14. T. Reps, "On the Algebraic Properties of Program Integration", Computer Sciences Technical Report 856, University of Wisconsin, Madison, 1989.

15. J. Stoy, *Denotational Semantics: The Scott-Strachey Approach to Programming Language Theory*, MIT Press, 1977.

16. M. Weiser, "Program Slicing", *IEEE Trans. on Software Eng. SE-10*, 4 (July 1984), 352-357.

17. W. Yang, S. Horowitz and T. Reps, "A Program Integration Algorithm that Accomodates Semantics-Preserving Transformations", in *Proc. 4th ACM Software Eng. Notes Symposium on SOftware Development Environments*, Irvine, CA, Dec. 1990, 133-143.

A Theory for Software Design Extraction

Ben A. Sijtsma[1] and Joseph W.L.J. Mager

Shell Research B.V.

Koninklijke/Shell-Laboratory, Amsterdam

P.O. Box 3003, 1003 AA Amsterdam, The Netherlands

Abstract

In this paper we consider the problem of extracting a design for an existing software system. This problem is clearly relevant to understanding and maintaining software systems. The basis of our approach is a formalization of top-down design with information hiding. This formalization allows an accurate and concise formulation of constructing an a posteriori design for a software system using only the source text. The theory predicts that in general there are many possible designs and that these designs can be partially ordered and form a lattice. The lattice has a smallest element and this element is the best top-down design in the sense that it has the most information hiding. We show how this element can be constructed.

A tool has been built on the basis of the theory developed here. It has been applied to many software systems, written in various programming languages. These applications have shown that the theory is successful and can be used for understanding, documenting, maintaining, and restructuring software systems, without requiring from the user a detailed knowledge of the underlying theory.

Keywords: Software Engineering, Reverse Engineering, Maintenance, Theory of Design Extraction.

1 Introduction

For software maintenance, as well as any other activity involving the understanding of a software system, it is important to know the underlying design. Unfortunately, the design of a system is often poorly documented. Moreover, the design evolves, or may even deteriorate, as the system is maintained, so, the original design documentation becomes obsolete. However, the maintainer needs to know the design so that he can safely adapt the system without introducing unwanted interactions or side effects.

In this paper we develop a theory for extracting the design from an existing software system using only the source text. The design that is extracted is a top-down design with information hiding [7]. It turns out that generally there are many possible designs and that these designs can be partially ordered and that they form a lattice [5]. The lattice has a smallest element and this element is the best top-down design in the sense that it has the most information hiding.

A great deal of research has been carried out in reconstructing or recovering the design. A common approach is to use the cross-reference information. In [4, 6, 8, 9] this information is used to define various (pseudo-)metrics, like "cohesion", "coupling",

---

[1]to whom correspondence should be addressed

"alteration distance", and "similarity". These metrics are then used to partition the units into clusters. The initial hierarchy of clusters thus obtained is in some cases improved upon by merging certain clusters. In [3] domain information too is employed to recover the design. In our approach we also use the cross-reference information but the difference is that we do not define any metric but develop a formalization of top-down design instead. As a result of this formalization we are able to give a concise and formal description of design extraction.

The structure of this note is as follows. In Section 2 we explain our notation for and operations on relations. Section 3 deals with a formalization of top-down design with information hiding. Section 4 contains the formal statement of what we mean by software design extraction. In Section 5 some properties of structure extraction are given and in Section 6 we briefly consider the set of all possible top-down designs for a system. The construction of the best top-down design is given in Section 7. Finally, the conclusions are presented in Section 8.

2 Relations

In the following we will use relations quite a lot. For completeness' sake some conventional notations are introduced below.

A relation on a set D is a set of pairs in $D \times D$, i.e. a relation is a subset of $D \times D$. If R is a relation on D and $a, b \in D$, then $a \, R \, b$ denotes $(a, b) \in R$. If it is clear from the context we will often omit "on D" in "a relation on D".

Note that relations are sets and hence usual set operations, such as $\cup$ and $\cap$, can be applied to them. The composition is another operation on relations. The composition of two relations, say R_1 and R_2, is denoted by $R_1 \circ R_2$, and is defined by $R_1 \circ R_2 = \{a, c : (\exists b :: a \, R_1 \, b \wedge b \, R_2 \, c) : (a, c)\}$. We assume that $\circ$ has higher binding power than $\cap$ or $\cup$, so $A \cup B \circ C$ means $A \cup (B \circ C)$.

Let R be a relation on D. Then R^n, where n is a natural number, is defined inductively by: $R^0 = \{a : a \in D : (a, a)\}$ and $R^{n+1} = R \circ R^n$.

A relation R is transitive if and only if $R^2 \subseteq R$. Note that $R^2 \subseteq R$ implies that $R^n \subseteq R$, for all $n > 0$. The transitive closure of a relation R, denoted by R^+, is defined by $R^+ = (\cup n : n > 0 : R^n)$. The transitive *reflexive* closure of a relation R, denoted by R^*, is defined by $R^* = R^0 \cup R^+$. Alternatively, R^+ can be defined by $R^+ = R^* \circ R = R \circ R^*$.

The inverse of a relation R, denoted by R^-, is defined by $a \, R^- \, b \equiv b \, R \, a$. Some straightforward properties of the inverse are: $(R_1 \circ R_2)^- = (R_2^- \circ R_1^-)$, $(R^+)^- = (R^-)^+$, and $(R^*)^- = (R^-)^*$. In view of this we will write R^{-+} to denote either $(R^-)^+$ or $(R^+)^-$; the same goes for R^*.

Let R be a relation on D and $d \in D$. The set $d \, R$ is defined by $d \, R = \{a \in D : d \, R \, a : a\}$. Similarly, the set $R \, d$ is defined by $R \, d = \{a \in D : a \, R \, d : a\}$, i.e. $d \, R = R^- \, d$.

A relation R is *cyclic* if and only if $(\exists d :: d \, R^+ \, d)$ and R is *acyclic* if it is not cyclic. Furthermore, a relation R on D is weakly connected if and only if $(\exists d :: (\forall a : a \in D : d \, R^* \, a))$. Such a d is called the root of R. A weakly connected relation R on D is a *tree* on D if the root has no parents and every element but the root has precisely one parent, i.e. if $R \, root = \emptyset$ and $(\forall a \in D : a \neq root : (\exists! b :: b \, R \, a))$.

3 Top-down design

The a posteriori generation of a design for an application will be a top-down design. This does not imply that we assume that the application has been developed top down. As is commonly known, hardly any substantial piece of software is designed in a top-down fashion. Quite frequently a design decision is revoked at a later stage and replaced by a more suitable one. However, once the software for an application has been completed, it is possible "to fake a rational design."

The principle of top-down design might be defined as follows.

> To build a system, or any part of it, decompose it into a number of subsystems and construct the system using these subsystems and possibly others which have already been defined. Each subsystem can be regarded as part of the system and can be built using the same principle.

In this definition a system is essentially the same as a subsystem and instead of using these terms, the term *module* will be used from now on. To be able to determine a top-down design for a piece of software, we have to formalize this notion.

According to the definition, the top-down design starts with a certain module. Moreover, at every stage of a top-down design new modules can be *introduced* and existing modules can be *used*. That modules introduce other modules can be considered as a relation on the set of all modules. Let D be the set of all modules. Since a design is finite the set D is finite. Assume that the top-down design starts with module $root \in D$. Let I be the following relation on D:

$$(\forall a, b \in D :: a \ I \ b \equiv \text{"module } a \text{ introduces module } b\text{"}).$$

The relation I has the following properties:

$$I^+ \ root = \emptyset, \text{ i.e. } root \text{ is not introduced,} \tag{1}$$

$$(\forall a : a \neq root : (\exists!b :: b \ I \ a)), \text{ every module but } root \text{ is introduced only once,} \tag{2}$$

$$I \text{ is acyclic, i.e. no module introduces itself whether directly or indirectly, and} \tag{3}$$

$$I \text{ is weakly connected, i.e. all modules contribute to the system.} \tag{4}$$

If (1) and (2) hold, then it can be shown that (3) and (4) are equivalent, so one of them suffices. Moreover, (1) to (4) are equivalent to the statement that I is a *tree* with root *root*.

The I relation models the introduction of modules. Another relation will be needed to model that modules use other modules which have already been introduced. This relation on D is called U and has the following meaning:

$$(\forall a, b \in D :: a \ U \ b \equiv \text{"module } a \text{ uses module } b\text{"}).$$

It is natural to assume that

$$I \cap U = \emptyset, \text{ i.e. no module is introduced and used by the same module.} \tag{5}$$

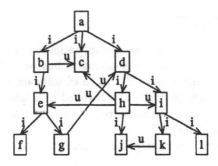

Figure 1: Example of a top-down design

More restrictions on U will be made. To exemplify these, consider the top-down design in Figure 1. The arrows marked with an "i" denote pairs in I; similarly, the arrows marked with a "u" denote pairs in U. The source of an arrow is the first element of a pair and the destination is the second one.

Note that in Figure 1 the relation $I \cup U$ is cyclic, since $d\ I\ h$, $h\ U\ e$, $e\ I\ g$, and $g\ U\ d$. The danger of circularities is that "the work never gets done." Module d delegates some of its functionalities to module h; module h achieves its functionality by using e. But e relies, indirectly via module g on the functionality of d. Hence if $I \cup U$ is cyclic, there is a danger that part of the functionality will never be implemented, due to infinite delegation. Hence, we assume that

$$I \cup U \text{ is acyclic} \tag{6}$$

If the u-arrow from g to d would be removed, then we could still add quite a few new u-arrows in Figure 1, without being in conflict with (5) and (6). Hence it is still possible that a top-down design deteriorates into a spaghetti-like structure.

One of the obvious ways of preventing "spaghetti" is to take $U = \emptyset$. This might be termed a *strict* top-down design: every module is used only where it is designed and there is no re-using of modules. This is of course too restrictive. If the relation U is considered as "reuse," a first lessening of the restriction $U = \emptyset$ is to allow that children of the same parent, with respect to the I-relation, can use each other. To give an example: if module a introduces $c_1, \ldots, c_n$ then the lessening would allow that c_i uses c_j. Note that the restriction "$(I \cup U)$ is acyclic" prevents cyclic use.

However, restricting U to children of the same parent is in conflict with the principle of top-down design. An example is given. At the design of a it is decided to introduce b and c and it is expected that b uses c. At the design of b it is decided to delegate some of its tasks to d. If U is restricted to children of the same parent, then b could use c, but d which performs some of the tasks of b, could not. This would be counterproductive. Such a U would discourage splitting a module into smaller ones and thus discourage top-down design. Hence we arrive at

$$(\forall a, b \in D : a\ U\ b : (\exists c :: c\ I^+\ a \wedge c\ I\ b)). \tag{7}$$

That is, a user (a) of a certain module (b) is directly or indirectly introduced by the introducer (c) of that certain module. Hence, the only modules that can use b must be introduced, directly or indirectly, by the I-parent of b. Thus every module is hidden from all other modules that are not contained in the I-tree starting at its introducer. Therefore, equation (7) has a nice intuitive content and forms another justification for the restriction. We call this restriction our version of the principle of information hiding [7]. Since

$$(\exists c :: c\ I^+\ a \wedge c\ I\ b) \equiv (\exists c :: a\ I^{-+}\ c \wedge c\ I\ b) \equiv (\exists c :: a\ I^{-+} \circ I\ b) \equiv a\ I^{-+} \circ I\ b,$$

equation (7) is equivalent to $U \subseteq I^{-+} \circ I$.

We will not place more restrictions on what we think is a good top-down design. The obtained properties are summarized in the following definition.

Definition 1 A top-down design on a set D is a pair (I, U), where I and U are relations on D, such that

    a) I is a tree on D,

    b) $I \cap U = \emptyset$,

    c) $I \cup U$ is acyclic, and

    d) $U \subseteq I^{-+} \circ I$.

A top-down design is implemented in a programming language. Every module will result in a unit of the programming language. The exact nature of a unit depends on the programming language used. For example, in the Fortran-77 programming language units are subroutines, functions, the main program, and common blocks. In the C programming language functions, global variables, and structures can be considered as units, although other choices are possible, e.g. files. In Pascal units are procedures, functions, the main program, user-defined types, and global variables.

So a module in a top-down design results in a unit in the source text. If in a top-down design module a introduces module b, then this generally means that in the source text the unit corresponding to module a refers to the unit corresponding to module b. If, in a Fortran example, module a corresponds to subroutine a and module b corresponds to subroutine b, then a introduces b generally results in a CALL to b from subroutine a. If module b corresponds to a common block, then subroutine a will generally use an element of common block b.

That module a *uses* module b also results in a reference from the unit corresponding to a to the unit corresponding to b. Thus in the source text the references resulting from I and the ones from U are *indistinguishable*. This implies that the source text does not contain the information of how the program was designed. Making again a distinction between these references is precisely the problem that is addressed in this paper.

4 The Problem

As stated at the end of the previous section, a source text can be considered as a set of units. The source text explicitly contains for every unit the information which other units it refers to. Hence an abstraction of the source text is a set and a relation on that set. If D is the set of units, then the relation R on D will have the following meaning:

$$(\forall a, b \in D :: a\ R\ b \equiv \text{"unit } a \text{ refers to unit } b\text{"}).$$

In the following we will not consider source texts any more, but assume the existence of a set and a relation on this set. As will be clear, R models the cross-reference information. However, we will make a simplifying assumption. We assume that the relation is weakly connected. That is, it is assumed that there is a root, which generally will be the main program. Furthermore, every unit makes some contribution to the program, i.e. we do not consider any dead code or variables that are never referred to.

We will like to make an additional remark on the relation between the cross-reference relation and the relation R. There are other relations than "refer," for example "instanciation," "implementation," and "inheritance." In principle one should include those pairs in R that are thought to be important for the design. The tool we have constructed based upon the theory presented here, extracts those pairs from the source text that can be considered as design decisions. The pairs are extracted depend on the programming language of the software system.

We are now able to state our problem.

Definition 2 A weakly-connected relation R on D *complies* with a top-down design (I, U) on D if and only if $U \subseteq R \subseteq I \cup U$.

A few remarks concerning this definition are in order. The requirement $U \subseteq R$ means that the top-down design does not contain U-pairs that cannot be found in R, i.e. there are no U-pairs that do not have their counterpart in the program text. The requirement that $R \subseteq I \cup U$ means that every R-pair must be either in I or in U, i.e. all R-pairs must have their counterpart in the top-down design.

From the definition it seems that the modules of the top-down design are the units from the program text. There is no objection to this view. However, notice that if R complies with a top-down design (I, U) then $R \subseteq I \cup U$ and $I \cup U$ is acyclic. Thus R is acyclic. This means that only for acyclic R we can hope to find a top-down design. Now, if R is a cyclic relation on D, then it is possible to consider the relation on the set of *strongly connected components* [1] induced by R. This induced relation is weakly connected if R is weakly connected and *acyclic* as well. Since the units in a strongly connected component are closely related, i.e. they all refer to each other, either directly or indirectly, it is save to assume that these units were introduced simultaneously. This is precisely the idea behind taking the strongly connected components. In the case that R is cyclic the modules are the strongly connected components and the relation is the one induced by R. Now the theory developed here becomes applicable, and it can also be argued convincingly that it is applied properly.

In other approaches to design recovery one considers a file as a module. It is then assumed that the source text is contained in a number of files and that a file consists of conceptually related units (see for example [4] and [8]). We, however, think that just because of maintenance this last assumption will often be violated. Therefore, we prefer the approach given above.

In the following we will use weakly connected and acyclic relations quite a lot and, therefore, we have defined a name for them.

Definition 3 A relation is a *refer* relation if and only if it is weakly connected and acyclic.

In the above it is shown that only for refer relations a top-down design might exist. In Section 7 it will be shown that every refer relation has a top-down design. Another important question is whether there is exactly one top-down design for a refer relation. The answer is NO! Generally there are quite a number of different top-down design for a refer relation. A simple example is given in Figure 2. Figure 2(i) depicts the refer relation. Figure 2(ii) and (iii) are two possible top-down designs. In Section 6 it will be shown that

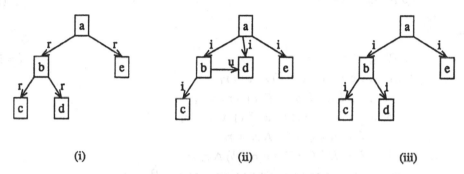

     (i)   (ii)   (iii)

Figure 2: Example of more than one top-down design

the set of all top-down designs has a structure. But before more can be said about this structure some properties concerning complies will be discussed.

5 Properties of comply

The goal of this section is to give a more simple characterization of *comply* than the one given in definition 2. Determining a top-down design for a refer relation R amounts to finding I and U such that they comply with R. The following lemma states that U is determined by R and I.

Lemma 4 If R complies with (I, U) then $U = R \setminus I$.

Proof.

$$
\begin{aligned}
&U \subseteq R \subseteq (I \cup U) \\
\Rightarrow\quad &U \setminus I \subseteq R \setminus I \subseteq (I \cup U) \setminus I \\
\Rightarrow\quad &\{I \cap U = \emptyset\} \\
&U \subseteq R \setminus I \subseteq U \\
\equiv\quad &U = R \setminus I \qquad\qquad\qquad \square
\end{aligned}
$$

The above lemma allows us to write "R complies with I" for "R complies with $(I, R \setminus I)$," as we will do in the following.

Our principle of information hiding is expressed in condition d) of definition 1. In proofs, however, alternative but equivalent conditions are handy in relation with the notion of comply.

Theorem 5 Let R be a refer relation on D with root r_r and let I be a tree on D with root r_i. Then

$$R \setminus I \subseteq I^{-+} \circ I \tag{8}$$
$$\equiv R \subseteq I^{-*} \circ I \tag{9}$$
$$\equiv (\forall a, b : a\ I\ b : R\ b \subseteq a\ I^*) \wedge r_r = r_i \tag{10}$$
$$\equiv I \circ R^- \subseteq I^* \wedge r_r = r_i \tag{11}$$

Proof.

$$I \circ R^- \subseteq I^* \wedge r_r = r_i \tag{= 11}$$
$$\equiv (\forall a, c : a\ I \circ R^-\ c : a\ I^*\ c) \wedge r_r = r_i$$
$$\equiv (\forall a, b, c : a\ I\ b \wedge c\ R\ b : a\ I^*\ c) \wedge r_r = r_i$$
$$\equiv (\forall a, b : a\ I\ b : (\forall c : c\ R\ b : a\ I^*\ c)) \wedge r_r = r_i$$
$$\equiv (\forall a, b : a\ I\ b : R\ b \subseteq a\ I^*) \wedge r_r = r_i$$
$$\equiv (\forall a, b : a\ I\ b : R\ b \subseteq I^{-*}\ a \wedge a\ I\ b) \wedge r_r = r_i \tag{= 10}$$
$$\equiv \{I \text{ is a tree, } R \text{ is acyclic and weakly connected}\} .$$
$$\quad (\forall b : b \neq r_i : R\ b \subseteq (I^{-*} \circ I)b) \wedge R\ r_r = R\ r_i = \emptyset$$
$$\equiv (\forall b :: R\ b \subseteq (I^{-*} \circ I)b)$$
$$\equiv R \subseteq I^{-*} \circ I \tag{= 9}$$
$$\equiv \{I \subseteq I^{-*} \circ I\}\ R \cup I \subseteq I^{-*} \circ I$$
$$\equiv R \setminus I \cup I \subseteq (I^{-+} \circ I) \cup I$$
$$\equiv \{I \text{ is a tree}\}\ R \setminus I \subseteq I^{-+} \circ I \qquad \square \tag{= 8}$$

The theorem above contains six different equivalent formulations of information hiding, The $(8) \equiv (10)$ is perhaps the most illustrative one. It states that R and I have the same root. Furthermore, it states that all the modules that refer to a certain module are members of the I-tree starting at the introducer of that specific module. Hence, that introducer hides this specific module from all modules that are not part of the I-tree starting at the introducer.

In proofs, equivalence $(10) \equiv (11)$ of theorem 5 will be used frequently. An example is contained in the following lemma. Theorem 5(11) states an upper bound for $I \circ R^-$; the next lemma gives upper bounds for $I^+ \circ R^-$ and $I \circ R^{-+}$.

Lemma 6 Let R be a refer relation on D and let I be a tree on D such that $R \subseteq I^{-*} \circ I$. Then (a) $I^+ \circ R^- \subseteq I^*$ and (b) $I \circ R^{-+} \subseteq I^* \cup R^{-+}$.

Proof. (a)

$$I^+ \circ R^- \subseteq I^* \circ I \circ R^- \subseteq \{\text{theorem 5}\}\ I^* \circ I^* = I^*.$$

(b) We only give an outline. It can be shown by induction on k that $(\forall k : k \geq 1 : I \circ (R^-)^k \subseteq I^* \cup R^{-+})$. The base case is implied by (a). The step case is obtained by applying the induction hypothesis and (a). $\qquad\square$

An interpretation for (b) of the previous lemma is as follows. A direct or indirect referrer to a certain module is either a member of the I-tree starting at the introducer of that certain module or it refers directly or indirectly to that introducer. The following lemma gives another upper bound, this time for I^*.

Lemma 7 Let R be a refer relation on D and let I be a tree on D, such that $R \subseteq I^{-*} \circ I$. Then $I^* \subseteq R^*$.

Proof. From theorem 5 it can be inferred that R and I have the same root; let *root* be that root. It is sufficient to show that $(\forall b :: I^* b \subseteq R^* b)$. This is done by proving with induction on k that $(\forall k : k \geq 0 : (\forall b : root R^k b : I^* b \subseteq R^* b))$. The base case is trivial and left to the reader. The step case is as follows. Let $root R^{k+1} b$ and assume that $a I^* b$. If $a = b$ then clearly $a R^* b$. Thus assume that $a \neq b$, i.e. $a I^+ b$.

$$a I^+ b \wedge root R^{k+1} b$$
$$\equiv \quad (\exists c, d :: a I^* d \wedge root R^k c \wedge d I b \wedge c R b)$$
$$\Rightarrow \quad \{\text{theorem } 5((9) \equiv (10)) \text{ and assumption}\}$$
$$(\exists c, d :: a I^* d \wedge d I^* c \wedge root R^k c \wedge c R b)$$
$$\equiv \quad (\exists c :: a I^* c \wedge root R^k c \wedge c R b)$$
$$\Rightarrow \quad \{\text{induction hypothesis}\}$$
$$(\exists c :: a R^* c \wedge c R b)$$
$$\equiv \quad a R^+ b \qquad\qquad\qquad\square$$

Corollary 8 If R and I satisfy the conditions of lemma 7 then $I \subseteq R^+$.

Proof. The proof follows immediately since $I \subseteq I^*$ and $\neg(a I a)$. $\qquad\square$

Now all the ingredients are there to show a simple relation between a refer relation and its top-down design.

Theorem 9 Let R be a refer relation on a set D and I a tree on D then

$$R \text{ complies with } I \equiv R \subseteq I^{-*} \circ I.$$

Proof. Due to theorem $5((8) \Rightarrow (9))$ the $\Rightarrow$ part is trivial. The $\Leftarrow$ part is as follows. The pair $(I, R \setminus I)$ is a top-down design because (a) I is a tree by assumption, (b) $I \cap R \setminus I = \emptyset$ by trivial inspection, (c) $I \cup R \setminus I$ is acyclic, since

$$I \cup R \setminus I \subseteq I \cup R \subseteq \{\text{Corollary } 8\} R^+,$$

and R is acyclic, and (d) $R \setminus I \subseteq I^{-+} \circ I$ holds due to theorem $5((9) \Rightarrow (8))$. Now that it has been established that $(I, R \setminus I)$ is a top-down design it is obvious that R complies with it. $\qquad\square$

The importance of the theorem above is that for finding a top-down design for R only trees that satisfy the information-hiding property need to be considered. All the other requirements such as $U \subseteq R \subseteq I \cup U$ and "$I \cup U$ is acyclic" are taken care of.

6 A lattice of top-down designs

In Section 4 we have shown that in general there are several top-down designs for a certain refer relation. That the set of all possible top-down designs has a nice structure itself is the topic of this section. For this set a notation is introduced.

Definition 10 Let R be a refer relation. Then T_R is defined by

$$T_R = \{I : I \text{ is a tree} \wedge R \text{ complies with } (I, R \setminus I) : I\}.$$

It is possible to define a meaningful partial ordering on T_R. A first step towards such an ordering is the following lemma. It states that if I_0 and I_1 are two top-down designs for a certain refer relation and module b is introduced by a in I_0 and by c in I_1, then either a introduces c in I_0 (in)directly or c introduces a in I_1 (in)directly.

Lemma 11 Let R be a refer relation. Let I_0, and $I_1 \in T_R$. Then

$$I_0 \circ I_1^- \subseteq I_0^* \cup I_1^{-*}$$

Proof.

$$
\begin{aligned}
& I_0 \circ I_1^- \\
= \; & I_0 \circ I_1^- \cap I_0 \circ I_1^- \\
\subseteq \; & \{I_i \subseteq R^+\} \\
& I_0 \circ R^{-+} \cap R^+ \circ I_1^- \\
\subseteq \; & \{\text{lemma 6(b) and calculus}\} \\
& (I_0^* \cup R^{-*}) \cap (R^* \cup I_1^{-*}) \\
= \; & (I_0^* \cap R^*) \cup (I_0^* \cap I_1^{-*}) \cup (R^{-*} \cap R^*) \cup (R_0^{-*} \cap I_1^{-*}) \\
= \; & \{I_i^* \subseteq R^* \text{ and } R \text{ is acyclic}\} \\
& I_0^* \cup I_1^{-*} \cup (I_0^* \cap I_1^{-*}) \cup R^0 \\
= \; & I_0^* \cup I_1^{-*} \qquad\qquad \square
\end{aligned}
$$

Consider the conclusion of lemma 11. Suppose that the second part of the union makes no contribution at all, i.e. suppose that $I_0 \circ I_1^- \subseteq I_0^*$. This implies, since I_0 and I_1 obviously have a common root, that I_0 is a top-down design for I_1 (see also theorems 5 and 9). Struck by this observation, we decided to choose this for defining a relation on top-down designs.

Definition 12 Let R be a refer relation. The relation $\sqsubseteq_R$ on T_R is defined by

$$I_0 \sqsubseteq_R I_1 \equiv I_1 \in T_{I_0}.$$

The expression $I_0 \sqsubseteq_R I_1$ can be read as "I_0 is a better top-down design than I_1." Space limitations prevent us from showing that $\sqsubseteq_R$ is indeed a partial ordering. However, the interested reader is probably able to produce the proof himself with the help of the following lemma. This lemma gives an equivalent definition of $\sqsubseteq_R$.

Lemma 13 Let R be a refer relation. Let $I_0, I_1 \in T_R$. Then

$$I_1 \in T_{I_0} \equiv I_1 \subseteq I_0^+.$$

Proof. That $I_1 \in T_{I_0}$ implies $I_1 \subseteq I_0^+$ is a direct consequence of corollary 8. To prove the $\Leftarrow$-part of the equivalence we use theorem 5. Since $I_0, I_1 \in T_R$ it is trivial that I_0 is an acyclic module structure, and that I_1 is a tree. We may also conclude from this that I_0 and I_1 have a common root. So, all we need to prove is that $I_1 \circ I_0^- \subseteq I_1^*$.

$$
\begin{aligned}
& I_1 \circ I_0^- \\
= & \{I_1 \subseteq I_0^+ \Rightarrow (I_1 = I_1 \cap I_0^+\} \\
& (I_1 \cap I_0^+) \circ I_0^- \\
= & (I_1 \circ I_0^-) \cap (I_0^+ \circ I_0^-) \\
\subseteq & (I_1 \circ I_0^-) \cap I_0^* \\
\subseteq & \{\text{lemma 11}\} \\
& (I_1^* \cup I_0^{-*}) \cap I_0^* \\
= & (I_1^* \cap I_0^*) \cup (I_0^{-*} \cap I_0^*) \\
\subseteq & I_1^* \cup I_0^0 \\
= & I_1^* \qquad\qquad \square
\end{aligned}
$$

The set T_R with partial ordering $\sqsubseteq_R$ is a lattice [5]. That is, every pair of top-down designs has a greatest lower bound and a least upper bound. Or, more formally, if I_0 and I_1 are two top-down designs, then there exists a top-down design I_l, the greatest lower bound, such that

$$I_l \sqsubseteq_R I_0 \wedge I_l \sqsubseteq_R I_1 \wedge (\forall I \in T_R : I \sqsubseteq_R I_0 \wedge I \sqsubseteq_R I_1 : I \sqsubseteq_R I_l),$$

and furthermore, there exists a top-down design I_u, the least upper bound, such that

$$I_0 \sqsubseteq_R I_u \wedge I_1 \sqsubseteq_R I_u \wedge (\forall I \in T_R : I_0 \sqsubseteq_R I \wedge I_1 \sqsubseteq_R I : I_u \sqsubseteq_R I).$$

The proof of this fact is too long to be included here. This fact gives us a nice clue which element of T_R we actually want to recover as the design. Since T_R is a finite set and is a lattice it has a maximal and a minimal element. That is, there is a top-down design that is larger, with respect to $\sqsubseteq_R$, than any other top-down design; and there is a top-down design that is smaller than any other. The maximal element of T_R is rather uninteresting; it is the top-down design where the *root* introduces all other modules, so it is the flattest possible tree. The minimal element, however, is more interesting and constitues the topic of the following section.

7 The minimal element of T_R

In this section we will give an explicit formulation for the minimal element of T_R in terms of R. To be able to do so some notions concerning *paths* in a relation have to be introduced.

If R is a relation then the sequence $a_0, a_1, \ldots, a_n$ is a *path* in R if and only if ($\forall i : 0 < i \leq n : a_{i-1} \ R \ a_i$). Furthermore, $PA_R(a, b)$ denotes the set of all paths in R from a to b and $\cap PA_R(a, b)$ denotes the set of elements that lie on all paths in R from a to b. Notice that if $a \ R^+ \ b$ then at least $a, b \in \cap PA_R(a, b)$ and if $\neg(a \ R^+ \ b)$ then $\cap PA_R(a, b) = \emptyset$.

The following theorem provides a major insight into the top-down designs for a certain relation.

Theorem 14 Let R comply with I and let *root* be the root of R and I.
Then $x \ I^+ \ y \Rightarrow x \in \cap PA_R(root, y)$.

Proof. Only an outline is given. Show by induction on k that $x \in \{root, x_1, x_2, \ldots, x_k\}$, where
$root \ R \ x_1 \ R \ \ldots \ R \ x_k \ R \ y$, i.e. show that x lies on every path from the *root* to y. The base case and the step case essentially amount to using lemma 6(a). □

We know that $I \subseteq I^+$, so if x introduces y then x is a member of all paths from the root to y.

Corollary 15 $x \ I \ y \Rightarrow x \in \cap PA_R(root, y)$.

In other terms, the corollary above means that x is a so-called *dominator* of y (see [2]). Let Figure 3 represent all paths in R from the *root* to d, where *root* a, b, c, and d are the only elements which lie on all paths from the *root* to d.

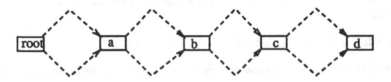

Figure 3: Paths in R

Corollary 15 implies that either *root* $I \ d$, $a \ I \ d$, $b \ I \ d$, or $c \ I \ d$. Moreover, it also implies that either *root* $I \ c$, $a \ I \ c$, or $b \ I \ c$, and *root* $I \ b$ or $a \ I \ b$, and *root* $I \ a$. Recall that our principle of information hiding is such that the deeper a module is placed in the I tree the less visible it is to other modules. Hence it is sensible to introduce modules as deep as possible in the I tree. Therefore, considering the choices above, it is reasonable to let $c \ I \ d$, $b \ I \ c$, $a \ I \ b$, and *root* $I \ a$. In the following we will indeed choose I as indicated above and show that this I is a top-down design.

In the following definition the choices made above are formalized.

Definition 16 Let R be a refer relation with root *root*. Define the relation I_R by

$$x \ I_R \ y \equiv x \neq y \wedge x \in \cap PA_R(root, y) \wedge \{x, y\} = \cap PA_R(x, y).$$

Readers might have recognised that I_R is the so-called *dominator tree* (see [2]), where every module is introduced by its *immediate dominator*. As is clear from this nomenclature, I_R is indeed a tree. That it is a top-down design as well will be shown below through some additional lemmata.

Lemma 17 Let $a \in \cap PA_R(root, b)$. Then $\cap PA_R(root, b) = \cap PA_R(root, a) \cup \cap PA_R(a, b)$.

Proof. As a is an element of every path from *root* to b, any path from *root* to b can be divided in a path from *root* to a and a path from a to b. Since R is acyclic these paths have only element a in common. Hence the intersection of all paths from *root* to b is the union of the intersection of all paths from *root* to a and the intersection of all paths from a to b. □

Lemma 18 Let R be a refer relation on D with root *root* and let $b \in D$. Then $I_R^* \, b = \cap PA_R(root, b)$.

Proof. An outline is given. Show by induction on k that $(\forall k : k \geq 0 : (\forall b : root \, I_R^k \, b : I_R^* \, b = \cap PA_R(root, b)))$. Since it has already been shown that I_R is a tree with root *root*, this induction proof is sufficient. The base case can be obtained by straightforward calculation. The step case uses the following observation: $a \, I_R \, b \Rightarrow I_R^+ \, b = I_R^* \, a$. □

Lemma 19 $c \, R \, b \Rightarrow \cap PA_R(root, b) \subseteq (\cap PA_R(root, c) \cup \{b\})$.

Proof. The proof is straightforward, since every path from the root to c can be extended to a path from *root* to b.

Now the stage has been set to show that R complies with I_R.

Theorem 20 R complies with I_R.

Proof. On account of theorem 9 and theorem 5 it now suffices to show that $(\forall a, b : a \, I_R \, b : R \, b \subseteq a \, I_R^*)$. Let $a \, I_R \, b$ and $c \, R \, b$. We have to show that $a \, I_R^* \, c$.

$$a \, I_R \, b \wedge c \, R \, b$$
$$\Rightarrow \quad \{\text{definition of } I_R\}$$
$$a \in \cap PA_R(root, b) \setminus \{b\} \wedge c \, R \, b$$
$$\Rightarrow \quad \{\text{lemma 19}\}$$
$$a \in \cap PA_R(root, c)$$
$$\equiv \quad \{\text{lemma 18}\}$$
$$a \in (I_R^* \, c)$$
$$\equiv \quad a \, I_R^* \, c \qquad\qquad □$$

We have now shown that I_R is a top-down design for R, i.e. $I_R \in T_R$. In the theorem below we show that it is the minimal element of T_R.

Theorem 21 Let R be a refer relation. Then $(\forall I : I \in T_R : I_R \sqsubseteq_R I)$.

Proof. Let $I \in T_R$. Then

$$a \ I \ b$$
$$\Rightarrow \quad \{\text{corollary 15}\}$$
$$a \in \cap PA_R(root, b) \wedge a \neq b$$
$$\equiv \quad \{\text{lemma 18}\}$$
$$a \ I_R^* \ b \wedge a \neq b$$
$$\equiv \quad a \ I_R^+ \ b$$
$$\equiv \quad \{\text{lemma 13 and definition 12}\}$$
$$I_R \sqsubseteq_R I \qquad\qquad\qquad \Box$$

In the above we have established that the *dominator tree* is the best top-down design. In [2] an algorithm can be found that efficiently computes this tree. Recall that if the I is known that the U relation simply is $R \setminus I$.

8 Conclusions

In this paper we have formalized the notion of a top-down design with information hiding. This formalization consists of two relations I and U. The relation I is a tree and denotes the introduction of modules. The relation U models that modules can be used more than once. The information hiding property limits the relation U such that modules are only visible in the I-tree starting at their introducers. Expressed the other way around, a certain module is invisible for modules that are not in the I-tree starting at the introducer of that certain module.

On the basis of the formalization we were able to express the problem of finding a top-down design for a so-called *refer* relation that can be extracted from the source text. We have indicated that the set of all possible top-down designs for a refer relation can be partially ordered and forms a *lattice*. We have shown that the minimal element of this lattice is the best top-down design and we have given an explicit formulation of this minimal element, which is in fact the dominator tree. The theory developed here is believed to be new.

We have constructed a tool which for a given a refer relation computes the best top-down design. The tool constructs graphs of the refer relation, the top-down design, and so-called "module graphs." For every module that introduces at least one other module a "module graph" is constructed that shows all the modules that are introduced together with their interrelations. Furthermore, the graph contains the relevant part of the U-pairs. Space limitations prevent us to discuss these module graphs is detail. We are currently preparing a paper discussing these module graphs and other outputs of the tool.

The tool has been applied to software written in various languages, such as Pascal, C, Fortran, Occam and others. Moreover, it has been applied to a large number of programs of varying size: from as small as 2000 lines of code to over 200,000 lines of code. From these applications we have seen that the design that is extracted and the module graphs that are constructed from it are of great help in understanding, documenting and maintaining the software. Furthermore, the graphs are also used to assess the structural complexity of the software.

That the set of top-down designs forms a lattice is helpful in the following way. It can be used to explain the differences between the actual and the anticipated design. It can be checked whether the anticipated design is an element of the lattice. If it is an element of the lattice then the software still has the correct design, although there is one with more information hiding. If the anticipated design is not an element of the lattice, then the minimal element of the lattice can be used to trace the error in the design.

The theory developed in this paper only works for *acyclic* relations. Cyclic relations are first made acyclic by considering the induced relation on the strongly connected components. In the future we hope to extend the theory to include cyclic relations as well.

References

[1] Aho, A.V., Hopcroft, J.E., Ullman, J.D. *Data structures and algorithms*. Addison-Wesley Publishing Company, Reading, Massachusetts, 1983, pp. 222-226.

[2] Aho, A.V., Ullman, J.D. *Principles of Compiler Design*. Addison-Wesley Publishing Company, Reading, Massachusetts, 1977, pp. 442-447.

[3] Biggerstaff, T. *Design recovery for maintenance and reuse*. IEEE Computer, Vol. 22-7, pp. 36-49.

[4] Choi, S.C. Scacchi, W. *Extracting and restructuring the design of large systems*. IEEE Software, Jan. 1990, pp. 66-71.

[5] Gilbert, W.J. *Modern Algebra with Applications*. John Wiley & Sons, New York, 1976, pp. 27-28.

[6] Maarek, Y.S., Kaiser, G.E., *Change management in very large software systems*. Phoenix Conference on Computer Systems and Communications, IEEE, Mar. 1988, pp. 280-285.

[7] Parnas, D.L. *On the criteria to be used in decomposing systems in modules*. Comm. of the ACM, Vol 15-2, Dec. 1972.

[8] Schwanke, R.W., Platoff, M.A. *Cross References are Features*. Proceedings of the Second International Workshop on Software Configuration Management, Princeton, NJ, Oct. 1989.

[9] Selby, R.W. Basili, V.R., *Error localization during software maintenance: Generating hierarchical system descriptions from the source code alone*. Conference on Software Maintenance, 1988, IEEE, Oct. 1988.

SESADA: An Environment Supporting Software Specialization[1]

Alberto Coen-Porisini

Flavio De Paoli

Dipartimento di Elettronica - Politecnico di Milano
P.zza Leonardo da Vinci 32, 20133 Milano (Italy)

Abstract

In this paper we present an example of customization of an Ada™ component by means of a tool (SESADA) that performs program *specialization*. Specializing a software component means to transform it into a component having the same functionality, but working only on a sub-domain of input data. Specialization is achieved by means of symbolic execution and static optimizations.

Specialization is motivated as a technique to improve reusability of software components. In fact, reusing software components involves complex problems; for example, we need to know where we shall look for components, and how to identify components that match our requirements. In addition, very often it is impossible to find a component that exactly matches requirements. Therefore, it is reasonable to suppose that some changes should be performed on existing components in order to reuse them.

Specialization is expected to produce software components that are smaller and more efficient than their original counterparts. As a consequence specialized components are likely to be more effective when employed in new environments.

SESADA has been implemented at Politecnico di Milano and runs under Unix operating system.

Keywords and phrases

Ada, program transformation, software reusability, software restructuring, source code optimization, symbolic execution

---

[1] Partially supported by CNR Progetto Finalizzato Sistemi Informatici e Calcolo Parallelo.

1. Introduction

The degree of reusability is high in all engineering disciplines, except for one: software engineering. The low degree of reusability in software design is partially responsible for high costs and low reliability of new products, compared with new products of other disciplines. Without reusability, a software product is always built from scratch and so it has to be carefully tested and debugged before reaching a suitable degree of reliability. Therefore, reusability is a major issue in software production, since increasing reusability will affect both costs and reliability of new software, decreasing the former and improving the latter [2].

Many reasons can explain the difficulties of reuse in software engineering occurred so far. The most important are due to the youth of the discipline and the lack or inadequacy of formal models to describe the process of software production. Nowadays, a lot of useful formal models have been introduced and therefore we observe a remarkable increase in reusing methodologies. However, there is little reuse of software components. It should be noted that it is much more difficult to build a new software system reusing existing components than, for instance, to build a new house using commercially available bricks and tiles. In fact, software component reuse involves problems much more complex than those arising in other disciplines. For example, we need to know where we shall look for components, and how to identify the components that match our requirements. In addition, even if we are able to overcome these problems, very often it is impossible to find a component that exactly matches our requirements. Therefore, it is reasonable to suppose that some changes should be performed on existing components in order to reuse them. This raises a new problem: modification of programs is an hard and error-prone activity to be performed by hands. Therefore, the degree of reuse of software components can be increased by means of tools that support designers in customizing existing components. Furthermore, since the modifications are accomplished (semi)automatically the degree of reliability of new components will be "similar" to that of the original ones.

Our contribution is in the area of program transformation tools supporting software changes [13]. The goal is to help restructure software components through a specific program transformation technique called, *specialization* [6]. Specializing a software component means to transform it into a component having the same functionality, but working only on a sub-domain of input data. Specialization is expected to produce software components that are smaller and more efficient than their original counterparts. In our approach specialization is applied to customize existing components by restricting their domain by means of predicates expressed in first order logic. Specialization is achieved by means of symbolic execution [11] and static optimizations [1]. Specialization extends Ershov's mixed computation [7] [8].

In this paper we present an example of specialization obtained by using SESADA, a tool which supports specialization of Ada™ [14] components; SESADA has been designed and implemented at the Politecnico di Milano, and it runs under Unix™ operating system.

The paper is organized in the following way: Section 2 gives an overview of the transformation technique called *specialization*; Section 3 describes the architecture of SESADA and its main features; Section 4 describes an example of specialization obtained using SESADA; finally, Section 5 draws some conclusions.

2. Specialization of programs

Given a program P working on an input data domain D, a specialized version of P is a program P' that works on an input data domain D' such that D' is included in D and for all input data belonging to D' the results computed by P' coincide with the results computed by P. This transformation is likely to improve effectiveness of reused components by reducing their size and increasing their speed.

Specialization of a given component is achieved by following a sequence of transformation steps. First, the component is symbolically executed in order to simplify its code, then a classical optimization, based on data flow analysis techniques, is performed in order to clean up the code obtained during the previous transformation; finally, the simplified-optimized code is processed to perform loop refolding. In what follows we provide a description of each transformation step accomplished during specialization.

2.1. Simplification by means of symbolic execution

In a symbolic execution of a program values are represented by symbols, i.e., variables are bound to symbolic expressions. Therefore, in order to describe the state of a symbolically executed program the set of variable-value pairs is not sufficient; for instance, when executing a conditional statement, values of variables could not suffice to choose along which branch the computation has to continue. Hence, some assumptions on values of variables have to be taken; such assumptions are represented by means of a first order predicate, which we refer to as path condition (PC). Initially PC has value **true**, i.e., no assumption has been taken on the values of variables.

Let us consider the following example[2]:

State:	$\{(x,\alpha), (y,\beta)\}$
PC:	true
Statement:	if x > 0
	then S1;
	else S2;
	end if

---

[2]The notation used in this example means that before the execution of **Statement** values of variables are those described in **State**, whereas **PC** represents the value of the path condition.

During symbolic execution of this statement it is necessary to assume that x is greater than zero, in order to follow the **then** branch, or less than or equal to zero, for the **else** branch. Therefore PC is equal to $(\alpha > 0)$ when executing S1 and equal to $(\alpha \leq 0)$ for S2.

After a conditional statement the new value of PC is obtained by composing both values that hold at the end of the **then** branch and at the end of the **else** branch: PC = (PC$_{then}$ $\vee$ PC$_{else}$).

By giving PC a suitable initial value representing the constraints on the input data domain, it is possible to examine how they are reflected in the code, just symbolically executing the program.

The information obtained during symbolic execution can be used to simplify the program. In the previous example, suppose that before the execution of the **if-then-else** PC equals $\alpha > 5$; this means that the assumptions made before (or deriving from input data constraints) ensure that only the **then** branch of the conditional statement will be followed. In this case we can simplify the program by eliminating both the test and the **else** branch. As a consequence, simplification yields the only statement S1.

A formal definition of the activity of symbolic execution-simplification has been provided in [6], for each basic statement of an Algol-like language. Let us note that during execution-simplification of loop statements, each time the path condition implies the truth of the loop test, simplification causes the substitution of the loop with its body, i.e., the loop is unfolded.

As a consequence of loop unfolding the size of the simplified program is usually greater than the size of the original program. Furthermore, some variables and some assignments of the original program, may become redundant in the simplified program. Thus, it is necessary to optimize the simplified program in order to obtain a suitable specialized program.

2.2. Optimization of the simplified code

Since during symbolic execution-simplification of a program some branches have been eliminated, some variables and some assignments may become useless. Therefore, using classical data flow analysis [1], the code obtained by symbolic execution-simplification is optimized.

For example consider the following piece of code:

```
State:          {(x,α), (y,β)}
PC:             α > 5
Statement:      y := 1;
                if x > 0
                        then
                                y := z;
                                x := x+z;
                        else S2;
                end if;
                x := 2;
```

After simplification the code becomes the following:

```
y := 1;
y := z;
x := x+z;
x := 2;
```

which can be transformed into:

```
y := z;
x := 2;
```

2.3. Loop refolding

After the optimization phase, the size of the simplified-optimized code can still be greater than the size of the original code; this is due to loop unfolding occurred during simplification. Therefore, a third kind of transformation is necessary to reduce its size. During this phase some sequences of statements are transformed into equivalent loop statements; this transformation is based on a heuristic technique, fully described in [6]. Here, we give the flavor of this technique by means of an example; let us consider the following piece of code in order to show how loop refolding occurs:

```
A(1) := 0;
A(2) := 1;
A(3) := 2;
A(4) := 3;
```

Looking at this sequence of statements it is possible to identify a fixed pattern that is present in each statement (A( ) := ;), and a variable part that is different in each statement (in this example the variable part is constituted by the right-hand side of each assignment and by the value of the index). As a consequence, it is possible to transform this sequence of assignments into a **for** loop, once we have found out the relationships between the values of the loop index, and the variable parts of each statement. In this example, said I the index of the **for** loop, we can represent the value of the array index as I, whereas the right-hand side of each assignment can be represented as I - 1. In such a way, the synthesized loop is the following:

```
for I in 1..4 loop
      A(I) := I - 1;
end loop;
```

At the end of this transformation step the resulting code is the actual specialized version of the original program.

3. SESADA: a tool for specializing Ada programs.

In this section we briefly describe the architecture of SESADA and its main features. SESADA provides an interactive environment which supports specialization of sequential Ada programs. It takes as input an Ada program and some constraints on its input variables and produces as output a specialized version of the program. SESADA has been developed under Unix operating system and it is composed essentially by three modules: the symbolic executor-simplifier, the theorem prover, the optimizer (see Figure 1). These three modules have been provided with a graphical interface, through which the user may interact with the system. Each module is described in the next section.

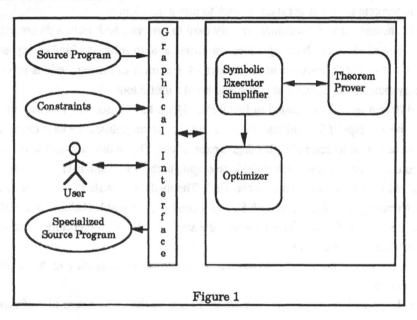

Figure 1

3.1. The Symbolic Executor-Simplifier

The symbolic executor-simplifier is the core of SESADA; it has been implemented on the basis of SYMBAD [5], a symbolic interpreter for a subset of Ada. In turn SYMBAD has been derived by modifying Unisex [10], a symbolic interpreter for Pascal programs. Ada's main features not handled by SESADA concern concurrency (task) and pointers (access types).

The symbolic executor-simplifier is made up of two parts: the first one is a translator that transforms Ada source code into an internal form written in Lisp; this translator has been implemented by using Lex and Yacc under Unix. The second one is a set of Lisp routines providing the run-time support needed for symbolic execution-simplification.

At the end of the symbolic execution-simplification the simplified program produced is given as input to the optimizer.

During symbolic execution-simplification, whenever a conditional statement, or a loop statement is reached the theorem prover is invoked in order to choose along which branch the computation has to continue.

3.2. The theorem prover

The theorem prover takes as input two predicates representing respectively, the path condition and the condition to be evaluated, and it tries to decide whether the path condition implies the condition or not. Since the question has the following form: Does PC imply C?, the answer can be *true*, *false*, or *neither*. *Neither* means that either PC is not strong enough to imply C or ¬C, or the theorem prover is not smart enough to take a decision.

In general, theorem proving activities are very hard to perform, both from a theoretical and a practical point of view. So, building a theorem prover able to solve any kind of expression is practically not realistic; however, under the remark that most of the expressions involve low degree polynomial inequalities, it is possible to build a useful tool.

Among different approaches found in literature, [4] we have based our theorem prover on Bledsoe's method *sup-inf* [3]. This method deals with linear inequalities; we have extended such method to some general cases of higher degree expressions. The method attempts to demonstrate a conjecture by contradiction. Each variable belonging to the conjecture is viewed as a constant characterized by a subrange (Skolem's constant). The method consists in solving inequalities, i.e., in determining the subrange of each Skolem's constant. If variables belong to an unfeasible subrange, i.e., its inferior limit is greater than the superior, then the conjecture is proven. The method consists of three major steps:

(1) rewrite the conjecture using only existential operators and regarding each variable as a Skolem's constant;

(2) put such expressions in a Disjunctive Normal Form so that only inequalities of type ≤ are involved;

(3) solve the inequalities with respect to the Skolem's constants.

The extension of the *sup-inf* method allows to reduce some expressions of higher degree so that the *sup-inf* method is still applicable. Experiences show that most of real programs decisions involve linear or sometimes second degree inequalities, so we believe that the class of problems our theorem prover can solve is large enough to handle most of the cases. Of course this remark does not hold for scientific algorithm where expressions often include operators like *log* or *cos*. Furthermore, whenever the theorem prover is invoked the path condition is simplified by eliminating redundant clauses.

3.3. The optimizer

The optimizer takes as input the simplified Ada program produced by the symbolic executor-simplifier and produces as output the specialized version of the original input program. It consists of two sub-modules: the first one is a classical optimizer based on data-flow analysis techniques, and the second one is a loop refolder.

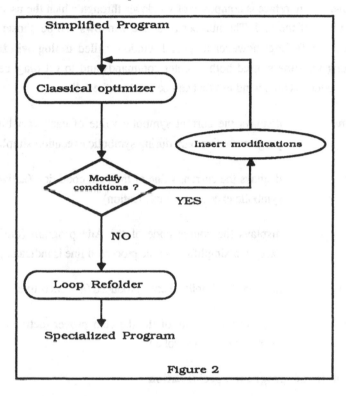

Figure 2

The first sub-module processes the code in order to eliminate redundant statements and reduces assignment sequences. After this phase, the user may introduce some changes in the code, i.e., some conditions of tests may be rewritten by the user to better capture the semantics of the program (see Figure 2); each time new modifications have been introduced the code is further processed by the classic optimizer.

In the next section we discuss an example in which this technique is applied (see Figure 11). Finally the code is processed by the loop refolder which synthesizes loops unfolded by the symbolic executor and/or may synthesize new loops deriving from previous transformation activities.

The user can create more than one specialized version of the original program interacting with the loop refolder: generalization can be introduced to modify the solutions proposed by the tool. However, this must be done carefully, because explicit modifications introduced by the user may yield defective code. In other words, it is left to the user's responsibility to verify the correctness of such transformations.

3.4. The graphical interface

The interaction between SESADA and the user is provided by a graphical interface developed on top of X-Window. The interface is composed of windows, through which the user may monitor the current activities of the tool. The number of active windows can be chosen by the user, depending on his/her feeling; however a special window called **dialog window** is always active. The **dialog window** is used both to enter commands and to get diagnostic messages from SESADA modules. Other windows that can be used are the following:

- **State window** displays the current symbolic value of each variable of the Ada program (active only during symbolic execution simplification).

- **PC window** displays the current value of the path condition (active only during symbolic execution-simplification).

- **SC window** displays the source code of the Ada program (during symbolic execution-simplification the processed line is indicated).

- **SSC window** displays the simplified code produced (always active).

- **THP window** displays the activity of the theorem prover (active only when the theorem prover is invoked).

4. An example of program specialization

In this section we provide an example of program specialization, obtained using SESADA. This example shows how SESADA works and, despite its size, it is complex enough to bring up the main capabilities of the tool. The program derives from an example described in [12].

4.1. Program Topsort.

The program Topsort takes as input an acyclic oriented graph, G, and produces as output a mapping between the nodes of G, N_G, and the set of natural numbers, $\mathbf{N}$, $L_G: N_G \rightarrow \mathbf{N}$, such that given two nodes N_i, $N_j \in N_G$, with $i \neq j$, if a path starting from N_i leading to N_j exists then $L_G(N_i) < L_G(N_j)$.

$L_G(N_i)$ gives the position of N_i in a list representing a topological sort of G. The list is such that for all nodes $N_j \in G$, with $i \neq j$, N_i precedes N_j if a path starting from N_i leading to N_j

exists. In other words, L_G describes an ordered list where each node occupies a position according to the topological sort of G.

G is described by means of a bidimensional matrix $A_{n \times n}$ of booleans, where n is the number of nodes of G, and each element a_{ij} belonging to A, $1 \leq i, j \leq n$, has value true if an arc starting from N_j and leading to N_i exists, otherwise it has value false.

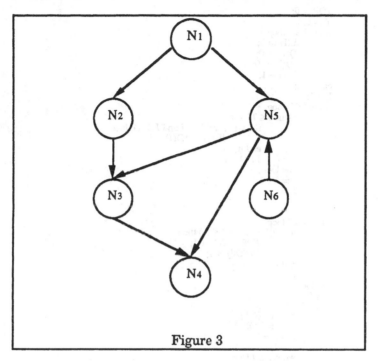

Figure 3

For example the graph of figure 3 is described by the following matrix:

$$A = \begin{bmatrix} F & F & F & F & F & F \\ T & F & F & F & F & F \\ F & T & F & F & T & F \\ F & F & T & F & T & F \\ T & F & F & F & F & T \\ F & F & F & F & F & F \end{bmatrix}$$

The program takes as input the matrix A and an integer N representing the number of nodes of G, and gives as output a vector L, representing the mapping of the nodes of G.

```
type GRAPH is array (1..49) of BOOLEAN;
type LIST is array (1.. 7) of INTEGER;

1          procedure TOPSORT(A: in GRAPH; N: in INTEGER,L: out LIST) is
2          I, J, Y ,TOP: INTEGER;
3          Q, ID: LIST;
4          begin
5                  I := 1;
6                  J := 1;
7                  TOP := 0;
8                  Y := 0;
9                  while I ≤ 7 loop
10                         L(I) := 0;
11                         Q(I) := 0;
12                         ID(I) := 0;
13                         I:= I + 1;
14                 end loop;
15                 I := 1;
16                 while I ≤ 7 loop
17                         while J ≤ 7 loop
18                                 if (A(I,J) and I ≤ N and J ≤ N) then
19                                         ID(J) := ID(J) + 1;
20                                 end if;
21                                 J := J + 1;
22                         end loop;
23                         I := I + 1;
24                         J := 1;
25                 end loop;
26                 I := 1;
27                 while I ≤ 7 loop
28                         if (ID(I) = 0 and I ≤ N) then
29                                 TOP := TOP + 1;
30                                 Q(TOP) := I;
31                         end if;
32                         I := I + 1;
33                 end loop;
34                 I := 1;
35                 while TOP /= 0 loop
36                         Y := Q(TOP);
37                         TOP := TOP -1;
38                         L(Y) := I;
39                         J := 1;
40                         while J ≤ 7 loop;
41                                 if (A(J,(Y -1)*N) and ID(J) > 0 and J ≤ N) then
42                                         ID(J) := ID(J) - 1;
43                                         if ID(J) = 0 then
44                                                 TOP := TOP + 1;
45                                                 Q(TOP) := J;
46                                         end if;
47                                 end if;
48                                 J := J + 1;
49                         end loop;
50                         I := I + 1;
51                 end loop;
52      end;
```

Figure 4

The example of Figure 3 has several solutions, three of them are:

list of nodes	output	sorted list

$$\cdot\ |1\ 2\ 5\ 6\ 4\ 3| \rightarrow |N_1\ N_2\ N_6\ N_5\ N_3\ N_4\ |$$

$$|N_1\ N_2\ N_3\ N_4\ N_5\ N_6\ | \cdots\ |1\ 3\ 5\ 6\ 4\ 2| \rightarrow |N_1\ N_6\ N_2\ N_5\ N_3\ N_4\ |$$

$$|2\ 4\ 5\ 6\ 3\ 1| \rightarrow |N_6\ N_1\ N_5\ N_2\ N_3\ N_4\ |$$

The actual mapping computed by the program depends on the implementation. Figure 4 reports the source code of the implementation of Topsort that we want to specialize; applying it to the above example the following output is produced: [2 4 5 6 3 1].

The high-level description of such implementation can be expressed as follows:

Let Q be the set containing the nodes of G such that
$\forall\ N_i \in Q$ there is not an arc of G, leading in N_i.
    Forall $N_i \subset Q$ do
        print(N_i)
        delete all arcs exiting from N_i
        $Q = Q/\{N_i\} \cup \{N_j \in G \mid$ no arc lead in N_j and N_j has not yet been printed$\}$
    done

4.2. A specialization of Topsort.

Let us specialize Topsort by imposing that the input graph, G, is connected, and each node of G has at most one incoming edge and one outgoing edge, that is, G is a "sequence of nodes". Figure 5 shows an example of such a graph.

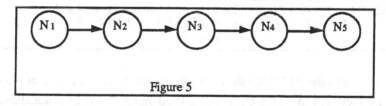

Figure 5

The input data domain constraint can be expressed by the following first-order predicate:

$$\forall\ (i, j): 1 \leq i, j \leq N, (i = j - 1 \Longrightarrow A(i, j)) \wedge (i \neq j - 1 \Longrightarrow \neg\ A(i, j))$$

Let us describe the activity of symbolic execution-simplification performed by SESADA, by illustrating the most significant points. When processing line 1 of the code in Figure 4, the user is asked to give an actual (symbolic) value and a predicate for each input parameter. Note that we do not take any assumption about the "length of G", i.e., the input parameter N has an unconstrained symbolic value val_N (see Figure 6).

*** Line 1: Insert value for variable N ***
SESADA> N = val_N;

*** Line 1: Insert conditions on variable N:
SESADA>;

Figure 6

If a parameter is of an array type, e.g. A, the user can give information by supplying values just for some elements (Figure 7a). In such a case, the remaining elements will have a symbolic value provided by SESADA; it is possible to use the keyword **all** to represent all elements, belonging to the same row or column (Figure 7b). If no information is supplied, SESADA initializes the array by providing a symbolic value for each element: the initial value of element $A(i,j)$ is represented by $A(i,j).0$. In our example, no value to any element of A is provided, instead, we use a predicate to represent the constraint on such elements (Figure 7c).

SESADA> A(1,1) = x, A(2,2) = y, A(3,3) = x+y;

Figure 7a

SESADA> A(all,1) = 0;

Figure 7b

*** Line 1: Insert values for array A:
SESADA>;

*** Line 1: Insert conditions on array A:
SESADA>FORALL I,J (1≤I and 1≤J and I≤val_N and J≤val_N and
(I=J-1 IMPLIES A(I,J).0)and (I /=J-1 IMPLIES not A(I,J).0))

Figure 7c

Note that the initial value of PC equals the constraint given for array A. Lines 2-15 are not relevant, since they contain only declarations of local variables and their initialization. From line 16 to line 25 there are two nested loops which are unfolded during symbolic execution. The body of the inner loop contains a conditional statement (line 18). In order to execute such statement, it is necessary to decide whether its conditional expression is implied by PC or not. The evaluation of the conditional expression produces the following expression:

$A(1,1).0$ and $1 \leq$ val_N and $1 \leq$ val_N

Figure 8 shows the question proposed to the theorem prover.

> Does
> FORALL I,J (1≤I and 1≤J and I≤val_N and J≤val_N and(I=J-1 IMPLIES A(I,J).0)and
>   (I≠J-1 IMPLIES not A(I,J).0))
>   Imply
> A(1,1).0 and 1 ≤ val_N and 1 ≤ val_N
>
> Figure 8

In this case the answer is *no*, and it is automatically found by SESADA. Therefore the assignment at line 19 is not executed. The second time statement of line 18 is executed the following question arises:

Does PC ⇒ A(1,2).0 and 1≤ val_N and 2 ≤ val_N ?

In this case the answer is *neither* and thus the predicate (A(1,2).0 and 1≤ val_N and 2 ≤ val_N) is added to PC. However, note that only the clause 2 ≤ val_N is relevant[3], thus only this clause is added to PC. At the end of the conditional statement (line 20) PC becomes:

[FORALL I,J (1≤I and 1≤J and I≤N and J≤N and (I=J-1 IMPLIES A(I,J).0)and(I≠J-1 IMPLIES not A(I,J).0)) and 2 ≤ val_N and ID(2).0 = 1]

or

[FORALL I,J (1≤I and 1≤J and I≤N and J≤N and (I=J-1 IMPLIES A(I,J).0)and(I≠J-1 IMPLIES not A(I,J).0)) and 2 > N and ID(2).0 = 0]

Since ID(2) has different values at the end of the **then** branch (ID(2) = 1) and at the end of the **else** branch (ID(2) = 0), its value after the conditional statement is represented by a new symbolic value: ID(2).0. The relationships between ID(2).0 and the values holding at the end of the **then** and **else** branches are added to PC.

Exiting the loop at lines 16-25 the value of PC is :

[FORALL I,J (1≤I and 1≤J and I≤N and J≤N and (I=J-1 IMPLIES A(I,J).0)and(I≠J-1 IMPLIES not A(I,J).0)) and 7 ≤ val_N and ID(2).0 = 1 and ID(3).0 = 1 and ID(4).0 =1 and ID(5).0 = 1 and ID(6).0 = 1 and ID(7).0= 1]

or

[FORALL I,J (1≤I and 1≤J and I≤N and J≤N and (I=J-1 IMPLIES A(I,J).0)and(I≠J-1 IMPLIES not A(I,J).0)) and 6 ≤ val_N and 7 > val_N and ID(2).0 = 1 and ID(3).0 = 1 and ID(4).0 =1 and ID(5).0 = 1 and ID(6).0 = 1 and ID(7).0 = 0]

or

[FORALL I,J (1≤I and 1≤J and I≤N and J≤N and (I=J-1 IMPLIES A(I,J).0)and(I≠J-1 IMPLIES

---

[3] Since (I ⇒ (P ∧Q ∧R)) ≡ ((I⇒ P) ∧ (I ⇒ Q) ∧ (I ⇒ R)), and since PC ⇒ A(I,J).0, then it is possible to reduce the question to: "Does PC ⇒ (1 ≤ val_N and 2 ≤ val_N). Obviously this question can be further reduced to
PC ⇒ 2 ≤ val_N.

not A(I,J).0)) and 5≤ val_N and 6 > val_N and ID(2).0 = 1 and ID(3).0 = 1 and ID(4).0 =1 and
ID(5).0 = 1 and ID(6).0 = 0 and ID(7).0 = 0]

or

[FORALL I,J (1≤I and 1≤J and I≤N and J≤N and (I=J-1 IMPLIES A(I,J).0)and(I≠J-1 IMPLIES
not A(I,J).0)) and 4 ≤ val_N and 5 > val_N and ID(2).0 = 1 and ID(3).0 = 1 and ID(4).0 =1 and
ID(5).0 = 0 and ID(6).0 = 0 and ID(7).0 = 0]

or

[FORALL I,J (1≤I and 1≤J and I≤N and J≤N and (I=J-1 IMPLIES A(I,J).0)and(I≠J-1 IMPLIES
not A(I,J).0)) and 3 ≤ val_N and 4 > val_N and ID(2).0 = 1 and ID(3).0 = 1 and ID(4).0 =0 and
ID(5).0 = 0 and ID(6).0 = 0 and ID(7).0 = 0]

or

[FORALL I,J (1≤I and 1≤J and I≤N and J≤N and (I=J-1 IMPLIES A(I,J).0)and(I≠J-1 IMPLIES
not A(I,J).0)) and 2 ≤ val_N and 3 > val_N and ID(2).0 = 1 and ID(3).0 = 0 and ID(4).0 =0 and
ID(5).0 = 0 and ID(6).0 = 0 and ID(7).0 = 0]

or

[FORALL I,J (1≤I and 1≤J and I≤N and J≤N and (I=J-1 IMPLIES A(I,J).0)and(I≠J-1 IMPLIES
not A(I,J).0)) and 2 > val_N and ID(2).0 = 0 and ID(3).0 = 0 and ID(4).0 =0 and ID(5).0 = 0 and
ID(6).0 = 0 and ID(7).0 = 0]

Lines from 27 to 33 contain another loop that is unfolded during symbolic execution-
simplification; let us examine the conditional statement of line 28; the first time it is executed
(i.e., I is equal to 1) the following question arises:

Does PC $\Rightarrow$ 0 = 0 and 1 ≤ val_N ?

The answer is *neither* since PC is not strong enough to imply that the value of N is greater,
equal or less than 1. The value of PC at line 31 contains information about values of variables
N, TOP, Q and ID; for example the first part of PC is:[4]

[FORALL I,J (1≤I and 1≤J and I≤N and J≤N and (I=J-1 IMPLIES A(I,J).0)and(I≠J-1 IMPLIES
not A(I,J).0)) and 7 ≤ val_N and ID(2).0 = 1 and ID(3).0 = 1 and ID(4).0 =1 and ID(5).0 = 1 and
ID(6).0 = 1 and ID(7).0= 1 and TOP.0 = 1 and Q(1).0 = 1]

The whole PC is reported in Appendix A1.

PC is now composed of eight different parts, representing the fact that N can have any permitted
value, i.e., N can be greater or equal than 0 and should not exceed the array size; as a
consequence, in what follows, it will be possible to evaluate all conditional expressions
encountered without adding new parts to PC, i.e., it will be always possible to split PC in two
parts PC$_{true}$, PC$_{false}$, such that PC$_{true}$ implies the truth of the conditional expressions, while
PC$_{false}$ implies the falsity.

---

[4]Since the value of PC when evaluating the test of line 28 for the first time is not strong enough to
imply neither the condition nor its opposite a new clause is added, to represent that N could be less
than 1. When reaching line 31 PC will have the following form:
PC : PC$_7 \vee$ PC$_6 \vee$ PC$_5 \vee$ PC$_4 \vee$ PC$_3 \vee$ PC$_2 \vee$ PC$_1 \vee$ PC$_0$
where each P$_i$ represents the fact that N ≤ i.

Since for I greater than 1 the test of line 28 evaluates to false, PC will be unchanged during the remaining iterations of the loop.

When the computation reaches the loop of line 35, the last part (See Appendix A1) of PC implies the falsity of the test TOP /= 0, while the other parts imply the truth; thus the simplifier produces a conditional statement; the **then** branch of this conditional statement contains code coming from the simplification of the loop body; since at each iteration it is possible to split PC in PC_{true} and PC_{false} the loop at lines 40-47 is completely unfolded. In appendix A2 the value of PC when the conditional expression of line 35 is reached for the second time is shown. After seven iterations PC implies the falsity of the test and thus the execution is completed. Appendix A3 describes the value of PC at the end of the execution.

```
      type GRAPH is array (1..49) of BOOLEAN;        35.3        if TOP /= 0 then
      type LIST is array (1..7) of INTEGER;          37.3            TOP := 0;
                                                     38.3                L(3) := 3;
1     procedure TOPSORT(A: in GRAPH,                 41.3.4      if 4 ≤ N then
               N: in INTEGER, L: out LIST) is         44.3.4          TOP := 1;
2     TOP: INTEGER;                                   47.3.4      end if;
4     begin                                           51.3        end if;
7               TOP := 0;                             35.4        if TOP /= 0 then
10.1            L(1) := 0;                            37.4            TOP := 0;
10.2            L(2) := 0;                            38.4                L(4) := 4;
10.3            L(3) := 0;                            41.4.5      if 5 ≤ N then
10.4            L(4) := 0;                            44.4.5          TOP := 1;
10.5            L(5) := 0;                            47.4.5      end if;
10.6            L(6) := 0;                            51.4        end if;
10.7            L(7) := 0;                            35.5        if TOP /= 0 then
28.1            if 1 ≤ N then                         37.5            TOP := 0;
29.1                TOP := 1;                         38.5            L(5) := 5;
31.1            end if;                               41.5.6      if 6 ≤ N then
35.1            if TOP /= 0 then                      44.5.6          TOP := 1;
37.1                TOP := 0;                         47.5.6      end if;
38.1                L(1) := 1;                        51.5        end if;
41.1.2          if 2 ≤ N then                         35.6        if TOP /= 0 then
44.1.2              TOP := 1;                         37.6            TOP := 0;
47.1.2          end if;                               38.6                L(6) := 6;
51.1            end if;                               41.6.7      if 7 ≤ N then
35.2            if TOP /= 0 then                      44.6.7          TOP := 1;
37.2                TOP := 0;                         47.6.7      end if;
38.2                L(2) := 2;                         51.6        end if;
41.2.3          if 3 ≤ N then                         35.7        if TOP /= 0 then
44.2.3              TOP := 1;                         37.7            TOP := 0;
47.2.3          end if;                               38.7                L(7) := 7;
51.2            end if;                               51.7        end if;
                                                     52     end;
```

Figure 9

Because of loop unfolding the code produced during simplification is longer than the original code; however, several static optimizations can be performed in order to reduce its size. In appendix B, we report the code produced during simplification, while the code in figure 9 represents the program simplified and optimized by means of classical data flow analysis techniques.

Each statement is labelled using the line number of the same statement in the original program, and the values of loop indexes whenever it comes from loop unfolding. For example the statement labelled with 44.3.4 comes from the statement of line 44, when the value of index of the extern loop was 3 and the index of the inner loop was 4.

It must be noted that variables I, J, Y, Q, and ID are no longer useful and then all statements referring to those variables have been eliminated by the optimizer. The size of the code has been reduced of a significant amount, however it can be still improved by transforming some sequences of statements into loops.

The loop refolder is able to identify two sequences of statements candidate to be transformed into loops; the first one is the sequence labelled from 10.1 to 10.7, while the second sequence is labelled from 35.1 to 51.6. Note that both sequences come from loop unfolding of the original program.

Figure 10 shows the specialized program obtained automatically.

```
type GRAPH is array (1..49) of BOOLEAN;
type LIST is array (1..7) of INTEGER;

1        procedure TOPSORT(A: in GRAPH, N: in INTEGER, L: out LIST) is
2        TOP: INTEGER;
3        begin
4                TOP := 0;
5                for I in 1..7 loop
6                        L(I) := 0;
7                end loop;
28.1             if 1 ≤ N then
29.1                     TOP := 1;
31.1             end if;
11               for I in 1..6 loop
35.1                     if TOP /= 0 then
37.1                             TOP := 0;
38.1                             L(I) := I;
41.1.2                          if I + 1 ≤ N then
44.1.2                                  TOP := 1;
47.1.2                          end if;
51.1                     end if;
19               end loop;
35.7             if TOP /= 0 then
37.7                     TOP := 0;
38.7                     L(7) := 7;
51.7             end if;
52       end;
```

Figure 10

The user can interact with SESADA in order to obtain a different[5] code; for example remarking that the test TOP /= 0 in figure 9 can be safely substituted by the test $1 \leq N$, $2 \leq N$ etc. it is

---

[5]Interacting with SESADA the user could try to obtain a "better" code; since the meaning of better code can not be stated formally, because of different needs of users, it is left to him/her to decide whether the code produced may be improved, by means of different optimizations.

possible to obtain a different (better, in this case) version of the simplified-optimized program (see figure 11).

type GRAPH is array (1..49) of BOOLEAN;		35.3	if 3 ≤ N then
type LIST is array (1..7) of INTEGER;		38.3	L(3) := 3;
		51.3	end if;
1	procedure TOPSORT(A: in GRAPH,	35.4	if 4 ≤ N then
	N: in INTEGER, L: out LIST) is	38.4	L(4) := 4;
4	begin	51.4	end if;
10.1	L(1) := 0;	35.5	if 5 ≤ N then
10.2	L(2) := 0;	38.5	L(5) := 5;
10.3	L(3) := 0;	51.5	end if;
10.4	L(4) := 0;	35.6	if 6 ≤ Nthen
10.5	L(5) := 0;	38.6	L(6) := 6;
10.6	L(6) := 0;	51.6	end if;
10.7	L(7) := 0;	35.7	if 7 ≤ N then
35.1	if 1 ≤ N then	38.7	L(7) := 7;
38.1	L(1) := 1;	51.7	end if;
51.1	end if;	52	end;
35.2	if 2 ≤ Nthen		
38.2	L(2) := 2;		
51.2	end if;		

Figure 11

Also in this case the loop refolder identifies two sequences of statements that can be refolded so that the program of figure 12 is obtained.

type GRAPH is array (1..49) of BOOLEAN;		type GRAPH is array (1..49) of BOOLEAN;	
type LIST is array (1..7) of INTEGER;		type LIST is array (1..7) of INTEGER;	
1	procedure TOPSORT(A: in GRAPH,	1	procedure TOPSORT(A: in GRAPH,
	N: in INTEGER, L: out LIST) is		N: in INTEGER, L: out LIST) is
4	begin	4	begin
10.1	for I in 1.. 7 loop	10.1	for I in 1.. 7 loop
10.2	L(I) := 0;	10.2	L(I) := 0;
	end loop;		end loop;
	for I in 1.. 7 loop		while I ≤ N loop
35.1	if I ≤ N then	38.1	L(I) := I;
38.1	L(I) := I;		end loop;
51.1	end if;	52	end;
	end loop;		
52	end;		

Figure 12   Figure 13

The user can interact with the loop refolder in order to produce other types of loops than **for** loop; in this example it is possible to produce a **while** loop, eliminating in such a way all conditional statements (See figure 13).

4.3. Some remarks about specialization technique

Comparing the original code of Topsort (figure 4) with the specialized program of figure 13 (or figure 12) we notice that the former has a complexity of $O(N^2)$, while the latter has a complexity of $O(N)$. The specialization has produced a program which is better from the point of view of size (it is smaller) and program complexity.

These improvements have been possible thanks to loop unfolding occurred during symbolic execution-simplification; if loop unfolding was not possible the results obtained using our technique would be different. For example look at the loop of lines 16-25, reported in figure 14, which can be rewritten as in figure 15. In such a case PC is not strong enough to unfold the extern loop and therefore lines 17-24, that is its body is executed once[6], adding to PC the clause I.0 ≤ N (I.0 represents the value of variable I within the loop). As a consequence, the inner loop can not be unfolded too, and since at line 18 PC equals to:

[FORALL I,J (1≤I and 1≤J and I≤N and J≤N and (I=J-1 IMPLIES A(I,J).0)and(I≠J-1 IMPLIES not A(I,J).0)) and I.0 ≤ val_N and J.0 ≤ val_N]

no simplification can be performed onto statements of lines 16-25, although we know that the conditional statement is executed only when the index of the extern loop equals the index of the inner loop minus 1. This is due to the fact that our technique simplifies one statement at a time, that is, each statement is simplified extracting it from the code. Local simplification is performed, i.e., the only knowledge taken into account comes from the information contained in the symbolic state; therefore the structure of the program can not be used to simplify a statement. As a consequence it is not possible to eliminate one of the two loops in figure 15 without unfolding it.

16	while I ≤ 7 loop		16	while I ≤ N loop	
17	while J ≤ 7 loop		17	while J ≤ N	
18	if (A(I,J) and I ≤ N and J ≤ N) then		18	if A(I,J) then	
19	ID(J) := ID(J) + 1;		19	- ID(J) := ID(J) + 1;	
20	end if;		20	end if;	
21	J := J + 1;		21	J := J + 1;	
22	end loop;		22	end loop;	
23	I := I + 1;		23	I := I + 1;	
24	J := 1;		24	J := 1;	
25	end loop;		25	end loop;	

Figure 14   Figure 15

5. Conclusions

Tools supporting program transformation activities are expected to improve both the productivity of software engineers and the quality of the produced software.

In this paper, we presented the SESADA system that specializes existing Ada components. Specialization has been motivated as a technique improving software reusability, but it can be

---

[6]Whenever a loop can not be unfolded, its body is symbolically executed-simplified once, starting from a new symbolic state which represents the fact that the loop may have been executed an arbitrary number of times. Exiting from the loop a new symbolic state is built in order to represent that the loop may or may not have been executed. As a consequence the loop will appear also in the simplified code.

effectively applied in other frameworks. For example, specialization may be used to restructure (long lived) software which has become (structurally) corrupted because of the modifications it has undergone during maintenance [9].

6. References

[1]   A.V. Aho, R. Sethi, J.D. Ullman *"Compilers: principles, techniques, and tools"*, Addison-Wesley (1986).

[2]   T.J. Biggerstaff and A.J. Perlis, *"Software Reusability voll.1-2"* ACM Press, 1989.

[3]   W.W. Bledsoe "The Sup-Inf method in Presburger Arithmetic." Tech. Rept. Department of Mathematics - University of Texas, 1974.

[4]   C.L. Chang, R.C. Lee *"Symbolic logic and mechanical theorem proving"*, Academic Press (1973).

[5]   A. Coen-Porisini, F. DePaoli "Symbad: a Symbolic Executor for sequential Ada programs." In Proceedings of the *SAFECOMP '90* (Symposium on sfety of computer control system), Gatwick, U.K. 30 October - 2 November 1990, Pergamon Press, pp. 105 - 111.

[6]   A. Coen-Porisini, F. DePaoli, C. Ghezzi, D. Mandrioli "Software Specialization via Symbolic Execution" to appear on *IEEE Transactions on Software Engineering*, September 1991.

[7]   A.P. Ershov "Mixed computation: potential applications and problems for study." *Theoretical Computer Science 18*(1982), 41-67.

[8]   A.P. Ershov "On the partial computation principle." *Information Processing Letters 6*, 2 (1977).

[9]   IEEE Software *"Maintenance & Reverse Engineering & Design Recovery"*, vol. 7, n. 1, 1990.

[10]   R. Kemmerer, S. Eckmann "UNISEX a UNIx - based Symbolic EXecutor for Pascal." *Software-Practice and Experience 15*, 5 (May 1985).

[11]   J.C. King "Symbolic execution and program testing." *Communications of the ACM 19*, 7 (1976).

[12]   J. Laski "Testing in the program development cycle." *Software Engineering Journal* (March 1989).

[13]   H. Partsch and R. Steinbruggen, "Program Transformation Systems" *Computing Surveys*, vol. 15, n. 3, pp. 199-236, 1983.

[14]   *"Reference Manual for the Ada Programming Language"*, USA-DoD, 1983, ANSI/MIL-STD-1815 A.

Appendix A1: The value of PC at line 31

[FORALL I,J (1≤I and 1≤J and I≤N and J≤N and (I=J-1 IPLIES A(I,J).0)and(I≠J-1 IMPLIES not A(I,J).0)) and 7≤val_N and ID(2).0 = 1 and ID(3).0 = 1 and ID(4).0 =1 and ID(5).0 = 1 and ID(6).0 = 1 and ID(7).0= 1 and TOP.0 = 1 and Q(1).0 = 1]

or

[FORALL I,J (1≤I and 1≤J and I≤N and J≤N and (I=J-1 IMPLIES A(I,J).0)and(I≠J-1 IMPLIES not A(I,J).0)) and 6≤val_N and 7>val_N and ID(2).0=1 and ID(3).0=1 and ID(4).0 =1 and ID(5).0 = 1 and ID(6).0 = 1 and ID(7).0 = 0 and TOP.0 = 1 and Q(1).0 =1]

or

[FORALL I,J (1≤I and 1≤J and I≤N and J≤N and (I=J-1 IMPLIES A(I,J).0)and(I≠J-1 IMPLIES not A(I,J).0)) and 5 ≤ val_N and 6 > val_N and ID(2).0 = 1 and ID(3).0 = 1 and ID(4).0 =1 and ID(5).0 = 1 and ID(6).0 = 0 and ID(7).0 = 0 and TOP.0 = 1 and Q(1).0 = 1]

or

[FORALL I,J (1≤I and 1≤J and I≤N and J≤N and (I=J-1 IMPLIES A(I,J).0)and(I≠J-1 IMPLIES not A(I,J).0)) and 4 ≤ val_N and 5 > val_N and ID(2).0 = 1 and ID(3).0 = 1 and ID(4).0 =1 and ID(5).0 = 0 and ID(6).0 = 0 and ID(7).0 = 0 and TOP.0 = 1 and Q(1) = 1]

or

[FORALL I,J (1≤I and 1≤J and I≤N and J≤N and (I=J-1 IMPLIES A(I,J).0)and(I≠J-1 IMPLIES not A(I,J).0)) and 3 ≤ val_N and 4 > val_N and ID(2).0 = 1 and ID(3).0 = 1 and ID(4).0 =0 and ID(5).0 = 0 and ID(6).0 = 0 and ID(7).0 = 0 and TOP.0 = 1 and Q(1).0 = 1]

or

[FORALL I,J (1≤I and 1≤J and I≤N and J≤N and (I=J-1 IMPLIES A(I,J).0)and(I≠J-1 IMPLIES not A(I,J).0)) and 2 ≤ val_N and 3 > val_N and ID(2).0 = 1 and ID(3).0 = 0 and ID(4).0 =0 and ID(5).0 = 0 and ID(6).0 = 0 and ID(7).0 = 0 and TOP.0 = 1 and Q(1).0 = 1]

or

[FORALL I,J (1≤I and 1≤J and I≤N and J≤N and (I=J-1 IMPLIES A(I,J).0)and(I≠J-1 IMPLIES not A(I,J).0)) and 1 ≤ val_N and 2 > val_N and ID(2).0 = 0 and ID(3).0 = 0 and ID(4).0 =0 and ID(5).0 = 0 and ID(6).0 = 0 and ID(7).0 = 0 and TOP.0 = 1 and Q(1).0 =1]

or

[FORALL I,J (1≤I and 1≤J and I≤N and J≤N and (I=J-1 IMPLIES A(I,J).0)and(I≠J-1 IMPLIES not A(I,J).0)) and 1>val_N and ID(2).0=0 and ID(3).0=0 and ID(4).0=0 and ID(5).=0 and ID(6).0=0 and ID(7).0=0 and TOP.0 = 0 and Q(1).0 =0]

Appendix A2: the value of PC when line 35 is reached for the second time.

[FORALL I,J (1≤I and 1≤J and I≤N and J≤N and (I=J-1 IMPLIES A(I,J).0)and(I≠J-1 IMPLIES not A(I,J).0)) and 7≤val_N and ID(2).1=0 and ID(3).0=1 and ID(4).0 =1 and ID(5).0 = 1 and ID(6).0 =¯1 and ID(7).0= 1 and TOP.1 = 1 and Q(1).1 = 2]

or

[FORALL I,J (1≤I and 1≤J and I≤N and J≤N and (I=J-1 IMPLIES A(I,J).0)and(I≠J-1 IMPLIES not A(I,J).0)) and 6≤val_N and 7>val_N and ID(2).1=0 and ID(3).0=1 and ID(4).0 =1 and ID(5).0 = 1 and ID(6).0 = 1 and ID(7).0 = 0 and TOP.1 = 1 and Q(1).1 =2]

or

[FORALL I,J (1≤I and 1≤J and I≤N and J≤N and (I=J-1 IMPLIES A(I,J).0)and(I≠J-1 IMPLIES not A(I,J).0)) and 5 ≤ val_N and 6 > val_N and ID(2).1 = 0 and ID(3).0 = 1 and ID(4).0 =1 and ID(5).0 = 1 and ID(6).0 = 0 and ID(7).0 = 0 and TOP.1 = 1 and Q(1).1 = 2]

or

[FORALL I,J (1≤I and 1≤J and I≤N and J≤N and (I=J-1 IMPLIES A(I,J).0)and(I≠J-1 IMPLIES not A(I,J).0)) and 4 ≤ val_N and 5 > val_N and ID(2).1 = 0 and ID(3).0 = 1 and ID(4).0 =1 and ID(5).0 = 0 and ID(6).0 = 0 and ID(7).0 = 0 and TOP.1 = 1 and Q(1) 1=2]

or

[FORALL I,J (1≤I and 1≤J and I≤N and J≤N and (I=J-1 IMPLIES A(I,J).0)and(I≠J-1 IMPLIES not A(I,J).0)) and 3 ≤ val_N and 4 > val_N and ID(2).1 = 0 and ID(3).0 = 1 and ID(4).0 =0 and ID(5).0 = 0 and ID(6).0 = 0 and ID(7).0 = 0 and TOP.1 = 1 and Q(1).1 = 2]

or

[FORALL I,J (1≤I and 1≤J and I≤N and J≤N and (I=J-1 IMPLIES A(I,J).0)and(I≠J-1 IMPLIES not A(I,J).0)) and 2 ≤ val_N and 3 > val_N and ID(2).1 = 0 and ID(3).0 = 0 and ID(4).0 =0 and ID(5).0 = 0 and ID(6).0 = 0 and ID(7).0 = 0 and TOP.1 = 1 and Q(1).1 = 2]

or

[FORALL I,J (1≤I and 1≤J and I≤N and J≤N and (I=J-1 IMPLIES A(I,J).0)and(I≠J-1 IMPLIES not A(I,J).0)) and 1 ≤ val_N and 2 > val_N and ID(2).1 = 0 and ID(3).0 = 0 and ID(4).0 =0 and ID(5).0 = 0 and ID(6).0 = 0 and ID(7).0 = 0 and TOP.1 = 0 and Q(1).1 =1]

or

[FORALL I,J (1≤I and 1≤J and I≤N and J≤N and (I=J-1 IMPLIES A(I,J).0)and(I≠J-1 IMPLIES not A(I,J).0)) and 1>val_N and ID(2).1=0 and ID(3).0=0 and ID(4).0=0 and ID(5).00 and ID(6).0=0 and ID(7).0=0 and TOP.1=0 and Q(1).1=0]

Appendix A3: the value of PC at the end of the symbolic execution

[FORALL I,J (1≤I and 1≤J and I≤N and J≤N and (I=J-1 IMPLIES A(I,J).0)and(I≠J-1 IMPLIES not A(I,J).0)) and 7 ≤ val_N and ID(2).1 = 0 and ID(3).1 = 0 and ID(4).1 =0 and ID(5).1 = 0 and ID(6).1 = 0 and ID(7).1= 0 and TOP.7 = 0 and Q(1).7 = 7]

or

[FORALL I,J (1≤I and 1≤J and I≤N and J≤N and (I=J-1 IMPLIES A(I,J).0)and(I≠J-1 IMPLIES not A(I,J).0)) and 6 ≤ val_N and 7 > val_N and ID(2).1 = 0 and ID(3).1 = 0 and ID(4).1 =0 and ID(5).1 = 0 and ID(6).1 = 0 and ID(7).1 = 0 and TOP.7 = 0 and Q(1).7 =6]

or

[FORALL I,J (1≤I and 1≤J and I≤N and J≤N and (I=J-1 IMPLIES A(I,J).0)and(I≠J-1 IMPLIES not A(I,J).0)) and 5 ≤ val_N and 6 > val_N and ID(2).1 = 0 and ID(3).1 = 0 and ID(4).1 =0 and ID(5).1 = 0 and ID(6).1 = 0 and ID(7).1 = 0 and TOP.7 = 0 and Q(1).7 = 5]

or

[FORALL I,J (1≤I and 1≤J and I≤N and J≤N and (I=J-1 IMPLIES A(I,J).0)and(I≠J-1 IMPLIES not A(I,J).0)) and 4 ≤ val_N and 5 > val_N and ID(2).1 = 0 and ID(3).1 = 0 and ID(4).1 =0 and ID(5).1 = 0 and ID(6).1 = 0 and ID(7).1 = 0 and TOP.7 = 0 and Q(1) 7= 4]

or

[FORALL I,J (1≤I and 1≤J and I≤N and J≤N and (I=J-1 IMPLIES A(I,J).0)and(I≠J-1 IMPLIES not A(I,J).0)) and 3 ≤ val_N and 4 > val_N and ID(2).1 = 0 and ID(3).1 = 0 and ID(4).1 =0 and ID(5).1 = 0 and ID(6).1 = 0 and ID(7).1 = 0 and TOP.7 = 0 and Q(1).7 = 3]

or

[FORALL I,J (1≤I and 1≤J and I≤N and J≤N and (I=J-1 IMPLIES A(I,J).0)and(I≠J-1 IMPLIES not A(I,J).0)) and 2 ≤ val_N and 3 > val_N and ID(2).1 = 0 and ID(3).1 = 0 and ID(4).1 =0 and ID(5).1 = 0 and ID(6).1 = 0 and ID(7).1 = 0 and TOP.7 = 0 and Q(1).7 = 2]

or

[FORALL I,J (1≤I and 1≤J and I≤N and J≤N and (I=J-1 IMPLIES A(I,J).0)and(I≠J-1 IMPLIES not A(I,J).0)) and 1 ≤ val_N and 2 > val_N and ID(2).1 = 0 and ID(3).1 = 0 and ID(4).1 =0 and ID(5).1 = 0 and ID(6).1 = 0 and ID(7).1 = 0 and TOP.7 = 0 and Q(1).7 =1]

or

[FORALL I,J (1≤I and 1≤J and I≤N and J≤N and (I=J-1 IMPLIES A(I,J).0)and(I≠J-1 IMPLIES not A(I,J).0)) and 1 > val_N and ID(2).1 = 0 and ID(3).1 = 0 and ID(4).1 =0 and ID(5).1 = 0 and ID(6).1 = 0 and ID(7).1 = 0 and TOP.7 = 0 and Q(1).7 =0]

Appendix B   The code of the simplified program

```
type GRAPH is array (1..49) of BOOLEAN;
type LIST is array (1..7) of INTEGER;

1        procedure TOPSORT(A: in GRAPH,
         N: in INTEGER, L: out LIST) is
2        I, J, Y, TOP: INTEGER;
3        Q, ID : LIST;
4        begin
5                I := 1;
6                J := 1;
7                TOP := 0;
8                Y := 0;
10.1             L(1) := 0;
11.1             Q(1) := 0;
12.1             ID(1) := 0
13.1             I := 2;
10.2             L(2) := 0;
11.2             Q(2) := 0;
12.2             ID(2) := 0
13.2             I := 3;
10.3             L(3) := 0;
11.3             Q(3) := 0;
12.3             ID(3) := 0
13.3             I := 4;
10.4             L(4) := 0;
11.4             Q(4) := 0;
12.4             ID(4) := 0
13.4             I := 5;
10.5             L(5) := 0;
11.5             Q(5) := 0;
```

```
12.1             ID(5) := 0
13.5             I := 6;
10.6             L(6) := 0;
11.6             Q(6) := 0;
12.6             ID(6) := 0
13.6             I := 7;
10.7             L(7) := 0;
11.7             Q(7) := 0;
12.7             ID(7) := 0
13.7             I := 8;
15               I := 1;
21.1.1   J := 2;
18.1.2   if 2 ≤ N then
19.1.2           ID(2) := 1;
20.1.2   end if;
21.1.2   J :=3;
21.1.3   J :=4;
21.1.4   J :=5;
21.1.5   J :=6;
21.1.6   J :=7;
21.1.7   J :=8;
23.1             I := 2;
24.1             J := 1;
21.2.1   J := 2;
21.2.2   J := 3;
18.2.3   if 3 ≤ N then
19.2.3           ID(3) := 1;
20.2.3   end if;
21.2.3   J :=4;
21.2.4   J :=5;
```

```
21.2.5  J :=6;
21.2.6  J :=7;
21.2.7  J :=8;
23.2              I := 3;
24.2              J := 1;
21.3.1  J := 2;
21.3.2  J := 3;
21.3.3  J := 4;
18.3.4  if 4 ≤ N then
19.3.4            ID(4) := 1;
20.3.4  end if;
21.3.4  J :=5;
21.3.5  J :=6;
21.3.6  J :=7;
21.3.7  J :=8;
23.3              I := 4;
24.3              J := 1;
21.4.1  J := 2;
21.4.2  J := 3;
21.4.3  J := 4;
21.4.4  J :=5;
18.4.5  if 5 ≤ N then
19.4.5            ID(5) := 1;
20.4.5  end if;
21.4.5  J :=6;
21.4.6  J :=7;
21.4.7  J :=8;
23.4              I := 5;
24.4              J := 1;
21.5.1  J := 2;
21.5.2  J := 3;
21.5.3  J := 4;
21.5.4  J :=5;
21.5.5  J :=6;
18.5.6  if 6 ≤ N then
19.5.6            ID(6) := 1;
20.5.6  end if;
21.5.6  J :=7;
21.5.7  J :=8;
23.5              I := 6;
24.5              J := 1;
21.6.1  J := 2;
21.6.2  J := 3;
21.6.3  J := 4;
21.6.4  J :=5;
21.6.5  J :=6;
21.6.6  J :=7;
18.6.7  if 7 ≤ N then
19.6.7            ID(7) := 1;
20.6.7  end if;
21.6.7  J :=8;
23.6              I := 7;
24.6              J := 1;
21.7.1  J := 2;
21.7.2  J := 3;
21.7.3  J := 4;
21.7.4  J :=5;
21.7.5  J :=6;
21.7.6  J :=7;
21.7.7  J :=8;
23.7              I := 8;
24.7              J := 1;
26                I := 1;
28.1              if 1 ≤ N then
29.1                      TOP := 1;
30.1                      Q(1) := 1;
31.1              end if;
32.1              I := 2;
32.2              I := 3;
32.3              I := 4;
32.4              I := 5;

32.5              I := 6;
32.6              I := 7;
32.7              I := 8;
34                I :=1;
35.1    if TOP /= 0 then
36.1              Y := 1;
37.1              TOP := 0;
38.1              L(1) := 1;
39.1              J := 1;
48.1.1  J:= 2;
41.1.2  if 2 ≤ N then
42.1.2            ID(2) := 0;
44.1.2            TOP := 1;
45.1.2            Q(1) := 2;
47.1.2  end if;
48.1.2  J := 3;
48.1.3  J := 4;
48.1.4  J := 5;
48.1.5  J := 6;
48.1.6  J := 7;
48.1.7  J := 8;
50.1              I := 2;
51.1    end if;
35.2    if TOP /= 0 then
36.2              Y := 2;
37.2              TOP := 0;
38.2              L(2) := 2;
39.2              J := 1;
48.2.1  J:= 2;
48.2.2  J := 3;
41.2.3  if 3 ≤ N then
42.2.3            ID(3) := 0;
44.2.3            TOP := 1;
45.2.3            Q(1) := 3;
47.2.3  end if;
48.2.3  J := 4;
48.2.4  J := 5;
48.2.5  J := 6;
48.2.6  J := 7;
48.2.7  J := 8;
50.2              I := 3;
51.2    end if;
35.3    if TOP /= 0 then
36.3              Y := 3;
37.3              TOP := 0;
38.3              L(3) := 3;
39.3              J := 1;
48.3.1  J:= 2;
48.3.2  J := 3;
48.3.3  J := 4;
41.3.4  if 4 ≤ N then
42.3.4            ID(4) := 0;
44.3.4            TOP := 1;
45.3.4            Q(1) := 4;
47.3.4  end if;
48.3.4  J := 5;
48.3.5  J := 6;
48.3.6  J := 7;
48.3.7  J := 8;
50.3              I := 4;
51.3    end if;
35.4    if TOP /= 0 then
36.4              Y := 4;
37.4              TOP := 0;
38.4              L(4) := 4;
39.4              J := 1;
48.4.1  J:= 2;
48.4.2  J := 3;
48.4.3  J := 4;
48.4.4  J := 5;
41.4.5  if 5 ≤ N then
```

```
42.4.5              ID(5) := 0;
44.4.5              TOP := 1;
45.4.5              Q(1) := 5;
47.4.5      end if;
48.4.5      J := 6;
48.4.6      J := 7;
48.4.7      J := 8;
50.4              I := 5;
51.4      end if;
35.5      if TOP /= 0 then
36.5              Y := 5;
37.5              TOP := 0;
38.5              L(5) := 5;
39.5              J := 1;
48.5.1      J:= 2;
48.5.2      J := 3;
48.5.3      J := 4;
48.5.4      J := 5;
48.5.5      J := 6;
41.5.6      if 6 ≤ N then
42.5.6              ID(6) := 0;
44.5.6              TOP := 1;
45.5.6              Q(1) := 6;
47.5.6      end if;
48.5.6      J := 7;
48.5.7      J := 8;
50.5              I := 6;
51.5      end if;
35.6      if TOP /= 0 then
36.6              Y := 6;
37.6              TOP := 0;

38.6              L(6) := 6;
39.6              J := 1;
48.6.1      J:= 2;
48.6.2      J := 3;
48.6.3      J := 4;
48.6.4      J := 5;
48.6.5      J := 6;
48.6.6      J := 7;
41.6.7      if 7 ≤ N then
42.6.7              ID(7) := 0;
44.6.7              TOP := 1;
45.6.7              Q(1) := 7;
47.6.7      end if;
48.6.7      J := 8;
50.6              I := 7;
51.6      end if;
35.7      if TOP /= 0 then
36.7              Y := 7;
37.7              TOP := 0;
38.7              L(7) := 7;
39.7              J := 1;
48.7.1      J := 2;
48.7.2      J := 3;
48.7.3      J := 4;
48.7.4      J := 5;
48.7.5      J := 6;
48.7.6      J := 7;
48.7.7      J := 8;
50.7              I := 8;
51.7      end if;
52      end;
```

Metric-Driven Classification Analysis

Richard W. Selby and R. Kent Madsen

Department of Information and Computer Science*
University of California, Irvine, California 92717
714-856-6326, selby@ics.uci.edu

Abstract

Metric-driven classification models identify software components with user-specifiable properties, such as those likely to be fault-prone, have high development effort, or have faults in a certain class. These models are generated automatically from past metric data, and they are scalable to large systems and calibratable to different projects. These models serve as extensible integration frameworks for software metrics because they allow the addition of new metrics and integrate symbolic and numeric data from all four measurement abstractions. In our past work, we developed and evaluated techniques for generating tree-based classification models. In this paper, we investigate a technique for generating network-based classification models. The principle underlying the tree-based models is partitioning, while the principle underlying the network-based models is pattern matching. Tree-based models prune away information and can be decomposed, while network-based models retain all information and tend to be more complex. We evaluate the predictive accuracy of network-based models and compare them to the tree-based models.

The evaluative study uses metric data from 16 NASA production systems ranging in size from 3000 to 112,000 source lines. The goal of the classification models is to identify the software components in the systems that had "high" development faults or effort, where "high" is defined to be in the uppermost quartile relative to

---

*This work was supported in part by the National Science Foundation under grant CCR–8704311 with cooperation from the Defense Advanced Research Projects Agency under Arpa order 6108, program code 7T10; National Aeronautics and Space Administration under grant NSG–5123; National Science Foundation under grant DCR–8521398; University of California under the MICRO program; Computer Sciences Corporation; Hughes Aircraft; and TRW.

past data. The models are derived from 74 candidate metrics that capture a multiplicity of information about the components: development effort, faults, changes, design style, and implementation style. A total of 1920 tree- and network-based models are automatically generated, and their predictive accuracies are compared in terms of correctness, completeness, and consistency using a non-parametric analysis of variance model. On the average, the predictions from the network-based models had 89.6% correctness, 69.1% completeness, and 79.5% consistency, while those from the tree-based models had 82.2% correctness, 56.3% completeness, and 74.5% consistency. The network-based models had statistically higher correctness and completeness than did the tree-based models, but they were not different statistically in terms of consistency. Capabilities to generate metric-driven classification models will be supported in the *Amadeus* measurement-driven analysis and feedback system.

1 Introduction

The development and maintenance of large-scale software systems require the efficient identification of potential problem areas. The "80:20 rule" suggests that a relatively small portion of a system causes a disproportionately large portion of its problems — 20% of the system is responsible for approximately 80% of the effort, faults, and rework [7]. Developers need to be able to identify the high-risk components, i.e., the "troublesome 20 percent," early in the development process so they can allocate resources accordingly and prevent problems later in the project.

We view this as a *classification problem*, and our approach uses metric-driven classification models to address it. In this paper we investigate an empirical modeling process for leveraging and integrating information from software products, processes, and personnel. The models are specified by "target classes" that reflect the goals and circumstances of a particular project. These user-specifiable target classes define the properties that developers want to predict about the system and its components, e.g., components likely to have a high number of faults, high development effort, or faults in a certain class. The model building process then characterizes software artifacts from previous systems, e.g., components, subsystems, or processes, which meet the target class criteria. The models use multiple software metrics, which are numeric and symbolic abstractions of software artifacts, to differentiate those past artifacts that would have been within or outside a target class. The resulting models can then be applied on a current or future project to identify artifacts likely, based on past data, of being in the target classes. These models guide software development and maintenance processes by identifying high-payoff problem areas.

Tree- and network-based classification models We have developed two model building techniques for analyzing large-scale systems. In earlier work, Selby and Porter developed and evaluated techniques for generating *tree-based classification models* [27]. The validation studies of these models used NASA software system data to identify two target classes, those components in the uppermost quartiles of development faults and effort. In this paper, we summarize an empirical validation study of *network-based classification models* and compare them to the tree-based models. The foundation of the tree-based models is the concept of partitioning, while the foundation of the network-based models is the concept of pattern matching. Tree-based models prune away metric information and can be decomposed, while network-based models retain all metric information and tend to be more complex. Both types of models are generated automatically from past metric data, and they are scalable to large systems and calibratable to different projects. Both models serve as extensible integration frameworks for software metrics because they allow the addition of new metrics and integrate symbolic and numeric data from all four measurement abstractions (nominal, ordinal, interval, and ratio).

Focus of the study This paper focuses on an empirical study to compare the effectiveness of tree- and network-based classification models in the domain of software engineering. Previous work has described general classification methods [23] [10] [25], and the specific application of tree- [27] [22] and network-based [18] models to large software systems [21]. The underlying research issue in this work is the investigation and application of measurement-based models to software engineering problems. Classification methods are not new, but they have not yet been applied extensively to large software systems. This paper is the first study to compare these two classification models on software engineering data.

Interaction with related software research The software development methodology for classification analysis and feedback defined in earlier work accommodates the use of either or both types of classification models [21]. The use of these model building techniques to identify target classes can be viewed as automating the steps of the *improvement paradigm* defined by Basili for the classification-related subset of improvement goals [4] [1]. Boehm and Ross have highlighted the importance of identifying and managing risks throughout software projects [8]. Classification modeling techniques can help support these risk management needs since they are applicable throughout the lifecycle and are driven by user-specifiable criteria for project risks. The classification models can incorporate metrics from the requirements [15] and design [16] [24] phases as well as later implementation, testing, and operational phases. The most advanced levels of the S.E.I. process maturity framework, "managed" and "optimizing" processes (levels 4 and 5), require the use of measurement techniques and highlight the need for measurement-based feedback methods, such as that provided by classification techniques [17]. Tree- and network-based classification models serve as metric integration frameworks that can incorporate metric data from software products, processes, and personnel. These models can leverage data from metric collection and analysis systems, such as *Amadeus* [29], *TAME* [1], *Ginger* [31], *SME* [13], and *AMS* [19], which can feed directly into the model building processes.

Section 2 outlines the research questions motivating this study. Section 3 gives a very brief introduction to tree- and network-based classification techniques. Section 4 describes a validation study that applies the classification modeling techniques to metric data from 16 NASA systems. Section 5 evaluates and compares the predictions from the two methods according to several parameters. The conclusions are summarized in Section 6.

2   Motivation

Earlier work has addressed research questions regarding the feasibility of classification analysis techniques for analyzing large software systems [27] [22]. This study is intended to address several other software research questions regarding classification analysis which leverage off this previous work, including:

- What is the predictive accuracy of network-based classification models?

- How does the predictive accuracy of tree- and network-based classification models compare?

- How does the predictive accuracy of the models compare on different target classes — high development faults or effort?

- How does the predictive accuracy of the models compare in terms of false positives (components predicted to be in the target class that are not)?

- How does the predictive accuracy of the models compare in terms of false negatives (components actually in the target class that are not predicted as such)?

- How is accuracy in the models affected by phase of prediction (using metrics available early in development versus a more complete set available later), amount of historical data, and grouping of metric values?

3 Classification Techniques

Classification techniques are centered on the notion of a target class. A classification technique distinguishes the objects in a particular set that are likely to be members of a target class (called positive or "+") from those objects that are unlikely to be members (called negative or "−"). The "objects" and the "target classes" are user-specifiable. In the software engineering problem domain, a useful example of objects to classify is the software components in a system. Examples of target classes to identify are those components with relatively high (or low) amounts of development faults, effort, or rework, or those components likely to be reusable on a future system.

The application of classification techniques basically requires a three-step process. A detailed explanation of a classification methodology appears in [21]. The first step is to define a target class, which is simply a binary membership function on the objects being classified. The second step builds (or "trains") a model to classify accurately a set of training objects according to whether or not they are in the target class. The training objects are known to be within or outside the target class, and they may be viewed as statistical samples of objects within and outside the target class. The training objects need to be representative of the population from which future objects will be selected, i.e., those objects whose target class membership is unknown and will be predicted by the model. Step three applies the model to previously unseen objects and predicts whether or not they belong to the target class.

We have developed automated tools to generate both types of classification techniques discussed, tree- and network-based models. Both tree- and network-based models classify objects by using their metric values to distinguish them. The models differ, however, in the way they approach the problem. The principle underlying the tree-based models is the concept of partitioning, while the principle underlying the network-based models is the concept of pattern matching. Tree-based models are constructed by classifying a set of previous (i.e., training) data by successively partitioning it. Each node in a tree-based model uses a particular metric and a particular set of data-thresholds to partition the objects it encounters. The network-based model treats the training objects as a set of paired, input-output patterns. Network-based models are constructed by iteratively modifying their empirical mapping of input patterns to output patterns while they are classifying a set of training data. A network-based model contains links that each map part of the input pattern to part of the output pattern. For more background on classification models, see [27] [21] [18] [23] [10] [25].

4 Validation Study

We conducted an extensive validation study using the network-based modeling techniques on metric data from NASA software systems.

Target Class Definition The two target classes selected provide useful information to developers and represent different software development issues. The two target classes are "high" development faults and "high" development effort. The objects being classified are software components, and a component is in the first target class if the number of development faults it had is in the uppermost quartile (25%) relative to past data. Analogously, a component is in the second target class if the number of hours of development effort spent on it is in the uppermost quartile (25%) relative to past data. The word high is in quotes because different environments can (and should) define their own target classes according to their particular goals.

Training Data We selected 16 moderate and large size software systems from a NASA production environment for this study [3] [11] [20]. The software provides ground support for unmanned spacecraft control. These systems range in size from 3000–112,000 lines of Fortran source code. They took from 5–140 person-months to develop over a period of 5–25 months. The staff ranged from 4–23 persons per project. The amount of software either reused or modified from previous systems averages 32 percent per project [26]. There are from 83–531 components in each system, where the term *component* is defined as a subroutine, function, main program, or block data. The 16 systems contain a total of over 4700 components.

There are 74 metrics (or attributes) associated with each component. The metrics capture information on the components' development effort, faults, changes, design style, implementation style, size, and static complexity [6] [5]. The metric data spans the beginning of design specification through the end of acceptance testing. The metric data was collected using a variety of data collection forms [3], developer interviews [2], and static analysis tools [14]. The data validation methods applied were described in earlier work [6]. Twenty-nine of the 74 metrics are available by the end of the design phase. In the study, these 29 metrics are called the metrics with "early" availability. The study constructs network-based models using all available metrics (74) as well as just those that are available early in development (29). The components and metrics are the same as those used in earlier work. For a complete list of the metrics and the itemization of "early" versus "all" metrics, see [27]. We are using the same metric data so that we can compare the results from the tree-based classification models described in [27] with the results from the network-based models in this study.

Recoding Data   The network-based modeling technique requires the metric data to be represented as nominal information. We use quartiles and octiles as the two methods for recoding the data in this study. Our related research is examining distribution-sensitive methods for data partitioning [22].

Training   The model training iterations end when the model correctly classifies 100% of the training components or when the network can no longer improve its correctness. The criteria used for the latter issue is as follows — if the network fails to improve its classification correctness during the last 50 training iterations, training is stopped.

An actual network-based model appears in [18]; an actual tree-based model appears in [27].

Application   We want to conduct our validation study using scenarios that could have actually happened in practice. Therefore, we order the 16 systems chronologically 1 through 16 — oldest to most recent — and successively apply the classification model constructed using the components in systems m through n as the training data and predicting those components likely to be in the target classes in system $n + 1$. The model constructed from metric data in system 1 is used to predict high-fault and high-effort components in system 2, the model constructed from systems 1 and 2 is used to predict system 3, and so forth. The components from one system are needed to evaluative the model predictions (which constitutes the "test set"), so the number of systems in the training sets ranges from 1–15. There are 120 combinations of training and test sets.

5   Data Analysis

There are numerous factors that affect the performance of classification models. In order to account for their individual contributions, an analysis of variance model is applied. A total of 1920 tree- and network-based models were automatically generated and evaluated using prototype tools. The full-factorial non-parametric analysis of variance model includes five primary factors and all two- and three-way interactions among the factors. The model generation and evaluation process is automated, and therefore, the increased sensitivity of a full-factorial design is preferred over the more economical fractional-factorial design [12] [9]. The primary factors and their levels are: model representation (network-based, tree-based); target

Correctness	$\dfrac{|correctly\ classified\ components|}{|total\ components|}$
Completeness	$\dfrac{|predicted\ in\ target\ class \cap actually\ in\ target\ class|}{|actually\ in\ target\ class|}$
Consistency	$\dfrac{|predicted\ in\ target\ class \cap actually\ in\ target\ class|}{|predicted\ in\ target\ class|}$

Table 1: Formulas for correctness, completeness, and consistency. The symbol | | means cardinality.

class (faults, effort); metric availability (early, all); number of training projects (1–15); and metric grouping (quartiles, octiles). Our earlier work helped focus this study on an appropriate set of model building parameters [27] [28] [22].

The predictive accuracy of the classification models generated from each combination of factors is evaluated in terms of three criteria: correctness, completeness, and consistency. *Correctness* is the percentage of components correctly classified as "+" or "−." Correctness measures the overall classification accuracy. *Completeness* is the percentage of components that are predicted to be "+" and actually are "+" relative to the total number of components that are *actually* "+." Completeness measures the extent to which the model identifies *all* the components that are actually in the target class — i.e., no false negatives. *Consistency* is the percentage of components that are predicted to be "+" and actually are "+" relative to the total number of components that are *predicted* "+." Consistency measures the extent to which the model identifies *only* the components that are actually in the target class — i.e., no false positives. Table 1 summarizes the formulas for correctness, completeness, and consistency.

The following two subsections summarize the statistical results from the network-based models only and the comparison between the tree- and network-based models.

Networks Table 2 summarizes the average classification accuracies for the network-based models. The overall F-tests for the three accuracy measures of correctness, completeness, and consistency were statistically significant ($\alpha < 0.0001$ for each). Metric availability and metric grouping had a statistically significant effect on both correctness ($\alpha < 0.0001$ for each) and completeness ($\alpha < 0.0001$; $\alpha < 0.02$). Target class and metric grouping had a statistically significant effect on consistency ($\alpha < 0.008$; $\alpha < 0.05$). The target class of faults had higher consistency than

Factor	Correctness (%)		Completeness (%)		Consistency (%)	
	Mean	Std.	Mean	Std.	Mean	Std.
(a) Target class						
faults	89.58	10.72	69.15	28.71	83.04*	20.81
total effort	89.67	7.86	69.03	26.09	75.95*	24.77
(b) Metric availability						
all	93.18*	5.47	81.80*	16.08	79.74	22.81
early	86.07*	11.02	56.38*	30.37	79.25	23.49
(c) Number of training projects						
1–3	89.48	9.09	71.64	27.24	81.47	23.06
4–6	89.28	9.90	67.06	28.39	79.56	22.73
7–9	89.78	9.46	68.90	27.44	78.09	24.29
10–12	89.68	9.75	69.06	25.84	76.36	23.42
13–15	91.77	7.32	63.22	26.18	78.68	19.90
(d) Metric grouping						
quartiles	86.00*	10.71	64.84*	29.78	82.08*	19.07
octiles	93.25*	5.98	73.34*	24.14	76.90*	26.36
Overall	89.63	9.40	69.09	27.42	79.49	23.14

Table 2: Classification accuracies for the network-based models. The means with asterisks (*) have differences that are statistically significant.

did the target class of effort, and the use of all metrics had higher correctness and completeness than did the use of early metrics. The metric grouping of octiles had higher correctness and completeness than did the quartile grouping, but quartiles had higher consistency.

There were several statistically significant two-way and three-way interactions among the factors ($\alpha < 0.05$). Target class x metric availability, metric availability x metric grouping, and metric availability x number of training projects were all statistically significant for correctness, completeness, and consistency. Target class x metric grouping was statistically significant for completeness and consistency. Target class x metric availability x metric grouping was statistically significant for correctness and consistency. Metric availability x metric grouping x number of training projects was statistically significant for correctness and completeness.

Figure 1 depicts the network-based model's correctness.

Figure 1: Mean correctness for all metrics available and varying number of projects in training-set using network-based models.

Comparison of Networks and Trees Table 3 summarizes the overall average classification accuracies for all the models, including both the network- and tree-based models. (Table 4 summarizes the average classification accuracies for just the tree-based models.[1]) For the combined data (Table 3), the overall F-tests for the three accuracy measures of correctness, completeness, and consistency were statistically significant ($\alpha < 0.0001$ for each). All five primary factors (model representation, target class, metric availability, number of training projects, and metric grouping) had a statistically significant effect on correctness ($\alpha < 0.0001$ for each, except $\alpha < 0.005$ for target class). All primary factors except number of training projects had a statistically significant effect on completeness ($\alpha < 0.0001$ for each). Only target class and metric availability had a statistically significant effect on consistency ($\alpha < 0.02$; $\alpha < 0.0001$). The network models had higher correctness and completeness than did the tree models, but they were not different statistically in terms of consistency. The target class of faults had higher correctness, consistency, and completeness that did the target class of effort. The use of all metrics had higher correctness, completeness, and consistency than did the use of early metrics. The metric grouping of octiles had higher correctness and completeness than did quartiles.

There were several statistically significant two-way and three-way interactions

---

[1]The tree-based models in Tables 3 and 4 are generated using 25% termination criteria and the information-theory evaluation function described in [27].

Factor	Correctness (%)		Completeness (%)		Consistency (%)	
	Mean	Std.	Mean	Std.	Mean	Std.
(a) Model representation						
networks	89.63*	9.40	69.09*	27.42	79.49	23.14
trees	82.19*	16.27	56.29*	31.44	74.49	27.60
(b) Target class						
faults	85.51*	15.88	65.93*	33.23	78.07*	26.94
total effort	86.31*	11.31	59.45*	26.40	75.91*	24.12
(c) Metric availability						
all	93.33*	6.44	80.43*	19.73	85.30*	20.54
early	78.49*	15.12	44.95*	28.33	68.69*	27.39
(d) Number of training projects						
1–3	84.82	14.34	63.92	30.79	76.37	27.21
4–6	85.66	14.09	62.78	30.24	76.95	25.31
7–9	86.60	13.29	61.82	30.14	76.59	25.64
10–12	86.88	13.15	62.01	29.19	78.24	23.49
13–15	89.70	10.61	58.77	28.12	80.08	19.68
(e) Metric grouping						
quartiles	83.80*	13.75	59.74*	30.90	76.88	24.39
octiles	88.02*	13.52	65.64*	29.15	77.10	26.75
Overall	85.91	13.79	62.69	30.18	76.99	25.59

Table 3: Classification accuracies for both model representations: network-based and tree-based models. The means with asterisks (*) have differences that are statistically significant.

Factor	Correctness (%)		Completeness (%)		Consistency (%)	
	Mean	Std.	Mean	Std.	Mean	Std.
(a) Target class						
faults	81.44	18.89	62.70	36.95	73.10	31.15
total effort	82.95	13.10	49.88	23.05	75.88	23.48
(b) Metric availability						
all	93.49	7.29	79.06	22.73	90.85	16.20
early	70.90	14.87	33.52	20.57	58.12	26.95
(c) Number of training projects						
1–3	80.16	16.90	56.21	32.21	71.26	29.98
4–6	82.04	16.54	58.49	31.46	74.33	27.44
7–9	83.42	15.63	54.73	31.10	75.09	26.90
10–12	84.07	15.38	54.96	30.71	80.12	23.51
13–15	87.64	12.86	54.32	29.54	81.47	19.57
(d) Metric grouping						
quartiles	81.59	15.93	54.64	31.20	71.67	27.79
octiles	82.79	16.59	57.94	31.63	77.31	27.15
Overall	82.19	16.27	56.29	31.44	74.49	27.60

Table 4: Classification accuracies for the tree-based models.

Evaluation Criterion	Model	Early Metrics Faults Quartiles	Early Metrics Faults Octiles	Early Metrics Effort Quartiles	Early Metrics Effort Octiles	All Metrics Faults Quartiles	All Metrics Faults Octiles	All Metrics Effort Quartiles	All Metrics Effort Octiles
Correctness	Net	**76.58%**	**91.97%**	**83.24%**	**92.50%**	94.52%	95.25%	**89.69%**	**93.27%**
	Tree	68.64%	68.56%	76.21%	78.21%	**96.20%**	**97.23%**	87.71%	89.24%
Completeness	Net	**41.82%**	**56.18%**	**42.22%**	**73.70%**	**88.90%**	76.07%	**82.40%**	**73.86%**
	Tree	26.85%	25.36%	28.42%	36.05%	88.72%	**92.73%**	63.82%	60.87%
Consistency	Net	**73.54%**	**80.32%**	**86.14%**	69.18%	87.04%	83.45%	78.84%	66.92%
	Tree	51.22%	56.00%	60.18%	**73.94%**	**92.09%**	**94.53%**	**79.57%**	**90.38%**

Table 5: Mean correctness, completeness, and consistency of network- and tree-based models for predicting target-class software components (bold type indicates the model with the higher value for each combination of parameters and evaluation criteria).

among the factors ($\alpha < 0.05$). Model representation x metric availability and target class x metric availability were statistically significant for correctness, completeness, and consistency. Model representation x metric grouping was statistically significant for correctness and consistency. Model representation x target class and target class x metric grouping were statistically significant for completeness. Model representation x number of training projects was statistically significant for consistency. Metric availability x metric grouping and metric availability x number of training projects were statistically significant for correctness and completeness. Target class x number of training projects was statistically significant for correctness. Model representation x metric availability x metric grouping and model representation x metric availability x number of training projects were statistically significant for correctness, completeness, and consistency. Model representation x target class x metric availability was statistically significant for correctness and completeness. Model representation x target class x metric grouping was statistically significant for completeness and consistency. Metric availability x metric grouping x target class and metric availability x metric grouping x number of training projects were statistically significant for correctness.

Table 5 summarizes the comparison between the network- and tree-based models.

6 Conclusions

Experience in industrial software development suggests that a relatively small portion of a software system is often responsible for a disproportionately large share of development resources and faults. Developers need to be able to identify these high-risk software components early in development if they wish to prevent them from dominating a project's resource consumption. In this paper we analyzed two methods for identifying components with user-specifiable properties: tree- and network-based classification models. These techniques have many advantages, including being scalable to large systems, calibratable to new projects, and extensible. They also serve as integration frameworks for software metrics. In the evaluative study using NASA system data, we automatically constructed 1920 classification models by varying several model building parameters: model representation, target class, metric availability, number of training projects, and metric grouping. The complete list of the metrics used appears in [27]. Actual network- and tree-based models generated from the data appear in [18] and [27], respectively. The empirical results presented in this study are intended to provide the basis for analysis of classification models — it is not implied that there is a direct extrapolation of these results to other environments and data sets.

The primary results from this study are as follows:

- Tree- and network-based classification models are feasible and useful for analyzing software systems.

- On the average, the predictions from the network-based models had 89.6% correctness, 69.1% completeness, and 79.5% consistency, while those from the tree-based models had 82.2% correctness, 56.3% completeness, and 74.5% consistency.

- The network-based models had statistically higher correctness and completeness than did the tree-based models, but they were not different statistically in terms of consistency.

- The following factors resulted in models with statistically significant increases in correctness and completeness: network-based model representations (as opposed to tree-based); high-faults as the target class (as opposed to high-effort); all metrics available (as opposed to only early metrics); and octiles as the metric grouping function (as opposed to quartiles).

- The following factors resulted in models with statistically significant increases in consistency: high-faults as the target class (as opposed to high-effort); and all metrics available (as opposed to only early metrics).

- There are many statistically significant interactions and important tradeoffs among the model building parameters, e.g., network-based models with octile metric-groupings had higher correctness and completeness, but those with quartile metric-groupings had higher consistency.

In our future work, we will develop techniques for optimizing model building toward either consistency or completeness. We are also characterizing the types of metrics effective for identifying different target classes such as error-proneness. We are formalizing feedback mechanisms and templates that leverage classification modeling techniques. Several companies and organizations are interested in using the classification techniques. We will integrate the classification model building tools and feedback mechanisms into the *Amadeus* metric-driven analysis and feedback system [29]. *Amadeus* is a system that defines software environment architecture mechanisms for enabling empirically guided software development and maintenance processes. The system defines an extensible integration framework for empirically based analysis techniques, such as the classification model building techniques described in this paper. *Amadeus* is integrated with and leverages components in the *Arcadia* process-centered software environment architecture [30].

7 Acknowledgments

We gratefully acknowledge Adam Porter and Doug Schmidt for their comments on previous versions of this article.

References

[1] V. R. Basili and H. D. Rombach. The TAME project: Towards improvement-oriented software environments. *IEEE Transactions on Software Engineering*, SE-14(6):758–773, June 1988.

[2] V. R. Basili and D. M. Weiss. A methodology for collecting valid software engineering data. *IEEE Transactions on Software Engineering*, SE-10(6):728–738, November 1984.

[3] V. R. Basili, M. V. Zelkowitz, F. E. McGarry, Jr. R. W. Reiter, W. F. Truszkowski, and D. L. Weiss. The software engineering laboratory. Technical Report SEL-77-001, Software Engineering Laboratory, NASA/Goddard Space Flight Center, Greenbelt, MD, May 1977.

[4] Victor R. Basili. Quantitative evaluation of software methodology. In *Proceedings of the First Pan Pacific Computer Conference*, Melbourne, Australia, September 1985.

[5] Victor R. Basili and Richard W. Selby. Calculation and use of an environment's characteristic software metric set. In *Proceedings of the Eighth International Conference on Software Engineering*, London, August 1985.

[6] Victor R. Basili, Richard W. Selby, and Tsai Y. Phillips. Metric analysis and data validation across Fortran projects. *IEEE Transactions on Software Engineering*, SE-9(6):652–663, November 1983.

[7] Barry Boehm. Industrial software metrics top 10 list. *IEEE Software*, 4(5):84–85, September 1987.

[8] Barry W. Boehm and Rony Ross. Theory-w software project management: Principles and examples. *IEEE Transactions on Software Engineering*, 15(7):902–916, July 1989.

[9] G. E. P. Box, W. G. Hunter, and J. S. Hunter. *Statistics for Experimenters*. John Wiley & Sons, New York, 1978.

[10] L. Breiman, J. Friedman, R. Olshen, and C. Stone. *Classification and Regression Trees*. Wadsworth, Monterey, CA, 1984.

[11] D. N. Card, F. E. McGarry, J. Page, S. Eslinger, and V. R. Basili. The software engineering laboratory. Technical Report SEL-81-104, Software Engineering Laboratory, NASA/Goddard Space Flight Center, Greenbelt, MD, February 1982.

[12] W. G. Cochran and G. M. Cox. *Experimental Designs*. John Wiley & Sons, New York, 1950.

[13] W. Decker and J. Valett. Software management environment (SME) concepts and architecture. Technical Report SEL-89-003, NASA Goddard, Greenbelt, Maryland, August 1989.

[14] W. J Decker and W. A. Taylor. Fortran static source code analyzer program (sap) user's guide (revision 1). Technical Report SEL-78-102, Software Engineering Laboratory, NASA/Goddard Space Flight Center, Greenbelt, MD, May 1982.

[15] W. E. Hall and S. H. Zweben. The cloze procedure and software comprehensibility measurement. *IEEE Transactions on Software Engineering*, SE-12(5):608–623, May 1986.

[16] S. Henry and C. Selig. Predicting source-code complexity at the design stage. *IEEE Software*, 7(2):36–45, March 1990.

[17] W. S. Humphrey. Characterizing the software process: A maturity framework. *IEEE Software*, 5(2):73–79, March 1988.

[18] R. Kent Madsen and Richard W. Selby. Metric-driven classification models for analyzing large-scale software. Technical report, University of California, 1990. (submitted for publication).

[19] J. A. McCall, P. Richards, and G. Walters. Factors in software quality. Technical Report RADC-TR-77-369, Rome Air Development Center, Griffiss Air Force Base, NY, November 1977.

[20] F. McGarry. Annotated bibliography of software engineering laboratory (sel)literature. Technical Report SEL-82-006, Software Engineering Laboratory, NASA/Goddard Space Flight Center, Greenbelt, MD, November 1982.

[21] Adam A. Porter and Richard W. Selby. Empirically guided software development using metric-based classification trees. *IEEE Software*, 7(2):46–54, March 1990.

[22] Adam A. Porter and Richard W. Selby. Evaluating techniques for generating metric-based classification trees. *Journal of Systems and Software*, 12(3):209–218, July 1990.

[23] J. R. Quinlan. Induction of decision trees. *Journal of Machine Learning*, 1(1):81–106, 1986.

[24] D. Rombach. Design measurement: Some lessons learned. *IEEE Software*, 7(2):17–25, March 1990.

[25] D. Rumelhart and J. McClelland, editors. *Parallel Distributed Processing*. MIT Press, Cambridge, MA, 1986. Volume 1.

[26] Richard W. Selby. Empirically analyzing software reuse in a production environment. In W. Tracz, editor, *Software Reuse — Emerging Technologies*. IEEE Computer Society Press, New York, September 1988.

[27] Richard W. Selby and Adam A. Porter. Learning from examples: Generation and evaluation of decision trees for software resource analysis. *IEEE Transactions on Software Engineering*, SE-14(12):1743–1757, December 1988.

[28] Richard W. Selby and Adam A. Porter. Software metric classification trees help guide the maintenance of large-scale systems. In *Proceedings of the Conference on Software Maintenance*, pages 116–123, Miami, FL, October 1989.

[29] Richard W. Selby, Adam A. Porter, Doug C. Schmidt, and James Berney. Metric-driven analysis and feedback systems for enabling empirically guided software development. In *Proceedings of the Thirteenth International Conference on Software Engineering*, Austin, TX, May 1991.

[30] Richard N. Taylor, Frank C. Belz, Lori A. Clarke, Leon Osterweil, Richard W. Selby, Jack C. Wileden, Alexander L. Wolf, and Michal Young. Foundations for the Arcadia environment architecture. In *Proceedings of ACM SIGSOFT '88: Third Symposium on Software Development Environments*, pages 1–13, Boston, November 1988. Appeared as *Sigplan Notices 24*(2) and *Software Engineering Notes 13*(5).

[31] Koji Torii, Tohru Kikuno, Ken ichi Matsumoto, and Shinji Kusumoto. A data collection and analysis system Ginger to improve programmer productivity on software development. Technical report, Osaka University, Osaka, Japan, 1989.

A Dynamic Failure Model For Predicting the Impact that a Program Location has on the Program

Jeffrey Voas

NASA-Langley Research Center

Mail Stop 478, Hampton, VA 23665 USA

Abstract

This paper presents a dynamic technique for predicting the effect that a "location" of a program will have on the program's computational behavior. The technique is based on the *three* necessary and sufficient conditions for software failure to occur: (1) a fault must be executed, (2) the fault must adversely affect the data state, and (3) the adverse effect in a data state must affect program output. In order to predict the effect that a location of a program will have on the program's computational behavior, the following characteristics of each program location are estimated: (1) the probability that a location of the program is executed, (2) the probability that a location of the program noticeably affects the program state created by the location, and (3) the probability that the data states created by a location affect the program's output. With estimates of these characteristics for each location in a program, we can predict those locations where a fault can more easily remain undetected during testing, as well as predict the degree of testing necessary to be convinced that a fault is not remaining undetected in a particular location.

Index Terms: Software testing, data state, sensitivity analysis, mutant, fault, failure probability.

1 Introduction

Software testing reveals failures. When an input distribution for a program is known, random testing has several advantages over other validation techniques; it does not rely on extensive analysis such as *proof of correctness*, it replicates operational behavior, and it has a statistical basis. However, testing has drawbacks: any predictions based on black-box random testing depend on an assumed input distribution. If an input distribution for a program changes, any predictions based on the previous input distribution may change dramatically. When testing reveals a failure, it provides little help in locating the fault. Finally, testing requires an *oracle*; since automated oracles are rarely available, human oracles (who require time and may introduce new faults) are required.

The dynamic technique presented in this paper complements software testing. It does *not* identify faults; correctness is never an issue. Instead, the technique identifies "locations" in a program where faults, *if they were to exist*, are more likely to remain undetected from tests. In this technique, a *location* is defined to be either an input statement, output statement, assignment statement, or the <expression> part of a while or if statement.

This technique requires no oracle nor specification, however it does require that inputs are selected at random consistent with an assumed input distribution. Preferably this input distribution will be the *operational distribution*, however there are certain instances where a uniform distribution may be substituted when the operational distribution is unknown and still produce valid results. The technique uses a program's input distribution, syntactic mutants, and changes injected into dynamically created data states to predict a location's ability to cause program failure *if the location were to contain a fault*. The technique can just as easily be applied to modules as programs; if this is done, the technique would predict the ability of a location in a module to cause module failure if the location were to contain a fault.

The technique makes predictions concerning future program behavior by estimating the effect that (1) an input distribution, (2) syntactic mutants, and (3) changed data values in data states have on current program behavior. More specifically, the technique first observes the behavior of the program when (1) the program is executed with a particular input distribution, (2) a location of the program is injected with syntactic mutants, and (3) a data state (that is created dynamically by a program location for some input) has one of its data values altered and execution is resumed. After observing the behavior of the program under these scenarios, the technique then predicts future program behavior if faults were to exist. These three scenarios simulate the three necessary and sufficient conditions for software failure to occur: (1) a fault must be executed, (2) a data state error must be created, and (3) the data state error must propagate to the output. Therefore the technique is tightly based on the conditions necessary for software failure.

Three analyses compose the technique: *Execution Analysis (EA)* estimates the probability that a location is executed according to a particular input distribution; *Infection Analysis (IA)* estimates the probability that a syntactic mutant affects a data state; and *Propagation Analysis (PA)* estimates the probability that a data state that has been changed affects the program output after execution is resumed on the changed data state. These analyses together form the technique that this paper presents—the technique is termed *PIE* (for *Propagation*, *Infection* and *Execution* analysis).

The remainder of the paper is organized as follows: Section 1 is responsible for presenting the three analyses: Section 1.1 relates and differentiates *PIE* from other software testing techniques, and Section 1.2 provides the algorithms of *PIE*. Section 2 shows (1) how to apply the estimates that the algorithms produce in order to make predictions about where faults can more easily remain undetected and (2) how to quantify the likelihood that a location will reveal a fault if one were to exist. Section 3 contains empirical results showing that the probability estimates that the algorithms produce do accurately reflect the effect that a location has on the program's computational behavior.

1.1 Survey of Related Techniques

Testing plays a significant role in analyzing software for faults. And as stated in the introduction, *PIE* can be used to complement the efforts of software testing even though *PIE* is fundamentally different than software testing.

PIE is a white-box analysis technique, i.e., its results are a function of the syntax and semantics of the code. Further, *PIE* is a dynamic technique—its results are also a function of an input distribution. Other white-box analysis techniques include coverage-based (or syntactic) testing techniques such as statement testing, branch testing, path testing, and mutation testing. *Statement testing* attempts to execute every statement at least once; *branch testing* requires that each branch be executed at least once; and *path testing* requires that each path be executed at least once; *EA* differs from statement, branch, and path testing because *EA* does not perform testing—it only estimates the probabilities that a particular location is executed. The results of *EA* can be useful, however, to persons performing statement, branch, or path testing, because *EA* estimates the probability of executing a particular location. For instance, if a person attempting to perform statement testing is having difficulty finding an input to execute a particular statement, then the person could look at the estimate of the probability that the statement is executed (from *EA*), and if it turns out that *EA* has produced a tiny estimate for this probability, then the person can decide whether statement testing is still a feasible goal.

Of all testing techniques, *PIE* is most closely related to mutation testing. It is related in the processes employed, not in the information produced. *Mutation testing* [1] is a testing strategy that evaluates inputs by taking a program P and producing n versions(*mutants*) of P, $[p_1, p_2, ..., p_n]$, that are syntactically different from P. If a set of inputs distinguish the mutants created from P, then it is assumed that if the actual program works with those inputs, the program is good. Mutation testing assumes the "competent programmer hypothesis" that states that a competent programmer produces code that is close to being correct, where "close" means only a few syntax changes are required to correct a program. Mutation testing also assumes that faults that interact can be caught with test data that reveals single faults, i.e., fault coupling is ignored [5]. Mutation testing tests input data; good test data kills all mutants.

IA uses mutation testing ideas in the following way: syntactic changes are made to program statements with the requirement that these syntactic changes must have semantic differences. Whereas mutation testing tests inputs, *IA* tests a location's ability to sustain a change in its semantics yet not change the data state. *PA* generalizes the applicability of mutation testing by allowing a data state to be mutated. *PA* tests to determine the frequency with which a change in a data state causes a change in the program's output. In short, *PA* and *IA*'s goal is significantly different from mutation testing's goals.

Another technique that *PIE* is closely related to is error-based testing. *Error-based testing* attempts to define certain classes of errors and the subdomain of the input space that should reveal any error of that class if that error type exists in the program. Morell

[4] proves properties about error-based strategies concerning certain errors that can and cannot be eliminated using error-based testing. Since error-based testing restricts the class of computable functions, the testing achievable by error-based testing is limited as well. This is because error-based testing defines errors in terms of their syntax, as does mutation testing. *PA* advances the concept of error-based testing by defining classes of errors in terms of their semantic effect in a data state.

In summary, *PIE* is a technique that is fundamentally different than software testing. Testing's goal is to detect faults through the production of failures; *PIE*'s goal is to estimate (1) the probability that a location of a program is executed, (2) the probability that a location of a program noticeably affects the data state created by the location, and (3) the probability that a data state created by a location affects the program's output. With these estimates, *PIE* complements software testing.

1.2 Definitions

The *PIE* technique is built in three levels. We begin with basic terminology in Section 1.2.1; then Section 1.2.2 describes the first level; Section 1.2.3 describes the second level, and Section 1.2.4 describes the third level. The third level contains the algorithms that are used in implementing the technique.

1.2.1 General Definitions

We view a *program* as a function g mapping a domain of possible inputs to a range of possible outputs. Another function, f (with same domain and perhaps different range), represents the desired behavior of g, and can be thought of as a functional specification of g. In practice, it is not necessary to have f explicitly, but it is necessary to be able to say whether a particular output of g is *correct* or *incorrect* for a particular input x, with the latter implying that $g(x) \neq f(x)$, and the former implying that $g(x) = f(x)$. The *failure probability* of program g, $\tau_{g,D}$, given that g's inputs $x_1, x_2, x_3, \ldots$ are drawn at random according to a fixed but known probability distribution D, is the probability that g results in failure for a randomly selected input, x_i. The probability that a specific input x_i is selected is just $D(x_i)$.

A variable is *live* if its current value may eventually affect the output. The program counter is considered live. Whether a variable is live or not is determined statically; this can be done using dataflow analysis. A *data state* between two consecutive locations (where consecutive is determined dynamically) is a set of mappings between all statically declared and dynamically allocated variables and their values at that point in execution. Also included in each data state are the input that began the execution and the program counter. The execution of a location is considered to be an atomic operation, hence data states can only be viewed *between* locations. An *data state error* is an incorrect variable/value pairing in a data state where correctness is determined by an assertion for that location. A data state error is frequently referred to as an *infection*, and these two terms are used interchangeably. If a data state error exists, the data state and variable with the incorrect value at that point are termed *infected*. A data state may have more than one infected variable. *Propagation* of a data state error occurs when a data state error affects the output.

In formalizing this technique, we will regularly mention "data state mutants." Recall that a data state is just a snapshot during execution of the values of all statically declared and dynamically allocated variables. Thus, a data state is a function of the location where it is taken, as well as the program input and the particular iteration of the location. A *data state mutant* is a change to a data state that would normally occur given an input, location, and iteration of that location.

In this paper, we will consider that data state mutants are created in one of two different ways: (1) either a forced change into a value in a data state (during *PA*), or a change that results from executing a syntactic mutant of the location (during *IA*). Note the difference between a data state error and a data state mutant: a data state error is defined with respect to the correct program, whereas a data state mutant is defined with respect to the current program. The current program that we have in our hands that we are applying this technique to may be correct, but we will not know whether this is true.

1.2.2 Definitions for known faults

Section 1.2.2 describes the first level of the *PIE* technique. The first level formalizes (1) the probability that a location is executed, (2) the probability that an infection occurs, and (3) the probability of an infection propagating to the output. To do so, we define three probabilities: (1) the execution probability, (2) the infection probability, and (3) the propagation probability. These probabilities are defined for a *known* fault, χ, injected into an otherwise correct program, ρ. Though these definitions are not directly usable in a conventional situation (where the faults, if any exist, are unknown), these definitions provide a foundation for understanding how faults affect the computational behavior of a program.

To define execution, infection, and propagation probabilities, we first introduce notation. Recall that this is a dynamic technique that collects information about what occurs during execution under certain circumstances; some of this information concerns the data states that are created as a program executes. It is therefore necessary to be able to uniquely identify a data state according to the input that the program is currently executing on, the location in the program where we are observing the data state, and which iteration of the location we are observing this data state on (if the location is executed more than once). Unfortunately, all of this identifying information complicates the notion but provides precision.

Let S denote a specification, ρ denote a correct version of S, x denote an input, $domain(S)$ be a set of all possible inputs to ρ for which S is defined, D be the probability distribution of $domain(S)$, l denote a program location in ρ, and let i denote a particular execution (or iteration) of location l caused by input x. Hence if $i > 1$, then l is in a loop or in a procedure that is called more than once. Let $\mathcal{B}_{l,\rho,i,x}$ represent the data state that exists prior to executing location l on the ith execution from input $x \in domain(S)$, and let $\mathcal{A}_{l,\rho,i,x}$ represent the data state produced after executing location l on the ith execution from input x. Note that before ρ begins execution on x, $\mathcal{A}_{l,\rho,i,x}$ and $\mathcal{B}_{l,\rho,i,x}$ equal the empty set for all i and all l. The execution of each location causes the data state that succeeds the location to no longer equal the empty set. Thus if after execution on x, some $\mathcal{A}_{l,\rho,i,x} = \emptyset$, then l was not executed an ith time by x.

It is important for us to be able to group data states into sets with similar properties. For instance, assume that location l is executed n_x times by input x. Then we might want to look at all of the data states that are created by this input immediately before l is executed or immediately after. The following sets allow us to do so:

$$\mathcal{B}_{l,\rho,x} = \{\mathcal{B}_{l,\rho,i,x} \mid 1 \le i \le n_x\}$$

$$\mathcal{A}_{l,\rho,x} = \{\mathcal{A}_{l,\rho,i,x} \mid 1 \le i \le n_x\}$$

We further group these sets into a single set for all $x \in domain(S)$:

$$\beta_{l,\rho,domain(S)} = \{\mathcal{B}_{l,\rho,x} \mid x \in domain(S)\}$$

$$\alpha_{l,\rho,domain(S)} = \{\mathcal{A}_{l,\rho,x} \mid x \in domain(S)\}$$

We let f_l denote the function that *is* computed at location l. The input to a function computed at a location is a data state and the output of such a function is also a data state. It is important to talk about the function that is computed at a particular location in order to see how individual locations map one incoming data state to an outgoing data state.

The *execution probability* of a known fault χ in location l is simply the conditional probability that a randomly selected input x will cause fault χ to be executed:

$$\varepsilon_{l,\rho,D} = \Pr[\mathcal{A}_{l,\rho,x} \neq \varnothing \text{ after } \rho \text{ executes on } x \mid x \text{ selected according to } D] \tag{1}$$

The *infection probability* of a known fault χ in location l is the conditional probability that a data state that location l creates becomes infected when location l is executed for a randomly selected input x:

$$\Pr[infected(\mathcal{B}_{l,\rho,x}, \chi, l) \mid \mathcal{A}_{l,\rho,x} \neq \varnothing \text{ after } \rho \text{ executes on } x] \tag{2}$$

where

$$infected(\mathcal{B}_{l,\rho,x}, \chi, l) = \begin{cases} \mathbf{T} & \text{if } \exists y \in \mathcal{B}_{l,\rho,x} \; f_l(y) \neq f_\chi(y) \\ \mathbf{F} & \text{otherwise} \end{cases}$$

(f_l denotes the function that *should be* computed at location l that instead contains fault χ, and f_χ denotes the function that *is* computed by location l when fault χ is inserted into it.)

The *propagation probability* of a known fault χ in location l is the conditional probability that a program will fail given that the fault at l has infected at least one of l's successor data states:

$$\Pr[\rho \text{ fails on input } x \mid infected(\mathcal{B}_{l,\rho,x}, \chi, l)] \tag{3}$$

1.2.3 Definitions for hypothesized faults and infections

When testing begins, the actual faults in a program are not known. Also, we do not know if our program is correct, which was an assumption in the definitions for the previous three probabilities. In other words, we do not know if we have a correct program ρ with a single fault χ injected at location l. Therefore the definitions for infection and propagation probabilities are not useful. However, estimation can be performed on the program that we *do* have, denoted by P, by "hypothesizing" that a fault or infection exists in P, and then estimating the effect of the "hypothesized fault" or "hypothesized infection." A hypothesized fault is simply a mutant of a location that is similar to those used in mutation testing [1]. This estimation based on a program P that we do have constitutes the second level of the *PIE* technique.

So in level two, we generalize the definitions of the previous probabilities for hypothesized faults, hypothesized infections, and the current program P. The *hypothesized execution probability* is the conditional probability that location l of program P is executed given an input x selected at random according to D:

$$\varepsilon_{l,P,D} = \Pr[\mathcal{A}_{l,P,x} \neq \emptyset \text{ after } P \text{ executes on } x \mid x \text{ selected according to } D] \qquad (4)$$

The *hypothesized infection probability* for a location l and hypothesized fault h is the conditional probability that hypothesized fault h produces a data state mutant in $\mathcal{A}_{h,P,i,x}$ for some input x and iteration i. $\mathcal{A}_{h,P,i,x}$ is the data state that occurs immediately after i^{th} execution of h—this data state is sampled after h is injected into l and execution of P begins on input x. The occurrence of a data state mutant is detected by comparing $\mathcal{A}_{l,P,i,x}$ with $\mathcal{A}_{h,P,i,x}$. The hypothesized infection probability for location l, hypothesized fault h, and input x selected at random according to D is:

$$\lambda_{h,l,P,D} = \Pr[infected'(\mathcal{B}_{l,P,x}, h, l) \mid \mathcal{A}_{l,P,x} \neq \emptyset \text{ after } P \text{ executes on } x] \qquad (5)$$

where

$$infected'(\mathcal{B}_{l,P,x}, h, l) = \begin{cases} \mathbf{T} & \text{if } \exists y \in \mathcal{B}_{l,P,x} \; f_l(y) \neq f_h(y) \\ \mathbf{F} & \text{otherwise,} \end{cases}$$

and f_h denotes the function computed by hypothesized fault h at location l. The estimate of the hypothesized infection probability is $\hat{\lambda}_{h,l,P,D}$ and is computed according to the algorithm in Section 1.2.4.

The *hypothesized propagation probability* for a location l in P is the conditional probability that if a data state mutant is injected into the data state immediately following l on l's i^{th} iteration, different program output occurs.

$$\psi_{a,i,l,P,D} = \Pr[\text{differing output from } P \text{ occurs on input } x \mid perturbed(a, \mathcal{A}_{l,P,i,x})]. \qquad (6)$$

where

$$perturbed(a, \mathcal{A}_{l,P,i,x}) = \begin{cases} \text{T} & \text{if } a \neq \Omega(a, \mathcal{A}_{l,P,i,x}) \\ \text{F} & \text{otherwise,} \end{cases}$$

and $\Omega(a, \mathcal{A}_{l,P,i,x})$ is a function that extracts the value of variable a in $\mathcal{A}_{l,P,i,x}$. The estimate of the hypothesized propagation probability is $\hat{\psi}_{a,i,l,P,D}$ and is computed according to the algorithm in Section 1.2.4

1.2.4 Algorithms for hypothesized infection probabilities and hypothesized propagation probabilities

We are now at the third level of the *PIE* technique. The third level contains the algorithms necessary for estimating the hypothesized propagation probability, estimating the hypothesized infection probability, and estimating the hypothesized execution probability.

It is necessary in these algorithms to sample internal data states. However the sets $\beta_{l,P,domain(S)}$ and $\alpha_{l,P,domain(S)}$ are not computable if there exists an element of $domain(S)$ on which P does not halt. We can, however, randomly select a finite set of inputs X according to D from $domain(S)$, and if on each $x \in X$ P halts, we can compute $\alpha_{l,P,X}$ and $\beta_{l,P,X}$. Although we cannot determine whether a program will halt for a specific input, we can set a time limit for termination, and if termination has not occurred in that interval, we will not include this input in X. This will be the scheme for creating X. Note also that some element, x_i, may occur more than once in X if $D(x_i)$ is large enough to cause it to be resampled when X is created. So with this we have the sets: $\alpha_{l,P,X}$ and $\beta_{l,P,X}$.

Propagation analysis is a technique that estimates the hypothesized propagation probability defined in equation 6. A *propagation estimate* is an estimate of the hypothesized propagation probability. In *PA*, a hypothesized data state error is created by a perturbation function. A *perturbation function* is a function that takes in a data value of a variable and changes it according to certain parameters. A perturbation function is a mechanism used by *PA* for upholding the condition $a \neq \Omega(a, \mathcal{A}_{l,P,i,x})$ in the definition of the function, *perturbed*. A variable whose value is changed by a perturbation function is said to have been *perturbed*.

The algorithm for finding $\hat{\psi}_{a,i,l,P,D}$ (see equation 6) is:

1. Set variable count to 0,

2. Randomly select an input x in X, and find the corresponding $A_{l,P,x}$ in $\alpha_{l,P,X}$. Select data state y to be $A_{l,P,i,x}$.

3. Perturb the sampled value of a if a is defined, else assign a a random value, and execute the succeeding code on both the perturbed and original data states,

4. For each different outcome in the output between the perturbed data state and the original data state, increment count; increment count if we believe that an infinite loop has potentially occurred (set a time limit for termination, and if execution is not finished in that time interval, assume an infinite loop occurred),

5. Repeat steps 2-4 n times,

6. Divide count by n yielding $\hat{\psi}_{a,i,l,P,D}$.

Note that the perturbation functions defined thus far in this research only perturb data values, however research is ongoing in creating perturbation functions to perturb data structures and the program counter. Since faults can create incorrect data structures and miscalculate the program counter as well as create incorrect data values, this research will eventually suggest perturbation functions to perturb data structures and the program counter. Without these additional perturbation functions, PA is an "incomplete" method.

Infection analysis is a technique that estimates the hypothesized infection probability defined in equation 5. The results of infection analysis are a function of the hypothesized faults used at a location and the distribution of $B_{l,P,x}$. The estimate of a hypothesized infection probability is termed an *infection estimate*.

The algorithm for finding $\hat{\lambda}_{h,l,P,D}$ (see equation 5) is:

1. Set variable count to 0,

2. Create a hypothesized fault for location l denoted h,

3. Randomly select an input x from X, and find the corresponding $B_{l,P,x}$ in $\beta_{l,P,X}$. Uniformly select a data state, y, from $B_{l,P,x}$.

4. Present the original location l and the hypothesized fault h with data state y and execute both locations in parallel,

5. Compare the resulting data states and increment count when $[f_l](y) \neq [f_h](y)$,

6. Repeat steps 3-4 n times,

7. Divide count by n yielding $\hat{\lambda}_{h,l,P,D}$.

The choice of which hypothesized faults to use in this algorithm determines the value gained from performing IA. The discussion is limited to hypothesized faults for arithmetic expressions and predicates, because this is where most of the empirical results thus far have come from (see Section 3). For arithmetic expressions, the hypothesized faults considered in this research are limited to single changes to a location: (1) a wrong variable substitution, (2) a variable substituted for a constant, (3) a constant substituted for a variable, (4) expression omission, (5) a variable that should have been replaced by a polynomial of degree k, and (6) a wrong operator. For predicates, the hypothesized faults we consider are limited to (1) substituting a wrong variable, (2) exchanging and and or, and (3) substituting a wrong equality/inequality operator.

Execution Analysis is a technique that estimates a hypothesized execution probability defined in equation 4. An *execution estimate* is an estimate of the hypothesized execution probability. The execution estimate of location l is denoted $\hat{e}_{l,P,D}$ and is computed according to the following algorithm. The input distribution used during EA is the same distribution that is used for creating the data state distributions used by PA and IA.

The algorithm for finding $\hat{e}_{l,P,D}$ for the current program P, location l, and probability distribution of the input domain D is:

1. Set array count to zeroes, where the size of count is the number of locations in the program being analyzed,

2. Instrument the program with "write" statements that signal when a particular location was executed, making sure repeated locations only print once per input,

3. Execute n inputs according to D on the "instrumented" program; this will produce n strings of location identifiers,

4. Increment the corresponding count[l] for each printed identifier stating location l was executed; if location l is executed on every input, then count[l] $= n$ at the completion of this step.

5. Divide each element of count[l] by n yielding $\hat{e}_{l,P,D}$.

1.3   Understanding the Resulting Estimates

When PIE is completed for the entire program, we have three sets of probability estimates for each program location l in P given a particular D:

1. Set 1: The estimate of the probability that program location l is executed, $\hat{e}_{l,P,D}$;

2. Set 2: The estimates of the probabilities, one estimate for each hypothesized fault in $(h_1, h_2, ...)$ at program location l, that given the program location is executed, the hypothesized fault will adversely affect the data state: $(\{\hat{\lambda}_{h_1,l,P,D}, \hat{\lambda}_{h_2,l,P,D}, ...\})$; and

3. Set 3: The estimates of the probabilities, one estimate for each variable in $(a_1, a_2, ...)$ at program location l, that given that the variable in the data state following location l is changed, the program output that results from this will too be changed: $(\{\hat{\psi}_{a_1,i,l,P,D}, \hat{\psi}_{a_2,i,l,P,D}, ...\})$.

Note that each probability estimate has an associated confidence interval, given a particular level of confidence and the value of n used in the algorithms. The computational resources available when PIE is performed will determine the value of the ns that are chosen in each algorithm. For example, for 95% confidence, the confidence interval is approximately $p \pm 2\sqrt{p(1-p)/n}$, where p is the $\dfrac{\text{number of occurrences of some event A}}{\text{total number of attempts of event A}}$ (p is the sample mean) [6, 3].

2   Sensitivity Analysis

The remainder of the paper focuses on making predictions. Remember that we want to show how the information of PIE can complement software testing. Section 2 shows (1) how to apply the estimates that the algorithms produce in order to make predictions about where faults can more easily remain undetected and (2) how to quantify the number of tests necessary to be convinced that a location is not protecting a fault from detection. Note the shift in emphasis in the paper—from estimation, that PIE performs, to prediction, that "sensitivity analysis" performs.

Sensitivity analysis (*SA*) is a tool for making predictions concerning where faults can more easily remain undetected during testing. Sensitivity analysis uses *PIE*'s estimates to predict the *minimum* effect on the failure probability that a particular location will have, i.e., *SA* quantifies the minimum effect that a program location has on the program. Note that program computational behavior is not dependent on an oracle; failure probability *is* dependent on an oracle.

With sensitivity analysis, a framework is created that can begin to answer the following questions: (1) Where can we get the maximum benefit from limited testing resources? (2) When should we use another validation technique other than testing? (3) What degree of testing must be performed to persuade ourselves that a location is probably not protecting a fault from detection? (4) When should we rewrite the software in a manner that makes it less likely to protect faults from detection?

Before we begin formalizing sensitivity analysis, consider the following analogy. If software faults were gold, then testing would be gold mining. The results of sensitivity analysis would be a geologist's survey performed before mining begins. It is not the geologist's job to dig for gold, but instead to establish the likelihood that digging at a particular spot would produce gold. A geologist might say, "This valley may or may not have gold, but if there is gold, it will be in the top 50 feet." At another location, the geologist might say, "Unless you find gold in the first 10 feet on this plateau, there is no gold. However, on the next plateau you will have to dig 100 feet before you can be confident that there is no gold."

When software testing begins, such an initial survey has obvious advantages over testing blind. From this analogy, sensitivity analysis is the "geologist." Sensitivity analysis predicts the required testing intensity for a particular confidence, whereas the geologist predicts the digging depth. Sensitivity analysis provides the degree of difficulty that will be incurred during random black-box testing of a particular location to detect a fault. If after random black-box testing to the degree specified by sensitivity analysis only to observe no failures, we then feel confident that the location is *correct.*

Sensitivity of a location *l* is a prediction of the minimum probability that a fault in *l* will result in a software failure under a particular program input distribution. If location *l* is assigned a sensitivity of 1.0 under a particular input distribution *D*, then it is predicted that each input in *D* that executes *l* will result in a software failure if *l* were to contain a fault. If l is assigned a sensitivity of 0.0 under D, then it is predicted that no matter what fault is present in l, no input in D that executes l will cause a failure. (Note that there is a continuum of sensitivities in $[0,1]$.) The greater the likelihood that a fault in location l will be revealed during testing, the greater the sensitivity that is assigned to l. A location with a low sensitivity is termed *insensitive*. A location with a high sensitivity is termed *sensitive*.

Testing either reveals or does not reveal faults; SA quantifies the significance of testing when testing reveals no faults. If testing's goal is to estimate the probability of failure, sensitivity *is not* an issue. Sensitivity *is* only an issue when testing's goal is to reveal faults. SA allows us to gauge how much trust we can place in testing for faults.

As an example, consider a simple program P:

```
{specification:  output 1 if a² + b² + c² < 900000 else output 0}
(1) read(a);
(2) read(b);
(3) read(c);
(4) d := sqr(a) + 1000;
(5) e := sqr(b);
(6) f := sqr(c);
(7) if ((d + e + f) < 900000) then
(8)     writeln("1")
    else
(9)     writeln("0");
```

P is supposed to perform the function described in the brackets but contains a fault in location 4. Assume that testing P under a particular input probability distribution D produces no failures. What does this testing say about the existence of faults in P? While we can make predictions about P's probability of failure under D, we do not have any assurances about an absence of faults in P. This is because: (1) D may not execute portions of P where the faults (if any) reside, (2) incorrect data states may not be produced, or (3) incorrect data states may be cancelled.

For P, Figure 1(i) and Figure 1(ii) contain input probability distributions that are not likely to reveal the fault in location 4; If the range of potential input values for variables a, b, and c are fixed in the interval $[545, 550]$, then the fault is more likely to be caught during testing. SA would warn that locations 4, 5, and 6 have the capacity to protect faults from detection if testing is performed according to Figure 1(i) or Figure

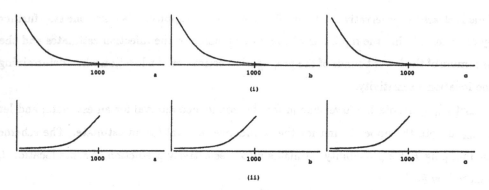

Figure 1: Probability distributions that are unlikely to reveal fault.

1(ii) (assuming $D =$ Figure 1(i) or $D =$ Figure 1(ii) when PIE is performed).

PIE's probability estimates for P given that $D =$ Figure 1(i) or $D =$ Figure 1(ii) follow:

1. EA reveals that there is a zero probability of a fault existing in locations 4, 5, and 6 and not being executed, and thus produce $\hat{\varepsilon}_{4,P,D} = 1.0$, $\hat{\varepsilon}_{5,P,D} = 1.0$, and $\hat{\varepsilon}_{6,P,D} = 1.0$.

2. IA reveals that locations 4, 5, and 6 produce high infection estimates, suggesting that actual faults in the locations would almost certainly produce infections.

3. Unlike the high probability estimates of IA and EA, PA tells something quite different. As an example, if the value of variable d is modestly altered after location 4, it is likely that P will still produce correct output. This is true of variable e after location 5, and variable f after location 6. PA will take this into consideration and indicate that locations 4, 5, and 6 are locations where infections can more easily remain undetected from testing, i.e., PA will produce low propagation estimates for variables d, e, and f at locations 4, 5, and 6.

Mapping the probability estimates for a location to a single sensitivity for that location is difficult, because determining the relative importance for each different set of probability estimates is difficult. Each estimate has an associated confidence interval, and we take the lower bound on the confidence interval. This assures that if bias occurs when finding a sensitivity, the bias causes underestimation of the sensitivity rather than overestimation.

This is clearly a conservative method. This conservative approach is taken one step further by only considering the minimum of the lower bounds of the infection estimates and the minimum of the lower bounds of the propagation estimates of a location when determining the location's sensitivity.

Let $(\cdot)_{min}$ denote the lower bound for the confidence interval for an estimate, and let $(\cdot)_{max}$ denote the upper bound for the confidence interval for an estimate. The scheme for mapping PIE's probability estimates into a sensitivity prediction of some location l, denoted by θ_l, follows:

$$\theta_l = (\hat{\varepsilon}_{l,P,D})_{min} \cdot \sigma(\min_h[(\hat{\lambda}_{h,l,P,D})_{min}], \min_a[(\hat{\psi}_{a,i,l,P,D})_{min}]) \qquad (7)$$

where

$$\sigma(a, b) = \begin{cases} a - (1 - b) & \text{if } a - (1 - b) > 0 \\ 0 & \text{otherwise.} \end{cases}$$

Equation 7 represents a prediction of the minimum probability that "if a fault were to exist in l, the existence of the fault will be revealed through testing."

With sensitivities in hand, we now return to the four proposed questions and explain how SA can begin to answer them.

1. *Where to get the most benefit from limited testing resources:*
   Sensitive locations require less testing than insensitive locations. By identifying sensitive locations, sensitivity analysis saves resources that can be applied to more critical insensitive locations.

2. *When to use some other validation technique other than testing:*
   Sensitivity analysis may show extreme insensitivity (frequent protecting of faults from detection), thereby pinpointing locations for which no reasonable amount of testing under an assumed distribution can be performed to gain confidence in such locations' lack of faults. At such locations, alternative techniques should be applied such as testing under a new distribution, proofs of correctness, code review, or exhaustive testing.

3. *The degree to which testing must be performed in order to be convinced that a location is probably not protecting a fault from detection:*
   Sensitivity analysis results may be used to determined how many test cases are

necessary to be convinced a location is correct with an acceptable confidence. θ_l can be used as an estimate of the minimum failure probability for location l in the equation $1 - (1 - \theta_l)^T = c$ [2], where c is the confidence that the actual failure probability of location l is less than θ_l. With this equation, we can obtain the number of tests T needed for a particular c. To obtain confidence c that the true failure probability of a location l is less than θ_l given the sensitivity of the location, we need to conduct T tests, where

$$T = \frac{\ln(1 - c)}{\ln(1 - \theta_l).} \tag{8}$$

When $\theta_l \approx 0.0$, we effectively have confidence c after T tests that location l does not contain a fault. To obtain confidence c that the true failure probability of a program is less than θ_l given the sensitivities of its locations, we need to conduct T tests, where

$$T = \frac{\ln(1 - c)}{\ln(1 - \min_l[\theta_l]).} \tag{9}$$

When $\min_l[\theta_l] \approx 0.0$, we effectively have confidence c after T tests that the program does not contain a fault. Note that for equation 8 and equation 9, θ_l can not be zero or one.

4. *Whether or not software should be rewritten:*
Sensitivity analysis results may be used as a guide to whether critical software has been sufficiently tested. If a piece of critical software is classified as having many insensitive locations, then the software may be rejected since too much testing will be required to achieve a sufficient level of confidence from testing.

3   Results

This section shows that *PIE*'s probability estimates are correlated to the actual effects that program locations have on the program's failure probability *when the locations were forced to contain faults*; this section contains both (1) empirical results and (2) examples. Section 3's results only expose the accuracy of the algorithms; a preliminary experiment showing that equation 7 is conservative is found in [9].

For the empirical results, we took the gold-version, G, of a battle simulation that was approximately 2000 lines in length and is specified in [7]. We

1. Made a copy of G, denoted by G',

2. Randomly selected some location l of G,

3. Injected a single fault F that virtually always infected into G' at location l (typically a fault was just a changed operator in an arithmetic expression),

4. Found $\hat{\tau}_{G',D}$ ($\tau_{G',D}$ represents the failure probability resulting from an injected fault F at location l in G', and $\hat{\tau}_{G',D}$ is an estimate of this probability),

5. Found $\hat{\varepsilon}_{l,G',D}$,

6. Found $\hat{\psi}_{a,i,l,G',D}$, where a is the variable on the left-hand side of the assignment statement at location l, and variable a was forcefully perturbed on *each* iteration i of l. In this experiment, $\hat{\psi}_{a,i,l,G',D}$ is a function of:

   (a) A perturbation function producing a uniformly selected value in the interval $[0.5x, 1.5x]$, where x is the original value variable a had before it was perturbed,

   (b) A uniform program input distribution,

   (c) 100 program inputs, and

   (d) Perturbation functions that were applied on each iteration i of l (if location l was executed more than once for some x).

7. Removed F from G', and

8. Went back to Step 2 and reperformed this analysis on a different l.

In these empirical experiments, we purposely injected faults with infection probabilities of approximately 1.0 so that the likelihood of low infection probabilities affecting the failure probability was negligible. This allowed correlation between $(\hat{\varepsilon}_{l,G',D} \cdot \hat{\psi}_{a,i,l,G',D})$ and $\hat{\tau}_{G',D}$ (see Table 1 and Table 2). The reason for multiplying the execution estimate and the propagation estimate is because propagation estimates are conditioned on executing a specific location; failure probability estimates are not. The correlation found from these 9 experiments is 0.995, meaning that the correlation found between the product of the propagation estimate and execution estimate and failure probability estimate was *high*. This preliminary result supports the claim that *PA* and *EA* produce probability estimates that are accurate enough to predict what effect a particular location has on the computation of the program.

Sixteen similar experiments using the same gold-version resulted in an overall correlation of 0.975 for all 25 experiments. The additional 16 injected faults were all *omission faults*, suggesting that PA can be used under certain circumstances as a debugging technique for omission faults.

For brevity, we will not include empirical results concerning IA and the gold-version, and will instead argue that IA's importance can be easily shown. There are locations that when injected with faults, do not affect the resulting data state; these are locations where faults can more easily remain undetected. Consider a correct location such as k := i *3, that is replaced by k := i * c. If i frequently has the value of 0 or c frequently has the value of 3 immediately before the location is executed, infection is not likely to occur. As another example, consider a correct location x := x mod 1000. If x is typically small (x < 500) before this location is executed, then a fault such as x := x mod 10000, if injected, would easily go undetected.

4 Concluding Remarks

This paper has presented two techniques that are based on the three necessary and sufficient conditions for software to fail; one technique, *PIE*, performs estimation, and the other, sensitivity analysis, performs prediction.

The first technique dynamically estimates program characteristics that affect a program's computational behavior. This technique does not require a specification nor oracle, however it requires an input distribution. *PIE* may be performed on incorrect programs and still reveal useful information. Since *PIE* is a code-based technique, it is expected that the program under analysis is "close" to being a correct implementation of the specification, both syntactically close and semantically close.

To date, *PIE* has only been applied to small programs, since no automated *PIE* system has yet been completed, and all results shown in this paper have been a combination of both manual and dynamic effort. In the future, *PIE* will be performed automatically— work on building a *PIE* system has begun. Once available, we recommend that *PIE* first be applied to the critical portions of a large-scale system. If resources allow for *PIE* to

trial	location l	fault F
1	XCorner := Batts[Beta][G].X - (((Army[Beta][G].Grow-1)/2)* Army[Beta][G].Squadsep);	XCorner := Batts[Beta][G].X - (((Army[Beta][G].Grow+1)/2)* Army[Beta][G].Squadsep);
2	A4 := (m+1)*((n+1)*Terrain[m,n]-n* Terrain[m,n+1])-m*((n+1)* Terrain[m+1,n]-n*Terrain[m+1, n+1]);	A4 := (m)*((n+1)*Terrain[m,n]-n* Terrain[m,n+1])-m*((n+1)* Terrain[m+1,n]-n*Terrain[m+1, n+1]);
3	Dist := sqrt(abs(sqr(x1-x)+ sqr(y1-y)));	Dist := sqrt(abs(sqr(x1-x)* sqr(y1-y)));
4	C1X := TX-TW/2;	C1X := TW-TX/2;
5	x1 := x+Batts[Beta][G].v* cos(Army[Beta][G].Theta);	x1 := x+Batts[Beta][G].v* sin(Army[Beta][G].Theta);
6	i := trunc(r);	i := trunc(round(r));
7	Xcorner := Batts[Beta][G].X- (((Maxi-1)/2)* Army[Beta][G].Squadsep);	Xcorner := Batts[Beta][G].X- (((Maxi-1)*2)* *Army[Beta][G].Squadsep);
8	TempI := 1+(k+m) mod Batts[Beta][G].NW[E,J];	TempI := (k+m) mod Batts[Beta][Ĝ].NW[E,J];
9	Af := Army[Beta][G].FixRate* Batts[Beta][G].Numfixers/cc;	Af := Army[Beta][G].FixRate+ Batts[Beta][G].Numfixers/cc;

Table 1: Injected Faults

trial	variable a	$\hat{\epsilon}_{l,G',D}$	$\hat{\psi}_{a,i,l,G',D}$	$\hat{\tau}_{G',D}$
1	XCorner	1.0	1.0	1.0
2	A4	0.98	1.0	0.85
3	Dist	1.0	0.98	1.0
4	C1X	0.98	0.0	0.08
5	x1	0.98	1.0	0.98
6	i	1.0	1.0	0.98
7	Xcorner	0.16	0.8125	0.09
8	TempI	0.01	1.0	0.01
9	Af	1.0	0.87	0.94

Table 2: Propagation Analysis Results

be performed on non-critical portions, that is beneficial as well.

The reason we mention performing *PIE* on specific program sections is *PIE*'s enormous costs: the sequential *PA* algorithm in this paper is of quadratic order. Therefore for large-scale systems, probably only sections of the program can have this analysis performed. One way of improving PIE's costs is parallelization; parallelization of the *PA* algorithm has been shown to produce near linear speed-ups [10].

When to apply *PIE* in the software life-cycle is an important concern—towards the end of the testing and validation phase appears to be the most appropriate time. Once program structure is certain to minimally change, which should be true at this point in the life-cycle, then *PIE* can be applied. If *PIE* were applied at the beginning of the testing phase, and major modifications were made to the program, then *PIE* would almost certainly need to be reperformed.

The second technique predicts whether locations are likely or unlikely to reveal faults. This technique, like *PIE*, is a function of the input distribution that *PIE* uses. It is expected that this input distribution will be the same one that the program will be tested according to. If the input distribution were to change, for example, to an input distribution based on some white-box analysis, then *SA* would predict the likelihood of faults remaining undetected if the program were tested according to this other input distribution. Thus for better predictions from *SA*, *PIE* should use the input distribution that the program is expected to be tested according to, which preferably is the operational distribution.

With *SA*, not only can we say that a program executed *k* inputs successfully, but if the program has many locations that are sensitive, we keep the confidence gained about the correctness of the program after testing is complete. If a program has many locations that are insensitive, we should realize that although it is possible that the program is correct, it is also possible that faults are remaining undetected, and thus the *k* successful tests do not offer an equivalent confidence.

Insensitive code is not necessarily bad. After all, correct code can be insensitive. The problem with insensitive code is that it suggests a greater ability to protect faults from detection, and that arguably is not a desirable characteristic. Research has been suggested that certain computable functions may have the misfortune of tending to result in insensitive code when implemented [8, 11]. This says that upper bounds may exist on the sensitivity that we can achieve for particular functions. We believe that there are design techniques that can be specified to create software that is "generally" more sensitive [11], however these techniques are only preliminary ideas requiring formalization.

5 Acknowledgements

The author expresses gratitude to Larry Morell for the help provided in formalizing these ideas in the years 1988 through 1990. This research was performed before the author accepted his current position as a National Research Council NASA/Langley Resident Research Associate, and during that time was funded as a graduate student under NASA grants NAG-1-824 and NAG-1-884 at the College of William and Mary.

References

[1] Richard A. DeMillo, Richard J. Lipton, and Frederick G. Sayward. Hints on Test Data Selection: Help for the Practicing Programmer. *IEEE Computer*, 11(4):34–41, April 1978.

[2] Richard G. Hamlet. Probable Correctness Theory. *Information Processing Letters*, pages 17–25, April 1987.

[3] Averill M. Law and W. David Kelton. *Simulation Modeling and Analysis*. McGraw-Hill Book Company, 1982.

[4] Larry Joe Morell. A Theory of Error-based Testing. Technical Report TR-1395, University of Maryland, Department of Computer Science, April 1984.

[5] L. J. Morell. A Model for Code-Based Testing Schemes. *Fifth Annual Pacific Northwest Software Quality Conf.*, pages 309–326, 1987.

[6] S. K. Park. Lecture notes on simulation, version 3.0. Department of Computer Science, College of William and Mary in Virginia, 1990.

[7] Timothy J. Shimeall. CONFLICT Specification. Technical Report NPSCS-91-001, Computer Science Department, Naval Postgraduate School, Monterey, CA, October 1990.

[8] J. Voas and K. Miller. Improving Software Reliability by Estimating the Fault Hiding Ability of a Program Before it is Written. In *Proceedings of the 9th Software Reliability Symposium*, Colorado Springs, CO, May 1991. Denver Section of the IEEE Reliability Society.

[9] J. Voas, L. Morell, and K. Miller. Predicting Where Faults Can Hide From Testing. *IEEE Software*, 8(2), March 1991.

[10] J. Voas and J. Payne. A Parallel Propagation Analysis Algorithm. Technical Report WM-91-2, College of William and Mary in Virginia, Department of Computer Science, March 1991.

[11] J. Voas. Preliminary Observations On Factors That Affect Program Testabilities. In *Proc. of the 9th Pacific Northwest Software Quality Conf.*, Portland, OR, To appear October 1991. Pacific Northwest Software Quality Conference, Inc., Beaverton, OR.

RELATION BETWEEN SOURCE CODE METRICS AND STRUCTURE ANALYSIS METRICS

Ivan ROZMAN, József GYÖRKÖS, Tomaž DOGŠA
UNIVERSITY OF MARIBOR, Faculty of Technical Sciences
Smetanova 17, YU-62000 Maribor, SLOVENIA

Abstract

The article suggests a hypothesis that a correlation between Source Code Metrics and Structure Analysis Metrics exists. For this purpose a definition of Structure Analysis Metrics which results are comparable with results of Source Code Metrics is given. Some presented examples made by different people involved into experiment (students) verify the hypothesis.

1. INTRODUCTION

Software metrics are one of the fundamental criteria on which the quality factors according to Boehm /Boeh76/ classification are based. The software metrics present the basis for the quantitative assessment of most quality factors. The greatest weakness of software metrics is the fact that the metrics results are obtainable mainly on a finished software product or seldom after a finished designing phase as explained in the article /McCa89/. Therefore we use the expression source code metric (SCM). This means that the measuring of software can be done backward - that is in later phases of software life cycle when our work on the software project is nearly concluded. An important progress can be achieved if metrics for earlier phases of software life cycle are developed.

On the other side software metrics (A survey and assessment research work is presented in literature /Rozm89b/.) are known especially as metrics of a product size and less as metrics of a style of program. For both types of metrics we must have a finished program first and then we can make software metrics. Thus, if we want to assess the time or effort needed to make a software, we should first develop this program, applied metric on it and on the basis of a given metric result we can estimate the time needed for the implementation of a program. Such process of usage SCM is in opposition to our wish that any metric and assessment of productivity is possible as soon as it can be performed, but no later than after the analysis phase.

SA (Structure Analysis) and SD (Structure Design) developed in the seventies. Much has changed within the domain addressed by software engineering, new programming tools have arisen, new concepts have developed, like object- oriented analysis and design and the systems nowadays are far larger and more complex than systems built 10-20 years ago. Adaptation of entire generation of programmers and analysts to these new tools and concepts will become an important thing, but however we see, SA still retain important methods for practical use in analyst practice nowadays, especially, because it has been completed in its "life time". It has attained the real - time extension as recommended the authors Hatley and Pirbhai /Hatl87/, it has also attained modification into object-oriented analysis /Coad90/ and such combinations with modern concepts as described in the article which connects SA with VDM (Vienna Development Method) based on object-oriented design /Toet90/.

From the conventional software life cycle model (e.g. waterfall) we know that the phases of analysis, design and implementation succeed one after another. The result of activities of all mentioned phases is to implement the requirements from target document on the computer. So, the designing phase maps the targets document into implementation document while the implementation phase maps the implementation document into programming language. From the general experience with CASE tools we know that the mapping of implementation document into the language is deterministic. Some CASE tools e.g. Yourdon's Cradle generate language code (Cobol, C, etc.) from implementation document (Structure Chart (SC) and pseudo code). If another mapping from the target document to the implementation document in our case from Data Flow Diagram (DFD) to SC is deterministic, too then the direct transformation from target document to language code should be deterministic. If so, then we can expect the great correlation between results of SCM and results given by Structure Analysis Metrics (SAM). The verification of suggesting hypothesis is the main aim of our article.

2. SA FORMALISMS

2.1. Data Flow Diagram

The DFD can be used on every level of system abstraction. It consists of four basic building blocks (external entity, process, data flow, data storage) /DeMa79/ from which fundamental system model is constructed first. Then it is decomposed into several more detailed and understandable diagrams. This is done until the functional primitive is reached. DFD has two parts: data dictionary and minispecification which describe the levelled graphical presentation of DFD in more detail.

One important weakness of SA is the fact that the SA presents only the statical picture of object. The dynamical properties remain hidden. The introduction of control flows is generally used to solve this problem. In our case we have used a specially defined language ACTESS as activation and validation media of system specification. The language is precisely described in article /Györ 90b/. For developing SAM we apply only the dynamic property of language ACTESS which is briefly described bellow.

Language ACTESS should fulfil three main aims. These are:
1. It must have all requirements for process activation.

2. It must display the activity of each process to user in such regular succession as it will be executed in a final program.

3. It must be easy to learn and user-friendly.

The second property is not ordinary. We have come to the fact that a user should have insight into results of SA. We think that the insight into results is the best if the user can see all processes as a display (minispecification) in regular succession as they will be executed. It is reasonable that the displaying of processes to the user should be user-friendly and easy to learn (requirentment three). The displaying should be incorporated into CASE tool as it is aSet /Rozm89a/, /Györ90a/(non-profit project which has been done at our university).

The succession of processes activation and presentation is determined by one module named ACTESS Module for each level of abstraction. ACTESS module is control specification in essence.

Language ACTESS is simple to learn especially for those who have some skills of programming. It is based on Pascal notation. A more detailed view into language ACTESS is evident by example on fig.1.

A reader perhaps wonders why is the activation of processes important. The succession of processes has to be determined in the process of transformation DFD into SC. For this purpose the transformation analysis is normally used. The language makes the determination of succession of processes more committed. The results given by language ACTESS express those part of final program which represent the sequence of modules separately (ACTESS module on fig.1) therefore we expect a greater correlation between proposed metrics.

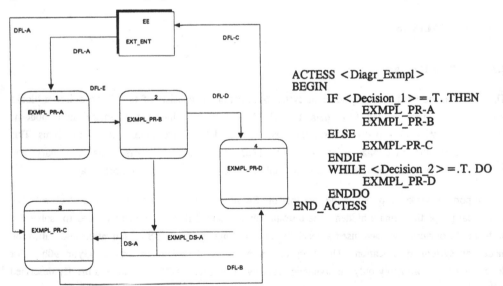

Fig. 1: DFD and corresponding ACTESS module

2.2. Data dictionary

Each arrow in the DFD means at least minimum one data element or usually more data elements that form data flow. A data element is a piece of information. Sometimes it is named data primitive - attribute because it cannot be decomposed into its components. In this case it forms a basic element of the data flow. For the decomposition of every data flow in the DFD into elements a special notation and operators are needed (equals, logical and, logical or, n iteration of bracket contents, optional data, comments).

2.3. Minispecifications

One of the meaningful activities in the system analysis phase is a decomposition of upper level of DFD. Normally, the decomposition is done until all the processes become atom or primitive processes. The atom process is not decomposed into small peaces because it represents an undivided unit. It is also possible to treat as an atom process one process in a higher level which depends on the level of abstraction and does not need further decomposition. In all example of abstraction the DFD must meet all necessities which are required from it. DeMarco recommended /DeMa79/ that all processes should be specified by minispecification. He and Peters /Pete88/ suggest the usage of Structure English in one of the following forms: pseudocode style, outline style or prose style.

Our experiences prefer the pseudocode with basic procedural constructs: sequence, if-then-(else), repeat-until, while-do and natural language for describing statement within. The utility of prose style gives good results in the English language but for any other language, if we use the same rules as in the English language are used, we can not say the same. (E.g. in the Sloven language we can not reach as good results as in the English language.) The outline style is already recommended by Peters /Pete88/ as a tool for first sketching the problem.

For SAM purpose we recommend minispecification based on prose style and restricted Pascal notation, using basic constructs.

3. PROPERTIES OF THE SAM

Before it is possible to define SAM their properties have to be defined. Some of these are the same as in any other metric but others have the specific character. These are:
1. Metric results between SCM and SAM have to be comparable because SAM should be defined on the SCM basis.
2. Metric must be executable almost from the beginning of software life cycle, just after a finished analyses phase. All processes have to be decomposed into functional primitives and all data flows must be decomposed, too.
3. Most significant properties are to confirm the intuition. This means, that object which are seemingly more complex should also be declared as more complex when the metric is applied.

4. It should be possible to use metric at the software life cycle when not all decisions (especially those, which are accepted in the designing phase) have been made.

4. Metric should have the properties of automation.

5. Most people can not manipulate with more than a small amount of information at the same time. Therefore visual tools should be available to assist them. It is convenient to incorporate metrics function into a CASE tool.

4. POSSIBILITY OF SAM

As we have said in the property one it is possible to proceed the SAM from the SCM. On fig. 2 and shortly described in literature /Rozm89b/ software metrics are mainly divided (in fig.2 all known metrics are not enumerated but only those which are important for proceeding the SAM) as follows:

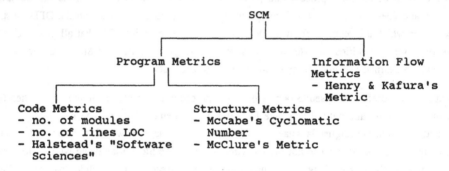

Figure 2: Division of SCM.

Like SCM division we can make a similar division for SAM (fig. 3).

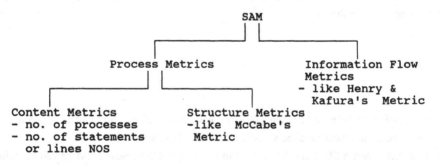

Fig.3: Possibilities of SAM

In our further explanation we shall describe all metrics mentioned in fig. 3 and derivations from metrics in fig.2.

4.1. Process metrics

As we see in fig.3 Process Metrics are divided into Content Metrics and Structure Metrics.

Content Metrics

In these metrics only the counting of processes and the counting of statements or lines in pseudo or prose style is significant.

The counting of processes in DFD is like the counting of modules or procedures (a program part with functional entirety with about between one half and one and half page source code) in a finished program. It is not simple to find similarity to the LOC in finished program. We have two possibilities. The first one is to use a brute-force approach and the second one is the usage of NOS (counting of statements or lines) instead LOC. The significant rules for brute-force approach are:

* every source code module, derived from a functional primitive has up to 70 or 100 lines of code,
* processes in DFD on the higher levels have mostly decision-making calling character, they cause short source code modules, perhaps only a few LOC.

It is not easy to assess how many LOC will contain the individual process in a finished program, especially, if we automate the assessment which must be done when such metric is applied in CASE tool.

A better approach than brute force approach is NOS. When NOS is used it is convenient to accept two rules which define it. These are:

* When the prose style without expressed key words is used counting of statements is more appropriate than counting of lines. If each statement has only one verb, the metric result will be more exact.
* When a pseudo code which is nearer to program language is used then counting the line of pseudo code is preferred, especially, when each statement has its own line.

Other more detailed Content Metrics of SAM are not applied because it is impossible to achieve more detailed reliable metric data made on the DFD. E.g.Halstead's "Software science" /Hals77/ metric which is most widely used on the source code.

Why is it not possible to apply Halstead's metric as SAM although no precise view may lead to opposite conclusion? In SAM it is true that we can determine all parameters (n_1, n_2, N_1, N_2) in the pseudo code, but it demands a pseudo code which is very determinate and therefore it is unappropriated for the usage in the analyzing phase. It has to be stressed here that the decision of the determination level of pseudo code is difficult. On one side the pseudo code must be understandable to the user because it must be close to the natural language while on the other side it must be fixed and also close to the program language what is required for easier design and implementation. The general conclusion is that the pseudo code in most cases is not so precisely determined. More precise results as obtainable by the NOS, generally, can not be achieved with other precise metrics.

Maybe someone tries to express the metric on data storage with Halstead's paradigm where the no. of distinct operators for connecting the data elements in data storages is taken as n_1, the no. of distinct data elements as n_2, the total no. of operators as N_1 and the total no. connecting data elements as N_2. Such metric we can do but we must know that the results obtainable by such metric are not comparable with results by Halstead's metric done on a finished program. Halstead's metric is code metric which measures the size of program or in SA terminology the size of processes, while metric described above measures the "size" of data storages.

Structure Metrics

For the evaluation of McCabe's Cyclomatic number $v_C(g)$ the following simplified equation, based on the graph theory is used /McCa76/:

$$v_C(g) = DE + 1$$
DE - decision elements

The application of this equation on the SAM is powerful and gives a real figure of analyzed problem complexity. We have two modified equations for the needs of SAM: the micro and the macro level equation.

The micro equation is simply the sum of all decision elements in the individual functional primitive plus one. These decisions are the pseudo code's decision operators in the suitable mini specification. This means that the decision elements should be in determined fashion that parser can recognize them.

The macro level equation is fusion of particular values for the micro complexity and added by the complexity of connections, defined by ACTESS between all processes in the lowest level of decomposition.

$$v_A(g) \text{ macro} = \sum_{i=1}^{no\_of\_AM} (DE_{ACTESS\ i} + 1) + \sum_{i=1}^{no\_of\_fp} (DE_i + 1)$$

DE_i - no. of decision elements in one functional primitive,
DE_{ACTESS} - no. of decision elements in ACTESS module,
no_of_AM - no. of ACTESS modules,
no_of_fp - no. of functional primitives.

4.2 Information Flow Metrics

Popular Information Flow Metric made on a finished program is Henry-Kafura metric /Henr81/. The authors suggest a formula for calculation metrics for each module in a program.

$$if\_SC = length * (fan\text{-}in * fan\text{-}out)^2$$

Fan-in and fan-out are defined:

The fan-in of a procedure A is the no. of local flows into a procedure A plus the no. of data structures from which a procedure A retrieves information. The fan-out for a procedure A is the no. of local flows from a procedure A plus the number of data structures which a procedure A updates.

The length is usually LOC.

For the application of Henry-Kafura formula as SAM we should change the rules for fan-in and fan-out. We have two possibilities. The first one is that we count the no. of incoming data flows to the process as fan-in and count the no. of outcome data flows from a process as fan-out. Such measure is very rough therefore we suggest another approach. In this approach we do not observe the incoming and outcome data flows as entirety but we count the incoming and outcome data elements of all data flows which pass the module. The changed rules are:

The fan-in$_{DF}$ of each process in DFD is the no. of data elements of all in data dictionary defined incoming data flows into a process. This means that we must count all data elements of all incoming data flows in the process irrespective how these data elements are connected with each other. Multiple appearance of data elements is omitted.

The definition of fan-out$_{DF}$ is the same as the definition of the fan-in$_{DF}$ but "incoming data flows into a process" are changed with "outcome data flows from a process".

We think that it is better (the results are lower and more suitable for further evaluation) if we change the multiplication in H-K formula with addition as suggested by W. Harrison and C.Cook in literature /Harr87/. Such modification is needed, especially, because in our suggestion we count data elements and not data flows as entirety.

Taking these changes mentioned above into account the proposed formula for making SAM is as follows:

$$if\_SA = no.\ of\ st.\ *\ (fan\text{-}in_{DF} + fan\text{-}out_{DF})^2$$

Another problem is how to weight expression in brackets The same problem is expressed in literature /Henry 81/, too. Authors recommended the weight square after analyzing the UNIX procedures. In our formula we retain the same suggestion to be comparable with SCM.

5. RESULTS

5.1. Examples

Examples presented below (table 1) are good for making comparison between SCM and SAM. Their aim is mainly to confirm our expectation that the high correlation between SCM and SAM exists. Unfortunately, we have only nine examples what is scarce for making statistical treatment. But in spite of this we did the statistical evaluation. We calculated Pearson's product moment correlation coefficient and Sperman's rank correlation coefficient of related metrics SCM and SAM

All examples in tab.1 present a different type of software (from predominant data oriented to predominant process oriented) and they were made by different people - students of our faculty. Each made one example entirety - analysis and coded in Pascal. The program METRIKA which was developed at our faculty was used for measuring SCM. The SAM was measured by the program which is incorporated in CASE tool aSet /Rozm89a/.

Table 1 Examples for SCM and SAM.

Example	No.of Mod.	LOC	$v_C(g)$ macro	$\overline{\text{if-SC}}$	No.of Proc.	NOS	$v_A(g)$ macro	$\overline{\text{if-SA}}$
			SCM				SAM	
Editor ACTESS	81	2631	748	7020	20	326	122	1140
Parser	38	1804	254	383	21	219	176	61
Linker	28	702	154	452	6	45	16	151
Patients diseases	12	449	83	832	12	30	34	155
Cars damages	11	438	48	1693	9	63	27	289
Flow Ch. Editor I	19	1187	153	2362	14	52	40	1037
Booking ticket	16	630	54	2890	14	85	42	357
Flow Ch. EditorII	41	1264	248	5520	14	90	52	2123
Picture topology	43	1803	83	5318	33	117	64	536

$\overline{\text{if-SC}}$ - arithmetic mean value if-SC of all mod.

$\overline{\text{if-SA}}$ - arithmetic mean value if-SA of all proc.

Table 2 Correlation between related metrics SCM and LOC.

	No.of No.of Mod, Proc.	LOC,NOS	$v_C(g)$ $v_A(g)$ macro, macro	$\overline{\text{if-SC}},\overline{\text{if-SA}}$
rp	0.511	0.893	0.582	0.724
rs	0.700	0.817	0.571	0.933

rp - Pearson's product moment correlation coefficient
rs - Sperman's rank correlation coefficient

5.2. Interpretation of results

Generally, Sperman's coefficient shows better results than Pearson's coefficient. The reason is that we do not know how the variables are distributed. But all Sperman's correlation coefficients, exceptionally the coefficient between $v_C(g)$ $v_A(g)$, are significant at level $\alpha = 0.05$ what is a general acceptable result. The same or better signification have only two Pearson's coefficients: between LOC,NOS and $\overline{\text{if-SC}}, \overline{\text{if-SA}}$.

Where are the reasons that our expectation about great correlations between SCM and SAM are not fully accomplished? First, we must remember that each example was made by different people, and second, that each designer - student uses its own intuition when he/she made transformation from DFD to structure chart. Unfortunately, the Transformation Analysis which is normally used for transformation DFD into structure chart is not a very deterministic process therefore a designer intuition becomes a decisive fact for this transformation. We are sure that all correlations could be greater if only one and the same person did all examples himself.

6. CONCLUSION

As we see from the examples, the correlation coefficients in some cases of our related metrics between SCM and SAM are not so high as we expected. It is true that we made comparison for only nine examples what is scarce for statistical treatment but in spite of this we can do some conclusions. These are:

We can define.the SAM on the base of SCM with consideration of most important properties, which have to be fulfilled for any software metric.

The correlation between SCM and SAM exists, especially in some cases of metrics e.g. between LOC and NOS but the designer intuition which is always present in transformation from DFD to SC damages the picture of general great correlation. So, it is hard to express SCM with SAM by a constant as we can do between metrics made on different programming languages /Cont86/.

It has to be stressed that the great correlation between $\overline{\text{if-SC}}, \overline{\text{if-SA}}$ gives a possibility to apply the measure of designa design measures early in the development, just after the analysis phase.

It is possible to achieve a greater correlation between SCM and SAM but this requires more rigorous rules as are normally applied in the Structure Designing Process. The introduction of stronger rules, into the designing process leads to decrease of designer's intuition, or designer's intuition moves from the designing phase to the earlier phases of software life cycle.

Literature

Boeh76   B.W. Boehm, "Software Engineering", IEEE Transaction on Computers, Vol. C-25, No. 12, December 1976, pp. 1226-1241.

Coad90   P. Coad, E. Yourdon, *Object Oriented Analysis*, Prentice Hall, 1990

Cont86   S.D. Conte, H.E. Dunsmore, V.Y. Shen *Software Engineering Metrics and Models*, The Benjamin/Cummings Publishing Company,Inc., 1986

DeMa79   T. DeMarco, *Structured Analysis and System Specification, Prentice Hall*, N.Y., 1979

Györ90a   J. Györkös, I. Rozman, T, Welzer, "A concept of an Efficient Computer Aided Software Engineering Tool" Management of Software Project 1988, Annual Review in Automatic Programming, Pergamon Press, Vol. 14, Part II, 1990.

Györ90b   J. Györkös, I. Rozman, T, Welzer "Dynamivcal System Specification as Validation Media", SIGPLAN Notices, Vol. 25, No. 9, Sept. 1990.

Hals77   M. Halstead, *Elements of Software Science*, Elsievier North-Holland, NY, 1977.

Harr87   Harrison,W., Cook,C.,"A Micro/Macro Measure of Software Complexity", The Journal of Systems and Software 7, 1987 pp. 213-219.

Hatl87   D.J. Hatley, I.A. Pirbhai, *Strategies for Real-Time System Specification*, Dorset House Publishing, New York, 1987.

Henr81   Henry,S., Kafura,D.,, "Software Structure Metrics Based on Information Flow", IEEE Trans. On SW Eng., vol. 7, 1981, pp. 509-518.

McCa76   T.J. McCabe, "A Complexity Measure". IEEE Trans. Software Engineering, Vol. Se-2, pp.308-320, 1976

McCa89   T.J. McCabe, C.W. Buler, "Design Complexity Measurements and Testing", Communicatin of the ACM, vol. 32, no. 12, Dec. 1989 pp. 1415-1425

Pete88   L. Peters,"Advanced Structured Analysisand Design", Prentice Hall, Englewood Cliffs, N.J., 1988.

Rozm89a   I. Rozman, J.Györkös, T.Dogša, K.Rizman, T.Welzer, "aSet - Automated Software Engineering Tool", 6th Syposium on Networksm Systems and Signal Processing, Zagreb, 1989.

Rozm89b   I.Rozman, J.Györkös, T.Welzer, T.Dogša, "The Quality of Software: A Survey and Assessment of Existing Research Works", Computer and Information Sciences - 3, Nova Science Publishers, New York, 1989, pp. 191-201.

Toet90   H. Toetenel, J. Katwijk, N. Plat, "Structured Analysis - Formal Design using Stream & Object Oriented Formal Specification", Proceedings of the ACM SIGSOFT, Napa,California, USA, May 9-11, 1990, pp. 118-127.

Algebraic validation of software metrics*

Martin Shepperd
Dept. of Computing and Cognition,
Bournemouth Polytechnic,
Talbot Campus,
Bournemouth, BH12 5BB, England

Darrel Ince
Dept. of Computer Science,
Open University,
Milton Keynes, MK7 6AA, England

Abstract

A method is described for the formal evaluation of a software metric and its underlying model. This is based upon the specification of the model as an algebra and its desired behaviour as an associated axiom set. If these axioms can be proved to be invariant across the model, then the model may be considered to be valid with respect to its axioms. Where an axiom cannot be shown to be invariant this implies that either the model is anomalous or that the axiom was inappropriate. This approach is applied to a design metric based upon inter-module coupling. It is argued that this method of metric validation is a general one, and one which is capable of increasing confidence in the correctness of a metric particularly during the early stages of its development when empirical data may either be sparse or unavailable. It is intended as a practical means whereby metrics workers can eliminate pathological metrics prior to embarking upon costly and time consuming empirical validation exercises. We do not intend that this method should supplant empirically based means of validation, rather that it is complementary technique.

Keywords: Software metrics, measurement, validation, algebraic specification, software design.

1. Introduction

Although there is no shortage of software metrics proposed over the past 20 years, validation of these metrics has proved difficult. However, without satisfactory evaluation it is unreasonable to expect widespread adoption by the software engineering industry. Yet this is a frustrating

---

*This work has been supported by British Telecom Research Labs., Martlesham Heath, Ipswich, IP5 7RE, England

situation, given the need to bring quantitative methods to bear upon the task of controlling large scale software engineering projects [deMa82, Boeh84, Gilb88].

There appear to be several barriers to metric evaluation. The first is the poor definition of a metric and its underlying model or theory. An example of a metric validation hampered by inadequately articulated model is given by Ince and Shepperd [Ince89] in their analysis of the classic Henry and Kafura information flow metric [Henr81]. Indeed, many of the peculiarities and anomalies within the information flow metric arise, precisely because the model is defined in extremely vague terms.

The second area of difficulty is that empirical analysis - the usual approach to metric validation - is often a difficult, expensive and protracted business. In [Ince88] we describe some of the ideal requirements for a convincing empirical study. These include large numbers of data points, use of industrial subjects in an industrial environment dealing with large scale artifacts and the need for appropriate statistics. The fact that many of these are difficult to achieve - other than the proper use of statistics - is borne out by our survey of approximately 50 published validations of design metrics. Of these 50 studies only four came close to fulfilling our desiderata. This not due to the perversity of metrics researchers but the difficulty of carrying out studies in industrial environments. Consequently, most work is of a passive or observational form which tends to suffer from factors that are outside the experimenter's control, or worse still outside his or her knowledge. Even the appropriate use of statistics to interpret empirical results, has lead to difficulties - *vide* the re-interpretation of many of the early "confirmations" of Halstead's software science by Hamer and Frewin [Hame82] or the re-appraisal of the support for McCabe's cyclomatic complexity metric [McCa76] by Shepperd [Shep88].

In this paper we present an alternative approach to metric validation based upon a formal specification of the metric model which eliminates much ambiguity. In addition the desired model behaviour is described as a set of invariants, for example one might stipulate that adding an additional entity to data design must always increase the value of the metric. The validation then consists of demonstrating that the axioms remain invariant for all model behaviours. This method is then applied to a design metric that captures some notion of inter module coupling [Stev74] and can be derived from a standard module hierarchy chart. Our findings suggest that this is a feasible approach and one which has potential for future metrics research.

2. Algebraic validation

Our method of algebraic validation of software metrics comprises three steps.

- formal definition of the model
- identification of desired model behaviour as an axiom set

- proving the axioms are invariant

Each of these steps will be described in turn.

First, the model behind the metric must be formally defined. The approach that we have adopted is to do this by means of algebra [Gutt77, Ehri85], which yields several advantages. The notation is unambiguous, it focuses attention upon the constructor or composition operations [Geha82] thereby providing a framework for defining meaningful and meaningless objects for measurement, and lastly it can easily be animated using OBJ[1]. The outcome of this step are the signatures defining the operations to build and manipulate a model of the object of measurement, coupled with a set of equations that define the meanings of these operations. The equations may be regarded as a term rewriting system.

Second, the desired behaviour of the metric and its model must be described as a set of axioms. An example of such an axiom is the removal of a shared data structure from a software design cannot increase a maintainability metric value. Isolating these axioms is a skilful process that requires some insight into the measurement domain, however, our method provides certain guide-lines to aid this process, which are described later in this section.

The third step is to formally prove whether the axioms are invariant over the model defined. When an axiom cannot be shown to be invariant one must infer either that the metric is flawed or that the axiom describing desired model behaviour was inappropriate.

We now examine the issue of identifying model axioms in more detail. There has been some work in the arena of axiomatic validation of software metrics, for example that of Prather [Prat84] and Weyuker [Weyu88]. The axioms proposed by Prather are rather weak and unrestricted whilst those proposed by Weyuker are on the contrary highly constraining. The problem with the former is that one tends to accept metrics that ought to be rejected, whilst with the latter the reverse pertains. Consequently our solution is to adopt a flexible approach whereby the axioms are specific to a given model and metric[2]. Given the potential diversity of software metrics it is hard to envisage any other alternative! Our approach is also novel in that whilst there is some interest in the axiomatic treatment of metrics [Zuse89, Melt90] no other work deals with a formal definition of the model.

---

[1]The algebra defining the coupling metric later in this paper, has been implemented with a minimum of effort.

[2]An alternative flexible approach has been presented by Zuse and Bollmann [Zuse89] in the form of viewpoints which allow for the specification of varying sets of fundamental requirements for different metrics, or even the same metric. The method described in this paper differs in that it employs an equational rewrite system to define and reason with the axioms.

Returning to the axioms, observe that measures must satisfy three classes of axioms:

- those axioms that are fundamental to all measurement;
- axioms necessary for the type of scale adopted;
- axioms specific to the model underlying the measure.

It will be noted that the axiom classes decrease in scope of application from universal to specific for a single, or small family of metrics. Each class will be reviewed in turn.

The following are axioms that must hold for all measurement for it to be meaningful.

Axiom 1: It must be possible to describe, even if not formally, the rules governing the measurement [Pfan68][3]. This axiom is somewhat difficult to apply in practice, but in essence, once the error-proneness of the measuring process has been accounted for, all measurements of the same object or process must assign it to the same equivalence class.

Axiom 2: The measure must generate at least two equivalence classes in order that, as Weyuker [Weyu88] points out, the measure be capable of discrimination.

Axiom 3: An equality relation is required[4]. Without an empirical equality operation each measurement, if it could be called that, would generate a new equivalence class with exactly one member.

Axiom 4: The previous axiom is further strengthened such that if an infinite number of objects or events are measured, eventually two or more must be assigned to the same equivalence class. This is a restatement of Weyuker's third axiom [Weyu88]. We note that some forms of measurement using a nominal scale, for example car number plates, do not satisfy this axiom - a hardly surprising observation when one considers that such a process must lie at the limits of what could reasonably be called measurement.

Axiom 5: The metric must not produce anomalies (i.e. the metric must preserve empirical orderings). In other words the Representation Theorem [Supp71, Kran71] must hold.

$$\forall \ p,q:\text{object} \cdot P \ r_e \ Q \rightarrow |P| \ r_n \ |Q|$$

where r_e is any empirically observable relation and r_n is the equivalent relation within the number or measurement system.

---

[3]This does not imply that the rules must always be applied correctly, since there is the possibility of error in the measurement process - a point eloquently made by Henry Kyberg [Kybe84] amongst others.

[4]This is not dissimilar in impact to Weyuker's third axiom [Weyu88].

To apply this axiom however, it does require that there is agreement upon the empirical orderings and that possibility of erroneous measurement is disregarded.

Axiom 6: The Uniqueness Theorem must hold [Supp71] for all permissible transformations for the particular scale type, that is, there exists a homomorphism between the transformed and the measurement structures.

Regarding the second class of axioms, those that are sufficient for different measurement scales are well documented in the classical measurement literature, for example Stevens [Stev59] and Krantz *et al* [Kran71]. Clearly our axiom set must be tailored to take account of scale and this is an important decision for any metric. Refer to [Zuse90] for a detailed discussion of the impact of scale upon software metrics.

The third class of axioms are those that relate to the specific model underlying the measure in question. Again, it is possible to provide categories under which axioms may be selected. These are:

- resolution;
- empirically meaningless structures;
- model invariants.

Under resolution it may be desirable to include Weyuker's second axiom that asserts that there only exist a finite number of objects of a given measurement score. This would be important if metrics that are insensitive, in certain respects[5], are to be avoided. One has certain reservations as to whether there is a practical distinction between infinite and a very large number but there are, nevertheless, occasions when the axiom may emphasise required metric behaviour.

Having chosen the axioms necessary for the type of measurement one must consider the composition operations available for the objects or processes under scrutiny. The importance of composition is that it is the constructor operator, and allows us to describe different objects or processes, in a recursive [Fent86] or hierarchical [Prat87] manner. What the existing approaches fail to embrace is the possibility of metrics where there is no composition closure[6]. It is an important aspect of any axiomatisation that we define meaningless structures for which measurement is undefined. In other words, we need to know when we should *not* measure in addition to when we should measure.

---

[5]The classic example, is of course, McCabe's cyclomatic complexity [McCa76] where one may infinitely vary the number of procedure nodes for a fixed number of predicate nodes, for a program flow graph.

[6]This will be the case for any syntactic software metric.

Model invariants are clearly going to be extremely diverse. Examples include Prather's [Prat84] second and third axioms which relate to measures of control flow structure. This is a difficult aspect of an axiomatic evaluation of a model, because in the end the choice of axioms will be dependant upon intuition and insight. Where it cannot be shown that a model satisfies such an axiom, two conclusions are possible. First, one might infer that the model is deficient in some respect, or second, that the axiom itself is inappropriate. Whatever, this axiomatic method at least draws the attention of the metrologist to such potential problem areas. It does not provide necessarily an answer.

In concluding this section, there are three points of note. Axiomatisations of software metrics are a vital tool for the theoretical validation of metrics and models, as they allow exploration of the model behaviour in a more rigorous fashion. Without doubt, they represent a step forward from merely using one's intuition. They may also permit a more thorough coverage of the model behaviour than the intuitive approach, or for that matter, than many empirical evaluations, particularly where cost or availability of data is a factor.

Second, they provide a mechanism to establish certain foundational properties of the model. These are:

- consistency, so that there exists one and only one outcome for any set of inputs;
- completeness, that the axiom set is sufficiently rich that there is no set of inputs for which no outcome is prescribed;
- the model is not rejected for violation of axioms for empirically meaningless structures.

Consistency is established by showing that the axiom set exhibits the Church-Rosser property. This is unfortunately an undecidable question. There are various notions of completeness, including the concept of sufficiently complete [Gutt78] which is weaker than the more usual mathematical definitions of completeness[7], but these are still undecidable.

Third, theoretical evaluation provides early feedback for the design and development of metrics and models. Given that empirical validation is a costly and time-consuming enterprise, any technique that helps identify models that are manifestly inadequate must be lauded.

3. A simple example of algebraic validation

The following is an algebraic specification of a simple design metric, C that is a measure of the degree of connectivity between modules within a system architecture. Such information

---

[7]An axiom set is usually said to be complete if it is impossible to add an independent axiom because *all* well formed formulae either follow from, or are inconsistent with, the existing axiom set.

will be of value to software designers since it will enable then to control these couplings, leading to more maintainable designs. This is similar in concept to the work on ripple analysis by Yau *et al* [Yau80], in that couplings are channels whereby the impact of a maintenance change propagates through a system. Designs with few couplings limit this propagation and are therefore regarded as more maintainable.

The C metric may informally be defined as follows. A *coupling* between two modules is defined to occur whenever a data structure is shared between the modules such that one module writes to the data structure and the other modules retrieves from the data structure - refer to Figure 1. Thus one module is able to influence the behaviour of the other. From an analysis of module couplings it is possible to compute the *fan_in* and *fan_out* of each module where the fan_in is the count of flows that terminate at a module and the fan_out the count of flows that emanate from a module. The product[8] of these two terms gives the C metric for the ith module.

$$C_i = \text{fan\_in} \cdot \text{fan\_out}$$

If these are summed across the system this gives a value for C,

$$C = \sum_{i=1}^{i=n} C_i$$

where there n modules in a system.

Although this coupling metric is clearly simplistic - for example it ignores parameterised communication between modules - it is still potentially useful for software designers, and in fact forms a major subset of system architecture metrics as IF4 [Ince89, Shep90] and is indirectly related to the information flow metric due to Henry and Kafura [Henr84]. In any case the simplicity is for reasons of brevity and elsewhere we have successfully applied this method to more complex metrics, for example the Information Flow metric and the 'work' metric [Shep91].

We will now develop a formal, algebraic specification [Gutt77, Ehri85] of the behaviour of the coupling metric and its underlying model in terms of equations. This will be defined step by step; for a complete specification refer to the Appendix. The first part of the algebraic specification defines the model operations. These include creating a new system architecture,

---

[8] A product is taken since this is equivalent to the number of information paths across a module linking the couplings in and out.

adding a module, adding a data structure access and so forth. First we consider the constructor operations. Informally we have:

new - creates a null system architecture
addm - adds a module to a system architecture
rd - defines a retrieval from a data structure by a module
wr - defines an update of a data structure by a module

These are necessary to build or define all possible system architectures for which our metric is defined. Note that some architectures are illegal, for instance we cannot have a design with two modules of the same name since this would create an ambiguity, nor can a non-existant module access a data structure. Consequently the operations *addm, rd* and *wr* can all fail and instead return an error condition. This can be seen by reference to their signatures.

$$\text{new: } \rightarrow \text{sys}$$
$$\text{addm: mod} \times \text{sys} \rightarrow \text{sys } \cup \text{ \{duplicate\_error\}}$$
$$\text{rd: mod} \times \text{ds} \times \text{sys} \rightarrow \text{sys } \cup \text{ \{missing\_mod\_error\}}$$
$$\text{wr: mod} \times \text{ds} \times \text{sys} \rightarrow \text{sys } \cup \text{ \{missing\_mod\_error\}}$$
$$\text{addm': mod} \times \text{sys} \rightarrow \text{sys}$$
$$\text{rd': mod} \times \text{ds} \times \text{sys} \rightarrow \text{sys}$$
$$\text{wr': mod} \times \text{ds} \times \text{sys} \rightarrow \text{sys}$$

The semantics of these operations are given by the following equations, where m and n are type mod and S is type sys:

1. exists?(m,new) = FALSE
2. exists?(m,addm(n,S)) = IF m=n THEN TRUE ELSE exists?(m,S)
3. exists?(m,rd(n,d,S)) = exists?(m,S)
4. exists?(m,wr(n,d,S)) = exists?(m,S)

5. addm(m,S) = IF exists?(m,S) THEN {duplicate_error} ELSE addm'(m,S)

6. rd(m,d,S) = IF exists?(m,S) THEN rd'(m,d,S) ELSE {mod_not_found}

7. wr(m,d,S) = IF exists?(m,S) THEN wr'(m,d,S) ELSE {mod_not_found}

By way of an example, Figure 2 illustrates a simple software architecture which can be unambiguously defined using the following sequence of constructor operations.

rd(A,d,rd(B,d,wr(A,d,addm(A,addm(B,new)))))

The operations fall into two categories, external and internal, the latter being indicated by a prime. The latter are required in order to restrict the range of the constructor operations although their presence is transparent to the behaviour of the model, hence their name. Equation 5 defines the relationship between the external, unrestricted add module operation and its internal, restricted counterpart. The latter is guaranteed to succeed because we have already tested for the possibility of duplicate modules. The next step is to define the metric operations C, for the entire system and C_i for a specified module. Both these operations have internal equivalents, to generate a dummy argument to mimic a state in the case of C and prevent a metric value being returned for a module that does not exist in the case of C_i.

C_i: mod $\times$ sys $\rightarrow$ nat $\cup$ {mod_not_found}

C: sys $\rightarrow$ nat

C_i': mod $\times$ sys $\rightarrow$ nat

C': sys $\times$ sys $\rightarrow$ nat

8. $C(S) = C'(S,S)$

9. $C'(new,S) = 0$

10. $C'(addm'(m,T),S) = C_i'(m,S) + C'(T,S)$

11. $C'(rd'(m,d,T),S) = C'(T,S)$

12. $C'(wr'(m,d,T),S) = C'(T,S)$

13. $C_i(m,S) =$ IF exists(m,S) THEN $C_i'(m,S)$ ELSE {mod_not_found}

14. $C_i'(m,S) =$ fan_in(m,S,S)*fan_out(m,S,S)

Equation 10 indicates that the system wide metric C is defined as the sum of the C_i for each module which in turn is the product of the fan_in and fan_out for each module. Next the fan_in and fan_out operations are given as:

fan_in: mod $\times$ sys $\times$ sys $\rightarrow$ nat

fan_out: mod $\times$ sys $\times$ sys $\rightarrow$ nat

15. fan_in(m,new,S) = 0

16. fan_in(m,addm'(n,T),S) = fan_in(m,T,S)

17. fan_in(m,wr'(n,d,T),S) = fan_in(m,T,S)

18. fan_in(m,rd'(n,d,T),S) = IF m=n THEN #wr(d,n,S) + fan_in(m,T,S) ELSE
fan_in(m,T,S)

19. fan_out(m,new,S) = 0

20. fan_out(m,addm'(n,T),S) = fan_out(m,T,S)

21. fan_out(m,rd'(n,d,T),S) = fan_out(m,T,S)

22. fan_out(m,wr'(n,d,T),S) = IF m=n THEN #rd(d,n,S) + fan_out(m,T,S) ELSE
fan_out(m,T,S)

These equations state that the fan_in of a module is a function of the number of data structures that it retrieves or reads from. It is also dependant upon the modules, other than itself that write to the data structure, which will be determined by the operation #wr. An advantage of a formal model definition is that it removes all ambiguity, so in this instance it is clear that global flow is not counted when a module both reads and writes to a data structure itself, since the operation explicitly tests for m≠n. It is also evident that this metric will count duplicate flows between modules, either via more than one shared data structure or by means of multiple reads and writes, to the same data structure. One might debate the desirability of such a counting strategy but at least it is made explicit.

#rd: ds × mod × sys → nat
#wr: ds × mod × sys → nat

23. #rd(d,n,new) = 0
24. #rd(d,n,addm'(m,S)) = #rd(d,n,S)
25. #rd(d,n,wr'(e,m,S)) = #rd(d,n,S)
26. #rd(d,n,rd'(e,m,S)) = IF d=e AND m≠n THEN 1 + #rd(d,n,S) ELSE #rd(d,n,S)

27. #wr(d,n,new) = 0
28. #wr(d,n,addm'(m,S)) = #wr(d,n,S)
29. #wr(d,n,rd'(e,m,S)) = #wr(d,n,S)
30. #wr(d,n,wr'(e,m,S)) = IF d=e AND m≠n THEN 1 + #wr(d,n,S) ELSE #wr(d,n,S)

This completes the definition of the metric and underlying model. Next, we turn to the *desired* model behaviour. To demonstrate the method of validation we will only consider two axioms, although clearly, in practice there are other model characteristics which one would wish to demonstrate.

Using the framework described earlier for identifying model axioms, we focus upon the third class of axiom - that is those specific to this model. A characteristic that one might demand for our *first axiom* is that as additional global flows or couplings are introduced to an arbitrary software design this must increase the value of the C metric. This may be more formally stated as:

∀S:sys; d:ds; m,n:mod • C(S) < C(wr'(n,d,S)) where #rd(m,d,S) ≥ 1 and m≠n

and:

∀S:sys; d:ds; m,n:mod • C(S) < C(rd'(n,d,S)) where #wr(m,d,S) ≥ 1 and m≠n

The *second axiom* that we will investigate is the requirement that the metric supports the development of designs that exploit reusable components, a characteristic that is not commonplace amongst design metrics as one might hope - *vide* the graph impurity measure due to Yin and Winchester [Yin78]. A formal restatement of this axiom is:

$$\forall m,n,r_1,r_2:mod; \; S:sys \; d,e:ds \; \bullet$$

$$C(wr'(r_1,d,rd'(r_1,d,wr'(r_2,e,rd'(r_2,e,wr'(m,d,rd'(m,d,wr'(n,e,rd'(n,e,addm'(r_1,addm'(r_2,addm'(n,addm'(m,S)))))))))))))) >$$

$$C(wr'(r_1,d,rd'(r_1,d,wr'(m,d,rd'(m,d,wr'(n,d,rd'(n,d,addm'(r_1,addm'(n,addm'(m,S))))))))))$$

where r_1 and r_2 are functionally equivalent.

The architecture of two such designs are given in Figure 3.

It goes without saying that there are many other axioms which one might derive for this model of module coupling. For instance one might wish to demonstrate that it is not a simple size measure by showing that the metric is not merely a positive monotonic function of the module count. Another possibility would be to show that adding modules to an arbitrary design can never decrease the metric value. However, in order to demonstrate our approach we will focus upon the above two axioms. Since the formal proofs are rather lengthy we give an abbreviated view in this discussion. For a more exhaustive treatment the reader is referred to [Shep91].

Returning to *Axiom One* we note that it is universal in nature, consequently we only need a single counter-example in order to refute the axiom. On the other hand, to establish a universal truth we will need to reason inductively. In this case the base case will be with fan_in_m, fan_in_n, fan_out_m and fan_out_n set to zero, and that by incrementing fan_in_m and fan_out_n the C metric will be increased. From Equation 14 we have that the C_i metric is the product of fan_in_i and fan_out_i and from Equation 10 that C is the sum of all C_i values. This means that we must show that at least one of C_m and C_n are increased by the action of incrementing fan_in_m and fan_out_n.

However, we see that for module m:

$$(0+1)*0 = 0*0$$

and that likewise, for n:

$$0*(0+1) = 0*0$$

Clearly, neither C_i value has been increased by the action of introducing an additional coupling between the two modules, and as a result the C metric value is not increased. Consequently, Axiom One does not hold.

The reason for the rather curious behaviour of our model is not hard to determine. Since the metric is founded upon the product of module fan_in's and fan_out's the effect of incrementing a fan_in, is in part dependent upon the value of the fan_out, and of course, *vice versa*. Thus if a module has a zero fan_in, then irrespective of the size of its fan_out, the value of C_i will always be zero. Should the reader consider this to be a rather contrived example, it is worth noting that such well known metrics as the Henry and Kafura information flow measure [Henr81] would also fail to satisfy this axiom.

Axiom Two is based upon the view that a design metric should not have the side effect of encouraging the duplication of modules when reuse is an alternative. In other words as a designer minimises module coupling he or she also minimises module redundancy. Figure 3 depicts two functionally equivalent architectures, the second one of which re-uses component r_1 instead of duplicating it as component r_2. As with Axiom One this is a universal axiom.

The simplest case - and also the base case for an inductive argument - is with S set to an empty design or equal to *(new)*. Adopting a similar approach to Axiom One we note that C is the sum of, in this case C_m, C_n, C_{r1} and C_{r2} for the first design and C_m, C_n, and C_{r1} for second design.

We now seek to show that the C metric for the first design is greater than that for the second. This we can do by tabulating the fan_in and out values for each module.

Duplication					Re-use			
Mod	F_I	F_O	C_i		Mod	F_I	F_O	C_i
m	1	1	1		m	2	2	4
n	1	1	1		n	2	2	4
r_1	1	1	1		r_1	2	2	4
r_2	1	1	1					
			C=4					C=12

By summing the C_i values for each system it is clear that the value for the design that duplicates r_1 as r_2 is lower than for the design that re-uses r_1, and therefore the second axiom falls. The reason for this anomalous behaviour is that the model behind the metric does not adequately distinguish between a module invocation and a module interface; a module has a single interface but may be invoked many times. Similar problems are discussed in respect of information flow metrics in [Incc89]. This is an example of a metric that has a potentially dangerous side effect built into it, if it were not applied with considerable caution in an industrial environment. Therefore, it is imperative that metrics be fully understood prior to their application and the algebraic approach described in this paper enables this to be accomplished in a rigourous and inexpensive fashion.

So, to recap. The algebraic approach is a method of formally validating a metric at an early stage in its development and may be employed to filter out weaker candidates prior to deploying costly empirical validation resources. It comprises three stages.

Stage One is to turn an informal description of metric and its supporting model into a formal specification by identifying the constructor operations and the measurement function; defining their signatures and by giving their semantics as a set of rewrite equations. This is a technique known as algebraic specification.

Stage Two is to determine the desired model behaviour using the various categories under which the behaviour may be described, for example measurement resolution. These must then be formally stated as axioms that characterise properties that are invariant over the model, for instance adding a data structure to a given system architecture must never result in a decrease in a metric value.

Stage Three is to demonstrate that the axioms are indeed invariant over the model. This can be accomplished by rigourous argument or by formal proof. Note that the use of term rewriting systems such as OBJ can considerably facilitate the derivation of such proofs. Where an axiom does not hold, one may draw one of two possible inferences: either the axiom was not well chosen and that the model behaviour is in actual fact acceptable, or that model is deficient in some respect and will need to be refined.

Having gained confidence in a model by means of our algebraic validation technique, it is still necessary to empirically validate the model, as it is probable that there are model properties that are important, yet that have been omitted from the set of model axioms due to oversight. Thus the two validation approaches are complementary. Last, it must be stressed that it is not intended that practising software engineers become involved in this process, rather it is the province of research and development staff, who need to satisfy themselves that a metric is well founded, before incorporating it into organisation and software engineering processes.

4. Summary

Clearly, further work is required to complete the algebraic validation of our example metric, particularly to explore such issues as the relationship between these metrics and other data metrics such as Henry and Kafura's metric [Henr81] and the type of design strategies that the metric favours, for instance when to hide information [Parn72]. Work using this technique on the design metric IF_4 has revealed three flaws previously unknown to its progenitor, notwithstanding the considerable amount of empirical evaluation that it had been subjected to [Shep91].

The theoretical evaluation has been stressed since it has not been given great attention in the past. Its particular value is, of course, that such techniques are almost invariably a good deal less resource consuming, than empirical studies. This is not to decry empirical work, but merely to observe that if we are expend considerable effort in an empirical validation of a model it should at least be internally consistent and satisfy certain criteria. Furthermore, theoretical analysis may uncover different problems with a model to those found by empirical investigation. Where it is possible to articulate a required model behaviour a mathematical proof may afford a higher degree of confidence than an empirical study, which in some ways is akin to sampling from a large and probably heterogeneous population, with no certainty that the sample is representative. On the other hand there are many situations where it is not possible to state *a priori* what model behaviour is required. In such circumstances empirical investigation is likely to be more effective. Empirical evaluation is also likely to be more effective at highlighting models that are insufficiently broad in scope or that make unrealistic assumptions. To repeat then, both forms of model evaluation are complementary and necessary.

One might also add, that as a by-product, an algebraic specification of metric is an effective way of unambiguously defining the counting rules for a metric. This alone has been the source of considerable confusion in the past, see for example [Lass81]. Likewise, it might also be argued that a formal specification provides a better foundation for the development of metric based software tools [Kitc86].

Although the flavour of this paper has been theoretical, formality alone is not sufficient. Indeed the essence of measurement is the mapping of empirical relations, drawn from an inherently informal world, into a formal model [Stev59]. However, the application of a little more rigour will make the development, refinement, validation and application of metrics a considerably less fraught process than is the present case.

References

[Boeh84] Boehm, B.W. 'Software engineering economics'. *IEEE Trans. on Softw. Eng.* 10(1) pp4-21. 1984.

[deMa82] deMarco, T. *'Controlling software projects. Management, measurement and estimation'.* Yourdon Press. NY. 1982.

[Ehri85] Ehrig, H. Mahr, B. *Fundamentals of algebraic specification,* EATCS, Vol.6 Springer-Verlag, 1985.

[Fent86] Fenton, N.E. Whitty, R.W. 'Axiomatic approach to Software metrification through program decomposition'. *Computer J.* 29(4) pp330-340. 1986.

[Geha82] Gehani, N.H. 'Specifications formal and informal - a case study', *Softw. Pract. & Experience,* 12, pp433-444, 1982.

[Gilb88] Gilb, T. *Principles of software engineering management,* Addison-Wesley, 1988.

[Gutt77] Guttag, J.V. 'Abstract data types and the development of data structures'. *CACM* 20(6) pp397-404. 1977.

[Gutt78] Guttag, J.V. Horning, J.J. 'The ALgebraic Specification of Abstract data types', *Acta Informatica,* 10, pp27-52, 1978.

[Henr81] Henry, S. Kafura, D. Harris, K. 'On the relationship among three software metrics' *ACM SIGMETRICS Performance Evaluation Review* 10, Spring pp81-88. 1981.

[Hame82] Hamer, P.G. Frewin, G.D. 'M.H. Halstead's Software Science - A Critical Examination'. *Proc. IEEE 6th Int. Conf on Softw. Eng.* pp197-206. 1982.

[Ince88] Ince, D.C. Shepperd, M.J . 'System design metrics: a review and perspective.' *Proc. IEE / BCS Conf. Software Engineering '88* July 12- 15, Liverpool University, pp23-27. 1988.

[Ince89] Ince, D.C. Shepperd, M.J. 'An empirical and theoretical analysis of an information flow based design metric'. *Proc. European Software Eng. Conf.,* Warwick, England. Sept. 12-15, 1989.

[Kitc86] Kitchenham, B.A. McDermid, J.A. 'Software metrics and integrated project support environments'. *Softw. Eng. J.* 1(1) pp58-64. 1986.

[Kran71] Krantz, D.H. Luce, R.D. Suppes, P. Tversky, A. *Foundations of measurement.* Academic Press, London. 1971.

[Kybe84] Kyburg, H.E. *Theory and measurement.* Cambridge Univ. Press, Cambridge, England. 1984.

[Lass81] Lassez, J-L. van der Knijff, D.J.J. Shepherd, J. Lassez, C. 'A critical examination of software science'. *J. of Syst. & Softw.* 2, pp105-112. 1981.

[Lisk86] Liskov, B. Guttag, J. *Abstraction and specification in program development.* MIT Press, MA.. 1986.

[McCa76] McCabe, T.J. 'A complexity measure' *IEEE Trans. on Softw. Eng.* 2(4) pp308-320. 1976.

[Melt90] Melton, A.C. Gustafson, D.A. Bieman, J.A. Baker, J.A. 'A mathematical perspective for software measures research', *Softw. Eng. J.* 5(4) pp246-254, 1990.

[Parn72] Parnas, D.L. 'On the criteria to be used in decomposing systems into modules'. CACM 15(2) pp1053-1058.

[Prat84] Prather, R.E. 'An axiomatic theory of software complexity metrics'. *The Comp. J.* 27(4) pp340-347. 1984.

[Prat87] Prather, R.E. 'On hierarchical software metrics'. *Softw. Eng. J.* 2(2) pp42-45. 1987.

[Shep88] Shepperd, M.J. 'A critique of cyclomatic complexity as a software metric' *Softw. Eng. J.* 3(2) pp30-36. 1988.

[Shep90] Shepperd, M.J. 'An empirical study of design measurement'. *The Softw. Eng. J.* Jan. 1990.

[Shep91] Shepperd, M.J. System Architecture Metrics: An Evaluation, PhD Dissertation, Open University, 1991.

[Stev59] Stevens, S.S. 'Measurement, psychophysics and utility' in Churchman, C.W. Ratoosh, P (eds.) *'Measurement: definitions and theories'.* Wiley, N.Y.. 1959.

[Stev74] Stevens, W.P. Myers, G.J. Constantine, L.L. 'Structured design' *IBM Sys. J.* 13(2) pp115-139. 1974.

[Supp71] Suppes, P. Zinnes, J.L. 'Basic measurement theory'. In Lieberman, B. (ed.) *'Contemporary problems in statistics'* O.U.P. 1971.

[Weyu88] Weyuker, E.J. 'Evaluating software complexity measures'. *IEEE Trans. on Softw. Eng.* 14(9) pp1357-1365. 1988.

[Yau80] Yau, S.S. Collofello, J.S. 'Some stability measures for software maintenance'. *IEEE Trans. on Softw. Eng.* 6(6) pp545-552. 1980.

[Yin78] Yin, B.H. Winchester, J.W. 'The establishment and use of measures to evaluate the quality of software designs' *Proc. ACM Softw. Qual. Ass. Workshop* pp45-52. 1978.

[Zuse89] Zuse, H. Bollmann, P. 'Software metrics: using measurement theory to describe the properties and scales of static complexity metrics'. *ACM SIGPLAN Notices* 24(8), pp23-33, 1989.

[Zuse90] Zuse, H. *Software Complexity, Measures and Methods*, deGruyter, Berlin, 1990.

Appendix - An Algebraic Specification of a Coupling Metric

syntax

external operations

```
new: → sys
addm: mod × sys → sys ∪ {duplicate_error}
rd: mod × ds × sys → sys ∪ {mod_not_found}
wr: mod × ds × sys → sys ∪ {mod_not_found}
C_i: mod × sys → nat ∪ {mod_not_found}
C: sys → nat
```

internal operations

```
exists?: mod × sys → boolean
addm': mod × sys → sys
rd': mod × ds × sys → sys
wr': mod × ds × sys → sys
fan_in: mod × sys × sys → nat
fan_out: mod × sys × sys → nat
```

#rd: ds × mod × sys → nat
#wr: ds × mod × sys → nat
C_i': mod × sys → nat
C': sys × sys → nat

semantics

vars

S, T: sys
m,n: mod
d,e: ds

equations

1. exists?(m,new) = FALSE
2. exists?(m,addm(n,S)) = IF m=n THEN TRUE ELSE exists?(m,S)
3. exists?(m,rd(n,d,S)) = exists?(m,S)
4. exists?(m,wr(n,d,S)) = exists?(m,S)

5. addm(m,S) = IF exists?(m,S) THEN {duplicate_error} ELSE addm'(m,S)

6. rd(m,d,S) = IF exists?(m,S) THEN rd'(m,d,S) ELSE {mod_not_found}

7. wr(m,d,S) = IF exists?(m,S) THEN wr'(m,d,S) ELSE {mod_not_found}

8. C(S) = C'(S,S)

9. C'(new,S) = 0
10. C'(addm'(m,T),S) = C_i'(m,S) + C'(T,S)

11. C'(rd'(m,d,T),S) = C'(T,S)
12. C'(wr'(m,d,T),S) = C'(T,S)

13. C_i(m,S) = IF exists(m,S) THEN C_i'(m,S) ELSE {mod_not_found}

14. C_i'(m,S) = fan_in(m,S,S)*fan_out(m,S,S)

15. fan_in(m,new,S) = 0
16. fan_in(m,addm'(n,T),S) = fan_in(m,T,S)
17. fan_in(m,wr'(n,d,T),S) = fan_in(m,T,S)

18. fan_in(m,rd'(n,d,T),S) = IF m=n THEN #wr(d,n,S) + fan_in(m,T,S) ELSE
       fan_in(m,T,S)

19. fan_out(m,new,S) = 0
20. fan_out(m,addm'(n,T),S) = fan_out(m,T,S)
21. fan_out(m,rd'(n,d,T),S) = fan_out(m,T,S)
22. fan_out(m,wr'(n,d,T),S) = IF m=n THEN #rd(d,n,S) + fan_out(m,T,S) ELSE
       fan_out(m,T,S)

23. #rd(d,n,new) = 0
24. #rd(d,n,addm'(m,S)) = #rd(d,n,S)
25. #rd(d,n,wr'(e,m,S)) = #rd(d,n,S)
26. #rd(d,n,rd'(e,m,S)) = IF d=e AND m≠n THEN 1 + #rd(d,n,S) ELSE #rd(d,n,S)

27. #wr(d,n,new) = 0
28. #wr(d,n,addm'(m,S)) = #wr(d,n,S)
29. #wr(d,n,rd'(e,m,S)) = #wr(d,n,S)
30. #wr(d,n,wr'(e,m,S)) = IF d=e AND m≠n THEN 1 + #wr(d,n,S) ELSE #wr(d,n,S)

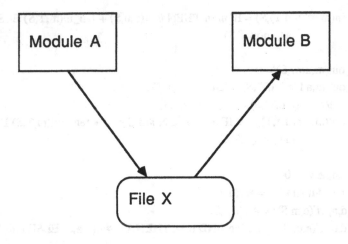

Figure 1: Example Module Coupling

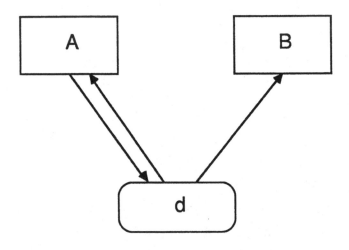

Figure 2: A Simple Software Architecture

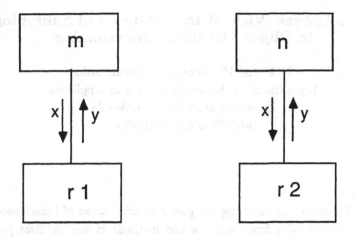

Architecture with duplication

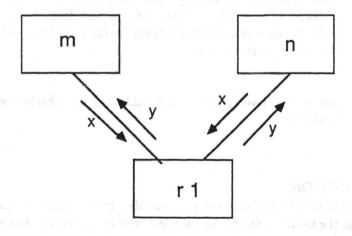

Architecture with re-use

Figure 3: The Impact of Re-use upon a Metric

An Algebraic View of Inheritance and Subtyping in Object Oriented Programming

F. Parisi Presicce, A. Pierantonio
Dipartimento di Matematica Pura ed Applicata
Università degli Studi - L'Aquila
I-67100 L'Aquila (Italy)

ABSTRACT

In Object Oriented Programming the powerful mechanism of inheritance allows the definition of classes starting from variables and methods of another class previously defined. Inheritance can be viewed as a relation between classes, which suggests how classes can be arranged in hierarchies. The hierarchies contain two kind of information: on the one hand, they indicate how programs are structured, how code is shared among classes; on the other hand, they give information about compatible assignment rules, which are based on subtyping.

In order to distinguish between code sharing, which is related to implementational aspects, and functional specialization, which is connected to the external behavior of objects, we introduce an algebraic specification based formalism, by which one can specify the behavior of a class and state when a class is to be considered subtype or inherits another one. It is shown that implementation inheritance can be reduced to specialization inheritance with respect to a virtual class.

Keywords

Objects, classes, message passing, inheritance, subtyping, code sharing, encapsulation, specifications, morphisms.

1 INTRODUCTION

It is expected that Object Oriented programming methodology and languages will be prevalent in the next decade. At the moment, different languages, like Smalltalk-80, C++, Eiffel and others, have become very diffused and often used as general purpose programming languages [Str86,Wiener88].

Often in such languages a program is considered as a collection of objects and messages. An object is intended as a single entity which integrates its data and the operations that can operate on these data (usually called methods).

The mechanism of message passing consists of sending a message to an object: if the object is able to answer it, there will be an appropriate method operation. Otherwise what results depends on whether the type checking system is static or not: in a typed language, like C++, sending an unknown message to an object corrisponds to an illegal notification at compile time, whereas in a language with dynamic type checking system or untyped, like Smalltalk-80, the unknown message will result in a run time error message. The inheritance and the message passing mechanism are not the only features of an Object Oriented programming language.

If the language provides support to encapsulation, we can access an object only by sending one of those messages declared public or specified in an external interface of the object. This mechanism protects the data against uncontrolled access from other objects and minimizes the amount of implementation details which are visible outside the object. Serious supports to encapsulation and data abstraction are requested but not always present in Object Oriented languages. Objects with the same features and properties are described by means the same "object pattern", called class. All the attributes of the objects are specified in their own class. Such objects are called instances of the class.

One of the Object Oriented programming hallmarks is inheritance. This mechanism appeared for the first time in SIMULA-67, is a very powerful tool to enhance some software quality factors like estendibility and reusability. The basic principle of inheritance is that sometimes, in order to define a new class, it is convenient to add new variables and methods to an existing class. The resulting class is said to "inherit" the variables and methods of the old one. In this way classes can be arranged in hierarchies, which indicate how code is shared among classes and how the program is structured. If the attributes of the instances of an inheriting class are at least those of the inherited one, we have also a subtyping relationship or a compatible assignment rule. This means that if a class T1 inherits a class T2, wherever we expect an instance of T2, an instance of T1 can be used. This is the reason why an inherinting classes is said a subclass and an inherited class is said a superclass.

In this paper we analyze more closely some of the main characteristics of Object Oriented methodology and in particular the interaction between encapsulation, with the induced interface, inheritance and subtyping, by using an algebraic formalism [Ehrig85] and by modelling a class using an extension of the notion of module specification [EW85,WE86,Ehrig90]. For semplicity of presentation, we will discuss the formalization using simple algebraic specifications, where properties of methods are expressed by equations. The approach can be immediately extended to other formalisms (i.e., institutions in the sense of [Goguen83,Sannella84]). In this model, we formally distinguish between implementation and specialization inheritance, as the existence of different sets of morphisms, subtype relation and its inverse "supertype".

2 INHERITANCE AND SUBTYPING

The notion of inheritance as it was introduced in the first Object Oriented programming languages can be considered according to different interpretations. Viewing inheritance as a technique to implement abstract data types the possibility of omitting some methods can be reasonable. In this way, the use of inheritance has to be retained as a private decision of the designer of a class. This kind of inheritance, implementation inheritance, is intended as an implementation technique in order to share and reuse code already written. On the other hand, the use of inheritance can also be regarded as a public declaration of the designer: it states that the instances of the subclass obey the semantics of the superclass. This notion of inheritance can be called specialization inheritance or enrichment.

In these two cases the visibility through the external interface is not the same depending on the different meanings given to the code sharing mechanism (this distinction was done in [Snyder86]). The first kind of inheritance, which is merely an implementation technique, does not lead to behavioral specialization of a class but to a flexible reuse of code already written. The other form of inheritance instead allows to reuse code in an incremental manner. Therefore we have code shared between two classes involved in the inheritance process and we have also a rule on compatible assignment since a subclass instance is a superclass instance too.

It is very important to point out that the relationship of subtyping between two classes does not depend on internal representations. For example, the class which implements the abstract data type stack can use an array or a linked list for its internal representation, but the functionalities this class provides are the same. We can consider an array based stack and a linked list based one as being of the same type, if the visible properties of the functionalities coincide.

This means that the subtyping is a more general relationship between classes than those present in the known languages. Actually, a code sharing mechanism does not always lead to a behavioral specialization while we can have the same functionalities by means of different representations.

Ideally, in order to specify the behavior (semantics) of a class we need a formal specification system. Such a system would probably require a theorem prover which represent an obstacle to its integration in a programming language.

A not fully satisfactory solution can be found if we restrict our attention to signatures only. In this case, we can verify the subtyping compatibility between two classes by means of an interface containment based approach [Card84]. There are no technological constraints to adopt this approach in a static language, but at the moment there are no languages that provide such a feature.

In [Pier90] we sketched an Object Oriented programming language kernel, called NDL, where a distinction can be found between an implementation inheritance and a specialization mechanism also called enrichment. In NDL there is an explicit subtyping declaration features. This declaration must be explicit because it is based only on signatures. The designer has the responsability of the meaningfulness of the subtype declarations.

3 INTERFACES AND PARAMETERS

Encapsulation is another very useful technique and sometimes referred to as the main features of Object Oriented programming languages [Am90]. The main goal of this mechanism is the protection of individual instances by means of access functions, setting the designer free to modify, in part or whole, the implementation of a class. For example, if a class provides appropriate access functions for its variables, then we can interpret, rename, or remove some of these without affecting any client of the class in question.

Inheritance introduces a new category of clients: the definition of classes [Snyder86]. Actually, inheritance compromises some encapsulation benefits such as the freedom of reinterpret, rename, or remove inherited variables. The designer of an inherited class cannot make changes on a variables which is directly referred to by the inheriting class. Checking all the inheriting classes to verify that a specific variable has not been used is prohibitively expensive. All this results in a reduction of flexibility provided by encapsulation. A solution is to provide another interface specifically for the class definition. All the attributes a class can view from its ancestor are specified in a explicit interface. So we have an interface for the instances of class users and another for the possible designers of descendant classes. We can call these interfaces instance and class interfaces, respectively. Furthermore we suppose that the instance interface is contained in the class interface since all the access function for the instance are also useful for a descendant class. The C++ language is the only Object Oriented programming language with such a capability [Str86].

In the process of developing software systems, implementation and specialization inheritance can be viewed as supporting two opposite "methodologies". In a bottom-up approach, existing classes are used to implement new classes which inherit the code of the superclasses to be used to realiza its methods. In a top-down approach, existing classes, reflecting previous design decisions, are refined, by way of specializing methods and properties of superclass, to obtain new classes which inherit the design decisions. Additional flexibility to this top-down approach can be achieved if we allow the definition of a class as an extension of features not yet implemented (or of which the implementation is not known).

An interesting case arises if we consider to extend an unimplemented signature. In order to do that we can use abstract classes but by doing so we have to implement all the features at each direct derivation of the classes. Then, it is preferable to use an import interface structure related with an combination mechanism. In this way, we can implement a whole specialization hierarchy in the opposite direction of enrichment. Moreover we can include classes which are partial implementations of what they specify in implementation or specialization processes.

The notion of import interface is inspired at the same structure present in [EW85]. The presence of an import interface allows the development of a system in a "middle-out" approach as follows:

- certain export interfaces can be realized assuming the existence of certain functionalities expressed in the import interface,

- the export interface are enriched or extended to obtain the desired overall system,

- the import interface is subsequently realized using other classes until all import interfaces are eliminated.

This approach is an adaptation of the rule-based approach to modular system design presented in [Parisi90], where such classes can be represented by productions $IMP \leftarrow PAR \rightarrow EXP$ and the objective is, having defined a notion of derivation, to use a set of such productions (each representing a partial realization) to generate from predefined functionalities (importless classes) the desired export interface. It would then be sufficient to "translate" such derivation into a sequence of allowed "operations" of classes.

Another interesting feature may be the genericity as it is proposed for example in the ADA language and analized in [Meyer86]. Genericity allows us to define software elements which can be extensible, reusable and compatible. Moreover, such software elements can have more than one interpretation according to some generic type parameters. There are two form of genericity depending on whether we require some operations, called constraints, on a type parameter or not (unconstrained and constrained genericity, respectively).

We agree with Meyer when he says that inheritance is more powerful than genericity because inheritance can simulate the genericity and the opposite is not true. Meyer suggests to combine inheritance and genericity. But he does not include the constrained genericity since a type parameter with constraints can be viewed as an abstract data type and classes are its implementations. But the price to pay in order to obtain such simulation is too high. So it is preferable to combine all forms of genericity with inheritance. In this algebraic approach, it is possible to include properties of the operations as constraints and not just a signature as in current languages.

4 ALGEBRAIC FORMALIZATION

To introduce a correctness notion in Object Oriented programming, we need an appropriate formal support. Such a support can be found in an approach based on algebraic specifications.

Now, we briefly review some basic notions. By algebraic specification $Spec$ we mean a triple (S, OP, E) consisting of a set S of sorts, a set OP of operation symbols and a set E of (positive conditional) equations. If $Sig_1 = (S_1, OP_1)$ and $Sig_2 = (S_2, OP_2)$ are signatures, a signature morphism $h : Sig_1 \rightarrow Sig_2$ is a pair of functions $(h_S : S_1 \rightarrow S_2, h_{OP} : OP_1 \rightarrow OP_2)$ such that for each operation symbol $N : s_1, .., s_n \rightarrow s$ in OP_1, $h_{OP}(N) : h_S(s_1), .., h_S(s_n) \rightarrow h_S(s)$.

A signature morphism automatically defines a forgetful functor $V_h : Alg(Sig_2) \rightarrow Alg(Sig_1)$ defined for each Sig_2-algebras A'' by $V_h(A'') = A' \in Alg(Sig_1)$ with $A'_S =$

$A''_{hs(s)}$ for each $s \in S_1$, $N_{A'} = h_{OP}(N)_{A''}$ for each $N \in OP_1$.

If $Spec_1$ and $Spec_2$ are two specifications, a <u>specification morphism</u> is a signature morphism $(fs, f_{OP}) : (S_1, OP_1) \to (S_2, OP_2)$ such that the translation of $f^\#(E_1)$ of the equations of $Spec_1$ is contained in E_2. Each specification morphism defines a forgetful functor $V_f : Alg(Spec_2) \to Alg(Spec_1)$ which intuitively translates models of $Spec_2$ into models of $Spec_1$ and which corrisponds to the restriction to models of $Spec_2$ of the forgetful functor of the related signature morphism.

The class we have described in the previous sections is composed of a certain number of parts: a parameter part, an import interface, an instance and a class export interface. All these components declare signatures and their properties.

4.1 Definition (Class specification and Semantics)

A class specification C_{spec} consists of five algebraic specifications PAR (parameter part), EXP_i (instance interface), EXP_c (class interface), IMP (import interface) and BOD (implementation related part) and five specification morphisms associated as in the following commutative diagram

$$PAR \xrightarrow{\;e_i\;} EXP_i \xrightarrow{\;e_c\;} EXP_c$$

$$\left. i \right\downarrow \qquad\qquad\qquad \left\downarrow v \right.$$

$$IMP \xrightarrow{\qquad\qquad\; s \;\qquad\qquad} BOD$$

The semantics of a class specification is a functor

$$SEM = V_v \circ Sem : Alg(IMP) \to Alg(BOD) \to Alg(EXP_c).$$

Interpretation

Each of the five parts consists not only of signatures, but also of equations, which describe some of the properties of the operations.

The interfaces EXP_i and EXP_c describe the external access functions and their behavior: the former describes the messages which can be sent to the objects which are instances of the class, while the latter contains the methods which can be used by other classes. The part of BOD not in EXP_c is hidden from other classes. The specification BOD describes an implementation of the exported methods using the ones provided by the IMP specification. The import specification IMP contains informations about <u>what</u> is needed by BOD to implement EXP_c, but not <u>which</u> can provide it: the latter task is provided by the interconnection mechanisms. The specification PAR models a simple version of genericity, unconstrained if the specification consists of sorts only, constrained in the general case where a potential parameter is required to have operations satisfying certain properties (such as the standard ring operations in a class which implements the usual methods to manipulate matrices over that ring).

Remark

For semplicity of presentation, a functorial semantics SEM is chosen. By choosing Sem as the free functor from $Alg(IMP)$ to $Alg(BOD)$, the semantics is the same as that of module specification [EW85]. The theory could easily be developped using a loose semantics, such as pairs (A_I, A_{E_c}) of algebras, provided that $A_I = V_s(A_B)$ and $A_{E_c} = V_v(A_B)$ for some $A_B \in Alg(BOD)$.

In our framework, a class is a couple that consists of a class specification and a class implementation. A class implementation is an algebra and may be written in a compatible language, where a compatible language is an Object Oriented programming language with at least the same feature as NDL and in which all the methods are functions.

4.2 Definition (Class)

A class $C = (C_{spec}, C_{impl})$ consists of a class specification C_{spec} and a class implementation C_{impl} such that $C_{impl} = SEM(A)$, where SEM is the semantics of C_{spec} and $A \in Alg(IMP)$

4.3 Example

In the following we introduce an example of simple class specification which corresponds to the commutative diagram. The morphisms are just inclusions. In the notation we use the keywords **Parameter, Instance Interface, Class Interface, Import Interface, Body** to declare the subspecification to be added to the parts already defined. For examples, since $PAR \subseteq EXP_i$, after the keyword **Instance Interface** only $EXP_i - PAR$ is listed. When a subspecification keyword is missing the relative specification is just the subspecifications in the diagram.

```
DICT is Class_Spec
Parameter
  sorts:
        record, key, item;
  opns:
        ERROR_record:  → record
        MAKE: key item → record
Instance Interface
  sorts:
        dict;
  opns:
        ERROR_dict:  → dict
        EMPTY:  → dict
        INSERT: record dict → dict
        DELETE: key dict → dict
        GET: key dict → record
  eqns:
        r,r_1,r_2 ∈ record; x,y ∈ key; a,b ∈ item; d ∈ dict;
        INSERT(r,INSERT(r,d)) = INSERT(r,d)
        INSERT(r_1,INSERT(r_2,d)) = INSERT(r_2,INSERT(r_1,d))
        GET(k,INSERT(MAKE(k,a),d)) = MAKE(k,a)
```

        DELETE(k,EMPTY) = EMPTY
        DELETE(k,INSERT(MAKE(k,a),d)) = d
Class Interface
eqns:
        INSERT(MAKE(k,a),INSERT(MAKE(k,b),d)) = $ERROR_{dict}$ (eq1)
        GET(k_1,INSERT(MAKE(k_2,a),EMPTY)) = $ERROR_{record}$
end Class_Spec

We aim at an approach to subtyping not only syntactic, but based on the behavior of a class as given by its specification. In this scenario, the subtyping relationship between two classes can be introduced more formally as follows

4.4 Definition (Subtyping)

Let $C1 = (C1_{spec}, C1_{impl})$ and $C2 = (C2_{spec}, C2_{impl})$ be two classes.

   i. C1 is weak subtype of C2, notation $C1 \preceq C2$, if there exist specification morphisms
$$f : EXP_{i2} \rightarrow EXP_{i1} \text{ and } p : PAR_2 \rightarrow PAR_1$$
   such that $f \circ e_{i2} = e_{i1} \circ p$ as in the following diagram

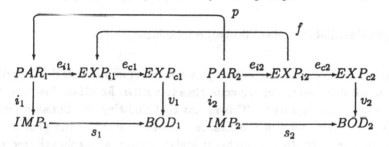

   ii. C1 is a strong subtype of C2, notation $C1 \sqsubseteq C2$, if, in addition,

$$V_f \circ V_{e_{c1}}(C1_{impl}) = V_{e_{c2}}(C2_{impl}).$$

The following class specification DICT+ is a subtype of the DICT class specification in the example 4.3 using inclusion morphisms. It is worth noticing that DICT+ is a subtype as well as an enrichment of DICT because the equation (eq1) of DICT is present in the body part of DICT+.

DICT+ is Class_Spec
Parameter
sorts:
        record, key, item;
opns:
        $ERROR_{record}$: → record
        MAKE: key item → record
Instance Interface

sorts:
  dict+;

opns:
  $ERROR_{dict+}$: → dict+
  EMPTY: → dict+
  INSERT: record dict+ → dict+
  DELETE: key dict+ → dict+
  GET: key dict+ → record
  MERGE: dict+ dict+ → dict+

eqns:
  $r,r_1,r_2 \in$ record; $x,y \in$ key; $a,b \in$ item; $d \in$ dict+;
  INSERT(r,INSERT(r,d)) = INSERT(r,d)
  $INSERT(r_1,INSERT(r_2,d)) = INSERT(r_2,INSERT(r_1,d))$
  GET(k,INSERT(MAKE(k,a),d)) = MAKE(k,a)
  DELETE(k,EMPTY) = EMPTY
  DELETE(k,INSERT(MAKE(k,a),d)) = d

Class Interface
eqns:
  $GET(k_1,INSERT(MAKE(k_2,a),EMPTY)) = ERROR_{record}$
  MERGE(EMPTY,d) = d
  $MERGE(d_1,d_2) = MERGE(d_2,d_1)$

Body
eqns:
  $INSERT(MAKE(k,a),INSERT(MAKE(k,b),d)) = ERROR_{dict}$
end Class_Spec

In the second section we have pointed out that the aim of implementation inheritance is the reuse, in a suitable manner, of the code already written for other classes, without resulting in behavioral specialization. This means that omitting functionalities and/or properties is allowed. This kind of inheritance is distinguished by the presence of a morphism to the body part BOD_2 of the inheriting class, in such a way that the morphism from the class interface EXP_{c2} to the body subspecification BOD_2 allows the omission of some functionalities.

4.5 Definition (Implementation Inheritance)
Let $C1 = (C1_{spec}, C1_{impl})$ and $C2 = (C2_{spec}, C2_{impl})$ be classes. Then

  i. $C2$ is weakly implemented by $C1$, notation $C2\ Winh\ C1$, if there exists a morphism

$$f : EXP_{c1} \to BOD_2,$$

  as in the following diagram

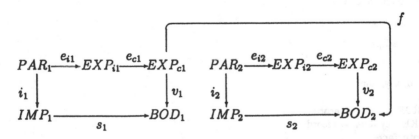

ii. C2 is strongly implemented by C1, notation C2 Sinh C1, if, in addition,

$$V_f(Sem(A)) = C1_{impl}$$

where $SEM(A) = V_{v_2}(Sem(A)) = C2_{impl}$ *for some* $A \in Alg(IMP_2)$.

4.6 Example

According to the above definition, we can show how a new class specification, say BAG, is implemented by DICT, the class specification just introduced in example 4.3. Indeed, what we need in order to do that is an appropriate morphism from the class interface part $EXP_{C_{dict}}$ of DICT to the body subspecification BOD_{bag} of BAG, as follows

f(record) = value	f(ERROR_{record}:→record) = ERROR_{value}:→value
f(key) = key	f(MAKE:key item→record) = MAKE:key item→value
f(item) = item	f(ERROR_{dict}:→dict) = ERROR_{bag}→bag
f(dict) = bag	f(EMPTY:→dict) = NEW:→bag
	f(INSERT:record dict→dict) = ADD:value bag→bag
	f(DELETE:key dict→dict) = DELETE:key bag→bag
	f(GET:key dict→record) = GET:key bag→value

```
BAG is Class_Spec
Parameter
 sorts:
        bool, value;
 opns:
        EQ: value value → bool
Instance Interface
 eqns:
        bag;
 opns:
        NEW:  → bag
        ADD: value bag → bag
        BELONGS?: value bag → bool
 eqns:
        v,v₁,v₂,x,y ∈ value; b ∈ bag;
        ADD(v₁,ADD(v₂,b)) = ADD(v₂,ADD(v₁,b))
        ADD(v,ADD(v,b)) = ADD(v,b)
        BELONGS?(x,ADD(y,b)) = EQ(x,y) or BELONGS?(x,b)
Body
 sorts:
        key,item;
 opns:
        ERROR_value:  → value
        MAKE: key item → value
        ERROR_bag:  → bag
        DELETE: key bag → bag
        GET: key bag → value
 eqns:
        a ∈ item; GET(v,ADD(MAKE(v,a),b)) = MAKE(v,a)
```

DELETE(v,NEW) = NEW
DELETE(v,ADD(MAKE(v,a),b)) = b
ADD(MAKE(v,a),ADD(MAKE(v,b),b)) = $ERROR_{bag}$
GET(v_1,ADD(MAKE(v_2,a),NEW)) = $ERROR_{value}$
end Class_Spec

Another tool found in Object Oriented programming languages to enhance the quality of software production is the possibility to inherit by specialization. Specialization inheritance allows the enrichment of the functionalities of a class and can be modelled by morphisms from the inherited class to the inheriting class in such a way that behavior is preserved. Note that in addition to the parameter part and the instance interface, also the class interface can be enriched (unlike subtyping, where we have seen that the example DICT+ has less "behavior" in the class interface than the DICT class specification).

4.7 Definition (Specialization Inheritance)
Let $C1 = (C1_{spec}, C1_{impl})$ and $C2 = (C2_{spec}, C2_{impl})$ be classes. Then

i. $C2$ is a weak specialization of $C1$, notation $C2$ W spec $C1$, if there exist morphisms

$$p : PAR_1 \rightarrow PAR_2,$$

$$f_i : EXP_{i1} \rightarrow EXP_{i2},$$

$$f_c : EXP_{c1} \rightarrow EXP_{c2},$$

such that $f_i \circ e_{i1} = e_{i2} \circ p$ and $e_{c2} \circ f_i = f_c \circ e_{c1}$, as in the following commutative diagram

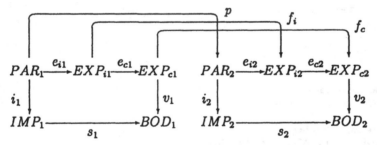

ii. $C2$ is a strong specialization of $C1$, notation $C2$ Sspec $C1$, if, in addition,

$$V_{f_c}(C2_{impl}) = C1_{impl}$$

4.8 Example

The class specification BAG turns out to be a specialization of the class specification SET which we are going to introduce; in fact all the visible parts of the class specification SET but the import interface are enriched in the BAG, by means of the following specialization morphism p and f_i (since the class interface is just the instance interface, f_c is equal to f_i)

$$p(\text{data}) = \text{value} \qquad\qquad f_i(\text{set}) = \text{bag}$$
$$f_i(\text{CREATE}:\to\text{set}) = \text{NEW}:\to\text{bag} \qquad f_i(\text{INSERT:data set}\to\text{set}) = \text{ADD:value bag}\to\text{bag}$$

SET is Class_Spec
Parameter
  <u>sorts</u>:
    data;
Instance Interface
  <u>sorts</u>:
    set;
  <u>opns</u>:
    CREATE: $\to$ set
    INSERT: data set $\to$ set
  <u>eqns</u>:
    $d, d_1, d_2 \in$ data;$s \in$ set;
    INSERT(d,INSERT(d,s)) = INSERT(d,s)
    INSERT(d_1,INSERT(d_2,s)) = INSERT(d_2,INSERT(d_1,s))
end Class_Spec

The implementation and specialization inheritance are introduced as relationships between classes. When $C2$ *Sinh* $C1$, we are able to implement $C2_{impl}$ with the code already written for $C1_{impl}$ without resulting in a behavioral specialization. If $C2$ *Sspec* $C1$, then $C2_{impl}$ has to satisfy the semantics of $C1_{spec}$.

There are a lot of implications formalized in the followings

4.9 Proposition

Let $C1 = (C1_{spec}, C1_{impl})$ and $C2 = (C2_{spec}, C2_{impl})$ be classes. Then

  i. if $C1$ Wspec $C2$ then $C1$ Winh $C2$ and

  ii. if $C1$ Sspec $C2$ then $C1$ Sinh $C2$.

4.10 Proposition

  i. Each of the four relationships $\preceq$, $\sqsubseteq$, Wspec , and Sspec is transitive.

  ii. If $C3$ Winh $C2$ and $C2$ Wspec $C1$ then $C3$ Winh $C1$ and
  if $C3$ Sinh $C2$ and $C2$ Sspec $C1$ then $C3$ Sinh $C1$.

Another important notion is that of Virtual Class which can be formalized in the following definition.

4.11 Definition (Virtual Classes)

A virtual class V consists of a triple (PAR, EXP_i, EXP_c) of specifications and two morphisms

$$PAR \xrightarrow{\ e_i\ } EXP_i \xrightarrow{\ e_c\ } EXP_c$$

The following result (which motivated the formalization of implementation and specialization inheritance as we did), shows that it is sufficient to consider specialization inheritance as the only relation generating a hierarchy of classes

4.12 Theorem

Let $C1 = (C1_{spec}, C1_{impl})$ and $C2 = (C2_{spec}, C2_{impl})$ be two classes. If $C2\ Winh\ C1$, then there exists a virtual class C such that

i. $C1\ Wspec\ C$,

ii. $C2\ Wspec\ C$.

The class C constructed in the previous theorem need not be abstract if $C2\ Sinh\ C1$ and can be implemented using the implementation of $C1$ and $C2$. By using the specialization inheritance (which implies subtyping) it is possible to represent the implementation inheritance (which usually reflects the development over time of the system) and keep the correctness under control.

As we have seen earlier the class specification BAG is weakly implemented by DICT (we have intentionally ignored the class implementation and dealt only with the specification for the sake of semplicity). Therefore the class specification SET is the largest, with respect to the relation $Wspec$ (and unique up to isomorphism) class specification such that DICT $Wspec$ SET and BAG $Wspec$ SET by using the morphism p', p'', f_i', f_i'' as follows

$p'(\text{data}) = \text{record}$	$p''(\text{data}) = \text{value}$
$f_i'(\text{set}) = \text{dict}$	$f_i''(\text{set}) = \text{bag}$
$f_i'(\text{CREATE:}\rightarrow\text{set}) = \text{EMPTY:}\rightarrow\text{dict}$	$f_i''(\text{CREATE:}\rightarrow\text{set}) = \text{NEW:}\rightarrow\text{bag}$
$f_i'(\text{INSERT:data set}\rightarrow\text{set}) =$	$f_i''(\text{INSERT:data set}\rightarrow\text{set}) =$
$\quad$ INSERT:record dict$\rightarrow$dict	$\quad$ ADD:value bag$\rightarrow$bag

Since the class interface of SET coincides with the instance interface, $f_c' = f_i'$ and $f_c'' = f_i''$.

The implementation and specialization inheritance relationships are based on interactions between what a class "produces" via its export interfaces and other classes. Other hierarchies can be defined based on the import interface and the generic parameters. Such specifications define what the class "needs" from the external world. In order to make these structures work for us we need some mechanisms, called attualization and combination, to relate a "producer" to a class in "need". The actualization and combination mechanisms will be introduced consistently with our formalism, so we will deal with a Strong and a Weak notion of such mechanisms, defined as relationships between classes and class specifications.

The notion of Strong Actualization states when a correct class $C1$ satisfies the behavior requested by the import interface subspecification of another correct class $C2$. In order to verify it, we have to check the existence of a morphism

$$h : PAR_2 \to EXP_{i1}.$$

By doing so, we obtain that all the class implementations of $C1$ are models of PAR_2 specifications (up to renaming). This result may be considered a global property. Actually, such notion states when a class implementation of a correct class $C1$ is a model (up to renaming) of the subspecifiaction PAR_2 of another correct class $C2$. We are not able to say something about other possible correct implementations of $C1$.

Similarly, the Combination mechanism is related to the import interface subspecification of a class. Here too we will have a Strong and a Weak notion. The Weak Combination states whether the specific implementation of a correct class $C1$ is a model for the subspecification IMP of another correct class $C2$. This is specified by the existence of a morphism

$$c : IMP_2 \to EXP_{c1}.$$

The actualization and Combination relations just mentioned define the availability of a class to satisfy the external need (parameter or import) of another class. The result of the matching of an import interface with a class export interface of another class, or of the parameter part with the export can be defined along the lines of the operations on module specifications described in [EW85] and [Weber86].

Such interconnections allow to define new inheriting classes whose behavior can be "predicted" and whose implementation can be constructed "explicitly" from those of the inherited classes.

5 CONCLUDING REMARKS

In this paper, we have proposed an approach to subtyping and inheritance in Object Oriented programming based on specification of the external behavior of classes. A class is composed of a class specification and an implementation. A class specification is treated as a model for the specification, in order to introduce the class correctness property, other properties and relationships between classes. The results obtained are intended as a formal support for the complete characterization of the main features of Object Oriented programming. We have discussed how we can distinguish between two form of inheritance, an implementative one and one based on an enrichment mechanism. We have also distinguished between two levels of relationships: strong, which is based on the formal specification and thus on global properties, and weak, which is based on local properties and in particular on the specific implementation.

In the main theorem, the implementation inheritance application results in a new class, which always exists and which is a more general specification (in the sense of specialization inheritance) than the two classes involved into inheritance step.

For a useful theory of software correctness and software reusability, it is important to be able to relate the behavior of parts which seem to be related by other criteria, such as code reuse for efficiency. This is the spirit of the Theorem of the last section.

For future work, it will be interesting to compare in more depth our formalized notion of implementation inheritance with the reusability in [Gaudel88] and with the notion of vertical refinement in [Clerici88] and in [Ehrig90].

Acknowledgments

Thanks are due to the anonymous referees for their useful criticisms and suggestions. This research has been supported in part by CNR under "Progetto Finalizzato: Sistemi Informatici e Calcolo Parallelo".

REFERENCES

[Am90]   P.America
            *A behavioural approach to subtyping in Object-Oriented Programming
            Languages*
            Proc. REX/FOOL, 1990

[Card84]   L.Cardelli
            A Semantics of multiple inheritance
            Proc. Semantics of Data Types, LNCS 173, 1984, pp.51-68

[Clerici88] S.Clerici, F.Orejas
            GSBL: an algebraic specification language based on inheritance
            Proc. ECOOP 1988, LNCS 322

[Ehrig85]   H.Ehrig, B.Mahr
            Fundamentals of Algebraic Specification 1
            EATCS, Springer Verlag, 1985

[Ehrig90]   H.Ehrig, B.Mahr
            Fundamentals of Algebraic Specification 2
            EATCS, Springer Verlag, 1990

[EW85]   H.Ehrig, H.Weber
            Algebraic Specification of modules in 'Formal Models in Programming'
            (Neuhold E.J., Chronist G.,eds)
            North-Holland, 1985

[Gaudel88] M.C.Gaudel,Th.Moineau
            A Theory of Software Reusability
            ESOP 88, LNCS 300, pp.115-130

[Gibbs90]   S.Gibbs, D.Tsichritzis, E.Casais
              Class Management for Software Communities
              Communication of the ACM,33,9 (Sept 90) pp.90-103

[Goguen83]   J.A.Goguen, R.Burstall
              Introducing Institutions
              Proc. Logics of Programming Workshop (E.Clarke, ed.) 1983

[Liskov87]   B.Liskov
              Data Abstraction and Hierarchy
              Addendum to the Proc. OOPSLA 87, 1987, pp.17-34

[Meyer86]   B.Meyer
              Genericity versus Inheritance
              Proc. OOPSLA '86, 1986, pp.391-405

[Parisi90]   F.Parisi-Presicce
              A rule-based approach to modular system design
              Proc. 12th ICSE, Nice 1990

[Pier90]   A.Pierantonio
              Problemi di ereditarietà e sottotipo in metodologie orientate agli oggetti
              Tesi di Laurea in Sc.Inf., Università de L'Aquila, December 1990

[Sannella84] D.Sannella, A.Tarlecki
              Building Specifications in an arbitrary Institution
              Proc. Semantics of Data Type, LNCS 173, 1984, pp.337-356

[Snyder86]   A.Snyder
              Encapsulation and Inheritance in Object-Oriented Programming Languages
              Proc. OOPSLA '86, 1986, pp.38-45

[Str86]   B.Stroustrup
              The C++ Programming Language
              Addison-Wesley,1986

[WE86]   H.Weber, H.Ehrig
              Specification of Modular Systems
              Transaction of Software Engineering, June 1986

[Wiener88]   R.Wiener, L.Pinson
              An introduction to Object-Oriented Programming and Smalltalk
              Addison-Wesley,1988

[Wirfs90]   R.J.Wirfs-Brock, R.E.Johnson
              Surveying Current Research in Object-Oriented Design
              Communication of the ACM,33,9 (Sept 90) pp.104-124

SCALING UP
RULE-BASED SOFTWARE DEVELOPMENT ENVIRONMENTS

Naser S. Barghouti   Gail E. Kaiser

Columbia University, Department of Computer Science
500 West 120th Street, New York, NY 10027

Abstract

Rule-based software development environments (RBDEs) model the software development process in terms of rules that encapsulate development activities, and assist in executing the process via forward and backward chaining over the rule base. We investigate the scaling up of RBDEs to support (1) multiple views of the rule base for multiple users and (2) evolution of the rule base over the lifetime of a project. Our approach is based on clarifying two distinct functions of rules and chaining: maintaining consistency and automation. By definition, consistency is mandatory whereas automation is not. Distinguishing the consistency and automation aspects of RBDE assistance mechanisms makes it possible to formalize the range of compatible views and the scope of mechanizable evolution steps. Throughout the paper, we use the MARVEL RBDE as an example application of our ideas.

1. Introduction

Process-oriented software development environments assist their users in carrying out the software development process [19, 16]. In order to accommodate long-term projects involving teams of software personnel, it is essential to support *multiple views* and *evolution.*

Multiple views are needed for several purposes. Individual users can express personal tailoring of localized aspects of the process; managers can impose their different management styles on their subgroups. Views for different user roles or lifecycle phases can emphasize the subset of functionality appropriate to those roles or phases, respectively. Evolution is inescapable due to changes in management philosophy and optimization of the development process, reorganization of the project components as their number and complexity grows, and changes to the tool set as new tools become available and older tools become obsolete.

The problems of multiple views and evolution are related, because they are both concerned with divergent versions of the process definition, the data format, and the tool set of an environment. But in the evolution case the divergence is over time, whereas there may be multiple views at the same point in time. Multiple views necessarily co-exist with one another, while evolution is not necessarily backward compatible and in fact may require upgrading or invalidation of previous views. Note that we are concerned here with the evolution of the process, schema and tool set, as opposed to the evolution of the product being developed or of the underlying environment framework.

Different process-oriented environments represent the process using different formalisms. Arcadia uses an extension of Ada as a process programming language [21]. HFSP employs a form of attribute grammars [15]. MELMAC combines several perspectives on the process into a representation similar to Petri nets [6]. It seems likely that the approach to multiple views and evolution will depend to a large extent on the process modeling formalism. This paper describes our investigation of the problems of multiple views and evolution in the context of process-oriented environments that use *rules* to define the software process.

Rule-based software development environments (RBDEs) are a subclass of process-oriented environments. In RBDEs, each step in the process is modeled by a rule that specifies the *condition* for initiating the step and the *effect* of completing the step. The schema (or data model) is typically specified in an object-oriented style, as a set of classes. The rules operate on objects, instances of the classes. Example RBDEs include Grapple [11], Darwin [17], CLF [5], Workshop [4], Oikos [1], ALF [3], and MARVEL [12]. In an RBDE, a view is a subset of the rules and/or classes, and the main problem introduced by adding multiple views to an RBDE lies in the inter-operability of views with respect to shared objects. Evolution consists of modifications to rules and/or classes, and the most significant difficulty is upgrading existing objects so they can continue to be manipulated in the environment.

We analyzed the RBDE paradigm, to find clues toward a solution of these problems. We discovered that rules serve two distinct purposes, to express, enforce and maintain *consistency* and to express and carry out opportunities for *automation*. Maintaining consistency is mandatory, whereas carrying out automation is optional. Distinguishing between these two functions of rules results in an elegant approach to supporting both multiple views and evolution. In particular, an RBDE can support multiple simultaneous views if they either share a common consistency model or reflect entirely disjoint models, while there are no such restrictions on overlapping notions of automation. Further, mechanical evolution of the consistency model is always feasible towards weaker levels of consistency or the addition of new constraints completely disjoint from the previous process and data models, but again there are no such limitations on evolution of the automation model.

We first give an overview of RBDEs, using our own MARVEL environment as an example, and describe a chaining algorithm for "enacting" software processes. We also present an example that we use throughout the paper. Next, we show how chaining has both consistency and automation aspects, and then introduce a "maximalist" chaining mechanism that formalizes the distinction between consistency constraints and automation opportunities. An extension of this mechanism is being implemented in the first multi-user MARVEL, version 3.0, while the previous single-user versions of MARVEL, culminating in version 2.6, did not distinguish these concerns [14]. In the next two sections, we explain how the separation of consistency from automation may be exploited to support multiple views and evolution. The paper ends with a comparison of related work concerned with multiple views and evolution in software development environments, and a summary of our contributions.

2. MARVEL Overview

Every software project assumes a specific development process and a particular organization for its components, as well as a set of software tools. Since these may be quite different for different projects, it is not appropriate to build a single software development environment, with a fixed development process employing a hardwired data model and a static tool set. Instead, RBDEs provide a common kernel that can be *tailored* to the particular project.

In the MARVEL RBDE, a project administrator specifies a model of the development process in terms of rules (the *project rule set*) and a model of the project's data in terms of object-oriented classes (the *project type set*), and writes envelopes that interface to external tools (the *project tool set*). These descriptions are then loaded into the MARVEL kernel, tailoring it as a MARVEL environment. The organization of the project components is abstracted into a hierarchy of complex objects, each an instance of one of the administrator-defined classes. These objects are manipulated by the software development tools installed on the operating system. The tools do not manipulate the objects' attributes directly, but operate on files and directories that are mapped to these attributes [13].

2.1. Rules

The development process of a project is modeled in terms of two kinds of rules: *activation rules* and *inference rules*. An activation rule controls the initiation of a development *activity*, typically the invocation of a tool. It specifies the condition under which it is appropriate to invoke the tool and the possible effects of the tool on the values of objects' attributes. Since activation rules invoke external tools that might either succeed or fail, they typically have multiple mutually exclusive sets of effects. For example, a compiler might succeed in producing object code, or fail and produce error messages. Thus, the activation rule encapsulating the compilation activity must specify two sets of effects, one to be asserted in case of success and the other in case of failure.

In contrast, inference rules are not associated with activities (i.e., the activity part is left empty) and each has a single effect, an expression that is a logical consequence of the condition of the rule. Inference rules define relations among attributes of the same or different objects and accordingly derive new values for attributes of the objects. Both activation and inference rules are parameterized to take as arguments one or more objects, each of which is an instance of some class. Three activation rules and an inference rule for C programming are shown in figure 2-1.

MARVEL's process and data models are strongly typed. The project type set must include definitions for all classes and attributes mentioned in the conditions and effects of the rules in the project rule set. Consider the edit rule in figure 2-1, which applies to instances of class CFILE, and whose condition checks whether the value of the reservation_status attribute is equal to CheckedOut. Thus, the definition of CFILE must contain an attribute called reservation_status of an enumerated type including the CheckedOut value. The rule set must be self-consistent in the sense that no two rules assume different types for the same attribute of the same class. For example, the rule set would not be self-consistent if it contains another rule that also applies to CFILE but assumes reservation_status is a string. The classes for the rules of figure 2-1 are shown in figure 2-2.

MARVEL analyzes the specifications of the project rule set and the project type set when they are loaded into the kernel. If these specifications are not both self-consistent and consistent with each other, they are rejected, with appropriate error messages. The administrator should debug the specifications and attempt to load them again. Thus, loading is analogous to

---

```
reserve[?f:FILE]:
    :
    (?f.reservation_status = Available)

    { RCS reserve ?f.contents ?f.version }

    (and (?f.reservation_status = CheckedOut)
         (?f.time_stamp = CurrentTime)
         (?f.locker = CurrentUser));

edit[?c:CFILE]:
    :
    (and (?c.reservation_status = CheckedOut)
         (?c.locker = CurrentUser))

    { EDITOR edit ?c.contents }

    (and (?c.compile_status = NotCompiled)
         (?c.time_stamp = CurrentTime));

compile[?f:CFILE]:
    :
    (?f.compile_status = NotCompiled)

    { COMPILER compile ?f.contents ?f.object_code
                       ?f.error_msg "-g" }

    (and (?f.compile_status = Compiled)
         (?f.object_time_stamp = CurrentTime));
    (?f.compile_status = Error);

dirty[?m:MODULE]:
    (forall CFILE ?c suchthat (member [?m.cfiles ?c]))
    :
    (and (?c.compile_status = Compiled)
         (?c.object_time_stamp > ?m.time_stamp)
         (?m.reservation_status = CheckedOut)
         (?m.locker = CurrentUser))

    { }

    (?m.archive_status = NotArchived);
```

Each rule has a name followed by a list of parameters enclosed in square brackets "[...]". Each parameter has a name beginning with "?" and a type, one of the classes defined in the project type set. Rule names can be overloaded. Following the parameter list is the condition, which consists of a set of bindings followed by ":" and a property list. Bindings attach a local variable to the set of objects that are of the type specified after the variable name and that satisfy the logical clause following "suchthat". The property list gives a complex clause of logical predicates that must be true of one (for existential) or all (for universal) of the objects bound to a variable. The activity invocation is enclosed in curly braces "{...}". Following is the set of effects, each terminated by ";". Each effect is a conjunction of logical predicates that assign values to named attributes of the parameter objects.

Figure 2-1: Example Rules

---

compilation with strong typing. When loading succeeds, the tailored RBDE presents the environment end-users (the software developers) with commands corresponding to the project rule set. Thus, environments for different projects are likely to have different user commands

```
RESERVABLE :: superclass ENTITY;
    locker : user;
    reservation_status : (CheckedOut,Available,None) = None;
end

FILE :: superclass RESERVABLE;
    time_stamp : time;
    contents : text;
end

HFILE :: superclass FILE;
    contents : text = ".h";
end

CFILE :: superclass FILE;
    contents : text = ".c";
    includes : set_of link HFILE;
    compile_status : (Archived,Compiled,NotCompiled,Error)
                        = NotCompiled;
    object_code : binary = ".o";
    object_time_stamp : time;
end

MODULE :: superclass RESERVABLE;
    archive_status : (Archived,NotArchived,INotArchived)
                        = NotArchived;
    cfiles : set_of CFILE;
    modules : set_of MODULE;
end
```

Each class definition starts with the name of the class followed by ":: superclass" and the list of its superclasses. Multiple inheritance is supported. Then follows a list of attribute definitions, each terminated by ";". A definition consists of a name followed by ":" and the type of attribute; the type may optionally be followed by "=" and an initialization value. MARVEL supports several built-in attribute types: string, integer, and real are self-explanatory. text and binary refer to text and binary file types, respectively, and the initializations in these cases give the file name suffixes used in the underlying file system. user represents a userid and time a time stamp. An enumerated type is a list of possible values enclosed in "()". The "set_of" construct allows an aggregate of arbitrarily many instances of the same class. A "link" attribute refers to a named and typed relation from an instance of this class to an instance or a set of instances of the given class. Each class definition is terminated by "end"

Figure 2-2: Example Classes

as well as different objectbase structures. When a user requests the execution of a command on a set of objects, MARVEL selects the rule that matches the command [2].

2.2. Chaining

RBDEs assist their users by applying forward and backward chaining to automatically fire rules, which in the case of activation rules initiate development activities. A rule's activity cannot be invoked unless its condition is satisfied. If the condition is not satisfied, the RBDE applies backward chaining to fire other rules whose effects might satisfy the condition. The result of this backward chaining is either the satisfaction of the original condition or the inability to satisfy it given the current objectbase state. In the latter case, the user is informed that the RBDE cannot execute her command.

When the condition is satisfied, the activity is initiated, and after it terminates, the RBDE asserts one of the rule's effects. This might satisfy the condition of other rules, collectively called the *implication set* of the rule. The RBDE fires these rules. The effects of these rules may in turn cause further forward chaining. In MARVEL, the parameters of rules fired through backward and forward chaining are bound through a heuristic mechanism [10].

Consider the edit rule in figure 2-1. Say a user requests to edit an instance of class CFILE but the reservation_status attribute of this object does not have the value CheckedOut, as required by the condition of the edit rule. Instead of rejecting the user's command, MARVEL tries to fire the reserve rule, one of whose effects changes the value of the reservation_status attribute to CheckedOut (only the success effect is stated since the failure effect results in no changes). If reserve succeeds, edit's condition becomes satisfied and its activity is invoked. Once the editing session terminates and its effect is asserted, MARVEL tries to fire all the rules whose condition became satisfied, including the compile rule. If compile terminates successfully, it triggers the dirty rule on the MODULE containing the original CFILE object.

3. Consistency and Automation

The simplistic chaining algorithm described above, which is implemented in MARVEL 2.6, does not reflect the administrator's intentions in specifying the various conditions and effects. There is no way for the administrator to state: (1) whether or not an unsatisfied condition of a rule warrants rejecting the user's command that triggered the rule, even though it might be logically possible to infer the condition; (2) whether or not an unfulfilled implication of the effect of a rule warrants rejecting the command, when it is not logically possible to automatically fulfill the implications; and (3) whether or not the actions performed during chaining are definite or tentative (i.e., can be undone). In particular, backward chaining is always attempted, forward chaining is treated as "best effort", and all actions are definite. The problem lies in the inability to distinguish between consistency and automation.

Considering the example of the previous section, the administrator might like to specify that compiling a C file after it has been edited is not mandatory, while outdating a module after one of its C files has been compiled is obligatory. The rules as given make it seem that both are optional, which is not the case. There is no way to specify that the former reflects an opportunity for automation but the latter is a consistency constraint.

3.1. A Maximalist Assistance Mechanism

Some RBDE rule languages, such as CLF's AP5 [5], distinguish between consistency rules and automation rules. The MSL rule language used in MARVEL 3.0 distinguishes between consistency predicates and automation predicates in both the condition and effects of rules, and a single rule may contain both kinds of predicates. Both AP5 and MARVEL 3.0 implement what we call a *maximalist* assistance mechanism. In the rest of this paper, we assume the maximalist mechanism implemented in MARVEL 3.0 (henceforth simply MARVEL), which subsumes the AP5 mechanism.

MARVEL combines consistency and automation as follows: (1) if an automation predicate in the condition of a rule is not satisfied, MARVEL tries to make it satisfied by backward chaining; (2) if a consistency predicate in the condition is not satisfied, MARVEL refuses to execute the activity; (3) the assertion of a consistency predicate in the effect of a rule mandates that MARVEL must either successfully fire all the rules in the implication set of this predicate or the entire chain including the original activity is rolled back (the rollback mechanism is outside the scope of this paper); and (4) the assertion of an automation predicate in the effect of a rule causes MARVEL to attempt to carry out the implications of the predicate on a "best effort" basis, but the chain may halt prematurely.

```
edit[?c:CFILE]:
    :
    (and (?c.reservation_status = CheckedOut)
         (?c.locker = CurrentUser))

    { EDITOR edit ?c.contents }

    (and (?c.compile_status = NotCompiled)
         [?c.time_stamp = CurrentTime]);

compile[?f:CFILE]:
    :
    (?f.compile_status = NotCompiled)

    { COMPILER compile ?f.contents ?f.object_code
                       ?f.error_msg "-g" }

    (and [?f.compile_status = Compiled]
         (?f.object_time_stamp = CurrentTime));
    (?f.compile_status = Error);
```

The predicates in the condition property list and effects enclosed in square brackets "[...]" are consistency predicates, whereas those in parentheses "(...)" are automation predicates.

Figure 3-1: Consistency and Automation Predicates

To illustrate, consider the modified rules in figure 3-1. The first predicate in the effect of the compile rule ("?f.compile_status = NotCompiled") is now marked as a consistency predicate. This causes the dirty rule to become a consistency implication of compile, meaning that the execution of the compile rule must be rolled back if this effect is asserted but for any reason it is not possible to execute the dirty rule. Similarly, the "?c.time_stamp = CurrentTime" predicate of the edit rule is changed to a consistency predicate. But since there is no rule whose condition depends on the value of a C file's timestamp, this does not result in any consistency implications.

The distinction between automation and consistency predicates is depicted by representing rules and chains as a graph. This graph consists of nodes that represent rules, and three kinds of edges: automation forward edges, consistency forward edges and automation backward edges; there are no consistency backward edges. An automation forward edge from rule R1 to rule R2 exists if one of the effects of R1 contains an automation predicate that implies a

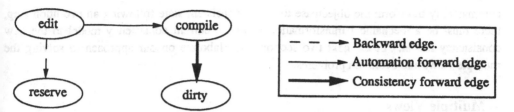

Figure 3-2: Rule Graph

predicate (of either kind) in the condition of R2. There is a consistency forward edge between rule R1 and rule R2 if there is a consistency predicate in one of the effects of R1 that implies a predicate in the condition of R2, and R2 is an inference rule. If R2 is an activation rule, however, then an automation forward edge appears instead. There exists an automation backward edge from R2 to R1 if an automation predicate in the condition of R2 is implied by a predicate (of either kind) in one of the effects of R1. The graph for the two unchanged rules of figure 2-1 and the modified rules in figure 3-1 is shown in figure 3-2.

Each rule R has a set of consistency implications consisting of all the rules that are connected to R via a forward consistency edge emanating from R. The set of loaded rules is *complete* if and only if for each rule loaded by the RBDE, <u>all</u> the rules in its consistency implication set are also loaded. It must also be the case that the loaded data model defines all of the classes and attributes accessed by these rules.

Consider the following scenario. A user requests to edit a C file "f.c". Once the editing session is terminated and the effect asserted, the RBDE fires all those rules whose condition became satisfied. One of these rules is compile, since there is an automation predicate in common between the effect of edit and the condition of compile. Thus MARVEL attempts to compile "f.c". If the compilation is successful, its first effect is asserted, and MARVEL fires all the rules in the implication set of this effect. The set includes the dirty rule, which is fired on the module "mod" containing "f.c". If the condition of dirty is not satisfied, say because "mod" has been reserved by another user, then the compile rule must be rolled back. The edit rule, however, is <u>not</u> rolled back since the compile rule was only an automation implication of edit, not a consistency implication.

Distinguishing between automation and consistency predicates enables us to define a *consistency model* for a development process. Given a rule set, the consistency model of the process is defined by the consistency forward edges in the rule graph. Thus, in order to preserve data consistency in a particular project, the RBDE must guarantee that for each rule, all the consistency implications of each rule's asserted effect will be carried out. All other rules in the rule graph define the *automation model* for the development process. These notions of consistency and automation form the basis for our approach to supporting multiple views and automating evolution in RBDEs.

Our approach is based on two observations: (1) all co-existing views must maintain either the same consistency model or disjoint consistency models; and (2) for the RBDE to be able to automatically transform the objectbase to a new consistent state following an evolution step, there must be a mechanical transformation from the current consistency model to the new consistency model. In the next two sections we elaborate on our approach to solving the multiple views and evolution problems.

4. Multiple Views

A *view* in an RBDE consists of subsets of the project rule set, the project type set and the project tool set. At any time, an RBDE must have some view loaded in order to function. Different views might be loaded by the same user during different phases of the development process; different users might also load different views at the same time to fulfill different roles. There are two correctness criteria for views: (1) the type set of the view must match the assumptions of its rule set; and (2) the set of rules in the view must be *complete* with respect to the project rule set. (A third criterion, compatibility of the rule and type sets with the project tool set, is outside the scope of this paper; see [8].)

The first criterion is local to a view in the sense that it determines whether or not the view is self-consistent. The conditions and effects of the rules in a view manipulate (read and update) the attributes of instances of the classes in the view's type set. Thus, each rule assumes that its view includes definitions of those attributes that the rule manipulates. If the view's type set does not meet the assumptions of the view's rule set, then there is a *discrepancy*.

A discrepancy can make it impossible for the RBDE to evaluate the conditions of some rules because the attributes manipulated in these conditions are either missing or of the wrong type, so these rules could never fire because their conditions would always be unsatisfied. This possibility can be tolerated only if none of the affected rules is in the consistency implication set of any rule in the rule set of the view. Similarly, a discrepancy could also make it impossible for the RBDE to assert the effects of some rules, resulting in a situation where the activity of a rule has terminated but the RBDE cannot assert the appropriate effect. This situation is not well-defined regardless of whether the predicates involved are consistency or automation, and in either case cannot be permitted.

Thus, an RBDE cannot load any view that does not meet at least the first of the criteria listed above (that the rule set and the type set match). The analysis is not affected by any other views, loaded or otherwise. The second criterion mentioned above, on the other hand, is greatly affected by the consistency model of the project rule set. A view is said to be complete if and only if for each rule R in the rule set of the view, the rule set includes all those rules that are members of the consistency implication set of R.

The notion of completeness is based on only the consistency forward edges in the graph of the project rule set. Automation forward edges are not relevant, since they represent optional behavior. For example, there is an automation forward edge between the two rules edit and compile. The inability to fire the compile rule after edit terminates successfully for any reason, including the non-existence of compile in the current view, does not invalidate the success of edit. Thus, a view containing edit but not compile is still complete.

A consistency forward edge, in contrast, is interpreted as a consistency implication. The consistency forward edge between `compile` and `dirty` means that if `compile` is fired and the relevant effect asserted, then the changes that its activity introduces in the objectbase cannot be made permanent unless `dirty` is also fired and terminates successfully (and so do any consistency implications of `dirty`). Thus, if a view contains `compile` but not `dirty`, the edge representing this consistency implication would be missing from the rule graph of the view. This could lead to inconsistencies if the changes introduced by `compile`'s activity become permanent (assuming all other implications are met) even though the `dirty` rule cannot be fired (because it is not in this view). Thus any other view that assumes that the module is marked as outdated whenever any of its C files is recompiled will see an inconsistent objectbase. The two correctness criteria for a view can be formalized as follows:

Definition 1: A view is said to be *complete* iff its rule set and type set are consistent with each other and if for each node in the rule graph of the view, the consistency forward edges are identical to the consistency forward edges for the corresponding node in the graph of the [complete] project rule set.

```
edit[?c:CFILE]:
    :
    (and (?c.reservation_status = CheckedOut)
         (?c.locker = CurrentUser))

    { EDITOR edit ?c.contents }

    (and [?c.compile_status = NotCompiled]
         [?c.time_stamp = CurrentTime]);
```

Figure 4-1: Incompatible View

Given this definition, the RBDE can determine that a view that includes the `edit` rule shown in figure 4-1 is not compatible with another view that includes the `edit` rule of figure 3-1. The new rule forward chains to the `compile` rule via a consistency predicate, whereas an automation predicate was employed in the original rule set of figure 3-1 (i.e., the "(...)" are replaced by "[...]"; note the predicates are identical). The two `edit` rules are incompatible, since an automation edge emanating from a node in the rule graph indicated by the earlier rule is replaced by a consistency edge in the later rule. But by the definition of completeness given above, either both rules must have a consistency forward edge for this predicate, or neither of them. One or the other rule could be employed in a project rule set, but both cannot be views for the same project rule set.

5. Evolution

When the process or data model is changed over time, the correctness criteria we required for views (that the data model matches the process model and that the process model is complete) must be reevaluated to ensure that they still hold. These restrictions must be enforced regardless of whether or not the rules that have been modified are in the consistency implication set of other rules. There are other aspects of evolution, however, whose correctness depends on the consistency model.

To illustrate, consider the compile rule of figure 3-1. This rule is connected by a consistency forward edge to the dirty rule of figure 2-1. The condition of the dirty rule contains four predicates that check if any C file contained in the module has been compiled more recently than the last archival of the module, and if the module is reserved by the user firing the rule. If the four predicates are satisfied, the module's archive is outdated by assigning the value NotArchived to the module's archive_status attribute.

```
dirty[?m:MODULE]:
    (forall CFILE ?c suchthat (member [?m.cfiles ?c]))
    :
    (and (?c.compile_status = Compiled)
         (?c.time_stamp > ?m.time_stamp)
         (?m.reservation_status = CheckedOut)
         (?m.locker = CurrentUser))

    { }

    (?m.archive_status = NotArchived);
```

Figure 5-1: Non-Mechanizable Evolution

Consider the scenario where the users of the environment tailored by these rules complain that the RBDE sometimes outdates module archives unnecessarily. The administrator discovers the reason is that the dirty rule outdates a module whenever any of its C files is recompiled, even though the source code had not been edited. So she modifies the dirty rule, as shown in figure 5-1. A new predicate "?c.time_stamp > ?m.time_stamp" replaces "?c.object_time_stamp > ?m.time_stamp" in the condition of dirty, so that the dirty rule outdates the module only when the source code has been edited in addition to being recompiled. This creates a new consistency forward edge between edit and dirty.

If this modified rule is loaded, then potentially all instances of MODULE might become inconsistent because the value of their archive_status attribute might not reflect the new consistency implication between edit and dirty. To upgrade the objectbase, the RBDE must fire the dirty rule on all instances of MODULE. For the cases where the condition is satisfied, the archive_status can be set to NotArchived and we can be confident that this is the correct value. However, in the cases where the condition is not satisfied, but the current value of archive_status is NotArchived, the RBDE must determine what is the correct value of archive_status. In general, this is impossible to do automatically (since there are two possible values, Archived and INotArchived). Therefore, this change to the dirty rule should not be allowed.

This example demonstrates the need for a concept of a *legal evolution step*. An evolution step is a change either to the definition of a single class or a single rule.

Definition 2: An evolution step is said to be *legal* iff (1) the resulting project type set and project rule set are self-consistent and consistent with each other; and (2) all objects in the objectbase can be mechanically transformed to meet the new consistency implications specified by the modified rule set.

The example above is not a legal evolution step in the general case since it is not always possible to mechanically transform an objectbase to a consistent state. However, this example may represent a legal evolution step on some objectbases, simply because the condition of the dirty rule happens to be satisfied for all instances of MODULE in that particular objectbase. There is no method for determining whether or not this evolution step is legal a priori; it is necessary to attempt the potentially very costly transformation of the objectbase.

A more realistic approach would be to restrict the kinds of changes allowed to those that can be statically analyzed to determine whether or not an evolution step should be attempted. Intuitively, if the consistency implications specified by the modified rules are weaker than the old ones, then all objects in the objectbase will definitely meet the new criteria. If the only change to the rule set is to relax a rule (i.e., make it apply to a narrower set of objects) or to completely remove it, then the objectbase would not violate any consistency requirements. Thus, a more useful definition is:

Definition 3: An evolution step is permitted iff the consistency implications specified by the rule set after the evolution step are either weaker than the implications before the evolution step is carried out, or are independent of them.

```
edit[?h:HFILE]:
    :
    (and (?h.reservation_status = CheckedOut)
         (?h.locker = CurrentUser))

    { EDITOR edit ?h.contents }

    (?h.time_stamp = CurrentTime);

compile[?f:CFILE]:

    (exists HFILE ?h suchthat (linkto [?f.includes ?h]))
    :
    (or (?h.time_stamp > ?f.object_time_stamp)
        (?f.compile_status = NotCompiled))

     { COMPILER compile ?f.contents ?f.object_code ?f.error_msg
                        "-g" ?h.contents }

    (and [?f.compile_status = Compiled]
         (?f.object_time_stamp = CurrentTime));
    (?f.compile_status = Error);
```

Figure 5-2: Mechanizable Evolution

The problem then reduces to defining "weaker" and "independent" consistency implications. The set of consistency implications specified by a rule set can be represented by the rule graph after removing all the automation edges from the graph, but keeping the consistency forward edges, to produce a *consistency graph*. For each set of consistency implications I, the corresponding graph is denoted by $G(I)$.

Definition 4: A set of consistency implications I' is said to be *weaker* than another set I iff $G(I')$ is a subgraph of $G(I)$. I' is said to be *independent* of I iff $G(I')$ and $G(I)$ are disjoint.

In an RBDE supporting only automation predicates, with no consistency predicates, there are no restrictions at all on modifying, adding and/or removing rules at any time. There is no notion of consistency in the objectbase that could become corrupted. The change in the rules simply causes a change in the optional automation behavior of the RBDE. In a maximalist RBDE with both automation and consistency predicates, automation rules can always be removed, but there are limitations on addition and modification since this might introduce a new forward consistency edge from some consistency rule to the automation rule.

To illustrate how an RBDE can decide whether or not an evolution step is permissible, consider the compile rule of figure 5-2. The condition of the rule was modified so that the compile rule is fired on a C file whenever one of the HFILEs it includes is edited. This change is necessary for practical programming in C, since any C source file might include several ".h" files. (The edit rule that applies to HFILE is also shown in figure 5-2, but would have been added in an earlier evolution step.)

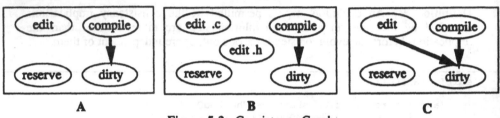

Figure 5-3: Consistency Graphs

The RBDE determines if this evolution step is legal by comparing the consistency graph of the rule set including the modified compile rule, shown in figure 5-3B, with the consistency graph of the original rule set, shown in figure 5-3A. The consistency edges in the two graphs are identical, which means that the evolution step fulfills the legality criteria and can be permitted. In contrast, the consistency graph of the rule set after the illegal evolution step discussed earlier in figure 5-1, shown in figure 5-3C, is not a subgraph of the original graph. Therefore, the evolution step should not be permitted.

6. Related Work
The RPDE[3] project has had substantial experience with supporting real changes [18]. The ease with which these changes were accommodated rests on three pillars: the system's architecture, its extended object-oriented technology, and structured representation of the programs manipulated by the system. RPDE[3] supports multiple display views, but these are hard-wired into the code of the system, as is the software process. Evolution of the process was one of the the several kinds of changes singled out as particularly difficult due to the limitations of their object-oriented technology [9].

The Field environment [20] integrates tools through a centralized message server that routes messages among tools. Tools send messages to the server to announce changes that other tools might be interested in, and the server broadcasts those messages to tools that have previously registered matching patterns. Existing tools are supported by adding an interface to each tool to send and receive messages. Field makes it relatively easy to evolve the tool set, but is not concerned with process modeling and there is no common project data model.

Forest [7] extends the Field approach by adding a policy tool to the message server. The policy tool supports a simple process model consisting of condition/action rules and a simple data model consisting of state variables. The policy tool fires the first rule whose condition matches each incoming message; the possible actions include sending a message on to a tool, sending a new message to the message server, or doing nothing. Forest enforces access control over which categories of users can change which rules, as well as the membership of these categories. It is not concerned with logical restrictions on evolution or the impact of changes on consistency of the global state reflected in the data accessed by the tools, and does not address multiple views.

In MELMAC [6], an object type and activity view, a process view, a feedback view and a project management view are combined into a common representation called a FUNSOFT net. These views represent different perspectives on the process, and are not related to our notion of multiple views for multiple users. The FUNSOFT net, essentially a hierarchical Petri net, consists of some nodes representing primitive activities while other nodes must be refined by recursive nets. The nodes may have preconditions and postconditions. MELMAC supports evolution of the process model by introducing the notion of modification points, which are attached to nodes whose refinements can be changed on the fly. It is not clear, however, whether there are any restrictions on what kinds of changes are allowed, to ensure consistency in the project database.

Darwin [17] uses laws, written as Prolog rules, to regulate the activities that users can carry out but it never initiates activities on behalf of users. A Prolog interpreter enforces these laws. The laws govern what changes can be made to the laws themselves as well as to programs, and thus a single elegant mechanism supports both process enactment and process evolution. But Darwin does not provide any mechanism for legislating that new laws are consistent with old ones with respect to the existing objectbase, and does not address the problem of multiple views.

APPL/A [21] is the process programming language used in the Arcadia environment. It extends Ada with persistent relations, triggers, predicates, and transaction statements. APPL/A is specifically concerned with accommodating inconsistency resulting from, among other things, evolution of the process program. A flexible consistency model, FCM [22], is defined in terms of predicates and transactions. Evolution of the process model may lead to adding new predicates, introducing inconsistencies in the project objectbase. The transactions may be used to control the enforcement of these predicates, by determining the conditions for relaxing consistency and providing a scope for restoring consistency. APPL/A seems to provide the closest match to MARVEL's consistency model. FCM defines a complementary framework for tolerating inconsistency. We suspect it would be relatively straightforward to extend our notions of compatible views and legal evolution steps to determine when this framework should be applied.

7. Conclusions

We considered the problems of scaling up rule-based software development environments to support multiple views and evolution. Our solution is based on distinguishing two functions of rules and chaining: (1) to express, enforce and maintain consistency constraints and (2) to express and carry out opportunities for automation. By definition, consistency is mandatory whereas automation is not. Our earlier work on MARVEL did not recognize any distinction between consistency and automation, and thus our original approach to multiple views and evolution [13] could lead to inconsistent objectbases. The new MARVEL 3.0 extends the maximalist assistance mechanism presented in this paper with additional directives to turn off forward and/or backward chaining in and/or out of individual predicates, to provide the administrator with powerful control over consistency implications. Now by separating the consistency and automation aspects of RBDE assistance mechanisms, we make it possible to formalize the range of compatible views and the scope of mechanizable evolution steps. However, neither multiple views or evolution has been implemented yet.

Acknowledgments

We would like to thank Israel Ben-Shaul, George Heineman and Timothy Jones, who are working with us on implementing the multi-user version of MARVEL. George Heineman also provided many suggestions to improve an earlier version of this paper. The Programming Systems Laboratory at Columbia University is supported by National Science Foundation grants CCR-9000930 and CCR-8858029, by grants from AT&T, BNR, DEC and SRA, by the New York State Center for Advanced Technology on Computer and Information Systems and by the NSF Engineering Research Center for Telecommunications Research.

References

[1]   V. Ambriola, P. Ciancarini and C. Montangero. Software Process Enactment in Oikos. In *4th ACM SIGSOFT Symposium on Software Development Environments*, pages 183-192. Irvine CA, December, 1990.

[2]   Naser S. Barghouti and Gail E. Kaiser. Modeling Concurrency in Rule-Based Development Environments. *IEEE Expert* 5(6):15-27, December, 1990.

[3]   K. Benali et al. Presentation of the ALF Project. In *9th International Conference on System Development Environments and Factories*. Berlin, May, 1989.

[4]   G. M. Clemm. The Workshop System — A Practical Knowledge-Based Software Environment. In *ACM SIGSOFT/SIGPLAN Software Engineering Symposium on Practical Software Development Environments*, pages 55-64. Boston MA, November, 1988.

[5]   Donald Cohen. Automatic Compilation of Logical Specifications into Efficient Programs. In *5th National Conference on Artificial Intelligence*, pages 20-25. AAAI, Philadelphia, PA, August, 1986.

[6]   W. Deiters and V. Gruhn. Managing Software Processes in the Environment MELMAC. In *SIGPLAN '90 4th ACM SIGSOFT Symposium on Software Development Environments*, pages 193-205. Irvine CA, December, 1990.

[7]   D. Garlan and E. Ilias. Low-cost, Adaptable Tool Integration Policies for Integrated Environments. In *4th ACM SIGSOFT Symposium on Software Development Environments*, pages 1-10. Irvine CA, December, 1990.

[8]   Mark A. Gisi and Gail E. Kaiser. Extending A Tool Integration Language. In *1st International Conference on the Software Process*. Los Angeles CA, October, 1991. In press. Available as Columbia University Department of Computer Science CUCS-014-91, April 1991.

[9]   W. H. Harrison, J. J. Shilling and P. F. Sweeney. Good News, Bad News: Experience Building a Software Development Environment Using the Object-Oriented Paradigm. In *Object-Oriented Programming Systems, Languages and Applications Conference Proceedings*, pages 85-94. New Orleans LA, October, 1989.

[10]   George T. Heineman, Gail E. Kaiser, Naser S. Barghouti and Israel Z. Ben-Shaul. Rule Chaining in MARVEL: Dynamic Binding of Parameters. In *6th Knowledge-Based Software Engineering Conference*. Syracuse NY, September, 1991. In press. Available as Columbia University Department of Computer Science CUCS-022-91, May 1991.

[11]   K. E. Huff and V. R. Lesser. A Plan-based Intelligent Assistant that Supports the Software Development Process. In *ACM SIGSOFT/SIGPLAN Software Engineering Symposium on Practical Software Development Environments*, pages 97-106. Boston MA, November, 1988.

[12]   Gail E. Kaiser, Peter H. Feiler and Steven S. Popovich. Intelligent Assistance for Software Development and Maintenance. *IEEE Software* 5(3):40-49, May, 1988.

[13]   Gail E. Kaiser, Naser S. Barghouti, Peter H. Feiler and Robert W. Schwanke. Database Support for Knowledge-Based Engineering Environments. *IEEE Expert* 3(2):18-32, Summer, 1988.

[14]   Gail E. Kaiser, Naser S. Barghouti and Michael H. Sokolsky. Experience with Process Modeling in the Marvel Software Development Environment Kernel. In Bruce Shriver (editor), *23rd Annual Hawaii International Conference on System Sciences*, pages 131-140. Kona HI, January, 1990.

[15]   Takuya Katayama. A Hierarchical and Functional Software Process Description and its Enaction. In *11th International Conference on Software Engineering*, pages 343-352. IEEE Computer Science Press, Pittsburgh PA, May, 1989.

[16]   Takuya Katayama (editor). *6th International Software Process Workshop: Support for the Software Process*. IEEE Computer Society Press, Hakodate, Hokkaido, Japan, 1990. In press.

[17]   N. H. Minsky and D. Rozenshtein. A Software Development Environment for Law-Governed Systems. In *ACM SIGSOFT/SIGPLAN Software Engineering Symposium on Practical Software Development Environments*, pages 65-75. ACM Press, Boston MA, November, 1988.

[18]   H. Ossher and W. Harrison. Support for Change in RPDE[3]. In *SIGPLAN '90 4th ACM SIGSOFT Symposium on Software Development Environments*, pages 218-228. Irvine CA, December, 1990.

[19]   Dewayne Perry (editor). *5th International Software Process Workshop: Experience with Software Process Models*. IEEE Computer Society Press, Kennebunkport ME, 1989.

[20]   Steven P. Reiss. Connecting Tools Using Message Passing in the Field Environment. *IEEE Software* 7(4):57-66, July, 1990.

[21]   S. M. Sutton, Jr., D. Heimbigner and L. J. Osterweil. Language Constructs for Managing Change in Process-Centered Environments. In *4th ACM SIGSOFT Symposium on Software Development Environments*, pages 206-217. Irvine CA, December, 1990.

[22]   S. M. Sutton, Jr. A Flexible Consistency Model for Persistent Data in Software-Process Programming Languages. In *4th International Workshop on Persistent Object Systems*, pages 297-310. Morgan Kaufmann, Martha's Vineyard MA, September, 1990.

Inference-Based Support for Programming in the Large

Gregor Snelting, Franz-Josef Grosch, Ulrik Schroeder

Praktische Informatik

Technische Hochschule Darmstadt

Magdalenenstr. 11c, D-61 Darmstadt

Abstract. We present interactive support tools for programming in the large which can handle incomplete, missing or inconsistent information about a software project. Our tool set comprises an incremental interface checker for incomplete component libraries, support for polymorphic component reuse, an inference-based interactive configuration system, and browsing algorithms based on usage patterns. We make heavy use of automated deduction techniques such as order-sorted unification or AC1 unification. All tools are generic and parameterized with language-specific information. The concepts described in this paper are currently under development as part of an interactive software development environment, which can automatically complete partial information and detect errors earlier than conventional tools.

Keywords: software development environment, interface checking, component reuse, pattern-based browsing, configuration management, automated deduction

1 Introduction

In a recent paper on the management of software projects, P. Elzer [El89] reports on an inquiry among the participants of a software engineering conference, who were asked for their wishes with respect to future software development tools. The majority of the interviewees voted for *intelligent tools*, but only a minority believed that such tools could be realized in the near future.

It is the aim of this paper to demonstrate that software tools which are based on inference techniques can indeed be constructed and be the basis of a software development environment. We will present a tool set which can

- handle incomplete and infer missing information in component libraries (*ambiguity tolerance*)
- temporarily allow inconsistent libraries (*fault tolerance*)
- allow fast and comfortable interaction (*incrementality*)
- be parameterized with language-specific information (*generateability*).

Our tool set comprises

1. an interface checker which is incremental and can handle incomplete or inconsistent software component libraries
2. support for reusable, polymorphic components even if the underlying programming language is not polymorphic
3. an interactive configuration management system which can handle partially specified configurations, infer missing information, and automatically construct makefiles.
4. an intelligent retrieval system which allows to search library components by usage patterns.

As we shall see, currently available tools for the above tasks are either not interactive, unable to cope with missing or inconsistent information, or unable to be parameterized with language-specific information, e.g. type systems or name resolution rules. Thus it is our aim to overcome these shortcomings of today's environments. Our inference-based tool kit can automatically complete information which has only partially been given by the programmers. Hence our tools can check consistency much earlier than traditional approaches, and can detect errors as soon as the globally inferred information becomes inconsistent. To achieve our goals, we make heavy use of techniques from automated deduction. Although the implementation of our system has just begun, we will present a running example which demonstrates how our tools interact and can derive information or detect errors which cannot be obtained using standard environment technology.

```
Fragment «Stack-Definition»
      DEFINITION MODULE stack;
        FROM x IMPORT elementtype;
        TYPE StackId;
        PROCEDURE newStack(): StackId;
        PROCEDURE push( s: StackId; e: elementtype );
        PROCEDURE pop( s: StackId );
        PROCEDURE top( s: StackId ): elementtype;
        PROCEDURE isEmpty( s: StackId ): BOOLEAN;
        PROCEDURE isFull( s: StackId ): BOOLEAN;
      END stack;
Fragment «Stack-Implementation»
      IMPLEMENTATION MODULE stack;
        CONST maxno = [constant];
        TYPE StackId = POINTER TO StackRepresentation;
             StackRepresentation = RECORD
                                      n: [ 0 .. maxno ];
                                      s: ARRAY [ 1 .. maxno ] OF elementtype
                                    END;
        ...
        PROCEDURE isFull ( s: StackId): BOOLEAN;
        BEGIN
          RETURN s↑.n = maxno;
        END isFull;
        ...
      END stack;
Fragment «Application 1»
      MODULE stackmain;
        FROM x IMPORT elementtype;
        FROM stack IMPORT StackId, newStack, push, pop, isFull;
        VAR s: StackId;
      BEGIN
        s := newStack();
        ...
        IF NOT isFull( s ) THEN
          push( s, 5 );
        END;
        ...
      END stackmain.
Fragment «Application 2»
      MODULE mystack;
        FROM x IMPORT elementtype;
        FROM stack IMPORT StackId, newStack, push, pop;
        VAR strbuffer: StackId;
      BEGIN
        strbuffer := newStack();
        push( strbuffer, "?" );
        ...
      END mystack.
```

Figure 1: Basic example

2 Inference-based Interface Control

Our tool set is centered around a *library of software components*. This is common practice, and it is standard that for components or modules which depend on each other, *interfaces* must be checked in order to guarantee correct component interaction. Traditional approaches support only a fixed language and are entirely batch-oriented, whereas more modern software engineering environments are interactive and integrate interface checking into system development [Na89], or are even generic tools which are parameterized with language-specific information [Pf86]. But none of the current approaches can handle incomplete or inconsistent interface information.

In order to illustrate our approach, we introduce a small example (shown on the previous page). The example gives a library of incomplete software components or *fragments* which contain definition, implementation and uses of a stack module[1]. Modula-2 is used as implementation language, but this choice is arbitrary. The fragments «Stack-Definition» resp. «Stack-Implementation» together constitute the module "stack". Both clients of "stack" as well as "stack" itself refer to an as yet undefined module "x". Our system can infer and check interface information despite the fact that "x" is not part of the library.

Our analysis algorithm is based on the central notion of a *context relation*, and before we demonstrate the analysis of our sample library, we recall basic facts about context relations. Context relations have originally been introduced as a device for incremental semantic analysis of incomplete program fragments. In contrast to traditional techniques (e.g. attribute grammars), they can handle and infer missing information and guarantee the detection of errors as soon as a fragment cannot be embedded into a correct program. There exists an elaborate theory and implementation, but due to lack of space we can only give some general remarks. The interested reader is referred to [BS86] for conceptual and methodological foundations and to [Sn89] for the underlying theory and optimal incremental analysis algorithms.

Relational analysis associates sets of attributes with nodes of a given abstract syntax tree. Attributes are terms of a free order-sorted algebra with sorted variables, where the signature of the algebra is language specific and therefore must be given by the language definer. Generally speaking, the use of an order-sorted algebra has the big advantage that many context conditions can be expressed as sortal constraints: for example, requirements like "the operands of an addition must have numeric type" or "the object on the left side of an assignment must be a variable" can easily be formulated.

Figure 2 gives basic definitions and properties of the relational calculus. Conceptually, context relations are very similar to the relations known from relational database theory. The main difference is that order-sorted terms are used as tuple components, and that a join operation has to *unify* corresponding tuple components instead of just testing them for equality. For purposes of semantic analysis, the domain of a context relation is always a set of syntactic entities resp. program objects. The language definer has to specify *basic context relations* for all terminals and rules of the language's syntax. A basic relation specifies sets of possible attributes (namely order-sorted terms according to the attribute algebra) for syntactic entities. It can be seen as an inference rule describing all context-sensitive constraints which apply to the syntax rule or terminal (see [BS86] for examples). A fragment can then be analysed by joining all basic relations of its constituents; the resulting relation describes exactly the (incomplete) semantic information associated with the fragment. This process is called *local semantic analysis*. As soon as a fragment is erroneous, that is, cannot be embedded into a correct program, an intermediate relation will become empty, signaling a semantic inconsistency.

---

[1] We apologize for using this example the 376912th time

Definition.
1. Let $(S, \leq)$ be a partially ordered set (called a *sort hierarchy*). Let F be a set of *function symbols* together with arities $\Delta = (\delta_f)_{f \in F}$, where $\delta_f \in S^* \times S$. Then $\Sigma = (S, \leq, F, \Delta)$ is called the *signature* of an order-sorted algebra.
2. Let a signature Σ be given. Let V be an infinite set of sorted variables, where $sort: V \to S$ gives the variable's sort; we require that for each sort there are infinitely many variables. The set of order-sorted terms T_Σ freely generated by V, together with the sort function for terms, is defined as follows:
   a. $V \subseteq T_\Sigma$
   b. if $f \in F$, $\delta_f = (s_1 s_2 .. s_n, s), n \geq 0, t_1 .. t_n \in T_\Sigma, sort(t_i) \leq s_i$ for $i \in 1..n$, then $t = f(t_1, t_2, .., t_n) \in T_\Sigma$ and $sort(t) = s$

By definition, terms are well-sorted. The set T_Σ is called the *attribute algebra*, since its elements are used as attributes of syntactic objects.

Definition.
1. A mapping $\sigma: V \to T_\Sigma$ with $\sigma(v) = v$ almost everywhere and $sort(\sigma(v)) \leq sort(v)$ is called a *substitution*.
   By definition, substitutions must be well-sorted. As usual, a substitution σ is extended canonically to T_Σ via $\sigma(f(t_1, .., t_n)) = f(\sigma(t_1), .., \sigma(t_n))$.
2. A substitution σ is called a *unifier* of two terms $t_1, t_2 \in T_\Sigma$ iff $\sigma(t_1) = \sigma(t_2)$. A unifier is called most general or an *mgu* if for all unifiers γ of t_1 and t_2, there exists a substitution ρ such that $\gamma = \sigma \circ \rho$.

Lemma. If each pair of sorts either has no lower bound, or a greatest lower bound, unifiable terms have an mgu.

Definition. Let N be a set. A *context relation* r over N is a set of mappings from N to T_Σ, thus $r \in 2^{N \to T_\Sigma}$. Each element of r is called a *tuple*. For a tuple t, the $(t(n))_{n \in N}$ are called the *tuple components*. The set N is also called the domain of relation r, $dom(r)$.

Usually, N is assumed to be a subset of a fixed "universal" set D (namely the set of all syntactic entities). The set of all context relations over domains $\subseteq D$ is denoted CR_D or CR for short. The subset of CR containing only ground tuple components is denoted CR^g.

Definition.
1. Let $r \in CR$ be context relation over N, and let $M \subseteq N$. The *projection* of a tuple $t \in r$ onto M is defined as $\Pi(t, M): M \to T_\Sigma$, $\Pi(t, M)(n) = t(n)$ for $n \in M$. The projection of r onto M is defined as

$$\Pi(r, M) = \{\Pi(t, M) \mid t \in r\}$$

Of course, $dom(\Pi(r, M)) = M$.
2. Let $r, s \in CR$ be context relations over N resp. M. The *union* of r and s is defined as

$$r \sqcup s = \Pi(r, N \cap M) \cup \Pi(s, N \cap M)$$

We have $dom(r \sqcup s) = N \cap M$.
3. Let $r, s \in CR$ be context relations over N, M. Let two tuples $t_1 \in r$, $t_2 \in s$ be given. If there is an mgu σ which simultaneously unifies $(t_1(n), t_2(n))_{n \in N \cap M}$, the tuples are called unifiable. For two unifiable tuples t_1, t_2,

$$\sigma(t_1, t_2): N \cup M \to T_\Sigma,$$

$$\sigma(t_1, t_2)(n) = \begin{cases} \sigma(t_1(n)) & n \in N \\ \sigma(t_2(n)) & n \in M \end{cases}$$

The *join* of r and s is then defined as

$$r \sqcap s = \{\sigma(t_1, t_2) \mid t_1 \in r, t_2 \in s, \exists \sigma : t_1, t_2 \text{ are unifiable via } \sigma\}$$

Obviously, $dom(r \sqcap s) = N \cup M$. The name "join" is due to the fact that for ground relations this operation is the same as the natural join operation known from relational data base theory.

Theorem. The algebra $(CR^g; \sqcup; \sqcap)$ is a complete lattice. $(CR^g; \sqcup; \sqcap)$ is a retract of $(CR; \sqcup; \sqcap)$ that is a subalgebra which is also a homomorphic image.
$\perp$ denotes the bottom element ("inconsistency"), and $\top$ denotes the top element ("ignorance") of the lattice.

Theorem. The context relation $cr(t)$ of a fragment with root node t is given by the formula

$$cr(t) = basicrelation(t) \sqcap \prod_{i=1}^{n} cr(t_i)$$

where the $t_1, \ldots, t_n$ $(n \geq 0)$ are the sons of t. $cr(t) = \perp$ iff the fragment cannot be embedded into a correct program.

Figure 2: Basic definitions and properties of the context relation calculus (from [Sn89])

Now we return to our example. Interface information is described by context relations. An interface relation of a component contains the attributes (as inferred so far) of those objects which are relevant for the library. In case of Modula-2, these are exported and imported objects, as well as undeclared objects which could be declared outside the component or module in question. For reasons of presentation, an object attribute gives just object class and type (the "real" attribute algebra is more complicated). For procedures, a list of argument types and a result type is given. In the relations below, "__" means "no type", and "i_o_c" stands for "integer or cardinal". Variables are written in uppercase letters (possibly with an additional index), where for simplicity a variable's name also gives its sort. The presence of variables in a relation indicates incomplete or polymorphic information. A relation which contains more than one tuple describes overloaded objects, which may have several (still possible) attributes.

Below we present the interface relation for module "stack", which is the basis for checking the interfaces to the (still nonexistent) module "x" and the clients of "stack". It has been derived by local semantic analysis of "DEFINITION MODULE stack" and "IMPLEMENTATION MODULE stack"[2]. Since nothing is known about "x", the actual element type is still unknown. Such "information holes" (either induced by missing components or by placeholders in a component's abstract syntax tree) prevent standard compilers from an analysis of internal or external consistency; in an interface relation they manifest themselves in form of uninstantiated variables ("TYPE" in our example).

stack	(module, __)
x	(module, __)
elementtype	(typeconst, TYPE)
StackId	(typeconst, opaque(117))
newStack	(procedure, (< >, opaque(117))
push	(procedure, (< opaque(117), TYPE >, __))
pop	(procedure, (< opaque(117) >, __))
top	(procedure, (< opaque(117) >, TYPE))
isEmpty	(procedure, (< opaque(117) >, bool))
isFull	(procedure, (< opaque(117) >, bool))

Local analysis of "Application 1" gives the left of the two relations on top of the next page. For the imported objects "pop" and "elementtype" no context information can be inferred, since they are not used. Note that the constant "5" in the call for "push" forces the second argument of "push" to be of type "integer_or_cardinal". In contrast to "Application 1", analysis of "Application 2" infers that the stack must have element type "char".

Now we come to the important step, namely checking the interfaces between "stack" and its clients. A necessary (but not sufficient) condition which must always be satisfied for a consistent library is that each component is consistent with any of its suppliers (*local consistency*). In our terminology this means that for each pair x and y of components, the join of their interface relations is not the bottom element: $cr(x) \sqcap cr(y) \neq \perp$[3]. If such a join results in $\perp$ (due to failed unifications of attributes of commonly used objects), a violation of local interface restrictions has been detected. The important point here is that such inconsistencies can be detected even if parts of a component's relation are uninstantiated, thus representing missing or incomplete information. But the necessary "local consistency" condition is not enough. We want to be able to guarantee that a global inconsistency is signalled as soon as an incomplete library cannot be made into a complete and consistent one by adding missing pieces. Adapting the final

---

[2] The inferred type of "StackId" is replaced by "opaque" in order to hide the implementation from the clients (opaque types are uniquely numbered). In the following, $cr(x)$ always denotes the interface relation of x, not the (slightly different) relation obtained by local analysis

[3] Remember that $\perp$ stands for any relation without tuples and denotes inconsistency. If x is neither a client nor supplier of y, the intersection of the domains of their relations is empty, hence the join is trivially $\neq \perp$

x	(module, __)
elementtype	(any_class, any_type)
stack	(module, __)
StackId	(typeconst, TYPE)
newStack	(procedure, (< >, TYPE))
push	(procedure, (< TYPE, i_o_c >, __))
pop	(any_class, any_type)
isFull	(procedure, (< TYPE >, bool)

x	(module, __)
elementtype	(any_class, any_type)
stack	(module, __)
StackId	(typeconst, TYPE)
newStack	(procedure, (< >, TYPE))
push	(procedure, (< TYPE, char >, __))
pop	(any_class, any_type)

theorem from figure 2 to component libraries, this requires that in an incomplete library all clients of a component must be consistent among themselves! In a complete library, this condition is a consequence from local consistency, but for incomplete libraries, it is not[4]; hence we must explicitly require the *Global library consistency condition:* For any component x

$$cr(x) \sqcap \prod_{x \succ y} cr(y) \neq \bot$$

where $x \succ y$ means: y is a direct or indirect client of x (or equivalently, y depends on x). The condition not only implies the "local consistency" condition, but implies in particular that for a component c with clients $c_1, ..., c_n$

$$cr(c) \sqcap \bigsqcup_{i=1}^{n} cr(c_i) \neq \bot$$

as can be shown easily using lattice-theoretic arguments. This condition can be interpreted as follows: In order to guarantee local consistency, all clients must stick to the supplier's interface, hence the union of all client's interfaces must be consistent with this interface as well. This union over the $cr(c_i)$ establishes a *lower bound*[5] for the incompleteness of the interface information of c: a component must at least have a grade of ambiguity which allows the needs of all clients to be satisfied and cannot be more specific than the lower bound. If new clients are added, this lower bound will increase, since the needs of more clients must be respected.

In our example, $cr(\text{stack}) \sqcap cr(\text{application 1}) \sqcap cr(\text{application 2}) = \bot$. This is due to the fact that "char" and "integer or cardinal" (which appear within the attributes of the procedure "push") cannot be unified and indicates a global inconsistency: no matter what element type ultimately will be choosen, one of the applications must become inconsistent with its supplier! This error is detected, although the module "x" containing the declaration of "elementtype" is still missing. On the other hand, the condition $cr(\text{stack}) \sqcap (cr(\text{application 1}) \sqcup cr(\text{application 2})) \neq \bot$ is not violated (as the reader can easily verify, the left hand side is a 2-tuple relation) – it is necessary but not sufficient for global consistency. This shows that although the library is already globally inconsistent, it is still locally correct: taken in isolation, both clients are consistent with its supplier.

In order to demonstrate incremental analysis, we add the following local procedure to the "IMPLEMENTATION MODULE stack":

```
PROCEDURE accumulate(s: StackId): elementtype;
...
    Sum := Sum + s↑.s[ i ];
...
END accumulate;
```

---

4 In complete libraries, all interface relations are fully instantiated and unification is just a test for equality. Equality is transitive, but unifiability is not

5 The reader should keep in mind that the lower we are in the lattice of context relations, the more we know

Since in Modula-2 the addition operator can be used only for arithmetic objects or sets, this procedure makes the interface information more precise: the stack's element type can only be an arithmetic type or a set. Local analysis of the new procedure and subsequent change propagation will therefore replace every "TYPE" in the interface relation by "ARITHMETIC_OR_SET". The consistency condition must be rechecked for all neighbours of "stack" in the component dependency graph, which – through use of procedure "push" in application 2 – leads to a unification of "ARITHMETIC_OR_SET" and "char". Since this unification fails, the use of "push" in application 2 is now inconsistent with the interface: the interface information of "stack" falls below the lower bound required by the clients. Thus before the modification, the library was globally inconsistent but locally consistent, now it is even locally inconsistent. Interface analysis does however not insist on an immediate correction of the inconsistent use of "push", but continues to check interfaces in the library as far as possible. This behaviour is called *fault tolerance*; we consider it a must in order to avoid complaints about the straight-jacket feeling which is caused by too restrictive tools.

Although our example is very small, it fully scales up to real-world situations. Since efficient algorithms for order-sorted unification are known today, inference-based interface checking is hardly more expensive than conventional techniques. During editing of a component, only local consistency will be checked; as soon as the component is written back to the library, interfaces to all neighbour components in the component dependency graph are checked or inferred.

3 Improving Reusability

Only some years ago, programming languages have been enriched with concepts which support reusability of software components. Two examples are generic packages in ADA and polymorphic functions in ML. Both concepts allow to fix the final types of e.g. function arguments not at definition site, but only at the usage of a package or function. This provides for reusable software components, which can be fed with objects of many different types (but these types must stick to a common pattern). Hence such reusable components can be used in different contexts – but the security of strong typing is still guaranteed. Some authors go even further and propose to use not complete function or package definitions, but *program schemes* or *templates* as basic software components, which must then be filled in and completed by the programmers. [En88] argues that a combination of template-based libraries with good retrieval techniques is the most promising approach for the future. But current tools cannot guarantee consistent use of such schemes, because incomplete programs cannot be analysed.

We will now demonstrate how we can provide for incomplete and reusable program schemes with secure interfaces even for non-polymorphic languages. In our terminology, a program scheme is just a fragment and – as we have seen above – may be incomplete and may have an ambiguous or overloaded interface. If such an interface relation contains uninstantiated variables (due to missing information), the component can be made polymorphic simply by ensuring that different clients may instantiate missing interface information differently. This is in contrast to the global consistency condition, which requires that all global objects must be used consistently in all clients. Thus, if for a certain component the global consistency condition is replaced by the weaker local consistency condition, we have what we want: every client must stick to the pattern specified in the interface relation, but different clients may instantiate this pattern differently. Technically speaking, we avoid that attributes of *all* occurences of an object are unified; instead each attribute of an object's use in a specific client is unified with a (conceptual) copy of the attribute from the supplier's interface relation.

In the above example, both clients of the stack definition are consistent with its supplier, because "type" and "arithmetic" is unifyable as well as "type" and "char". Thus we can use the stack definition module as a generic, reusable component: the stack's element type is purposefully left open, in order to allow programmers to use this stack definition as a program scheme, where the element type may be filled in (thereby instantiating the scheme). But even with the element type missing, consistent use of the scheme can be guaranteed. Hence a slight change in the analysis algorithm results in reusable, polymorphic components: the programmers must just state which objects or components should behave polymorphicly! In fact, we obtain a reusability mechanism for free which is very similar to ADA or ML, but useable for languages which do not explicitly support reusability.

There are some additional mechanism in order to improve reusability. Library components are named; they can be used by other components simply by providing their name. Thus, components may be decomposed into named pieces. In the next section we will see how this mechanism can be used in order to avoid the well-known problems with redundant program text in the presence of variants. In addition, we provide for components that are *parameterized* in the sense that named "holes" (missing parts of a fragment) can be instantiated by the user of a component; this is done just by providing program text or component names.

4 Inference-based configuration control

Configuration control deals with the management and consistent configuration of *system families*, whose members differ only in some components (*variants*); it has recently received much attention. Most of today's tools are extensions of Make [Fe79] or RCS [Ti85]. The shape system [ML88] allows variants for Make targets; additional attributes can be used to specify a particular configuration thread. A different approach can be found in [Est88]: here, component dependencies are computed (rather than specified) from language-specific rules; again, additional attributes are then used to compose a particular configuration. Other authors proposed to extend programming languages with constructs which allow the description of system families [WS88]. Again, all these approaches are batch oriented and neither incremental nor ambiguity tolerant.

In our system, any library component may exist in several variants. A *variant editor* is used to visualize the system dependency graph. Dependencies are determined by the system, hence no specification (e.g. a makefile) is necessary. For each component, the editor will offer the available variants in a menu, thus the user may interactively construct a particular configuration. Although the basic dependency graph cannot be modified[6], the editor allows to compose or decompose a component into subfragments and to add or delete variants. As in the above-mentioned systems, we use additional attributes to distinguish variants of a component. By using these attributes, the editor can check immediately whether a configuration is consistent. The consistency check in the variant editor makes again use of context relations, and this has some important consequences:

— the editor can partially infer attributes itself: if, for example, one variant with the attribute "X-Windows" (in contrast to "SunView") has been selected, the unification-based mechanism will conclude that all relevant clients and suppliers also must have this attribute

— inconsistencies can be detected even if a configuration thread is not completely specified: if in the above scenario a user tries to select a "SunView" variant, this inconsistency will be detected even if other attributes are still unknown

— by filtering the menus for variants with respect to the attributes inferred so far, the editor can even guarantee that inconsistent configurations cannot be constructed.

According to the calculus of context relations, attributes may be structured and grouped into conceptual classes. This is a simple consequence of the use of order-sorted terms and imposes a taxonomy on variant attributes. For any library, inference rules must be given which describe constraints on the

---

[6] dependencies are computed by language-specific rules and thus cannot be changed arbitrarily

variant attributes of dependent components. Such inference rules are just basic context relations; if the system structure changes, new basic relations must be provided.

Note that attributes used for variants and attributes used for interfaces are different and in principle completely orthogonal. For practical reasons, it is even necessary to allow that different variants of a component have different interfaces. In such a case, the interface analysis will first filter out all variant combinations which have inconsistent interface relations. The variant editor will then display only variants which passed this test; the variant attributes are used as an additional device. Once a (partial) configuration has been determined (because attributes have been supplied or inferred), the editor can automatically generate appropriate makefiles.

```
Fragment «Stack-Implementation» (variant attribute: STACK-ORGANIZATION)
    IMPLEMENTATION MODULE stack;
      FROM x IMPORT elementtype;
      FROM Storage IMPORT Allocate;
      <optConstant>
      TYPE StackId = POINTER TO StackRepresentation;
      <StackType>
      PROCEDURE newStack(): StackId;
        VAR id: StackId;
      BEGIN
        Allocate( id, SIZE( StackRepresentation ) );
          <EmptyStack>
        RETURN id
      END newStack;
      ...
        <isFull>
    END stack;
Fragment «optConstant» (variant attribute: <static>)
    CONST maxno = [constant];
Fragment «optConstant» (variant attribute: <dynamic>)
    (* empty fragment *)
Fragment «StackType» (variant attribute: <static>)
    TYPE StackRepresentation = RECORD
                                    n: 1..maxno;
                                    s: ARRAY [ 1..maxno ] OF elementtype
                                  END;
Fragment «StackType» (variant attribute: <dynamic>)
    TYPE StackRepresentation = POINTER TO eList;
        eList = RECORD
                    e: elementtype;
                    pre: StackRepresentation
                  END;
Fragment «EmptyStack» (variant attribute: <static>)
    id↑.n := 0;
Fragment «EmptyStack» (variant attribute: <dynamic>)
    id↑ := NIL;
Fragment «isFull-Imp» (variant attribute: <static>)
    PROCEDURE IsFull( s: StackId ): boolean;
    BEGIN
      RETURN s↑.n = maxno
    END IsFull;
Fragment «isFull-Imp» (variant attribute: <dynamic>)
    PROCEDURE IsFull( s: StackId ): boolean;
    BEGIN
      RETURN false
    END IsFull;
```

Figure 3: Variants of basic example

Before we discuss the lattice-theoretic aspects of consistent variant libraries, we demonstrate our concepts by extending our small example library. We introduce a variant attribute

stack-organization = { ‹dynamic› | ‹static› }

As shown in figure 3, some of the original fragments have been split up into subfragments (subfragments are referenced by «name»). In addition, some of the fragments exist in two variants; the variants with attribute ‹static› realize an array implementation of the stack, the variants with attribute ‹dynamic› realize a linked list implementation. Note that the "Stack Implementation" fragment does not exist in variants and has an uninstantiated variant attribute, but all implementation dependent parts exist as subfragments, where each subfragment exists in two variants. This minimizes duplication of code and avoids the well-known difficulties with redundant program text.

The variant editor will display the component dependencies either in graphical or textual form. The example below uses a textual representation of part of the dependency graph. The editor offers menus for all components which exist in variants, and the user can choose between ‹dynamic› or ‹static›.

```
configuration of module "stack" consisting of
    fragment «Stack-Definition» consisting of
        fragment «isFull-Def»            [ static | dynamic ]
    end
    fragment «Stack-Implementation» consisting of
        fragment «optConstant»           [ static | dynamic ]
        fragment «EmptyStack»            [ static | dynamic ]
        fragment «...»
        fragment «isFull-Imp»            [ static | dynamic ]
    end
end
```

In our example there is an inference rule (realized as set of basic context relations) which states that the variant attribute of all variants of a configuration must be equal. Thus it is sufficient to select just one menu item: once the static variant of «optConstant» has been selected, the editor knows that all other fragments must be ‹static› as well. All remaining menus are filtered such that the "dynamic" item can no longer be selected: the editor gurantees consistency of the configuration. Note that our example is very simple; it is possible to use more than one variant attribute and to specify dependencies between attributes. It is also possible to store (partial) configurations and load them when the variant editor is invoked, thereby establishing working environments. Such environments can be named (e.g. "fast access" for a partially specified "static" configuration), hence a configuration with certain global characteristics can be made available immediately.

The interface analysis treats variants as overloadings of fragment interfaces. The relational calculus allows to describe such overloadings using the union operation, and (as mentioned above) the analysis will automatically filter out inconsistent variant combinations – which is actually the same as overloading resolution, a standard relational facility. The library is considered consistent as long as there is at least one consistent configuration possible. This is expressed in the

Library consistency condition with variants: For any component x with variants $x^1, ..., x^k$,

$$(\bigsqcup_{\nu=1}^{k} cr(x^\nu)) \sqcap \prod_{x \succ y} (\bigsqcup_{\nu=1}^{j} cr(y^\nu)) \neq \bot$$

where the y^ν are variants of y. If c is a component with variants $c^1, ..., c^k$ and clients $c_1, ..., c_n$, the local consistency condition becomes

$$(\bigsqcup_{\nu=1}^{k} cr(c^\nu)) \sqcap (\bigsqcup_{i=1}^{n} cr(c_i)) \neq \bot$$

which implies in particular that for any client c_i there must be a variant c^ν fulfilling its needs: $cr(c^\nu) \sqcap cr(c_i) \neq \bot$. A symmetric condition holds for variants of clients with respect to suppliers.

If in our example the newly added "PROCEDURE accumulate" (see section 2) exists only in the static variant, this condition is violated for the static variant of application 2, hence interface analysis will determine that application 2 can only be configured in the dynamic variant, because it uses "char" as the stack's elementtype. But still, module "x" is missing!

5 Improving component retrieval

Component retrieval in a library deals with effective search procedures for components which obey a certain given (possibly incomplete) specification. Besides classical tables of contents, two techniques have recently been used to obtain more intelligent retrieval. The first approach tries to (hand-)construct a taxonomy of software components in a library. This allows to build special expert systems, which can find components with given characteristics or attributes [CK87, EW87, ZW89]. The second approach evolved in the world of functional programming: here, some systems allow to search for functions not by name or attributes, but by usage patterns, thus using a type scheme as a search key. The type scheme is inferred from intended uses of a function, and the retrieval component will find function definitions with equal or similar type characteristics [RT89, Ri89]. It turned out that usage patterns are a much better filter than one might think, and we therefore generalized the approach to arbitrary languages.

The general idea is to allow context relations as search patterns. Such relations can be supplied by the user, or computed by the system itself. For example, a list of all library objects which can be used at a given point in a fragment can simply be achieved by inferring the attributes of the object at the point of use, and unifying this information with attributes of objects available in the library. The former attributes are a by-product of local relational analysis, and the latter are part of interface relations. It is also possible to search for combinations of attributes: "give me all pairs of functions, where either the result type of the first is equal to the argument type of the second, or the second has five parameters of type real". Hence we can use polymorphic or overloaded search patterns, by simply coding them as context relations.

The unification-based join operation is used to implement the search: if a join between a search pattern and an object's interface relation does not fail, the object is considered as qualified. Other systems use just matching instead of unification, but in our context matching of attributes is not enough, because attributes can be incomplete. Since users often forget the order of parameters, we provide to use associative-commutative unification [Fa84] for certain subattributes, such as parameter lists. A final example shall demonstrate the technique:

Imagine a user who thinks that our sample library contains something like a "stack", but does not know the names of the corresponding functions, not to speak of parameter types and order. However he believes that there are two functions "add an element" and "remove an element", which both take an argument of type "stack", and the first one takes an additional argument, the stack element. The user does not know anything about the realization of stacks, all he knows is that both functions must accept an argument of the same type. This rather unprecise search pattern can be described by the following context relation:

"add"	(procedure, (< TYPE_2, TYPE_1 >, __))
"remove"	(procedure, (< TYPE_1>, __))

Although the user has mixed up the order of parameters, the relational inference engine (enhanced with AC1–unification for parameter lists) will find the module "stack" in our sample library, since the interface relation for "stack" has columns for "push" and "pop" which contain attributes compatible with the search pattern. The search result will be displayed in a pretty-printed style:

Fragment «Stack-Definition»

```
DEFINITION MODULE stack;
  PROCEDURE push( s: StackId; e: elementtype );
  PROCEDURE pop( s: StackId );
```

Component search directed by usage patterns will usually find more than one candidate, and in order to increase accuracy, it can be combined with traditional retrieval techniques. Indeed, pattern-based browsing should be considered a complement to traditional techniques, not an alternative. Hence, our retrieval component also offers searching for component names, text fragments or variant attributes. Interface information, inconsistencies, inferred attributes of program objects etc. can be displayed conveniently. In addition, the fragment mechanism gives us hypertext-like cross-referencing for free: as described above, fragments may refer to each other, and a mouse click onto a fragment reference immediately shows its definition.

6 Conclusion

We have seen that use of automated deduction techniques allows to build more intelligent and flexible software development tools. Unification-based interface analysis and variant control allows to handle incomplete information and can detect errors earlier than conventional systems. As a by-product, component reuse and search for appropriate components is enhanced; consistent reuse of program schemes can be guaranteed even for non-polymorphic languages.

The tools described in this paper grew out of efforts to generalize concepts which had been used in a generic environment for programming-in-the-small. This environment, the PSG system [BS86], already used fragments as basic components and inference-based algorithms for static program analysis, and our excellent experiences in using these algorithms finally led us to believe that they can be applied to a more general domain.

Due to space restrictions, our presentation was sometimes sketchy. The interested reader can find more details on the inference calculus in [BS86, Sn89]; additional features of the variant control system are described in [Sch89]. The relational inference engine is in use since four years, whereas the implementation of the tools described in this paper (which are based on this engine) has just begun. We hope to be able to report in more detail in the near future.

Acknowledgements. Wolfgang Henhapl contributed important ideas; his support is gratefully acknowledged.

The work described in this paper is funded by the Deutsche Forschungsgemeinschaft, grant He 1170/4–1.

7 References

[BS86]   Bahlke, R. and Snelting, G.: The PSG System: From Formal Language Definitions to Interactive Programming Environments. ACM TOPLAS 8, 4 (October 1986), pp. 547-576.

[CK87]   Collberg, C.S. and Krampell, M.G.: A Property-Based Method for Selecting among Multiple Implementations of Modules. Proc. ESEC 87, LNCS 289, pp. 193–201.

[El89]   Elzer, P.: Management von Softwareprojekten. Informatik Spektrum 12, 4 (August 1989), pp. 181 – 197.

[EW87]   Embley, D.W. and Woodfield, S.N.: A Knowledge Structure for Reusing Abstract Data Types. Proc. 9th Intern. Conference on Software Engineering, IEEE 1987.

[En88]   Endres, A.: Software-Wiederverwendung: Ziele, Wege und Erfahrungen. Informatik Spektrum 11, 2 (April 1988), pp. 85 – 95.

[Est88]   Estublier, J. : Configuration Managment. Proc. International Workshop on Software Version and Variant Control, Grassau 1988.

[Fa84]   Fages, F.: Associative-Commutative Unification. Proc. 7th CADE, 1984, LNCS 170, pp. 194 – 208.

[Fe79]   Feldmann, S. I.: Make - A program for maintaining computer programs. Software Practice and Experience, Vol. 9, April 1979.

[ML88]   Mahler A. and Lampen, A.: An Integrated Toolset for Engineering Software Configurations. Proc. Practical Software Engineering Environments, SIGPLAN Notices 24, 2 (February 1989).

[Na89]   Nagl, M.: Eine integrierte Softwareentwicklungsumgebung – ein alternativer konzeptioneller Ansatz. Proc. Software Entwicklung, Marburg 1989, Informatik Fachberichte 212, pp. 21 – 42.

[Pf86]   Pfreundschuh, M.: A Model for Building Modular Systems Based on Attribute Grammars. PhD thesis, University of Iowa, Dept. of Computer Science, 1986.

[Ti85]   Tichy, W. F.: RCS - A System for Version Control. Software Practice and Experience 15, 7 (Juli 1985), pp. 637 – 654.

[RT89]   Runciman, C. and Toyn, I.: Retrieving Re-usable Software Components by Polymorphic Type. Proc. Functional Languages and Computer Architecture, ACM 1989, pp. 166 – 173.

[Ri89]   Rittri, M.: Using Types as Search Keys in Function Libraries. Proc. Functional Languages and Computer Architecture, ACM 1989, pp. 174 – 183.

[Sch89]   Schroeder, U.: Incremental Variant Control. Proc. 2nd International Workshop on Software Version and Variant Control, Princeton 1989, pp. 145 – 148.

[Sn89]   Snelting, G.: The Calculus of Context Relations. ACTA INFORMATICA Vol. 28 (May 1991), pp. 411 – 445.

[WS88]   Winkler, J. and Stoffel, Ch.: Program-Variations-in-the-Small. Proc. 1st International Workshop on Software Version and Variant Control, Grassau 1988, pp. 1 – 20.

[ZW89]   Zimbel, R. and Weber, P.: Ein Expertensystem zur Auswahl von wiederverwendbaren Programmoduln. Informatik Forschung und Entwicklung 4, 4 (1989), pp. 174 – 192.

TICKLE: Object-Oriented Description and Composition Services for Software Engineering Environments.

Tim Collins, Kevin Ewert, Colin Gerety *, Jon Gustafson, Ian Thomas

Hewlett-Packard Company.
3404 East Harmony Road,
Ft. Collins, Colorado 80525
USA

Abstract

Providing support for object-oriented descriptions of software engineering environment facilities has received considerable interest in recent times. The TICKLE (Tool Inter-communication and Composition Kernel for Large Environments) system provides services for the definition of SEE objects with their associated operations, and the description of the tools and the functions they offer as implementations of operations. Novel features in TICKLE include the separate definition and manipulation of the associations between operations and tool functions in a *composite*, scoping of the mapping associations to within the composite, and the integration of these object-oriented notions with recent ideas on the use of broadcast mechanisms for tool communication.

Keywords: Software engineering environments, frameworks, object-oriented interfaces, tool communication, tool composition, mapping, scope.

1 Introduction.

The importance of explicit description of the data that is managed in a software engineering environment (SEE) has been widely recognized for some time. More recently, there has been a focus on enhancing these descriptions with definitions of the operations that are associated with data objects. Some of these operations are implemented as tools.

Our objectives for TICKLE (Tool Inter-communication and Composition Kernel for Large Environments) were to support:

- the separation of the logical/conceptual descriptions of the SEE's data objects and operations on them from the implementations of the operations;

- the description of both the logical/conceptual level and the implementations explicitly, in a way that can be read and manipulated by both humans and tools;

- communication and composition mechanisms for tools in a SEE built on a broadcast mechanism.

These areas of concern have been called *data* and *control integration* [WASS90, THOM91].

The objective of this paper is to show how the TICKLE system supports the definition of SEE data, the definition of the tools (some of which already exist and were written before the

---

*Please address correspondence to this author.

development of the TICKLE system described in this paper), and the association of the tools with an object's operations. Novel features include the separate definition and manipulation of the mapping information associating an operation with its implementation, the scoping of the mapping from operations to their implementations, and the unification of this object-oriented idea with more recent notions of broadcast mechanisms for communication between tools [REIS90, CAGA90].

TICKLE provides a set of services that are defined so as to complement the existing services in both Unix and PCTE [BOUD88]. We are not interested in using these systems purely as implementation vehicles for the system we are proposing. We are concerned with complementing and extending their facilities. We believe it is important that, when complementary services define concepts, these have a clearly defined relationship with the concepts and philosophy of the base systems on which the services run. This has been a key motivating factor in several of the design decisions for TICKLE.

The alternatives to the definition of complementary services are to define a "complete" interface (the PCTE solution) which represents a very large effort, or to define a set of services whose concepts have an undefined relationship with those of the base systems on which it will run. This leads to difficulties in understanding of the total set of facilities available to the tool writer, and their inter-relationships. We have also designed the services so that they respect the "spirit" and rationale of PCTE and Unix. Examples of this include the use of multiple schemas, the way in which tools are described, etc.

The result is not an object-oriented database definition. It was not our objective to create such a definition. The TICKLE system allows the integration of existing tools as operation implementations in a clear and clean way (see also [MAHL90] and [NANA90] for comparable approaches), specifies a well-defined relationship between the concepts and facilities available to a tool writer (for example, the interaction with base system process management), and provides an open system that allows the addition (and modification) of data object types, operations, and implementations, without requiring modifications in the existing implementations.

2 Overview.

This section presents a brief overview of the TICKLE system. There is a more detailed discussion, including rationale, of each of these issues in the following sections.

Figure 1 shows a **source_file** data type which has four associated operations, **compile**, **edit**, **check_out**, and **check_in**. Data types and their associated operations are described in schemas in TICKLE.

The implementations of those elements are shown in Figure 2. There is a Builder tool that offers the two functions **compile_file** and **build_target**. The Editor tool offers the **create_window** and **insert_string** functions. The Configuration Manager tool offers the **check_out** and **check_in** functions. Note that the names of the logical *operations* in the environment may be different from the names of the *functions* offered by tools. Tools provide the implementations of operations in TICKLE and have explicit, manipulable, descriptions.

Figure 3 shows the mapping between the *operations* associated with the object type and the *functions* offered by the tools that are the implementations of the operations. This mapping is explicit and manipulable in TICKLE.

In TICKLE, the mapping from operations to tool functions is not global for the whole set of types and implementations in the environment. The mapping is scoped. TICKLE provides a static description of a scope and also precise execution semantics for the scope. TICKLE introduces the notion of a composite tool, whose definition includes object and operation definitions, and the mapping of operations to tool functions. A composite tool defines a scope for the mapping of operations to implementations as well as for events.

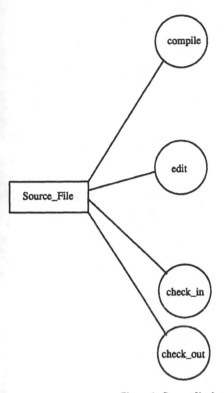

Figure 1: Source file data type with four associated operations.

The existence of the scope facilitates the implementation of broadcast semantics and monitoring of operation invocations and events. TICKLE supports the definition of events, and the monitoring of events (including operation invocations) within a scope.

3 Schema Management Facilities.

Schemas are used in the database and SEE database world to describe the properties of the data managed by the databases and repositories. In TICKLE, schema information conveys logical/conceptual information about some of the elements in the SEE. The TICKLE schema mechanism is modeled closely on the PCTE mechanism. Readers familiar with the PCTE schema management mechanisms will find many similarities between the two mechanisms.

In this section, we introduce some general background on schemas and then describe TICKLE schemas in more detail. We then define the underlying model that supports TICKLE's multiple schema facilities and show how importation facilities allow sharing of type information between schemas. Inheritance is discussed next and then schema evolution. Finally, the notion of TICKLE working schemas is described. TICKLE goes beyond the PCTE schema model in its treatment of operations associated with object types but several TICKLE mechanisms are based on generalizations or adaptations of existing PCTE solutions. Section 3.4 on the importation mechanism gives some examples.

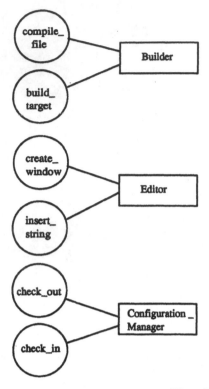

Figure 2: Functions offered by the tools.

3.1 Schemas and multiple schemas.

Schemas describe the properties of the data stored in a database. Some of the reasons why schemas are important in SEE databases include (i) the expression of agreement among the tools that use the schemas on the structure and some of the semantics of the data they share, (ii) they exemplify the trend of migration of the semantics of the data from the tools to the data management systems, and (iii) they allow enforcement of certain aspects of data manipulation that might otherwise have to be achieved by convention among the tools.

TICKLE does not have a single global schema for a TICKLE environment, it supports multiple schemas. Each schema is defined in a Schema Definition Set (SDS). A type definition may appear in several SDSs, allowing sharing of type information among SDSs. This is explained more fully in section 3.4 on importation of types.

Multiple schema systems have a number of advantages:

1. they may allow evolution of one schema independently of the other schemas in the system;

2. they may allow different schemas to provide different name mappings for different tools;

3. they may provide views that are subsets of the information in the database relevant or restricted for users of the database.

This latter point is unusual in object-oriented systems. Stefik and Bobrow discuss the concept of perspective [STEF86] which is defined as "a form of composite object interpreted as different views

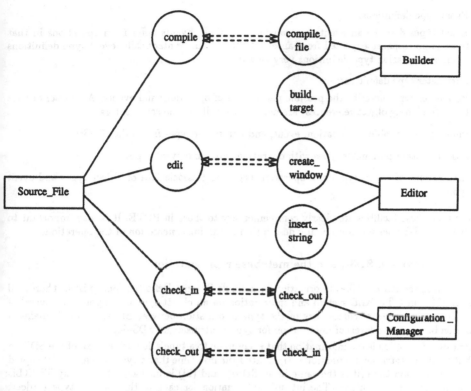

Figure 3: The mapping from operations to tool functions.

on the same conceptual entity". The perspectives they define are actually separate view objects which have associated methods and manipulate state variables of the single conceptual object.

Harrison et al [HARR89] comment that the classical object-oriented models do not apply well in software engineering because the set of operations available on an object changes during the life cycle of the object. Also, Penedo has reported experience on use of an object oriented database for the Project Master Data Base implementation that indicated that some view mechanism for capturing the different sets of interfaces available on an object was necessary [PENE89]. We believe that TICKLE's working schema and composite tool facilities support the view requirements uncovered in the work described above.

3.2 TICKLE schemas.

In TICKLE, each Schema Definition Set (SDS) is an object, encapsulated by a set of operations that manipulate it. The information managed by the object includes:

1. Object type definitions;

   Object types correspond to the items of interest in the SEE. They have names (local to a SDS), parent types, etc.

2. Operation type definitions;

   Operation types describe some operation in terms of its name (local to a SDS), the type of its return value (if any), its parameter names, their types, etc.

3. Event type definitions;

   Event types describe an event that can be generated. Events differ from operations in that there is no response expected from an event generation. Syntactically, event type definitions resemble operation type definitions very closely.

4. Parameter type definitions;

   Parameter types describe the possible parameters of operations and events. A number of base types (including object references) are defined, as well as type constructors.

5. Importations of object, operation, event, and parameter types from other SDSs;

6. Associations of parameter types with operation types and event types;

7. Associations of object types and operation types, and associations of object types and event types.

Note that these facilities are clearly complementary to those in PCTE. It is also important to note that the SDS does not contain any description of the *implementation* of the operations.

3.3 Types, type_in_SDSs, and the metabase representation.

The preceding section describes information in a single Schema Definition Set (SDS). There will be many SDSs in a TICKLE system and information on an object type may appear in several of these. To resolve issues of consistency of the type information between SDSs, TICKLE makes a distinction between two levels of information for types: intrinsic and SDS-dependent.

Intrinsic information is the information that is common to a type's definition in all of the SDS' in which it appears. Intrinsic information is (i) created the first time that a type is defined; (ii) copied at type importation time (it is the same in all SDSs); and (iii) is unchangeable by any TICKLE schema management primitive. The intrinsic information for each of the sorts of type (object, operation, event, and parameter) is different and defined in the TICKLE specifications. Examples are the number and types of parameters of an operation, the parent types of an object type, etc.

SDS-dependent information is additional, supplementary information on the type that depends on the view of that type in a particular SDS. Examples are the name of an operation, which operations are associated with an object type, etc.

The schema modification primitives may only modify the SDS-dependent information on a type. They operate on a single SDS and modify the properties of types etc. within that SDS - they change the "view" described in that SDS but have no effect on the "views" provided by other SDSs or those properties of the type that are intrinsic. Since the intrinsic information on a type is unchangeable, and because the schema management operations have been carefully defined to have only local effect, it is not possible to introduce inconsistencies in type definitions between SDSs.

In TICKLE, all of the type information in a SDS is represented as a pre-defined object type in the object base. It may also be represented as a structure in the object base composed of related objects, where types are themselves represented as objects and associations between types, between operation types and object types for example, are represented as relationships. The collection of this information is known as the metabase and, since the objects may themselves managed by TICKLE, the structure is described by a schema called the metaschema.

3.4 Importation of types.

Sharing of type information is required in multiple schema systems. In TICKLE it is achieved, as in PCTE, by the importation of type information from one schema to another. The importation operation specifies a type within some other originating SDS that is to be imported into the SDS that is the destination parameter of the import operation.

Imported type definitions are *copied* from the originating SDS into the destination SDS. Importation is not achieved by maintaining a *reference* from the importing SDS to the type definition in its original SDS. The difference between copying and reference does not appear as a difference in semantics (since the referenced intrinsic information is immutable in the original SDS in any case), but rather as a practical issue. Copying means that the SDS contains all relevant information about the type and is a self-contained, independent, unit of information. The advantages of making it self-contained relate to the ease of transfer of schema information between environments, and the accessibility of schema information in a distributed network subject to partitioning. A feature of this solution is that there is no propagation of change information from the originating SDS to the importing SDS. This means that the user of a SDS can use it predictably and be isolated from changes that occur elsewhere.

Importation in PCTE operates according to a certain number of rules. These rules reflect the semantics of how PCTE distinguishes the intrinsic properties of a type from the way that the type manifests itself in a particular SDS. Examples of the PCTE importation rules include:

- importation of an object type from a SDS S also implies importation of all of the ancestor types of the object type (because the parent types of an object type are intrinsic to the type);

- importation of an object type from a SDS S does not imply importation of any of the attribute types that are associated with that object type in S, nor the importation of their association (if the attribute types have already been imported, for example). This is because this information is SDS-dependent;

- importation of an enumerator attribute type T from a SDS S implies the importation of the enumeration item types defined for T;

- importation of a link type of cardinality *many* implies the importation of the key attribute types for that link type, and also their association as key attribute types of the link type.

Similar rules have been devised for importations in TICKLE. Some example rules include:

- importation of an operation type from a SDS S implies importation of the parameter (and possibly result type) for the operation. Importation of operation types and event types is closely modeled on the importation of enumerator types in PCTE.

- Importation of an operation type and its parameter types also imports the association between the operation type and the parameter types. This is analogous to the importation of the association between a link type and its key attribute types in PCTE.

3.5 Inheritance.

Object types are arranged in a DAG (Directed Acyclic Graph) in TICKLE and PCTE. The graph defines a subtype relationship between the object types that indicates what is commonly called inheritance. The association of operation and event types with an object type in a TICKLE SDS means that all child types of that object type in that SDS also have that operation type or event type associated with them. This definition means that TICKLE supports interface inheritance.

Implementation inheritance can be subdivided into support for code or tool reuse, and definition of object structure. Code reuse is supported, with the identification of the implementation being mediated by the mapping information described in section 5. Structure inheritance may also be supported in a PCTE-based implementation of TICKLE. This depends on whether the TICKLE object types, and especially their subtype relationship, correspond to PCTE object types and their parent/child relationships.

3.6 Schema evolution.

Flexible schema evolution is an essential requirement for software engineering databases. The long life of many projects and much software means that it must be possible to extend and modify the schemas that were in use at the beginning of a project many times during the project lifetime, and to be able to do this in a way that does not require manipulation of data created with existing schemas when those schemas are updated.

Using the distinction between the intrinsic SDS-dependent properties of types, it is possible to provide a wide range of primitives that allow schema modification without the overhead of expensive data migration. For example, schema evolution primitives operating on a SDS allow the definition of new operation or event types as well as the deletion of operation and event types defined in the SDS (subject to certain integrity conditions). It is also possible to add and delete associations between operation or event types and an object type. In contrast, it is not possible to extend or modify the set of parameters for an operation type, for example, as the set of parameters is considered an intrinsic property of the operation or event type.

Replacement of an implementation for an operation does not involve a modification of a SDS. It is achieved by modifying the mapping information, as described in section 5.

Zdonik [ZDON86] has examined the problem of type evolution in object-oriented databases, a problem similar to the one faced in TICKLE. He focuses on two problems: (i) the compatibility of data structure for an object code and code of the methods that access it, and (ii) the compatibility of the values written and returned by methods as the constraints governing a type's state evolve from version to version.

In TICKLE, some forms of type evolution are supported by the SDS mechanism that allows the evolution of the set of operations defined for a type. The relationships between operations available on the "view" of a type T in one SDS and the "view" of T, possibly considered as a different version of T, in a different SDS is clear and well-defined. The flexibility of allowing the same operation name to refer to different implementations using the working schema and mapping facilities (see section 5) also eases the problems of type evolution.

Nevertheless, it is clear that an implementation and an object's data structure have to be consistent, however, and the solutions proposed by Zdonik apply equally well for TICKLE.

3.7 Working Schemas.

Operations are implemented by tools. Several operations may be implemented by the same tool. Tools, as operation implementations, may invoke TICKLE operations and generate TICKLE events. Each tool will execute as a process (either a Unix process or a PCTE process). Each executing process has a TICKLE *working schema* (by analogy with PCTE's working schema) that is a union of TICKLE SDSs. The working schema of a tool defines the object types, operation types, parameter types, and their associations, that are visible to the executing tool.

A tool may be represented as an object and have some SDSs associated with it that define its characteristics (see section 4), including its initial working schema and may also change its working schema during its execution.

4   Tool Description Facilities.

One of the motivations behind TICKLE was to make explicit descriptions of elements in the environment available to the environment's users and administrators. This applies to the tools in the environment as well. Tool descriptions are provided by a tool writer as they describe features of the tool and its implementation. This information is also installed in the environment with the tool.

One of the other objectives was to support the development of independent tools that could act as components of larger tool compositions. We would like tool writers to be able to develop component tools and support their combination into customized tool compositions. We would like writers of component tools to be able to prepare them independently (as far as possible) of the way in which they will be used, and their environment of execution. Unix filters and the pipe composition mechanism provide a simple example of this sort of philosophy, where each filter is designed independently of how it will be composed with others in a pipe.

It is therefore necessary to be able to describe tools and tool components so that their users and tools who compose them with other tools have detailed descriptions of the tools' interfaces. This composition is achieved by the connections between the operations and the tools that provide their implementations.

This section describes how tools are characterized in TICKLE. A tool's description is essentially split into two parts, an "export" interface that describes the services that the tool offers to its environment, and an "import" interface, that describes the services that the tool requires from its execution environment.

Most of these concepts are already familiar from the work on module interconnection languages and reusable component description techniques and there is little novel in the concepts presented here. The fact that we describe components that will not be processed by some language tool after composition (as it would if we were combining source language components) simplifies the problem for us. We do not need to deal with such complexities as parameterization of generic components, etc.

A description of an installed tool is actually an object in the object base, encapsulated by operations. An example of the operations is add_an_exported_interface, etc. We have not defined a textual tool description language, though this would be possible. A textual language would be useful for the transfer of tool descriptions between environments. A compiler for a textual language would call the operations on a tool description object.

4.1 A tool's external "export" interface.

In this context, the "export" interface of a tool is related to the set of services that the tool offers to other tools/implementations in the environment.

In addition to the tool executable that acts as the focal point for the collection of information on the tool, information associated with "export" interface of a tool includes:

1. the tool's entry points, each of which is characterized by a signature including a description of its parameter types. This is a list of functions offered by the tool. There may be a formal description of the interface's semantics also associated with an entry point.

2. schemas containing suggestions for object type, operation type and event type definitions that could correspond to the entry points of the tool. This may be delivered in text form with the tool and be represented by the schema objects in the installed form. This is essentially documentation for the users who are building schemas, including object, operation and event definitions, which will need to be associated with implementations.

3. some definitions of event classes (descriptions of events that may be generated by other tools) and a suggested entry point for each entry class.

4.2 A tool's external "import" interface.

A component tool is not required or expected to implement all of its required functions itself. The tool writer may decide to use some service that is provided by some other tool that will be present in the environment in which the component tool will execute or with which it will be composed. It is this notion of what the component will need from its environment that we call the "import" interface of the tool.

There is no explicit description of this information in most object-oriented programming languages, though it is more common in module interconnection languages and characterizations of reusable components.

Information associated with the "import" interface of a tool includes:

1. the operation types that the tool calls using the TICKLE operation invocation mechanism. Note that a tool writer may choose to use the TICKLE invocation mechanism even if he is providing all of the components of the tool. The advantage would be that the invocation would then be subject to the dispatching mechanism, including event monitoring, (as described in section 6.2).

2. the event types that the tool can generate. Like the operation invocations, these events are generated on objects whose types need to be included in the set of object types described above. By analogy with some programming languages, this might correspond to a description of exception conditions raised within a module.

4.3 Working schema information for a tool.

This is an ordered list of SDSs that should be included in the working schema of the tool when it starts executing. The working schema is used in the interpretation of the tool's use of TICKLE services.

5   Creating A Composite Tool.

The preceding sections have described the logical descriptions of objects and operations in the environment, and the descriptions of tools that can implement operations. TICKLE supports the composition of tools to create a *composite* tool. This represents a significant extension of current ideas on broadcast mechanisms for communicating between tools.

A composite tool to support the edit-compile-debug phase of software development would include a builder, editor, configuration management tool, etc.

The description of a composite includes the mapping from operations to their implementations as tool functions. In TICKLE, this mapping is separate and distinct from the definition of the operations (part of the logical structure) and the description of the tools. There are two main purposes for the separation of the mapping information in TICKLE. The first is to make the mapping explicit and manipulable, rather than assuming some implicit link between operations and implementations based on a name character string or a unique identifier. The second is to be able to modify mappings without having to modify either (i) the schema information that describes the logical structure of parts of the environment, or (ii) the implementations that will effect the operations in many different environments, or the descriptions of these implementations.

Novel features of TICKLE's management of mappings are (i) the separation of the mapping; (ii) the scoping of a mapping; and (iii) the association of a scope with a *composite tool* obtained by composing tools.

The composite includes a *static description* of the connection between operations and implementations for a particular scope. It links invocation and event generations in some tools to others that act as their implementations. The composite defines a scope for mapping information.

Any definition of scope needs to deal with interaction and communication between scopes. In TICKLE, the definition of a composite tool includes a description of the events within the composite that will generate events that are visible *outside* the scope defined by the composite. For example, the definition of a composite supporting the edit-compile-debug phase may define that all file-modified events are made visible outside the composite.

5.1 Scoping of mappings.

Most object-oriented systems assume a *global* mapping between operations and implementations. All operation invocations use the same mapping information to establish the implementation for the operation. While this may be appropriate for a single program (which implicitly has a clearly defined notion of scope related to the process that will execute it) we do not believe it is appropriate or necessary to have a single global mapping from operations to implementations in a SEE.

The arguments that apply are similar to those for the existence of multiple schemas in section 3.1. Scopes provide a mechanism for isolation of the composite from changes that occur outside the scope, and isolation of the composite's environment from details of the composite's implementation. Within a composite, it is possible to present those operations that are important to its users without presenting unnecessary and irrelevant operations.

The ATIS system [ATIS90] provides the concept of a Method Map for operations and implementations. ATIS defines a classical binding algorithm that selects a method based on a message and the type of the element to which the message is sent. The algorithm takes the type hierarchy into account in identifying a method. The mapping from **message x element type – > method** is global to the environment. The Method Map (defined on a user/role basis) is not integrated into this algorithm. It behaves much as a cache of **message x element type** mappings which is searched before the global structure. We believe the choice of defining a map on a per user/role basis represents a particular policy choice and the TICKLE mechanism provides a more abstract, policy-free mechanism than the ATIS Method Map. In TICKLE, each role would have an associated composite tool which defined the operations and mappings to implementations for that role.

The mapping information is therefore a *static description* of the connection between operations and implementations for a particular scope. It defines a composition of tools and links invocation and event generations in some tools to others that act as their implementations. A composite tool's description is an object in the object base and can be examined and manipulated through a set of operations.

5.2 The mapping information in a composite.

There are several sorts of information represented or referenced in a composite. They include:

1. the implementations that are components of the composite;

2. the object types and associated operations for all of the operation invocations and event generations that any of the component implementations can generate;

3. the map from object types and operation identifiers to identifications of implementation entry points;

4. the definition of event classes (patterns of event occurrences) and their associations with implementation entry points that will process the events;

5. parameter mapping information. Since there may be differences between the calling format of the operation invocation and the calling format of the entry point of an implementation, each particular association in the map may also indicate parameter transformations;

6. for each entry point and implementation, an indication of the circumstances under which a new instance of the tool (a new tool process) will be started to respond to an operation invocation or event generation.

Operations provided on the objects that represent composite tools include import of type definitions; identification of the implementations; association of operation identifiers and implementation identifiers; definition of parameter mappings; and definition of event classes (for defined event types).

In SoftBench [CAGA90], there is an initialization file that captures which tools react to which messages. This is a simple forerunner of this sort of mapping information.

6 Execution Model.

Providing support in a SEE for the descriptions of the static structures described in the preceding sections is relatively easy. There are many object management systems that have been proposed for SEEs that are capable of managing these static descriptions.

The real test of the relationship between the concepts of the model and those of the underlying system on which it is implemented is in the description of the execution model. This is where we realize the importance of a well-defined relationship between the concepts and services of TICKLE and those of the base systems on which it runs. This is where we need to identify how the TICKLE services add value in a *compatible* way to Unix and PCTE.

It is important in this discussion to distinguish between the *statically* defined members of a composite (the implementations described in the preceding sections), and the *dynamic* members of an executing composite - the processes that correspond to instances of execution of the tools that are the static components of the composite. A static component may be instantiated in several dynamic components at composite execution time.

6.1 The representation of an executing composite.

In TICKLE, an executing composite is represented as a process (that is additional to any dynamic components of the composite). This process manages the mapping information described in section 5 and the information on the dynamic components of the composite. We call this process a Dynamic Context Manager (DCM).

The characterization of an executing composite as a process provides a convenient hook to define several execution time characteristics of the composite. Initiating a composite involves initiating the DCM process and this will have all of the characteristics of processes in the base system on which this runs, either PCTE or Unix. The dynamic components of a composite may inherit certain characteristics from the DCM process of the composite tool in which they are started; they may also adopt certain other characteristics when they begin execution; and they may also change some of these during execution.

Note that this model says that the dynamic components of a composite derive some of their characteristics from the DCM process, not from the process that invokes the operation (or generates the event) that results in the initiation of the dynamic component. We discuss this point further in the conclusion of this paper as it has repercussions on some of the transaction semantics of operation invocation and event monitoring.

6.2 Operation invocation and event generation.

It is important to recall that an operation invocation in TICKLE is not the same as a remote procedure call, although, as far as the process invoking the operation is concerned, the semantics are very similar. The intervention of the DCM to manage the mapping allows the monitoring of events, including operation invocations within the composite.

When an operation invocation (or event generation) is written in the source code of a tool, it appears in the text as a character string reference to the name of the operation, the parameter names, etc.

At execution time, as the tool is executing as a dynamic component of a composite, this name is interpreted using the working schema of the executing tool to yield an identifier for the operation (event). This interpretation is independent of the composite to which the tool belongs and is solely determined by its working schema.

The operation identifier, and certain other information contained in the operation invocation (or event generation) are then used with the mapping information of the composite in which the invocation (generation) is being made. They identify an entry point of an implementation, a static component of the composite.

There may be a dynamic component (process) of the composite corresponding to the static component that can service the request and if this is so, the invocation (generation) information is passed to the appropriate entry point of that process. Each dynamic component is characterized by an expression that indicates the classes of events and operation invocations to which it may respond. If there is no current dynamic component that can respond, a new one is initiated.

6.3 Events and monitoring.

Monitoring of invocations and event generations is also supported. Within a composite, a static component may have associated patterns that describe *event classes*. Whenever an event (which may include operation invocation) described by an event class occurs, one or more entry points of implementations associated with the event class are identified.

These entry points can then be called using the method for identification of suitable dynamic components that has been already described.

This mechanism allows a single event to be received by many tools. TICKLE allows the list of receiving tools to be managed outside and independently of the tool which invokes the operation or generates the event. The same is true for tools that implement operations, they need not know about the characteristics of the tools that request services from them. TICKLE therefore allows flexible extension of a composite without perturbation of the existing components.

This is different from most rpc mechanisms that support a point-to-point semantics for communication between a caller and the called program.

7 Discussion.

TICKLE provides a tool inter-communication and composition mechanism. It supports the composition of implementations (tools) with other implementations, with the result of the composition being another implementation. It uses descriptions in and of the environment to support the composition and these descriptions are organized using the object-oriented paradigm.

Other efforts have adopted similar approaches. Mahler and Lampen [MAHL90] have also adopted the approach of describing the data of interest in an environment using object-oriented techniques. In their STONE system, the binding of a message received from the user interface component to the unchanged Unix tools that correspond to the associated method is performed by a modified shell that has access to the equivalent of TICKLE's schema and mapping information.

In [NANA90], the intention was to support the construction of a flexible object-oriented superstructure encapsulating elementary tools and making it possible to dynamically build new tools. Their system has a Tool Manager that corresponds in many ways to TICKLE's DCM.

In both of these systems, there is an emphasis on the composition of elementary tools, that is, existing Unix tools that do not use the message passing system that is used to invoke the tools.

There is little discussion of the support for tools that do use message passing to inter-communicate, and little description of the results of a composition.

There are several aspects of TICKLE that are also found in Reality [BELZ90]. Reality's objectives are to support prototyping of distributed software systems. In Reality, a communication architecture defines how events generated by one design unit instance (dui) is received by other duis (each dui is simultaneously active). Within a dui, there may be processes whose invocation is determined by a pattern associated with the process.

Reality has two models for communication and invocation. Communication of events between duis is by connection of event ports between them (fan-out connections are also possible), rather then by a pattern describing whether a dui is interested in receiving the event. Dispatching of events (within a dui) to processes that will execute some body is handled by a different mechanism, pattern-directed invocation.

One of the closest approaches to the one presented here is $RPDE^3$ [HARR87]. The stated goal of $RPDE^3$ was " .. to support both the integration of tools constructed from many small fragments and the construction of tools that can be extended to process new types of data without source code changes. Pursuit of this goal led to us to use an object-oriented style to define interfaces among tool parts". Our investigations led us to a similar conclusion about the contribution of object-oriented technology. In fact, the $RPDE^3$ and TICKLE approaches are complementary. $RPDE^3$ is concerned with flexible construction and extension of a tool, which will often run as a single processs, (composition of fine-grain tool fragments), whereas TICKLE is concerned with the composition of coarse-grain tools, running in separate processes, into task-oriented composite tools.

The TICKLE approach to tool composition shows up some interesting problems in the specification of transaction services for SEE frameworks, and the semantics of operation invocations and events in a composite. Consider the case of an executing tool, a dynamic component, that starts a transaction and then invokes an operation that is actually performed by some other tool in the composite. This other tool may also use data management services. We need to support semantics for transactions that say (i) that the invoked tool's data management service accesses also form part of the transaction, and (ii) that they take place outside the invoking tool's transaction.

TICKLE provides comprehensive facilities for the description of data and operations within an environment. It also provides facilities for the description of the tools in the environment. Novel features of TICKLE include: the mapping from operations to implementations is separately defined and manipulated, giving a greater degree of flexibility to the designers of composite tools in the environment; the mapping is not global to the whole environment in TICKLE, it is scoped (scoping is important in large environments to allow local customization of composite tools, and isolation of the work of users from changes made elsewhere). The composite tool idea, which is closely tied to the idea of scope in TICKLE, also means that monitoring of events and the implementation of broadcast semantics becomes feasible in large-scale environments.

8 Acknowledgements.

Despite our sympathy with the advice of an anonymous reviewer, we have retained the use of object-oriented terminology in this paper.

Several people contributed to the conception of the TICKLE system. They include: Allan Cantos, Phil Debello, Jerry Duggan, Gary Fritz, Jussi Ketonen, Dave Leblang, Bryan Lockwood, Sam Sands, and David Yon.

Alan Snyder provided extremely valuable input as a reviewer.

9 References.

ATIS90 ANSI X3H4 Working Draft, Information Resource Dictionary System, ATIS, February 1990.

BELZ90 Belz F., Luckham D., "A New Approach to Prototyping Ada-based Hardware/Software Systems", in Proceedings of Tri-Ada 90, Baltimore, December 1990.

BOUD88 Boudier G., Gallo F., Minot R., Thomas I., "An Overview of PCTE and PCTE+", in Proceedings of the ACM Sigsoft/Sigplan Software Engineering Symposium on Practical Software Development Environments, Boston, November 1988, in ACM Sigsoft *Software Engineering Notes*, Vol. 13, No. 5, November 1988.

CAGA90 Cagan M., "The HP SoftBench Environment: An Architecture for a New Generation of Software Tools", Hewlett-Packard Journal, Vol. 41, No. 3, June 1990.

HARR87 Harrison W.H., "The $RPDE^3$ Environment - A Framework for Integrating Tool Fragments", IEEE Software, November 1987.

HARR89 Harrison W.H., Shilling J.J., Sweeney P., "Good News, Bad News: Experience Building a Software Development Environment Using the Object-Oriented Paradigm", in Proceedings of OOPSLA 89, New Orleans, October 1989.

MAHL90 Mahler A., Lampen A., "Integrating Configuration Management into a Generic Environment", in Proceedings of the Fourth ACM SIGSOFT Symposium on Software Development Environments, Irvine, December 1990, in ACM Sigsoft *Software Engineering Notes*, Vol. 15, No. 6, December 1990.

NANA90 Nanard M., Nanard J., Pingand P., "An object-oriented kernel for dynamical software integration", in Proceedings of the 1st International Conference on Systems Integration, Morristown, New Jersey, April, 1990, published by IEEE Computer Society.

PENE89 Penedo M.H., Personal Communication.

REIS90 Reiss S.P., "Interacting with the FIELD environment", Software - Practice and Experience, Vol. 20(S1), June 1990.

STEF86 Stefik M., Bobrow D.G., "Object-Oriented Programming: Themes and Variations", AI Magazine, Vol. 6, No. 4 (Winter), 1986.

THOM91 Thomas I., Nejmeh B., "Tool Integration in Software Engineering Environments.", Soft-Bench Technical Note SESD-91-11, Hewlett-Packard, June 1991, submitted for publication.

WASS90 Wasserman A.I., "Tool Integration in Software Engineering Environments", in "Software Engineering Environments: International Workshop on Environments", Long F. (ed), Springer-Verlag, Berlin 1990.

ZDON86 Zdonik S., "Maintaining Consistency in a Database with Changing Types", in Proceedings of the Object-Oriented Programming Workshop, June 1986, published in ACM SIGPLAN Notices, Vol. 21, No. 10, October 1986.

Integrated Project Support Environments, text generation and technical writing

Colin Tattersall
Computer Based Learning Unit
Leeds University
United Kingdom
colin@cbl.leeds.ac.uk

Abstract

The acceptance and usability of application software is enhanced by its supporting documents. This documentation is expensive to produce, requiring a thorough understanding of the capabilities of the software, an awareness of user needs and adequate consideration of the scope and aims of individual documents. Though much effort is expended in the documentation process, texts often fail to achieve the quality required by the user community. Manuals may not reflect the workings of an application accurately or may be out of step with particular versions of the software. By attempting to write documentation for large, heterogeneous groups of users, manuals may fail to support the tasks with which particular organisations are involved and the learning requirements of particular users. Though the different types of document—from exhaustive technical specifications to quick reference sheets—are targeted to achieve different goals, their production is often simply viewed as the provision of varying amounts of the same material. This paper argues that the quality of user manuals would be improved by exploiting text generation techniques in the technical writing process. Using models of the various aspects of software production within the generation process, a tight bond is made between software and documentation. This allows manuals to be tailored to particular working practices and learning differences. The reduction in document development time afforded by text generation relaxes the traditional restriction to a single set of documentation, so that a range of bespoke, accurate user manuals becomes available with each software system. Moreover, the approach may be used to produce manuals in a range of different languages without additional translation costs.

Keywords: technical writing, software engineering environments

1 Introduction

User documentation is an integral part of the total software package. However, manual production is often isolated from the software development process and performed by a team of technical writers divorced from the design and development environment. Haselkorn's [6] examination of likely future developments in technical writing notes the "increasing dissatisfaction with documentation created as an isolated, final stage of product development", and concludes that documentation considerations should be involved earlier in the development process. Thus, the prediction is that issues of usability and readability, traditionally viewed as the concern of technical writers, will feature during the software development process. Such an approach would help ease the problems of accuracy and completeness of user manuals. Dye [3] highlights the importance of these attributes, which depend upon a thorough understanding of the scope and workings of an application. Such information is difficult to capture outside the design and development process.

Though an integration of document development with software development would assist in addressing some of the problems of user manual production, many difficulties remain. Since no tie exists between software and documentation, maintaining manuals in the context of software upgrades and extensions becomes a complex activity. Tight control is needed to ensure a mirrored development of both application and manual.

The problems of managing complex documentation projects have long been apparent, and a number of attempts have been made to ease the burden of document production. Walker's account [19] of the Concordia system identifies many of the key issues and describes a system which attempts to support technical writers. The WE system [14] uses labelled graphs to assist in the structuring of documents. More recent work by Garg and Scacchi [4] on the use of hypertext techniques in document production shows continued interest in the development of technical writing support tools.

Though these systems have dramatically reduced the effort expended in development and maintenance of technical documentation, a tight bonding of software and manual is still lacking and the onus remains on the documentation team to accurately reflect the application.

These issues have many similarities with those found in the production of system documentation. Accuracy and completeness are of paramount importance, since the software engineers involved with system production must be provided with a clear picture of the state of development of an application. System documents are highly technical in nature since their content is aimed at supporting the software developer. Many software engineering research teams were quick to appreciate that such documents could be generated straightforwardly from the models which are central to advanced development environments (see, for example, [8]).

However, this approach is not suitable for the production of user manuals, since it relies on a simple reformatting of detailed technical descriptions. User documentation requires an interpretation of such models to meet the needs of the user community, producing an account which is more acceptable in terms of readability and usability. It is important to note the difficulty of addressing this level of user acceptability with only one set of documentation, since the needs of different user groups varies widely. In this respect, off-line documentation suffers from many of the deficiencies as its online counterpart[1]. Help

---

[1] Indeed, many software developers simply provide a machine-readable form of the user manual as an application's only online help facility.

systems research is clear on the need to provide different help for different users [11] and on the need to assist users in task accomplishment in addition to supporting learning [2]. What is required is the ability to provide cost-effective, bespoke, accurate and complete user documentation for particular organisations. In this way, a stock control system used by a brewery, and the same application used in a paper mill would be supported by different documentation reflecting the variations in working practices of the two user communities. This paper outlines the use of text generation techniques within advanced software engineering environments aimed at providing such a capability.

2 What does automatic generation offer?

Text generation systems revolve around the selection and organisation of information from an underlying domain representation to address particular discourse goals. These goals may be requests for instructions, justifications of courses of action or explanations of problem diagnoses. The texts are guaranteed to accurately reflect this underlying model, and a complete account of the capabilities and functioning of an application may be produced by iterating through the various discourse goals which may be input to the generator (eg all questions forms). The capacity to address these issues automatically has many advantages over current approaches, such as the use of hypertext or structured editing techniques, where considerable effort is required to create the necessary frames of text.

In the generative approach, any changes to the underlying model are immediately reflected in the associated texts. Thus, since generation is automatic, both initial document production and subsequent maintenance costs are reduced. Furthermore, by setting different discourse goals to the system, different documents can be generated. *"How to do it"* guides can be produced which relate the actions users must undertake to accomplish tasks. Command reference sheets may be generated to describe the arguments and syntax of each application command. Mixes of task-based and explanatory information can be used to reveal the workings of an application within manual entries. The underlying representation can be changed to model different views of a given domain, with these variations being accommodated in the texts generated from the model.

The level of flexibility offered by the generative approach goes beyond what can be produced with hypertext systems, while sharing the ability to present information both on and offline. Indeed, an online version of an automatically generated manual offers further prospects for tailoring and adaptation in a similar vein to that found in Intelligent Help Systems research [17]. Possibilities are raised for comparing unknown information with previously used concepts, guiding the introduction of new facilities and expanding on misconceived topics, together with the ability to dynamically restructure a manual to reflect the user's task context. The central point is that only the generative approach is able to offer a cost-effective method of providing the level of tailoring required in technical documentation.

3 How do the techniques integrate with advanced software engineering environments?

The domain representations which underlie text generation systems are expensive to create. Moreover, these models are often built solely for use in generation, and liberties are taken in representing the world in order to facilitate the generation process. Thus, the accuracy and completeness required of user manuals cannot be taken for granted in the traditional knowledge representation context. However, the attraction of the Information Processing world as a setting for text generation techniques revolves around the increasing use of models and modelling techniques within the software development process. As Haine [5] notes "models have become the very stuff of systems analysis", and a number of commentators are highlighting the need for deeper models of software (eg [13]), anticipating an increase in the use of knowledge representation techniques within advanced software engineering environments. The Integrated Project Support Environments (IPSEs), Integrated Software Development Environments (ISDEs) and Software Factories which spearhead European research in software engineering all exploit formal models of software design and development.

The relationship between a software model and the Information Processing world is interesting from an AI perspective since the world (the application) is derived from a representation (the model), thus ensuring accuracy and completeness[2]. The move towards total coverage of the software life-cycle in IPSEs means that, in terms of the model, nothing is left unsaid, thereby guaranteeing what McKeown and Swartout [9] term "generational adequacy". The unique feature of the information processing domain is that it offers complete and consistent models as a side-effect of the software development process.

The structure of software models in terms of concepts and relations need not be dictated by the requirements of the text generation component, since object-oriented techniques can be employed to specialise the process for particular representations (see [18]), allowing a range of information sources to be exploited in the generation of texts. Thus,

---

[2]How well this application matches the world of office practices is a separate issue which the systems analyst must address.

the debate as to whether a single formalism can adequately represent the many aspects of a software project is not a determining factor in the application of these techniques within technical writing.

4 How are technical documents generated automatically?

Initial exploration of these ideas revolves around the PORSCHE (Producer Of Rhetorically StruCtured HElp) system, a prototype question-answering component based on work carried out in ESPRIT project EUROHELP.[3] Although originally designed as an on-line help facility, PORSCHE has a "batch-mode" which allows all questions to be put to the system in order to generate exhaustive sets of documentation.

The underlying representation used by PORSCHE during answer generation is the Application Model (AM) formalism [16] evolved during EUROHELP and designed to model, generically, a range of application software. Though the representation is not (currently) used in the design process, many of the issues it addresses also feature in modelling for software engineering environments. Indeed, the formalism has similarities with the Unified Model developed in the ESPRIT AMADEUS project [1] from ten of the most popular software development methods.

The AM captures three primary sources of information:

The User Task Space: representing the users, the objects they manipulate, and the tasks which can be undertaken using the application.

---

[3]EUROHELP was an ESPRIT project (number 280), 50% funded by the European Commission.

A Dialogue Model (or Interaction Space): representing how the user is to accomplish these tasks in terms of, for example, the commands which are used.

The System Space: representing how the system functionality supports the execution of the defined user tasks.

Thus, it is primarily concerned with "lower CASE" issues, though the formalism has been extended to support a requirements capture methodology [15]. The model shares features with other software development methodologies, such as a hierarchical decomposition of tasks, which is related to the goal oriented decomposition of the ESPRIT PIMS project [12]. This is illustrated in Figure 1, below:

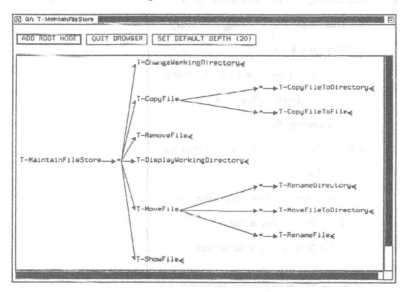

Figure 1: Browsing a hierarchical task decomposition

The figure shows part of the Task Space for the Unix shell, modelling a subset of the file system maintenance functionality. Beyond their value in the software development process, such hierarchies are ideally structured for use in technical writing. Smith et al. [14] note that "organizing expository information into a hierarchical structure and then signalling that structure is a particularly effective strategy for writers to follow". Horton [7] emphasises the need to "mirror the organization of the subject" within documentation, and the hierarchical organisation of tasks can be reflected in a hierarchical sectioning of user manuals. In this way, the above decomposition could be used to give the following table of contents:

1 Maintaining the file structure

  1.1 Changing the working directory

  1.2 Copying files

    1.2.1 Copying files to a directory

    1.2.2 Copying a file to a file

  1.3 Removing files

  1.4 Displaying the working directory

  1.5 Moving files

    1.5.1 Moving files to a directory

    1.5.2 Renaming a file

    1.5.3 Renaming a directory

  1.6 Showing files

For each task, the goal of "how to do it" can be put to the generation system to produce a response. This text is generated by querying the underlying model and organising the resulting content to form an internal representation of an answer. This data structure is then associated with lexical information to produce the final response. Thus, the manual section under heading **1.1 Changing the working directory** would be:

1.1 Changing the working directory

  To change the working directory in Unix, use:

  cd unix-directory-specification

The corresponding section in the Mail manual would be:

2.3.2 Changing the working directory

  To change the working directory in Mail, use:

  cd directory-specification
or
  chdir directory-specification

This text generation is performed by mapping linguistic structures onto the domain model. Associated with each generation goal (Inform, Instruct, Evaluate, ...) is a series of generic discourse relationships, or *rhetorical predicates*. These predicates capture the general types of information to be expressed in an answer (Membership, Attribution, InstrumentAchievement, ...) and are mapped onto specific relationships in the domain model during the generation process. The above responses were generated from the underlying Application Model structure shown in Figure 2, below:

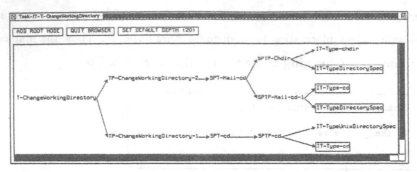

Figure 2: The AM structure capturing *change directory* functionality

Since the model formalism captures information in three spaces, it is possible to change one space without modifying the others. Thus, upgrading an application with a menu-based front-end modifies only the Interaction Space. The user manuals may then be regenerated to reflect these changes. In this way, different task spaces may be used with an application to capture different working practices, and the appropriate documents reproduced automatically. This leads to the user manual tailoring referred to earlier, and offers clear benefits over the traditional documentation production process. Rather than using a team of technical writers to reproduce the documentation, automatic regeneration could be performed, thereby lowering the cost of manual production and allowing software producers to provide customised documentation.

This can be illustrated with the following example. An invoicing system used by a brewery is modelled in Figure 3 below:

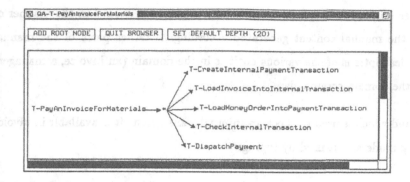

Figure 3: A task space decomposition for an invoicing system

This functionality could be realised in a number of ways in the system and interaction levels, perhaps using an email system. Supplying the same software to a paper mill operating different working practices would be supported with a different task level. If the company requires all payments to be authorised by a manager, the task space might be:

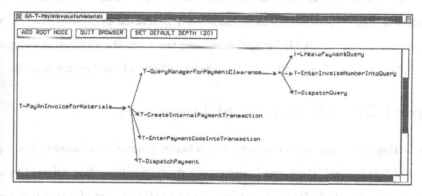

Figure 4: Tailoring the task space

Bespoke user documentation for each company would be sectioned in the manner of Figure 4, and the manual content generated accordingly. Other parts of the manual would provide descriptions of the various entities in the domain (an invoice, a manager) and details of the domain commands:

~p is a command which is used to check an internal transaction. It is available in invoice processing mode and is used by typing:

$$\tilde{p}$$

In addition to the straight translation of domain content shown above, automatic generation allows a variety of factors to influence the content of a text. Instructions and descriptions can be mixed to generate longer texts from the representation. Manual entries may expand upon concepts within a text or highlight the similarities and differences between domain concepts. By maintaining a model of what has already been included in the manual, answers may refer to information previously related using a comparison.

The text show in figure 5, overleaf, was automatically generated by PORSCHE. Since two alternative methods are available for accomplishing the task, the generation component supplies further information capturing the differing effects of the two commands.

5   Support for other natural languages

The previous section noted the explicit separation between generation of answer content and translation of this content into natural language, a decomposition often referred to as *what to say vs. how to say it*. As far as is possible, the semantic content of a text is determined prior to consideration of syntactic issues, allowing the possibility of generation in

---

9.2 Loading an invoice into an internal transaction

To load an invoice into an internal transaction in
invoice processing mode, use:

~f <*invoice-number*>

or

~m <*invoice-number*>

~f and ~m are similar. Both are available in
invoice processing mode, both take an invoice
number as argument, and both have the effect of
loading an invoice into the working transaction.
However, ~m also has the effect of indenting the
invoice.

An invoice number refers to an invoice.

Figure 5: Generation of longer manual entries

different languages. This capacity makes automatic generation of documentation particularly attractive in the European context, and is dependent upon knowledge of word order
and lexical information. To illustrate the possibilities, the answer structure generated in
response to a request for a description of the Unix mail delete command is shown below:

((INSTRUMENTACHIEVEMENT

(HASPLAN (IT-TypeDelete IT-TypeMailSpecification)))))

As yet, no tie exists between this content and the final English text—this translation is
achieved using phrasal forms such as the following:

subject	task phrase	infinitive
verb	*to use*	imperative
object	interaction sequence	singular

The subject is a verb phrase associated with the task and its arguments (*"to delete messages"*) and the object is the interaction sequence required to achieve the task. Thus, the following phrase can be produced:

To delete messages, use: *delete* <mail-specification>

Similar phrasal forms and vocabulary can be used to give:

Pour effacer des messages, tapez: *delete* <description du message>

PORSCHE is capable of generating responses to requests for instructions in both English and French, and this capability is being extended to cover further types of text and other European languages.

6 Supporting both on and offline document production

One of the future directions for the research involves an examination of the relationship between static (offline) and dynamic (online) versions of the same document. Though traditionally viewed as identical documents (both in terms of content and structure) delivered on different media, generating both types of manual relaxes this restriction, allowing the flexibility of online information to be exploited. An online manual integrated with a software system opens up many possibilities for increasing user support. Error messages from an application could be used to "turn the pages" of the online manual to the appropriate section. If information about the user's ongoing task were available, this could be used in a similar manner, allowing the manual to track the user's progress.

Online documentation could be dynamically restructured to accommodate differences in knowledge. In this way, information with which the user is familiar would appear earlier in the manual, allowing supportive comparisons to be made in the later material detailing new information.

The use of diagrams and screen snaps within offline documentation could be exploited online. By making snaps active and permitting interaction with the application under controlled conditions, the user could explore the consequences of particular actions. Tailored help would be available within these contexts to assist the user in formulating the correct model of system behaviour. Such a facility has similarities with the use of "insets" in the Andrew system [10], though the embedded application context would be generated from the underlying model.

Alternatively, screen snaps could be captured dynamically from the user's environment and animated to illustrate where menus should be clicked, what icons are used for and how mouse-based interaction is performed with a system. Though the issue of multimedia coordination is still in its infancy, the possibilities for enhancing the quality of online documentation are clear.

7   Conclusions

This paper examined the use of text generation techniques embedded within advanced software engineering environments and designed to assist in the production of user documentation. The work draws upon a number of research areas to challenge the status of user documentation as expensive to produce, inadequate with respect to user needs and inflexible in delivery mechanism.

Deriving user documentation automatically from the model used to produce an application ensures the accuracy of the resulting manual and avoids the cost of a separate knowledge representation phase to support generation. Moreover, the tight binding of software and documentation eases the problem of maintaining the accuracy of user manuals.

Using text generation techniques in document production allows a variety of factors to influence the process. Thus, different versions of the offline manual can be produced by varying aspects of the underlying model, such as task information. Likewise, online documentation can be tailored using information supplied dynamically by the application, such as error messages, or information from other sources, such as the user.

In this way, documentation can be provided which is accurate, complete, tailored to the application user and cheap to produce.

Acknowledgements

The expertise and comments of A.J. Cole and J.R. Hartley of the Computer Based Learning Unit and Mick Smith of ICL Strategic Systems Services were invaluable to this work.

References

[1] W.J. Black, A.G. Sutcliffe, P. Loucopoulos, and P.J Layzell. Translation between pragmatic software development methods. In *Proceedings of ESEC '87—the first European Software Engineering Conference*. Springer-Verlag, 1987.

[2] J.M. Carroll and J. McKendree. Interface design issues for advice-giving expert systems. *Communications of the ACM*, 30(1):14–31, 1987.

[3] K.L. Dye. When is a document accurate and complete? In *Proceedings of the Pacific Rim Conference on Professional Technical Communication (IPCC 1988)*, pages 269–272. IEEE, 1988.

[4] P.K. Garg and W. Scacchi. A Hypertext System to Manage Software Life-Cycle Documents. *IEEE Software*, 7(3):90–98, May 1990.

[5] P. Haine. Selecting CASE Tools for business use. In R. Williams, editor, *Using CASE Tools in Systems Development*, pages 15–18. Gower Publishing Company, 1990.

[6] M.P. Haselkorn. The Future of "Writing" for the Computer Industry. In E. Barrett, editor, *Text, ConText, and HyperText*, pages 3–14. MIT Press, 1988.

[7] W.K. Horton. *Designing and Writing Online Documentation*. Wiley, 1990.

[8] S. McGowan. IPSEs—a Tool Writer's Point of View. In K.H. Bennett, editor, *Software Engineering Environments*, pages 299–306. Ellis Horwood, 1989.

[9] K.R. McKeown and W.R. Swartout. State of the art: Language generation and explanation. In M. Zock and G. Sabah, editors, *Advances in Natural Language Generation*, volume 1, pages 1–51. Ablex Publishing, 1988.

[10] J.H. Morris, M. Satyanarayanan, M.H. Conner, J.H. Howard, D.S. Rosenthal, and F.D. Smith. Andrew: A distributed personal computing environment. *Communications of the ACM*, 29(3):184–201, March 1986.

[11] C.L. Paris. Tailoring object descriptions to a user's level of expertise. *Computational Linguistics*, 14(3):64–78, September 1988.

[12] J. Paris. Goal Oriented Decomposition—Its Application for Process Modelling in the PIMS Project. In F. Long, editor, *Software Engineering Environments: International Workshop on Environments*, pages 69–78. Springer-Verlag, 1990.

[13] C. Rich and R.C. Waters. *The Programmer's Apprentice*. Addison Wesley, 1990.

[14] J.B. Smith, S.F. Weiss, G.J. Ferguson, J.D. Bolter, M. Lansman, and D.V. Beard. WE: A writing environment for professionals. In *AFIPS Conference Proceedings Volume 56: 1987 National Computer Conference*, pages 725–736. AFIPS Press, 1987.

[15] M. J. Smith, M. W. Reeder, A. T. F. Hutt, and R. V. Evans. The process, task and object modelling workbench—functional requirements specification. Technical Report HCI/SAM/351, ICL, Strategic Systems Services, 1990.

[16] M.J. Smith, M.W. Reeder, C. Duursma, C. Tattersall, A.J. Cole, F. Ravn, and B. Koza. Application model definition. Technical Report ICL-ULE/EUROHELP/041, ICL, Knowledge Engineering Business Centre, Manchester, July, 1989.

[17] C. Tattersall. Exploiting text generation techniques in the provision of help. In *Proceedings of the Seventh Conference on Applications of Artificial Intelligence (CAIA-91)*. IEEE, 1991.

[18] C. Tattersall. Generating help for users of application software. *User Modeling and User Adapted Interaction*, 1991.

[19] J.H. Walker. Supporting Document Development with Concordia. *IEEE Computer*, 21(1):48–59, January 1988.

The Arcs Experience

Dick Schefström, Telesoft, Aurorum 6, 951 75 Luleå, Sweden.

**Reporting from a large innovation driven
software development project.**

Arcs is a programming environment. A child of the 80's booming interest for software
tools, "environments", and computer aided software engineering. Like any child, it went
through a continuous evolution and growth, learning by experience, mistakes, and observing the surrounding world. Now, however, is the time to go out into real life. She is ready,
and is entering the market as a software product.

This paper describes Arcs 2.0: its current shape and the lessons learned on how to design
and architect such a system. Some of those experiences will then be generalized into a
model of software environments, together with some predictions on the future in the area of
which Arcs has been a member. And finally, we will discuss the road there, which was full
of less technical issues, but which anyway were most important in practice.

1.0   The Arcs vision.

Over time, the goal of the project was expressed in different ways, emphasizing different
aspects like the benefits of integration and the need for bringing overview and configuration management down to the work of individual programmers. With some perspective,
however, the probably most persistent underlying theme was a strive for supporting the
understanding of large and complex software systems. The finding of a remedy for the frus-
tration we feel when being confronted with a large piece of software that we want to modify, extend, or otherwise evolve, but cannot since we do not understand its structure and the
possible effects of a change.

This process is probably very typical, since most development is not of the kind that we
create something from scratch. Rather, software development is usually a question of
extending systems, or building new systems in close connection to existing ones. The classical observation that 70-80 percent of a systems life-cycle cost is in "maintenance"
directly supports this view, (Corbi 1989, Chikoffsky & Cross 1990, Parikh & Zvegintsov
1983).

So, the most urgent problem to solve should be that of helping a user to quickly understand,
and with confidence and success, modify a large software system.

In other areas, the concept of *Hypertext*, (CACM 1988), has been used to support the learning and exploration of information using computers. Put simply, hypertext can be summarized in two points:

- Structure the information as a *network of nodes*. Let *nodes* represent pieces of information, and let the *links* represent references between them.

- Use all available computing devices and user interface technology to provide efficient means for browsing back and forth in such information networks.

An important part of Arcs is therefore the *Software Hypertext Engine*, which applies this idea to software. Navigation in, and overview of, the software is the key thing.

However, Hypertext systems are almost always very static. The information is not changing once it has been made a Hypertext network. *Change* is however one of the most characteristic attributes of software, and can not be avoided. Rather, change is the sign of life. The problem is that change disturbs the *order* that is needed before any system can be investigated and understood. Therefore, a number of services had to be introduced with the purpose of making the original vision possible. This second part could therefore be called the *Disorder Combat Engine*, since its purpose is that of ensuring that change, and the thereby generated partial chaos, can be kept under control.

All the different services of Arcs can now be associated with one of those two engines:

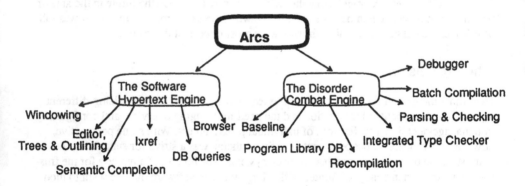

The rest of this chapter describes the role and contents of the services indicated in an abstract and compact way. Further sections will go into details with how they were implemented in Arcs.

1.1 The Software Hypertext Engine

The Interactive Cross Referencer, *IXRef*, views software as a network of implicit hypertext links, between the declaration of an entity and every place where it is used.

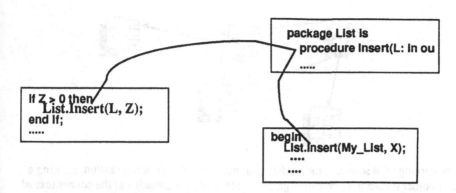

IXRef provides the ability to explore those links, and is therefore at the very heart of the vision.

The *Semantic Completion* service can be viewed as a direct extension of IXRef. Whenever the user types a prefix of a package or procedure, it could be viewed as there already exist hypertext links to all the entities that match the prefix typed this far.

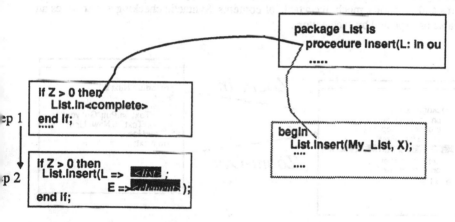

Consequently, Arcs can present, fill in, or navigate to any of the potential completion alternatives.

The *Browser* is an unavoidable component of the Software Hypertext vision. Graphical expression of hypertext nodes and links is so natural that we use it without even thinking about it.

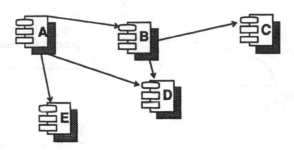

When working with software, the *module* is a most natural unit of iconization, creating a natural border between the browsers graphic presentation approach and the editors textual format. As will be developed later, not too much imagination is needed for seeing the potential of evolving the browser into traditional Design tool territory. The advantage of guaranteed correct graphical presentation relative to underlying, real, software is invaluable.

To navigate within a software hypertext node, and for presenting and changing its contents, there is a *Software Sensitive Editor*. This editor takes on at the level below the browser, presenting the inner structure of the modules. It does so by initially showing available procedures and functions, much like a table of contents. Syntactic checking and services are available as expected by such editors.

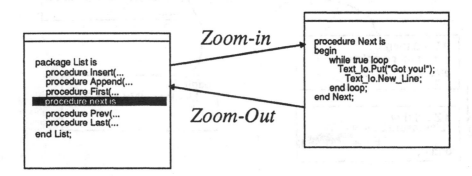

The Arcs Editor is however also the framework for many semantic services, like IXRef and semantic completion, and is also used for all other textual information presentation and manipulation.

The *Database Queries* is another natural part of the software hypertext engine. They allow the user to express complex and set oriented queries over the network that is made up of the modules and their access paths.

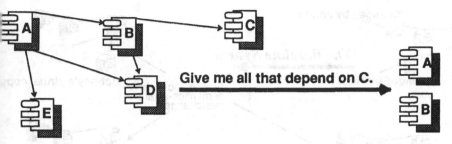

Many services in Arcs, like dependency analysis and recompilation checks are just special cases of queriesin this language.

.2 The Disorder Combat Engine

The most typical example of disorder occurring when developing software is the ripple effects introduced in other modules when changing one of them. Suddenly then, we do not feel confident in whether the modules still fit together. The remedy is usually called "recompilation", a word which however in this context usually refers to a desire to reestablish the order and confidence that was before a change. *Recompilation*, or *"rechecking"*, is therefore the most basic role of the disorder combat engine.

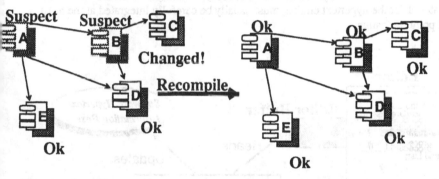

The situation is in practice even more complex. Not only do different parts of the software system affect each other when being changed, but it also takes place in parallel by different people. In Arcs, the component addressing this problem is called the *Baseline System*, and its role is to provide a systematic way of allowing a set of programmers to modify a common baseline of software, and help to administrate the resulting continuous reintegration of change.

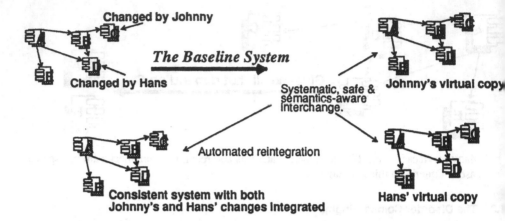

The baseline system combats the disorder that is generated by the multitude of people, modules, and versions.

The *Integrated Type Checker* is the basic component to fight disorder at the detailed level. Here, things must be fast, since for the software hypertext engine to work, the program edited by the user must be in some reasonably semantically correct state. To achieve the quite extreme performance required in this case, the type checker, which also builds the basic material for the hypertext engine, must usually be carefully integrated at the most detailed point of change.

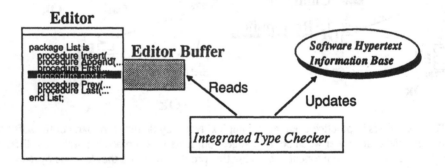

Therefore, the type checker is working incrementally in close cooperation with the editor.

The information base of the software hypertext engine must be stored in a way that allows for efficient access, multiple views, multiple versions, and concurrent multiperson access and change. This is a tremendous challenge for any database. The *Program Library Database* of Arcs provides the basic mechanisms needed for solving those problems, and is an example of applying the ideas of the "environment database" that was so thoroughly researched during the last decade.

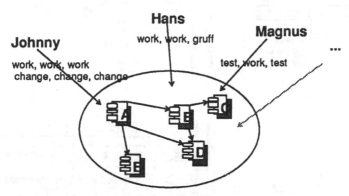

The Program Library Database

Visions must be abstract and compact, acting as generators of ideas while still directing development so that the result is kept homogeneous. The above concepts worked well in that respect.

2.0 Implementing the Vision - an Overview

This vision was finally implemented, and is now facing the market as a software product. Some key characteristics from the implementation effort are the following:

- Arcs was mostly implemented in Ada, made for supporting Ada, and was used for its own development over a long period of time. This turned out to be an essential source for validation of concept, usefulness, and new requirements.

- The user interface was built on X windows and the Motif toolkit, using the TeleUSE user interface management system, (Telesoft 1991). Early efforts with Arcs showed that a system of such an ambition level very easily can turn into a complexity close to being unfriendly to the user. An extensive effort was therefore invested, utilizing both the latest technology and careful UI design, to ensure an easy to use system.

- It was a rather large effort, involving between ten and fifteen people for a number of years. The total amount of software written was in the order of several hundred thousand lines of mostly Ada. This context further helped us validating the scalability of the approach, which otherwise often passes without serious test. Using the system ourselves in this non-trivial problem size context, made us more confident in being able to keep Arcs value while facing the size of application projects.

The result is a very extensive system, embedding a richness in functionality and concept that requires a major document to report. This paper can only give a flavour, of which the Arcs session screendump below is an example:

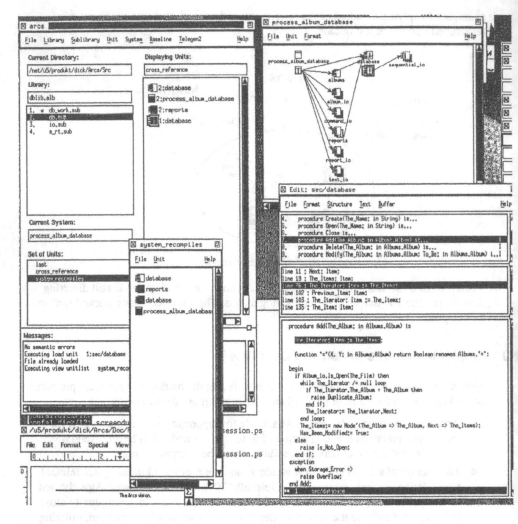

To the upper left we see the *Main Window*, from which the different subsystems can be reached. The main window also acts as the initial basic interface to the program library database. The subwindow labeled "Library" shows the first level of this database, the different segments, ("db_work, db, io, s_rt" in the example above), which together make up the users complete database. Those segments also act as the basis for the version management scheme.

The database may then be further explored using the *Browser*, several instances of which are shown on the screen. At this level, compilation units are represented as graphical icons of different shape and colour depending on their type and state.

The library database supports a rather general query mechanism, the results of which are reported in terms of lists of units, stored in a working area labeled "Set of Units" in the figure above. The user may then further manipulate those lists by pointing at its name and selecting the appropriate command from a menu.

Many commands in Arcs are reporting their result in terms of such lists, and in the figure above we can see two such examples:

- *cross_reference*, which is a list that is generated when the user asks for all usages of a given entity. Arcs then responds by computing the list of units where this entity is actually used. If a unit of this list is then loaded into the editor, (by double clicking on its unit icon), a list is shown representing every place in the unit where the given entity is used. Clicking at any of those lines representing the found usages causes the editing window to show the corresponding part of the program.

  This is exemplified in the editor window to the lower right in the screendump above.

- *system_recompiles*, which is a list containing all units that are currently "not trusted" in the sense that their contexts have changed since the last time those modules were checked for consistency with respect to this context. Traditionally, this corresponds to "recompilation", sometimes using tools like "make" for doing the work. In Arcs, however, this list is just there, like the air in the room, at every moment reflecting the true state of the system. The units are of course listed in correct order of recompilation, so that the user can just point at the list and select the "compile" command to get a consistent system.

Several other lists are generated as the result of different events and actions taken. The general principle of using the lists as a flexible means for communicating both between tools and between tools and the user, should however be clear.

The Browser view, shown in the upper right part of the screendump, shows the interconnection patterns between the modules of the program. In the figure, some units are marked with an exclamation mark, which means that they must be recompiled. This does, of course, directly correspond to the units that are in the *system_recompiles* list.

In general, visualizing module interconnection structures is a very frustrating task, since there is a tendency that the complete network includes so many connections and modules that the information contents is lost. In addition, it is difficult to automatically find a layout that fulfills the goal of efficiently communicating much and relevant information to the user. Available algorithms are often made for minimizing connection crossings, which however turns out to be a different thing than what we are looking for here.

The simple solution in Arcs is to let the user take control, allowing him to specify which units should be shown at the screen, and where to place them. This is done by providing commands to show or hide using or used units for any given unit. In addition, the user can move around the icons to get a convenient layout.

Much more could be said about functionality in Arcs, such as the...

- The *semantic completion*, which turns out to be the most convenient support for helping users to quickly know which procedures are available and what are a their parameter profiles.

- The *structure orientation* of the editor, which provides for overview of large documents or packages.

- The different presentation modes and features of the *browser*, which is felt like the maybe most rewarding area to further develop. Removing any technical obstacles which today unnecessarily separate design from programming is a challenging next step.

- The role of the *query language*, which although not for the beginner user was surprisingly much used by advanced users.

- The *user interface uniformity* achieved by generating all command boxes out of an abstract command definition, thereby making completions, matchings, wildcarding, and other UI aspects completely uniform. A similar unification can be seen in the editor where all sorts of.lists, be it cross reference hits, completion alternatives, compilation errors, buffers, sections of the module edited, etc, are presented and manipulated in the same way.

- The *reference-robustness* of the editor, which makes references to positions in the source, like cross reference hits and compilation errors, still be correct while the user changes the same source.

- The central role of the *baseline system*, which acts as the overall project pump, establishing new fresh baselines out of the contributions of a dozen developers at ever higher pace. The resulting automation of reporting of change, and administration of versions, was usually claimed to be one of the most important contributions of Arcs.

- The rather sophisticated *help-system*, which avoids burdening the user with tiring pages of manuals, but instead provides short and context sensitive help hints at a fine granularity. Whenever a field is to be filled in or a set of options may be selected, the user may point at the corresponding place and push a button to get information on exactly this aspect.

- The extremely fast *type-checker*, which provides instant semantic check and update of internal forms. The nice performance characteristics were however in this case as much achieved by means of smart integration technology as by means of incremental approaches.

- The generality of use, with no limitations imposed on the number of instances of browsers and editors available at the same time.

But we will not discuss those points. Instead we will further develop two other points of development environments, and how they were addressed in Arcs, namely

- the importance of immediate state change reflection and the synchronization of views
- the need for a certain level of openness.

2.1 Synchronization of views

In a rich development environment like Arcs, which furthermore emphasizes software presentation and understanding, there is a tendency that several different representations of the same items are present at the same time. The most obvious example is the editor and the browser: they often show the same software, (however at different levels of abstraction), and when changing this software in one place, all other places showing it must be updated. When the user changes a with clause, importing another unit, this must be shown immediately at the graphical level.

This property is especially important for the browser, since it means that the graphical view presented is always guaranteed to reflect the actual source. The user can rely on that it shows the "truth", and is thereby relieved of the tedious maintenance of at least certain kinds of design diagrams. The truly seamless integration of design with programming is the challenging long term goal. To achieve this, one must view "design" and "programming" as different views of the same underlying representation, (Schefström 1989b, Schefström 1990).

This does however require much care in the design of the software to achieve the necessary performance characteristics, and the most important aspects can be summarized in two points:

- *Precision* in catching change.
- *Incremental* update of datastructures.

Although the actual update of the datastructures is an issue, the most serious problem seems to be that of systematically collecting the change events in a way that does not destroy the structure of the software. Different strategies have been proposed to design software for meeting those needs, such as database triggers and callback approaches like the "dependency chain" of Smalltalk. At the macro level, approaches like HP Softbench and its message broadcast server, (Cagan 1990), and the Telesoft Postmaster, (Gustavsson & Madsen 1990), have been implemented.

Within Arcs, a simple and very straightforward approach was instead used, where the basic primitives for doing changes were instrumented to call a central "notifier" package, which in turn embedded the knowledge on which subsystems to further notify. Although less general and simple, it works very well, was cheap to implement, and very efficient to execute.

One of the components called upon change is the "graph management" subsystem, which provides high level operations on the network of interconnected modules that makes up a program. It provides the basic information for browser views, recompilation, configuration management, and database query services. To get the necessary performance characteristics, this "graph" datastructure was made to be incrementally updated. However, as an initially unexpected side-effect, we then also got the automatically maintained recompilation lists mentioned previously, which in turn removed the need for a whole class of commands related to consistency checking. In this way, the implementation technique implied by performance needs had effects on the way the user interface turned out.

2.2 Openness

In recent years there has been a growing tendency to emphasize the importance of "openness". In fact, the concept has sometimes almost reached the status of buzzword. The Arcs development was of course also under continuous pressure to respond to this trend. The problem was however that it is seldom completely clear what is demanded for a system to be "open". Usually, it includes ingredients such as building on standards, the ability to work together with other systems, adaptability, and the availability of some of the internal interfaces for public use.

General broad interfaces to basic mechanisms are however quite costly to publish, since they expose much of the internal structure, (contrary to ideas of information hiding), and imply rather high maintenance costs. They must also be kept very stable, which introduces further limitations on the development team. It is furthermore a rather passive way of stimulating integration, saying "here are some interfaces: do something with them".

In Arcs, openness is instead addressed by providing "application specific protocols", where a concrete and precise *integration idea* is first developed, which is then manifest in the ability of Arcs to respond to a corresponding protocol. The approach is nicely illustrated in the way Arcs provides for foreign editors to be integrated without losing any of the specific services provided by the built in editor. The provision of this ability was especially important due to the sometimes almost religious user affection to a particular editor.

The principal architecture is as follows:

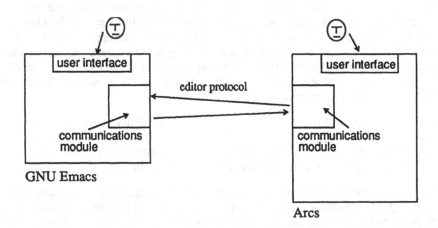

GNU Emacs

Arcs

Arcs and the foreign editor, here exemplified by GNU Emacs, are executing in different processes, and communicate using a socket. The *editor protocol* is a specification of what information must be passed between the systems to implement the services of interactive cross referencing, semantic completion, semantic check, compilation, etc. There is no static client-server relationship: sometimes Arcs acts as the client, such as when the user double clicks on a unit icon which causes the corresponding source to be loaded into the editor. In other situations Arcs acts as the server, such as when the editor asks for cross reference information or want to semantically check the source.

This solution worked surprisingly well, and was simple and straightforward to implement. Some of the conclusions or lessons learned were the following:

- Tools must be made to work with "split vision", being able to respond at any time both to user interface actions and to message requests.

- In terms of the client-server model, tools must be able to dynamically change their roles. Statically assigned roles as server or client therefore seem less relevant.

- High level protocols, close to the end user functionality, are much cheaper and more efficient to implement than broad and general interfaces. It seems to be a better approach to implement a new such protocol when the need arises than to maintain a broad lower level interface.

The last point may be especially rewarding to further develop, which was especially obvious from the work on integrating Emacs. This editor has an "extension language" which can be used by anyone to add new commands and functionality as equal right citizens. In our case, this extension language was used to very quickly implement the Emacs side of the editor protocol, which immediately leads the thoughts to the idea of instrumenting all tools with such extension languages. In this way one could view it as a "component interaction description language", providing for a very flexible user controlled integrability.

Finally, we propose the following definition of the concept of "openness" in the context of software tools:

> The *openness* of a tool or toolset is a measure of the cost for replacing any of its subsystems with a new, external, one, without losing the original functionality.

According to this definition, Arcs proved to be quite open. The editor example above worked in a man-month of implementation effort.

3.0 Generalizing the Architecture

In this chapter, we will generalize the experiences of the Arcs project and suggest a general model of software tools, finally arriving at a proposed architecture for software development environments.

3.1 A Model of Software Tools

The smallest entity of concern is called a *service*. The concept does not need to be further defined except that it should be an action performed by the computer that is of interest to a software developer. The services are partitioned into subsets that are called *tools*. Each tool should provide a well delimited set of services that are regarded as strongly related to each other while showing little overlap or dependency on other tools. The problem of designing tools is therefore similar to that of designing software modules in general, and we now arrive at the following definition:

A *Tool* is a set of services that show strong internal *cohesion* and low external *coupling*.

The concepts of cohesion and coupling are well known from the area of software design, (Yourdon & Constantine 1979). Informally, *cohesion* is a measure of the strength of the arguments on why certain entities should be grouped together, while *coupling* denotes the extent to which entities that we choose *not* to group together anyway depend on each other.

In the context of development environments, the word *integration* is often used instead of cohesion, while the requirement for low coupling is often talked about in terms of *pluggability*, *extensibility*, and *composability*.

Examples of tools are editors, formatters, graphics design tools, compilers, etc.

Just as related services are grouped into tools, certain sets of tools are more closely related than others. Examples include a compiler and its associated debugger; a project plan drawing tool and its critical path analyzer; a graphical design editor and its associated analyzer and code generator; a document editor, its spelling checker, and picture drawing subsystem, etc. Although being clearly identified as distinct tools according to the definition above, they are made to work closely together with certain other tools. We call this a *toolset*, and define it in a way similar to that of tools:

A *Toolset* is a set of tools that show strong internal *cohesion* and low external *coupling*.

The concept of an *environment* can now be explained in the same way:

An *Environment* is a set of toolsets that show strong internal *cohesion* and low external *coupling*.

There are fewer examples of environments than of tools and toolsets. The reason being that the task is bigger and therefore more costly.

As in every software system, it is always a good thing to factor out common routines into separate reusable modules. This idea of avoiding duplication of code has always been one of the most basic driving ideas behind any software design. Tools are no exception in this case, and we therefore need an element in our model that explicitly identifies such basic pieces of software that we expect to be of use to many different tools. We call this part the *framework*.

A *Framework* is set of software modules that is expected to be of interest to several tools, and is therefore especially well documented and supported.

Utilizing a framework has the same advantages as reuse of software in general: It is economic and imposes uniformity among its users.

The model can now be summarized graphically:

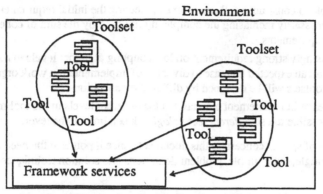

Levels of abstraction in development environments

So, we have a hierarchical view of software tools, consisting of *services, tools, toolsets,* and *environments*, where a latter entity is composed of a set of former ones. Parts of the tools are implemented by reusing services as provided by a *framework.*

3.1.1 The Integration Dilemma

The definitions above embed a potential contradiction: The requirement for low external coupling at one level, such as between *tools*, is at the next higher level contradicted by the requirement on strong internal cohesion, such as within a *toolset*. We call this problem the *Integration Dilemma*, since it reflects the eternal tension between the desire to make independent modules while meeting the need for close cooperation between the same modules. The word *integration* has even sometimes come to represent this problem, and the area of *integration techniques* is emerging as an independent subject where systematic solutions are sought.

Part of the solution to this dilemma is in observing that the concepts of coupling and cohesion are relative, having slightly different meaning depending on which level they are applied. The "strength" of the requirement on cohesion is usually higher at lower levels in the model, while the need for low coupling is increasing at higher levels:

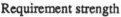

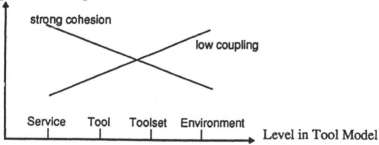

This observation can be used to draw a number of further conclusions:

- It is possible to construct a full *environment*, meeting the initial requirements above, without necessarily increasing the complexity imposed by the sum of cohesion and coupling requirements.
- The increasingly strong requirement on low coupling at higher levels in the model fits well with an expected increase in diversity of implementation work organization. Different toolsets will be designed by different organizations.
- The difference in requirement emphasis at the different levels in the tool model makes it possible to use *different technologies* depending on the level.

The last point is of special concern to this document, since it points at the need for identifying not only a single, but multiple, problem definitions and solution techniques in the area of integration.

3.1.2 Dimensions of Integration.

In recent years, it has gained increased acceptance to discuss the subject of integration in terms of three "dimensions" usually called *control, data,* and *user interface,* (Schefström 1989, Atmosphere 1990). Using a slightly modified version of (Schefström 1989), the definitions are as follows:

> The *control* integration aspect of a tool determines its communicational ability, i e the degree to which it communicates its findings and actions to other tools, and the degree to which it provides means for other tools to communicate with it. This includes the *temporal* aspect of immediate notification; the *selective* aspect of communication with a particular tool; and the *granularity* aspect of communicating changed circumstances with high precision.

> The *data* integration aspects of tools determines the degree to which data generated by one tool is made accessible and is understood by other tools.

> The *user interface* integration aspect is the degree to which different tools present a similar external look-and-feel, and behave in a similar way in similar situations.

The idea that those three aspects are independent dimensions of the same underlying concept of integration is sometimes emphasized by presenting them as a three dimensional diagram:

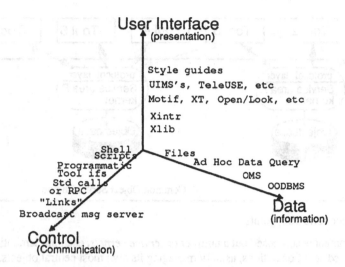

Projects and proposals in the area of development environments have often had different focus with respect to the dimensions above. Some of the large European efforts are good examples of this: while the Eureka Software Factory project has stressed aspects of the Control dimension with its emphasis on a Software Bus (Fernström & Ohlsson 1989), other joint European efforts, such as the PCTE/PACT and EAST projects, (Thomas 1989), have mostly worked in the data dimension. The "market" seems to take care of the UI dimensions by means the standardization around X-windows and associated toolkits like OSF/Motif and OpenLook.

However, in a well balanced environment all three dimensions must be explicitly cared for. In the following sections, we discuss techniques for addressing those dimensions at different levels in the tool model.

.2 A proposed environments architecture

The model and definitions above do not imply a single actual architecture. Rather, a number of different ones fit into the picture. In this section, we will present one such architecture, and select a few points to discuss further.

The following gives an overview of the involved components:

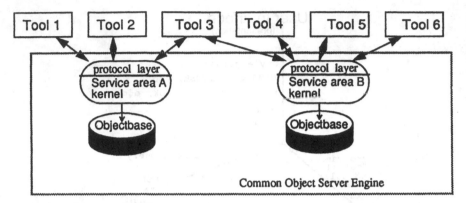

One could note the following points:

- The environment is composed out a number of *service kernels*, each implementing a closely related set of operations, usually managing its own most central objects.

- The service area kernels are utilized both by each other, but maybe more typically by a number of *tools*. The kernels may include finally packaged functionality, but are also communicating with the tools using *specialized tool protocols*.

- The kernels, and most often also the tools, are permanently activated. This avoids the otherwise quite inefficient and state destroying start-process-terminate cycle.

- Although there is not a single global database, there is a strong need for unifying the object access implicit in the tool protocols. The commonalities together make up the *common object server engine*.

The "kernels" in the architecture is a response to the practical need for parallel work with less coordinated developments. Functionality and tools should be brought tighter together only after that a strong "integration idea" has been developed. Before that, they are probably better evolved in isolation. Within a kernel, the traditional idea of database integration can be applied with success. Approximately, the "kernel' and the tools accessing it corresponds to the level of a toolset in the model of the previous section.

The Arcs experience showed that general and broad public tool interfaces often require high bandwidth, are complex to specify, expose more of the lower level services, and are harder to maintain. The problems are especially obvious when tools and the kernel are implemented in separate virtual spaces, in which case it seems even more of an advantage to use specialized high level protocols that are close to the end user functionality desired. The specialized nature does however generate a need for quickly and even user-implementable new protocols, leading to the need for providing both kernels and tools with an easy to access extension facility for doing this work.

It also seems clear that future environments and operating systems will have to leave the traditional start-process-terminate cycle, and instead invoke services by sending messages to already activated instances of components. In the Arcs experience, the repeated start-process-terminate has been one of the most serious reasons for efficiency losses and lack of interactiveness. The reason could be visualized by the following diagram:

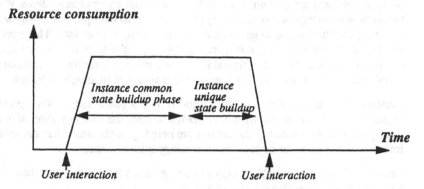

Many tools, such as the compiler used in Arcs, repeatedly perform the same operations and build up the same datastructures each time they are invoked. We call this phase the *instance common state buildup*. As an often smaller part of the work, the purely *instance unique* work is performed, followed by a throw away of the state at termination. In addition to repeatedly wasting the energy corresponding to the area of the first part of the diagram, the opportunities for user interaction are usually limited to before start and after termination.

Future environments can gain much from avoiding this cycle. When making the compiler that is used in Arcs work this way, the response time was in most cases improved by an order of magnitude.

The architecture above avoids imposing a single central database as the means for integration and unification. This is not due to that the idea of the central database can be shown to involve any principal flaws, but is rather a recognition of the fact that it has proven to be hard to implement it in practice. The central database has a tendency of becoming a development bottleneck and often experience continuous problems in reaching the extremely high quality and maturity that is required by such a central basic component.

Therefore, it seems more practical to accept a certain multitude of databases, although the final goal of a single homogeneous one remains. It also seems clear that the needs for unifying the way we access the now different databases will have to be addressed, causing a return of the global database concerns at the level of the tool protocols. Experience will show whether it is easier to deal with this time.

.0   The Road There

The Arcs project started in 1985. During this time, it passed through a large number of organizational contexts, a multitude of management policies, and a bunch of different roles spanning from being a research framework and testbed to that of an important strategic product. It took too long time, however, and in this chapter we will take a look at what obstructed and what helped.

The most important driving force behind innovation intensive development is usually the personal spirit and engagement of a usually rather small group of individuals. We call them the *technology intrapreneurs* since they often work in an entrepreneurial way within a larger organization, trying to get room for implementing a given idea. Those people are usually self-directed and motivated, and need little push or help in taking the necessary initiatives. This is usually where original ideas are born, which are then transformed and massaged into the necessary shape with respect to market and funding constraints.

Another role is usually played by the traditional *line organization*, which represents a slightly different culture usually more oriented towards the administration of mature routine operations. Predictability and control are here keywords rather than the sometimes intuitive and eager action style of the technology intrapreneurs.

Lots of resources and valuable energy can be lost in the friction between those forces. And yes, indeed, such was also the case with Arcs.

While the intrapreneurs want an integrated organization, with little barriers between subprojects, the line organization works in the other direction. The reason is that the former sees the challenge and benefit of the integrated whole, and has no problem of overviewing the project anyway, the latter feels that it is impossible to control unless split into independent parts that can be administrated separately.

While the line organization needs detailed and long plans to feel secure, the intrapreneurs are confident in their ability to navigate through the landscape based on rather abstract and principal plans. With its view on man-hours and headcounts as interchangeable and equivalent units, the line organization contrasts to the intrapreneurs deeply contents oriented view, where even large variations in man-hours are absorbed in the order of magnitude differences observed depending on who does the work and how.

While the line organization thinks about the project as yet another activity to administrate for a while, the intrapreneurs feel that they have a long term mission they must take to completion.

While the intrapreneurs leader style is informal and based on convincing and motivating people, the line organization is more oriented towards directives and formal orders.

Intrapreneurs want "action now", while the line organization is more cautious and often prefers waiting.

The problem above is a classical one, and the experience from the Arcs project is that the resulting power struggle between the two factors is the largest single source of efficiency loss and delay. It was the major reason why Arcs took six years and not three.

The solution is probably just as well known as it seems hard to implement. Innovation driven developments must be freed from the traditional line organizational culture, which has its role in running mature routine operations, but is often lost and confused in other contexts. Alternatively, the line organization must be well educated and experienced with the nature and limitations of larger innovation driven efforts. Managing innovation intensive development is a profession of its own, distinct from other tasks. Unless this problem can be firmly addressed, one should think very carefully whether to actually start any development of new technology and concepts. It will probably be too costly.

5.0 Acknowledgements

Arcs was a large and long term project. It acted as the generator for a long series of reports and results, thesises and papers. It constituted large parts of the contribution of Telesoft, (formerly TeleLOGIC), in several R&D cooperations like Eureka Software Factory, (Fernström & Ohlsson 1989), and ESPRIT II/Atmosphere, (Boarder, Obbink, and Schmidt 1989).

Many people were involved and made important contributions. The original startup kernel team of me, Mikael Bäckman, Johnny Widen and Hans Öhman is still there, but was soon extended (and taken over!) by a number of talented software engineers. I would like to mention Lars Anderson, Petter Bengtsson, Agneta Carlström, Lena Fridlund, Nils-Olof Forsgren, Mats Halvarsson, Anders Johansson, Börje Johansson, Sture Jonsson, Nils-Åke Klittby, Leif Larsson, Håkan Lennestål, Magnus Lindgren, Nils Livingstone, Anders Lundqvist, Arne Nilsson, Björn Nordgren, K-H Närfelt, Jarl Sandberg, Pär Törnqvist, and Ola Strömfors. At the San Diego branch Bruce Bergman, Karen Fraser, Tom Halliley, Buffy Hyler, Richard Kaufmann, Nancy McConlogue, and Jack Schwartz all contributed in various ways over the years.

Thank you all, you engaged commandos of software technology. It was a great experience. When we now start a new phase of development, possibly under the name ArCs++, an extensive amount of experience and results is at our disposal.

I would also like to thank Henk Obbink of the Atmosphere project, and Christer Fernström of ESF for many interesting discussions.

6.0 References

(Atmosphere 1990), *Atmosphere - Advanced Tools and Methods for System Production in Heterogeneous*, Extensible, Real Environments. ESPRIT II Subproject, area II.1.1 ASEE, Proposal nr 2565.

(Agresti 1986), *The Conventional Software Lifecycle: Its Evolution and Assumptions*, in New Paradigms For Software Development, IEEE Computer Society 1986.

(Boarder, Obbink & Schmidt 1989), *ATMOSPHERE - Advanced Techniques and Methods of System Production in a Heterogeneous, Extensible, and Rigorous Environment*. Proceedings of the International Conference on System Development Environments and Factories, Berlin 9-11 May, 1989.

(CACM 1988), *Special Issue on Hypertext*, Communications of the ACM, July 1988.

(Chikofsky & Cross 1990), *Reverse Engineering and Design Recovery: A Taxonomy*. IEEE Software, January 1990.

(Corbi 1989), *Program Understanding: Challenge for the 1990s*, IBM Systems Journal Vol 28 no2 1989.

(Cagan 1990), *The HP SoftBench Environment: An Architecture for a New Generation of Software Tools*, Hewlett-Packard Journal, June1990.

(Fernstrom et al 1988), *Eureka Software Factory Design Guidelines and Architecture*, ESF Consortia, Hohenzollerndamm 152, 1000 Berlin 33, West Germany.

(Fernstrom & Ohlsson 1989), *The ESF Vision of a Software Factory*, Proceedings of the International Conference on System Development Environments and Factories, Berlin 9-11 May, 1989.

(Gustavsson & Madsen 1990), *The Postmaster Model - The SDT Tool Integration Mechanism*. Telesoft, Box 4148, 20312 Malmö, Sweden.

(Schefstrom 1989), *Building a Highly Integrated Development Environment Using Preexisting Parts*, in Proceedings of IFIP'89 XI World Computer Congress, San Francisco, CA, 28 Aug-1 Sep 1989.

(Schefström 1989b), *Visualizing Designs Based on Ada*. Telsoft AB, Aurorum 6, 951 75 Luleå, Sweden.

(Schefström 1990), *Projections From a decade of CASE*, proceedings of the Ada Europe International Conference, Dublin 12-14 June 1990. Cambridge University Press.

(Telesoft 1991), *TeleUSE User's Guide*, Telsoft AB, Teknikringen 2, 583 30 Linköping, Sweden.

(Thomas 1989), *Tool Integration in the PACT Environment*, 11:th Conference on Software Engineering, May 1989, Pittsburgh, Pennsylvania.

(Yourdon & Constantine 1979), *Structured Design*, Prentice-Hall 1979.

(Parikh & Zvegintsov 1983), *The World of Software Maintenance*, Tutorial on Software Maintenance, Parkikh & Zvegintsov, eds., CS Press, Los Alamitos, Calf., 1983, pp1-3.

Panel presentation
Impact of Software Engineering Researches on Industrial Practice

Alfonso Fuggetta
CEFRIEL
Via Emanueli, 15
20126 Milano (Italy)
Tel.: +39-2-66100083 - Fax: +39-2-66100448
E-Mail: alfonso@mailer.cefriel.it

Panelists:

1. Marie Claude Gaudel (Univ. Paris Sud, France)

2. Valente Frasca (TECSIEL, Italy).

3. Charles Jackson (British Telecom, United Kingdom).

4. Robert Troy (Verilog, France).

During the last 20 years many efforts have been devoted to the study, design, and development of new techniques, methodologies and tools to better support the production of software applications. This is due to several well-known facts:

- Software is becoming more and more complex and therefore difficult to design and build: moreover, most applications require high levels of dependability.

- According to Belady and Lehman [1], to be useful an application must evolve in order to take into account all the new requirements deriving from the real world. The so-called software maintenance is not seen as a bug fix activity anymore, but as a complex process that must continuously re-analyze the requirements of the real problem and modify the application software accordingly.

- Software is going to be even more used in most of the new products that will be developed in these years (consider for example the hi-fi market or the new generation of cars that is appearing or going to appear in the near future).

In general, the development of software is becoming a more and more costly and critical activity that needs to be turned as much as possible into an efficient, highly automated, industrial process.

To tackle these problems effectively, a large number of techniques, methodologies, tools and environments have been studied, designed, developed and offered to the users.

But how many of these techniques, methodologies and tools are really used in the industrial community? To what extent have these technologies contributed to improve the way people are developing software?

Let us consider the following sample of technologies produced during the last years:

- Formal methods.

- Expert systems and AI.

- Object-oriented design and programming.

- CASE tools.

- Executable specifications.

- Testing and verification techniques.

- Rapid prototyping.

- Evolutionary life-cycle.

- Configuration management.

- Project management and control.

If we look at the research carried out at the Software Engineering Institute on the level of maturity of the organizations producing software, we can easily realize that it is quite low: almost all of the studied organizations are positioned in the two lower levels of maturity identified by SEI [2]. At these levels, the software process is based on very simple methodologies and environments, already well know and adopted in the 60s and 70s, and almost none of the above-mentioned technologies have been adopted and used on a large scale. Most of the new tools or methologies have been bought, but they are only used in small scale, trial projects, or are not used by the developers at all. According to SEI, therefore, the impact of software engineering research on industrial practice has been substantially low, at least during the past years: to cope with this situation, they propose a model of organization evolution in which the level of maturity of an organization can be increased by progressively introducing tools, techniques and methodologies into the production process.

This point leads, however, to another provocative question: is technology enough or even necessary? During the last ICSE [3], held last may in Austin, Texas, Watts Humphrey presented the results of a study conducted in Japan by a SEI team, who applied the SEI assessment procedure to a significant number of organizations developing software. The results are quite surprising: in spite of the high productivity and quality that Japan organizations producing software have been demonstrating during the last years, their SEI level of maturity is in many cases lower than the level of similar american and european companies.

One more point: if we look at people who are producing the software engineering technology (universities, research centres, tool vendors, ...), it seems that they are not using their own products to develop their new technology. Are we using formal methods and CASE tools to specify and design expert systems or new CASE tools?

To summarize, I would like to provoke the panelists on the following questions:

- Are we producing the *right* technology?

- Are we producing and transferring technology *right*?

- Are we *really* using the technology we are producing?

References

[1] M.M. Lehman and L.A. Belady. *Program Evolution, Processes of Software Change*, New York: Academic Press, 1985.

[2] W.S. Humphrey. *Managing the Software Process*, SEI Series in Software Engineering, Addison-Wesly Publishing Company, Reading (MA), 1989.

[3] W.S. Humphrey, D.H. Kitson and J. Gale. A comparison of U.S. and Japanese Software Process Maturity, *Proceedings of 13th Internationl Conference on Software Engineering*, IEEE Computer Society, 1991.

The Production of Software in the FINSIEL Group

Valente Frasca
TECSIEL S.p.A. - I.R.I.-FINSIEL Group
Via del Ponte di Piscina Cupa, 43
00128 Roma (Italy)

Some premise

Those who assert to possess the *right* software engineering technology exhibit the best clue that they are on the wrong direction. This means that they do not understand the complexity of the reality and then the actual essence of the software development problems.

- "The amateur software engineer is always in search of some sort of magic, some earthshaking technological innovation whose application will immediately make the process of software development easy"; but "It is the mark of the professional software engineer to know that no such panacea exists" [1]. In other terms we must handle with care the suggestions of two dangerous metaphors: "software factory" and "software engineering". A factory is devoted to reproduce again and again the *same* product in the most efficient and effective way; the engineer applies scientific and technological rules in order to satisfy the *will* of a user that has just previously recognized her/his objective, understood her/his problem, found a solution. No such situations occur in software design and development.

- The solution of the software analysis and design problems cannot be reduced to the realization of a "cookbook", because "software design today remains a very labor-intensive business; to a large extent, it is best characterized as a cottage industry" [1]. The quality of software depends on the quality of the developers.

Anyway 10% of USA GNP is devoted to the expenses for hardware/software, 47% of software code was never delivered because obsolete before the release, 29% was delivered but never used, 95% of the expenses for software are devoted to maintenance (Gartner Group):

- software production in an industrial environment cannot be based on an un-manageable, un-controllable process.

The FINSIEL approach

We do not claim to have and produce the *right* technology, but we do hope to have chosen a good starting point, i.e. the right fundamental issues and a good approach:

- to face the problem with a global approach
  . the main issue: the **organization** of the production process
  . a "complete" analysis of the production process (strategic planning, Software Life Cycle and cross life cycle activities)
  . a **methodology** for all aspects of the process
  . **integrated software tools** for all phases of the process (starting from the SLC)
  . analysis of the impact of the tools on the organization

- to start to apply the method to the kind of systems that we better know (the Information Systems)

- to systematically check and verify the results of the methodology application.

The organization

- Theoretical level; the perspective: against taylorism, the management of the production (of software systems) as the organization of "dialogs" and of consensus for an "ontological" design (see [2]).

- Structural level; the macro-organization of a network of business sites and competence (production) sites; the micro-organization of communications via software tools.

  The FINSIEL Group has been making for many years "experiments" about the organization of software production: good results have been achieved partitioning the software production process into the three main phases (e.g. analysis, design and coding) to be performed by two different laboratories: one for the analysis, and the other for design and coding. The concept has been extended to the overall structure of the Group, which is subdivided into "vertical" and "horizontal" companies. The vertical ones are devoted to the management of market segments, and their production units are subdivided into laboratories; while the horizontal ones are specific competence laboratories (i.e. design&code labs for information systems, package production labs, etc.)

  According to this approach a vertical company constitutes mainly a filter toward the customer (interpreting his "real" needs), with a function of system integrator; whereas the second type constitutes the site of the code production and reuse.

The methodology

- A proprietary methodology has been developing during the last ten years: DAFNE^{TM}; continuous revisions and new versions are planned; some high skilled resources are fully devoted to such tasks.

- DAFNE basic issues: to understand the environment (the "enterprise") in which the automatic system has to be embedded; to envisage the transformation of the target organization due to the introduction of the system; to allow the final user to participate and verify the partial results; to propagate the gathered information and choices from the preliminary analysis to the code ("traceability"); to use semantically unambiguous formal languages.

- Some data (Italsiel SpA): 1000 (1987), 1500 (1991) developers have been using the methodology, producing approximately 20.000.000 lines of code. DAFNE was applied to a wide range of applications: small scale and large scale projects; information systems and system software; ...

- Some result; observations at Italsiel SpA, data comparison of years 1982 (without DAFNE), 1988 (using DAFNE). Productiveness increase: development +28% (loc/m-y); maintenance: +30+48% lines of code in charge of one person, -15+20% debugging time; total effort at fixed lines of code: -35%, analysis effort ==, design effort: -20%, coding & test effort: -51%; shift of effort distribution: analysis +50%, design +33%, coding & test -22%;

- The FINSIEL CASE tools are specified and designed using DAFNE.

- A "dream" under continuous verification: a unique methodology for all kind of applications (including KBS, O-O systems, ...).

- The FINSIEL approach has allowed the standardization of the communications among marketing teams and development teams and among the developers themselves, so that the highest parallelism of the development activities, the subdivision of big projects into geographically distributed units and the attribution of precise roles, including the separation of development from maintenance, has been made available.

The CASE tools

- A proprietary CASE product has been developing during the last seven years: DAFNE TOOLS^{TM}; an AD/CYCLE compliant version of the tool is in progress; tens of high skilled resources are devoted to the production of DAFNE TOOLS.

- CASE tools modify the work process (as any other software tool does in a host environment), therefore the design of a CASE tool affects the design of an organization: the "physiognomy" of a tool must be both:

    a) closely tied to the methodology (simple diagram or text editors do not provide a guideline for the designers, and therefore do not represent a significant support); and

    b) significantly flexible (designer discovery and invention, i.e. creativeness, have not to be killed; project standards and leader will have to be considered; slight transformations of the production process have to be envisaged; ...).

- CASE tools provide the best performance (in terms of "intelligent" management and manipulation) if the results of each phase of the SLC are formalized (DAFNE does provide it).

- The reuse: a key issue also at analysis/design level.

- FINSIEL new generation CASE tools, an overview: an environment devoted to support the creation, manipulation, inquiry and multiform (usually graphical) display of project information and the generation of related documents, providing all the automatic mechanisms able to perform every derivation, transformation and validation of the information that can be done without any human intervention (including code generation, reverse engineering, forward engineering, etc.).

- The platform: an editor generator for context-sensitive graphical languages.

- The challenge: to follow a methodology through the CASE tool is more graceful than to develop without constraints.

The technology transfer

- Internal and external courses are available on both the methodology and tools (data of 1990; N° of attendees: 2704, N° of training days: 9094) .

- Each step of the professional progression is marked by specific courses.

- Almost the whole body of developers of the main FINSIEL companies is trained and practised in DAFNE and DAFNE TOOLS (current version).

References.
[1]   Booch G. - Object Oriented Design - Cummings 1991
[2]   Winograd T. - Flores F. - Understanding Computers and Cognition - Ablex 1986

The Impact of Software Engineering Researches on Industrial Practice – a Personal View

Charles Jackson
British Telecom Laboratories
Ipswich IP5 7RE, UK

It is fashionable, in some industrial quarters, to state that software engineering reseach has not delivered the commercial benefits that other fields of research are thought to have achieved. It is certainly true that, when we examine industrial software practice, we find that there is a very wide disparity between the methods and techniques being used – ranging from the apparently primitive to the exceedingly sophisticated. It is also true that productivity improvements have been unable to match the explosive demand for software-based products. The problem with this analysis is that it in no way compares like with like. The average software system being produced today far exceeds those of previous decades in terms of size, complexity and criticality.

Technological Trends in Software Engineering

Over the past 3 decades the size of software based systems has grown exponentially with telecomms ranking second only to military systems.

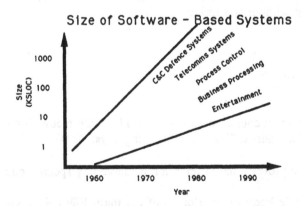

Size of Software - Based Systems

At the same time , and of course not unrelated, the complexity has grown at an even faster rate. To some extent this has been 'managed' through the introduction of high level design concepts such as processes and services but the 'global' complexity continues to grow broadly in concert with system size.

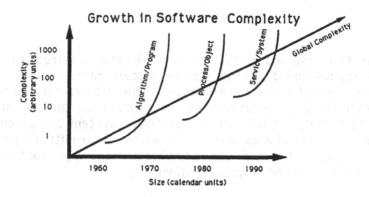

More recently, criticality has become a key issue for industrial software. As software becomes increasingly embedded in all our key activities it penetrates applications in which its reliable operation is essential to safety, security, financial viability, environmental protection and the operation of the organisations, systems and networks.

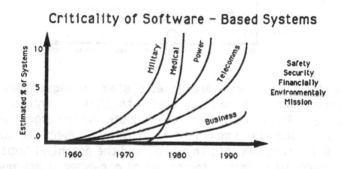

When measured in these global terms, software technology <u>has</u> undoubtedly been very successful. At least, we have survived! The problem, however, is whether we can continue to survive. The answer to this depends upon resolving a crisis of confidence between those who pay for and develop software based systems, and the software engineering research community. This crisis is in the large part due to two factors. Firstly, there is a very marked communication gap between software researchers and industrial management. Secondly, Industry is by no means convinced that software research is tackling the real problems. Industry has seen the movement of the centre of gravity from "program generation" to Systems Design and Requirements Engineering. This has not been mirrored by software research.

An Industrial Perspective

Looked at from the industrial perspective, the development of the software engineering discipline can be crudely characterised by the historical pattern of where value is added in the life cycle ie which phase really determines competitiveness. This has been moving steadily upwards such that, for the average software system being developed today, the most critical area does not lie within the traditional phases of software development (design and coding), but in the uppermost levels of requirements capture and customer engineering.

Value Added in the Life Cycle

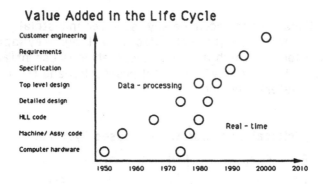

As the nature of the use of software-based systems changes from that of replacing clerical and mechanical tasks to that of enhancing and extending the capability of equipment, individuals and the organisation, it is increasingly (exponentially more) difficult for customers and suppliers to predict what the requirements should be and the potential impact that a new system might have. This is the result of our dynamic and uncertain environment. Historically, poor requirements capture has contributed substantially to the shortcomings of the software industry.

- On average, large software systems are delivered 1 year behind schedule
- 1% of projects finish on time, to budget
- 25% of software intensive projects never finish

The fundamental difficulty which is facing industry is that, whilst key software parameters, both in terms of demand and technical content, have been growing exponentially, the general level of software productivity has not.

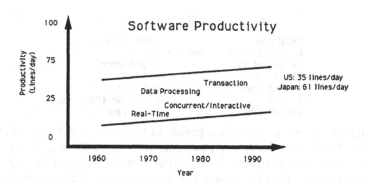

The shortfall has been the obvious cause for the rapid growth in numbers of software active personnel. Another is less apparent. As systems have become more sophisticated / higher "tech" and the base hardware technology cheaper, the balance in new systems development costs between software and hardware has swung until it is dominated by software. As we move into the area of intelligent services, the pressure for yet more software domination will continue.

The Software / Hardware Balance

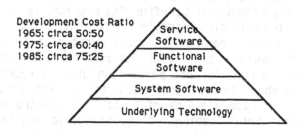

Thus Industry perceives a headlong flight into software – it already dominates the cost and duration of most telecommunications R&D projects.

And when Industry looks at the increase in size, complexity and criticality of systems it doesn't see a technical success story – it sees a number of exponentially increasing problems.

The Limits of Current Software Technology

The conclusion that is drawn is that there is an "envelope of capability" which currently limits our capacity to exploit software's potential for the future. However, the pressure for more software remains largely unabated. Very roughly the current limits are defined as follows.

Limits in Software

Total size:	1 million lines
Number of major components:	1000
Component size:	10 000 lines
Design Life:	10 years
Project Team:	100 staff
Quality:	1 error per 1000 lines
Productivity:	50 lines per day

These limits represent exponential break-points which are very difficult to exceed without some radically new approach to software. A top team, applying current best practice across the board may well better these figures by perhaps a factor of two but a low grade team is unlikely to even approach them.

The Role of Software Research

We can now begin to assess the role and success of software research in its relevance to industrial need.

1. To help industry to "navigate" within this "envelope of capability". This implies developing engineered technology based upon current software concepts and transferring that technology into use. The evidence suggests that the best teams have taken up new ideas, but the wide disparity is a testamony to a either poor communication or a lack of sufficiently strong evidence of benefits. The problem has certainly been compounded by the exclusive approach inherent in most techniques which implies teams and organisations must adopt a single method rather than using that which is appropriate for each part of the project. Additionally, there is a well-founded perception that the researchers aren't knowledgeable about the reality of industrial software production - its variety, its skill base, its financial and time constraints, and (vitally) its systems level problems. Many academic and research institution software research projects, although technically excellent, presume an industrial environment that does not exist. Clearly such work is likely to prove difficult to transfer into use.

2. To extend the "envelope of capability". The software limits are in effect technological barriers. If we are to move forward into a new era of software engineering and to have the capability to develop new generations of information services, systems and networks, we must somehow "tunnel through" the barriers of size, complexity, criticality and customer requirements definition. This is not going to be achieved simply by improving on existing concepts but requires new approaches to be found. These approaches must have the potential for large 'leverage' on software costs and to genuinely "punch holes in the "envelope of software capability". The difficulty is identifying software research which is genuinely directed towards radically new approaches to software creation. Too much academic work falls into the category of being marginal in potential.

There is no doubt that technical success has been achieved in the automation of well established areas such as dataflow, databases, development environments, and configuration management. These have been successful because they address a large potential user base. In other areas such as formal specification, functional languages, verification, and high-level design there has been little evidence of any real take-up. I believe this to be because of a poor understanding of the industrial domain and particularly the emphasis of software research on the logical as opposed to the performance and reliability aspects.

It is worthwhile noting that when a radically new approach to software which is well focussed on the user, eg spreadsheets, has appeared it has been taken up enthusiastially.

Industrial Adoption of Software Technology

The acceptance of new software technology is strongly dependent on the value that industry perceives it to have, set against the costs of introducing it and tempered by its significance in the whole context of software production. Industry is, by and large, ready to adopt new software technology whenever it can see the benefit. This means that software researchers will have to work a lot harder at selling their ideas in terms which are meaningful to industrial management.

However, management is not the only, nor is it the greatest, factor in the equation. The key to take-up of software research lies with the individual software developer and preferably the professional of a few years standing. As with all technology, it is really the users that matter. The majority of software engineers enjoy doing what they do and are remote from the hard economics. They perceive their job as an intellectual task. To change the way they do it requires some personal motivation. Their motivations are not the same as those of their management. In addition, a significant proportion have been preconditioned in universities to see their role as the "production of programs". This "culture" needs change for it is substantially reducing the potential impact of reuse technology and metrics and it encourages a single paradigm attitude. It is also clear that the academic curricula are weak in systems concepts and non-functional (performance, reliability, etc) aspects. The growing acceptance of object oriented techniques demonstrates the importance of the academic teaching world in achieving technology transfer.

One of the reasons for poor take-up of software research is that its benefits have not been practically demonstrated on <u>industrially</u> relevant problems. The fact that the researchers may be using the technology themselves is by no means sufficient. Often they are not even doing that. Where, in my experience, researchers have gone into the industrial environment to try out their ideas the results have usually been positive in either direct impact or in highlighting real deficiencies.

It is also important to distinguish between methods and tools in considering the introduction of new software technology. From a software research viewpoint it is argued that the primary improvements in software come from the methods not the tools. In this case it is questionable whether we need more technology unless it is to extend our "envelope of capability". Clearly the differences between the best and worst software teams are due to the use of good methods (that does not necessarily imply rigid and formal methods) which suit the particular problems and culture. It is often the case that quite simple techniques, entirely without tool support, can make a big difference in, for example, software quality and timeliness. If software researchers are to make an impact they must understand that by upgrading the "less effective" areas of software production the "average effectiveness" of an organisation may be substantially improved. Nevertheless, tool support is important to individuals and organisations in transferring methods.

Conclusion

This paper describes the context within which software research may make an impact. It is clear that it is difficult to gain acceptance for new technology unless it very well directed towards identifiable and significant problems. From the industrial standpoint a piece of software research can be assessed in terms of three quality criteria.

1. Relevance: Does it address an identifiable and real industrial problem domain.

2. Significance: If the research is brought to fruition and successfully transferred, will it either significantly reduce costs or will it enable one or more of our current limitations to be substantially extended.

3. Excellence: Is the research both of sufficient understandability and potential standing to be independently recommended by industrial and academic colleagues.

Where these have not been met there have been serious difficulties in achieving any impact.

Finally, it is vitally important to industry that software research is directed not only to optimising the use of the current software paradigm but also to seeking radically new approaches. These will not be found unless the "systems dimension" becomes a driving force in future research.

"No Silver Bullets" - Fred Brooks

However, there have been major breakthroughs which have been instrumental in changing the course of computing - the compiler, the operating system, the database, logic programming. To deny the possibilty of further breakthroughs is to consign software to a predetermined, arduous and marginal evolution. But to find them we must look for them and they will not be found on the well trodden paths. There may be no silver bullets but somewhere there are the materials from which to manufacture them.

In the meantime, we had better make the best use of our current technology by ensuring that software research and industry work closely together to reduce the gap between best and worst practice. We must pay a little less attention to the "top of the market" and much more to the average, poorly trained and inexperienced software developer.

IMPACT OF METHODS ON PRODUCTIVITY & QUALITY

(Panel: Impact of Software Engineering Research on Industrial Practices)

Robert TROY – Président Directeur Général

VERILOG – 150 rue Vauquelin – 31081 TOULOUSE – FRANCE

Phone: (33) 61.19.29.39 – Fax (33) 61.40.84.52

It is clear that industrial practices in terms of software development have to progress. Despite the few advances made in the methods and techniques used, the breathtaking increase in the size of applications, and above all the criticalness of the functions performed, result in deadlines and costs frequently being overshot. Now the cost of software is the largest expense in the IT industry making the use of CASE tools and methods a strategic element for many companies.

The battle must simultaneously be fought on two fronts: **productivity and quality.**

Improved **productivity** can be obtained in two ways:

- automation, which consists in working more efficiently with the assistance of tools;
- re-use, which avoids the need for redoing the same things in development again and again.

Automation, as it stands today, is disappointing, only the clerical tasks are automated. Just as in other industries, major gains in productivity will only be possible if profound changes are made to current practices.

Despite the high expectations of re-use, today industrial applications are not significant.

Improving **quality** is possible by adopting standards and by early detection of errors throughout development.

- Widespread use of standards and common techniques allow practices to be harmonized and experience to be capitalized.

- Quality must be built in as a continuous process. Indeed, the type of errors and the moment at which they are detected have a major influence on the overall cost of a project. The later an error is detected, the more it costs in terms of time and effort.

In order to make current practices progress, not only a technology (for automation, early error detection) is required, but also suitable methods, standards and organizations (for re-use, quality process).

The technology exists today. There are more than 400 CASE tools available on the market. The distinction is usually made between three major categories:

- front-end: analysis and design
- back-end: coding, testing, maintenance
- support: data, documentation and process management

Back-end and support tools generally meet the requirements fairly well, except perhaps, for maintenance and testing. As far as front-end tools are concerned, the following distinctions have to be made:

- "informal" tools that only require a small investment but which cannot provide a great deal more than documentation and communication assistance;

- "formal" tools, that require a large investment in terms of training, which cannot be generalized to the industry as a whole in the current state of Software Engineering culture;

- "semi-formal" tools which offer the best investment/ improvement trade-off by combining the rigour of the formal with the ease-of-use of the informal. Evidence of the benefits provided by this approach can be seen today in many industrial projects.

But tools are nothing without methods and human organizations, and large scale software development is not taught at school. Engineers and technicians learn their profession on the job, and the lack of a culture grounding, both at the technical and management levels, is putting a brake on the dissemination of new methods. It is more difficult to change human organizations than technology. Therefore, it is vital that the training provided by the suppliers of tools be relayed in the organizations.

The standards in the area of software development are still very rarely applied outside the most advanced sectors (defence, aerospace, ...), except some technical norms such as: SQL, Posix, PostScript ...

Consequently the use of software engineering technology is still slight. CASE tools have only recently started to find their place and only within the last three years have significant inroads been made. Total market penetration is estimated to be slightly more than 10%. At the moment there are approximately 4 million software developers in the world, which led to a total development cost of 250 billion dollars. If the generalized use of CASE allowed only a 10% improvement in overall productivity, savings of 25 billion dollars could be achieved, which represents 10 times the investment in CASE tools this year. However major companies are now making large corporate investment in CASE. The experiments of the pioneers in the '80s are therefore evolving into major implementations by large organizations supported by special internal CASE task forces.

This rapid evolution shows that the software crisis creates an enormous need for methods and tools to improve productivity and quality. CASE is not just a technology for its own sake, it is satisfying a real need. However, many improvements are still to be made. Now that companies are starting to use CASE throughout their organizations, they are becoming more knowledgeable and are asking for more support, better visibility of results, better training and significant consulting assistance.

CASE suppliers must propose tools that will provide users with real benefits, that is to say tools that must be easy to use, yet formal enough to be effective. CASE must in fact be part of the solution to the software crisis, and not become part of the problem. The danger now is that many methodologies originally designed for the end-user, providing a standard approach to projects, may become too technical for that end-user. The future success of CASE will depend on the suppliers' ability to establish the balance between the need for formal methods and the need for providing easy-to-use tools to the end-users. At present, it seems that such technology and tools are already available.

Consequently, the success of CASE now mainly depends on the users' commitment. The real benefits of CASE will not be seen if there is not a profound change in culture and organization. Technology is not everything in a project, it must be completed by a real management involvment, and the creation of the right structures. The priority today lies in a higher level of education and training allowing project managers and software developers to acquire better skills in using the principles of software engineering. The earlier CASE culture is acquired – starting at university –the easier and the greater will the return on CASE be.

Finally, what seems to be highly needed is a consistent reference model and some standards, capable of evolving, in critical areas such as integration frameworks and repositories. These standards are far from complete, one can feel that they should not be pushed too fast until sufficient experience has been gained to estimate all the trade-offs and optimum solutions. The current trend is towards a few competing standards which represent a compromise between total inconsistency and unacceptable rigidity. The setting up of these standards is the responsibility of everyone involved in CASE: suppliers, hardware manufacturers and users. At the moment standards depend either on hardware manufacturers or on consortiums and special interest groups, usually leaving the end user by the wayside. Moreover, the length of time required for standards to get well-established leads to the emergence of *de facto* standards, imposed by one or a few players. If valid standards are to be obtained, all the parties involved in the CASE industry, including users, must work together. The goal being to define technological standards, as well as professional practices and the respective obligations of the users and suppliers to ensure the success of CASE.

For the coming years, all these ever-growing needs are expected to command significant improvements in the areas of tools, methods, standards and organizations.

The software industry cannot wait any longer.

REQUIREMENTS ENGINEERING - GETTING RIGHT FROM WRONG

Martin S. Feather

USC / Information Sciences Institute

4676 Admiralty Way, Marina del Rey CA 90292, USA

feather@isi.edu

The scruffies: proponents of bottom-up development of tools and techniques to help the present-day requirements process. The scruffy approach works: it has immediate payoff, we can see how to make progress, and it can be incrementally introduced. Because of these alluring features, it *is* being pursued.

The neats: proponents of formal-based, knowledge-intensive smart systems to revolutionize the requirements process. The eventual success of the neat approach is less certain. There are several opinions of the answer to: 'Can the neats ever play a significant role in requirements engineering?':

a. Never — the extra effort of doing things the neat way will always exceed the payoff.

b. Hardly ever — only in very special circumstances, and/or for a minor portion of the overall development task.

c. Eventually — sufficient advances in requirements work will result in neat tools that provide support for a revolutionized development process.

d. Completely — AI systems will dominate the entire software process (and everything else).

Some people, myself included, believe in c, and that it is attainable long before d (or, to put it another way, that significant 'neat'-style requirements engineering support does not presume tremendous advances in AI in general). The question, however, is not whether we are right or wrong (if we could answer that now, it wouldn't need research), but whether we should devote our necessarily finite research efforts into pursuing c. My position is that we, the research community, *should* be working on c, for the following reasons:

— no-one else will: the uncertainty and short-term dynamics dissuade extensive commercial pursuit of this avenue;

— potentially large pay-off: while 'scruffy' approaches will incrementally improve what human requirements engineers can achieve, they are inherently limited by their reliance upon humans to interpret everything. In contrast, the 'neat' approach seeks to have the computer *reason* with the requirements, not just serve as a glorified notepad.

— analogous indications of success: the use of formal methods within the later stages of software development (for example, the use of program transformation to derive efficient code from lucid specifications) has followed an analogous course, and *is* beginning to bear fruit.

I do, however, believe that we need a shift in thinking in order to develop useful neat tools. Most formal methods have made the assumption that what they are dealing with is correct. In contrast, I suggest that the distinguishing feature of *requirements* engineering is that it deals primarily with the *incorrect*; its very purpose is to discover and respond to 'errors'. In other words, requirements engineering is the process of *getting right from wrong*.

To understand this in more detail, contrast the end product of requirements engineering, a specification, with the input, requirements. Specifications, while free from certain efficiency concerns, nevertheless impose a number of expectations, for example that they be complete, consistent and unambiguous. In contrast, the expressions of requirements will typically be fragmentary, contradictory, incomplete, inconsistent and ambiguous. Furthermore, their expression may employ widely varying levels of abstraction (e.g., concrete examples, scenarios, general properties) styles (e.g., textual, graphical, formulae, domain-specific notations) and viewpoints (e.g., system-wide properties, single user viewpoints, snapshots of the entire state at one moment in time, historical traces of ongoing activity).

Requirements that exhibit these properties don't necessarily reflect failings or errors of the producer of those requirements; in fact, it is often advantageous to make use of the freedoms from specification concerns that they provide. Because they are the antithesis of desired properties of specifications, however, the task of developing a specification from such requirements (and ultimately a program, whether or not a this is by route of a specification) may be complex and lengthy. Tools and techniques that support this task should be the goal of requirements engineering research. Such tools must not only be tolerant of requirement freedoms, but must actively assist in the removal of these freedoms in order to produce specifications.

I continue by considering each of these 'requirement freedoms', to identify the opportunities for the neats to provide useful support for requirements engineering.

Incompleteness — requirements can provide partial descriptions of tasks. Particularly for large and complex tasks, it is important to be able to provide requirements incrementally, so that at any intermediate point there they may be incomplete. It is also useful for several people to be separately preparing or extending sets of requirements, which later may be combined into a single whole; for maximum advantage, each of those people should not be constrained to be working with a complete set of requirements. During construction, incompleteness may direct the acquisition of further requirements information, or modification of already acquired requirements. The information that is imparted in an incomplete set of requirements must be retained and manipulated, even if it remains disjointed and cannot be coalesced into a single whole. Analysis and explanation tools must handle incompleteness gracefully. They should do reasoning about, and presentation of, the information that is available, while indicating the limits. Modification of requirements may introduce further incompleteness, or be applied to remove it. Tools should make plausible guesses when appropriate, and be able to gracefully retract those guesses when they are determined to be incorrect.

Inconsistency — requirements can be mutually contradictory. This is particularly useful for the statement of an idealized requirement, which we may recognize as being unrealizable, but which we nevertheless wish to express. This is also useful for representing contradictory viewpoints, in order to describe them as a precursor to negotiation. Finally, multiple sources of requirements should not need to be tightly coupled so as to constrain them to generating only completely consistent sets of requirements. These various sources of inconsistency should be used to identify and drive a conflict resolution process. Trade-offs must be made, negotiation techniques will be brought to bear. Analysis must appropriately limit the propagation of inconsistency so that an inconsistency amongst the requirements does not render all other analysis results worthless!

Redundancy — requirements need not avoid stating the same thing multiple times. Indeed, it may be advantageous to be able to state the same thing from multiple points of view, e.g., the cash register's point of a transaction view as compared with the customer's point of view of a transaction. Both viewpoints may overlap, stating the same thing in different ways. Furthermore, redundancy permits cross-checking, a form of validation of the accuracy of the emerging specification. A single formalization of the information will be selected for inclusion in the specification, but linked back to the multiple requirements that led to it. Analysis and explanation techniques can make good use of redundancy when presenting information to the user, since alternative presentations of the same information may emphasize different aspects that would otherwise be easily overlooked. Indeed, analysis is the activity of presenting redundant information, although presumably information that would be hard to immediately deduce from a given form of the specification (e.g., proving some property holds of a specification is 'merely' a deduction from the existing specification, yet arbitrarily complex reasoning may be required to make that deduction).

Ambiguity — requirements may be ambiguous. In particular, holding to an attitude of "all or nothing" is often counter-productive during the requirements process. This can be addressed in several ways. A client should be allowed to state requirements in an ideal fashion, but at the same time list acceptable alternatives. If it is difficult to know alternatives ahead of time, a client should be allowed to state flexible requirements (e.g., try hard to meet this goal) or preferences of one requirement over another (e.g., always choose safety over cost if both can't be met). Ambiguity indicates the need for choice among alternatives. Our tools must be able to navigate in a sea of choices, preferences and trade-offs. It may no longer be possible to say that a requirement can or cannot be met. Instead, achievement becomes relative to a client's preferences or to some allowable range of behavior. Further, during construction there should be no pre-ordained dogma that insists choices be resolved when they arise. It is useful to retain a record of alternatives, and justifications for choices when they are made, so that the resulting system can be justified, and so that future changes can induce a reconsideration of those choices as appropriate.

Non-uniformity of abstraction — requirements may express knowledge anywhere within a broad spectrum of generality. This range goes from very general-purpose domain independent, through domain-specific, task-specific, to concrete examples. This allows the use of general-purpose information suitably instantiated for the task in hand. Similarly, specific but paradigmatic behaviors may be stated as requirements, the intent being to construct a specification that exhibits those, and similar, behaviors; thus generalization from examples occurs during construction. Analysis and explanation likewise make use of this flexibility, presenting information in general terms (e.g., a traffic light controller is an instance of a scheduling system), very specific cases that the user can relate to (e.g., car-1 enters the intersection while its traffic light is green), and even in qualitative terms (e.g., an increase in traffic will cause a decrease in a throughput requirement). Modification comes in to play not only to move between levels of abstraction in the traditional sense of refinement/generalization but also as a means to tailor, customize and incrementally construct something 'similar' without being restricted to pure refinement or abstraction.

Heterogeneous forms of expression — statements of requirements should be free to use whatever form of expression is most natural to the aspect of the task being described. This might be textual, formulae, graphical, a domain-specific notation, etc. Furthermore, different aspects of the same task should be able to utilize different forms of expression. This is convenient for both human understanding (presentation in those terms that individual is most comfortable with), and reasoning (expression that suppress details irrelevant to the particular form of reasoning). These varied forms must be acceptable as input forms of requirements, and require translation into some common (internal) representation. Support for user-defined languages and notations permit task- and domain-specific extension of the notations available. The external, user-provided expressions should be used where possible as the means to present analysis information, so that translation must go both ways. Modifications expressed in terms of any of the representations must be appropriately conducted in the internal representation.

Summary and Acknowledgements

I see plenty of opportunities for the use of neat-style tools and techniques in what I consider to be the core activity of requirements engineering, namely addressing the mismatch between the typical and desirable properties of requirements, and the mandatory properties of specifications (and implementations). Credit for the 'requirement freedoms' notion is shared with Stephen Fickas, however blame for my (mis)use of it here rests upon me alone. There follow several references to work that I have found representative of these ideas.

References

[1] R. Balzer, N. Goldman, and D. Wile. Informality in program specifications. In C. Rich and R. Waters., editors, *Readings in Artificial Intelligence and Software Engineering*, pages 223–232. Morgan Kaufmann, 1986. Originally published in IEEE Transactions on Software Engineering, 4(2), pp. 94-102, March 1978.

[2] S. Fickas and P. Nagarajan. Critiquing software specifications: a knowledge based approach. *IEEE Software*, November 1988.

[3] C. Rich, R.C. Waters, and H.B. Reubenstein. Towards a requirements apprentice. In *Proceedings, 4th International Workshop on Software Specification and Design Monterey, California*, pages 79–86. Computer Society Press of the IEEE, 1987.

A (Neat) Alphabet of Requirements Engineering Issues

Anthony Finkelstein
Imperial College, Department of Computing
180 Queens Gate, London SW7 2BZ
acwf@doc.ic.ac.uk

A is for Abstraction. Classically software development is seen as a process by which an abstract requirement is, through a process of reification, made progressively more concrete. We have built support for this process based on some formal understanding of it. Unfortunately users have a habit of presenting their requirements already embodied in some fashion - either in terms of a preexisting technology or, worse, in terms of their vision of an appropriate technological solution. Stripping away the additional detail is an important part of requirements engineering for which we do not as yet have appropriate tools. To create such tools we need an adequate theory of what is happening in this process.

B is for Boundaries. It is widely accepted that, as part of requirements engineering, we need to model the environment into which the designed system will be placed. We still have to resolve the problem of how widely to set the boundaries for that modelling. This depends in turn on having a manipulable and analysable representation scheme.

C is for Cooperation. Requirements engineering is cooperative work and the solution of many of the pressing issues in requirements engineering is dependent on the resolution of issues in support for group work. To achieve this, experience suggests, we need well founded models of cooperative activity.

D is for Design. The primary role of requirements engineering is, in the last analysis, to provide the information necessary to proceed with design. This means linking the products of requirements engineering to design methods and hence an alignment between the means of expression that each deploys.

E is for Elicitation. One of the weak links in requirements engineering. It is often crudely assumed that this is the bridge from the "informal" to the "formal". Yet both interview protocols and large texts, the stuff of elicitation, have formal structural properties which we can exploit in the development of tool support.

F is for Formal. It seems incontrovertible that we should use representation schemes with a well understood semantics for writing descriptions in requirements engineering, particularly if we seek to reason about those descriptions. There is no point in writing a specification if we cannot determine interesting consequences from it. Logic and discrete mathematics are the best available foundation for such representation schemes. However, only small and very tentative steps have so far been made in devising appropriate formal tools for requirements engineering. The well known limitations of existing techniques do not signal a failure of the approach per se but rather suggest that it is a lot more difficult to devise languages, notations and practical reasoning strategies for realistic representation schemes than might at first have been thought.

G is for Genericity. A clear divide can be discerned in research strategy between those who favour requirements engineering support that uses domain knowledge and those who favour generic tools and techniques. I favour the generic approach largely because of a general feeling that successful software engineering tools are usually: small; tightly focused in terms of the task they perform; not life-cycle phase specific; and, critically, based on a sound theoretical foundation. None of these are possible with a domain based approach.

H is for Hot topics. Software engineering seems particularly prone to fads and fashions - hypertext, object orientation with inheritance and so on. Without an agenda of the sort provided by the "neat perspective" it is easy to be carried along by the tide and to adopt unproven or patently inappropriate techniques.

I is for Insecurity. There is little value in presenting a validation model which is not securely derived from the underlying statement of requirements nor where the comments and observations made during the process of validation cannot be securely associated with changes to the requirements.

J is for Jargon. To move forward any discipline needs to achieve a common vocabulary. This is singularly lacking in requirements engineering. Formality gives us the first elements of such a vocabulary

K is for Knowledge engineering. The observation that there is a close similarity between the activities of knowledge engineering and software engineering is now a commonplace. This similarity rests on shared concern with reasoning and formal expression. It should allow us to borrow, from the practice of knowledge elicitation/acquisition, techniques which might be appropriate for requirements elicitation.

L is for Life-cycle. The software life-cycle has been pronounced dead many times but still remains an important reference point in almost any discussion of requirements engineering. The control of iteration in requirements engineering - when and how to "freeze" specifications - remains for most practical approaches to software development a key issue. Achieving that control means understanding, in as rigorous, a fashion as possible the consequences of change and the relations between successive representations.

M is for Method. Methods (JSD and the like) remain among the most successful contributions of software engineering to the practitioner community. Their success rests upon the selection of appropriate representation schemes, the careful definition of the relations between them and the description of the process by which such specifications are built within those representation schemes. Extending the success of these methods to requirements engineering and providing tool support for them demands a principled, and hence I would argue a formal, understanding of the way these methods are constructed.

N is for Non-functional requirements. Non-functional requirements is a catch all term denoting, broadly, those requirements in which there is no direct route from the specification of a property to its implementation and no way, short of testing, to show that it has been achieved. The generally cited example of this is "performance". A couple of years ago however if asked to give an example of a non-functional requirement most people would have said "user-friendliness". The work on formal specification of user interfaces suggests that properties such as the consistency and cognitive complexity of a user interface can be expressed formally and proven to hold from a specification. This suggests that a requirement is not inherently non-functional but rather that labelling it non-functional reflects the state-of-the-art. The consequence is obvious, rather than worry about how to manage non-functional requirements we ought to be trying to make them into functional requirements.

O is for Organisational issues. It should not blindly be assumed that organisational issues like "culture", "policy", "commitment" and "authority" are impervious to formal analysis or modelling

P is for Problem. Good problems are as difficult to find as good solutions. It is not unfair to suggest that a good deal of the recent advance in formal specification techniques is attributable to the development of good problems - lift systems, libraries and the like. Such problems both focus work and provide a common reference point and evaluative framework. There is as yet no equivalent for requirements engineering.

Q is for Quantitative. Metrics tend to excite strong feelings among software engineers either of passionate support or of deep mistrust. Whatever ones views about the merits or otherwise of existing work in this area it is fair to observe that the bulk of it has concentrated on design and implementation rather than requirements engineering where, I would argue, cost and effort estimation most naturally fits. Tying quantitative measures to the products of requirements engineering and deriving estimates from them is a natural "neat" issue.

R is for Reuse. Setting aside the question of how appropriate reuse is to requirements engineering, most reuse strategies depend on what people do worst in software engineering - understanding what other people have written. Reimplementing or respecifying a "component" is often the easiest way to guarantee that it does what you want. The best route to supporting reuse is therefore to produce tools which aid rapid understanding of existing components - in other words validation tools. At this point the insecurity argument rehearsed above clearly applies. If we find effective and safe means of validating requirements specifications, chances are that reuse will be a by-product.

S is for Specification. Specification is the central activity of requirements engineering. We cannot expect to be able to support, manage or to teach requirements engineering without understanding that activity. This means we need a model of the activity that is explicit and analysable. At the very least we need such a model to evaluate what we achieve by piecemeal "scruffy" tool development.

T is for Traceability. The problem of achieving traceability from a design, and its associated documentation, through to a requirements specification is well understood and the means for resolving it is known - establishing formal relation between successive representations. Less frequently discussed is the problem of tracing back from the requirements specification into the domain which gave rise to those requirements. The tendency, in practice, is to stop traceability with the procurer's signature on the requirements specification. In some senses this leaves the really hard problem of establishing the formal relation between the requirements specification and the tangled collection of perspectives and statements which are the product of requirements elicitation.

U is for User interfaces. There has been considerable advance in the area of user interface development methods including work in the area of task analysis. There is a clear need to integrate this with "conventional" requirements engineering. Formal specification provides an avenue for that integration.

V is for View. Requirements engineering takes place in the context of multiple overlapping and inconsistent views of the underlying domain. Integrating these views depends on achieving a precise understanding of the ways in which they are expressed and the nature and scope of the inconsistencies between them.

W is for Wicked problems. Incompleteness and inconsistency do not of themselves rule formal analysis out of court. They simply mean that great care has to be taken in the selection of the appropriate tools.

X is for eXotic representation schemes. We do not, as yet, understand what concepts are appropriate for representing requirements. Exotic representation schemes are a means of finding out. Even if they are unlikely to be of value as specification languages in their own right they can inform the development of improved specification languages.

Y is for Rationale. There seems little point in devoting a large amount of effort to documenting specification rationale if all you can do with it is read it. Reasoning about and replaying development is only possible with a formal representation of rationale.

Z is for ZZZZ. The general level of interest among the software engineering community in requirements engineering.

The Scruffy Side of Requirements Engineering

Sol Greenspan

GTE Laboratories Incorporated
Computer and Intelligent Systems Lab
40 Sylvan Road, Waltham, Massachusetts 02254

Introduction

We have been asked to take sides in a "neat vs. scruffy" debate in the Requirements Engineering arena, and I have been asked to represent the scruffies. It is quite clear that the world of Requirements Engineering is fraught with scruffy problems, and later I will list some requirements problems that have a high "scruff factor." I also happen to think there is a place for neat ideas (being myself a neat at heart). However, I will argue that much of requirements engineering is quite scruffy, and to have an impact, the neats will have to find useful niches in a scruffy world. What is needed, one might say, is embedded neatness.

But first let us try to map the essence of the original neat vs. scruffy debate in Artificial Intelligence (AI) onto the Requirements Engineering realm. The main goal in AI is to reproduce or imitate human intelligence through computational means. The neats plan to succeed by applying formal methods (i.e., logic). The scruffies would like to succeed in demonstrating intelligent behavior by any effective means, and they aren't placing their bets on formal logic. The neat approaches are generally criticized for being too simplistic and for working only on toy problems ("The real-world is more complicated than that, you know."). The scruffy approach is generally criticized for being *ad hoc*, ill-defined, and for lacking an underlying theory ("Sure, it works, but we don't understand why.").

It follows, then, that the neat vs. scruffy argument in Requirements Engineering has something to do with reproducing the intelligent problem-solving behavior of a Requirements Engineer (heretofore, RE). The neats will make promises about formal methods, while the scruffies will claim that the "real" problems are not amenable to formal treatment and will let pragmatism be their guide.

Hard Requirements Issues

The central question, then, is what are the important problem-solving behaviors of the RE? I issue a warning to the neats that a lot of the expertise and responsibilities of the RE are pretty scruffy, i.e., resistant to formalization. I challenge the neats to find neat niches, i.e., specific forms of analysis where formalization is practical and valuable. (I urge the scruffies to cooperate in the identification of these opportunities.)

Let's try to characterize the problem-solving behavior of the RE. The focus of the job is concerned with how to get a requirements statement that characterizes system concepts that are (a) best for satisfying organizational objectives, and (b) attainable with existing or feasible technologies. Thus, the RE's problem-solving is concerned with understanding and communicating business objectives and (existing and proposed) systems, and how the former can be satisfied with the latter. We add to this (c) satisfying a number of other types of constraints, such as conformance to standards, legal constraints, physical laws, and other worldly concerns. This is the core activity of requirements definition and analysis.

To illustrate the scruffiness of this job further, let us consider the interesting and exciting domain of systems in the emerging world of so-called intelligent networks, which are being introduced by telecommunications companies in order to provide new services as well as to automate operations. Some of the difficult tasks that the RE encounters in this domain (which I assume apply to other kinds of system as well) have to do with the following situations:

- The business objectives that the systems must support, in addition to being hard to articulate, may be the subject of negotiations across organizational boundaries to determine requirements. Individual objectives may be fuzzy (e.g., make lots of money, be safe), and the logistics of the communication and negotiation process may be severe.

- There is a large embedded base of systems. The RE must understand and perhaps model systems that are not neatly designed.

- Systems are usually composed of an integration of components from multiple vendors (developers). The RE must solicit and evaluate vendor proposals, and make decisions which are technically difficult, unmanageable detailed, and often not based on technical criteria.

- There are a large number of external sources of requirements, including policies, standards, and regulations stemming from the company, the industry, and government. These are often difficult to quantify or precisely state, and not easy to check for conformance.

- A number of nonfunctional requirements are imposed but it is difficult to ascertain whether solutions systems (or system components) meet these requirements.

- Both functional and nonfunctional requirements have various degrees of importance (i.e., mandatory, desired) and different parties have different priorities. Criteria for tradeoffs are hard to define.

- Systems will be composite, i.e., consisting of hardware, software, and people. Can one adequately specify the behavior and goals of the human components? How is this different from solving the general AI problem?

I do not mean to convey that the RE's situation is so hopeless that we should not bother trying to develop (neat and/or scruffy) methods and tools for him/her. What I do mean is that there are a number of very challenging issues that are not being addressed or obviously addressable by formal methods. The scruffies can try to help by providing productivity tools to facilitate communication and document preparation, by specifying informal guidelines as to the form and content of a requirements specification, and by prescribing methodologies for managing the process of gathering requirements.

Although I am representing the scruffy point of view in this position paper, my heartfelt desire is that neats will identify here an opportunity to develop formal frameworks for formulating theories and developing models of systems and of the various kinds of domain knowledge implied in the list above. A neat approach to some of these problems can be characterized as representing and reasoning about the relationships between the various kinds of knowledge. However, I entreat the neats to correct the sins of the past.

- Get out of the representation tar pit! Or "My representation is better than your representation!" The purpose of constructing a theory/model must go beyond the purposes of understanding and communication. They must support useful kinds of analysis, e.g., dealing with some of the issues listed above.

- Apply formal methods to key requirements problems! Key problems are those that significantly reduce risk, cost, and uncertainty.

- Address doable problems! Assess how much knowledge is needed to perform particular kinds of analysis; if the work involved in gathering the requirements information is too great, it won't be worth the benefit of doing the analysis.

Conclusion

In conclusion, the world of the RE is scruffy indeed. Many of the obstacles to success in Requirements Engineering are not amenable to formal methods. Even if some aspects of the problems could be formalized, it may not be worth doing, because the amount of knowledge needed may be too great.

However, research on formal methods for specifying and reasoning about systems and their requirements have had and will continue to have great value for their role in increasing our understanding of system development. (I will not mention any of this work here, since it is the job of those advocating the neat position to toot their own horn.) I would like to see this research focus on the high-leverage problems.

An example of relevant formal work is investigation of deontic and temporal logics. The former is (or at least *could be*) applied to the RE's task of considering which system components are responsible for which system functions. Temporal logics have mostly been used to specify system behavior but not to describe user requirements in natural terms.

If we want to improve the state of the art in Requirements Engineering, we certainly can't wait for the neats to formalize all the important things. However, we can try to get some leverage on a few important problems. Perhaps the neats and scruffies (who may not be so clearly separable anyway) need to work together to identify the high-payoff problems and applicable formalisms.

Expediency and Appropriate Technology:

An agenda for requirements engineering research in the 1990s

Colin Potts

MCC, Software Technology Program

Over the past few years, I have become increasingly scruffy in my thinking about system requirements. I would, of course, prefer to use a more neutral word, such as 'expediency', than 'scruffiness', because there is nothing sloppy or unprofessional about scruffiness as I am going to use the term. Quite the contrary: if engineering is the judicious application of theory to practical ends, then one can just as easily have too much of it as too little. I wish to argue that in the case of system requirements, it is better to err on the side of too little theory rather than too much.

Requirements engineering is about the communication of human intent. The profound practical difficulties that arise in requirements engineering can all be stated in simple, non-technical language, and they all come back to breakdowns in communication of one form or another: people often don't know what they want, and when they do they often can't explain it very well; people often disagree about values and plans of action; complex systems and phenomena are difficult to understand and envisage, especially when they are not immediately to hand for observation and experiment; people often misunderstand what they hear or read, particularly when they have to assimilate large volumes of information from different sources, over time, or from a large body of text.

These commonplace observations can all be recast in terms of system requirements. Instead of talking about people changing their minds, one can talk about 'requirements volatility'. Instead of talking about differences of intent, one can talk about 'viewpoint analysis'. But such translations miss the point that few of the significant problems in requirements engineering are specific to system requirements per se; they are issues general to ill-formed problem solving situations in many walks of life. Furthermore, they are so fuzzy and ill-defined that they bring to mind Von Neumann's quip (pointed out to me by Julio Leite) that you can't formalize anything until you know what you're talking about. And that, I claim is the trap that the 'neats' fall into: premature formalization.

'Neat' approaches to requirements engineering have had little effect beyond the research lab to date. This is not itself a criticism, because many valuable innovations are adopted only after an incubation period of many years. Most 'neat' requirements engineering research seems to me to have been conducted because the people involved wished to apply techniques already developed for 'downstream' software development phases further 'upstream'; for example, the application of plan-based program skeleton recognition and reuse techniques to domain model schemas, or the application of program transformations to requirements volatility. This is fundamentally a high-technology approach. Just as we have power tools for programmers, so we should have power tools for systems analysts. What this leads to is research dominated by the construction of language-sensitive editors and transformational systems, interpreters and debuggers for executable specification languages, and the like. There is a focus on automation.

In contrast, the 'scruffy' approach is to regard requirements definition and analysis as a specialization of open-ended intellectual work in general. Appropriate technology, therefore, includes specializations of more general enabling technologies, such as hypertext systems, spreadsheets, outline, or 'idea' processors, document formatters, and presentation and storyboard scripting systems. Rather than automation, the focus is on intellectual empowerment.

None of this is to say that the high-technology, 'neat' strategy is wrong. However, it is vital to understand that neatness has limitations which are more significant and instructive than its benefits. There are self-contained sub-problems and application-specific scenerios of use where neatness could pay off handsomely once the technology is mature. But these are not, and never will be, the whole story. For example, executable specifcications are a good basis for prototyping in domains where the requirements are stable enough that the effort to conduct a sufficiently detailed executable model is worthwhile. Where customers or a product team are floundering to come up with a vision of what the new system will be, a more appropriate technology might be one that facilitates the rapid construction of several ad hoc mockups. Transformational systems may be appropriate in situations where application generators are widely used today, namely where there is a detailed theory of the application and a restricted number of satisfactory target implementation architectures. But where the application is unfamiliar or cuts across several domains (a very common situation), such technology may only get in the way.

Does all this mean that requirements engineering is merely the exercise of intellectual and communication skills and that requirements engineering research is almost a contradiction in terms? I don't think so. There are many challenges to be addressed in requirements engineering that require innovative techniques and the application of appropriate technology. In Potts (1991), I describe these in greater detail and cite recent research that looks promising:

Bridging the gap from concept to essential model: Most useful techniques do not stem from computer science research, but from organizational theory, group interaction research, ethnological interviewing techniques, and seat-of-the-pants experience. A good example is the issue-based approach of Horst Rittel.

Bridging the gap from essential model to system architecture: The principal breakthroughs in this area are more likely to be methodological than technological. The strongest heuristics come from methods which emphasise domain structure rather than behavior.

Validating the model: Here is one area in which powerful technology is appropriate. Many representational techniques either have an operational semantics or could have their semantics specified without major revisions to the spirit of the technique.

Abandoning the tabula rasa assumption: Few systems are new systems. Advances in specifying and analyzing requirements for evolution and integration depend on the development and adoption of better abstraction mechanisms. A longer-term challenge is to develop techniques for predicting the impact of required changes. Traceability would be greatly aided by hypertext technology. To infer consequences of changes requires more formal models of design components and change than are currently used, which might cross the threshold from appropriate scruffiness to neat unusability. A granularity tradeoff must also be addressed: smaller components enable greater precision, but higher update overhead whenever changes are made.

Integrating requirements engineering with system planning: Requirements include cost and development time constraints, and the requirements phase of a project is also the time when the project is planned. However, few requirements techniques address the connection between project and product features.

In conclusion, the most significant challenges in requirements engineering are all best addressed by 'scruffy', hands-on, field-tested, low-technology innovations.

References

Potts, C., 'Seven (plus or minus two) challenges for requirements analysis research', *Proc. 6th Int. Workshop Software Specification and Design.*, IEEE Comp. Soc. Press, 1991.

CASE Support For The Software Process

Peter Hruschka

Systemhaus GEI
Pascalstraße 14, D-5100 Aachen, Germany
hruschka@gei-aachen.de

Many methods have been suggested over the last 20 years to improve the process of developing software . Within the last decade lots of tools have appeared on the market supporting one or other method. In about 1986 the term CASE (Computer Aided Software Engineering) was coined for such tools. Using a wide interpretation, CASE covers any computer-aided tool supporting any activity during software development, from system planning and analysis to coding and testing, from estimating to controlling, from communication support to version and configuration control, etc.

In this panel we will examine how helpful CASE can be in supporting the process of creating software and systems **today**. Potential users find themselves in a complicated situation. Not only that there are hundreds of CASE tools available. It has been said that selecting CASE is at least as complicated as buying a new car because many parameters have to be taken into account. And introducing CASE into a company could be the largest project that the company has undertaken, since it involves nearly all of the staff over a long period of time (maybe 5 to 10 years!)

The panelists have been selected to represent a broad spectrum: CASE users are represented, whose goal mainly is the engineering of **end-user systems** in time and within budget. CASE developers are represented, providing state-of-the-art **CASE products** and introductory support and guidance. CASE researchers complete the panel, providing **basic research results** in various important areas.

They all have been asked to answer the same two questions from their respective viewpoints:

1) What are the three major advances in CASE today? What has CASE really achieved so far and why do you think that this has improved the software development process?

2) What are the three major open issues? What has to be solved in the future? What are the largest handicaps and obstacles for CASE users today? What are the

areas that need more basic research? Why aren't we n-times more productive and why haven't we improved quality by m percent?

We have definitely achieved some benefits with CASE, since about 10 percent of all system developers **are currently using** some CASE tools and are providing success stories about their projects. So we have already passed the 5 percent hurdle, where a technology is still considered to be in its infancy and only used by brave pioneers and true believers. Some market researchers claim that by the mid 90s every second developer will have access to CASE.

But we definitely have some problems, too, since 90 percent of the developers are **currently not using** CASE to develop their systems. Is it just lacl of awareness, lack of education, lack of appropriate hardware and infrastructure in their companies or are there serious problems inhibiting successful use of CASE in their environments?

It is my firm believe that CASE is here to stay: some of the software engineering achievements of the last 20 years are already effectively supported by tools. Any further "SE" advances will only become fully effective when "CA" tools are provided for them. The panel will hopefully contribute to setting the expectations of potential users of CASE to the right level and to guiding developers and researchers to provide the results urgently requested by users in the near future.

CASE Support for the Software Process: A Research Viewpoint.

Jeff Kramer

Department of Computing,
Imperial College of Science, Technology and Medicine,
180 Queen's Gate, London SW7 2BZ, UK.
jk@doc.ic.ac.uk

1. INTRODUCTION

The process of software production involves many stages, from requirements elicitation and specification through to system construction and maintenance. A large number of methods can be used during this process, each covering different stages of the process. Each method generally consists of one or more representation schemes (notations) together with a set of recommended procedures and heuristics as to how to complete each representation and guidance on how to move to the next representation. These methods may overlap or be disjoint. It is generally left to the project team to try to convert information to a suitable form for the next stage, to ensure consistency and to try to bridge the gaps between the different methods and notations required for each stage of the process. Even at a single stage, it is necessary to represent different aspects of the application, not only in terms of a partitioning of the application domain but also to provide different views (such as functional, performance, fault tolerance, safety and others). In addition, different companies and project personnel will need to tailor individual methods and the overall software process according to their experience and the particular application domain.

These are the requirements of the software development process. The vision is of a CASE framework for method integration, which supports distributed development by teams of personnel, provides tool support for the entire software lifecycle and which can be customised to suit both the particular application domain and the particular user environment. How far are we from achieving this goal? We address this by first assessing the current achievements of CASE technology, and then by examining what are believed to be some of the major research issues which are outstanding. Although of critical importance, the area of management is largely neglected in this paper as it lies beyond the expertise of the author.

2. ACHIEVEMENTS

One of the major advances in CASE technology has been in the support for **graphics**. Users expect and CASE tools readily provide an integration of textual and graphical means for data entry and display. Aided by advanced hardware technology, graphics are no longer slow and painful to produce. This advance in graphics has contributed greatly to current acceptance and use of CASE tools in the marketplace. For example, Software Though Pictures STP [13] is a CASE tool which supports multiple graphical editors.

It has been recognised that, in the development of specifications, designs and systems, users require **feedback** to raise the confidence they have in their work. This ranges from formal verification (in the case of formal specifications) and analysis (of aspects such as performance), to animation and simulation as a means of interpreting the possible consequences of their designs or specifications. The result is that appropriate feedback tools have also been integrated into the specification/design tool, thereby enhancing its utility and extending its use over a larger part of the development process. Some have even taken this further by the provision of generators for prototype software. A good example of such a CASE tool is Statemate [6], which provides good graphics support for its notation, statecharts [7], integrated simulation for analysis and feedback, and generators for fast prototyping.

A third achievement has been more recent, and is a natural consequence of the early CASE work in syntax-directed editors. These evolved from the early provision of support for one notation or language to the provision of generalised editors which could generate a specific editor by the provision of its grammar, rules or set of graphical symbols. These provided the basis for **meta-CASE** tools from which customised CASE tools can be generated. Meta-CASE tools are now commercially available (eg. [1,11]), providing support for a range of notations for methods. Besides the obvious advantage in the ability to derive many tools from one metatool, a particular advantage is the ease with which one can tailor or modify a tool by modifying its grammar or rules. An interesting result is the ability to define the metatool itself in the grammar, and hence provide a sound and easy means for bootstrapping a new version from an old!

3. CHALLENGES

Current CASE tools still tend to be focussed on a particular stage of the development process. The need to provide multiple views and to extend the coverage over a larger part of the process requires **integration** of methods, notations and tools. This work is largely dictated by the means for information exchange which is generally provided by the use of a common data model, usually supported by a common, centralised data base or repository. This has the advantage of providing a uniform basis for consistency checking. Multiview facilities and extensions [10] are then supported by the provision of mappings to/from the common data model, as in STP [13]. Although one could identify such integration as one of the major achievements of CASE support, I feel this to be unjustified. The use of centralised data bases at the heart of much of the early IPSE work was one of the major causes in the limited success of that technology. General data models are difficult to design and tend to be difficult to modify and extend if radically different new tools are to be integrated. It is analogous to the search for "universality". Therefore, although this approach has enabled us to make good progress in the provision of current CASE tools, I believe that the centralised repository approach is too tightly integrated, and will be one of the major restrictions in the provision of tools which integrate more methods and notations, cover a larger part of the lifecycle and support use by large teams of software engineers.

Besides the need for multiple notations, methods and views as expressed earlier, there is the need to support multiple users. Personnel on a project will generally be at different stages of development, working independently but communicating to transfer information and coordinate their efforts. Loose coupling between users and between their methods and tools is preferable for facilitating change. Although this seems to be an ideal application for distributed computing techniques, **distribution** is yet to have a major impact on the CASE world. Perry [12] has identified evolution, complexity and scale as three major concerns in the provision of software development environments for multiple users. Distribution has much to offer to all three areas through its support for partitioning and decentralisation, with loose coupling as the form of composition. Information exchange between distributed tools and views can then be provided by direct mappings or transformations rather than through some centralised repository.

One of the drawbacks cited for distribution is the problem of consistency. It is generally more difficult to check and maintain consistency in a distributed environment. On the other hand, I believe that we should reexamine this obsession with consistency, and perhaps make more provision for **inconsistency**. Inconsistency is inevitable as part of the development process. Forcing consistency tends to restrict the development process and stifle novelty and invention. Furthermore, if consistency is required at all times, it can also make tool support less responsive. Consistency is a relative notion, and should perhaps be considered as a piecemeal process, to be checked incrementally between particular parts or views of a design or specification. Also, it should only be checked at particular stages rather than enforced as a matter of course. Consistency resolution and the need for human intervention are also challenging aspects.

Dealing with inconsistency is part of a more general need to provide real support for **method guidance**. Methods are intended to supplement rather than replace a user's skill. Methods include rules, recommended procedures and heuristics which need to be encoded in the CASE tools in some way. Rules and constraints in method use are easily provided, but help and guidance which cater for users of widely varying degrees of expertise are usually not provided. Advice needs to support both normal and unconventional use of the method. A support tool that could not deal with deviations from the recommended method and treated them as 'errors' from which it could not recover, would be unacceptable. For instance, a crucial part of any active guidance system for a method is the remediation mechanism whereby possible repair procedures are deduced and recommended to the practitioner. In addition, the guidance system should perhaps include some ordering or prioritisation of advice between alternative actions, such as corrective actions before method steps. Early steps in this direction were provided in the TARA project on Tool Assisted Requirements Analysis [3,9].

4. CONCLUSIONS

Thus, under the major concern for **integration,** the issues which I believe need promotion for the advance of CASE support are **distribution,** the need to cope with **inconsistency** and the need for real **method guidance.** Our current work on ViewPoints aims to facilitate distributed development and the use of multiple representation schemes. The approach is based on partitioning the application domain, the notations and the method steps into separate distributable ViewPoints [2], with a configurable framework for method and tool integration [5]. Our intention is that this framework will also provide an environment for the examination of the inconsistency and method guidance issues. The ViewPoint approach is also strongly related to Jackson's recent work on views and implementations [8] in which he copes with "complexity in terms of separation and composition of concerns".

REFERENCES

[1]   A. Alderson. "Meta-CASE technology", Software Development Environments and CASE Technology, European Symposium, Königswinter, June 1991, LNCS 509 (Endres and Weber eds.), Springer Verlag, 81-91.

[2]   A. Finkelstein , J. Kramer, and M. Goedicke. " ViewPoint Oriented Software Development", Proc. of 3rd International Workshop on Software Engineering and its Applications, Toulouse, France, December 1990.

[3]   A. Finkelstein and J. Kramer. " TARA: Tool Assisted Requirements Analysis", to appear in Conceptual Modelling, Databases and CASE: An Integrated View of Information Systems Development, Loucopoulos and Zicari (eds), McGraw Hill, 1991.

[4]   J. Kramer, K. Ng, C. Potts, K. Whitehead, "Tool Support for Requirements Analysis" IEE Software Engineering Journal, Vol. 3,3, May 1988.

[5]   J. Kramer and A. Finkelstein, "A Configurable Framework for Method and Tool Integration", Software Development Environments and CASE Technology, European Symposium, Königswinter, June 1991, LNCS 509 (Endres and Weber eds.), Springer Verlag, 233-257.

This is joint work with Anthony Finkelstein of Imperial College, and Michael Goedicke of the University of Essen

[6] D. Harel, H. Lachover, A. Naamad, A. Pnueli, M. Politi, R. Sherman, A. Shtul-Trauring and M. Trakhtenbrot, "STATEMATE: A Working Environment for the Development of Complex Reactive Systems", IEEE Trans. on Software Engineering, Vol.16, 4, April 1990, 403-414.

[7] D. Harel. "Statecharts: A Visual Formalism for Complex Systems", Science of Computer Programming, 8, 1987, 231-274.

[8] M.A.Jackson. "Some Complexities in Computer-Based Systems and their implications for System Development", Proc. of IEEE Int. Conf. on Computer Systems and Software Engineering (CompEuro 90), Tel-Aviv, Israel, May 1990, 344-351.

[9] J. Kramer, K. Ng, C. Potts, K. Whitehead. "Tool Support for Requirements Analysis", IEE Software Engineering Journal, Vol. 3,3, May 1988.

[10] S. Meyers. "Difficulties in Integrating Multiview Development Systems", IEEE Software, Vol. 8,1, Jan. 1991, 49-57.

[11] J. Pocock. "VSF and its relationship to Open Systems and Standard Repositories", Software Development Environments and CASE Technology, European Symposium, Königswinter, June 1991, LNCS 509 (Endres and Weber eds.), Springer Verlag, 53-68.

[12] D.E. Perry. "Industrial Strength Software Development Environments", Information Processing 89, G.X.Ritter (ed), Elsevier (North Holland), 1989, 195-203.

[13] A.I. Wasserman and P.A. Pircher. "A Graphical, Extensible Integrated Environment for Software Development", Proc. of 2nd Symposium on Practical Software Development Environments, SIGPlan Notices, Vol. 22, 1, Jan. 1987, 131-142.

CASE Support For Large Systems

Dave Robinson

SD-Scicon UK Limited
Pembroke House, Pembroke Broadway
Camberley, Surrey GU 15 3XD

1. Introduction

This paper presents the view of the author and members of the AIMS project, a European Aerospace initiative funded under the EUREKA programme. I am subcontractor to the project and have been its system architect for three and a half years. Five European Aerospace companies have taken part in the initiative; Aerospatiale, Alenia, British Aerospace, CASA, and MBB (now Deutsche Aerospace). We are currently in its third phase; the Demonstration Phase, with Aerospatiale, Alenia and British Aerospace actively involved, while Deutsche Aerospace is negotiating re-entry after its company's recent restructuring.

The advantages and open issues discussed below are based on feedback and actual benefits derived from specific Embedded Computing System development experience gained by one or more of the project partners. Specifically, the IPSE technology employed on the Experimental Aircraft Project (EAP) was instrumental in providing quantifiable evidence of cost savings and quality improvements. Published results show that for an investment of £30,000 per person, a return of £180,000 per person was achieved. Significantly this investment cost encompassed training, education, equipment, and method investment, as well as software product investment.

Today, four of the AIMS partners are collaborating on developing the European Fighter Aircraft (EFA). This is a multimillion pound project, which has on board more complex Embedded Computer Systems than any previous aircraft. With the returns already seen on the EAP development, the partners were keen to capitalise and enhance the practices and support technologies that gave the six to one return on investment. The resultant IPSE technology chosen is known as the Eurofighter IPSE. The major advances described in this paper are based on the technology of the EAP environment and the Eurofighter IPSE. The open issues are based on the leading edge drive of these European Aerospace companies, that are being addressed by the AIMS project.

2. Major Advances in CASE Today

2.1 Modelling and its Integration Effects

Successes, when they happen, always seem to be inevitable. So one of today's successes in IPSE capabilities seem to be secondary to the support technology that enables it to happen. We refer to the practice of modelling. There are three areas of modelling.

1) *The Modelling of the Product under Development.* This includes the history or derivation trail of its development from requirements through to operational use and maintenance.
2) *The Modelling of the Development Process.* This is the working practices or activities carried out in order to develop the product.
3) *The Modelling of the Organisation carrying out the Development.* This is the representation of the organisational roles which carry out the development, together with delegation and authority assignments.

To the European Aerospace industry, all three aspects listed above need to be integrated in order that they can effectively manage and control its ECSs development and maintenance, while meeting their stringent certification and safety critical demands. However, in the industry at large, we see many products coming onto the market which support one or two of these concepts, or part of the concepts embodied in full scale IPSEs. These products help smaller development users who may not be able to afford the extra costs which such high quality demands bring, but who can gain from the ability of using modeling techniques.
Certainly, data modelling has been around in the industry for a long time. But the advent of IPSEs and PTI technology has brought about the widening of the technique to be applied to the Development Process and Organisational concepts of System and Software Development. This brings about the real payback in focusing on the key aspects of integration across these development project concepts. Today, modelling enables this to happen, but the support technology and company culture in the industry leaves this as an open issue we will discuss below.
But what of the support technologies that enable such modelling to take place. Repositories get the majority of attention. Great debates on repositories are passionate and frequent among supplier specialists; Entity Relationship, Object-Oriented, Extented Relational, and Semantic models all have their protagonists. But all of these models enable good modelling practices to be carried out, and let people think about what integration they really want from the three aspects of product, process and organisation. We shall see later that this is an area where improvement is required.

2.2 Controlled Team Working

Today's Eurofighter IPSE supports a controlled environment where the tasks carried out on the development, the delegation of tasks, and the authorisation (and assurance) of the items developed by the tasks are all automatically supported by an integrated version, variant and configuration model. This provides the following advantages:

- tasks assigned to developers ensure that only the information needed to carry out the task is provided.
- project management has development control over the consistent development of the right versions of items, and the correct configuration of developed items.

- project management has control over delegation of tasks and the levels of authorisation required to approve development work carried out.
- no version of a development item can be accidentally deleted.

This then is the second major advance that IPSEs have given the European Aerospace developers today. An integrated set of facilities to do with controlled team working. These capabilities allow a large development project to be managed and monitored, with the organisational aspects of information control fully automated. The way in which the version, variant and configuration capabilities are integrated with the task allocation and return scheme means that developers do not need to concern themselves with these details. The creation and level control of versions of development items, and the appropriate grouping of items for a task is automatically controlled. The tasking scheme is integrated with the organisational roles to control who is allowed to delegate tasks, and who receives the results, while it prevents development of items other than those defined to be developed.

2.3 Controlled Change

During the development of an Embedded Computing System modifications to the original development are made. This is either brought about by software, rig or flight testing. In addition, changes to the original requirements may bring about modifications. Utilising the controlled team working scheme described above, change control is brought under the same degree of management control·as the original development. This then, while utilising the same support technology, gives the development user its third major advantage.

3. Open Issues in CASE Today

3.1 Introducing Change into an Organisation

Under the sponsorship of NATO's SWG on APSE, the PCIS initiative is looking at the next generation of IPSE/PTI standards. They have held two public workshops at which users confirmed that their biggest problem today was introducing new technology into their organisations. They stated that they did not need more new technology, they needed help in introducing existing technology. For example, the supplier driven initiatives of the Eighties had produced the PCTE PTI technology, but users found they could not convince their companies strategic decision makers to make the high initial investment, or take the high degree of risk that introducing such major changes brought about.

The users at the PCIS workshop identified four major hurdles to introducing change

1) Identify the problem they are trying to solve in terms that the strategy decision makers (of their companies) can understand.

2) Demonstrate to the strategy decision makers the benefits they will get from the introduction of the change. These benefits should be quantified in terms to which they can relate.
3) Handle the resistance to change on the shop floor.
4) Manage the actual introduction of the change in technology.

So this is the first open issue, how do the suppliers of CASE technology who have been instrumental in the technology push of the Eighties respond to the User Pull demands of the Nineties.

3.2 True Integration for Development

While we discussed today's capabilities to model process, product and organisational aspects of developement above, one of the most common mis-uses of the word integration applies to tool integration. Many of today's solutions when boasting of an integrated tool set, mean that they have entities in an environment that have a file attribute, and in that file attribute, resides the information and knowledge produced by a tool. The underlying support environment has no knowledge of, or control over that tool information. Further, while a number of tools have been integrated in this way the methods they suport may be incompatible and the user is still left with the problem of resolving that incompatibility.
What is requried is to perform method integration rather than tool integration. In addition, the method should be compatible (i.e. integrated) with the Development Model.
One issue associated with this is highlighted by the technology push, user pull difference. Currently there is an initiative to develop a reference model. This is infamously referred to as the Toaster Model. However this model is a solution oriented architecture, featuring design type components. Should there be a user driven initiative to define Development Models? The focus on this would be what are the important elements that a user requires technology support for. This would feature the product, process, and organisation modelling semantics referred to above.
This then is the second open issue, what do we really mean be integration, should it be the user driven interpretation, or the solution driven interpretation? What are the semantics of system development that govern integration.

3.3 Environments and the Role of Tools within Them

This topic is related to the integration issue above. What we are seeing happening today is that CASE/IPSE environments are taking over much of the work traditionally carried out by tools.

1) *Interface Management.* Already tools no longer need to handle the complexities of user interface details. Windows and tool builders kits (TBK, VSF, Object Maker) are now available to do this.

2) *Information (Data) Management.* Many tools effectively define a data model and manage the information produced by the tool. However as we see in the previous item, in the future this information can no longer be knowledge known only to the tool. Users require this information for traceability, maintenance, quality assurance, and other reasons. Environments are providing powerful modelling and management capabilities, and these will be steadily improving.

3) *Process Management.* Tools manage the sequence of operations and the integrity rules associated with these operations. At the moment these operations are of such low a level that an IPSE would not require such detailed modelling of activities. However, if Formal Methods are incorporated into environments and formal proofs become part of the development process then this situation may change.

4) *Integrity Rules.* While the integrity of the data transformation a tool carries out may be left with the tool, there is a requirement that the environment hold the knowledge of that transformation and has a knowledge of any integrity rules that should persist outside the lifetime of the tool invocation. Again this is guaranteed be the tool as only by invocation of the tool can the information be accessed. With the information being held in the environment repository this task will no longer be the responsibility of the tool.

The open issue for discussion here is how will the emergence of support environments governing more and more aspects of the total Developement Process affect the traditional role and function of individual tools.

In this paper I have used the term IPSE rather then CASE. I think the term reflects how you look at, and approach, system development: from an "in the large" or an "in the small" position. This is reflected in the evolution taking place at the moment CASE has started firmly from the tool camp and is moving out. IPSE has started from the green fields of PTI et al. Will they arrive at the same place? Which will get there first?

CASE Seen From Both Sides Of The Fence

Wolf E. Fischer

debis Systemhaus GEI
Pascalstr. 14, D 5100 Aachen, Germany

1. The Dual Role

As an early CASE user in the area of developing medical X-ray systems I have had the opportunity of working with Upper CASE tools since 1985. I have continued being a user over the last three years, during which time I have been in charge of developing GEI's CASE products. Developing CASE tools is a large software project itself, under extreme time pressure because of the international competition and of course under budget limitations. So my position is influenced by my experience both as a user and as a CASE developer, where market needs and trends determine the requirements and priorities for the next versions.

2. Achievements

Among the initial requirements for our ProMod environment was the **support of the full life cycle**, not just the support of a single activity. Ten years ago that meant bridging the gap between **one** selected requirements methodology (i.e. Structured Analysis) and **one** selected design methodology (i.e. Modular Design). This was limited to **one** specific platform (i.e. VAX/VMS). We consider it a major achievement that the support of the process from the first ideas to the final code has been improved in various ways. Meanwhile multiple views for modeling requirements have been integrated, allowing information system analysts as well as embedded real-time system analysts to emphasize the dominant view in their models. Using these results one can either work towards modular system architectures and implementation in classical 3GLs like Fortran and C or one can generate data base schemas and 4GL code for data-driven applications. All the integrated tools are available on 7 different platforms, including UNIX workstations and SAA-compliant architectures.

Most problems in software development become harder as the size and the scope of the projects increase. Therefore, Software Engineering methods and CASE are most effective in medium to large projects, not in supporting a single person's activities. Most methods have been developed in such a way that work breakdown structures are supported. Such methods ensure that everybody in the project is "talking the same language". Some of the early CASE tools already supported teamwork in the sense that submodels (developed by different people or groups) could be combined into larger models and checked for global consistency and completeness. Since the early tools were most often built on top of file systems, merging the results of different users often was a tedious, time-consuming and an error-prone process. Today we have client/server architectures allowing **effective cooperation in teams** based on structural object-oriented data base systems, which can be used online from different users in the project.

A large handicap of early CASE tools was their handling. In addition to learning the software engineering methods, users often had to take 3 - 5 day courses just to learn how to use the tool. Software developers spent a lot of time not working on the problem, but just figuring out how to input and output their ideas to the tools. Today window-oriented, icon-driven, graphical user interfaces are the state-of-the-art. We have spent a lot of effort to go one step further: on every platform users of CASE tools should find a **familiar look and feel**. This could be DecWindows, OpenLook, Motif or CUA. One can use the CASE tools in the same way as all the other tools that comply with the style guides provided by the manufacturers. So, training and learning efforts can concentrate on methods and problem solving techniques again. One of the major acceptance problems for CASE has been eliminated.

3. Open Issues

In each area of software engineering methods we find a multitude of approaches, often with very similar concepts. Nevertheless many different notations and different terminologies are used. New notations and new terminologies are added constantly hardly changing much of the essential concepts. In Europe especially we still see national standards like Merise or SSADM competing, but the same is true for methods like SA, SSA and SADT. We see a definite need to come to **more method convergence** internationally (at least for some "kernel methods"). The advantage for users would be less uncertainty about which method they should select. It would be much easier to cooperate internationally in large projects. CASE manufacturers would also benefit, because they could provide exchange formats between tools on a more sophisticated level. GEI supports these standardisation efforts in multiple ways. For real-time & embedded systems, e.g., the ESPRIT project COMPLEMENT aims at harmonizing the existing methods and tools and setting up a large technology transfer programme.

As mentioned above we have seen a lot of progress in integrating the development portion of the software process. Other areas of large projects like planning, version control, or office automation functions still have to be integrated with the technical development. Most companies have basic mechanisms for these administrative activities in place (independent of their use of CASE). Even if CASE tools offer these functionalities one can not expect users to change their environment. Therefore

CASE tools have to become more open and more flexible. They have to provide **better interfaces and integration mechanisms for administrative services,** so that they can be combined with planning and estimating systems, with mail and documentation systems, etc. Such flexible architectures are currently being developed at GEI, partially within the Eureka Software Factory programme and partially within vendor-specific frameworks like IBM's AD/Cycle or DEC's Cohesion.

More and more activities of the development process are supported by CASE. Although good integration has been achieved, for example between requirements, design and implementation methods, we see a need for **faster and more efficient traceability mechanisms** in CASE tools. The software life cycle is changing. Many CASE tools are principally based on the waterfall model. Projects are rarely working according to it. Instead we have to take into account prototyping methods, maintenance of existing systems, reuse, reengineering and much more. We are working towards flexible process models to allow project-specific or company-specific tailoring of the activities and steps in the development process. Such process models will only be successful when we have more flexible means of tracing information collected by one tool in one step to the many other places where this information is also used. Method convergence and better links to administrative services - as discussed above - are prerequisites to reach this goal.

4. Conclusions

We have reached a maturity in methods and CASE tool support, that allows teams to efficiently cooperate in the development of systems. Predefined sets of methods assist them, from requirements analysis to coding and integration. Tools today are user friendly and intuitive to handle; and since familiar, graphical user interfaces are offered little or no user interface training is needed.

Further advances can be achieved if the number of conceptually similar, but in details different methods converge and become more standardized. CASE tools need more flexible tool-to-tool interfaces; especially better links to existing administrative tools. This would also enable tools to be combined under tailorable process models and support better traceability of all the information collected in the development process.

CASE Support for the Software Process:
Advances and Problems

Bernard Lang

INRIA
B.P. 105, 78153 Le Chesnay CEDEX, France
bernard.lang@inria.fr

Je maintiendrai
Motto of the House of Nassau

There are many facets to the software process, and much controversy over their identification or importance. However it seems obvious to me that we can at least distinguish between the technical and the managerial aspects. Being an academic, I am of course biased towards the technical issues, but even management has its techniques.

1. Achievements or Advances.

There have been many major advances in the technical aspects of the software process. To begin with, lets us recall that the problems predate their identification as a Software Engineering discipline, and complex software, presenting to a large extent similar problems, was already developed in the sixties. These problems were addressed as they emerged and were understood, with a varying degree of success. Though now a popular acronym, CASE is not a new concept, and we have been building tools since the inception of Computer Science.

Bearing this in mind, I would assert that one of the greatest achievement of CASE technology has been in the realm of reuse. Indeed, early advances in software technology have been based on the development of operating systems and of languages and compilers. Operating systems actually started as a systematization of various routines commonly used by programs, and which were standardized both to regulate the use of the machine and to avoid repetitious programming tasks. Similarly, programming languages were developed to embody in a systematic way programming techniques that had been identified as useful. There is only a difference of degree between a simple reusable component, a parameterized component, a component generator, and a compiler (for a language). This trend is far from abating: many languages have been and are being developed embodying new programming knowledge either w.r.t. coding technology or w.r.t. problem domain technology.

One of the best example is the current development of synchronous real-time languages that simplify the programming of large classes of reactive systems by embodying in a compiler advanced knowledge of the problem domain. An older example concerns parameterized components, and component generators such as Yacc and Lex to cite the most well known. A last example is the development of new extensions to operating systems that provide collections of ready made components for various purposes, most notably the creation of man-machine interfaces.

Finally, I would note that the so-called "*object oriented*" techniques that have gained so much recognition lately — and are essentially expressed as new structures in programming languages or data-bases — have and will considerably improve reuse technology.

I believe the second major achievement is the development of new operating system layers and tools, most notably in *networking, data-bases and man-machine interfaces*. To be effective, computerized support has to properly integrate all the services offered by the machine, and also to integrate the contributions of all the people involved in the software process. Indeed such integration mechanisms are one of the foremost and most difficult research topics at this time. However, none of the essential work would be possible without the fantastic evolution of the available **platforms**.

Similarly, the progress in graphical interfaces has considerably improved the responsiveness and usability of our tools. Indeed, one of the major difficulties for the software engineer or the programmer is the very mass of facts, commands, rules (etc...) that have to be learned and memorized in order to cope with current computer environments. Self explicative modern tools, as pioneered by the Macintosh, considerably relieve this load, and graphics considerably increase the communication bandwidth. Also the quality of graphical interface generators makes it easier to create and customize new tools.

The third achievement I would like to mention concerns the evolution of the **architecture of CASE tools and environments**, which should not, as is sometimes the case, be confused with the architecture of the supporting platform (e.g. distributed implementation). Monolithic systems are now being replaced by open architectures aiming at the integration of independently produced CASE tools. Simultaneously, many tools are now replaced by parameterized tools, or tool generators. Though far from over, this evolution already brings many benefits to users (if also some losses to manufacturers):

- creation of a competitive market of integratable tools, that can be produced by the most competent companies in each concerned area.

- customization of tools, and of environments built from tools to adapt to the need of companies and software projects.

- ability of tools and environments to evolve with the needs of users, and with the progress of technology.

- disappearance of scale factor preventing the contribution of smaller companies or countries as producers or consumers of CASE environments.

- better integration of CASE tools, w.r.t. functionality, and particularly w.r.t. to look and feel (see also previous point).

Another benefit of this architectural evolution is that it positively influences the design and architecture of the software systems produced.

The development of numerous methods that assist the design and development of complex software project might also be seen as an essential achievement, considering their crucial role in most industrial projects. It is not clear to me whether these tools are fundamental, or whether there are only (*very necessary*) crutches intended to compensate for the current inadequacy of other tools (that could well be changed, e.g. programming languages), or worse to compensate for the inadequacy or limited ability of the people involved (whom we have to live with).

2. Open issues.

Since one of the roles of a panel is to be controversial, I shall state that what I consider a major success, namely reuse, is also a major open issue, if only because of its remaining potential for increasing productivity. The problem is still open in many respects:

- we are more demanding and expect to reuse all types of documents/data that occur in the software process: code of course, but also design, development history, etc.

- the interaction between reuse and software certification is not too well understood.

- we are now aiming for very large data bases of reusable components, opening many hard research problems w.r.t. the organization of these data bases and the component retrieval algorithms.

- the problem is further compounded by the availability of component generators, and by mechanized combination of components, leading to higher order problems.

Possibly, an analysis of how reuse has been dealt with in the past, through its implicit contribution to the evolution of systems and languages could give us some hints for new paths to follow.

Another glaring open problem is **modularity and standards**. Considerable progress has been made from procedures, to modules and Abstract Data Types (ADT), to "object oriented" techniques. But many issues are still not well understood and raise complex theoretical problems, many of which are being addressed by the research on type systems. In this respect, software engineering could benefit from a more mature attitude towards programming techniques. The community focuses too much on fashion, religion and buzz-words like logic programming, ADT, object orientation, with very little respect, attention and connection to the actual mechanisms and constructions they offer and permit. I found this lack of clear identification of technical concepts to be a major problem in large team work.

More specifically related to the architecture of CASE environments is the issue of properly identifying the useful CASE functionalities, and even more importantly of characterizing their interfaces and the (logical or physical) types of data/structures and control they should exchange. A typical example, still seeking consensus after 15 years, is the representation of programs. Identifying, and standardizing these interfaces is crucial for the success of open and customizable CASE environments or software factories.

This leads me to what I believe to be one of the most controversial and open problem, though it is not strictly speaking a technical one: **patents** and **interface copyright** laws.

It is not my intention here to take sides on this issue. However I am surprised how little serious discussion there has been in the community to determine what kind of laws would be the most appropriate to protect the interest of creators, and of users, without preventing progress. I have seen little response to the very cogent (if controversial) positions of the founders of the Free Software Foundation.

Considering the importance of standards, and the fact that they often correspond to marketed products, this issue will certainly bear on the progress of CASE environments.

Concerning the managerial aspects of the software process, it seems to me that much work has been done in other areas for automating production processes, but this work seems seldom taken into account in the SE literature. Are there specific reasons that justify this?

I would also like to point out that software production is to a large extent the production and management of complex inter-related documents. Hence the development of office automation should have a notable impact on software production technology. Though I cannot assess myself whether that is the case, I believe this issue should be raised.

3. Conclusion

My own work being more with design and implementation techniques for CASE tools for advanced users, I am moderately qualified to actually assess their effectiveness in general industrial environments, and this has certainly biased my choices.

I have tried to strictly adhere to the panel topic as stated, namely CASE support. However, it is my strong belief that much of the progress in software engineering stems for other, often unexpected, sources. CASE is only a way to mechanize technical knowledge that has been previously acquired. Experiments and theoretical research are still much needed to increase this knowledge.

Vol. 505: E. H. L. Aarts, J. van Leeuwen, M. Rem (Eds.), PARLE '91. Parallel Architectures and Languages Europe, Volume I. Proceedings, 1991. XV, 423 pages. 1991.

Vol. 506: E. H. L. Aarts, J. van Leeuwen, M. Rem (Eds.), PARLE '91. Parallel Architectures and Languages Europe, Volume II. Proceedings, 1991. XV, 489 pages. 1991.

Vol. 507: N. A. Sherwani, E. de Doncker, J. A. Kapenga (Eds.), Computing in the 90's. Proceedings, 1989. XIII, 441 pages. 1991.

Vol. 508: S. Sakata (Ed.), Applied Algebra, Algebraic Algorithms and Error-Correcting Codes. Proceedings, 1990. IX, 390 pages. 1991.

Vol. 509: A. Endres, H. Weber (Eds.), Software Development Environments and CASE Technology. Proceedings, 1991. VIII, 286 pages. 1991.

Vol. 510: J. Leach Albert, B. Monien, M. Rodríguez (Eds.), Automata, Languages and Programming. Proceedings, 1991. XII, 763 pages. 1991.

Vol. 511: A. C. F. Colchester, D.J. Hawkes (Eds.), Information Processing in Medical Imaging. Proceedings, 1991. XI, 512 pages. 1991.

Vol. 512: P. America (Ed.), ECOOP '91. European Conference on Object-Oriented Programming. Proceedings, 1991. X, 396 pages. 1991.

Vol. 513: N. M. Mattos, An Approach to Knowledge Base Management. IX, 247 pages. 1991. (Subseries LNAI).

Vol. 514: G. Cohen, P. Charpin (Eds.), EUROCODE '90. Proceedings, 1990. XI, 392 pages. 1991.

Vol. 515: J. P. Martins, M. Reinfrank (Eds.), Truth Maintenance Systems. Proceedings, 1990. VII, 177 pages. 1991. (Subseries LNAI).

Vol. 516: S. Kaplan, M. Okada (Eds.), Conditional and Typed Rewriting Systems. Proceedings, 1990. IX, 461 pages. 1991.

Vol. 517: K. Nökel, Temporally Distributed Symptoms in Technical Diagnosis. IX, 164 pages. 1991. (Subseries LNAI).

Vol. 518: J. G. Williams, Instantiation Theory. VIII, 133 pages. 1991. (Subseries LNAI).

Vol. 519: F. Dehne, J.-R. Sack, N. Santoro (Eds.), Algorithms and Data Structures. Proceedings, 1991. X, 496 pages. 1991.

Vol. 520: A. Tarlecki (Ed.), Mathematical Foundations of Computer Science 1991. Proceedings, 1991. XI, 435 pages. 1991.

Vol. 521: B. Bouchon-Meunier, R. R. Yager, L. A. Zadeh (Eds.), Uncertainty in Knowledge-Bases. Proceedings, 1990. X, 609 pages. 1991.

Vol. 522: J. Hertzberg (Ed.), European Workshop on Planning. Proceedings, 1991. VII, 121 pages. 1991. (Subseries LNAI).

Vol. 523: J. Hughes (Ed.), Functional Programming Languages and Computer Architecture. Proceedings, 1991. VIII, 666 pages. 1991.

Vol. 524: G. Rozenberg (Ed.), Advances in Petri Nets 1991. VIII, 572 pages. 1991.

Vol. 525: O. Günther, H.-J. Schek (Eds.), Advances in Spatial Databases. Proceedings, 1991. XI, 471 pages. 1991.

Vol. 526: T. Ito, A. R. Meyer (Eds.), Theoretical Aspects of Computer Software. Proceedings, 1991. X, 772 pages. 1991.

Vol. 527: J.C.M. Baeten, J. F. Groote (Eds.), CONCUR '91. Proceedings, 1991. VIII, 541 pages. 1991.

Vol. 528: J. Maluszynski, M. Wirsing (Eds.), Programming Language Implementation and Logic Programming. Proceedings, 1991. XI, 433 pages. 1991.

Vol. 529: L. Budach (Ed.), Fundamentals of Computation Theory. Proceedings, 1991. XII, 426 pages. 1991.

Vol. 530: D. H. Pitt, P.-L. Curien, S. Abramsky, A. M. Pitts, A. Poigné, D. E. Rydeheard (Eds.), Category Theory and Computer Science. Proceedings, 1991. VII, 301 pages. 1991.

Vol. 531: E. M. Clarke, R. P. Kurshan (Eds.), Computer-Aided Verification. Proceedings, 1990. XIII, 372 pages. 1991.

Vol. 532: H. Ehrig, H.-J. Kreowski, G. Rozenberg (Eds.), Graph Grammars and Their Application to Computer Science. Proceedings, 1990. X, 703 pages. 1991.

Vol. 533: E. Börger, H. Kleine Büning, M. M. Richter, W. Schönfeld (Eds.), Computer Science Logic. Proceedings, 1990. VIII, 399 pages. 1991.

Vol. 534: H. Ehrig, K. P. Jantke, F. Orejas, H. Reichel (Eds.), Recent Trends in Data Type Specification. Proceedings, 1990. VIII, 379 pages. 1991.

Vol. 535: P. Jorrand, J. Kelemen (Eds.), Fundamentals of Artificial Intelligence Research. Proceedings, 1991. VIII, 255 pages. 1991. (Subseries LNAI).

Vol. 536: J. E. Tomayko, Software Engineering Education. Proceedings, 1991. VIII, 296 pages. 1991.

Vol. 537: A. J. Menezes, S. A. Vanstone (Eds.), Advances in Cryptology – CRYPTO '90. Proceedings. XIII, 644 pages. 1991.

Vol. 538: M. Kojima, N. Megiddo, T. Noma, A. Yoshise, A Unified Approach to Interior Point Algorithms for Linear Complementarity Problems. VIII, 108 pages. 1991.

Vol. 539: H. F. Mattson, T. Mora, T. R. N. Rao (Eds.), Applied Algebra, Algebraic Algorithms and Error-Correcting Codes. Proceedings, 1991. XI, 489 pages. 1991.

Vol. 540: A. Prieto (Ed.), Artificial Neural Networks. Proceedings, 1991. XIII, 476 pages. 1991.

Vol. 541: P. Barahona, L. Moniz Pereira, A. Porto (Eds.), EPIA '91. Proceedings, 1991. VIII, 292 pages. 1991. (Subseries LNAI).

Vol. 543: J. Dix, K. P. Jantke, P. H. Schmitt (Eds.), Nonmonotonic and Inductive Logic. Proceedings, 1990. X, 243 pages. 1991. (Subseries LNAI).

Vol. 544: M. Broy, M. Wirsing (Eds.), Methods of Programming. XII, 268 pages. 1991.

Vol. 545: H. Alblas, B. Melichar (Eds.), Attribute Grammars, Applications and Systems. Proceedings, 1991. IX, 513 pages. 1991.

Vol. 547: D. W. Davies (Ed.), Advances in Cryptology – EUROCRYPT '91. Proceedings, 1991. XII, 556 pages. 1991.

Vol. 548: R. Kruse, P. Siegel (Eds.), Symbolic and Quantitative Approaches to Uncertainty. Proceedings, 1991. XI, 362 pages. 1991.

Vol. 550: A. van Lamsweerde, A. Fugetta (Eds.), ESEC '91. Proceedings, 1991. XII, 515 pages. 1991.

Lecture Notes in Computer Science

For information about Vols. 1–461
please contact your bookseller or Springer-Verlag

Vol. 462: G. Gottlob, W. Nejdl (Eds.), Expert Systems in Engineering. Proceedings, 1990. IX, 260 pages. 1990. (Subseries LNAI).

Vol. 463: H. Kirchner, W. Wechler (Eds.), Algebraic and Logic Programming. Proceedings, 1990. VII, 386 pages. 1990.

Vol. 464: J. Dassow, J. Kelemen (Eds.), Aspects and Prospects of Theoretical Computer Science. Proceedings, 1990. VI, 298 pages. 1990.

Vol. 465: A. Fuhrmann, M. Morreau (Eds.), The Logic of Theory Change. Proceedings, 1989. X, 334 pages. 1991. (Subseries LNAI).

Vol. 466: A. Blaser (Ed.), Database Systems of the 90s. Proceedings, 1990. VIII, 334 pages. 1990.

Vol. 467: F. Long (Ed.), Software Engineering Environments. Proceedings, 1989. VI, 313 pages. 1990.

Vol. 468: S.G. Akl, F. Fiala, W.W. Koczkodaj (Eds.), Advances in Computing and Information – ICCI '90. Proceedings, 1990. VII, 529 pages. 1990.

Vol. 469: I. Guessarian (Ed.), Semantics of Systems of Concurrent Processes. Proceedings, 1990. V, 456 pages. 1990.

Vol. 470: S. Abiteboul, P.C. Kanellakis (Eds.), ICDT '90. Proceedings, 1990. VII, 528 pages. 1990.

Vol. 471: B.C. Ooi, Efficient Query Processing in Geographic Information Systems. VIII, 208 pages. 1990.

Vol. 472: K.V. Nori, C.E. Veni Madhavan (Eds.), Foundations of Software Technology and Theoretical Computer Science. Proceedings, 1990. X, 420 pages. 1990.

Vol. 473: I.B. Damgård (Ed.), Advances in Cryptology – EUROCRYPT '90. Proceedings, 1990. VIII, 500 pages. 1991.

Vol. 474: D. Karagiannis (Ed.), Information Systems and Artificial Intelligence: Integration Aspects. Proceedings, 1990. X, 293 pages. 1991. (Subseries LNAI).

Vol. 475: P. Schroeder-Heister (Ed.), Extensions of Logic Programming. Proceedings, 1989. VIII, 364 pages. 1991. (Subseries LNAI).

Vol. 476: M. Filgueiras, L. Damas, N. Moreira, A.P. Tomás (Eds.), Natural Language Processing. Proceedings, 1990. VII, 253 pages. 1991. (Subseries LNAI).

Vol. 477: D. Hammer (Ed.), Compiler Compilers. Proceedings, 1990. VI, 227 pages. 1991.

Vol. 478: J. van Eijck (Ed.), Logics in AI. Proceedings, 1990. IX, 562 pages. 1991. (Subseries in LNAI).

Vol. 479: H. Schmidt, Meta-Level Control for Deductive Database Systems. VI, 155 pages. 1991.

Vol. 480: C. Choffrut, M. Jantzen (Eds.), STACS 91. Proceedings, 1991. X, 549 pages. 1991.

Vol. 481: E. Lang, K.-U. Carstensen, G. Simmons, Modelling Spatial Knowledge on a Linguistic Basis. IX, 138 pages. 1991. (Subseries LNAI).

Vol. 482: Y. Kodratoff (Ed.), Machine Learning – EWSL-91. Proceedings, 1991. XI, 537 pages. 1991. (Subseries LNAI).

Vol. 483: G. Rozenberg (Ed.), Advances in Petri Nets 1990. VI, 515 pages. 1991.

Vol. 484: R. H. Möhring (Ed.), Graph-Theoretic Concepts in Computer Science. Proceedings, 1990. IX, 360 pages. 1991.

Vol. 485: K. Furukawa, H. Tanaka, T. Fuijsaki (Eds.), Logic Programming '89. Proceedings, 1989. IX, 183 pages. 1991. (Subseries LNAI).

Vol. 486: J. van Leeuwen, N. Santoro (Eds.), Distributed Algorithms. Proceedings, 1990. VI, 433 pages. 1991.

Vol. 487: A. Bode (Ed.), Distributed Memory Computing. Proceedings, 1991. XI, 506 pages. 1991.

Vol. 488: R. V. Book (Ed.), Rewriting Techniques and Applications. Proceedings, 1991. VII, 458 pages. 1991.

Vol. 489: J. W. de Bakker, W. P. de Roever, G. Rozenberg (Eds.), Foundations of Object-Oriented Languages. Proceedings, 1990. VIII, 442 pages. 1991.

Vol. 490: J. A. Bergstra, L. M. G. Feijs (Eds.), Algebraic Methods II: Theory, Tools and Applications. VI, 434 pages. 1991.

Vol. 491: A. Yonezawa, T. Ito (Eds.), Concurrency: Theory, Language, and Architecture. Proceedings, 1989. VIII, 339 pages. 1991.

Vol. 492: D. Sriram, R. Logcher, S. Fukuda (Eds.), Computer-Aided Cooperative Product Development. Proceedings, 1989 VII, 630 pages. 1991.

Vol. 493: S. Abramsky, T. S. E. Maibaum (Eds.), TAPSOFT '91. Volume 1. Proceedings, 1991. VIII, 455 pages. 1991.

Vol. 494: S. Abramsky, T. S. E. Maibaum (Eds.), TAPSOFT '91. Volume 2. Proceedings, 1991. VIII, 482 pages. 1991.

Vol. 495: 9. Thalheim, J. Demetrovics, H.-D. Gerhardt (Eds.), MFDBS '91. Proceedings, 1991. VI, 395 pages. 1991.

Vol. 496: H.-P. Schwefel, R. Männer (Eds.), Parallel Problem Solving from Nature. Proceedings, 1990. XI, 485 pages. 1991.

Vol. 497: F. Dehne, F. Fiala. W.W. Koczkodaj (Eds.), Advances in Computing and Information - ICCI '91. Proceedings, 1991. VIII, 745 pages. 1991.

Vol. 498: R. Andersen, J. A. Bubenko jr., A. Sølvberg (Eds.), Advanced Information Systems Engineering. Proceedings, 1991. VI, 579 pages. 1991.

Vol. 499: D. Christodoulakis (Ed.), Ada: The Choice for '92. Proceedings, 1991. VI, 411 pages. 1991.

Vol. 500: M. Held, On the Computational Geometry of Pocket Machining. XII, 179 pages. 1991.

Vol. 501: M. Bidoit, H.-J. Kreowski, P. Lescanne, F. Orejas, D. Sannella (Eds.), Algebraic System Specification and Development. VIII, 98 pages. 1991.

Vol. 502: J. Bārzdiņš, D. Bjørner (Eds.), Baltic Computer Science. X, 619 pages. 1991.

Vol. 503: P. America (Ed.), Parallel Database Systems. Proceedings, 1990. VIII, 433 pages. 1991.

Vol. 504: J. W. Schmidt, A. A. Stogny (Eds.), Next Generation Information System Technology. Proceedings, 1990. IX, 450 pages. 1991.